Reintroduction of Top-Order Predators

Conservation Science and Practice Series

Published in association with the Zoological Society of London

Blackwell Publishing and the Zoological Society of London are proud to present our new *Conservation Science and Practice* volume series. Each book in the series reviews a key issue in conservation today. We are particularly keen to publish books that address the multidisciplinary aspects of conservation, looking at how biological scientists and ecologists are interacting with social scientists to effect long-term, sustainable conservation measures.

Books in the series can be single or multi-authored and proposals should be sent to:

Ward Cooper, Senior Commissioning Editor, Wiley-Blackwell, John Wiley & Sons, 9600 Garsington Road, Oxford OX4 2DQ, UK
Email: ward.cooper@wiley.com

Each book proposal will be assessed by independent academic referees, as well as by our Series Editorial Panel. Members of the Panel include:

Conservation Science and Practice Series

Reintroduction of Top-Order Predators

Edited by

Matt W. Hayward and Michael J. Somers

A John Wiley & Sons, Ltd., Publication

Blackwell Publishing was acquired by John Wiley & Sons in February 2007. Blackwell's publishing program has been merged with Wiley's global Scientific, Technical and Medical business to form Wiley-Blackwell.

Registered office: John Wiley & Sons Ltd, The Atrium, Southern Gate, Chichester, West Sussex, PO19 8SQ, UK

Editorial offices: 9600 Garsington Road, Oxford, OX4 2DQ, UK
The Atrium, Southern Gate, Chichester, West Sussex, PO19 8SQ, UK
111 River Street, Hoboken, NJ 07030-5774, USA

For details of our global editorial offices, for customer services and for information about how to apply for permission to reuse the copyright material in this book, please see our website at www.wiley.com/wiley-blackwell.

Library of Congress Cataloguing-in-Publication Data

Reintroduction of top-order predators / edited by Matt W. Hayward and Michael J. Somers
p. cm. – (Conservation science and practice series)
Includes bibliographical references and index.
ISBN 978-1-4051-7680-4 (pbk. : alk. paper) – ISBN 978-1-4051-9273-6 (hardcover : alk. paper) 1. Top predators–Reintroduction. 2. Wildlife reintroduction. 3. Wildlife conservation. I. Hayward, Matt.
QL758.R45 2009
639.9′87–dc22

2008042547

A catalogue record for this book is available from the British Library.

Set in 10.5 on 12.5 pt Minion by SNP Best-set Typesetter Ltd., Hong Kong
Printed and bound in Malaysia by Vivar Printing Sdn Bhd

1 2009

Dedications

MWH

To Gina and the two little humans she helped reintroduce (supplement) to this world, Madeleine and Zoë.

MJS

To my folks Daphne and John and the immediate clan, Michele, Sebastian and Ethan.

Contents

Contributors

Som B. Ale, Biological Sciences, University of Illinois, 845 W. Taylor Street, Chicago, IL 60607, USA. Email: sale1@uic.edu.

Edward E. Bangs, US Fish and Wildlife Service, Northern Rocky Mountain Wolf Recovery Coordinator, 585 Shepard Way, Helena, MT 59601, USA.

Urs Breitenmoser, KORA, Thunstrasse 31, CH-3074 Muri, Switzerland.

Christine Breitenmoser-Würsten, KORA, Thunstrasse 31, CH-3074 Muri, Switzerland.

Sarah Christie, Zoological Society of London, Regent's Park, London NW1 4RY, UK. Email: sarah.christie@zsl.org.

Deon Cilliers, De Wildt Wild Cheetah Project, De Wildt Cheetah and Wildlife Trust, PO Box 16, De Wildt 0251, South Africa.

Joseph D. Clark, US Geological Survey, Southern Appalachian Field Laboratory, 274 Ellington Plant Sciences Building, University of Tennessee, Knoxville, TN 37996, USA. Email: jclark1@utk.edu.

Harriet T. Davies-Mostert, Carnivore Conservation Group, Endangered Wildlife Trust, and Wildlife Conservation Research Unit (WildCRU), Oxford University, Post Bag X11, Parkview, 2122, South Africa. Email: harrietd@ewt.org.za; http://www.ewt.org.za.

Chris R. Dickman, Institute of Wildlife Research, School of Biological Sciences, University of Sydney, NSW 2006, Australia. Email: cdickman@bio.usyd.edu.au.

Richard Frankham, Department of Biological Sciences, Macquarie University, NSW 2109, Australia, and Australian Museum, College Street, Sydney, NSW 2010, Australia.

Alistair S. Glen, Western Australian Department of Environment and Conservation, and Invasive Animals CRC, Dwellingup Research Centre, Banksiadale Road, Dwellingup, Western Australia 6213, Australia. Email: Al.Glen@dec.wa.gov.au.

Markus Gusset, Wildlife Conservation Research Unit, Department of Zoology, University of Oxford, Tubney, Abingdon OX13 5QL, UK. Email: mgusset@bluewin.ch.

Matt W. Hayward, Marie Curie Research Fellow, Mammal Research Institute, Polish Academy of Science, 17-230 Bialowieza, Poland. Email: hayers111@aol.com.

Philipp Henschel, Forest Leopard Study, Wildlife Conservation Society—Gabon Program, BP 7847, Libreville, Gabon. Email: phenschel@uuplus.com.

Luke T.B. Hunter, Great Cats Program, Wildlife Conservation Society, 2300 Southern Blvd, Bronx 10460, USA. Email: l.hunter@panthera-foundation.org.

Rodney M. Jackson, Snow Leopard Conservancy, 18030 Comstock Ave, Sonoma, CA 95476, USA. Email: rodjackson@mountain.org.

A.J.T. Johnsingh, Eminent Wildlife Biologist, Nature Conservation Foundation, Mysore, and Honorary Scientific Advisor, WWF-India. Email: ajt.johnsingh@gmail.com.

Marcella J. Kelly, Associate Professor, Department of Fisheries and Wildlife, Virginia Tech, 146 Cheatham Hall, Blacksburg, VA 24061-0321, USA. Email: makelly2@vt.edu.

Hans Kruuk, Honorary Professor, Department of Zoology, University of Aberdeen, Tillydrone Avenue, Aberdeen AB24 2TZ, UK.

Mike Letnic, Institute of Wildlife Research, School of Biological Sciences, University of Sydney, NSW 2006, Australia. Email: mletnic@bio.usyd.edu.au.

Peter A. Lindsey, Mammal Research Institute, University of Pretoria, Pretoria 0002, South Africa. Email: palindsey@gmail.com.

John D.C. Linnell, Norwegian Institute for Nature Research, Tungasletta 2, N-7485 Trondheim, Norway. Email: john.linnell@nina.no.

David W. Macdonald, Wildlife Conservation Research Unit, Department of Zoology, University of Oxford, Tubney House, Tubney, Oxon OX13 5QL, UK.

M.D. Madhusudan, Nature Conservation Foundation, 3076/5, IV Cross, Gokulam Park, Mysore 570002, India.

Kelly Marnewick, Centre for Wildlife Management, University of Pretoria, Pretoria, and De Wildt Wild Cheetah Project, De Wildt Cheetah and Wildlife Trust, PO Box 16, De Wildt 0251, South Africa.

M. Gus L. Mills, Tony and Lisette Lewis Foundation and Mammal Research Institute, University of Pretoria, Private Bag X5890, Upington, 8800, South Africa.

John Odden, Norwegian Institute for Nature Research, Tungasletta 2, N-7485 Trondheim, Norway.

Stephanie S. Romañach, Tropical Resource Ecology Programme, University of Zimbabwe, PO Box 1060, Mount Pleasant, Harare, Zimbabwe.

Scott Silver, Facility Director/Curator of Animals, Queens Zoo, Wildlife Conservation Society, 53–51 111th Street, Flushing, NY 11368, USA.

Rob Slotow, School of Biological and Conservation Sciences, University of KwaZulu-Natal, Westville Campus, Private Bag X54001, Durban, 4000, South Africa. Email: slotow@ukzn.ac.za.

Douglas W. Smith, Leader—Yellowstone Wolf Project, YCR, PO Box 168, Officer's Row, Building 27, Yellowstone National Park, WY 82190, USA. Email: doug_smith@nps.gov; http://www.nps.gov/yell/naturescience/wolves.htm.

Michael J. Somers, Centre for Wildlife Management, Centre for Invasion Biology, University of Pretoria, Pretoria 0002, South Africa. Email: michael.somers@up.ac.za.

Manuela von Arx, KORA, Thunstrasse 31, CH-3074 Muri, Switzerland.

Foreword

As a conservation measure, reintroduction of any species should always be a last resort. It has much public appeal, and may be scored in the media as a glorious triumph of hands-on conservation, overcoming all the practical problems involved. But it also marks a failure, a mismanagement of our environment, which failed to ensure previous survival of populations. However, once reintroduction is accepted as the only method to ensuring the presence of a particular species in an area, it becomes a test of our science—of our knowledge—of an animal.

As many of the chapters in this remarkable volume demonstrate, that knowledge of behaviour and ecology is still full of gaps. And if any group of animals can show the acute need of research to back practical conservation measures, it must be the carnivores. I feel very pleased to introduce this book, since this collection of research papers is such a neat follow-up of my *Hunter and Hunted* (Cambridge University Press, 2002), dealing with the enigmatic relationship between carnivores and mankind.

Why should carnivores be singled out as a group, and this volume dedicated to them? Perhaps there are three main reasons for this. Firstly, we and the public at large appear to like them more than many other mammals. Secondly, there is the ambiguous nature of the interaction between carnivores and ourselves (especially the threats they pose and damage they cause, versus strong emotional appeal). Thirdly, there are the highly significant top-down effects of carnivores within ecosystems, posing fascinating ecological problems, particularly for reintroductions.

The complexities of top-down effects of top-order predators in ecosystems, and the role they play after reintroductions, have been beautifully illustrated in recent studies. Amongst others, there are those reported in this book on the wolf in Yellowstone, where wolves reduced populations of elk, which enabled willow to spread to feed increasing numbers of beavers and provide habitat for song birds (Smith *et al.* this volume). Equally important, it is suggested that reintroduction of the dingo would reduce the lethal effects of exotic smaller predators on native Australian prey (Dickman *et al.* this volume). These studies demonstrate the almost universal occurrence of such effects, after the highly detailed research for instance in marine environments, where sea otters depress prey populations, which in turn enable gigantic kelp beds to grow and create habitats for diverse fish populations (whereas sea otter populations themselves are in places decimated by predation by killer whales).

In programmes of reintroduction of carnivores, one has become acutely aware of the human dimensions of such undertakings. The pre-eminent importance of considering people's reactions to receiving previously absent wild carnivores in their environment shines through in many of the contributions here. The need to involve people whose livelihoods may be affected is a *sine qua non*, but all too often ignored in the past, with disastrous consequence. Even now, there still are conservationists who consider reintroducing wolves into the upland sheep grazings of Scotland without consulting local farmers, who would have to radically change their husbandry methods.

As pointed out by the editors of this book (Hayward & Somers, this volume), reintroduction requires an ability to forecast how releases will behave and how they will affect local ecology. To predict such influences, one needs data from many different habitats on the natural history of carnivores. As an example of what is involved, it is only for a few common species (e.g. lion, wolf, coyote, red fox, Eurasian badger and otter) that we have sufficient diet data from different areas to be able to predict with some confidence what newly released animals will feed on in a new habitat. Similarly, we are hugely data-deficient on social behaviour and organization of carnivores to be able to predict the optimal sex/age composition of groups of releases in reintroductions. Exposed in this book is a dearth of basic (and in itself not very exciting or ground-breaking) information, and predictably, academia is not inclined to fund studies to meet such needs.

The present volume provides a fascinating forum for some of the foremost experts on carnivores, in conservation and reintroduction, to discuss the problems involved. As presented here, many others will be able to learn from the splendid successes of re-populating areas of Europe with lynx, of South Africa with wild dogs and of North America with wolves. We are dealing with multi-disciplinary exercises, involving genetics, diseases, human social aspects, population ecology, animal social behaviour, feeding ecology, habitat analyses and other fields. It is ecology at its most appealing, and challenging.

None of the cases and arguments in this volume are cut and dried; they are an intriguing and essential part of ongoing discussion. Thus, I may be very impressed with the case put forward for preventing inbreeding in small introduced populations (Frankham, this volume), but cannot help remembering that if one introduces only a couple of cats or goats on an island, they produce thousands of bothersome and healthy offspring. The last word has not been spoken, nor has it in any of the other issues.

In several situations, however dire for the species concerned, authors argue cogently against a reintroduction under present conditions, usually because the main causes of extirpation have not been removed. Tiger in India, leopard, hyaena or wild dog in Congo, snow leopard in the Himalaya, jaguar in South America—in all of these cases, a reintroduction would only add more victims to the slaughter. A tremendous amount of conservation work needs to be done before the field is clear for a reintroduction—a last resort after our failed *modus vivendi* with these other occupants of the planet.

In the end, perhaps the most important message of this collection is the dire need for more basic data on the natural history of carnivores, such as food, behaviour and habitat. This we need not just for the almost-extinct ones, but for virtually all of them. Not Nobel-prize winning studies, but basics, and lots of it, to make sure that we can forecast animals' needs in situations where conservation management is called for—especially where such management involves reintroduction.

Hans Kruuk

Acknowledgements

MWH thanks the Society for Conservation Biology for a travel grant to the 2007 annual meeting at the Nelson Mandela Metropolitan University, Port Elizabeth, South Africa. Preparation for this book was funded by a Marie Curie Transfer of Knowledge Fellowship BIORESC of the European Community's Sixth Framework Programme under contract number MTKD-CT-2005-029957.

The following people generously provided their time and expertise to review various chapters: Anders Angerbjorn, Sumanta Bagchi, James Blignaut, Paulette Bloomer, Mark Boyce, Elissa Cameron, Chris Carbone, Tim Caro, Peter Crawshaw Jr., Barbara Croes, Fredrik Dalerum, Harriet Davies-Mostert, Sarah Durant, Hans de Ilongh, Paul Funston, Josh Ginsberg, Matthew Gompper, Markus Gusset, Gina Hayward, David Hetherington, Markus Hofmeyr, Djuro Huber, Luke Hunter, Bogumiła Jędrzejewska, Włodzimierż Jędrzejewski, Chris Johnson, Devra Kleiman, Robert Lacy, Wayne Linklater, Tom McCarthy, Bethan Morgan, Justina Ray, Richard Reading, Terry Robinson, Eric Sanderson, Krzysztof Schmidt, Phil Seddon, Debra Shier, Jeff Short, Rob Slotow, James L. David Smith, Pritpal Soorae, Penny Spiering, Mel Sunquist, Jon Swenson, Micaela Szykman and Bettine van Vuuren. The following people from Wiley-Blackwell happily and expertly helped with the production of the book: Angela Bailey, Rosie Hayden, Delia Sandford and Ward Cooper.

1

Reintroduction of Top-Order Predators: Using Science to Restore One of the Drivers of Biodiversity

Matt W. Hayward[1] and Michael J. Somers[2]

[1]Mammal Research Institute, Polish Academy of Science
[2]Centre for Wildlife Management, Centre for Invasion Biology, University of Pretoria

Top-order predators is a broad phrase that we have intentionally chosen to describe carnivorous mammalian predators with a range of body sizes that occur at the upper end of the food chains of each continent. This definition is not limited by body mass or taxonomic clade, as it was intended to compare the actual or potential reintroduction of a diverse range of species from grey wolves, *Canis lupus,* to marsupial predators, such as Tasmanian devils, *Sarcophilus harrisi.*

By their very nature, top-order predators are relatively rare in natural ecosystems—be they African lions, *Panthera leo,* preying upon the vast herds of wildebeest, *Connochaetes taurinus,* in the Serengeti; wolves preying upon the large elk, *Cervus elaphus,* herds of Yellowstone; or dingoes, *Canis lupus dingo,* preying upon the millions of kangaroos in the Simpson Desert. This inherent scarcity lends itself to difficulty and insecurity in conservation efforts (Weber & Rabinowitz, 1996), as small declines in already small populations can set into motion unpredictable and uncontrollable stochastic forces as part of the small-population paradigm (Caughley, 1994).

Reintroduction of Top-Order Predators, 1st edition. Edited by M.W. Hayward and M.J. Somers.
 ISBN 978-1-4051-7680-4 (pb) and 978-1-4051-9273-6 (hb)

While a range of threatening processes affect top-order predators (IUCN, 2007), ultimately they are mostly incompatible with human existence (Kruuk, 2002). Valuable attempts to integrate top-order predators into human landscapes are underway (e.g. Ogada *et al.*, 2003) but, wherever pastoralism provides an easy source of meat for carnivores, the risk of human–wildlife conflict will remain (Treves & Karanth, 2003). Since the advent of early hominids, there has been conflict (Brain, 1981) and competition for the top-order predator niche (Kruuk, 2002). Consequently, we have been present at, and often responsible for, the extinction of numerous large carnivores in Europe, North America, South America and Australia (Martin, 1967; Martin & Guilday, 1967; Flannery, 1994; Flannery & Roberts, 1999; Stuart, 1999). The number of carnivore species driven extinct during the Pleistocene was disproportionately high (Martin & Steadman, 1999). Even today, those top-order predators that persist continue to be persecuted by humans—be they brown bears, *Ursus arctos,* in Europe (Gentleman, 2004; Hunter, 2006); snow leopards, *Uncia uncia,* in the Himalayas (Bagchi & Mishra, 2006); or jaguars, *Panthera onca,* in Venezuela (Polisar *et al.*, 2003). Direct persecution may not be the sole threat, as a decline in prey will invariably lead to a decline in predator abundance through bottom-up limitation (Karanth *et al.*, 2004; Hayward *et al.*, 2007d).

This simplification of the diverse threats to top-order predators may ultimately benefit their conservation. If scientists can successfully identify the key extinction threats to a species and agree upon them, they can work towards removing those threats. Where conservation biologists continue to disagree on the causes of endangerment of threatened species, little action can occur. Such disagreement between conservation practitioners may be the key to identifying why some countries have implemented numerous reintroduction programmes, while other countries have not bothered.

Top-order predators are amongst the most studied wild organisms on the planet, and we know the natural history of many species in great detail. Therefore, we have a deep understanding of their behavioural and evolutionary ecology (see Somers & Gusset, this volume). As a consequence, there is general agreement as to the ultimate extinction threats facing many top-order predators, such that conservation management actions can be based on sufficient knowledge to achieve satisfactory conservation goals. Yet, despite popular perceptions to the contrary, other top-order predators are more difficult to study or have simply been neglected by researchers, resulting in insufficient ecological understanding to develop confidence in conservation management actions.

Reintroduction is one action available to conservation managers. Sadly, such actions can only occur after other conservation strategies have failed. Throughout this book, we define reintroduction as an attempt to establish a species within its historical range but where it has since been extirpated, and translocation as the deliberate movement of wild individuals between parts of their extant range (IUCN, 1998). Although top-order predators have declined globally (Weber & Rabinowitz, 1996), they are still amongst the most frequently reintroduced group of organisms (Seddon *et al.*, 2005). There are multiple reasons for this, including assisting with a species' conservation (Hayward *et al.*, 2007a), the degree of knowledge about these charismatic species, the restoration of ecosystem functioning (Terborgh *et al.*, 1999; Sinclair *et al.*, 2003), the financial benefits of their presence in ecotourism ventures (Lindsey *et al.*, 2005, and this volume), or that they were the first and only species to have been made locally extinct.

Determining the success of reintroductions is an essential practice. For most species, definitions of success include an unsupported, self-sustaining population of >500 individuals (Griffith *et al.*, 1989) or a local categorization as vulnerable or better according to IUCN (International Union for the Conservation of Nature and Natural Resources) Red List criteria (Breitenmoser *et al.*, 2001). Top-order predator populations that exceed 500 individuals are rare in today's world of fragmented landscapes. Indeed, the Vulnerable category of the IUCN Red List requires >1000 mature individuals (IUCN, 2001), which means that supposedly natural populations, such as the cheetahs, *Acinonyx jubatus*, of the Serengeti Plains (~60 adult females, which are 25% more common than males) (Kelly *et al.*, 1998), would be deemed unsuccessful had they stemmed from a reintroduction. Thus, in the short term, reintroduction success can be more satisfactorily defined as breeding by the first wild-born generation or a 3-year breeding population with natural recruitment exceeding mortality (Griffith *et al.*, 1989), particularly in small, enclosed reserves (Hayward *et al.*, 2007b). In all but the largest reserves, populations of top-order predators that are self-sustaining (i.e. that do not require some form of human interference such as genetic rescue) or exceed 500 individuals are likely to be very unusual (see Frankham, this volume; Gusset, this volume).

It is universally recommended that continuing, long-term monitoring should occur after reintroductions have taken place to ensure continued population growth or stability (Mills, 1991; Weber & Rabinowitz, 1996; Hunter, 1998; Breitenmoser *et al.,* 2001; Hofmeyr *et al.,* 2003; Moehrenschlager & Somers, 2004; Gusset, this volume). Furthermore, on-going management is also likely to be necessary to ensure survival of reintroduced stock, manage their increases or avoid genetic and other stochastic problems (Frankham, this volume; Gusset, this volume).

It is timely that this diverse array of conservation biologists collectively recorded their experiences, results and opinions regarding the reintroduction of top-order predators. There are plans to reintroduce tigers, *Panthera tigris,* to Sariska, India (Q. Qureshi, Wildlife Institute of India, Dehra Dun, India; personal communication), and a second population of Asiatic lions, *Panthera leo persica,* may soon be reintroduced to Madhya Pradesh (Johnsingh *et al.* 2007). The world's most endangered canid, the Ethiopian wolf, *Canis simiensis,* will also soon be reintroduced to parts of its former range to reduce the risk associated with catastrophes striking its few remaining sanctuaries (C. Sillero-Zubiri, University of Oxford, UK; personal communication).

But what of other top-order predators? Will Tasmanian devils that are currently being decimated by facial tumour cancer ever be returned to the Australian mainland, despite existing there as little as 450 years ago (Butler, 1968)? And what about the eastern quoll, *Dasyurus viverinus,* which was last observed on the Australian mainland in the 1960s (Strahan, 1995)? Poland's Białowieża Primeval Forest is the most pristine example of the mixed deciduous forests that once covered most of continental Europe, but the absence of brown bears illustrates that this area is not completely intact (Jędrzejewska *et al.*, 1995; Clark, this volume). Can this species potentially be reintroduced successfully, considering that the attempts made prior to the 1960s failed (Clark, this volume)?

This book aims to identify the top-order predators that have been studied sufficiently for conservation managers to have confidence in attempting reintroductions, and those for which we need more information. For those species that are frequently reintroduced, the book will identify the information that is essential to give confidence in achieving a successful reintroduction. The book will also identify those top-order predators that are rarely reintroduced and will determine whether the absence of reintroduction is due to insufficient ecological knowledge of the species or to a lack of need for reintroduction.

For example, recent reviews of carnivore reintroductions (Breitenmoser *et al.*, 2001) illustrated great disparities between the reintroduction of top-order predators. It is notable that five African top-order predators have been reintroduced during 30 projects, while two Asian species have been reintroduced in just two projects. In North America, six species have been reintroduced in 28 projects (Breitenmoser *et al.*, 2001).

In order to achieve these goals, the book is broken up into three sections. The first section provides reviews of reintroduction programmes of wolves, bears, African lions, African wild dogs (*Lycaon pictus*), tigers, snow leopards, leopards (*Panthera pardus*), jaguars and cheetahs. The second section provides reviews of the ecology of individual species, which highlight that there is no current need for reintroduction to occur. This may be because existing populations are able to recolonize vacant habitats naturally; because a species still exists throughout its range, albeit at dangerously low densities; or because we lack a sufficient understanding of the species ecology to risk such a programme. The final section provides examples of recent advances in our understanding of top-order predator ecology that should enable us to predict their behavioural or ecological responses to the reintroduction process.

This book is not intended to describe the methods by which a reintroduction programme should be undertaken, as there are many publications available that provide this information (Hofmeyr & van Dyk, 1998; Bothma, 2002). Rather, we hope this book will highlight recent advances in our understanding of top-order predator behavioural and evolutionary ecology that improve the likelihood of success of reintroduction programmes, or highlight deficiencies that require further research.

If nothing else, we hope this book will illustrate the necessity of a detailed understanding of the basic natural history of species from sites throughout their range and in different time periods. Without such knowledge, scientists can have little confidence in recommending a conservation strategy to managers. Such simple natural history is largely spurned by the scientific, or perhaps just the academic, world (Wilcove & Eisner, 2000), but is fundamental to the successful conservation of threatened species (Belovsky *et al.*, 2004). Indeed, the 31 researchers who continued to describe the diet of the lion following the first description (Bourliere, 1963) provided essential information that resulted in an ability to predict the diet of lions at reintroduction or at unstudied sites (Hayward *et al.*, 2007c). Similarly, multiple publications assessing reintroductions and translocations of wild dogs have yielded substantial breakthroughs in our understanding of the essential requirements for a successful reintroduction (Gusset *et al.*, 2008). Repeated descriptions of the natural history of a species in different ecosystems and in different times (seasons, years, climatic variations) provide the necessary replication to yield causal explanations to the theoretical complexities of conservation ecology (Belovsky *et al.*, 2004).

Large-scale, replicated and controlled manipulation experiments are far more attractive to the academic world, however top-order predators, particularly those that require reintroduction, are largely incompatible with such actions given the small sample sizes of sites or individuals that are often available. It is rare that a reintroduction programme is designed as an appropriately replicated experiment, but increasing cooperation between researchers and managers may see this occurring more frequently. Furthermore, new modelling techniques enable us to use a limited amount of data and then to simulate replicated reintroduction experiments (e.g. Gusset, this volume). We hope this book will illustrate that conservation scientists must persist in describing the natural history of threatened species in the knowledge that this is an essential requirement of successful conservation management. Given the high frequency of reintroduction programmes occurring in some places (Hayward *et al.*, 2007b), there may now be opportunities to consolidate the research via some *post hoc* meta-analysis to further establish and refine the emerging science of reintroduction biology.

Acknowledgements

This book is a result of a symposium held during the annual conference of the Society for Conservation Biology held in Port Elizabeth, South Africa, in July 2007. We thank the Society for providing financial support for many of our presenters. We thank Elissa Cameron and Markus Gusset for commenting on earlier drafts of this chapter.

References

Bagchi, S. & Mishra, C. (2006) Living with large carnivores: Predation on livestock by the snow leopard (*Uncia uncia*). *Journal of Zoology* 268, 217–224.

Belovsky, G.E., Botkin, D.B., Crowl, T.A. et al. (2004) Ten suggestions to strengthen the science of ecology. *BioScience* 54, 345–351.

Bothma, J.D.P. (2002) *Game Ranch Management* (Fourth Edition). van Schaik, Pretoria.

Bourliere, F. (1963) Specific feeding habits of African carnivores. *African Wildlife* 17, 21–27.

Brain, C. (1981) *The Hunters of the Hunted? An Introduction to African Cave Taphonomy*. University of Chicago Press, Chicago, USA.

Breitenmoser, U., Breitenmoser-Wursten, C., Carbyn, L.N. & Funk, S.M. (2001) Assessment of carnivore reintroductions. *Carnivore Conservation.* (eds J.L. Gittleman, S.M. Funk, D.W. Macdonald & R.K. Wayne), pp. 241–280. Cambridge University Press and The Zoological Society of London, Cambridge.

Butler, W.H. (1968) Remains of *Sarcophilus* the "Tasmanian" Devil (Marsupialia, Dasyuridae) from coastal dunes south of Scott River, Western Australia. The *Western Australian Naturalist* 11, 87–89.

Caughley, G. (1994) Directions in conservation biology. *Journal of Animal Ecology* 63, 215–244.

Flannery, T.F. (1994) *The Future Eaters: An Ecological History of the Australasian Lands and People.* Reed Books, Sydney.

Flannery, T.F. & Roberts, R.G. (1999) Late Quaternary extinctions in Australasia: An overview. *Extinctions in Near Time.* (ed R.D.E. MacPhee), pp. 239–255. Kluwer Academic/Plenum Publishers, New York.

Gentleman, A. (2004) Bavaria's bear exterminated. *The Guardian* p. 22. London, UK.

Griffith, B., Scott, J.M., Carpenter, J.W. & Reed, C. (1989) Translocation as a species conservation tool: Status and strategy. *Science* 245, 477–480.

Gusset, M., Ryan, S.J., Hofmeyr, M. et al. (2008) Efforts going to the dogs? Evaluating attempts to re-introduce endangered wild dogs in South Africa. *Journal of Applied Ecology* 45, 100–108.

Jędrzejewska, B., Bunevich, A.N. & Jędrzejewski, W. (1995) Observation of brown bear *Ursus arctos* in Białowieża Primeval Forest from 1948–1950. *Parki Narodowe i Rezerwaty Przyrody* 14, 87–90.

Johnsingh, A.J.T., Goyal, S.P. & Qureshi, Q. (2007) Preparations for the reintroduction of Asiatic lions *Panthera leo persica* into Kuno Wildlife Sanctuary, Madhya Pradesh, India. *Oryx* 41, 93–96.

Kruuk, H. (2002) *Hunter and Hunted.* Cambridge University Press, Cambridge.

Hayward, M.W., Adendorff, J., O'Brien, J. et al. (2007a) Practical considerations for the reintroduction of large, terrestrial, mammalian predators based on reintroductions to South Africa's Eastern Cape Province. *The Open Conservation Biology Journal* 1, 1–11.

Hayward, M.W., Adendorff, J., O'Brien, J. et al. (2007b) The reintroduction of large predators to the Eastern Cape Province, South Africa: An assessment. *Oryx* 42, 205–214.

Hayward, M.W., Hofmeyr, M., O'Brien, J. & Kerley, G.I.H. (2007c) Testing predictions of the prey of the lion (*Panthera leo*) derived from modelled prey preferences. *Journal of Wildlife Management* 71, 1567–1575.

Hayward, M.W., O'Brien, J. & Kerley, G.I.H. (2007d) Carrying capacity of large African predators: Predictions and tests. *Biological Conservation* 139, 219–229.

Hofmeyr, M. & van Dyk, G. (1998) Cheetah introductions to two north-west parks: Case studies from Pilanesburg National Park and Madikwe Game Reserve. *Cheetahs as Game Ranch Animals.* (ed B.L. Penzhorn), pp. 60–71. Wildlife Group of the South African Veterinary Association, Onderstepoort.

Hofmeyr, M., Davies, R., Nel, P. & Dell, S. (2003) Operation Phoenix—The introduction of larger mammals to Madikwe Game Reserve. *Madikwe Game Reserve: A Decade of Progress.* (ed M. Brett), pp. 8–20. North West Parks & Tourism Board, Rustenburg.

Hunter, L.T.B. (1998) Early post-release movements and behaviour of reintroduced cheetahs and lions, and technical considerations in large carnivore restoration. *Cheetahs as Game Ranch Animals.* (ed B. L. Penzhorn), pp. 72–82. Wildlife Group of the South African Veterinary Association, Onderstepoort.

Hunter, X. (2006) Hunters kill France's last brown bear. *The Guardian.* London, UK.

IUCN (1998) *IUCN Guidelines for Re-introductions.* IUCN, Gland, Switzerland.

IUCN (2001) *IUCN Red List Categories and Criteria: Version 3.1.* IUCN, Gland, Switzerland.

IUCN (2007) *2007 Red List of Threatened Species.* IUCN, Gland, Switzerland.

Johnsingh, A.J.T., Goyal, S.P. & Qureshi, Q. (2007) Preparations for the reintroduction of Asiatic lions *Panthera leo persica* into Kuno Wildlife Sanctuary, Madhya Pradesh, India. *Oryx* 41, 93–96.

Karanth, K.U., Nichols, J.D., Kumar, N.S., Link, W.A. & Hines, J.E. (2004) Tigers and their prey: Predicting carnivore densities from prey abundance. *Proceedings of the National Academy of Science, USA* 101, 4854–4858.

Kelly, M.J., Laurenson, M.K., Fitzgibbon, C.D. et al. (1998) Demography of the Serengeti cheetah (*Acinonyx jubatus*) population: The first 25 years. *Journal of Zoology* 244, 473–488.

Lindsey, P.A., Alexander, R.R., du Toit, J.T. & Mills, M.G.L. (2005) The potential contribution of ecotourism to African wild dog *Lycaon pictus* conservation in South Africa. *Biological Conservation* 123, 339–348.

Martin, P.S. (1967) Prehistoric overkill. *Pleistocene Extinctions: The Search for a Cause.* (eds P.S. Martin & H.E. Wright), pp. 75–120. Yale University Press, New Haven.

Martin, P.S. & Guilday, J.E. (1967) A bestiary for Pleistocene biologists. *Pleistocene Extinctions: The Search for a Cause.* (eds P.S. Martin & H.E. Wright), pp. 5–66. Yale University Press, New Haven.

Martin, P.S. & Steadman, D.W. (1999) Prehistoric extinctions on islands and continents. *Extinctions in Near Time.* (ed R.D.E. MacPhee), pp. 17–55. Kluwer Academic/Plenum Publishers, New York.

Mills, M.G.L. (1991) Conservation management of large carnivores in Africa. *Koedoe* 34, 81–90.

Moehrenschlager, A. & Somers, M.J. (2004) Canid reintroductions and metapopulation management. *Canids: Foxes, Wolves, Jackals and Dogs. Status Survey and Conservation Action Plan.* (eds C. Sillero-Zubiri, M. Hoffman & D.W. Macdonald), pp. 289–298. IUCN/SSC Canid Specialist Group, Gland, Switzerland.

Ogada, M.O., Woodroffe, R., Oguge, N.O. & Frank, L.G. (2003) Limiting depredation by African carnivores: The role of livestock husbandry. *Conservation Biology* 17, 1521–1530.

Polisar, J., Maxit, I., Scognamillo, D., Farrell, L., Sunquist, M.E. & Eisenberg, J.F. (2003) Jaguars, pumas, their prey base, and cattle ranching: Ecological interpretations of a management problem. *Biological Conservation* 109, 297–310.

Seddon, P.J., Soorae, P.S. & Launay, F. (2005) Taxonomic bias in reintroduction projects. *Animal Conservation* 8, 51–58.

Sinclair, A.R.E., Mduma, S.A.R. & Brashares, J.S. (2003) Patterns of predation in a diverse predator–prey system. *Nature* 425, 288–290

Strahan, R. (1995) *Mammals of Australia.* Reed Books, Sydney.

Stuart, A.J. (1999) Late Pleistocene megafaunal extinctions: A European perspective. *Extinctions in Near Time.* (ed R.D.E. MacPhee), pp. 257–270. Kluwer Academic/Plenum Publishers, New York.

Terborgh, J., Estes, J.A., Paquet, P. et al. (1999) The role of top carnivores in regulating terrestrial ecosystems. *Continental Conservation: Scientific foundations of Regional Reserve Networks.* (eds M.E. Soule & J. Terborgh), pp. 39–64. Island Press, Washington, DC.

Treves, A. & Karanth, K.U. (2003) Human–carnivore conflict and perspectives on carnivore management worldwide. *Conservation Biology* 17, 1491–1499.

Weber, W. & Rabinowitz, A. (1996) A global perspective on large carnivore conservation. *Conservation Biology* 10, 1046–1054.

Wilcove, D. & Eisner, T. (2000) The impending extinction of natural history. *The Chronicle of Higher Education* 15 September.

2

A Critical Assessment of South Africa's Managed Metapopulation Recovery Strategy for African Wild Dogs

Harriet T. Davies-Mostert[1], *M. Gus L. Mills*[2] *and David W. Macdonald*[3]

[1]Carnivore Conservation Group, Endangered Wildlife Trust, and Wildlife Conservation Research Unit (WildCRU), Oxford University
[2]Tony and Lisette Lewis Foundation and Mammal Research Institute, University of Pretoria
[3]Wildlife Conservation Research Unit, Department of Zoology, University of Oxford

Summary

The only viable population of African wild dogs, *Lycaon pictus* (Temminck 1820), in South Africa occurs in the Kruger National Park. In 1997, a panel of experts identified the establishment of a second viable population as a conservation priority. However, the absence of suitable large conservation areas required that this population be established as what we call a managed metapopulation: namely a series of small, isolated subpopulations that would be managed as a single population by moving wild dogs between areas. Between 1998 and 2006, 66 founder animals were used to establish nine such subpopulations, and the metapopulation reached a peak of 264 animals in 17

Reintroduction of Top Order Predators, 1st edition. Edited by M.W. Hayward and M.J. Somers.
 ISBN 978-1-4051-7680-4 (pb) and 978-1-4051-9273-6 (hb)

packs in June 2005. Pup survival was 64% and yearling survival 71%. Mean annual wild dog densities were 3.3 animals·100 km^{-2} and approached the upper limit of wild dog densities reported from larger conservation areas. Although the metapopulation strategy was successful in terms of enriching species assemblages and stimulating ecotourism, the process of establishing subpopulations was management intensive. A number of management challenges were revealed, including managing conflict with neighbours following breakouts, addressing concerns over the ability of prey populations to sustain wild dog predation, and the necessity of overcoming stochastic processes that affect small populations, and which curtail natural population dynamics. Experiences gained over the past 10 years have improved technical capacity to capture and translocate wild dogs, and this is likely to inform wild dog conservation management elsewhere in Africa. The managed metapopulation approach might be successfully applied to other large mammal species occupying fragmented habitats and, in some cases, this may be a necessary last resort to stave off extinction. However, such an approach requires considerable inputs of time and money and, where they are an option, priority should be given to conservation strategies that will promote natural dispersal and population self-regulation.

Introduction

Human population growth and the associated loss, fragmentation and degradation of natural wildlife habitats are the most important cause of global extinctions of wild plant and animal species (Barbault & Sastrapradja, 1995). Many species with large historical ranges have been reduced to small, fragmented populations. The deleterious effects of habitat destruction, and concomitant loss of resources, have been well documented for large mammals, which appear to be particularly vulnerable to changes in habitat availability and quality. Well known examples include the African elephant, *Loxodonta africana* (Barnes, 1999); the Sumatran rhinoceros, *Dicerorhinus sumatrensis* (Kinnaird *et al.*, 2003); the Ethiopian wolf, *Canis simensis* (Sillero-Zubiri *et al.*, 2002); the giant panda, *Ailuropoda melanoleuca* (Liu *et al.*, 1999); and the Iberian lynx, *Lynx pardinus* (Rodriguez & Delibes, 2003).

Occasionally, the trend towards fragmentation and isolation is somewhat mitigated by expansion of some conservation areas (Hanks, 2001; van der Merwe & Saayman, 2003). However, most habitat loss is irreversible and many species are unlikely ever to recover their former ranges (Gaona *et al.*, 1998). The conservation and management of small, fragmented populations has therefore become an unavoidable necessity. Reintroduction and translocation have been used as conservation tools for a number of medium- to large-sized carnivore species, both as a means of population recovery (Eurasian lynx, *Lynx lynx* [Breitenmoser *et al.*, 2000]; grey wolf, *Canis lupus* [US Fish & Wildlife Service, 1987]; red wolf, *Canis rufus* [Phillips *et al.*, 2003], and also to prevent human–carnivore conflict outside protected areas (cheetahs, *Acinonyx jubatus* [Marnewick *et al.*, this volume]; leopards, *Panthera pardus* [Hayward *et al.*, 2006a]). In this chapter, we present a critical assessment of a recovery strategy to improve the conservation status of the endangered African wild dog *Lycaon pictus* in South Africa.

Conservation status of African wild dogs

African wild dogs represent a monotypic genus that once occurred throughout sub-Saharan Africa (Schaller, 1972; Fanshawe *et al.*, 1991; Woodroffe *et al.*, 2004) but now occupies a fraction of that range. Habitat fragmentation and isolation, exacerbated by direct persecution by humans, have been recognized as the ultimate causes contributing to the overall decline of wild dog populations (Childes, 1988; Fanshawe *et al.*, 1991; Ginsberg *et al.*, 1995a; Woodroffe *et al.*, 1997). Countries where wild dogs have been extirpated are characterized by high human population densities (Woodroffe *et al.*, 1997). There are currently thought to be 5500–6000 wild dogs left in the wild, living in ~600–1000 packs (Woodroffe *et al.*, 2004), and the species is listed as Endangered by the IUCN (International Union for the Conservation of Nature and Natural Resources; C2a[i], Ver 3.1 2001; IUCN 2006). At present, only a handful of countries contain viable wild dog populations, with the largest populations occurring in northern Botswana, Tanzania and northern Mozambique (Woodroffe *et al.*, 2004).

Wild dogs present a particular challenge to conserve because they naturally range widely and occur at low densities, with the effect that even the largest protected areas are able to support only small populations (Woodroffe & Ginsberg, 1998). The effects of habitat loss, consequential prey loss and direct persecution, combine to worsen the species' plight (Schaller, 1972), with the result that they generally persist only as small populations that are vulnerable to stochastic events such as disease outbreaks.

Population and habitat viability assessment for the African wild dog: 1997

The only viable population of wild dogs in South Africa occurs inside the Kruger National Park (Kruger). Several free-ranging and highly persecuted packs occur in Limpopo Province, and their status is precarious (Lindsey *et al.*, 2004b). A workshop to assess wild dog population and habitat viability (PHVA) was held in Pretoria, South Africa, in October 1997, against the backdrop of the extinction of the Serengeti wild dog population in the early 1990s (Ginsberg *et al.*, 1995b, Woodroffe *et al.*, 1997) and growing evidence that concerted conservation intervention would be necessary to ensure the continued survival of the species. A key outcome of this workshop was the decision to establish a second viable wild dog population in South Africa (Mills *et al.*, 1998). However, wild dogs are likely to require areas of more than 10,000 km^2 in order to maintain natural viable populations (Woodroffe *et al.*, 1997), and no such areas exist in South Africa outside Kruger. Recognizing that it would probably be several years—if ever—before this shortage of space would be alleviated, for example through the development of new private game conservancies and the proclamation of large trans-frontier conservation areas, a metapopulation approach towards wild dog conservation was adopted (Mills *et al.*, 1998).

The relevance of metapopulation theory to conservation in general, and wild dogs in South Africa in particular, is summarized by Akçakaya *et al.* (2007). In South Africa, the metapopulation approach involved developing a network of protected areas outside Kruger capable of supporting at least nine packs of wild dogs (Mills *et al.*, 1998). The recommended minimum number of packs was determined through a VORTEX population modelling exercise (VORTEX 7.4, Lacy, 1993) using a combination of wild dog life history data from existing populations in Kruger and northern Botswana. The intention was that wild dog subpopulations would be established through a series of reintroductions in small (<1000 km^2) predator-fenced areas. These would be managed as a single metapopulation by capturing and transferring individuals between reserves in order to mimic natural processes of immigration and emigration. The Wild Dog Advisory Group of South Africa (WAG-SA), comprising an association of scientists and managers, was established to guide and implement the metapopulation strategy.

The term *metapopulation* has a particular usage in the context of the South African wild dog recovery strategy. Classical metapopulation theory describes a set of spatially discrete subpopulations that display asynchronous population dynamics, and where migration between one or more patches is possible (Levins, 1969; Hanski & Simberloff, 1997). Non-classical models have also been proposed, including: patchy populations, in which rates of recolonization are so high that the population is essentially panmictic (Harrison, 1994); source-sink metapopulations, where one subpopulation provides a continuous source of founders for colonization of the other sites, which act as sinks; and non-equilibrium (declining) metapopulations, in which extinction exceeds recolonization (Harrison, 1994).

The isolated and confined (i.e. predator-fenced) nature of potential wild dog reintroduction sites in South Africa meant that rates of natural dispersal and colonization were likely to be extremely low. Unmanaged, these subpopulations would likely exhibit the characteristics of a non-equilibrium metapopulation, rendering metapopulation extinction highly probable. However, we wanted the South African wild dog recovery programme to be as well founded as possible in relevant conservation biology theory, and felt that the best way to achieve this was to draw on metapopulation biology. We therefore refer to the programme as the establishment of a managed metapopulation, but we do so in the realization that the parallels, while helpful, are only approximate. The approach taken was to establish a series of subpopulations, within which some aspects of natural metapopulations would be simulated by artificially balancing extinction with recolonization. Translocations (playing the role of dispersal) would balance mortality caused by environmental and demographic stochasticity, and also greatly improve dispersal success. The spatial dimensions that are important to the operating of natural metapopulations, and central to models that simulate them, were rendered irrelevant insofar as management interventions dictated the mixing of individuals between subpopulations in the managed metapopulation.

The large distances between subpopulations were considered likely to increase resilience of the metapopulation as a whole to stochastic events. For example, the extinction of a sizable wild dog population in the Serengeti ecosystem in 1991 was attributed to a rabies outbreak, although this was never proven (Burrows, 1992; Kat *et al.*, 1995). The impacts of such catastrophic events would be partially avoided in a managed metapopulation by spreading risks among several discrete subpopulations (Shafer, 2001).

Development of the metapopulation

The South African wild dog recovery strategy commenced with the clearly defined and measurable goal of establishing at least nine packs of wild dogs within 10 years (Mills *et al.*, 1998). In January 1998, two reserves already contained populations of reintroduced wild dogs. Wild dogs were first introduced into the 900-km^2 Hluhluwe-iMfolozi Park in KwaZulu-Natal Province in 1980. By early 1998, the population contained 12 individuals in three groups (Maddock, 1999, Somers *et al.*, 2008). Wild dogs were first reintroduced into the 600-km^2 Madikwe Game Reserve in the Northwest Province in 1995. Although the population grew to 24 animals in 1997, only three survived a rabies outbreak in early 1998 (Hofmeyr *et al.*, 2000). Between January 1998 and December 2006, seven additional subpopulations were established (Figure 2.1). Key management decisions required to develop the metapopulation included those associated with site selection, the selection of founder animals for reintroduction and the nature of post-reintroduction management (Mills *et al.*, 1998).

Site selection

The PHVA process provided a framework for prioritizing reintroduction sites based on 29 criteria identified as important for wild dog population persistence through a ranking process. The most critical variables were available biomass of potential prey, vulnerability to disease, potential for site expansion and connectivity, human population density, habitat size and the density of other competing predators (Mills *et al.*, 1998). Of the nine subpopulation sites incorporated into the metapopulation by 2006, only five were assessed at the time of the workshop, and several fulfilled only some of the criteria (Table 2.1). Details of how each criterion was assessed are not provided in the workshop report, making it impossible to retrospectively determine the usefulness of the ranking exercise, and preventing any evaluation of new sites by the same criteria. Decisions to reintroduce wild dogs into new areas were sometimes based on factors other than the *a priori* criteria prioritized at the workshop. Faced with practical and political realities, the steering group (WAG-SA) decided that, pragmatically, the willingness of reserve managers to participate in the metapopulation management process was an overwhelmingly important consideration.

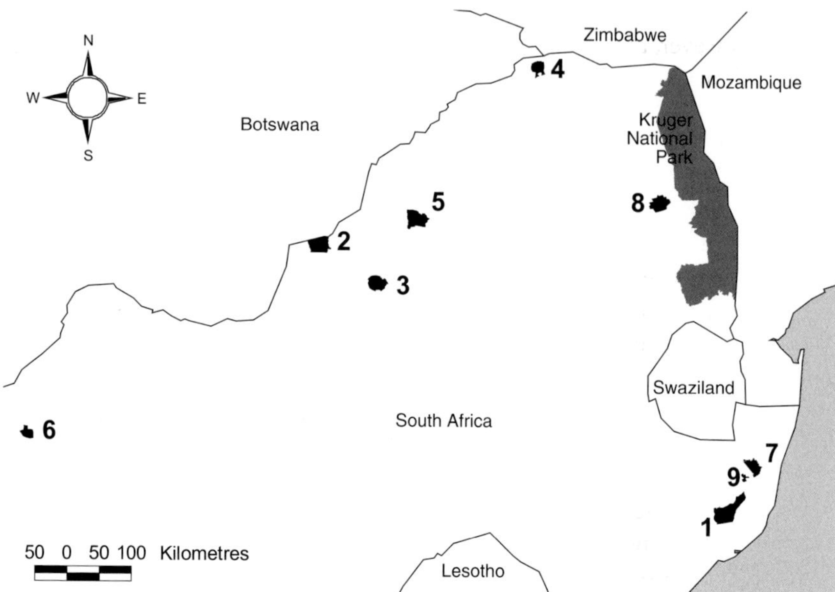

Figure 2.1 **Map showing the location of the nine wild dog subpopulations comprising the South African metapopulation. Numbers depict reserves in order of participation: 1. Hluhluwe-iMfolozi Park; 2. Madikwe Game Reserve; 3. Pilanesberg National Park; 4. De Beers Venetia Limpopo Nature Reserve; 5. Marakele National Park; 6. Tswalu Kalahari Reserve; 7. Mkhuze Game Reserve; 8. Balule Game Reserve; 9. Thanda Private Reserve.**

In addition to their inherent "suitability" for wild dogs, some subpopulation reserves were required to undergo substantial on-site preparations prior to reintroduction. All of the metapopulation reserves occurred in areas of mixed game/livestock ranching, where the potential for conflict with neighbouring communities was high. Therefore pre-reintroduction public relations programmes were an important component of release site preparation (Mills *et al.*, 1998). Government-legislated minimum fence specifications were required in order to receive permits for wild dog reintroduction, and holding enclosures were necessary to contain founding animals. The costs associated with establishing and maintaining subpopulations were considerable: mean expenditure on initial reintroductions was US$36,880 and mean annual maintenance expenditure was US$10,753 (Lindsey *et al.*, 2005a). These costs did not, however, appear to provide a major disincentive to metapopulation participation.

Founder animal selection

The selection of founder animals was based on age, sex, and immune and genetic status, as well as established hunting skills and previous exposure to competing carnivores (Mills *et al.*, 1998). Simulations using VORTEX models (Lacy, 1993), populated with field data from Kruger and Moremi Game Reserve, created confidence that animals could be captured from the wild in Kruger, Zimbabwe and Namibia in sufficient numbers to stock the subpopulations without jeopardizing source populations (Mills *et al.*, 1998).

All founder reintroductions were into areas where wild dogs had been previously extirpated and therefore contained no existing populations. A total of 66 founder individuals were used for these reintroductions (Figure 2.2a). However, only three were sourced from Kruger between 1998 and 2006. A high proportion of founders (n = 38) were wild-caught dogs captured on private farmland where conflict with livestock and game farmers threatened their survival. Ten captive-bred animals were also used. These captive animals were bonded with wild-caught stock to improve the aggregate hunting skills of reintroduced packs (Scheepers & Venzke, 1995; Gusset *et al.*, 2006). The mean size of founding packs was 9.6 ± 1.5 ($n = 9$), which comprised an average 7.0 ± 0.6 adults and yearlings with their dependent pups (<1 year-olds, Figure 2.2b). This was larger than the minimum founding pack size of six individuals recommended at the PHVA (Mills *et al.*, 1998).

Population dynamics

The mean size of litters born in the metapopulation was 8.6 ± 0.41 ($n = 50$), falling within the range of litter sizes reported elsewhere (Fuller *et al.*, 1992; Creel *et al.*, 2004). Litter size did not differ among the five subpopulation reserves with sample sizes adequate to make this comparison (Kruskal-Wallis Test, H = 1.59, 4 df, $p = 0.810$; Table 2.2). Overall pup survival was 0.64 (exact binomial CI: 0.60–0.69) and yearling survival was 0.71 (CI: 0.65–0.76). These too did not differ among sites (H = 3.24, 4 df, $p = 0.52$ and H = 2.03, 3 df,

Table 2.1 **Site attributes and founding population sizes for the nine metapopulation reserves established between 1998 and 2006.**

	Subpopulation reserves								
Details	**Hluhluwe-iMfolozi Park**	**Madikwe Game Reserve**	**Pilanesberg National Park**	**Venetia Limpopo Nature Reserve**	**Marakele National Park**	**Tswalu Kalahari Reserve**	**Balule Game Reserve**	**Mkhuze Game Reserve**	**Thanda Private Reserve**
Year joined metapopulation	1980	1995	1999	2002	2003	2004	2005	2005	2006
Protected area status	Provincial	Provincial	Provincial	Private	National	Private	Private	Provincial	Private
Assessed at PHVA?	Yes	Yes	Yes	No	Yes	Yes	No	No	No
Total biomass of potential prey (kg km^{-2})	High	Medium	High	Low	Low	Medium	Medium	High	High
Vulnerability of wild dogs to disease	High	Medium	Low	Low	Low	Low	Low	High	High
Potential expansion of the area	Yes	Yes	No	Yes	Yes	Yes	Yes	Yes	Yes

Human population density inside the area	Low	Low	Low	Low	Low	Low	Low	Low	Low
Potential linkage to other areas through corridors	Yes	Yes	No	Yes	Yes	Yes	Yes	Yes	Yes
Habitat size available (actual km^2)	900	620	500	320	740	200	200	400	50
Density of other competing carnivores (km^{-2})[a]	L < 0.1; H = 0.3	L = 2.5; H = 4.0	L = 4.5	L = 5.7; H?	0	ND	ND	L = 0; H?	ND
Number of founders	14	20	13	20	17	16	7	13	4
New individuals	8	11	11	16	16	4	0	0	0
From elsewhere in metapopulation	6	9	2	4	1	12	7	13	4

[a]L, lion; H, spotted hyena.

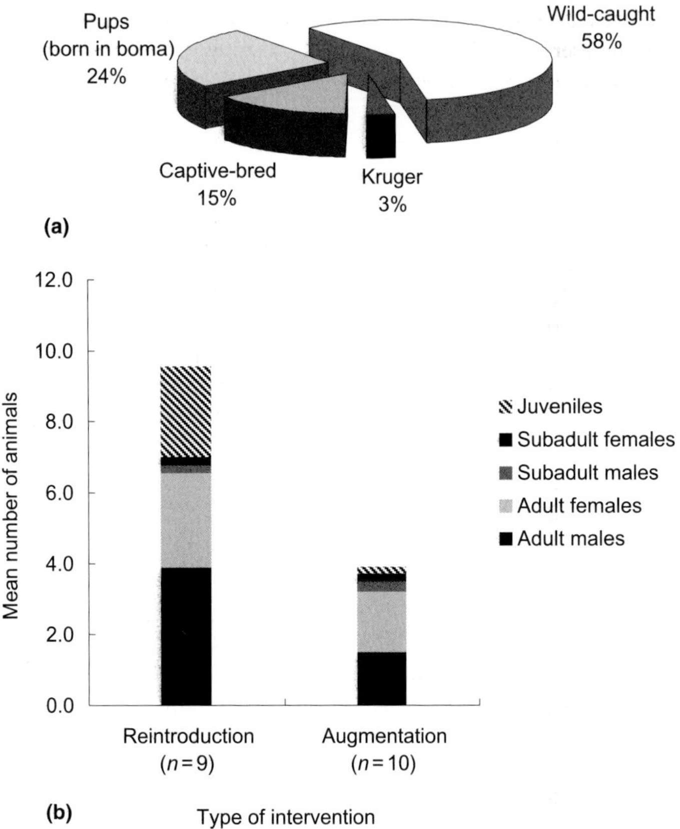

Figure 2.2 **Details of animals used in the South African wild dog metapopulation programme, including: (a) source of founders for new populations, and (b) mean group sizes for reintroductions and augmentations.**

$p = 0.57$, respectively). Altogether, 45% of pups survived to adulthood. The metapopulation reached a peak of 264 individuals in 17 packs in June 2005—at which time numbers were higher than in Kruger (120 individuals in 15 packs; Kemp & Mills, 2005; Figure 2.3). This was likely a result of the successful 2005 breeding season, in which more than 90 pups were born. This population spike was short-lived and only 60 pups were born the following season. The propensity for wild dog populations to fluctuate has been observed in

Table 2.2 **Litter size, pup survival and yearling survival statistics for the nine subpopulation reserves within the managed metapopulation. Pup survival refers to the proportion of pups surviving to 1 year; yearling survival is survival from 1 to 2 years.**

Subpopulation	Number of litters[a]	Mean litter size (±SE)	Mean pup survival (exact binomial CI)	Mean yearling survival (exact binomial CI)
Hluhluwe	18	8.3 (0.79)	0.66 (0.58–0.73)	0.67 (0.56–0.76)
Madikwe	10	9.8 (1.04)	0.60 (0.49–0.69)	0.69 (0.56–0.80)
Pilanesberg	6	8.3 (0.56)	0.76 (0.58–0.89)	0.91 (0.75–0.98)
Venetia	6	8.3 (0.71)	0.72 (0.57–0.83)	0.78 (0.61–0.90)
Marakele	5	9.8 (1.59)	0.72 (0.61–0.86)	0.60 (0.44–0.75)
Tswalu[b]	1	4.0	0.00	—
Balule[b]	2	8.0	0.25	—
Mkhuze[b]	2	7.0	0.36	—
Thanda[c]	—	—	—	—
Metapopulation	50	8.6 (0.41)	0.64 (0.61–0.86)	0.71 (0.65–0.76)

[a]Excludes litters with more than one breeding female.
[b]Sample sizes too small to conduct statistical tests.
[c]No data available as the population was only established in 2006, during which two females bred.

larger systems such as Kruger (Kemp & Mills, 2005), where it is related to rainfall (Buettner *et al.*, 2007).

Population management interventions—in which animals were translocated from one subpopulation to another—took place on 20 occasions and involved a total of 67 individuals. These translocations were undertaken to establish new subpopulations (n = 12), address demographic and genetic concerns at the subpopulation level (n = 4), promote new pack formation at release sites (n = 3), or remove dispersal groups from areas offering no further breeding opportunities (n = 1). Average group sizes for such translocations tended to be smaller (3.4 ± 0.4 adults and yearlings) than for founding packs (Figure 2.2b) and, with one exception, all involved single-sex groups. The exception occurred when a female and her mixed-sex six-month-old pups were translocated from Marakele National Park to form a founding group in Mkhuze Game Reserve in early 2005.

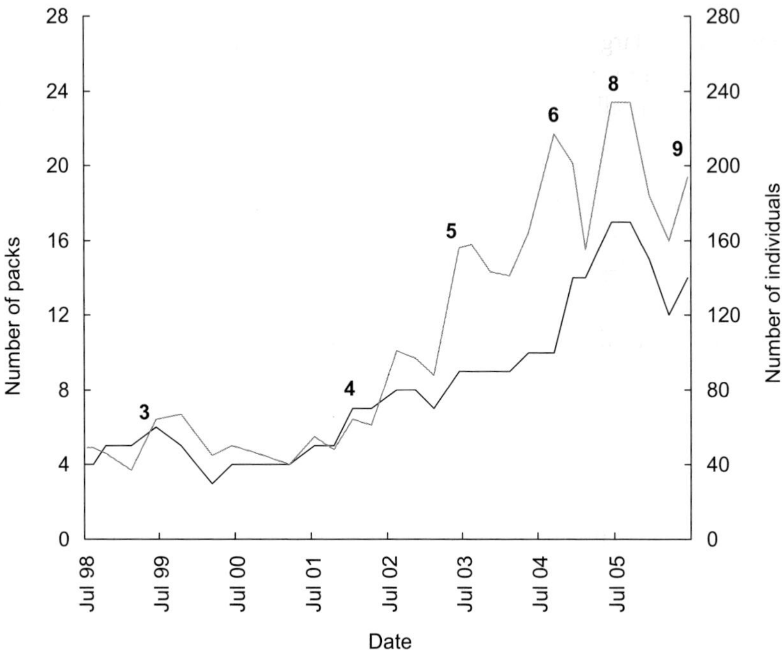

Figure 2.3 **Changes in the number of packs (solid line) and individuals (dashed line) in the South African wild dog metapopulation between 1998 and 2006. Bold numbers above the trend lines indicate the number of subpopulations in the metapopulation. Axes are scaled at 1:10, indicating a mean pack size of 10 when trend lines are aligned.**

In addition to intra-metapopulation translocations, animals were completely removed from the metapopulation on two occasions. The first was in March 2005 when one (containing 18 animals) of the two packs in Pilanesberg National Park was removed to alleviate perceived predation pressure on ungulate populations. The second involved the removal of seven males from Marakele in October 2006. These cases are discussed in more detail below.

By the end of 2006, the metapopulation encompassed a total land area of 3,930 km^2 and wild dog densities stood at 3.2 wild dogs·100 km^{-2}. This was 5.7 times higher than densities in Kruger at the beginning of 2005, when numbers were the lowest on record (0.55 wild dogs·100 km^{-2}; Kemp & Mills, 2005), and 1.6 times higher than the peak densities recorded during the census of 1995 (2.0 wild dogs·100 km^{-2}; Wilkinson, 1995). Mean wild dog densities in the metapopulation approached the upper limit of wild dog densities reported from larger conservation areas elsewhere in Africa (range: 0.2–3.5 wild dogs·100 km^{-2}; Fuller *et al.*, 1992). This was probably because the wild dogs were artificially confined and also because they effectively use fences for hunting (van Dyk & Slotow, 2003; Rhodes & Rhodes, 2004).

There was a non-significant tendency for wild dog and lion, *Panthera leo*, densities to be inversely related in the four metapopulation reserves where populations of both species were successfully established ($r_s = -0.8$, $n = 4$, $p > 0.05$). The direction of this relationship was consistent with that found in larger systems where wild dog densities are low when those of their competitors are high (Creel & Creel, 1996; Figure 2.4). Lion densities in

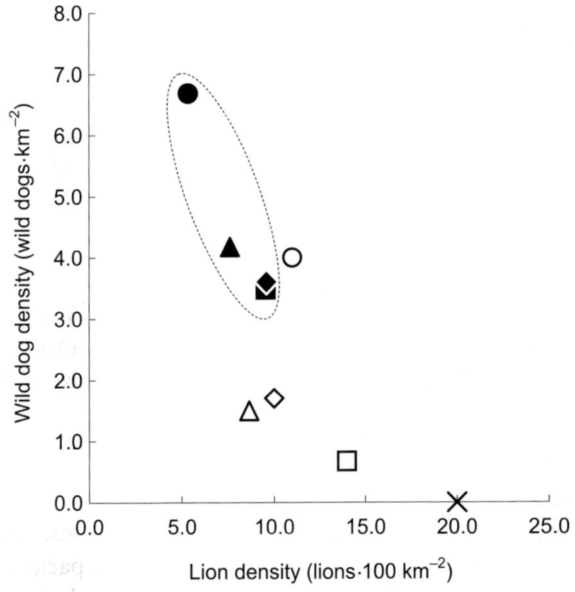

Figure 2.4 **Relationship between wild dog population density and lion population density in the four metapopulation sites where populations of both species have been established (solid symbols) and across five larger systems (open symbols). Metapopulation sites include: De Beers Venetia Limpopo Nature Reserve (●), Madikwe Game Reserve (▲), Pilanesberg National Park (◆), and Hluhluwe-iMfolozi Park (■). Densities from larger systems are sourced from Creel & Creel (1996) and include: Selous Game Reserve (○), Kruger National Park (◇), Serengeti National Park pre-1979 (△), Serengeti National Park 1979–1991 (□), and Ngorongoro Crater (×).**

metapopulation reserves tended to be lower than in larger systems and this may plausibly have contributed to the elevated wild dog densities.

Only one subpopulation extinction was experienced between 1998 and 2006. This occurred at Tswalu Kalahari Reserve ~18 months after reintroduction. Several wild dogs displayed symptoms of disease and, within a few months, all had died or disappeared. Later tests confirmed an outbreak of canine distemper (G. van Dyk, Tswalu Kalahari Reserve, South Africa; personal communication). Management interventions staved off two other inevitable subpopulation extinctions at Tswalu and De Beers Venetia Limpopo Nature Reserve. The former occurred when supplementation with additional males was necessary after all the founding males in the second reintroduction were killed by lions in September 2006 (WAG-SA minutes, 1998–2006). The latter involved the reintroduction of new adult females to Venetia 4 years after the population was first established, when the attrition of all unrelated founder adults rendered the pack unviable.

The principles of metapopulation management

The history of the managed metapopulation was fraught with questions concerning the maximum number of wild dogs that could be sustained at a given reintroduction site (WAG-SA minutes, 1998–2006). In response to this, WAG-SA issued a set of principles and guidelines emphasizing the importance of implementing the strategy within the context of biodiversity conservation that incorporates compositional, structural and functional attributes of ecosystem organization (WAG-SA, 2005). These principles stipulated that population intervention should simulate natural conditions for wild dogs as closely as possible, insofar as naturally dispersing groups form the units for new pack formation (Fuller *et al.*, 1992; Creel *et al.*, 2004). Subpopulations should be managed for the number of packs they contain, as opposed to the number of individuals within packs.

The use of natural dispersing groups for population management interventions was not always practical. The timing of dispersals was unpredictable, and dispersal events were sometimes out of synchrony with opportunities to absorb groups into existing or new subpopulations. As a result, dispersing wild dogs were occasionally placed in holding enclosures for extended periods awaiting translocation to suitable release sites (WAG-SA minutes, 1998–2006). This resulted in additional financial and personnel inputs to provision the captive packs and maintain holding enclosures (Lindsey *et al.*, 2005a). Removing dispersal groups also had the undesirable effect of curtailing natural pack formation within subpopulations, which was largely reduced to a series of "arranged marriages", with little opportunity for individual choice.

Major considerations for the managed metapopulation approach

By its nature, the managed metapopulation strategy is, as its name makes clear, managed. It demands human intervention, with its logistical challenges and occasional shortcomings and, as circumstances change, often in unforeseen ways, inevitably management has to adapt. Interventions have taken many forms, from infrastructural inputs, such as construction of holding enclosures and the erection and maintenance of perimeter fences, to monitoring populations and translocating animals (Lindsey *et al.*, 2005a; see also Table 2.3 for a general summary of challenges experienced and interventions undertaken). Sometimes, relatively minor changes in circumstances in a subpopulation have necessitated a management upheaval. Despite the diversity of these eventualities, some general experiences emerge and we discuss these below.

Managing conflict within subpopulations

Wild dog predation within subpopulation boundaries has created conflict with managers due to perceived impacts on prey populations (WAG-SA minutes, 1998–2006). The facts that most reserves rely on ecotourism to generate income and that wild dogs are highly sought-after by tourists has not offset this resentment (Davies, 1998; Lindsey *et al.*, 2005b; Gusset *et al.*, 2008a; H.T. Davies-Mostert, PhD thesis, in preparation). Wild dogs have disproportionately high daily nutritional requirements for their body size (Gorman *et al.*, 1998), and adult wild dogs require between 1.8 and 3.5 kg·dog^{-1}·day^{-1} to meet their energy demands (Fuller & Kat, 1990; Mills & Biggs, 1993; Creel & Creel, 1995). A pack of 12 individuals, which is the average size of packs in Kruger (Fuller *et al.*, 1992), preying mainly on impala, *Aepyceros melampus*, can be expected to consume 280–300 animals each year (Lindsey *et al.*, 2004a). Preliminary guidelines from the PHVA workshop suggested that reintroduction sites should contain at least 1200 impala (or prey equivalents) for each

Table 2.3 **An overview of the broad management challenges experienced, targeted concerns, and subsequent management interventions undertaken by metapopulation reserves between 1998 and 2006. Counts provide the number of reserves implementing an intervention strategy in response to a specific challenge, and therefore the maximum value for any cell is 9.**

		Broad management challenges: Targeted concerns								
		Internal conflict		External conflict		Stochastic events		Biological limitations		
Management interventions		**Perceived negative impacts on prey**	**Pressure to maintain dog numbers for tourism**	**Temporary (accidental) breakouts**	**Permanent breakouts**	**Disease outbreaks (confirmed or suspected)**	**Other mortality, rendering pack unviable**	**Unsuccessful pack bonding**	**No breeding opportunities for single-sex groups**	**Number of reserves applying intervention**
No action taken		1	0	Unknown	4	1	2	1	3	5
Reactive	Introduce additional wild dogs	—	1	0	0	2	1	2	4	5
Reactive	Manipulate pack structure	0	0	0	0	—	1	3	1	3
Reactive	Return to source subpopulation (capture or lure)	—	0	6	3	—	—	—	—	7
Reactive	Capture and remove to elsewhere within metapopulation	1	—	0	5	—	—	—	4	6

Reactive	Capture and remove dogs from metapopulation	1	—	0	1	—	—	—	0	2
	Hold dogs in quarantine	—	—	—	—	1	—	—	—	1
	Supplement prey populations	2	2	—	—	—	—	—	—	2
Preventative	Vaccinate wild dogs	—	—	—	—	2	—	—	—	2
	Improve perimeter fence integrity (structural improvements, increase patrol frequency)	—	—	2	0	—	—	—	—	2
	Fit anti-snare collars	—	—	—	—	—	2	—	—	2
	Anti-poaching patrols	—	—	—	—	—	2	—	—	2
Number of reserves experiencing management challenge ($n = 9$)		3	2	≥6	7	3	3	4	5	

pack of wild dogs they support. This estimate was refined upwards by Lindsey *et al.* (2004a), who predicted that nearly 3000 impala would be required per pack in areas where impala form a high proportion of wild dog diet. Although most metapopulation reserves met these requirements, they also contained populations of other large predators, which complicated the determination of overall "carrying capacity" for the large carnivore guild.

Wild dogs as coursing predators play an important ecological role by removing the weak and sick from prey populations (Pole *et al.*, 2004; H.T. Davies-Mostert, PhD thesis, in preparation). However, there is mounting evidence that electrified perimeter fences—such as those found on all subpopulation reserves—provide a hunting advantage to reintroduced packs, enabling them to capture prey that would otherwise have managed to escape (van Dyk & Slotow, 2003; Rhodes & Rhodes, 2004; H.T. Davies-Mostert, PhD thesis, in preparation). The diet of wild dogs within the metapopulation appears to be skewed towards larger prey animals (van Dyk & Slotow, 2003; H.T. Davies-Mostert, PhD thesis, in preparation). This might be due to a combination of fence-hunting techniques and decisions to manage for larger ungulates on small reserves (P. Funston, Tshwane University of Technology, Pretoria, South Africa; personal communication), thereby shifting the size ratio of prey populations away from buffer prey species (e.g. impala) towards larger ungulate species (e.g. zebra, *Equus burchelli* or blue wildebeest, *Connochaetes taurinus*). Greater kudu, *Tragelaphus strepticeros*, represent a possible exception to this rule as they are selected by wild dogs in a range of systems despite their large size (Hayward *et al.*, 2006b).

Predation impacts are further compounded by the managed removal of ungulates through live sales (Pilanesberg, Madikwe) and meat and trophy hunting (Venetia). Concern over declining ungulate populations led to an entire pack being removed from Pilanesberg in 2005 (WAG-SA minutes, 1998–2006) despite the absence of any evidence that low ungulate densities have a detrimental impact on ecotourism income. Concerted research efforts to assess the relationship between animal densities and ecotourism potential would help to clarify this issue.

Resolving external conflict

Subpopulation reserves are characterized by high perimeter: area ratios and hard external boundaries, so that potential for conflict between reintroduced wild dogs and neighbouring landowners is high (Woodroffe & Ginsberg, 1998). Electrified perimeter fences designed to contain predators, although useful in this regard, rarely form a completely impenetrable barrier and, where breakouts occurred, conflict often ensued (WAG-SA minutes, 1998–2006).

Breakouts took one of two forms. *Temporary* or *accidental breaches* typically occurred when wild dogs broke through boundary fences in pursuit of fleeing prey or when the integrity of the boundary fence was compromised (for example, during flooding). *Permanent breaches* occurred when natural dispersing groups deliberately broke out, seemingly as part of the process of establishing new packs outside of their natal range. In the former, it was often possible to lure packs back into the reserve (H.T. Davies-Mostert, PhD thesis, in preparation). In the latter, however, groups travelled vast distances in short periods of time (H.T. Davies-Mostert, unpublished data) and were therefore more difficult, if not impossible, to recapture.

At least eight of the nine subpopulation reserves experienced temporary or permanent breaches between 1998 and 2006 (Table 2.3). Differing levels of monitoring intensity among subpopulations made it difficult to determine the exact number of breaches that were experienced at each site, but what we do know is that breakouts led to higher levels of management intervention in some reserves than others. For example, 13 separate breaches were recorded at Marakele in the 4 years between May 2003 and April 2007 (H.T. Davies-Mostert, unpublished data). These included six permanent breakouts of single-sex dispersing groups and seven temporary breakouts of the entire pack. In contrast, Tswalu did not suffer any breakouts during this period. The factors contributing to these differences in breakout rates are poorly understood, but are likely to include frequency of fence-hunting (leading to accidental breaches), intraspecific and intraguild pressure, and the propensity of dispersers to travel long distances in search of breeding opportunities (Fuller *et al.*, 1992). Even the most "wild dog–proof" perimeter fences have suffered breaches when dispersing wild dogs have decided to leave.

Conflict resulting from breakouts may have a significant impact on reintroduced populations. In June 2004, seven yearling wild dogs from Marakele, representing 32% of all adults and yearlings in the population, were shot by a neighbouring landowner after the wild dogs broke through the perimeter fence in pursuit of a blue wildebeest. Perhaps more detrimental was the negative perception that breakouts generated among reserve neighbours and the negative effect that this had on the attitudes of managers towards participation in the metapopulation programme. The particularly high breakout rates and subsequent reputational damage to the project (and the park itself) led South African National Parks to recapture and remove the entire population from Marakele in late 2006. Conflict with neighbours ultimately reduced the number of subpopulations from nine to eight.

Strategies to reduce conflict with reserve neighbours were broadly divided into two types: those strategies that were preventative or designed to reduce the frequency of breakouts, and those aimed at managing the impacts of breakouts after they occurred. The former strategy included maintaining the integrity of perimeter fences by improving their structural impermeability—for example, by installing trip wires and fortifying river crossings, or by increasing patrol frequency to ensure that damaged fences were quickly repaired.

Strategies to minimize conflict *after* the wild dogs had escaped ranged from relatively simple tactics, such as intensifying wild dog monitoring frequency in order to reduce management response time to breakouts, to more complex and long-term strategies such as fostering public awareness of the reintroduction programme among neighbouring communities (Gusset *et al.*, 2008a). Although the latter has been suggested as a means of reducing carnivore–human conflict during large-scale reintroduction programmes (Yalden, 1993; Gusset *et al.*, 2008b), a metapopulation-wide study of factors influencing reintroduction success found that these programmes had little influence on post-reintroduction survival of wild dogs. It was postulated that this was due to the existence of predator-proof fences that limit contact between wild dogs and people living adjacent to subpopulations (Gusset *et al.*, 2008b)—in other words, the *preventative* strategies discussed above did generally work.

Other "coping" strategies to conflict mitigation included the purchase of insurance policies to cover the costs of damage inflicted upon people or property by wild dog escapees. Liability cover was not restricted to livestock, and in one case (at Venetia) payment was made after escaped wild dogs preyed on wild ungulates (H.T. Davies-Mostert, PhD thesis, in preparation). A slightly different approach was adopted by Ezemvelo KZN Wildlife—the authority responsible for wild dog subpopulations in KwaZulu-Natal Province—in which compensation was awarded to local communities neighbouring Hluhluwe and Mkhuze for proven livestock (not wildlife) losses to wild dogs. This scheme was not immune to the pitfalls that inflict compensation programmes worldwide (Nyhus *et al.*, 2003): it relied on rapid and accurate assessment of the extent of losses and, in some cases, pay-outs were perceived to be insufficient and delayed (B. Whittington-Jones, Endangered Wildlife Trust, Johannesburg, South Africa; personal communication). Perceptions among communities neighbouring Hluhluwe actually deteriorated between 2000 and 2003 (Gusset *et al.*, 2008a) and, as with similar schemes elsewhere, it is not yet clear whether compensation has significantly reduced conflict over wild dog predation in the province (Naughton-Treves *et al.*, 2003). Further investigation is required to assess the efficacy of this approach.

Stochastic events affecting small populations

With the exception of Hluhluwe, wild dog subpopulations within the managed metapopulation typically contained only one or two packs and were vulnerable to demographic stochasticity and catastrophic events (MacArthur & Wilson, 1967; Caughley, 1994). Furthermore, when no more breeding opportunities existed, they were at risk of inbreeding depression, or pack dissolution and subpopulation extinction.

Small, isolated populations are more vulnerable to disease-related mortality, not least because impacts at the pack level are disproportionately large at the population level. PHVA participants recommended the adoption of standard pre-reintroduction rabies vaccinations. However, the management challenges (including extended pre-release confinement) imposed as a result of unbonded and potentially dispersing single-sex groups led to the decision in 2004 to abandon this strategy, on the grounds that the managed metapopulation was deemed capable of absorbing subpopulation extinctions from time to time (WAG-SA, 2005).

Biological considerations

Wild dogs have social characteristics that lend themselves well to a managed metapopulation approach. The establishment of new subpopulations has been simplified by the relative ease with which new social groupings can be artificially formed (Gusset *et al.*, 2006). Despite this, wild dog social dynamics have occasionally confounded post-reintroduction population management. The reluctance of some individuals to form pack bonds has thwarted human-assisted pack formation in four of the metapopulation reserves and has required either the reintroduction of additional wild dogs, or the artificial manipulation of pack structure (through removal of individuals) to promote the formation of strong intra-pack bonds (Table 2.3).

The mechanisms of dispersal and new pack formation specific to wild dogs have also occasionally confounded metapopulation management. During the 1998–2006 period, at least five subpopulations contained single-sex groups with no breeding opportunities (Table 2.3). Methods of dealing with this ranged from taking no action, introducing additional wild dogs to stimulate new pack formation, or removing the single-sex group to another subpopulation with potential unrelated pack mates. Decisions over which interventions were most appropriate were highly dependent on conditions within the specific subpopulation (and the metapopulation overall) at the time. For example, a lone male at Venetia was left to roam freely on the reserve for 2 years because he was a single male, and at the time other subpopulations did not require augmentation. Conversely, when a group of three 2-year-old females dispersed from the Venetia pack in mid-2004, they were promptly captured and used as founding females for Tswalu. For the most part, management issues were discussed on a case-by-case basis among WAG-SA members and were solved collaboratively.

Technical and financial aspects of metapopulation management

Recovery programmes to restore large mammalian carnivores through reintroduction are logistically and technically complex (Reading *et al.*, 1997), and the South African wild dog recovery strategy was no exception. Metapopulation management was intensive and expensive and required considerable outlays in terms of expertise, materials, time and personnel (Lindsey *et al.*, 2005a). Mean expenditure on initial reintroductions was as much as US$36,880 per site and mean annual maintenance costs were US$10,753, excluding the potential costs of wild dog predation should prey populations require augmentation (Lindsey *et al.*, 2005a). Despite this, the direct costs of the programme were readily absorbed by the subpopulation reserves, several of which are privately owned and therefore received no government assistance or substantial donor funding. Participation in the metapopulation held the promise of tangible rewards: wild dogs are a high-profile game viewing species and can contribute to the income-earning potential of reserves (Lindsey, 2005b; Gusset *et al.*, 2008a). Although there is some evidence that tourism income can partially offset the costs of fence maintenance and other wild dog–related management interventions (Hayward *et al.*, 2007), this has yet to be proven across a range of systems. It might therefore seem surprising that several private reserves—whose key focus was the direct generation of profits—were so willing to invest in the programme. However, the reputational value—and subsequent indirect benefits—of publicly contributing to the conservation of South Africa's most endangered large carnivore is likely to have offset the investment costs.

Organizational continuity has been shown to improve the success of species-recovery programmes elsewhere (Phillips *et al.*, 2003). The implementation of the South African metapopulation programme has benefited from close collaboration among metapopulation managers. Quarterly WAG-SA meetings provided opportunities for in-depth discussions on various management options, while reinforcing the view of the metapopulation as a single population that needed to be collectively managed.

The value of the managed metapopulation approach for the recovery of wild dogs and other endangered large carnivores elsewhere

Less than 10 years after its inception, the primary goal identified in the wild dog PHVA workshop of 1997 had been achieved: namely to establish a series of wild dog subpopulations in South Africa outside of Kruger containing at least nine wild dog packs. Inevitably, some of the challenges that had been anticipated in the PHVA proved to be more serious than others. For example, total prey biomass available at metapopulation sites emerged as a recurrent topic of prolonged discussions at several WAG-SA meetings, while the density of competing carnivores appeared to be less problematic in practice than had been anticipated during the PHVA and in our results (Figure 2.4) (Gusset *et al.*, 2008b).

One unexpected challenge arose from the frequently rapid population increases that followed initial wild dog reintroductions. Despite evidence from larger conservation areas that wild dog populations are highly dynamic and prone to large fluctuations (Fuller *et al.*, 1992), managers were sometimes reluctant to accept similar dynamics in subpopulation reserves. By 2002, concerns were being raised at nearly every WAG-SA meeting about the capacity of some reserves—most notably those in the northern part of the country—

to support high wild dog densities (WAG-SA minutes, 1998–2006). Research to determine the extent to which small fenced reserves can absorb fluctuations in predator and prey populations—in the context of what is both ecologically and economically acceptable—will help to further refine the minimum size and prey thresholds for future wild dog reintroductions, and for those of other large predators.

In addition to achieving the primary goal, there have been other benefits from the programme. The 10 years of experience managing small wild dog populations has given us a better understanding of how to deal with specific challenges. For example, although the broad parameters of capture and translocation were well understood by a few individuals in the late 1990s, repeated interventions as demanded by the growth of the metapopulation have increased the number of skilled personnel able to carry out these activities. Similarly, we have learned that although packs can be artificially bonded with relative ease, situations sometimes arise that require additional pack manipulation to ensure that bonding is successful (Gusset *et al.*, 2006). These skills will benefit wild dog conservation activities elsewhere in Africa, wherever direct management intervention is called for. The programme has also improved understanding of factors influencing wild dog reintroduction success (Gusset *et al.*, 2008b).

The managed metapopulation approach is most obviously applicable for species inhabiting fragmented landscapes with little opportunity for natural dispersal—circumstances that are particularly likely to apply to large mammals. For example, the identification and protection of a few critical tiger, *Panthera tigris*, habitats in India has been identified as a conservation priority (WCS, 1995). Tiger populations risk a high probability of local extinction when they occur in protected areas that are too small to support viable populations of tigers in the long term, and surrounded by patches of unsuitable matrix within which successful dispersal is unlikely, and thus where unmanaged metapopulation dynamics are frustrated (Hanski, 1994; Wikramanayake *et al.*, 2004). Conservation efforts have aimed at improving dispersal probabilities to maintain a larger metapopulation of protected tiger populations (Wikramanayake *et al.*, 2004). However, with ever-increasing human population pressure, there may be cases where this is impossible, and intervention through translocation is the only means by which to ensure gene flow. Similarly, lions in South Africa are unable to persist outside conservation areas and, for them too, the managed metapopulation approach may become essential (Slotow & Hunter, this volume). In such fragmented environments, and especially in the case of large carnivores, an essential element of any conservation intervention will be conflict mitigation, and this is conspicuously so for metapopulation management. This will require not only ingenuity but also funding. For example, Gusset *et al.*, (2008b) found impermeable perimeter fences to be particularly important for the survival of reintroduced wild dogs, and these are expensive.

A further example might be cheetahs in South Africa, which also provoke conflict beyond protected areas (Marnewick *et al.*, this volume). Inevitably, compromising the "naturalness" of protected populations engenders controversy (Athreya, 2006). However, translocated populations (which are often small and isolated) will require ongoing intensive management to ensure genetic vigour and, reluctantly, the unavoidable conclusion may be that translocations may increasingly be the least detrimental option for salvaging demographic viability.

Future strategies for wild dog conservation in South Africa

The managed metapopulation approach has been successful in increasing the number of free-ranging wild dogs in South Africa, making innovative use of an existing network of fenced private reserves. However, the maintenance of this metapopulation requires an open-ended commitment to skilled management, consuming both time and money in perpetuity (Woodroffe & Ginsberg, 1999). It is, metaphorically, a functional analgesic relieving the chronically disrupted natural processes of the wild dog's biology in South Africa. A greater hope, therefore, lies in remedying the fundamental ailment through restoring connected landscapes—for example, through the formation of trans-frontier conservation areas that may facilitate natural metapopulation dynamics. Similarly, large-scale wildlife conservancies, whose members tend to be more tolerant of predators than are single-tenant landowners (Lindsey *et al.*, 2005), also have the potential to provide important refuges for wild dogs and other predators (Lindsey *et al.*, this volume). We recommend that the continued management and expansion of the managed wild dog metapopulation should run in parallel with such fundamental and innovative large-scale restoration. Significantly, the important palliative care provided by the managed metapopulation should not be mistaken for the final goal, and certainly should not become an excuse for neglecting restoration. A combination of education and awareness programmes, tax incentives for conservancy formation, innovative management of human–wildlife conflict, and the identification and protection of suitable dispersal corridors will be needed to restore natural processes to wild dog biology in South Africa beyond Kruger. In the meantime, the quasi-experiment of the managed metapopulation approach has doubled the numbers of free-ranging wild dogs in the country and has enhanced their protection (insofar as not all the conservation eggs are in one basket), while providing both pleasure, and some revenue, to a growing number of people who may in future therefore place a higher value on these beautiful creatures.

Conclusions

1. The primary goal identified in the 1997 wild dog PHVA workshop was achieved less than 10 years after its inception, through an approach that we call "the managed metapopulation". In short, a constellation of nine wild dog subpopulations, each comprising one or two packs, was established outside of Kruger.
2. The process of establishing and managing wild dog subpopulations was highly management intensive, demanding considerable input of both finance and skilled personnel.
3. The experiences gleaned through delivering this outcome over the past 10 years have increased the technical capacity to manage wild dogs, and this has the potential to contribute to improved wild dog management practices elsewhere, and perhaps to offer lessons more widely to similar schemes in Africa.
4. Managed metapopulations could be a useful tool for the conservation of some other carnivore species in fragmented landscapes where natural dispersal processes are impeded by human activities.
5. Although the quasi-experiment of the South African managed metapopulation has delivered its primary aim, this approach should not distract effort from restoring natural metapopulation processes by recreating connectivity to facilitate natural population dynamics and to reduce the intensive management required to ensure metapopulation viability.

Acknowledgements

HDM is supported through grants from Fauna & Flora International and from Siren, and through funds provided by Land Rover South Africa and by De Beers Consolidate Mines, both through the Endangered Wildlife Trust. We are grateful to the various Wild Dog Advisory Group of South Africa members who have provided subpopulation details over the years. Peter Lindsey and Markus Gusset provided useful comments on the manuscript.

References

Akçakaya, H.R., Mills, M.G.L. & Doncaster, C.P. (2007) The role of metapopulations in conservation. *Key Topics in Conservation Biology.* (eds D. Macdonald & K. Service), pp. 64–84. Blackwell Publishing, Oxford.

Athreya, V. (2006) Is relocation a viable option for unwanted animals? The case of the leopard in India. *Conservation and Society* 4, 419–423.

Barbaut, R. & Sastrapradja, S.D. (1995) Generation, maintenance and loss of biodiversity. *Global Biodiversity Assessment.* (ed W.H. Heywood), pp. 193–274. Cambridge University Press, Cambridge.

Barnes, R.F.W. (1999) Is there a future for elephants in West Africa? *Mammal Review* 29, 175–199.

Breitenmoser, U., Breitenmoser-Würsten, C., Okarma, H. et al. (2000) *The Action Plan for the Conservation of the Eurasian Lynx (*Lynx lynx*) in Europe.* Council of Europe, Bern Convention Meeting, Bern, Switzerland.

Buettner, U.K., Davies-Mostert, H.T., du Toit, J.T. & Mills, M.G.L. (2007) Factors affecting juvenile survival in African wild dogs (*Lycaon pictus*) in Kruger National Park, South Africa. *Journal of Zoology, London* 272, 10–19.

Burrows, R. (1992) Rabies in wild dogs. *Nature* 359, 277.

Caughley, G. (1994) Directions in conservation biology. *Journal of Animal Ecology* 63, 215–244.

Childes, S.L. (1988) The past history, present status and distribution of the hunting dog *Lycaon pictus* in Zimbabwe. *Biological Conservation* 44, 301–316.

Creel, S.R. & Creel, N.M. (1995) Communal hunting and pack size in African wild dogs, *Lycaon pictus. Animal Behaviour* 50, 1325–1339.

Creel, S.R. & Creel, N.M. (1996) Limitation of African wild dogs by competition with larger carnivores. *Conservation Biology* 10, 1–15.

Creel, S.R., Mills, M.G.L. & McNutt, J.W. (2004) Demography and population dynamics of African wild dogs in three critical populations. *Biology and Conservation of*

Wild Canids. (eds D.W. MacDonald & C. Sillero-Zubiri), pp. 337–350. Oxford University Press, Oxford.

Davies, H.T. (1998) *The Suitability of Matusadona National Park as a Site for Wild Dog* (Lycaon pictus) *Reintroduction.* MSc thesis, University of Zimbabwe.

Davies-Mostert, H.T. (in preparation) *The Utility of the Metapopulation Approach for Wild Dog (*Lycaon pictus*) Conservation in South Africa.* PhD thesis, University of Oxford.

Fanshawe, J.H., Frame, L.H. & Ginsberg, J.R. (1991) The wild dog—Africa's vanishing carnivore. *Oryx* 25, 137–146.

Fuller, T.K. & Kat, P.W. (1990) Movements, activity, and prey relationships of African wild dogs (*Lycaon pictus*) near Aitong, southwestern Kenya. *African Journal of Ecology* 28, 330–350.

Fuller, T.K., Kat, P.W., Bulger, J.B. et al. (1992) Population dynamics of African wild dogs. *Wildlife 2001: Populations.* (eds D.R. McCullough & H. Barrett), pp. 1125–1139. Elsevier Science Publishers, London.

Gaona, P., Ferreras, P. & Delibes, M. (1998) Dynamics and viability of the endangered Iberian lynx (*Lynx pardinus*). *Ecological Monographs* 68, 349–370.

Ginsberg, J.R., Alexander, K.A., Creel, S., Kat, P.W., McNutt, J.W. & Mills, M.G.L. (1995a) Handling and survivorship of African wild dog (*Lycaon pictus*) in five ecosystems. *Conservation Biology* 9, 665–674.

Ginsberg, J.R., Mace, G.M. & Albon, S.D. (1995b) Local extinction in a small and declining population: Wild dogs in the Serengeti. *Proceedings of the Royal Society of London B* 262, 221–228.

Gorman, M.L., Mills, M.G.L., Raath, J.P. & Speakman, J.R. (1998) High hunting costs make African wild dogs vulnerable to kleptoparasitism by hyaenas. *Nature* 391, 479–481.

Gusset, M., Maddock, A.H., Gunther, G.J. et al. (2008a) Conflicting human interests over the re-introduction of endangered wild dogs in South Africa. *Biodiversity and Conservation* 17, 83–101.

Gusset, M., Ryan, S.J., Hofmeyr, M. et al. (2008b) Efforts going to the dogs? Evaluating attempts to re-introduce endangered wild dogs in South Africa. *Journal of Applied Ecology* 45, 100–108.

Gusset, M., Slotow, R. & Somers, M.J. (2006) Divided we fail: The importance of social integration for the re-introduction of endangered African wild dogs (*Lycaon pictus*). *Journal of Zoology, London* 270, 502–511.

Hanks, J. (2001) Conservation strategies for Africa's large mammals. *Reproduction Fertility and Development* 13, 459–468.

Hanski, I.A. (1994) A practical model of metapopulation dynamics. *Journal of Animal Ecology* 63, 151–162.

Hanski, I. & Simberloff, D. (1997) The metapopulation approach, its history, conceptual domain and application to conservation. *Metapopulation Biology: Ecology, Genetics and Evolution.* (eds I. Hanski & M.E. Gilpin), pp. 5–26. Academic Press, San Diego, California.

Harrison, S. (1994) Metapopulations and conservation. *Large-Scale Ecology and Conservation Biology.* (eds P.J. Edwards, R.M. May & N.R. Webb), pp. 111–128. Blackwell, Oxford.

Hayward, M.W., Adendorf, J., Moolman, L., Hayward, G.J. & Kerley, G.I.H. (2006a) The successful reintroduction of leopard *Panthera pardus* to the Addo Elephant National Park. *African Journal of Ecology* 45, 103–104.

Hayward, M.W., Adendorf, J., O'Brien, J. et al. (2007) Practical considerations for the reintroduction of large, terrestrial, mammalian predators based on reintroductions to South Africa's Eastern Cape Province. *The Open Conservation Biology Journal* 1, 1–11.

Hayward, M.W., O'Brien, J., Hofmeyr, M., & Kerley, G.I.H. (2006b) Prey preferences of the African wild dog *Lycaon pictus* (Canidae: Carnivora): Ecological requirements for conservation. *Journal of Mammalogy* 87, 1122–1131.

Hofmeyr, M., Bingham, J., Lane, E. P., Ide, A. & Nel, L. (2000) Rabies in African wild dogs (*Lycaon pictus*) in the Madikwe Game Reserve, South Africa. *Veterinary Record* 146, 50–52.

IUCN (2006) *2006 IUCN Red List of Threatened Species.* Available: <www.iucnredlist.org>. Accessed 26 August 2007.

Kat, P.W., Alexander, K.A., Smith, J.S. & Munson, L. (1995) Rabies and African wild dogs in Kenya. *Proceedings of the Royal Society of London* 262, 229–223.

Kemp, L. & Mills, M.G.L. (2005) The 4th Wild Dog and 2nd Cheetah Photographic Census in Kruger National Park. SANParks, unpublished report.

Kinnaird, M.F., Sanderson, E.W., O'Brien, T.G., Wibisono, H.T., & Woolmer, G. (2003) Deforestation trends in a tropical landscape and implications for endangered large mammals. *Conservation Biology* 17, 245–257.

Lacy, R. (1993) Vortex: A computer simulation model for population viability analysis. *Wildlife Research* 20, 45–65.

Levins, R.A. (1969) Some demographic and genetic consequences of environmental heterogeneity for biological control. *Bulletin of the Entomological Society of America* 15, 237–240.

Lindsey, P.A., Alexander, R., du Toit, J.T. & Mills, M.G.L. (2005a) The cost efficiency of wild dog conservation in South Africa. *Conservation Biology* 19, 1205–1214.

Lindsey, P.A., Alexander, R.R., du Toit, J.T. & Mills, M.G.L. (2005b) The potential contribution of ecotourism to African wild dog *Lycaon pictus* conservation in South Africa. *Biological Conservation* 123, 339–348.

Lindsey, P.A., du Toit, J.T. & Mills, M.G.L. (2004a) Area and prey requirements of African wild dogs under varying habitat conditions: Implications for reintroductions. *South African Journal of Wildlife Research* 34, 77–96.

Lindsey, P.A., du Toit, J.T. & Mills, M.G.L. (2004b) The distribution and population status of African wild dogs (*Lycaon pictus*) outside protected areas in South Africa. *South African Journal of Wildlife Research* 34, 143–151.

Lindsey, P.A., du Toit, J.T. & Mills, M.G.L. (2005) Attitudes of ranchers towards African wild dogs *Lycaon pictus*: Conservation implications on private land. *Biological Conservation* 125, 113–121.

Liu, J., Ouyang, Z., Taylor, W.W., Groop, R., Tan, Y. & Zhang, H. (1999) A framework for evaluating the effects of human factors on wildlife habitat: The case of giant pandas. *Conservation Biology* 13, 1360–1370.

MacArthur, R.H. & Wilson, E.O. (1967) *The Theory of Island Biogeography.* Princeton University Press, Princeton, New Jersey.

Maddock, A. H. (1999) Wild dog demography in Hluhluwe-Umfolozi Park, South Africa. *Conservation Biology* 13, 412–417.

Mills, M.G.L. & Biggs, H.C. (1993) Prey apportionment and related ecological relationships between large carnivores in Kruger National Park. *Symposium of the Zoological Society of London* 65, 253–268.

Mills, M.G.L., Ellis, S., Woodroffe, R. et al. (1998) *Population Habitat and Viability Assessment for the African Wild Dog* (Lycaon pictus) *in Southern Africa.* Unpublished IUCN/SSC Conservation Breeding Specialist Group workshop report, Pretoria.

Naughton-Treves, L., Grossberg, R. & Treves, A. (2003) Paying for tolerance: Rural citizens' attitudes toward wolf depredation and compensation. *Conservation Biology* 17, 1500–1511.

Nyhus, P.J., Osofsky, S.A., Ferraro, P., Madden, F. & Fischer, H. (2003) Bearing the costs of human–wildlife conflict: The challenges of compensation schemes. *People and Wildlife, Conflict or Coexistence?* (eds R. Woodroffe, S. Thirgood, A. Rabinowitz), pp. 107–121. Cambridge University Press, Cambridge.

Phillips, M.K., Henry, V.G. & Kelly, B.T. (2003) Restoration of the Red Wolf. *Wolves: Behaviour, Ecology and Conservation.* (eds L.D. Mech & L. Boitani), pp. 272–288. University of Chicago Press, Chicago.

Pole, A., Gordon, I.J., Gorman, M.L. & MacAskill, M. (2004) Prey selection by African wild dogs (*Lycaon pictus*) in southern Zimbabwe. *Journal of Zoology, London* 262, 207–215.

Reading, R.P. Clark, T.W. & Griffith, B. (1997) The influence of valuation and organisational considerations on the success of rare species translocations. *Biological Conservation* 79, 217–225.

Rhodes, R. & Rhodes, G. (2004) Prey selection and use of man-made barriers by African wild dogs while hunting. *South African Journal of Wildlife Research* 34, 135–142.

Rodriguez, A. & Delibes, M. (2003) Population fragmentation and extinction in the Iberian lynx. *Biological Conservation* 109, 321–331.

Schaller, G.B. (1972) *The Serengeti Lion.* University of Chicago Press, Chicago.

Scheepers, J.L. & Venzke, K.A.E. (1995) Attempts to reintroduce African wild dogs *Lycaon pictus* into Etosha National Park, Namibia. *South African Journal of Wildlife Research* 25, 138–140.

Shafer, C.L. (2001) Inter-reserve distance. *Biological Conservation* 100, 215–227.

Sillero-Zubiri, C., Macdonald, D.W. & the IUCN/SSC Canid Specialist Group (2002) *The Ethiopian Wolf: Status Survey and Conservation Action Plan.* IUCN, Gland, Switzerland. 123pp.

Somers, M.J., Graf, J.A., Szykman, M., Slotow, R. & Gusset, M. (2008) Dynamics of a small re-introduced population of wild dogs over 25 years: Allee effects and the implications of sociality for endangered species' recovery. *Oecologia* 158, 239–247.

US Fish & Wildlife Service, (1987) Northern Rocky Mountain Wolf Recovery Plan. US Fish & Wildlife Service, Denver, Colorado. 119pp.

van der Merwe, P. & Saayman, M. (2003) Determining the economic value of game farm tourism. *Koedoe* 46, 103–112.

van Dyk, G. & Slotow, R. (2003) The effects of fences and lions on the ecology of African wild dogs reintroduced to Pilanesberg National Park, South Africa. *African Zoology* 38, 79–94.

WAG-SA (1998–2006) *Minutes of WAG-SA Meetings, 1998–2006.* Johannesburg, South Africa.

WAG-SA (2005) *Principles and Guidelines for the Management of the South African Wild Dog Metapopulation.* Unpublished document, May 2005.

WCS (Wildlife Conservation Society) (1995) *Saving the Tiger.* WCS, Bronx, New York.

Wikramanayake, E., McKnight, M., Dinerstein, E., Joshi, A, Gurung. B. & Smith, D. (2004) Designing a conservation landscape for tigers in human-dominated landscapes. *Conservation Biology* 18, 839–844.

Wilkinson, I. (1995) *The 1994/1995 Wild Dog Photographic Survey.* South African National Parks report, South African National Parks, Skukuza.

Woodroffe, R. & Ginsberg, J.R. (1998) Edge effects and the extinction of populations inside protected areas. *Science* 280, 2126–2128.

Woodroffe, R. & Ginsberg, J.R. (1999) Conserving the African wild dog *Lycaon pictus*: II. Is there a role for reintroduction? *Oryx* 33, 143–151.

Woodroffe, R., Ginsberg, J.R., Macdonald, D.W. & the IUCN/SSC Canid Specialist Group (1997) *The African Wild Dog—Status Survey and Conservation Action Plan.* IUCN, Gland, Switzerland. 166p.

Woodroffe, R., McNutt, J.W. & Mills, M.G.L. (2004) African wild dog (*Lycaon pictus*). *Canids: Foxes, Wolves, Jackals and Dogs: Status Survey and Conservation Action Plan.* (eds C. Sillero-Zubiri, M. Hoffman & D.W. Macdonald). IUCN, Gland, Switzerland.

Yalden, D.W. (1993) The problems of reintroducing carnivores. *Symposia of the Zoological Society of London* 65, 289–306.

3

Reintroduction Decisions Taken at the Incorrect Social Scale Devalue their Conservation Contribution: The African Lion in South Africa

Rob Slotow[1] *and Luke T.B. Hunter*[2]

[1]School of Biological and Conservation Sciences, University of KwaZulu-Natal
[2]Great Cats Program, Wildlife Conservation Society

Summary

Owing to the complexity of social–ecological systems, decision-making for conservation outcomes is difficult. Successful conservation decisions are compromised by mismatches in the social (human) versus ecological versus conservation scale. We assess this problem using the reintroduction of a top-order predator, the African lion, *Panthera leo*, into 37 different small reserves in South Africa. Using a survey of reserves, published information and personal experience, we describe and document this ongoing reintroduction process, which began in 1991. We evaluate the contribution that this reintroduction effort makes to global and national conservation of this threatened (Vulnerable) species. We then assess the social (human) drivers influencing the decisions that were taken, including the effects of personal perspective and the institutional scale at which decisions were taken (i.e. individual, reserve, agency, national and global levels). Although the introductions have

Reintroduction of Top-Order Predators, 1st edition. Edited by M.W. Hayward and M.J. Somers.
 ISBN 978-1-4051-7680-4 (pb) and 978-1-4051-9273-6 (hb)

largely met the objectives of individual reserve management, this massive reintroduction process makes little contribution to conservation of this threatened species. This is because of the lack of integrity of origin of populations, and fragmentation of non-viable individual populations that are not linked in any metapopulation framework. Personal perspective, institutional complexity (private, state, state–private partnership), institutional structure (civil service versus parastatal), institutional age and institutional size all affected decisions. Inappropriate decisions were taken because of mismatches in the social scale versus the scale of the ecological or conservation problem. This mismatch in scaling continues, and we highlight particularly the absence of a national conservation agency—which is the appropriate scale at which some national or globally relevant conservation decisions need to be taken and implemented. We encourage similar multi-scale evaluations that focus on linkages, as well as system elements, particularly by incorporating social aspects.

Introduction

Conservation practice involves managing natural resources within an intricate human context. In seeking conservation solutions in the face of ever-increasing human threat and disturbance, and particularly in the context of sustainable use of natural resources (e.g. Ripple & Beschta, 2006), the social component is increasingly incorporated (Carpenter & Folke, 2006). However, the effects of the social context on broader conservation success is poorly formulated or studied (see Walker *et al.*, 2006). Social–ecological systems are a mechanism for incorporating social drivers into an ecological framework (Walker *et al.*, 2006) and, although a relatively recent development, progress in categorizing key system drivers is helpful in assessing the outcomes of conservation projects (e.g. Biggs *et al.*, 2008). Here, we evaluate (*sensu* Kleiman *et al.*, 2000) a broader conservation issue—the reintroduction of African lions, *Panthera leo,* throughout South Africa—and examine drivers of the decision-making process and thus of successful management, particularly the issue of mismatches in scales (*sensu* Cumming *et al.*, 2006; see Manson, 2008 for a theoretical contextualization of scaling in such systems).

Terrestrial top-order predator reintroductions take place in a particularly complex ecological and social environment. This is because they tend to be keystone ecological species within the system (Mills *et al.*, 1993), and their loss or addition to the system may cause significant effects on ecosystem structure through, for example, trophic cascades or mesopredator release (or control) (Ray *et al.*, 2005; Schmitz *et al.*, 2006; Ripple & Beschta, 2007; Carpenter *et al.*, 2008,). In addition, they tend to be dangerous cultural keystone species (*sensu* Garibaldi & Turner, 2004), the presence of which may have both negative outcomes, such as increased conflict with people (e.g. Packer *et al.*, 2005), and positive outcomes, for example ecotourism potential (Boshoff *et al.*, 2007) (and vice versa). In a conservation context, terrestrial top-order predators tend to be threatened, and therefore require a broader approach with regard to social and biodiversity issues in order to promote larger, and a greater number of, populations.

Except for the odd vagrant, by the late 1980s, lions had been exterminated from all of South Africa outside the Greater Kruger National Park and the Kgalagadi Transfrontier Park. From the early 1990s, political opportunities, economic shifts and increasing international tourism in South Africa favoured a shift in land use from livestock to nature-based tourism (Wells, 1996; Hunter *et al.*, 2007). As such, a large number of relatively small (<600 km^2), and mainly privately owned, game reserves were established in what were historically livestock and game-farming areas. Chiefly to increase their appeal to tourists, complete suites of the original large-mammal fauna, including large predators (e.g. wild dog, *Lycaon pictus*, Gusset *et al.*, 2008; and cheetah, *Acinonyx jubatus*, Hayward *et al.*, 2007a), and megaherbivores (e.g. elephant, *Loxodonta africana*, Garaï *et al.*, 2004; Slotow *et al.*, 2005) were reintroduced. The lion, the largest and arguably most charismatic of these predators, is also in demand as a tourist animal (e.g. Mbenga, 2004), and their reintroduction was planned as part of the process for many reserves. Apart from their ecotourism agenda, most reserves additionally claim biodiversity conservation as a key objective and market their product as contributing to the conservation of large mammals, including lion (various reserve managers, personal communications; Hayward *et al.*, 2007a). Note that the lion is currently classified as vulnerable on both a global assessment (IUCN, 2007) and regionally within South Africa (Friedman & Daly, 2004).

Rather than assessing whether individual lion reintroductions have been successful (which they have, see General Discussion below), we focus here on evaluating (*sensu* Kleiman *et al.*, 2000) the broader contribution of this programme to conservation *per se*. Our discussion focuses on assessing linkages among system elements rather than on the individual components only (i.e.

individual reserves)—an approach that is suitable for highlighting meaningful insights into human–environmental systems (Bennett & McGinnis, 2008). In terms of evaluating whether the reintroduction of lions has made a contribution to broader conservation, we assess whether these populations meet IUCN (International Union for the Conservation of Nature and Natural Resources) reintroduction criteria (IUCN/SSC, 1998). Specifically, we assess issues of origin and ongoing integrity of populations, plus population viability. Given that they are all small populations that would not on their own be viable, we question whether there are any metapopulation aspects (see Armstrong, 2005; Gusset *et al.*, 2008) emerging from the reintroduction process. We focus on the process, emphasizing organizational structures (*sensu* Kleiman *et al.*, 2000).

The specific objectives of this chapter are to:

1 To document the history of lion reintroductions into South Africa;
2 To assess patterns of reintroduction in order to discern key drivers of decisions;
3 To assess the current situation from an ecological, social and conservation perspective;
4 To interpret the scale at which drivers were, and are now, operating;
5 To assess the consequences of mismatches in scale on conservation best practice.Based on the insights gleaned from this study, we then make broad recommendations.

Methods

We conducted an e-mail survey of all known reintroduced, free-ranging, lion populations in South Africa as of August 2007 ($n = 37$ reserves). This excluded the naturally occurring populations in the Greater Kruger National Park reserves (private conservancies that are contiguous with Kruger) and the South African portion of the Kgalagadi Transfrontier Park (formerly Kalahari Gemsbok National Park). Our survey also excluded, Hluhluwe-iMfolozi Park (HiP) to which lions were reintroduced in the mid-1960s, when the drivers were very different; however, we have included details of a recent supplemental reintroduction to this population taking place within the time frame of the study period (1991 onwards). Eleven reserves did not complete the e-mail survey, and these were targeted, again by email, with a few key questions from the survey or were queried through telephone interview. Respondents were informed that we were performing a broad analysis of lion reintroductions in South Africa, but were not informed of our specific aims and objectives as detailed in this chapter. All reserves are fenced and are maintained as discrete, owner-operated units in which management decisions and activities typically stop at the reserve boundary (see Hayward *et al.*, 2007a; Hunter *et al.*, 2007; R. Kettles, Makalali Private Game Reserve, Hoedspruit, South Africa & R. Slotow, unpublished data, for descriptions of the typical context).

In addition to asking questions about reintroduction, population history, composition and origin of founders, the survey requested information on management interventions. Managers provided information on whether they had implemented translocation, hunting, female contraception, male vasectomy, culling (including for breakouts), male replacement, and/or prey supplementation as part of their population-management strategy. In addition, for each of female contraception, male vasectomy and culling, managers were asked their opinion on the ease of implementation of that intervention on a scale of 1 (very easy) to 5 (very difficult), as well as whether they considered it a viable option (yes/no). With regard to the latter query, managers assessed their subjective personal perspective on how appealing they viewed that option in the longer term. By contrasting their opinion on ease of implementation (i.e. their experience) with their opinion on viability, we could assess the influence of personal perspective on decision-making at this level. Managers also provided information regarding a number of concerns, including breakouts from reserves, whether a prey species had gone locally extinct because of lion predation, and whether lion had killed cheetah or wild dog.

In addition to the results of the survey, we bring to this chapter our personal experience of collaborating closely with the conservation managers on all reintroductions that took place prior to 2002. Subsequent to 2002, while we have not been associated with all reintroductions, particularly those to the Eastern Cape, we have continued to advise (*gratis*) managers of existing major reintroduced lion populations (e.g. Phinda, Pilanesberg, Madikwe, Makalali, Tembe and Welgevonden), and have been consulted on some recent reintroductions, including Thanda and Nambithi. Our discussions here also draw on relevant publications where available.

Results and discussion

Reserve ownership

Reserve ownership is a key social driver because it governs the scale at which decision-making about reintroduction takes place. Decisions for state-owned reserves may be motivated by reserve managers, but the actual decision-making takes place at a centralized, higher level in the organization. Decisions about private reserves tend to be taken at the local scale of the reserve owner. Although some private reserves are multi-owner, the majority, particularly those in the earlier reintroductions, were single-owner reserves. State–community and state–private reserves are more complex, with decision-making within the organization removed from the reserve level, and further complicated by inter-organizational agreements. The vast majority of reserves that reintroduced lions were privately owned (81%), two were state reserves, and five reserves were state–community or state–private partnerships (Table 3.1).

Table 3.1 **Ownership of reserves that have reintroduced lions by Province. Social scale of decision-making increases from private through to state–private (see text).**

Province	Private	State	State–community[a]	State–private[a]	Total
Kwazulu-Natal	5	—	1	—	6
Eastern Cape	9	1	—	—	10
Limpopo	11	—	—	1	12
Western Cape	1	—	—	—	1
North West	—	1	—	1	2
Northern Cape	2	—	—	—	2
Mpumalanga	2	—	1	1	4
Free State	—	—	—	—	0
Gauteng	—	—	—	—	0
Total	30	2	2	3	37

[a]State–community reserves are those owned by communities, but run by government agencies. State–private reserves involve partnerships, with some private land incorporated within the fence-line around the larger government-owned reserve, and the whole are is managed by the state agency.

Patterns of establishment

The first reintroduction of lions was into the state-owned HiP in the mid-1960s. A single male lion had moved naturally into the area from Mozambique, and rangers released two females in an unauthorized movement of lions from a site near Kruger National Park (Anderson, 1981). Although HiP is a state reserve, the decision at the time was taken at the level of the reserve, despite senior management objection (P. Hartley, Ezemvelo KZN Wildlife, South Africa; personal communication). This was a "hard release" with no acclimation period (see van Dyk, 1997 for a description of the alternative soft-release method, which was the approach used in all other reserves considered here). The HiP lions successfully established themselves, with the population reaching 140 animals in 900 km^2 (Maddock *et al.*, 1996). This population was intensively managed through culling during the 1980s, with all lions being removed from the northern Hluhluwe Game Reserve to enhance a herbivore reintroduction programme (Maddock *et al.*, 1996). Owing to inbreeding depression, additional lions were reintroduced into that population in four releases between 1999 and 2001 (Trinkel *et al.*, 2008). This decision was motivated by reserve management, but was authorized by the central executive (R. Slotow, personal observations).

The first properly planned and legally authorized reintroductions (i.e. with an approved reintroduction plan assessed and permitted by the relevant legislative authority) took place into privately owned reserves, Thornybush (Limpopo) in 1991 and Phinda (KwaZulu-Natal) in 1992. The major driver of reintroductions in South Africa was economic, i.e. the financial incentives associated with the ecotourism industry (Hayward *et al.*, 2007a). Even state reserves that have reintroduced lions have been largely motivated by tourism rather than by ecological factors (e.g. Addo, Hayward *et al.*, 2007a; Pilanesberg, Madikwe and Tembe, R. Slotow, personal observations), although they generally give consideration to the ecological role of lions in planning restoration (e.g. Hayward *et al.*, 2007a). Since 1994, reintroductions have continued with at least one new population established each year, with peaks in 1998, 2004 and 2005 (Figure 3.1).

The two populations in North West Province (Figure 3.1), the state-owned Pilanesberg and Madikwe, were established very early compared with other state reserves, and there were no subsequent reintroductions to that province (Table 3.1). There have also been no reintroductions of wild lions to reserves in the Free State or Gauteng Provinces. Reintroductions to the Eastern Cape

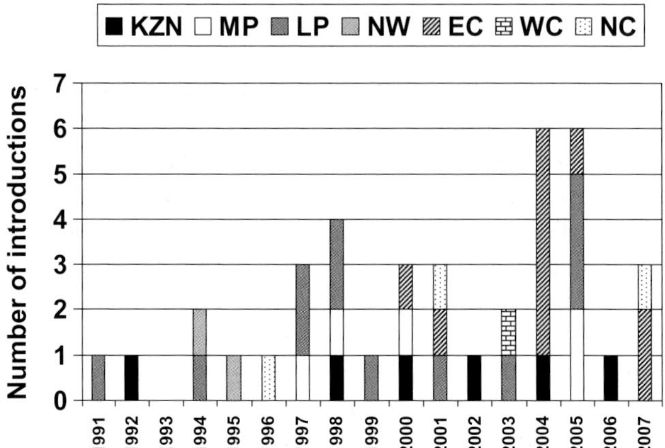

Figure 3.1 **History of reintroduction of lions into small, fenced reserves in South Africa. The first reintroduction, to Hluhluwe-iMfolozi Park (HiP) in 1965, is not shown. Additional lions were released into HiP in four groups from 1999 to 2000, but this is not shown as it was an established population. Province abbreviations: KZN, KwaZulu-Natal; MP, Mpumalanga; LP, Limpopo; NW, North West; EC, Eastern Cape; WC, Western Cape; NC, Northern Cape.**

have been a recent development, with the first release in 2000 (Hayward *et al.*, 2007b). This delay relative to other provinces was partly caused by the need to establish contiguous areas that were sufficiently large for reintroductions. The first two Eastern Cape reserves to release lions, Shamwari and Kwandwe, were both single-owner reserves. Based on the example and success of the initial reintroduction sites, landowners elsewhere in the province subsequently collaborated through the formation of conservancies to form areas sufficiently large for lion reintroductions, a process that took many years to complete.

The reintroduction of lions into a reserve in a region appeared to serve as a catalyst for larger land-use shifts to ecotourism, as well as for subsequent enlarging of fenced units to enable lion reintroductions. These "catalyst" reserves were Phinda in KwaZulu-Natal; Makalali and Welgevonden in Limpopo; and Shamwari and Kwandwe in the Eastern Cape. The original reserve was enlarged by other owners joining (e.g. Phinda, Hunter *et al.*, 2007; Makalali, Druce *et al.*, 2004), or other reserves were formed in the region, often adjacent or close to the catalyst (e.g. Eastern Cape, Hayward *et al.*, 2007b).

At the time of writing, there are no wild lions in Gauteng or Free State, or on private reserves in North West Province, but there are many captive-bred lions in private hands (used mostly for "canned-hunting" operations, where they are kept in confined areas and therefore cannot escape) in all these provinces. These lions are maintained in enclosures and are not part of larger ecosystems (for example, they do not selectively remove prey [e.g. Druce *et al.*, 2004], nor cause prey to respond to predation risk [e.g. Hunter & Skinner, 1998]). We have not included these properties in our survey, although some general patterns are obvious and noteworthy. In particular, private land use and lion ownership in those provinces focused on consumptive use through game farming and hunting, rather than non-consumptive ecotourism. Furthermore, these landowners did not pursue the pattern seen elsewhere of consolidation and development of larger, contiguous, conservancies.

Social contextualization of the decision to reintroduce lions

The social scale of decision-making ranged from the level of the individual (or a small group) in HiP (in the 1960s) and in private reserves to the institutional level in state reserves, or to the multi-institutional level in state–partnership reserves. The decision to reintroduce was clearly "easier" at the lower level of the social scale, which we consider below.

Regarding the main reason for reintroducing lions, private individuals were essentially divided into two groups: consumptive versus non-consumptive use. In three provinces, the predominant driver was for consumptive use (i.e. captive lion operations generating hunting income; Gauteng, Free State and North West Province), whereas in other areas the decision was made primarily for non-consumptive use (i.e. free-ranging, reintroduced populations). This area dichotomy is very strong and is probably related to an economic scaling. Requiring a far greater capital investment than captive lion breeding and hunting, the establishment of free-ranging lions demands extensive land, expensive fencing, maintenance and infrastructure development (tourist camps, lodges, roads etc.). Furthermore, free-ranging lions require a sustainable prey base of naturally occurring herbivores, which must often be reintroduced themselves on a massive scale prior to lion releases (e.g. Hofmeyr *et al.*, 2003), whereas captive-bred lions can be fed on livestock (donkeys etc.) that can be shipped in as carcasses. The scale of the operation therefore dictates whether or not it is feasible to reintroduce free-ranging lions. A region's aesthetic appeal may also have been a factor, effectively dictating those areas in which private developers were interested in investing, with the open areas of the flat Free State and Gauteng grasslands historically holding less appeal for tourism than the woodland savannahs dominating the rest of South Africa. Personal perspective (aesthetic appeal) could thus have determined the region into which lions were reintroduced.

Further evidence of the importance of individual perspective in deciding where reintroduction should take place is suggested by the pattern of development near and around catalyst reserves. Once a successful reintroduction had taken place, that area effectively was elevated onto the development radar of other individuals—in other words, the risk was regarded as being lower where someone had already tested the water. It is worth noting however, that ecotourism ventures tend to increase beyond tourist carrying capacity before rationalization occurs, organizations sell-up or merge and the number of ventures stabilizes (Langholz & Kerley, 2006).

In large institutions, individual perspective plays a diminished role. When contrasting private versus state reserves, those managed by larger, older institutions (South African National Parks Board [SANParks] and Ezemvelo KwaZulu-Natal Wildlife) took longer to reintroduce lions to an area relative to time taken by private owners (Table 3.2), if we take the first reintroduction in each province as the start date. Where state reserves were first to reintroduce lions to a region, they were small, relatively young institutions (North West Parks and Tourism Board [NWP]; and Mpumalanga Parks Board—Table 3.2). However, there have been no private reintroductions of lions to those provinces (although both institutions were involved in public–private partnerships). In provinces with suitable state-owned reserves, but which have not reintroduced lions (Gauteng, Free State and Eastern Cape), all are managed by a provincial government department rather than by autonomous parastatal Parks Boards. The former are completely civil servant–run institutions, which may make such decisions particularly difficult to effect because they have to be taken at such a high level in the organization. These government departments are also responsible for implementation of broader environmental legislation and are not focused on biodiversity conservation (as the parastatal organizations are). Core conservation agendas may thus be lower priorities within such agencies.

Table 3.2 **Effect of social scale of institution on decision to reintroduce lions.**

Region	First reserve	Year of reintroduction	Owner	Second reserve	Year of reintroduction	Owner
Waterberg	Welgevonden	1998	Private	Marakele	2005	SANParks
Eastern Cape	Shamwari	2000	Private	Addo	2004	SANParks
Northern Zululand	Phinda	1992	Private	Tembe	2002	EKZNW
North West Province	Pilanesberg	1994	NWP	None	—	—
Mpumalanga	KwaMadwala	1997	MPB	None	—	—

Large, old parastatal institutions: SANParks, South African National Parks Board. EKZNW, Ezemvelo KwaZulu-Natal Wildlife.
Small, young parastatal institutions: NWP, North West Parks and Tourism Board. MPB, Mpumalanga Parks Board.
Note that reserves in Gauteng, Free State and Eastern Cape are run by civil service provincial government departments, and there are no introductions to any of the reserves that they manage, despite some reserves being suitable for free-ranging lions.

Origin of lions

Lions reintroduced to South Africa came from three source populations: the Kruger National Park and surrounding areas, the Kgalagadi Transfrontier Park and surrounding area, and Etosha National Park, in Namibia. Two populations, Pilanesberg National Park (19 lions, three pride bloodlines and one separate male bloodline; 1994) and Madikwe Game Reserve (16 lions, one additional different male bloodline from those in Pilanesberg, 1995) were established with lions imported directly from Etosha. All other parks with Etosha bloodlines reintroduced animals translocated at a later time from the small Pilanesberg and Madikwe populations.

There are five geographic clusters of reserves that have reintroduced lions (clockwise in Figure 3.2):

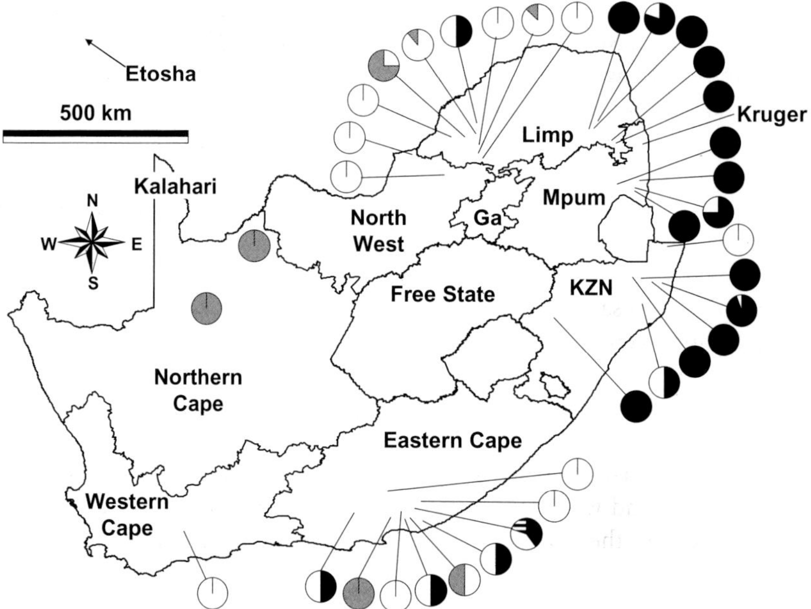

Figure 3.2 **Location and genetic origin of lions reintroduced to small fenced reserves in South Africa. Province abbreviations: Ga, Gauteng; Limp, Limpopo; Mpum, Mpumalanga; KZN, KwaZulu-Natal. Shading for pie charts indicates origin: black, Kruger Park/Lowveld; white, Etosha, Namibia, via Pilanesberg/Madikwe; grey, Kalahari. The one pie chart in the Eastern Cape with horizontal lines indicates white lions of Kruger/Lowveld origin. The indicator lines point to approximate location.**

1 Kalahari;
2 North-west savannah;
3 North-east savannah;
4 KwaZulu-Natal savannah;
5 Eastern and Western Cape.

Both reserves in the Kalahari have reintroduced lions of local, Kalahari origin (but see below). The nine reserves in the north-west savannah all have some lions of Etosha origin, with three reserves also having some Kalahari stock, and one reserve having Kruger stock. The nine reserves in the north-east all contain Kruger stock, but two reserves additionally have some Etosha stock. Five of the six reserves in the KwaZulu-Natal savannah have Kruger stock, with the other having Etosha stock; two reserves have some Etosha stock mixed with Kruger. Of the 10 reserves in the Cape cluster, the origin of lions in one was unknown, eight had Etosha stock, two had Kalahari stock and three had Kruger stock. Note that Tswalu, in the Kalahari, originally (1996) reintroduced lions of Kruger origin as they were easily available through an ownership linkage to another private reserve. However, these were removed, and local Kalahari lions, which were by then available, were reintroduced in 2001.

If we consider the potential genetic linkages of populations in the short term:

1 The north-west savannah linkage will include lions originating from Etosha and Kalahari across three reserves;
2 The north-east savannah linkage will include Etosha and Kruger stock across three reserves;
3 The Cape linkage will include Etosha, Kalahari and Kruger stock across five reserves. Longer-term potential linkages will add Kruger stock to the north-west linkage and will link Etosha and Kruger stock in KwaZulu-Natal. All clusters, except the Northern Cape, will therefore have mixed origins.

In considering the origin of reintroduced lions, there are three key factors to consider from a conservation perspective (IUCN/SSC, 1998):

1 The appropriateness of the source;
2 Retaining the genetic integrity of the source genes within the release site;
3 The potential for linkages between reserves and for retaining the source integrity through linkages.

Lions from the three original source populations are thought to be genetically closely related, with all belonging to a southern African geographic subpopulation (Barnett *et al.*, 2006), although their respective behaviours and ecology differ considerably (Packer & West, in press). Assuming animals are available from the most appropriate source (i.e. closest naturally occurring population), this argues for conservatism in planning lion reintroductions. An assessment of state-owned reserves indicates that, generally, the early reintroductions avoided mixing lions from different origins, while later reintroductions have not (Table 3.3). It is noteworthy that later reintroductions were by larger, older conservation agencies. In terms of private reserves, 19 have retained the integrity of their populations, while 10 have not (Figure 3.2). Most private reserves in the Kruger area and KwaZulu-Natal reintroduced

Table 3.3 **Assessment of conservation practice of state-managed conservation areas.**

				Good conservation practice (source population concerns[a])		
Reserve	**Year**	**Agency**	**Existing lions in region**	**Origin[b]**	**Integrity**	**Linkage**
Pilanesberg	1992	NWP	No	No[b]	Yes	Yes
Madike	1994	NWP	No	Yes	Yes	Yes
KwaMadwala	1998	MPB	No	Yes	No	No
HiP	1999	EKZNW	Yes	No[c]	No	No
Tembe	2001	EKZNW	Yes	No[d]	Yes	No
Addo	2004	SANParks	Yes	No[e]	Yes	No
Marakele	2005	SANParks	Yes	No[e]	No	No
Bongani	2005	MPB	Yes	No[d]	No	No

[a]Origin refers to the source, which should be closest to the place of reintroduction. Integrity refers to consistency in retaining the source stock. Linkage refers to consideration for reserve expansion and subsequent retention of integrity.

[b]Lions should have come from Kalahari, not Etosha. No Kalahari lions were available at the time, so the next best option (Etosha) was selected.

[c]HiP, Hluhluwe-iMfolozi Park. The reintroduction was deliberately of different stock because of severe inbreeding. In terms of integrity, the lions should have come from Kruger.

[d]Lions should have come from Kruger stock.

[e]Lions should have come from Etosha stock, given the already existing surrounding populations (although Kalahari or Kruger [whichever was closer] should have been used to found those surrounding populations).

animals from the nearest source population, i.e. Kruger (Figure 3.2). However, the main stock for both the north-western cluster and the Eastern Cape originated from Etosha via NWP. If geographic proximity and ecological similarities between origin and release sites were considered, then more appropriate stock was probably Kalahari for both the north-western cluster and Eastern Cape. In terms of linkages, private reserves have tended to retain similar stock to surrounding reserves (when lions from different sources have not been mixed). This has the advantage of creating a local genotype (see Hayward *et al.*, 2007a), but is potentially undesirable in the longer term if that genotype is not derived from the closest, more appropriate, source population.

Decision-making on the origin of lions

Decisions about genetic integrity of the populations were primarily motivated by economics and availability. SANParks sourced lions from a population under their own control (Kalahari). Ezemvelo KwaZulu-Natal Wildlife sourced lions from NWP, who donated them, verified origin and health, enhanced outbreeding (relative to their existing inbred Kruger-origin lions; Trinkel *et al.*, 2008), and provided release expertise. Mpumalanga Parks Board sourced lions from nearby Kruger, or from NWP to promote outbreeding. Private reserves sourced lions primarily according to availability. Initially, lions were available from Kruger only. In 1994, lions were imported from Etosha into NWP reserves, and offspring from these lions became available for sale to private reserves from 1996 onwards. Lions were not available from Kruger from about 1999 onwards because of the identification of bovine tuberculosis in that population. Most reserves then sourced from the readily available NWP stock, which was certified as tuberculosis-free (required for permits for translocation to be issued), and were also marketed as being:

1. Feline Immunodeficiency Virus–free (FIV is present in Kruger-origin lions except HiP);
2. Very large and attractive individuals;
3. Habituated to tourism vehicles;
4. Not prone to hunting buffalo (valuable disease-free buffalo were present on many reserves reintroducing lions).

This marketing, combined with the reintroduction expertise provided as part of the package by NWP staff successfully prioritized these Etosha-origin animals for reintroductions (over Kruger-stock animals that were available from some smaller reserves, such as Phinda and Makalali), although this was unfortunate from a genetics perspective. While reintroductions started to include Kalahari-origin lions in 2001, access to stock from SANParks is still relatively limited, with reintroductions occurring in SANParks-managed parks (Addo and Marakele) and supplementation at Welgevonden (which SANParks plans in the future to consolidate into Marakele) and Tswalu. Other Kalahari-origin lions have been obtained following removals from Tswalu.

Population parameters and management

The minimum area into which lions were released was 4 km^2 (total n = 37 reserves). However, that was a temporary measure awaiting (for 3 years) approval for release into a larger, 58 km^2, reserve (survey comments). Excluding that instance, the smallest reserve to which lions were reintroduced was 15 km^2 (Power, 2002) and the largest was 750 km^2 (Marakele). The cumulative area of the 37 reserves is 6467 km^2, an area almost one-third of the size of the Kruger National Park. The median reserve size was 122 km^2.

The mean number of lions released to a reserve was 6.1 (median = 5; range = 2–19; n = 35 reserves), giving a mean release density of 0.08 lions/km^2 (range = 0.01–0.75; n = 35 reserves). A total of 214 lions were released into these reserves. The 2007 average population size was 12.9 (total = 438; median = 8.5; range = 2–19; n = 35 reserves), giving a mean 2007 density of 0.13 lions/km^2 (median = 0.087; range = 0.01–1.25; n = 34 reserves).

There was a significant effect of reserve size on the number of lions reintroduced, as well as the current (2007) population, with both increasing with reserve size (Figure 3.3). Given that the current population is limited by management in all cases (with recent reintroductions including females under contraception), there is a relatively tight relationship between reserve size and current population. The two outliers are the largest two reserves (both state reserves), with Madikwe having a very much higher population size than predicted by the overall relationship (more than double), and Marakele having a very much lower population size than predicted by simple area requirements (but see Hayward *et al.*, 2007c for caution on simply using area rather than carrying capacity). Of the reserves that responded to our survey, nine indicated that they were above carrying capacity, six indicated that they were below carrying capacity, three indicated that they were at carrying capacity

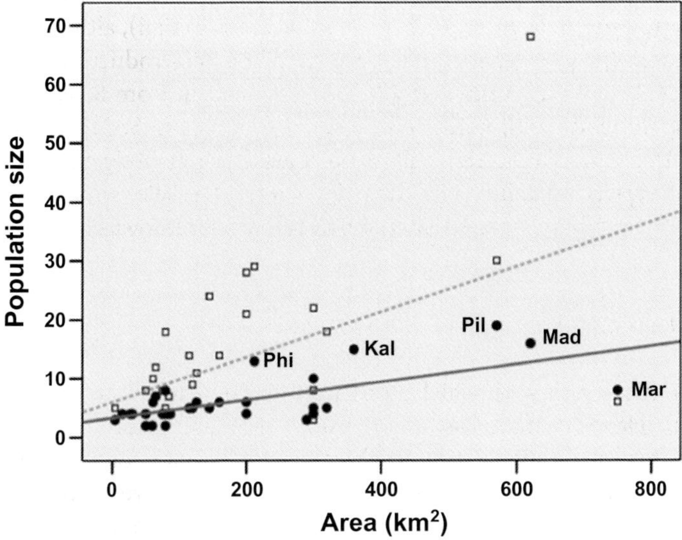

Figure 3.3 **Effect of reserve size on the decision regarding starting-population size (solid line, circles) and current (2007) population size (dashed line, squares). There was a significant positive relationship between both the reintroduced (regression analysis: $F_{1,33} = 27.05$, $p < 0.001$) and the 2007 (regression analysis: $F_{1,32} = 12.8$, $p = 0.001$) population sizes and area. Reserve abbreviations: Kal, a private reserve in the Kalahari; Mar, Marakele; Mad, Madikwe; Phi, Phinda; Pil, Pilansberg. The 2007 values for named reserves are at the same area value.**

(based on their reserve-specific ecological assessment with varying degrees of objectivity), and two indicated that they did not know. Note that even those reserves that indicated that they were above carrying capacity do manage their populations through intervention.

About half of the reserves responding ($n = 24$) indicated that they had used translocation, contraception, and culling to control lion numbers and had supplemented the prey base by additional reintroductions (Table 3.4). Six reserves had implemented hunting, eight reserves had implemented vasectomies, and seven reserves had removed and replaced (through reintroducing unrelated males) the resident adult male coalition in the population to reduce inbreeding (Table 3.4) (see Druce *et al.*, 2004; Kettles & Slotow, 2009). The range of responses for ease of implementation was from 1 (very easy) to 5 (extremely difficult) in each case, but the averages were fairly similar, with

Table 3.4 **Management interventions and concerns on 24 of the reserves that have reintroduced lions.**

Primary issues	Control methods and problems	Number of reserves	Ease of implementation[a]	Considered viable
Interventions	Translocation	13	—	—
	Hunting	6	—	—
	Female contraception	12	2.4	yes = 16; no = 2
	Male vasectomy	8	2.2	yes = 11; no = 6
	Culling (including for breakouts)	12	3	yes = 14; no = 6
	Male replacement	7	—	—
	Prey supplementation	12	—	—
Concerns	Breakouts (n = 30 responding)	17	—	—
	Prey locally extinct	3	—	—
	Lions killed cheetah	11	—	—
	Lions killed wild dog	8	—	—
	Total responding	24	—	—

[a]Ease of implementation based on responses to the survey. Average value presented from respondent scale of 1 = very easy; 5 = extremely difficult.

vasectomies being easiest, contraception next, and culling the most difficult (Table 3.4). In terms of whether managers considered the interventions viable, it is clear that personal appeal was a driver because, although vasectomies were the easiest to implement, only 65% considered it viable, and it was implemented in only two-thirds of the reserves relative to female contraception or culling. Although contraception was considered viable by almost 90% of managers, and culling by 70% of managers, they had been implemented in an equal number of reserves.

In terms of management concerns, 57% of reserves (of 30 respondents) indicated that a lion had broken out of the reserve (n = 30 reserves) (Table 3.4). In terms of other species on the reserve, a prey species had been driven to local extinction on 13% of reserves (attributed to lion predation, although empirical data are unavailable in most cases), and lions had killed cheetah on 46% of reserves and wild dogs on 33 % of reserves (Table 3.4; note that wild dog are not present on all reserves).

Decision-making about population establishment and management of reintroduced lions

Decisions about establishing lion populations generally fell into two categories. A few reserves, generally those earlier in the process, tried to establish a number of different prides and, in larger reserves, released multiple male coalitions. This meant that the starting populations were relatively large, for example Madikwe and Pilanesberg (Figure 3.3, all above the regression line). Marakele on the other hand, released a very small founding population in 2005 (Figure 3.3). Among private reserves, Phinda (1992) released a relatively large population, but subsequently private reserves have tended to reintroduce the bare minimum founding population regardless of reserve size (Figure 3.3, with the exception being a recent reintroduction into the Kalahari). If the outliers mentioned above are excluded, the regression line would be effectively flat, i.e. the founding population was as small as possible, regardless of reserve size. The main reason for this is that such decisions are technical ones, taken primarily by reserve managers at the site, who want as small a population as possible to mitigate the management issues arising from rapid population growth (Hunter *et al.*, 2007), while allowing advertising as a "big five" tourism destination (Hayward *et al.*, 2007a).

In terms of containing the population size over time, all reserves have actively controlled lion populations. The extent of that control differs substantially, with some reserves retaining as small a population as possible (e.g. Marakele, Figure 3.3), while others have allowed the population to increase substantially (e.g. Madikwe, Figure 3.3). Nine reserve managers feel that they are above carrying capacity, with their current populations indicating that they are not able to control the population as much as they would like. Furthermore, while managers have an idea of the number of lions that they desire on their reserve, this is not based on scientific assessment (Hayward *et al.*, 2007a)—i.e. personal perspectives, rather than independent science, drives decisions at this level. Note that Hayward *et al.* (2007c) provide a scientific basis to assessing carrying capacity for lion (and other predators) for some of these small reserves, and highlight that many have, at various times, exceeded carrying capacity, with resultant crashes in some prey populations.

The belief of managers that they are above carrying capacity, and their sense of inability to control numbers, is probably linked to the recent, much reduced market for live, wild lions (Hayward *et al.*, 2007a; Kettles & Slotow, 2009), reflecting the diminishing area into which it is desirable/feasible (see section above on consumptive use) to reintroduce the species in South Africa. Accordingly, the only additional technique for many reserve owners to reduce populations further is euthanasia. Euthanasia is relatively unappealing, largely because establishing lions is expensive and individual animals formerly held high value for re-sale, so managers are reluctant to simply dispose of them. Additionally, euthanasia would have to be approved both at the reserve management level (who may find it more appropriate) and at a higher social system level (who might find it more unappealing because of the broader context of their concern, e.g. retaining high ecotourism income). The same broader societal inputs may also constrain hunting of lions (Hayward *et al.*, 2007a; Kettles & Slotow, 2009). Such mismatch may lead to inaction when the higher social level decision-makers find the intervention unappealing and consider the threat relatively low (see Hill & Thompson, 2006). For now, Marakele is able to retain its population at a low level because it started with a small population and has ensured, through contraception, that the population has not increased.

All possible population-management tools have been used to manage reintroduced lion populations, and interestingly, at about the same frequency. Many reserves have used multiple approaches (see also Kettles & Slotow, 2009). It is clear from the results presented above that there was a mismatch between the experience of managers (ease of implementation) and the appeal of alternative interventions (whether they considered them viable). This mismatch highlights the role of personal perspective in decision-making. Kettles & Slotow (2009) assessed the viability of various management interventions, with similar results in terms of ease of implementation—values are given in parentheses for a range of 1 (very easy) to 5 (extremely difficult)) of interventions: Artificial takeover (male replacement) (2); live removal for translocation (2.6); female contraception (3); and male hunting (3). They conclude that interventions are more constrained by social (human) factors than by technical factors, or by the effect on the lions *per se* (e.g. behaviour) (Kettles & Slotow, 2009). Decisions about management interventions are therefore as strongly influenced by societal inputs (including personal perspective) as by technological constraints.

General discussion

This case study summarizes the scope of efforts to restore lions in South Africa and clearly indicates that populations can be successfully re-established in areas from which they have been extirpated (e.g. Druce *et al.*, 2004; Hayward *et al.*, 2007b; Hunter *et al.*, 2007; Trinkel *et al.*, 2008). However, it is clear that personal perspectives, rather than any coordinated approach, have greatly influenced both the reintroduction process and the subsequent management of lion populations. Decisions have been influenced by the relative appeal of a particular approach to an individual or small group (*sensu* Hill & Thompson, 2006). This is a problem if the context of that individual or group is broader or narrower than it should be for best-practice decisions for that particular circumstance, i.e. where there is a mismatch in the social–ecological–(conservation) system (*sensu* Cumming *et al.*, 2006). An important outcome of this assessment, therefore, is to highlight the effect that the l evel at which decisions are taken in the social system has on conservation outcomes. Mismatches in scale (Cumming *et al.*, 2006) resulted in delays in lion reintroductions, and also in errors in choosing the source of founders or replacements.

Accordingly, although reintroduced populations (including HiP) now contain more than 500 lions outside of the two naturally occurring populations of Kruger and Kalahari, each remains largely isolated from all others and each is managed as an individual, separate unit. This is clearest when reviewing the approach taken by reserves towards genetic considerations in establishing and managing lions. Although there is now scant evidence for genetic differences between the main source populations (Barnett *et al.*, 2006), this was not known at the time of most of the reintroductions. Furthermore, at that time, there was no perceived global threat to lion, making conservation of lion a relatively low priority. However, broader-level conservation genetics does not appear to drive decision-making in the ongoing management of re-established populations. Seven reserves have replaced lions (removed existing male coalitions and reintroduced new, unrelated ones, e.g. Druce *et al.*, 2004; Kettles & Slotow, 2009), and supplemented populations without removal (Trinkel *et al.*, 2004) because of genetic considerations. Such decisions continue to be taken at the reserve level, focusing on local agendas (availability or cost of founders, etc.), rather than giving attention to broader conservation goals for the species. This lack of coordination even has impacts at the level of the individual site where there has been no large-scale planning for such issues as inbreeding. Reserve managers have typically responded to such management challenges on an *ad hoc* basis as they arise, even though a coordinated effort among reserves would probably be more effective in addressing these challenges or avoiding them in advance.

The mismatch between the potential actions that could be taken if national conservation priorities were to drive decisions and the actual decisions that were taken is symptomatic of the fragmented nature of conservation planning and decision-making in many countries. Although South Africa has a national Department of Environment and Tourism, which is responsible for legislation and national regulations, the governmental agencies responsible for conservation implementation include the SANParks and nine different provincial agencies. We have identified a mismatch in the practice of these agencies based on their status (parastatal versus civil service department), and institution age and size. When private landowners are added to the milieu, this mismatch is even more significant, particularly as each province has different legislation and regulations governing translocation, release, and management of wild animals. Where national species-level conservation strategies exist, they have been formulated largely by the private and NGO sector, for example the South African Wild Dog Advisory Group (WAG-SA) and the Rhino Management Group (RMG).

The formation of these groups has resulted in national strategic plans, which have tended to drive local decisions, resulting in improved conservation outcomes. For example, WAG-SA has developed a metapopulation-management plan for wild dogs (Mills *et al.*, 1998; Davies-Mostert *et al.*, this volume), which has been successfully implemented (Gusset *et al.*, 2008) in the same country, and with a subset of the same reserves reintroducing lions. WAG-SA identifies appropriate areas, selects founder stock from appropriate wild and captive (managed through a stud-book) origins, and plans removals from reserves based on the needs of the national programme. This approach indicates success at the level of individual reserves, which now have wild dogs to contribute to achieving reserve-level objectives (as with lions) but, more importantly, the national wild dog metapopulation provides a strong contribution to conservation at the species level at both a national and global scale.

In terms of black rhinoceros, *Diceros bicornis*, the RMG made a broad assessment of habitat that would be suitable for establishment of new populations and specifically targeted those areas for reintroduction. As all suitable state reserves already have populations, they have recently established new populations on one community and three private reserves. This rhino expansion project was the key driver for a group of private reserves to form a larger conservancy in order to be eligible for rhino reintroduction and for a community reserve to be established on an area returned under a restitution land claim (R. Blok, Ezemvelo KZN Wildlife, South Africa; personal communication). All of these new populations are very productive in terms of offspring (S. Morgan, University of KwaZulu-Natal, South Africa & R. Slotow, unpublished data; T. Conway, Ezemvelo KZN Wildlife, South Africa; personal communication).

The lack of a national-level coordinating body for lion conservation (i.e. with the higher social level of decision-making absent) has resulted in *ad hoc* reserve-level decisions and has precluded the development of altruistic decisions at the lower social level of individual reserves, or even at the intermediate level of multi-reserve-managing conservation agencies. For wild dog and rhino, reserve managers are secure in the knowledge that there is a larger plan (contractual for rhino) for excess animals, and therefore a framework in which they take decisions to maximize productivity of those species in order to contribute to the broader conservation goals. We highlight here the need for integrated national-level conservation planning, both for the conservation of a particular species, such as the lion, but also to integrate such plans across species, e.g. including consideration of the potential impact of lions on threatened wild dogs (killed by lions on nine reserves) and cheetahs (killed on 12 reserves). Besides the lack of a national-level plan, at a local scale, managers do not have reserve-specific plans to mitigate these impacts (Slotow and Hunter, personal observations).

Thus, despite a massive, costly effort which comprises the single largest attempt to restore a felid to its historic range anywhere, the contribution to regional and global conservation priorities for the species remains in question (IUCN/SSC, 2006a,b; Hunter *et al.*, 2007). This is particularly disappointing given that lions are classified nationally as Vulnerable (Friedman & Daly, 2004), and that these reintroduced populations now comprise about 15% of the total national population. We hope this review fosters a process of planning and dialogue to enhance the conservation outcomes of this effort. As the first small step, we recommend the formation of a national action group for lion owners, using similar groups to those created for wild dogs and rhinos as a model. Ideally, we recommend planning to take place at a higher social scale than at the reserve level, with formulation of an integrated national lion metapopulation-management plan, and buy-in by individual reserves to this. Such a plan could provide a sensible framework for future management to achieve conservation objectives for lion, as well as more broadly for habitats and the species that they contain. For example, planning for consolidation of reserves into larger areas (e.g. Eastern Cape, Hayward *et al.*, 2007a), linkages (corridors, e.g. Northern Zululand, P. Goodman, Ezemvelo KZN Wildlife, South Africa; personal communication) and formation of trans-frontier conservation areas (e.g. Phongolo [Kwazulu-Natal] and Royal Jozini [Swaziland], R. Slotow, personal observations), with lion as one of the flagships. Furthermore, consolidation, linkages and planned relocations among reserves could lead to the establishment of viable, locally adapted genotypes (*sensu* May, 1991) (see Hayward *et al.*, 2007c).

We have presented a retrospective description of the reintroduction programme for lion in South Africa, an approach that has been criticized by Armstrong & Seddon (2007). We acknowledge the shortcomings of our approach in terms of the detailed understanding of each reintroduction event. However, we want to highlight what we believe is a very important concept to emerge: across broad-scale reintroduction programmes (i.e. many established populations), such a retrospective, descriptive approach provides insight into broader-scale drivers, particularly at the social level. Our focus on linkages, as well as on system elements, provides insights into this complex social (human)–environmental system (Bennett & McGinnis, 2008).

We believe that multi-scale assessments, including retrospective descriptive approaches, should be encouraged for other multi-population reintroduction programmes. Furthermore, as well as proposing a total of 10 questions for assessment, Armstrong and Seddon (2007) highlight three key questions at the metapolulation level: harvesting rates, allocation between sites and compensation for isolation. These, and their remaining questions, all highlight their focus on the biological aspects of reintroduction. Our assessment highlights the social aspects of reintroductions, and the outcomes that we have suggested above (consolidation, linkages, transfrontier conservation areas) all emerge from a social perspective of decision-making. We suggest that questions relating to social aspects of reintroductions should be included in addition to Armstrong and Seddon's (2007) 10 proposed questions for assessment. We strongly support the call by Armstrong and Seddon (2007) for more integrated analyses, particularly as they also emphasize the importance of higher levels of biological organization (metapopulation and ecosystem), but we emphasize the necessity for including aspects at all levels of the social scale as well.

As well as informing priorities and processes for ongoing and planned lion restoration in South Africa, a national lion-management group could also take an on advisory role for potential lion reintroductions elsewhere. South African practitioners have accumulated extensive technical experience in reintroducing and managing lions, which might be useful in areas undergoing similar land-use changes, for example in Namibia (Stander, 2003) and in countries in post-conflict recovery such as Angola, Rwanda and West Africa (see Henschel, this volume), which have suitable protected areas where lions are now extinct or relict. Similarly, lion populations closed to natural process such as dispersal and immigration because of anthropogenic barriers, such as the Ngorongoro Crater population, may benefit from the release of new founders. Finally, the proposal to restore Asiatic lions to the Palpur-Kuno Wildlife Sanctuary in northern Madhya Pradesh, India (Johnsingh *et al.*, 2007) could benefit from the depth of South African knowledge and experience.

Our results and interpretation highlight some cautions for top-order predator reintroductions. Although individual-based agendas can result in local successes (a free-ranging lion population that is meeting local management objectives regardless of whether it has to be more or less intensively managed for persistence), broader-level national or regional conservation value can only be ensured through decision-making and collaboration at the appropriate higher social scale. As such, reintroduction programmes should initially consider whether decisions are being taken at the appropriate level for long-term conservation value. In addition, the burdens and costs of top-order predator management could be alleviated through economies of scale by merging adjacent, or linking nearby, reserves (Hayward *et al.*, 2007a). This would result in larger contiguous conservation areas, which would be better practice for both the top-order predators, but also for the habitats and all associated species that would be protected (see Hunter *et al.*, 2007). Both of these modified approaches would require decision-making at a higher social level than current activities indicate, preferably a national-level strategy driven by a national-level collaboration.

Acknowledgements

We thank all the reserves mentioned here for providing information used in this chapter. Gus van Dyk has provided major inputs into both the practice of reintroductions and into our thinking about lion management. Craig Packer has continually encouraged, supported and enhanced our involvement with lion management. We thank the National Research Foundation (Grant 2004050400038 to RS) and the University of KwaZulu-Natal for funding. We thank Matt Hayward for the invitation and encouragement to complete this chapter and for very helpful comments on the manuscript.

References

Anderson, J.L. (1981) The re-establishment and management of lion *Panthera leo* population in Zululand, South Africa. *Biological Conservation* 1, 107–117.

Armstrong, D.P. (2005) Integrating the metapopulation and habitat paradigms for understanding broad-scale declines of species. *Conservation Biology* 19, 1402–1410.

Armstrong, D.P. & Seddon, P.J. (2007) Directions in reintroduction biology. *Trends in Ecology and Evolution* 23, 20–25.

Barnett, R., Yamaguchi, N., Barnes, I. & Cooper, A. (2006) The origin, current diversity and future conservation of the modern lion (*Panthera leo*). *Proceedings of the Royal Society B* 273, 2119–2125.

Bennett, D. & McGinnis, D. (2008) Coupled and complex: Human–environment interaction in the Greater Yellowstone Ecosystem, USA. *Geoforum* 39, 833–845.

Biggs, H.C., Slotow, R., Scholes, B. et al. (2008) Towards integrated decision-making for elephant management. *Assessment of South African Elephant Management.* (eds R.J. Scholes & K.G. Mennell), pp. 530–578. Witwatersrand University Press, Johannesburg.

Boshoff, A.F., Landman, M., Kerley, G.I.H. & Bradfield, M. (2007) Profiles, views and observations of visitors to the Addo Elephant National Park, Eastern Cape, South Africa. *South African Journal of Wildlife Research* 37, 189–196.

Carpenter, S.R. & Folke, C. (2006) Ecology for transformation. *Trends in Ecology and Evolution* 21, 309–315.

Carpenter, S.R., Brock, W.A., Cole, J.J., Kitchell, J.F. & Pace, M.L. (2008) Leading indicators of trophic cascades. *Ecology Letters* 11, 128–138.

Cumming, G.S., Cumming, D.H.M. & Redman, C.L. (2006) Scale mismatches in social-ecological systems: Causes, consequences, and solutions. *Ecology and Society* 11, 14.

Druce, D., Genis, H., Braak, J. et al. (2004) Population demography and spatial ecology of a reintroduced lion population in the Greater Makalali Conservancy, South Africa. *Koedoe* 47, 113–118.

Friedman, Y. & Daly, B. (eds) (2004) *Red data book of the mammals of South Africa: A conservation assessment.* CBSG Southern Africa, Conservation Specialist Group (SSC/IUCN), Endangered Wildlife Trust, Johannesburg.

Garaï, M.E., Slotow, R., Reilly, B. & Carr, R.D. (2004) History and success of elephant re-introductions to small fenced reserves in South Africa. *Pachyderm* 37, 28–36.

Garibaldi, A. & Turner, N. (2004) Cultural keystone species: Implications for ecological conservation and restoration. *Ecology and Society* 9, 1.

Gusset, M., Ryan, S.J, Hofmeyr, M. et al. (2008) Efforts going to the dogs? Evaluating attempts to re-introduce endangered wild dogs in South Africa. *Journal of Applied Ecology* 45, 100–108.

Hayward, M.W., Adendorff, J., O'Brien, J. et al. (2007a) Practical considerations for the reintroduction of large, terrestrial, mammalian predators based on reintroductions to South Africa's Eastern Cape Province. *The Open Conservation Biology Journal* 1, 1–11.

Hayward, M.W., Adendorff, J., O'Brien, J. et al. (2007b) The reintroduction of large carnivores to the Eastern Cape, South Africa: An assessment. *Oryx* 41, 205–214.

Hayward, M.W., O'Brien, J. & Kerley, G.I.H. (2007c) Carrying capacity of large African predators: Predictions and tests. *Biological Conservation* 139, 219–229.

Hill, S.D. & Thompson, D. (2006) Understanding managers' views of global environmental risk. *Environmental Management* 37, 773–787.

Hofmeyr, M., Davies, R., Nel, P. & Dell, S. (2003) Operation Phoenix—The introduction of larger mammals to Madikwe Game Reserve. *Madikwe Game Reserve: A Decade of Progress.* (ed M. Brett), pp. 8–20. North West Parks and Tourism Board, Rustenberg.

Hunter, L.T.B. & Skinner, J.D. (1998) Vigilance behaviour in African ungulates: The role of predation pressure. *Behaviour* 135, 195–211.

Hunter, L., Skinner, J.D., Pretorius, K. et al. (2007) Reintroducing lions *Panthera leo* to northern Kwazulu-Natal, South Africa: Short-term biological and technical successes but equivocal long-term conservation. *Oryx* 41, 196–204.

IUCN (2007) *IUCN Red List of Threatened Species*. Available: www.iucnredlist.org. Accessed 21 September 2008.

IUCN/SSC (1998) *IUCN Guidelines for Reintroduction*. IUCN, Gland, Switzerland.

IUCN/SSC Cat Specialist Group (2006a) *Regional Conservation Strategy for the Lion* Panthera leo *in Eastern and Southern Africa*. IUCN—Regional Office of Southern Africa, Gaborone.

IUCN/SSC Cat Specialist Group (2006b) *Regional Conservation Strategy for the Lion* Panthera leo *in West and Central Africa*. IUCN—Regional Office of Central Africa (BRAO) and the West and Central African Lion Conservation Network (ROCAL), Yaoundé.

Johnsingh, A.J.T., Goyal, S.P. & Qureshi, Q. (2007) Preparations for the reintroduction of Asiatic lion *Panthera leo persica* into Kuno Wildlife Sanctuary, Madhya Pradesh, India. *Oryx* 41, 93–96.

Kettles, R. & Slotow, R. (2009) Management of free-ranging lions on an enclosed game reserve. *South African Journal of Wildlife Management*. (in press)

Kleiman, D.G., Reading, R.P., Miller, B.J. et al. (2000) Improving the evaluation of conservation programs. *Conservation Biology* 14, 356–365.

Langholz, J.A. & Kerley, G.I.H. (2006) *Combining Conservation and Development on Private Lands: An Assessment of Ecotourism Based Private Game Reserves in the Eastern Cape*. Centre for African Conservation Ecology Report 56, Nelson Mandela Metropolitan University, Port Elizabeth.

Maddock, A., Anderson, A., Carlisle, F. et al. (1996) Changes in lion numbers in Hluhluwe Umfolozi Park. *Lammergeyer* 44, 6–18.

Manson, S.M. (2008) Does scale exist? An epistemological scale continuum for complex human–environment systems. *Geoforum* 39, 776–788.

May, R.M. (1991) The role of ecological theory in planning re-introduction of endangered species. *Symposia Zoological Society of London, B* 62, 145–163.

Mbenga, E. (2004) *Visitor Wildlife Viewing Preferences and Experiences in Madikwe Game Reserve, South Africa*. MSc Environmental Development dissertation, University of KwaZulu-Natal.

Mills, M.G.L., Ellis, S., Woodroffe, R. et al. (1998) *Population and Habitat Viability Assessment for the African Wild Dog (*Lycaon pictus*) in Southern Africa*. Final Workshop Report. IUCN/SSC Conservation Breeding Specialist Group, Apple Valley.

Mills, L.S., Soulé, M.E. & Doak, D.F. (1993) The keystone-species concept in ecology and conservation. *Bioscience* 43, 219–224.

Packer, C. & West, P. (in press) *Panthera leo*. The Mammals of Africa Vol 5. Carnivora, Pholidota, Perissodactyla. (eds J.S. Kingdon & M. Hoffmann). Academic Press, Amsterdam.

Packer, C., Ikanda, D., Kissui, B. & Kushnir, H. (2005) Lion attacks on humans in Tanzania—Understanding the timing and distribution of attacks on rural communities will help to prevent them. *Nature* 436, 927–928.

Power, R.J. (2002) Prey selection of lions *Panthera leo* in a small, enclosed reserve. *Koedoe* 45, 67–75.

Ray, J.C., Redford, K.H., Steneck, R.S. & Berger, J. (eds) (2005) *Large Carnivores and the Conservation of Biodiversity*. Island Press, Washington.

Ripple, W.J. & Beschta, R.L. (2006) Linking a cougar decline, trophic cascade, and catastrophic regime shift in Zion National Park. *Biological Conservation* 133, 397–408.

Ripple, W.J. & Beschta, R.L. (2007) Restoring Yellowstone's aspen with wolves. *Biological Conservation* 138, 514–519.

Schmitz, O.J., Kalies, E.L. & Booth, M.G. (2006) Alternative dynamic regimes and trophic control of plant succession. *Ecosystems* 9, 659–672.

Slotow, R., Garaï, M.E., Reilly, B., Page, B. & Carr, R.D. (2005) Population ecology of elephants re-introduced to small fenced reserves in South Africa. *South African Journal of Wildlife Research* 35, 23–32.

Stander, P.E. (2003) *The Ecology of Lions and Cheetahs Re-introduced to the Kalahari Game Lodge, Namibia*. PCT Research Paper No.2, Unpublished Report, Predator Conservation Trust, Windhoek.

Trinkel, M., Ferguson, N., Reid, A. et al. (2008) Introducing fresh genes into an inbred lion population in the Hluhluwe-Umfolozi Park, South Africa. *Animal Conservation* 11, 138–143.

van Dyk, G. (1997) Reintroduction techniques for lion (*Panthera leo*). *Proceedings of a Symposium on Lions and Leopards as Game Ranch Animals.* (ed J. van Heerden), pp. 82–91. Wildlife Group of the SA Veterinary Association, Onderstepoort.

Walker, B.H., Gunderson, L.H., Kinzig, A.P., Folke, C., Carpenter, S.R. & Schultz, L. (2006) A handful of heuristics and some propositions for understanding resilience in social-ecological systems. *Ecology and Society* 11(1), 13.

Wells, M.P. (1996) The social role of protected areas in the new South Africa. *Environmental Conservation* 23, 322–331.

4

Recovery of Eurasian Lynx in Europe: What Part has Reintroduction Played?

John D.C. Linnell[1], Urs Breitenmoser[2], Christine Breitenmoser-Würsten[2], John Odden[1] and Manuela von Arx[2]

[1]Norwegian Institute for Nature Research
[2]KORA

Summary

The distribution of Eurasian lynx, *Lynx lynx*, in Europe is currently far wider than it has been for several centuries. This recovery has been brought about through both natural recovery and by reintroduction. Of four remnant populations, three (Scandinavia, eastern Baltic and Carpathian Mountains) have shown strong recoveries. These populations have only had short periods of protection, so most recovery happened under a regime of regulated harvest. The fourth (southern Balkan) population has not shown any signs of recovery, potentially a result of its small size and isolation. There have been 15 different reintroduction attempts throughout Europe since 1971, using both wild and captive animals. Of these, six clearly failed, four are of uncertain status and five appear to have been successful. Most of these reintroduction projects have used relatively few animals, have had little follow-up and did not maintain present-day IUCN (International Union for the Conservation of Nature and Natural Resources) standards, although in their time some were clearly pioneering projects. Despite this rather *ad hoc* approach, lynx now have a solid distribution in Central Europe that would have been impossible to achieve through natural expansion. The sum total of this experience underlines the

Reintroduction of Top-Order Predators, 1st edition. Edited by M.W. Hayward and M.J. Somers.
 ISBN 978-1-4051-7680-4 (pb) and 978-1-4051-9273-6 (hb)

need to consider carnivore conservation at very large spatial and temporal scales, and to adopt a systematic conservation-planning approach, where reintroduction and natural recovery are complementary tools.

Introduction

The early to mid Holocene distribution of Eurasian lynx, *Lynx lynx*, covered all of Europe, including the British Isles, with the exception of the Iberian Peninsula (Sommer & Benecke, 2006). However, by the end of the 19th century and early 20th century, lynx distribution had been greatly reduced through a combination of direct persecution, deforestation and the loss of wild ungulate prey (Breitenmoser, 1998). By the mid-20th century, their distribution was at an all-time nadir (Kratochvil, 1968 a,b), and lynx were extinct throughout the continental part of Western Europe. Only four nuclei survived. These were: (1) Scandinavia, (2) the eastern Baltic drainage, (3) the Carpathian Mountains, and (4) the south-western Balkans. (Kratochvil, 1968a,b; Breitenmoser & Breitenmoser-Würsten, 1990; von Arx *et al.*, 2004).

The future of these surviving populations would have been bleak if it had not been for the dramatic reversals in public attitudes and wildlife-management policy that appeared in the mid-20th century. A wide range of national and international legislation provided lynx with far greater protection, and policies of extermination gave way to policies aiming at recovery or sustainable harvest. Bounties were removed and restrictions were placed on many forms of killing, such as bans on the use of poisons. Public pressure also grew for the active recovery of lynx populations through human assistance. In parallel, better management of wild ungulate species (mainly motivated by hunters seeking to increase game populations) led to a dramatic increase in prey base, and post-Second World War forestry practices rapidly increased the area of woodland across the continent (Breitenmoser, 1998; Vera, 2000; Breitenmoser & Breitenmoser-Würsten, 2008).

As a result, the present situation at the start of the 21st century is very different from that of the mid-20th century (von Arx *et al.*, 2004). The present-day distribution (Figure 4.1) and size of lynx populations is probably far greater than it has been in Europe for centuries. Our goal here is to analyse the role that reintroduction has played in this development, comparing and contrasting it to the role of natural expansion.

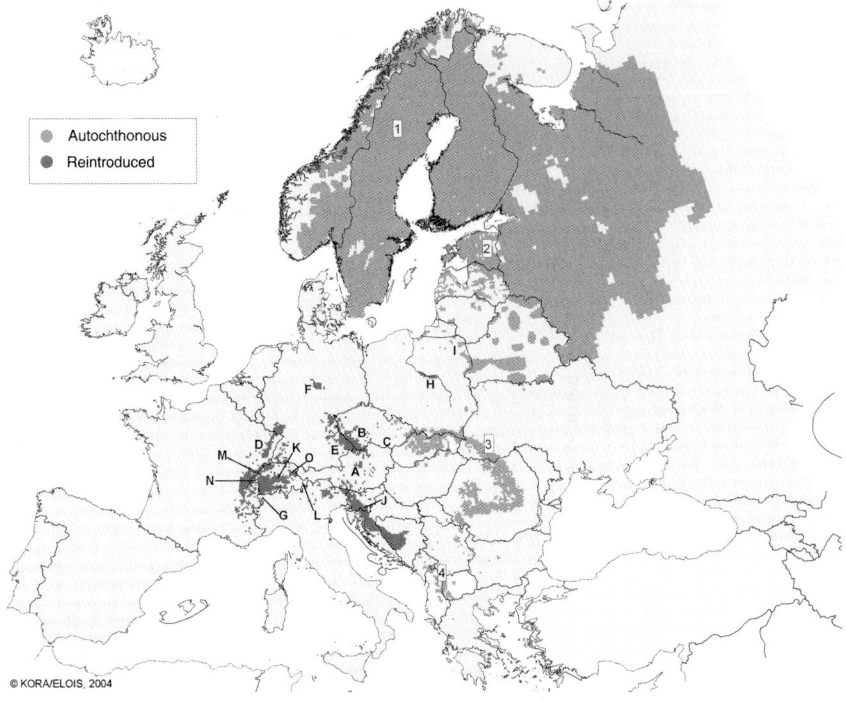

Figure 4.1 **Present distribution of Eurasian lynx in Europe, showing autochthonous and reintroduced populations in different shading (see key). Numbers 1–4 refer to the Scandinavian, Eastern Baltic, Carpathian and Balkan populations, respectively, while letters A–O refer to the 15 reintroduction sites listed in Table 4.1. Source: KORA/ELOIS.**

Overview of reintroductions

In Europe, reintroductions involving 170–175 lynx have been carried out at 15 different sites in eight countries during the past 37 years (Table 4.1; Figure 4.1). Unfortunately, very few of these reintroductions have been well studied, so our ability to evaluate them is somewhat limited. The following text provides a brief summary of those for which we have some information.

Table 4.1 **List of lynx reintroductions in Europe 1970–2007.**

ID	Country	Release location	Years	Male	Female	Total	Source	Status	Fate	Size	Reference
A	Austria	Turrach, Styria	1977–1979	6	3	9	Wild	O	F	—	1
B	Czech Republic	Bohemian Forest	1982–1989	11	7	18	Wild	O	S	75	2
C	Czech Republic	Podyji NP	1993–1994	2	2	4–6	Captive	U	F	—	3
D	France	Vosges	1983–1989	12	9	21	Wild and captive	O	S	30	4
E	Germany	Bavarian Forest	1970–1974			5–10	Wild and unknown	U	F	—	5
F	Germany	Harz	2000–2006	9	15	28	Captive	O (24) and U (4)	U	?	6
G	Italy	Gran Paradiso NP	1975	2	0	2	Wild	O	F	—	7
H	Poland	Kampinos	1992–1999	14	17	31	Captive	O	U	>10	8
I	Poland	Pisz Forest	2003–2006		2	4	Captive	O	U	?	9
J	Slovenia	Dinaric Mountains	1973	3	3	6	Wild	O	S	130	10
K	Switzerland	Western Alps	1971–1976	7	5	12	Wild	O (6) and U (6)	S	100	7, 11
L	Switzerland	Engadin	1972–1980	2	2	4	Wild	U	F	—	7, 11
M	Switzerland	Jura	1972–1975	5	5	10	Wild	O (4) and U (6)	S	80	7, 11, 12
N	Switzerland	Jorat Plateau	1989			3	Unknown	U	F	—	11
O	Switzerland	Eastern Alps	2001–2007	5	6	11	Wild	O	U	?	11

Status: O, officially sanctioned reintroduction; U, unofficial or clandestine reintroduction.

Fate: F, failed; S, success; U, uncertain; ?, unknown population size at present.

References for Table 4.1 (see References list for full details): 1. Gossow & Honsig-Erlenburg 1986; 2. Bufka & Cerveny 1996; Koubek & Cerveny 1996; 3. Reiter 1996; 4. Vandel et al. 2006; 5. Wölfl et al. 2001; 6. Anders & Sacher 2005; 7. Breitenmoser & Breitenmoser-Würsten 1990; 8. Böer et al. 1994, 1995; 9. Krzysztof Schmidt, personal communication; 10. Cop & Frkovic 1998; 11. Breitenmoser et al. 2007; 12. Breitenmoser & Baettig 1992.

Vosges (France)

This is one of the best documented reintroductions of lynx (recently summarized in Vandel *et al.*, 2006). Lynx were exterminated from the region by the 17th and 18th centuries. Between 1983 and 1993, 21 lynx were taken from zoos in the Czech Republic, Slovakia, Slovenia and the United Kingdom; although the original intention was that all lynx should have been originally wild-caught and not habituated to people. The animals were released into four separate mountain massifs within the region, in 11 different operations, using both soft- and hard-release methods. Animals were followed using telemetry. Of the 21 released, a maximum of four females and six males survived long enough to potentially breed. Of the other 11, five were lost to the population in the immediate release phase. Two were recaptured because they appeared to be too habituated to people, one died of starvation and two were illegally killed. In the following period, four more individuals were illegally shot and two died of unknown causes. There may have been some additional clandestine releases of captive lynx across the border in the German Pfälzerwald, but it does not seem that these have established a breeding population. In the Vosges, the first reproduction was confirmed in 1987, and since then at least 12 other reproductive events have been identified. By 2000–2002, lynx appeared to have a permanent presence in 2000–3000 km^2 out of a total of 5000 km^2 of potential habitat. There is no direct estimate of population size but, from the distribution area, it is estimated that there could potentially be 30 lynx in the region.

Jura (Switzerland)

Between 1972 and 1975, 10 lynx were reintroduced into the Swiss part of the Jura Mountains in a combination of officially sanctioned and clandestine releases. The animals were reportedly of wild origins (Slovakian portion of the Carpathian Mountains) and were hard-released with no follow-up, although Breitenmoser & Baettig (1992) attempted to reconstruct the development until the period of systematic monitoring started (Capt, 2007). Lynx expanded to fill a large portion of the available habitat on both sides of the Swiss–French border. At present, there are an estimated 70 lynx (66% in France), occupying an area of 7000 km^2 in the mountain range (von Arx *et al.*, 2004; Breitenmoser *et al.*, 2007; Breitenmoser-Würsten *et al.*, 2007).

Alps (Switzerland)

Between 1971 and 1976, 12 lynx were reintroduced into four areas of the western Swiss Alps in a combination of officially sanctioned and clandestine releases. The animals were reportedly of wild origin (from the Slovakian portion of the Carpathian Mountains) and were hard-released with no follow-up. Additional clandestine releases into the south-eastern Alps and the Swiss Plateau appear to have failed immediately. The lynx population in the western Swiss Alps expanded and now occupies a large portion of the north-western Alps. This distribution has been more or less stable for more than a decade, although there have been localized fluctuations. Substantial areas of habitat remain unoccupied. The recent, 2001–2007, translocation of lynx to the eastern Alps has led to a significant expansion of lynx distribution. There are currently an estimated 60–90 lynx occupying 12,000 km^2 in the Swiss Alps (Breitenmoser & Breitenmoser-Würsten, 1998, 1999; Molinari-Jobin *et al.*, 2001, 2006). Lynx have also extended their distribution into the French Alps, where there are potentially 10–15 lynx occupying 1200 km^2 (Stahl & Vandel, 2001; Marboutin *et al.*, 2006). The recent translocation of lynx from western Switzerland to the eastern Swiss Alps is in too early a stage to evaluate, although initial data indicate that lynx have survived and become established (Ryser *et al.*, 2004). This reintroduction aims to bridge the gap between the western and eastern occurrences in the Swiss Alps, as well as contributing to connectivity within the Alpine arc as a whole.

Northern Dinaric Mountains (Slovenia, Croatia)

Lynx disappeared from the northern part of the Dinaric Mountains in the early 20th century. In March 1973, six lynx were released in the Kocevje region of southern Slovenia (Cop & Frkovic, 1998). The lynx had been caught in the wild in Slovakia in January and spent 2 months in acclimatization enclosures before release. Reproduction was documented in the year of release and in all the subsequent 5 years. From 1978, the population was open for hunting and its development was monitored by the distribution of shot lynx. The population appears to have rapidly expanded, colonizing the Dinaric range throughout southern Slovenia, western Croatia and into north-western Bosnia. Some animals even spread northwards to the Alps on the borders with Italy and Austria. By the early 21st century, the expansion appears to have stagnated and possibly begun to decline, and the population is believed to be at around 130 individuals today (Stanisa *et al.*, 2001; Kos *et al.*, 2004; von Arx *et al.*, 2004).

Kampinos (Poland)

Between 1993 and 2000, 30 lynx were released in Kampinos National Park (Böer *et al.*, 1994, 1995, 2000). The lynx were all of captive origin (from zoos in Germany, Sweden and Finland). Lynx were maintained at the release site in enclosures, where they were exposed to wild prey before release. All lynx were radio-collared prior to release. Of those released, at least 13 died during the following 3 years, of which six were killed in vehicle collisions, two were killed by poachers and five died in undetermined circumstances. At least one of the released animals failed to develop hunting skills and persisted in killing livestock. At least six of the released females reproduced. By 2000, there were at least 19 lynx in the area, of which 10 were released individuals and at least five were wild-born. Released animals dispersed up to 60 km, so that lynx established themselves in at least two neighbouring forest complexes.

Harz Mountains (Germany)

Between 2000 and 2006, 24 lynx were officially released in the Harz Mountains National Park (Anders & Sacher, 2005). The animals were all of captive origin and were kept for 6–8 weeks in an acclimatization enclosure before release. The released animals were not radio-collared. Two of the released animals had to be recaptured because of a lack of shyness towards people, and seven other lynx were documented as having died following release (only one, with a broken leg, was in the immediate post-release phase; four others died from a combination of starvation and sarcoptic mange, one died in a collision with a train and one cause of death was undetermined). At least four lynx have been detected that were clandestinely released in the same area. Reproduction, of one to four litters, has been detected each year from 2002 to 2006.

Bohemian Forest/Sumava Mountains (Czech Republic, Germany)

The original reintroduction of lynx into the Bavarian National Park in Germany in the 1970s was poorly monitored and its fate is unknown. Between 1982 and

1989, 18 lynx that were wild-caught in the Slovakian Carpathians were released on the Czech side of the border (Koubek & Červeny, 1996). These animals have established themselves throughout the forest complex on the border, covering a range of approximately 18,000 km^2. The population is roughly estimated to contain 70 individuals. Reproduction is regularly observed. The main cause of death that is documented is illegal killing (Wölfl *et al.*, 2001).

Other sites

Styria, Austria

Nine lynx of wild origins were reintroduced into southern Austria between 1977 and 1979. Although the animals were radio-collared, these all malfunctioned soon after release. Records of lynx observations were kept for the next 4–5 years, and these showed that lynx spread out from the release site and survived for a number of years. There were also records of reproduction close to the release site (Gossow & Honsig-Erlenburg, 1986; Huber & Kaczensky, 1998). There are still confirmed reports of lynx presence in various parts of Austria, although it is clear that there is not a well-established population descending from the original reintroduction (Laas *et al.*, 2006).

Podyji, Czech Republic

This unofficial reintroduction involved six animals from Czech zoos that were released in, or close to, Podyji National Park in 1993–1994. One of the lynx was found dead from malnutrition 2 months after release. However, a number of kills made by lynx were found, confirming that at least some of the animals acquired predatory behaviour. No signs of lynx presence were seen after 1995, indicating that the reintroduction was a failure (Reiter, 1996).

Gran Paradiso, Italy

Two male lynx were released in 1974. One was found dead across the border in France 8 months later, while the other vanished.

Pisz Forest, Poland

So far, four lynx of zoo origin have been released during the past few years. To date, there is no information on the success of this reintroduction as there is little follow-up.

Perspectives on reintroductions

From the 15 reintroductions that have occurred in Europe, there are a number of interesting perspectives.

1 Most of these reintroductions have been badly planned and poorly followed-up, as judged by today's standards for reintroductions. Few, if any, of the guidelines provided by such international bodies as the IUCN/SSC's (Species Survival Commission) Reintroduction Specialist Group (IUCN, 1998) have been followed, despite the fact that some reintroduction projects have made claims to the contrary. The motivations for reintroductions varied enormously—although systematic conservation planning was not a feature of any, apart from the most recent in eastern Switzerland. Many were done clandestinely, and even officially sanctioned reintroductions have found that private people have been "supplementing" the reintroduction with their own animals. This reflects the somewhat chaotic status that existed in Central European legislation concerning the keeping of wild animals. This poor planning and lack of follow-up makes it hard to evaluate the reintroductions, and has certainly contributed to the high number of failed attempts. The failure to effectively monitor many reintroductions implies that it is both impossible to react in an adaptive manner to developments and to learn from the exercise (Breitenmoser *et al.*, 2001).

2 There has been widespread use of both captive-born lynx and wild lynx that have experienced extended periods in captivity, even when wild animals were potentially available. This is very controversial amongst both conservation and animal welfare groups (Jule *et al.*, 2008; Christie, this volume). However, as the examples show, it appears that at least some captive lynx are able to adapt to the wild, and have been shown to kill wild prey and to reproduce. On the other hand, in several cases, captive-born animals have starved to death and some have had to be recaptured because they did not show the desired level of shyness towards people.

3 No attention has been paid to the genetic origins of the lynx being released. Most wild lynx have come from the Carpathian Mountains which, although being geographically close to many of the release sites in Central Europe, have a distinct genetic profile compared with the former alpine and extant Balkan lynx (C. Breitenmoser-Würsten, unpublished data). When it comes to the captive lynx, these have come from a wide range of sources, including

Baltic, Carpathian and Scandinavian countries; however, many are of unknown origin as stud books are not always kept.

4 There has been very little pre-release public-relations work or release-site evaluation.

5 There has been no attempt to coordinate activities, such that lynx reintroductions contribute to restoring an interconnected metapopulation. For example, areas such as the Harz Mountains are small and isolated, implying that it is unlikely that they will ever manage to achieve a viable population or to contribute to the viability of other populations (Kramer-Schadt *et al.*, 2005). Furthermore, virtually all lynx populations are isolated and are below the threshold that will protect them from losing genetic diversity (based on Frankham, this volume). This small-scale thinking is related to both the fragmented nature of the habitat into which some lynx have been released and to the fragmented nature of the administrative divisions. Similar conservation planning and organizational problems have led to the numerous successful lion, *Panthera leo*, reintroductions being of little value for the conservation of the species in South Africa (see Slotow & Hunter, this volume).

6 Many of the reintroductions involved very small numbers (in one case, only two males were released!). Although the reintroduction into Slovenia appears to have succeeded (in the short term) when based on only six individuals, all the other successful reintroductions involved 10 or more individuals. Even this is a very small number compared with what would be recommended today. The issue of long-term genetic viability remains an open question for these populations based on small numbers of founders (Breitenmoser-Würsten & Obexer-Ruff, 2003 for lynx; Liberg *et al.*, 2005 for an example with wolves; and Frankham, this volume).

In general, the reintroduction of lynx into Europe has been an *ad hoc* affair, seemingly more motivated by idealism and a "let's see what happens" attitude rather than a coordinated, science-based approach to make the best contribution to lynx restoration in Europe. Many of these problems can be excused by the fact that many releases were conducted in the 1970s, before either the science or the guidelines were in place and, as such, these reintroductions were pioneering projects. Despite their lack of scientific rigour, the present distribution of Eurasian lynx in Western Europe owes its presence to these "amateur" efforts. However, we still see recent examples of reintroductions (e.g. Harz, Kampinos and Pisz), which contrast sharply with, for example, the translocation of lynx to the eastern Swiss Alps in terms of their flawed rationale and design. Against this background, it is surprising that so many of the reintroductions have actually been a success, at least in the short term. This being said, standards have changed, and there is a desperate need to establish and enforce good practice guidelines across Europe to ensure that future efforts are held to professional standards and are focused on a coordinated conservation goal (Breitenmoser *et al.*, 2001).

Overview of natural recoveries

Scandinavia

The decline of lynx in Scandinavia was probably driven mainly by direct persecution. A wide range of local and state bounty systems operated, starting in the 17th and 18th centuries. Most of these stayed in place in some form until the early 20th century. The lynx population reached its all-time low in the period from 1920 to 1940, when it was basically confined to an area in central Norway and central Sweden, with perhaps a few survivors in the south. During the 20th century, lynx have been subject to constantly changing hunting regulations, most of which led to greater restrictions being placed on hunters. In Sweden, the bounty was removed in 1912 and this was followed with a period of protection from 1927 to 1943. Lynx were harvested again for the next four decades, until a new phase of protection was expanded from southern areas in 1986 to the whole country in 1991. This protection was then removed in northern areas in 1995, and in all areas in 1997, to be replaced by a period of very closely controlled quota-regulated harvest/lethal control. In Norway, bounties were paid at various times by the state and the municipalities up until the 1980s, and there were no restrictions on harvest season, numbers or methods until 1982, when lynx became a game species. They have remained a game species until the present, apart from a brief period of protection from 1992 to 1994.

The Scandinavian population appears to have responded to this successively more restrictive hunting legislation and began expansion in the 1940–1960s (earlier in Sweden than in Norway) and has more or less continued until the present. The dramatic increase in the distribution and density of roe deer, *Capreolus capreolus*, during the 20th century has probably also been of great importance in helping this expansion (Andersen *et al.*, 2004). Today, there are approximately 1800–2000 lynx on the Scandinavian peninsula, distributed throughout most of Norway (except the south-western coast) and most of Sweden (there are still very few in the extreme south, although reproduction has been documented in the past few years). The population distribution and density in both countries is partly regulated by hunter harvest and by the use of lethal control in response to conflicts with livestock herders and ungulate hunters.

Eastern Baltic drainage

The timing of lynx decline in this region was similar to Scandinavia. Finland, Estonia, Latvia, north-eastern Poland and Lithuania all had critically low populations in the 1920s and 1930s. Although populations may have increased during the Second World War (Jędrzejewska & Jędrzejewski, 1998), they were rapidly suppressed after the war so that, by the 1950s, they were on the edge of extinction, only remaining in a few eastern parts of Finland, Estonia and Latvia that border onto western Russia and in a few forests in north-eastern Poland that bordered Belarus. In response, Poland gave lynx game status from 1927, and Finland removed bounties and protected lynx from 1962 to 1982, after which time they became game. Estonia, Latvia and Lithuania gradually introduced more restrictive harvest legislation. Apart from Lithuania and Poland, which protected lynx in 1978 and 1995, respectively, lynx have remained a harvested game species until the present in Finland, Estonia and Latvia. Again, lynx appear to have rapidly responded to the cessation of bounties and restrictions on harvest, and have expanded. Lynx are now found throughout most of central and southern Finland, most of Estonia and Latvia. There are now between 2500 and 3000 lynx in these countries. The proximity to large populations in neighbouring Russia and Belarus, and the expansion of roe deer and the increase in forest cover, are also likely to have greatly facilitated this recovery. It is only in the highly fragmented landscapes of Lithuania and north-eastern Poland that lynx have not recovered (Jędrzejewska & Jędrzejewski, 1998; Bluzma, 2000; Valdmann, 2000; Ozolins, 2001; Pohja-Mykrä *et al.*, 2005; Anonymous, 2007).

Carpathian Mountains

Lynx decline in the Carpathians was most advanced in Poland, reaching its lowest in the 1850s. The species achieved a partial recovery under the status of a game species until their protection in 1995. Throughout the rest of the range, the population's greatest decline was in the 1930s. As a response, lynx were protected in Czechoslovakia from 1936 to 1956 and in Romania from 1933 to 1961. There are really few concrete data available on the actual extent of this decline, although it appears that lynx remained present throughout most of the mountain range, but at very low density. Following protection, they received game-species status where their harvest was regulated. Ukraine protected lynx in 1980. These actions seem to have allowed a rapid recovery of lynx. In this region, there was also a recovery of prey populations during this period. At their all-time low, lynx maintained much of their distribution throughout the range but at greatly reduced numbers, probably in the region of a few hundred animals. There are now probably more than 2000 lynx present in the mountain range. Lynx have also recently re-expanded into eastern parts of the Czech Republic (Kratochvil, 1968b; Salvatori *et al.*, 2002).

Balkans

Lynx became functionally extinct throughout the northern parts of the Dinaric Mountains (present-day Slovenia, Croatia, Bosnia and Herzegovina) in the late 19th century. They persisted in small numbers in the mountains on the borders of western Macedonia, eastern Albania, Kosovo and Montenegro. Although there are few hard data from this region, it appears that little has changed during the 20th century, despite the species being protected in Macedonia in 1973 and in Albania in 1994. Lynx still exist in the same restricted range at very low numbers (probably less than 100).

Natural recovery versus reintroduction

Lynx distribution past and present

On the surface, Europe may seem like an unlikely place to look for a success story in the field of large-carnivore conservation. With its highly modified and fragmented habitats, and a population of 500 million people, it is a far cry from wilderness. Despite this, the changes in the distribution and density of large carnivores (and their prey) that have occurred during the mid and late 20th century can only be called dramatic. Lynx are now found in more areas and in greater numbers than they have been for several centuries. There are now in the region of 8000 lynx in 25 European countries (not counting those in Russia). This turn-around has occurred through both active reintroduction and natural recovery. In this section, we shall briefly compare and contrast the success of the two approaches.

Reintroductions

Despite the *ad hoc* nature of many of the reintroductions, there is no doubt that they have succeeded in greatly expanding the distribution of lynx into Central and Western Europe. The populations in the northern Dinarics, Vosges, Jura, Western Alps and Bavaria/Bohmeia are all currently at a size where they should persist for the short term at least. These areas could not have been recolonized naturally, either in the past 30 years or into the foreseeable future, as they are not connected to extant populations through suitable corridors. However, the growth rates of most of these populations appear to be very slow despite the fact that unoccupied, but suitable, habitat remains. Some, such as the Dinaric population, may even be in decline. The reasons for this are complex as there are (1) biological, (2) habitat and landscape, (3) procedural and (4) anthropogenic (conflict-associated) factors that are at work. Firstly, lynx are relatively slow breeders and poor dispersers (at least when compared with species like wolves). The narrow genetic basis of these populations is also a potential problem, given the spectre of inbreeding depression, although the development of connections between the reintroduced populations (e.g. between the Vosges, Jura and Western Alps) may ease this problem somewhat. Secondly, the habitat of these reintroduced populations tends to consist of small patches, which are both internally and externally fragmented by human infrastructure and unsuitable modified habitat (e.g. intensive farmland). Thirdly, reintroduction procedures were far from optimal. Finally, lynx are universally controversial in areas where they have been reintroduced. Controversy is based on two main issues. On the one hand, lynx are associated with depredation on livestock (Stahl *et al.*, 2001) while, on the other hand, hunters are concerned about the impact of lynx on wild ungulate populations (Breitenmoser *et al.*, 2007). The result of these conflicts is the widespread illegal killing of lynx throughout the areas where they have been reintroduced (Koubek & Červeny, 1996; Wölfl *et al.*, 2001;

Červeny *et al.*, 2002; Schmidt-Posthaus *et al.*, 2002; Vandel *et al.*, 2006; Breitenmoser-Würsten *et al.*, 2007). This illegal killing is probably the most severe of the proximate factors limiting the expansion of these populations. The combination of these four factors means that, although these reintroduced populations may be secure in the short term, their long-term fate is still an open question.

Natural recovery

Three out of four surviving relict populations have demonstrated clear recoveries during the past 70 years. These recoveries in Scandinavia, the Eastern Baltic drainage and the Carpathian Mountains have been generally coincident with the removal of state-sponsored bounties, the introduction of some restrictions on harvest following their designation as game species (as opposed to being classed as pests or vermin) and, in some cases, short periods of protection. They have also been coincident with recoveries of prey populations, primarily roe deer, owing to improved regulation of harvest and, in many cases, with increased forest cover. All three of these populations appear to have reached a level where they are viable and able to sustain continued regulated harvest, although there are some areas on their edges where local subpopulations may be threatened. However, the Balkan relict has probably not changed its status during this period, merely persisting in critically low numbers. The reasons for this are not altogether clear, but it appears that hunting (both legal and illegal) has continued and that prey populations are relatively low. This is probably due to the fact that this region has only recently seen the relaxation of human pressure on rural landscapes that began to occur much earlier in Western Europe. In addition, the population was very small and was totally isolated from any neighbouring populations.

The main lessons from this are that, given a relaxation (but not necessarily a cessation) of hunting pressure and a suitable habitat with adequate prey, lynx populations have been able to make rapid recoveries. It is an interesting aspect that many of the first movements to limit hunting pressure and to introduce protection stem from the 1920s and 1930s, long before the modern conservation movement began. That being said, lynx are not without controversy in the areas of natural recovery. Again, the two main conflicts are caused by depredation on livestock (e.g. Odden *et al.*, 2002) and perceived competition with hunters for wild ungulates. The fact that lynx are managed as *de facto* game species in most countries where they have naturally recovered allows the regulation of population size at levels that minimize conflicts. However, illegal killing is still widespread in some areas (Andrén *et al.*, 2006).

Common lessons

The wide distribution that lynx currently enjoy in Europe is the result of natural recovery and reintroductions. We have examples of successes and failures from both approaches, and it is likely that both will be needed in the future given the present, fragmented distribution of lynx in Europe. From the experience that we have gained from both approaches, we can identify some main lessons which should be heeded in all future recovery activities:

1 Lynx restoration must be carefully planned, and evaluating its success must be carried out over the long term following IUCN reintroduction guidelines (IUCN, 1998). Even 30 years after initiation, it is hard to determine whether some reintroductions will lead to a population that is viable in the long term. This also reflects a need to invest in robust monitoring programmes that follow the development of the population, human attitudes, and eventual conflicts.

2 There is a need to plan for restoration on wide spatial scales. This concerns both the habitat in an area of many thousands of square kilometres around a release site into which a reintroduced population might expand and the connection within and between other populations, both autochthonous and reintroduced.

3 The human dimension is the most important. Although large-carnivore conservation and reintroduction will always be controversial, this controversy can be reduced through effective communication, good public consultation and stakeholder involvement and the definition of clear long-term management plans before any activity is initiated. The widespread occurrence of poaching is alarming and requires a focus on both good public consultation and on law enforcement.

4 The above mentioned issues present somewhat of a conundrum, as the intensive conservation activity needed is very hard to achieve at large spatial scales. In effect, a form of "think global, act local" hierarchy of action is needed, where one works intensively on a local scale around the release sites or recovery sites, but keeps an eye on the larger scale when planning. This requires the use of systematic conservation planning and the use of GIS systems to model potential expansion at landscape scales. The need for this large-scale effort and focus, and the associated costs, is probably the single most important reason why population-recovery efforts should be well planned and well funded.

References

Anders, O. & Sacher, P. (2005) Das luchsprojekt Harz-ein Zwischenbericht. *Naturschutz im Land Sachsen* 42, 3–12.

Andersen, R., Herfindal, I., Linnell, J.D.C., Odden, J., Liberg, O. & Sæther, B.E. (2004) When range expansion rate is faster in marginal habitats. *Oikos* 107, 210–214.

Andrén, H., Linnell, J.D.C., Liberg, O. et al. (2006) Survival rates and causes of mortality in Eurasian lynx (*Lynx lynx*) in multi-use landscapes. *Biological Conservation* 131, 23–32.

Anonymous (2007) *Management Plan for the Lynx Population in Finland.* Ministry of Agriculture and Forestry 1b/2007, Helsinki.

Bluzma, P. (2000) Large predatory mammals in Lithuania: Abundance dynamics, distribution, population density. *Folia Theriologica Estonica* 5, 35–41.

Breitenmoser, U. (1998) Large predators in the Alps: The fall and rise of man's competitors. *Biological Conservation* 83, 279–289.

Breitenmoser, U. & Baettig, M. (1992) Reintroduction and expansion of the lynx (*Lynx lynx*) in the Swiss Jura Mountains. *Revue Suisse de Zoologie* 99, 163–176.

Breitenmoser, U. & Breitenmoser-Würsten, C. (1990) *Status, Conservation Needs and Reintroduction of the Lynx (*Lynx lynx*) in Europe.* Council of Europe, Nature and Environment Series No. 45, Strasbourg.

Breitenmoser, U. & Breitenmoser-Würsten, C. (1999) The reintroduction of Eurasian lynx in the European Alps. *Reintroduction News* 18, 13–14.

Breitenmoser, U. & Breitenmoser-Würsten, C. (2008) *Der Luchs—ein Grossraubtier in der Kulturlandschaft.* Salm Verlag, Bern.

Breitenmoser, U., Breitnemoser-Würsten, C. & Capt, S. (1998) Re-introduction and present status of the lynx (*Lynx lynx*) in Switzerland. *Hystrix* 10, 17–30.

Breitenmoser, U., Breitenmoser-Würsten, C., Capt, S., Molinari-Jobin, A., Molinari, P. & Zimmermann, F. (2007) Conservation of the lynx *Lynx lynx* in the Swiss Jura Mountains. *Wildlife Biology* 13, 340–355.

Breitenmoser, U., Breitenmoser-Würsten, C., Carbyn, L.N. & Funk, S.M. (2001) Assessment of carnivore reintroductions. *Carnivore Conservation.* (eds J.L.

Gittleman, S.M. Funk, D.W. Macdonald & R.K. Wayne), pp. 241–281. Cambridge University Press, Cambridge.

Breitenmoser-Würsten, C. & Obexer-Ruff, G. (2003) Population and conservation genetics of two re-introduced lynx (*Lynx lynx*) populations in Switzerland—A molecular evaluation 30 years after translocation. *Proceedings of the 2nd Conference on the Status and Conservation of the Alpine Lynx Population* (SCALP).

Breitenmoser-Würsten, C., Vandel, J.M., Zimmermann, F. & Breitenmoser, U. (2007) Demography of lynx *Lynx lynx* in the Jura Mountains. *Wildlife Biology* 13, 381–392.

Bufka, L. & Cerveny, J. (1996) The lynx (*Lynx lynx* L.) in the Sumava region, southwest Bohemia. *Journal of Wildlife Research* 1, 167–170.

Böer, M., Reklewski, J., Smielowski, J. & Tyrala, P. (2000) Reintroduction of the European lynx (*Lynx lynx*) to the Kampinoski National Park, Poland—A field experiment with zooborn individuals. Part III: Demographic development of the population from December 1993 until January 2000. *Der Zoologische Garten* 70, 304–312.

Böer, M., Smielowski, J. & Tyrala, P. (1994) Reintroduction of the European lynx (*Lynx lynx*) to the Kampinoski National Park, Poland—A field experiment with zooborn individuals. Part I—Selection, adaptation and training. *De Zoologische Garten* 64, 366–378.

Böer, M., Smielowski, J. & Tyrala, P. (1995) Reintroduction of the European lynx (*Lynx lynx*) to the Kampinoski National Park, Poland—A field experiment with zooborn individuals. Part II Release phase, procedures, and activities of lynxes during the first year. *De Zoologische Garten* 65, 333–342.

Capt, S. (2007) Monitoring and distribution of the lynx *Lynx lynx* in the Swiss Jura Mountains. *Wildlife Biology* 13, 356–364.

Červeny, J., Koubek, P. & Bufka, L. (2002) Eurasian lynx (*Lynx lynx*) and its chance for survival in Central Europe: The case of the Czech Republic. *Acta Zoologica Lithuanica* 12, 428–432.

Cop, J. & Frkovic, A. (1998) The re-introduction of the lynx in Slovenia and its present status in Slovenia and Croatia. *Hystrix* 10, 65–76.

Gossow, H. & Honsig-Erlenburg, P. (1986) Management problems with reintroduced lynx in Austria. *Cats of the World: Biology, Conservation and Management.* (eds S.D. Miller & D.D. Everett), pp. 77–84. National Wildlife Federation, Washington, DC.

Huber, T. & Kaczensky, P. (1998) The situation of the lynx (*Lynx lynx*) in Austria. *Hystrix* 10, 43–54.

IUCN (1998) *Guidelines for Re-introductions* IUCN/SSC Reintroduction Specialist Group, Gland, Switzerland.

Jędrzejewska, B. & Jędrzejewski, W. (1998) *Predation in Vertebrate Communities: The Bialowieza Primeval Forest as a Case Study.* Springer, Berlin.

Jule, K.R., Leaver, L.A. & Lea, S.E.G. (2008) The effects of captive experience on reintroduction survival in carnivores: A review and analysis. *Biological Conservation* 141, 355–363.

Kos, I., Potocnik, H., Skrbinsek, T., Majic-Skrbinsek, T., Jonozovic, M. & Krofel, M. (2004) *Ris v Sloveniji: Strokovna izhodisca za varstvo in upravljanje*. University of Ljubljana Press, Ljubljana.

Koubek, P. & Červeny, J. (1996) Lynx in the Czech and Slovak Republics. *Acta Scientiarum Naturalium Academiae Scientiarum Bohemicae Brno* 30, 1–78.

Kramer-Schadt, S., Revilla, E. & Wiegand, T. (2005) Lynx reintroductions in fragmented landscapes of Germany: Projects with a future or misunderstood wildlife conservation? *Biological Conservation* 125, 169–182.

Kratochvil, J. (1968a) History of the distribution of the lynx in Europe. *Acta Scientiarum Naturalium Academiae Scientiarum Bohemoslovacae Brno* 2, 1–50.

Kratochvil, J. (1968b) Recent distribution of the lynx in Europe. *Acta Scientiarum Naturalium Academiae Scientiarum Bohemoslovacae Brno* 2 (5/6), 1–74.

Laas, J., Fuxjäger, C., Huber, T. & Gerstl, N. (2006) Lynx in the Austrian Alps 2000 to 2004. *Acta Biologica Slovenica* 49, 43–49.

Liberg, O., Andrén, H., Pedersen, H.C. et al. (2005) Severe inbreeding depression in a wild wolf (*Canis lupus*) population. *Biology Letters* 1, 17–20.

Marboutin, E., Duchamp, C., Rouland, P. et al. (2006) Survey of the lynx distribution in the French Alps: 2000–2004 Population status analysis. *Acta Biologica Slovenica* 49, 19–26.

Molinari-Jobin, A., Zimmermann, F., Angst, C., Breitenmoser-Würsten, C., Capt, S. & Breitenmoser, U. (2006) Status and distribution of the lynx in the Swiss Alps 2000–2004. *Acta Biologica Slovenica* 49, 3–11.

Molinari-Jobin, A., Zimmermann, F., Breitenmoser-Würsten, C., Capt, S. & Breitenmoser, U. (2001) Present status and distribution of the lynx in the Swiss Alps. *Hystrix* 12, 17–27.

Odden, J., Linnell, J.D.C., Moa, P.F., Herfindal, I., Kvam, T. & Andersen, R. (2002) Lynx depredation on domestic sheep in Norway. *Journal of Wildlife Management* 66, 98–105.

Ozolins, J. (2001) Status of large carnivore conservation in the Baltic States: Action plan for the conservation of Eurasian lynx (*Lynx lynx*) in Latvia. *Council of Europe, T-PVS (2001) 73 addendum* 1, 1–18.

Pohja-Mykrä, M., Vuorisalo, T. & Mykrä, S. (2005) Hunting bounties as a key measure of historical wildlife management and game conservation: Finnish bounty schemes 1647–1975. *Oryx* 39, 284–291.

Reiter, A. (1996) Lynx (*Lynx lynx*) in the Podyji National Park. *Acta Scientiarum Naturalium Academiae Scientiarum Bohemicae Brno* 30, 51–57.

Ryser, A., von Wattenwyl, K., Ryser-Degiorgis, M.P., Willisch, C., Zimmermann, F. & Breitenmoser, U. (2004) Luchsumsiedlung Nordostschweiz 2001–2003. *KORA Bericht* 22, 1–60.

Salvatori, V., Okarma, H., Ionescu, O., Dovhanych, Y., Findo, S. & Boitani, L. (2002) Hunting legislation in the Carpathian Mountains: Implications for the conservation and management of large carnivores. *Wildlife Biology* 8, 3–10.

Schmidt-Posthaus, H., Breitenmoser-Würsten, C., Posthaus, H., Bacciarini, L.N. & Breitenmoser, U. (2002) Causes of mortality in reintroduced Eurasian lynx in Switzerland. *Journal of Wildlife Disease* 38, 84–92.

Sommer, R.S. & Benecke, N. (2006) Late Pleistocene and Holocene development of the felid fauna (Felidae) of Europe: A review. *Journal of Zoology, London* 269, 7–19.

Stahl, P. & Vandel, J.M. (2001) Lynx distribution in the French Alps (1995–1999). *Hystrix* 12, 11–15.

Stahl, P., Vandel, J.M., Herrenschmidt, V. & Migot, P. (2001) Predation on livestock by an expanding reintroduced lynx population: Long term trend and spatial variability. *Journal of Applied Ecology* 38, 674–687.

Stansia, C., Koren, I. & Adamic, M. (2001) Situation and distribution of the lynx (*Lynx lynx* L.) in Slovenia from 1995–1999. *Hystrix* 12, 43–51.

Valdmann, H. (2000) The status of large predators in Estonia. *Folia Theriologica Estonica* 5, 158–164.

Vandel, J.M., Stahl, P., Herrendschmidt, V. & Marboutin, E. (2006) Reintroduction of the lynx into the Vosges mountain massif: From animal survival and movements to population development. *Biological Conservation* 131, 370–385.

Vera, F.W.M. (2000) *Grazing Ecology and Forest History.* CABI Publishing, Waltingford.

von Arx, M., Breitenmoser-Würsten, C., Zimmermann, F. & Breitenmoser, U. (2004) Status and conservation of the Eurasian lynx (*Lynx lynx*) in Europe in 2001. *KORA Bericht* 19e, 1–330.

Wölfl, M., Bufka, L., Cerveny, J. et al. (2001) Distribution and status of lynx in the border region between Czech Republic, Germany and Austria. *Acta Theriologica* 46, 181–194.

5

Reintroduction of Wolves to Yellowstone National Park: History, Values and Ecosystem Restoration

Douglas W. Smith[1] *and Edward E. Bangs*[2]

[1]Yellowstone Wolf Project
[2]US Fish and Wildlife Service

Summary

Wolves, *Canis lupus*, were present when Yellowstone National Park (YNP) was established in 1872, but were eradicated by 1926 because of a Congressionally-mandated policy. There was no wolf population present until they were reintroduced from Canada. Wolves were reintroduced because the Endangered Species Act (ESA) of 1973 called for their restoration, and US National Park Service policy called for restoring natural conditions. After nearly 20 years of acrimonious public debate, wolves captured in Canada were reintroduced to central Idaho and YNP in 1995 and 1996. By late 2007, there were an estimated 1500 wolves in Montana, Idaho and Wyoming, 171 of which were in YNP. The focus of our paper is YNP, the most intensively studied area. Individual young adult wolves were released in remote areas of public land in central Idaho. Wolf family groups were acclimated for 10 weeks in pens constructed in YNP and were released directly from their pens. Reintroductions were planned to take place over the course of 3–5 years, but unpredicted success necessitated only 2 years. The population grew rapidly, approximately 17% each year, pup survival was high—in some cases, more

Reintroduction of Top-Order Predators, 1st edition. Edited by M.W. Hayward and M.J. Somers.
 ISBN 978-1-4051-7680-4 (pb) and 978-1-4051-9273-6 (hb)

than one female per pack produced pups—and human-caused mortality was low. Two disease outbreaks in 1999 and 2005 temporarily slowed population growth. Lifetime female reproductive success ranged from 2 to 35 pups born/female, with the average being 14.

The age structure and composition of wolf packs changed through time, owing primarily to wolves living longer and becoming older. Genetic relatedness between packs was high, especially in the northern region of YNP, and breeding relationships in packs varied greatly from multi-year stability to year-to-year breeder overturn. Despite high genetic relatedness between packs, overall the genetic diversity of the population was high and equal to other wild North American wolf populations. Wolves preyed primarily on elk, *Cervus elaphus*, but mule deer, *Odocoileus hemionus*, were preyed upon in summer, when they seasonally migrated back into YNP, and bison, *Bison bison*, were preyed upon in winter, when they were most vulnerable to wolf predation. Wolf predation was highly selective, preying on elk calves in early winter and on older females throughout the year but, more recently, bull elk have increased in the wolf kill, possibly due to condition declines related to a multi-year drought. Wolves interacted with the other large carnivores, lowering numbers and altering the social structure of coyote, *Canis latrans*, populations, and aided grizzly bears, *Ursus arctos*, by providing ungulate carcasses that bears usurped. Wolves appeared to have little effect on cougars, *Felis concolor*, despite some interspecific killing. Wolves may be a factor in a trophic cascade involving wolves–elk–willow, as willow, *Salix* spp., height has increased since about 3 years post wolf reintroduction, after being suppressed for decades by elk browsing. Response of aspen, *Populus tremuloides*, is less clear as some evidence indicates increased aspen growth at the elk wintering-range periphery, but not in the core winter range. Population increases of beavers, *Castor canadensis*, and songbirds are associated with the willow increase.

Overall, wolf reintroduction was deemed a success, but political opposition is still strong, creating continuing controversy for federal and state wildlife managers. Wolf issues are highly symbolic to people, and scientific information is only one of many factors, and sometimes a minor one, in management outcomes. YNP has proven to be a biologically exceptional wolf habitat, but their reintroduction remains controversial, owing to livestock depredation and perceptions that wolves are affecting wild ungulate populations and the hunter harvest adjacent to YNP. Here, we compare predictions against outcomes of wolf restoration.

Introduction

Yellowstone National Park (YNP) was established in 1872 as the world's first national park. At that time, wolves, *Canis lupus*, were present, but a congressional mandate by government led to their eradication. By 1926, the last wolf pups were killed, and packs remained absent until reintroduction in 1995 and 1996 (Weaver, 1978). Beginning in the late 1950s and 1960s, several long-term wolf studies eventually portrayed wolves as something different than wanton beasts (Rutter & Pimlott, 1968; Mech, 1970; Allen, 1979). These changing public attitudes about the environment cleared the way for the Endangered Species Act (ESA), under which wolves were listed as endangered species. The ESA required that threatened or endangered plants and animals should be restored. Wolf restoration was always controversial, as wolf eradication was locally perceived as a successful solution to livestock depredation. Environmental groups, with increased support from the general public, began to push to restore wolves, creating strongly competing human values. Although not easily simplified, the debate largely boiled down to urban pro-wolf versus rural anti-wolf forces, with each side marshalling as much money and political support as they could muster. Gridlock was common, as were legal challenges. In some ways, YNP was the flashpoint because of its high profile and recognition to the public.

The controversy lasted for decades. In the early 1960s, YNP raised the issue but was quickly silenced by western politics and attitudes. As wolves began to naturally recolonize and expand their range in north-western Montana in the mid-1980s, the issue gathered a public profile and political attention. In 1988, the US Congress mandated the "Wolves for Yellowstone?" studies of wolf restoration to the Park (National Park Service, 1990; Varley & Brewster, 1992), partly to investigate its potential effect, but also to delay reintroduction. In 1991, Congress established a multi-federal and state agency and a special interest committee, in a failed attempt to politically resolve the issue of wolf restoration to YNP as well as to central Idaho (Wolf Management Committee, 1991). In 1992, Congress mandated preparation of an intensive environmental review—a legal milestone toward wolf reintroduction.

During the 2-year preparation of the Environmental Impact Statement (EIS), the US Fish and Wildlife Service (USFWS), National Park Service (NPS) and other cooperating agencies conducted unprecedented public outreach: 130 public meetings and hearings were held, nearly 750,000 pamphlets and newspaper inserts were distributed, hundreds of media interviews were conducted and almost 180,000 public comments were analysed. The EIS was published in early 1994 and special regulations, which included even more public outreach and comment, were finalized in late 1994 (US Federal Regulation, 59 FR 60252). Ultimately, and despite litigation from both pro-wolf (wanting more legal protection) and anti-wolf groups (wanting no action), 66 wolves were captured in Canada, and 10 in north-western Montana, and transported into Idaho and YNP in 1995 and 1996 (Bangs & Fritts, 1996; Phillips & Smith, 1996; Bangs *et al.* 1998). The wolves were reintroduced under Section 10j of the ESA, which allowed for extra management flexibility for species reintroduced as experimental populations (e.g. ranchers could legally shoot wolves seen attacking their livestock). If there are any take-home messages from the entire effort 12 years later, it is that attention to public outreach, human values, legitimate conflict resolution and policy formulation, involving all stakeholders, cannot be slighted.

Background

Wolves are seen as pawns in a larger cultural and philosophical battle that has been ongoing since the settlement of the American West. In part, predator eradication was "how the West was won". The range was made more profitable for livestock production through predator removal. Early in YNP's history, manipulation of wildlife populations was frequent, and most large carnivores (e.g. wolves, cougars [*Felis concolor*], coyotes [*Canis latrans*] and lynx [*Lynx canadensis*]) were removed early in the 20th century (Pritchard, 1999). Bears (*Ursus arctos* and *Ursus americanus*) were not culled as they were fed and preserved for visitor enjoyment. The elk, *Cervus elaphus*, population erupted following carnivore removal. Agency control of elk began from the early 1930s until 1968, and bison and pronghorn antelope populations were also manipulated (Houston, 1982). Debate about proper elk management was keen and, after 1968, elk increased again to high levels, spawning renewed debate about wolf restoration (Weaver, 1978; Houston, 1982). A new policy, however, was in place (Leopold Report, 1963 [Leopold *et al.*, 1963]), which stated that wildlife populations on NPS lands would be "naturally regulated", therefore limiting many intrusive management activities, with the added caveat of restoring "vignettes of primitive America". Therefore, from 1968 until about the time of wolf reintroduction, elk numbers grew to record numbers (Wagner, 2006), and a small hunting industry established itself in the adjacent state of Montana (when the elk migrated from the Park and were considered to be surplus). It was under these ideal conditions that wolves were reintroduced to YNP.

Study site

YNP (8991 km^2) is at the centre of the Greater Yellowstone Area (GYA), which is 76% federal land. The GYA is primarily mountainous coniferous forest, has more than 95,000 wild ungulates (primarily elk, mule deer [*Odocoileus hemionus*] and bison [*Bison bison*], but also moose [*Alces alces*], pronghorn antelope [*Antilocapra americana*], bighorn sheep [*Ovis canadensis*], mountain goat [*Oreamnos americanus*] and white-tailed deer [*Odocoileus virginianus*]), is grazed in summer by approximately 412,000 livestock, has a US$4200 million local economy, and receives about 14,500,000 recreational visits annually (Varley & Brewster, 1992). Human visitation to YNP is more than 3 million people per year, making it one of the most frequently visited parks in the United States. Most wildlife species present at YNP establishment are still present, and the Park is one of the few North American ecosystems with a full suite of natural ungulates and carnivores.

Initially, all released wolves were radio-collared, and collars have been maintained in all YNP packs as well as in most packs forming outside the Park. Typically, about 35%–40% of the individuals in YNP were collared. Capture and collaring of >300 wolves from 1995 to 2007 was accomplished exclusively through helicopter darting or netting (only 21 were captured this way) in winter. Radio-collared wolves were relocated weekly and daily during two intensive 30-day winter-predation study periods (15 November to 14 December, and 1–30 March, with both investigations being held from 1995 to 2007; Smith *et al.*, 2004).

Wolf reintroduction

The actual reintroduction began in January 1995, 21 years after ESA listing and fierce debate and controversy. Despite vocal opposition, the USFWS and a host of co-operators captured 31 wolves in Canada and shipped them to the Park. Fourteen came from Alberta in 1995 and 17 from British Columbia in

1996. At the same time, 35 wolves from the same locations were shipped to central Idaho's Frank Church-River of No Return Wilderness. The Canadian source areas were situated along the Rocky Mountains and had similar terrain and prey to Yellowstone and Idaho (Fritts *et al.*, 2001). In 1997, 10 wolf pups, orphaned because their pack killed livestock, from north-western Montana, were also less successfully reintroduced (eight out of 10 were dead within 9 months).

Release strategies differed between the Park and central Idaho (Bangs & Fritts, 1996, Fritts *et al.*, 2001). In the Park, wolves were acclimated as family groups (packs) in pens of >1 acre, and were "soft" released 10 weeks later. In Idaho, yearling and other young individual wolves were "hard" released directly onto the landscape to mimic natural dispersal. The reason for the different reintroduction techniques was the differing attributes of each area. Lone wolves were immediately released into 54,000 km^2 of contiguous rugged, largely road-less, public land in central Idaho because it accommodated wide-ranging post-release movements. The YNP road system and availability of Park staff made acclimation pens accessible, and therefore more feasible and much less expensive than was possible in Idaho.

Acclimation was a crucial part of YNP's soft-release strategy to keep packs intact and to minimize post-release movements outside YNP, where conflicts with adjacent people and livestock were most likely. In 1995, the first three groups were placed in separate pens on YNP's elk-rich northern wintering range. In 1996, four groups were placed in pens, two on the northern range, one in the Park's interior, and one near its south-east corner. Park staff fed the penned wolves road-killed deer, elk, moose and bison, twice a week. Pen acclimation worked in YNP, as did the hard release in Idaho. Confinement reduced post-release movements, maintained familial ties between wolves and facilitated same-year reproduction. While the original plan predicted 3–5 years of releases, only 2 years were needed to establish several resident packs. By 2000, with 177 wolves in the GYA, the reintroduction project was labelled a complete success "ahead of schedule and under budget" with more benefits and fewer problems than predicted.

Territoriality and population expansion

Wolf packs quickly established themselves inside and outside of the Park (Figure 5.1). Pack cohesiveness varied, with some wolves showing strong

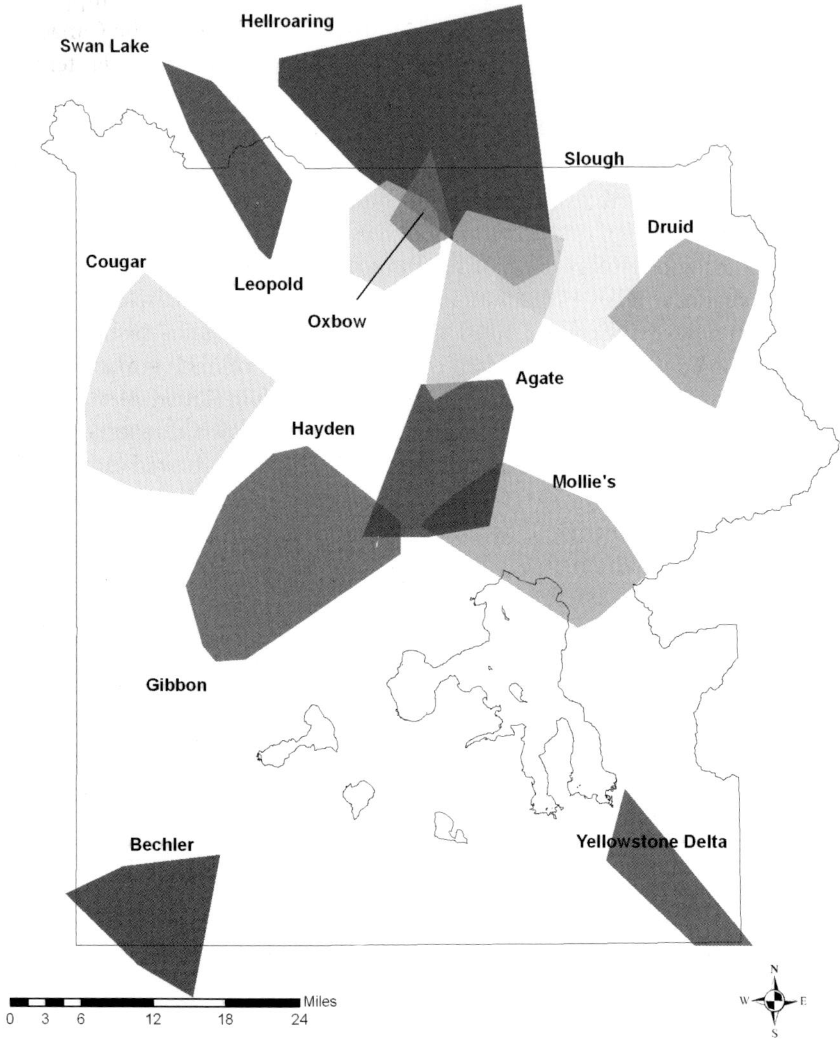

Figure 5.1 **Wolf pack territories in Yellowstone National Park 2006. Most areas in the Park that can be settled by wolves have been.**

social bonds while others dispersed immediately, but most remained in the Park and quickly established territories. The first wolf was illegally killed outside of the Park within 6 weeks of the first release, but such killing was not common and did not impede population growth or expansion. In general, wolf movements during the first year overlapped broadly for about 3 months, with some conflict between wandering packs, until they settled into a territorial pattern closely resembling extant wolf populations. Packs released during the second year wandered longer, probably due to the presence of already established packs, and wolf conflict was greater, with one recently released pack displacing a settled pack and killing its pups.

Territory size ranged from 140 to 1430 km^2. Packs occupying the prey-rich northern range tended to have the smallest territories, averaging only 293 km^2 ($n = 56$), while packs occupying areas where prey is less abundant had larger territories, averaging 880 km^2 ($n = 52$). Such disparity makes it misleading to estimate an "average size" of a pack territory. Some of the variability is probably due also to the migratory behaviour of elk. Seven out of the eight elk herds that use the Park are migratory and, except for the northern and Madison-Firehole herds, most elk leave the Park in the winter, strongly affecting wolf movements and, ultimately, territory size—but most wolf packs did not follow migrating elk. Occasional extra-territorial movements did occur, as wolves left YNP in search of prey (Smith *et al.*, 2003). This was common enough; typically, three or four packs would leave YNP at least once a year, exposing them to livestock, agency control of problem wolves and illegal killing.

The wolf population growth rate averaged about 17% per year (Figure 5.2) and, by 2000, all YNP was settled. Peak numbers were reached in 2003 at 174 wolves in 14 packs. Since 2003, the total number of packs has remained at more than 13 but, the YNP population crashed in 2005 because of a disease outbreak involving at least three diseases (canine parvo-virus, canine distemper and adeno-virus), but the mortality was probably due mostly to distemper (Smith & Almberg, 2007). Wolf density was highest in the northern portion of the Park, known as the northern elk wintering-range, because of a large elk population. About half the wolves lived on about 15% of the Park's total area. Park-wide pack size varied from two to 37 wolves, but averaged 11—an expected pack size given the moderately sized main prey of elk and the low rates of human-caused morality.

Wolf pack composition changed over time as some young wolves survived and did not disperse, shifting the pack structure from simple packs with a

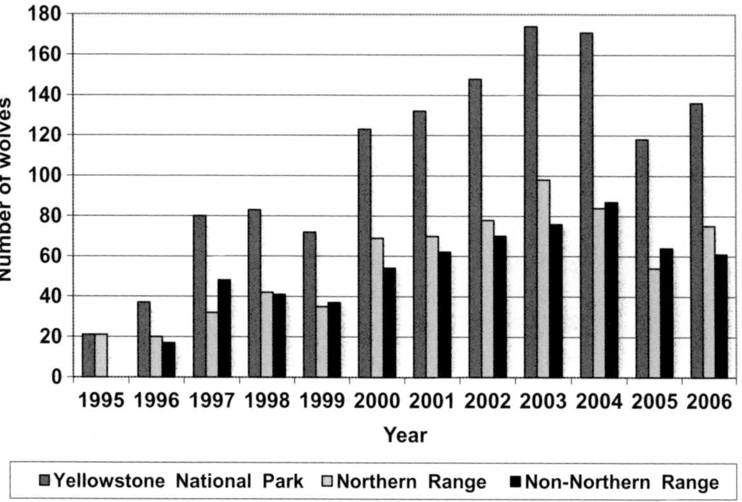

Figure 5.2 **Population growth of wolves in Yellowstone National Park by area within the Park, 1995–2006. More than half of the wolves live in the northern portion of the Park on only about 15% of the Park's land area. This is due to the high density of elk in this area.**

breeding pair and young to multi-generational complex packs with many older and experienced individuals. Territorial clashes became important, with some large packs usurping ground from smaller ones.

Pup production

Four of the seven reintroduced packs bred in the pens and had pups shortly after release. This was unexpected as we had initially planned the acclimation and release to occur before the February breeding season. However, legal battles delayed the capture and transport of the wolves to pens, delaying the releases until late in the wolf courtship and breeding season. Combined with wolves' natural abilities, the fact that they bred in the pens jump-started the population, giving it an immediate and secure foothold in the Park.

Pup production was initially high (Figure 5.3), with an average litter size of five pups and a pup survival of 80%–90%. As of 2007, there have been 143

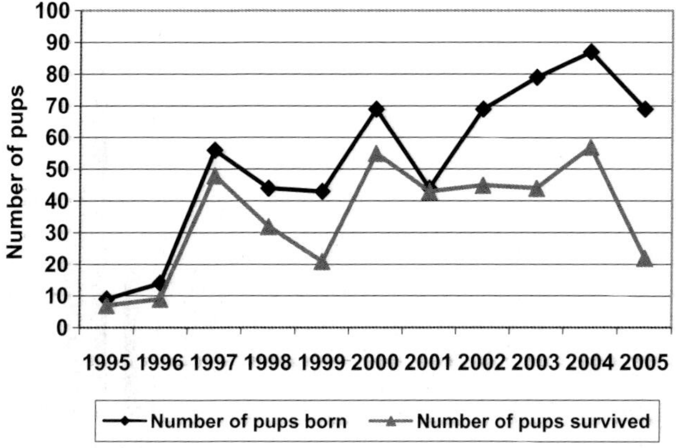

Figure 5.3 **Number of pups born and survived in Yellowstone National Park 1995–2006. High mortality in 1999 and 2005 were due to disease outbreaks.**

documented litters of pups born in YNP since reintroduction. Wolves also took advantage of the favourable conditions in YNP by having multiple litters per pack. About 15% of breeding attempts involved more than one litter. These packs averaged more pups over-winter than packs having only one litter. Another condition contributing to multiple litters was the presence of several unrelated adults in the same pack. Because wolves avoid inbreeding, and most members in a pack are related, the adult male breeder usually has only his unrelated mate to breed with (Von Holdt *et al.*, 2007). This limits the number of litters per pack.

Match-made packs in pens (both complete packs and pairs of unrelated wolves or females with pups with an introduced male were used), and changes in leadership can change this dynamic, and result in an alpha male that is not related to any of the females in the pack. As a result, he bred with multiple females. This circumstance produced spectacular numbers of pups—21 in three litters for the Druid Peak pack in 2000, increasing their pack size to 37 wolves and making them one of the largest wolf packs ever recorded (Fuller *et al.*, 2003). In 2005, the Slough Creek pack had four litters and 17 pups (only three survived), and the Leopold pack had at least 19 pups (only two survived) in at least three litters. A few other packs also produced double litters, and a least one pack did so every year in the northern portion of YNP, but only one pack in the interior of YNP had more than one litter.

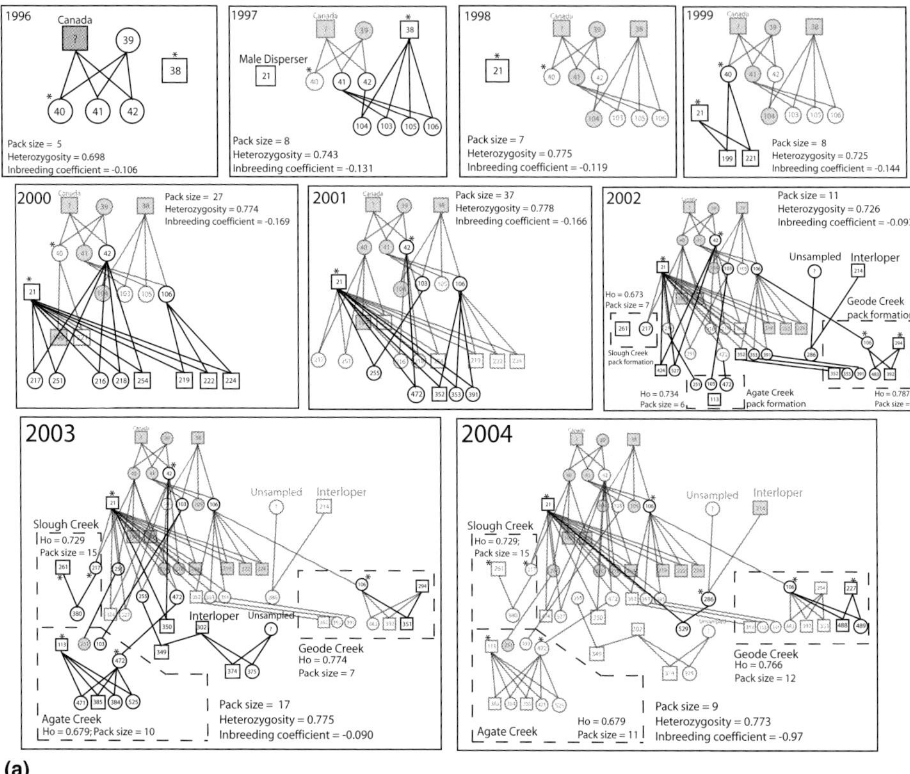

Figure 5.4 **Pedigrees from two different wolf packs in Yellowstone National Park showing both (a) stable (Leopold) and (b) high turnover (Druid Peak) mating behaviour (from Von Holdt *et al.*, 2007).**

The number of pups produced per female lifetime varied from two to 35 and averaged 14. Pups surviving to winter ranged from 0 to 25 per female and averaged 11. Most pair bonds were 1–3 years, but several were >5 years, with one being 7 years (Figure 5.4; Von Holdt *et al.*, 2007). Interpack relatedness was high, owing to proximity of territory vacancies and dispersal from the few reintroduced packs (Figure 5.5), but overall average heterozygosity was comparable to other wild wolf populations (Von Holdt *et al.*, 2007). Overall tolerance between adjacent packs and dominant–subordinate breeding behaviour is hypothesized to have a strong genetic underpinning.

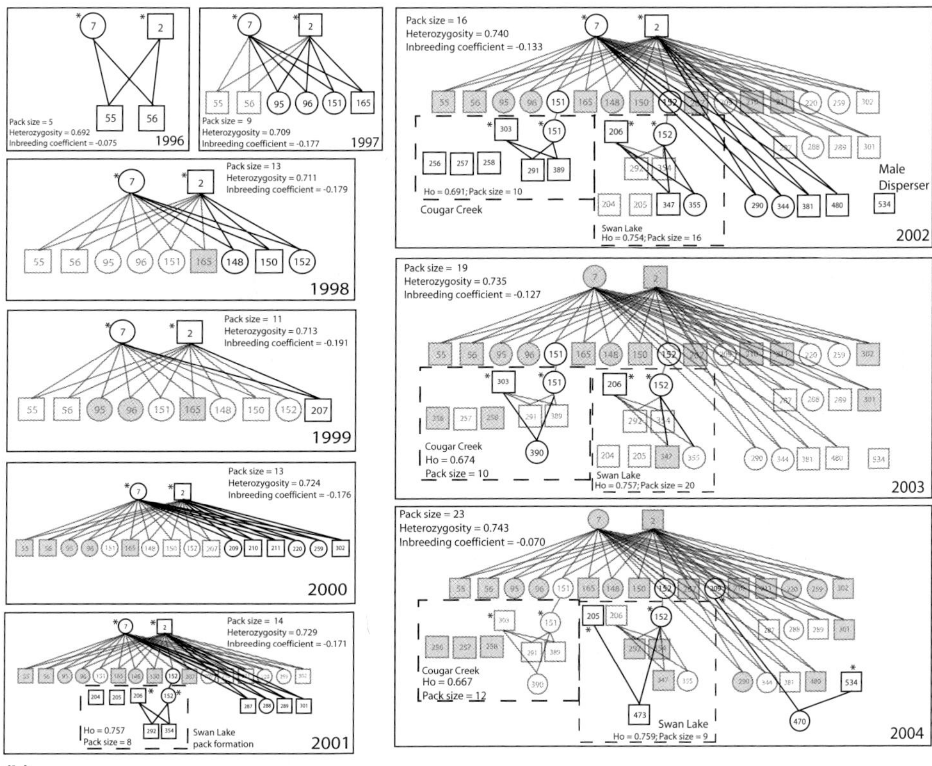

Figure 5.4 ***Continued***

Despite this high productivity, reproductive failure was also documented. Most years, at least one pack—and sometimes up to three—produced no pups at all. Reasons for these failures included disease, lack of a mate during the breeding season and den abandonment or pups being killed by adjacent packs in territorial disputes. Pup survival was poor in 1999 and 2005, likely due to disease (see above; Figure 5.3). In 1999, most diseased animals were pups whereas in 2005 both pups and adults died.

Previously only documented in captivity, we recorded two instances of pups successfully breeding. Normally reaching sexual maturity at 22 months of age (Mech, 1970), one male and female pup bred at 10 months and

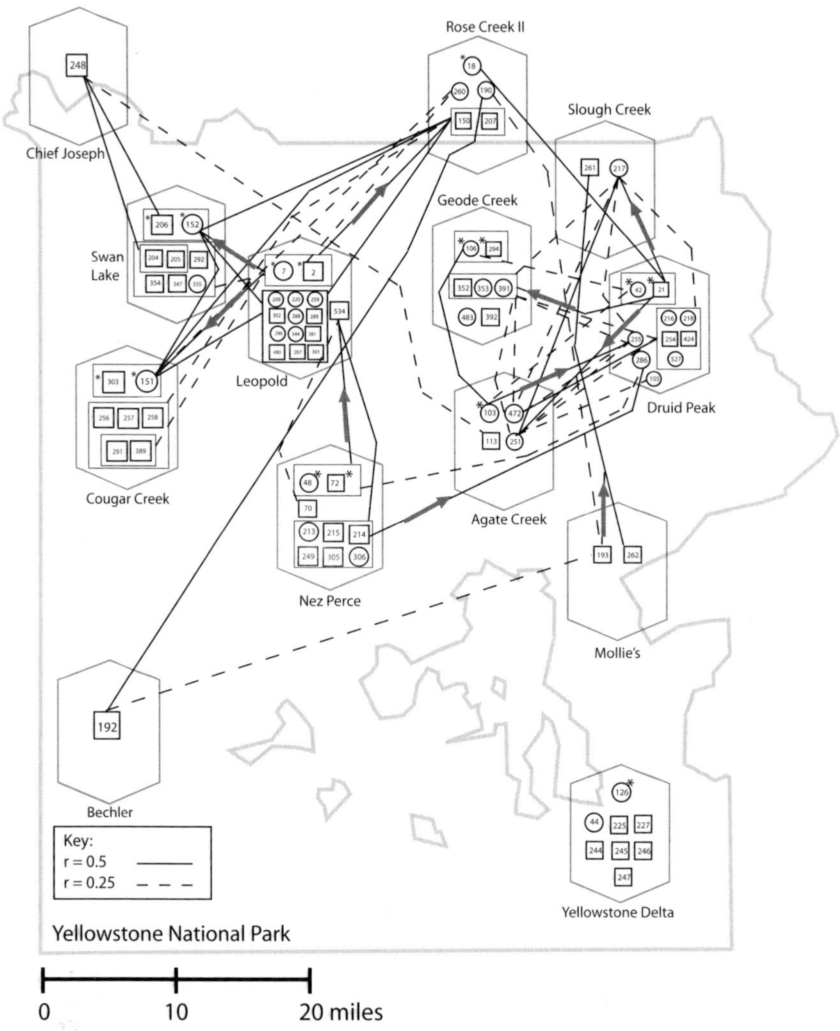

Figure 5.5 **Relatedness between wolf packs in Yellowstone National Park (from Von Holdt *et al.*, 2007).**

produced offspring (they did not breed with each other but with adults >22 months of age). We attribute this early breeding to a shortage of mates. Although vacant breeding territories were available in these first years, mates largely were not. The circumstances under which one would predict such an occurrence were present: abundant food, available territories, and few other adult wolves with which to breed.

Mortality and survival

Overall, annual wolf survival for all sex and age classes, except for young pups, was about 80%. We found increasing survival with age: 74% for pups ($n = 6$), 86% for yearlings ($n = 12$), 81% for adults (2–5 years, $n = 55$), and 68% for old adults (>5 years, $n = 17$). Males and females had approximately equal survival rates (males = 79%, $n = 49$; females = 81%, $n = 41$). However, these data represent only information gathered from radio-collared adult-sized wolves and collaring does not take place until about 9 months. Wolf survival inside YNP (80%, $n = 203$) was consistently higher than outside YNP (68%, $n = 198$), where wolves were significantly more exposed to human-caused mortality. Initially human-caused mortality outside YNP typically accounted for most mortality, but later intraspecific killing became the leading cause of mortality inside YNP.

As population density increased, especially on the northern range, intraspecific killing became more common as did territorial trespasses (Smith, 2005). According to Fuller *et al.*, (2003), wolf density on the northern range should have been higher because of available biomass, but it was not. We hypothesize that this may be due to social strife occurring at high density. In other words, the biomass hypothesis of Fuller *et al.*, (2003) predicts wolf density at low-to-moderate densities accurately but, at high density, wolf–wolf killing becomes the limiting factor despite greater prey biomass. Regardless, higher density and interpack conflict led to wolves leaving Yellowstone, whereupon they were then exposed to higher mortality due to human causes. This source-sink dynamic has had important implications for management, as approximately 20% of the radio-collared wolves outside YNP are killed annually due to conflicts with people, creating opportunities for settlement for YNP-born wolves (US Fish and Wildlife Service, 1995–2006).

Wolf–elk relationships

Wolf impacts on elk, even considering livestock depredations, may be the most controversial aspect of wolf recovery to the GYA. This is because human hunting is allowed outside the Park and elk hunting is culturally and economically important to the surrounding states. Many local residents fear that the return of the wolf will have a significant impact on elk numbers and, consequently, reduce hunting and guiding opportunities and income.

Elk have been the primary year-round prey of wolves since the reintroduction. Of the eight species of ungulates that live in YNP, wolves overwhelmingly choose elk. Of 2365 documented winter kills by wolves, 88% have been elk (Figure 5.6), and the majority of prey killed in summer (as determined from faeces) are also elk (Smith *et al.*, 2006). The proportion of elk calves, cows and bulls killed on the northern range in winter by wolves is 28%, 33% and 26%, respectively, with 13% unknown, (Figure 5.7). This shows strong selection for calves, which comprised only about 18% of the available elk on the northern range between 1995 and 2000 (Smith *et al.*, 2004). It also represents strong selection against cows, as they comprised roughly 60% of the available

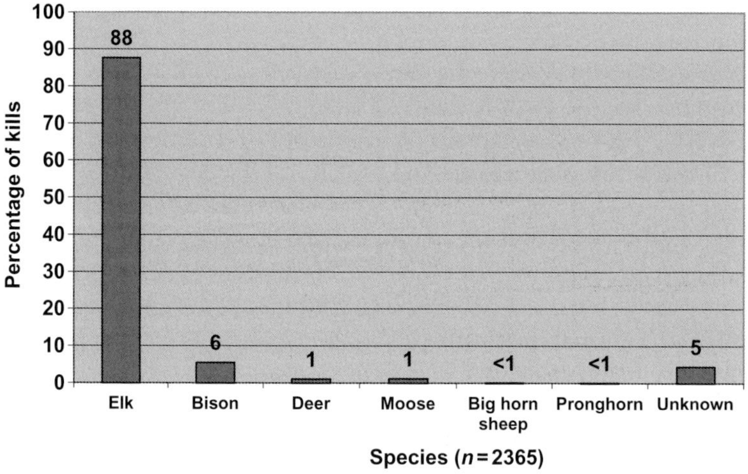

Figure 5.6 **Prey selection of wolves in Yellowstone National Park 1995–2006. The proportion of bison taken has increased in later years, although this is not seen in the graph, owing to the large sample size.**

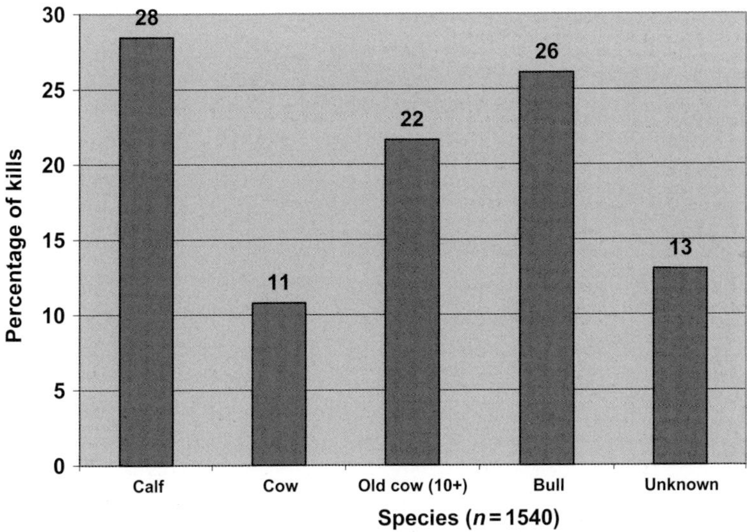

Figure 5.7 **Sex and age of wolf-killed elk in Yellowstone National Park 1995–2006. Wolves select for calves and old cows and take bulls in proportion to availability. Recent trends, however, indicate increased use of bulls in early winter.**

elk from 1995 to 2000. Wolves killed bulls in proportion to their availability during this time period (Smith *et al.*, 2004).

This pattern of prey selection has changed over time and underscores the value of long-term research (Sinclair *et al.*, 2007). From 1995 to 2003, wolves preyed primarily on elk calves in early winter when adult elk were less vulnerable. In early winter 2004 and 2005, the majority of the wolf kill switched to bulls, whereas previously bull elk were killed in late winter. We hypothesize that the current drought, of more than 10 years, is affecting elk condition entering winter, and is primarily affecting bulls. Less winter and summer precipitation has reduced the quantity and quality of forage for elk and has affected their condition going into winter. We speculate that this is especially acute for bull elk because of the demands for peak body condition prior to the rut. Entering the rut in less than optimal condition further weakens the bulls, making them particularly vulnerable to wolf predation, and wolf prey selection has changed accordingly. This relationship is a high priority for future study.

Furthermore, wolves typically kill the older, senescent cow elk; the average age of wolf-killed cow elk 1995–2007 was 14 years old (Wright *et al.*, 2006; YNP, unpublished data), which is about the age that elk begin having a calf every other year instead of every year (Wright *et al.*, 2006). The average age of a cow elk killed by human hunters was 6 years old, and the reproductive value of these prime-age elk was much higher than of old wolf-killed elk (Wright *et al.*, 2006).

Kill rates also varied across years and seasons. Overall in early winter, a wolf killed 1.4 elk/30 days and 2.2 elk/30 days in late winter for an overall winter kill rate of 1.8 elk/wolf/30 days (Figure 5.8; Smith *et al.*, 2004). Kill rates were elevated during snowier winters (Figure 5.8). From 2000 to 2007, preliminary data indicate that kill rates have declined compared to the 1995–2000 period. This could be due to several factors such as drought, behavioural learning by elk, less vulnerable prey and wolf–wolf competition to name some possibilities. Success at killing elk per encounter has declined, suggesting that at least some of the explanation is elk behaviour/experience (MacNulty, 2007).

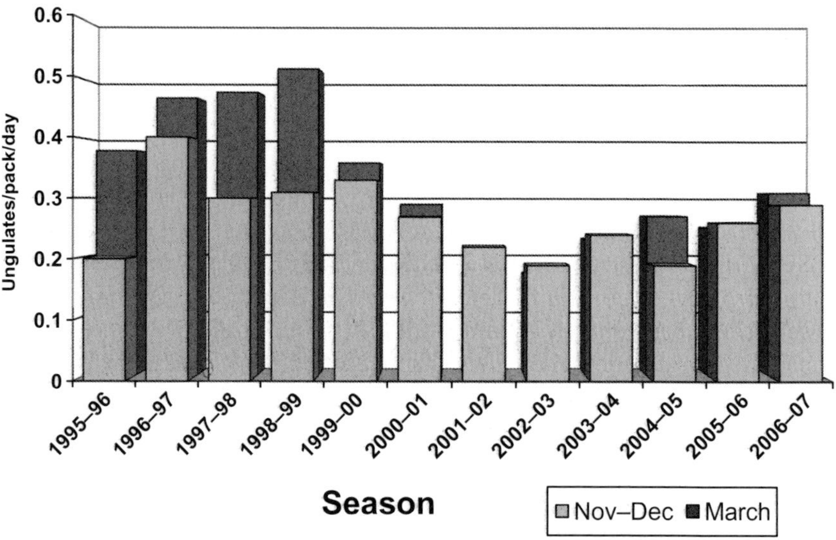

Figure 5.8 **Ungulates killed/pack in early and late winter in Yellowstone National Park, 1995–2006. Early-winter kill rates are always lower than those in late winter. Average-to-severe winters (1994–1995, 1996–1997 and 2004–2005) see increases in wolf kill rates.**

Interestingly, any variation in kill rate was due to bulls, calves or older females and not to prime-aged females (aged 2–10 years). Wolf predation on prime-aged cows was constant and low compared to the other sex and age classes, which varied seasonally and annually (Vucetich *et al.*, 2005). This at least suggests that weather and forage may be important drivers to the elk–wolf interaction as we hypothesize the non-prime cows were more susceptible to environmental stress. Their vulnerability to predation may therefore be less influenced by environmental variables.

Data collection on kill rates and prey selection in summer have been less successful, mainly due to failure of Global Positioning System (GPS) satellite radio-collars designed to locate wolves at 30-min intervals throughout the day and night. However, preliminary data from some successful GPS tracking indicates that prey selection and kill rates differ from winter and that, overall, wolves probably consume less biomass in summer compared to winter. Wolves do not prey extensively on elk calves when they are born, around June 1, as do other carnivores, particularly bears (Barber-Meyer, 2006).

The debate of wolf impacts on elk has been intense and is far from resolved. Some would argue that most of the wolf predation on elk in the northern portion of the Park is additive owing to the fact that elk are estimated to be well below carrying capacity, so resources are plentiful contributing to good elk condition (Taper & Gogan, 2002; White & Garrott, 2005). An alternative viewpoint is that elk carrying capacity has been reduced due to a decade-long drought, causing elk condition to decline and therefore making them more vulnerable to wolf attack and the effect of predation being more compensatory (Vucetich *et al.*, 2005). Obviously, no mortality is ever entirely additive or compensatory and may switch back and forth based on numerous factors. Whether or not the presence of bison will exacerbate elk declines or buffer against them is an open question (Garrott *et al.*, 2007; Hebblewhite & Smith, in press). Wolf effects on bison at this time are minimal. Mule deer, an important summer prey of wolves, are similarly affected little, owing to migration outside of YNP in winter and thereby avoiding year-round predation pressure.

Part of the controversy and debate about wolf effects on prey revolves around the wolf kill rate at different prey densities, e.g. the functional response (Messier, 1995; Eberhardt, 2000). A significant effort has gone into understanding this relationship, and to a degree it is still unresolved. Although our YNP studies are not yet sufficiently long term to inform this debate as prey density has not varied enough over time, wolf kill rates did not vary across a range of prey densities across the Park, suggesting that wolves kill at a minimal rate commensurate with caloric needs, only killing at higher rates when prey become more vulnerable (e.g. late winter; Smith *et al.*, 2004). Supporting this view is the observation that wolves killed by prey were not uncommon.

Besides kill rate, prey selection was not uniform across the Park, suggesting two wolf–prey systems across YNP: one on the northern elk-wintering range and one in the interior (Smith *et al.*, 2004). Compared to the interior, the northern range is lower in elevation, has less snow, geothermal areas are rare and elk are abundant all year. Conditions in the interior are the opposite: elevation is higher, snow is deep and more persistent, thermal features are abundant (providing very small refugia from otherwise deep snow) and most elk migrate out of the area, making them rare in winter. Wolves have adapted to these different conditions. On the northern range, elk are the primary prey of wolves throughout the winter. In the interior in winter, after many of the elk have left the Park, wolves must also kill bison and moose (Smith *et al.*, 2000, 2004). Wolves in the interior are also able to use thermal areas to their advantage (Bergman *et al.*, 2006). Prey that reside in small snow-free thermal areas are faced with deep snow outside the area, making them abnormally vulnerable to predation (Bergman *et al.*, 2006). Consequently, this small segment of the elk population that utilizes high-elevation thermal features to over-winter, is declining and could eventually disappear (Garrott *et al.*, 2007).

Finally, factors other than elk behaviour and vulnerability may play a role in which elk get killed. Some landscape features were associated with wolf kills, for example disproportionate numbers of wolf-killed carcasses were found near streams and roads, and valley bottoms in general had a higher predation risk (Kauffman *et al.*, 2007). Both on the northern range and in central Yellowstone, kills were more associated with landscape features than with elk density (Bergman *et al.*, 2006; Kauffman *et al.*, 2007).

Effects on scavengers

Average wolf pack size in YNP is 11, so wolves can immediately eat about 110 kg of a cow elk carcass that weighs 230 kg, which results in a lot of left-over meat. Even more is left from bull elk (320 kg), moose (410 kg) or bison (680 kg) carcasses. As wolves sleep off their meal, a suite of species move in to consume as much as they can. Studies in YNP as well as Canada's Yukon

Territory (Kaczensky *et al.*, 2005) and Isle Royale National Park (Vucetich *et al.*, 2004), have shown that scavengers consume a large proportion of a wolf kill. In fact, small packs have to compete with scavengers to such an extent that they may have kill rates as high as larger packs in order to make up for what scavengers take (Kaczensky *et al.*, 2005). Unlike cougars and bears, which conceal and cover their kills, wolves must out-eat the voracious scavengers.

We have documented 12 different scavenger species that utilize wolf kills, not including the many invertebrates that ultimately clean up the carcass (Wilmers *et al.*, 2003). Ravens, *Corvus corax*, are the most common scavenger found at wolf kills and a subset of ravens follow the wolves (Stahler *et al.*, 2002). Ravens quickly recruit more ravens and, within minutes, there would be a cacophony of raven cries. An easy way to locate a wolf kill is to look for raven activity. The average number of ravens per kill on the northern range is 28, but 135 ravens were once seen at one kill site (Stahler *et al.*, 2002).

Almost every wolf kill also attracts magpies (*Pica hudsonia*), bald eagles (*Haliaeetus leucocephalus*), golden eagles (*Aquila chrysaetos*), and coyotes. Coyotes visit wolf kills at their peril. Virtually every coyote killed by a wolf was in the vicinity of a wolf kill (Ballard *et al.*, 2003). Black and grizzly bears also visit wolf kills when they are not hibernating, and grizzlies dominate wolves at kill sites (Hebblewhite & Smith, in press). Although all GYA wolf packs must deal with bear competition, one pack, Mollie's, in YNP's interior, is particularly vulnerable to bear raids (Ballard *et al.*, 2003). Typically, grizzly bears emerge from their dens in March. Upon emergence they are ravenous, and tend to search out wolf kills. In the past 5 years, every kill made by Mollie's pack from March to October was taken over by grizzly bears. Our observations of these interactions show that within a few hours of wolves killing an elk or bison, bears detect it and chase the wolves away. We expect this wolf–bear–carcass situation to be an important aspect of the grizzly bear story in GYA in future years.

In the future, we expect more rare animals to take advantage of wolf kills and perhaps increase their populations. Wolverines, *Gulo gulo*, for example, typically do not migrate to lower elevations like other animals do in winter, and they rely primarily on carrion to survive. Wolves often make kills on high ridges in winter because bull elk often stay high on windblown slopes, surrounded by deep snow. These kills could serve as food sources to the currently rare wolverine or the equally rare red fox, *Vulpes vulpes*. Examples like this and others show the effects that wolves may have on numerous other species, increasing the overall biodiversity of an area like YNP.

Surplus killing

We have only documented surplus killing one winter, the severe winter of 1996–1997, considered one of the most severe of the 20th century (Mech *et al.*, 2001). Heavy snows in November–December were followed by rain on New Year's Day 1997, followed by below-zero temperatures acting together to virtually seal-out ungulate access to forage. Thousands of elk died, and vulnerability to wolves was high (Smith *et al.*, 1999). Wolves made many kills but also scavenged many others. One pack (Druid Peak) was observed making five kills in one day. We watched these five kills for several weeks after they were made and, interestingly, the wolves returned to all of them and, combined with the scavengers, fully consumed all five carcasses. We believe this is typical and that the occasionally reported carcass that is not eaten stems from inadequate time to consume the kill and/or being disturbed from it.

Other carnivores

Yellowstone and the surrounding public land have one of the most unique assemblages of large carnivores in North America. Few other places have such a grouping of carnivores—black and grizzly bears, cougars, coyotes and wolves—that all feed on elk at some point during the year. Lynx, wolverine and red fox are present but very rare. Only one of the eight elk herds that use Yellowstone is non-migratory, so human hunters should be included in this carnivore assembly. To understand carnivore–carnivore interactions, we have involved other researchers and initiated cooperative studies.

The most dramatic effects of wolf reintroduction on the carnivore community have been on coyotes. Pre-wolf reintroduction, large packs (range = 5–8) of coyotes were common, but they virtually vanished soon after wolves became established (Crabtree & Sheldon, 1999). Coyote populations declined by 50% after wolf recovery, but have recently rebounded to pre-wolf levels but with much smaller pack size (R. Crabtree, Ecological Research Center, USA; personal communication). A 2005 drop in wolf numbers and social adaptation by coyotes were speculated to be the causes (R. Crabtree, personal communication).

Effects on large carnivores other than coyotes have been less dramatic. Early results indicate that wolves may be beneficial to grizzly bears. Grizzly bears are dominant to wolves at carcasses about 80% of the time and utilize wolf kills during times of food shortage (Hebblewhite & Smith, in press). Wolf interactions with black bear have been fewer: wolves seem to dominate black bears but have had no impact on their behaviour or population level.

Wolf–cougar interactions have rarely been observed (Ruth, 2004). Displacement of cougars to more rugged and forested terrain by wolf packs has occurred, and a few cougars have been killed by wolves, but the population seems relatively unaffected by wolf population recovery, at least at this point in time (Ruth, 2004).

A pilot study by a host of co-operators involving wolves, cougars and grizzly bears showed a differing response by each carnivore to the human elk-hunting season north of YNP (Ruth *et al.*, 2003). Bears, primarily a scavenger, seemed to be attracted to hunting activity, leaving YNP to take advantage of elk remains, while cougars, primarily a hunter, followed the elk that retreated into YNP at the onset of the hunting season. Wolves, which readily hunt and scavenge, seemed to be unaffected by the hunting season, travelling in and out of YNP just as before and after the onset of the elk-hunting season. A study of the fate of hunter- versus wolf-killed ungulate carcasses indicated that wolf kills are used by a much larger and more diverse scavenger guild than ungulate carcasses left by hunters (Wilmers *et al.*, 2003).

Ecosystem effects

Because of YNP's long history and written records back to 1872, monitoring over periods of time when wolves were both present and absent offers a unique opportunity to examine the link between wolves and biodiversity in this North American temperate ecosystem. Will wolves restructure the YNP ecosystem? What will it be like in 30 years, after the full ecological effects of wolves have manifested themselves?

Indirect effects of wolves on vegetation have been recorded in other ecosystems (McLaren & Peterson, 1994; Hebblewhite *et al.*, 2005), and preliminary observations indicate that the same may be happening in YNP (Ripple *et al.*, 2001; Beschta, 2003; Beyer *et al.*, 2007).

Biological communities are often dynamic. Such dynamism has characterized a 100,000-ha region of northern YNP where aspen, *Populus tremuloides*, recruitment has declined during the past 100 years—a reduction that coincides with decades of high elk densities (Houston, 1982; Larsen & Ripple, 2003; Wagner, 2006). However, abiotic and biotic factors have also been implicated in the decline of aspens and other mesic or riparian plant communities (Romme & Despain, 1989; Singer *et al.*, 2002, 2003). Regardless of the cause of the decline, aspen stands are biodiversity hotspots across the west, especially for songbirds (Turchi *et al.*, 1995). A widespread aspen response since wolf reintroduction has not been recorded (Ripple *et al.*, 2001), but unpublished data indicate that aspen growth has increased at the periphery of the elk wintering-range, whereas aspen is still suppressed in the elk core wintering area (E. Larsen, University of Wisconsin, Stevens Point, USA, personal communication.). This preliminary finding suggests that any recovery in vegetation may be linked to the number of elk present and not to changes in elk behaviour (e.g. numerical versus behavioural response), but this has yet to be established, and Kaufmann *et al.*, (2007) and Bergman *et al.*, (2006) did find a landscape effect on wolf predation.

Willow growth has increased more dramatically since wolf reintroduction. However, it is important to note that this response has not been uniform across the northern range, supporting the theory that a predation effect exists (Beyer *et al.*, 2007). However, we feel that the most parsimonious explanation is that elk have reduced their use of areas where predation pressure was high (behavioural), and also there are fewer elk on the landscape (numeric response). As a consequence, the intensity of browsing on aspens and willows was relaxed (Beyer *et al.*, 2007; Hebblewhite & Smith, in press). Why willow has responded sooner than aspen is unknown, but it may be no more complex than the fact that willow is a shrub and aspen a tree, and the former therefore better able to withstand heavy browsing pressure.

Restoration of aspen and willow following wolf reintroduction, even if wolves are only one of several causes, could have far-reaching effects. It is likely that wolves are necessary, but not on their own sufficient, for woody vegetation recovery. Preliminary data from a songbird study comparing abundance and diversity in recovered versus suppressed willow stands show a significant songbird response where willow was lush (Table 5.1; Baril & Hansen, 2007). Evidence to include beavers in this mix is also accumulating as beavers, after decades of only transients and few colonies, increased 10-fold coincident with wolf and willow recovery (Smith *et al.*, 2004).

Table 5.1 **Riparian songbird abundance, species richness and diversity in willow sites that were completely protected from herbivory, sites that were recently released from herbivory and sites with no recent growth under heavy herbivory in Yellowstone National Park, 2003. The log response ratio X_{p+}/X_{p-} of released (X_{p+}) to suppressed (X_{p-}) sites is also shown for comparison (from Hebblewhite & Smith, in press).**

Factor	Protected sites—willow (SE)	Released sites—recent willow growth (SE)	Suppressed sites—no recent growth (SE)	*p*-Value	Log response ratio
Mean number of birds	12.2 (0.9510)	12.6 (0.7546)	9.6 (0.6602)	0.016	+0.12[a]
Richness	6.9 (0.5232)	6.3 (0.3293)	4.8 (0.3717)	0.0013	+0.16[a]
Shannon index	1.7 (0.1203)	1.7 (0.0513)	1.3 (0.0886)	0.004	+0.12[a]

SE, Standard error of the mean.
[a]All response ratios are statistically significantly different from 0, $p < 0.05$.

It is important to note that grasses drive the northern Yellowstone system (and are not suppressed by ungulate grazing; Frank & McNaughton, 1992), as only 2%–4% of the entire area is deciduous woody vegetation (Smith *et al.*, 2003). However, there is evidence that the importance of woody vegetation is disproportionate to its abundance. Therefore, any increase may increase biodiversity—for example as we are beginning to see with beavers responding to increased willow, which in turn provides aquatic habitat for other plants and animals (Baker & Hill, 2003).

All of these possible ecosystem effects will take many more years of study to sort out, and other hypotheses like climate change have not been fully incorporated into any overarching theory. Data are accumulating, however, that human hunters do not serve as surrogate wolf hunters; the spatio-temporal effects of wolf hunting are vastly different to those of human hunters, even though this claim has been one rationale for massive global predator extermination.

Livestock depredation

Within YNP, commercial operators and Park staff travel by horseback and hobble or tether horses overnight near wolves but, so far, only minor problems have occurred (there were several incidents where wolves chased horses but with no attacks). Outside YNP, livestock are common. Before wolves were reintroduced to the GYE, livestock producers within the area where most wolf packs were expected to live, reported that they lost an estimated 8340 cattle, *Bos taurus*, and 12,993 sheep, *Ovis aries*, annually (National Park Service, 1990). Prior to wolf reintroduction, predation accounted for only about 3% of all cattle losses and 30% of all sheep losses. We predicated that, on average, 100 wolves in the GYE would kill 19 cattle and 68 sheep annually, with damage at an estimated value of US$2000 to US$30,000 annually. From 1995 to 2006, wolves in the GYA were confirmed to have killed 415 cattle and 610 sheep (US Fish and Wildlife Service, 2007). This rate is at predicted levels as only approximately 35 cattle and 51 sheep were confirmed killed per year, even though the annual wolf population averaged 200 wolves over that same 12-year period. Wolf depredations were dispersed and sporadic and only a few livestock producers incurred multiple losses. While unimportant to the regional livestock industry, wolf depredations could affect the economic viability of a few small ranches, primarily those dependent on remote public land grazing allotments closest to YNP. Interestingly, human tolerance in the GYA ecosystem is less than human tolerance for carnivores in other areas (e.g. Africa or India) where human population density is higher and economic well being is considerably lower (Jhala & Giles, 1991; Creel & Creel, 2002). This disparity is interesting and counter-intuitive.

Thirty-three domestic dogs, *Canis lupus familiaris*, mainly livestock-herding and guarding dogs and hunting hounds, have been killed by wolves, but over perceived territorial disputes, rather than hunger (Bangs *et al.*, 2006a). In an attempt to maintain local social tolerance of wolves and to reduce illegal killing, the USFWS wolf-control policies consider any wolf attack on livestock to be a serious issue that requires an aggressive agency response. We relocated problem wolves 42 times and killed 267 problem wolves to reduce conflicts in the GYE. Agency-initiated research with radio-collared livestock indicated that wolf depredation was rare, but suggested that confirmed losses may be a fraction (perhaps only one in eight confirmed) of actual wolf-caused losses near active dens in densely forested and remote public land grazing allotments

(Oakleaf *et al.*, 2003). Even then, livestock depredations by wolves could still only be significant to a few ranches. USFWS regulations allow livestock producers to kill wolves attacking their livestock and allow any wolf that threatens human safety to be killed (US Fish and Wildlife Service, 1994; US Federal Regulation 59 FR 60252; US Federal Regulation 70 FR 1286; Bangs *et al.*, 2004, 2006a). In addition, a host of lethal and non-lethal tools are used to reduce the rate of wolf–livestock conflict (Bangs *et al.*, 2006b).

Human impacts

No one predicted that people would often see wolves after they were reintroduced to the Park. Elsewhere, few people catch even a fleeting glimpse of a wild wolf. But now in YNP, dedicated people can see wolves most days. In fact, more than 20,000 people directly report that they see a wolf in YNP each year, but another survey estimates that 150,000 visitors/year may see wolves (Duffield *et al.*, 2006). YNP is probably the best place in the world to easily view wild wolves. Their high visibility has also made YNP wolves the most photographed and reported upon in the world.

The economic activity and visitor enjoyment generated by wolf viewing has been a surprise. Before wolves, winter was not considered by many to be a prime wildlife-viewing season in the YNP, but now it is, and summer viewing is also more popular. The economic benefit derived from this is estimated to be US$32,000,000 annually and, using a standard economic multiplier, may reach US$85,000,000 annually (Duffield *et al.*, 2006). Providing people with the opportunity to experience Park wolves either first-hand or through the popular media is one of the remarkable achievements of the restoration programme. The high visibility of YNP wolves also offered unprecedented scientific opportunities to study various aspects of wolf behaviour that had been rarely observed.

The EIS predicted that wolf restoration would decrease opportunities to harvest some ungulates, primarily cow elk, and that this reduced hunting opportunity would roughly result in US$200,000–US$450,000 in hunter benefits and in US$200,000–US$400,000 in hunter expenditures annually (US Fish and Wildlife Service, 1994: Table 5.2). Many hunting camps are situated on the Park boundary with the intent to harvest elk moving from YNP. On the north boundary of YNP, there has been, according to hunting outfitters, a sharp decline in hunter success and the number of elk. On the south boundary, no such decline in either measure has been stated by hunters. On the east and west boundaries, there are fewer outfitters and less discussion has occurred. This downturn in hunting activity on the north boundary was not included in the Duffield *et al.*, (2006) study. The cause of the decline in the north but not in the south is debated. The decline of elk in the north is probably due to wolves and other factors (e.g. multi-causal decline), but another consideration should be the ability of the range to support elk, and this may have declined owing to multi-year drought and/or elk numbers exceeding carrying capacity during the decade preceding wolf recovery. In the south, such an overshoot may not have occurred pre-wolf (winter feeding is still practised in the state of Wyoming), resulting in less of an elk decline post-wolf. Wolf and bear densities are high along both boundaries, and human hunting might be slightly more intense along the southern boundary. Issues of wolves affecting big-game hunting have become more of an issue in recent years compared to livestock depredation and may not be as easily solved (e.g. livestock-killing wolves are not tolerated). Overall, predictions about the impacts of wolf recovery have been correct, but there are some notable exceptions that many would not consider minor (Table 5.2).

Conclusion

Wolf extermination took place because of negative human values about wildlife in deference to other social values, even in National Parks. As a result of those values, government programmes encouraged wildlands to be modified for direct human use; in other words, wildlife and indigenous people to be replaced by settlers, crops and livestock, with predator extermination. Without large blocks of livestock-free habitat or abundant prey to minimize conflicts, and facing extreme human prejudice and persecution, wolves had no future in the early 1900 American West.

Largely because of reintroduction, wolf packs currently occupy areas where only 20 years ago biologists believed wolves could not exist because the level of conflict would be intolerable. Wolf restoration in YNP and other areas of the northern Rocky Mountains has become a resounding success story. But without the core refugium provided by large blocks of public land such as YNP, such success would have not been possible. Because of land-use changes during the past century, we predict that wolves will only be an ecological force in relatively small areas of their once vast historic range, as a certain minimal

Table 5.2 **Assessment of wolf impacts from the EIS: Predictions compared to 10-year appraisal (Smith, 2005).**

Predictions[a]	Appraisals
No wolves existed in the Yellowstone ecosystem	None have been found after reintroduction, except for reintroduced wolves and their offspring born in the Yellowstone ecosystem
Wolves would travel outside the experimental area	Yes wolves have travelled outside the experimental area
Wolf packs would kill 120 ungulates per year	Based on estimated wolf kill rates from winter data (no summer data), wolf packs kill 168–264 elk per year
Wolves would kill an annual average of 19 (range 3–32) cattle and 68 (range 38–110) sheep each year	As of the end of 2001, wolves in the Yellowstone ecosystem have killed an annual average of six cattle (range 0–22) and 37 sheep (range 0–117) each year
Land-use restrictions would occur around dens only	Land-use restrictions have occurred around dens only inside Yellowstone National Park
State management would occur before delisting	States will not manage wolves before delisting
Few visitors to Yellowstone National Park would see wolves	More than 100,000 people had seen wolves in Yellowstone National Park as of August 2002

[a]Made before wolf reintroduction.

wolf density must be achieved before the strong ecological effects found in YNP are manifested (Berger & Smith, 2005). These minimal wolf densities will probably not be realized outside of parks and large areas of public land as wolf densities will be held low owing to conflicts with humans (Garrott *et al.*, 2005).

YNP has become a more complete landscape with the return of wolves. It has provided the public with a fascinating look at an "American Serengeti" and with unparalleled opportunities for scientific inquiries into the nature of ecosystems and top-down trophic cascades. That success should be appreciated and relished, but it could not have occurred without YNP being preserved more than 125 years ago. Successful wolf restoration was inevitable once human values changed, because the biological requirements for a viable wolf population, space and prey, had already been restored. There was enough remote habitat and wild prey so that, with agency management, conflicts between wolves and people were rare. The majority of the publicly perceived conflicts were sufficiently rare, and the presence of wolves sufficiently valuable, that local people should tolerate wolves. Given some minimal level of secure habitat, wild prey and human tolerance, wolf populations will persist. Wolves will eventually spread to adjacent areas as the changing social values, which allowed recovery in parts of the northern United States, continue to manifest themselves elsewhere. The USFWS has proposed to remove the wolf from ESA protection in early 2008. That would mean that, outside the National Parks like YNP, wolves would be managed by the state Fish and Game Agencies—much as are black bears, mountain lions, deer and elk—and that management would include public hunting as long as it did not threaten the Northern Rocky Mountain wolf population. Some think that this is the most appropriate form of conservation for recovered wildlife populations, including wolves (Bangs & Smith, in press). The only certain outcome is more public controversy. Wolves may not make everyone's life better, but they always make people's lives more interesting.

Acknowledgements

We appreciate the efforts of all those people working for the Yellowstone Wolf Project, both past and present. More than 150 people have volunteered, and many have worked as technicians, and we are eternally grateful. We especially thank D. Guernsey, D. MacNulty, R. McIntyre, M. Metz, K. Murphy and D, Stahler. Financial support came from many sources. The National Park Service provided government support, and private support came through the Yellowstone Park Foundation in the form of grants and/or donations. We are particularly grateful to an anonymous donor, the Tapeats Foundation, Frank and Kay Yeager, the California Wolf Center, Masterfoods, Patagonia Inc, the wolf radio-collar donors and many others who have contributed toward wolf studies in Yellowstone National Park. Part of this work was supported by NSF grant DEB-0613730. Finally, we are thankful for safe and capable piloting by R. Stradley of Gallatin Flying Service, M. Duffy of Central

Copters, and B. Hawkins, G. Brennan and D. Williamson of Hawkins and Powers Aviation.

References

Allen, D.L. (1979) *Wolves of Minong: Their Vital Role in a Wild Community*. Houghton Mifflin Co., Boston, Massachusetts.

Baker, B. & Hill, E.P. (2003) Beaver. *Wild Mammals of North America*. (eds G.A. Feldhamer, B.C. Thompson. & J.A. Chapman), pp 288–310. JHU Press, Baltimore.

Ballard, W.B., Carbyn, L.N. & Smith, D.W. (2003) Wolf interactions with non-prey. *Wolves: Ecology, Behaviour and Conservation*. (eds L.D. Mech & L. Boitani), pp. 259–271. University of Chicago Press, Chicago.

Bangs, E.E. & Fritts, S.H. (1996) Reintroducing the gray wolf to central Idaho and Yellowstone National Park. *Wildlife Society Bulletin* 24, 402–413.

Bangs, E.E. & Smith, D.W. (in press) *Reintroduction of the Gray Wolf to Yellowstone National Park and Central Idaho, USA*. IUCN Reintroduction Specialist Group.

Bangs, E.E., Fontaine, J., Meier, T. et al. (2004) Restoration and conflict management of the gray wolf in Montana, Idaho, and Wyoming. *Transactions of North American Wildlife and Natural Resources Conference* 69, 89–105.

Bangs, E.E., Fritts, S.H., Fontaine, J.A. et al. (1998) Status of gray wolf restoration in Montana, Idaho, and Wyoming. *Wildlife Society Bulletin* 26, 785–798.

Bangs, E.E., Jimenez, M., Niemeyer, C. et al. (2006a) Livestock guarding dogs and wolves in the Northern Rocky Mountains of the United States. *Carnivore Damage Prevention News* 8, 32–39.

Bangs, E.E., Jimenez, M., Niemeyer, C. et al. (2006b) Nonlethal and lethal tools to manage wolf/livestock conflict in the northwestern United States. *Proceedings of the Vertebrate Pest Conference* 22, 7–16.

Barber-Meyer, S.M. (2006) *Elk Calf Mortality Following Wolf Restoration to Yellowstone National Park*. PhD thesis, University of Minnesota.

Baril, L. & Hansen, A. (2007) *Avian Response to Willow Height Growth (Salix spp.) in Yellowstone's Northern Range*. Report to Yellowstone National Park.

Berger, J. & Smith, D.W. (2005) Restoring functionality in Yellowstone with recovering carnivores: Gains and uncertainties. *Large Carnivores and the Conservation of Biodiversity*. (eds J.C. Ray, K.H. Redford, R.S. Steneck & J. Berger). pp. 100–108. Island Press, Washington, DC.

Bergman, E., Garrott, R., Creel, S., Borkowski, J.J., Jaffe, R. & Watson, F.G.R. (2006) Assessment of prey vulnerability through analysis of wolf movements and kill sites. *Ecological Applications* 16(1), 273–284.

Beschta, R.L. (2003) Cottonwoods, elk, and wolves in the Lamar valley of Yellowstone National Park. *Ecological Applications* 13(5), 1295–309.

Beyer, H.L., Merrill, E.H., Varley, N. & Boyce, M.S. (2007) Willow on Yellowstone's northern range: Evidence for a trophic cascade? *Ecological Applications* 17, 1563–1571.

Crabtree, R.L. & Sheldon, J.W. (1999) Coyotes and canid coexistence in Yellowstone. *Carnivores in Ecosystems.* Eds T.W. Clark, A.P. Curlee, S.C. Minta & P.M. Kareiva), pp. 127–163. Yale University Press, New Haven.

Creel, S. & Creel, N.M. (2002) *The African Wild Dog: Behaviour, Ecology, and Conservation.* Princeton University Press, Princeton.

Duffield, J., Neher, C. & Patterson, D. (2006) *Wolves and People in Yellowstone: Impacts on the Regional Economy.* University of Montana, Missoula. Final Report to NPS.

Eberhardt, L.L. (2000) Reply: Predator–prey ratio dependence and regulation of moose populations. *Canadian Journal of Zoology* 78, 511.

Frank, D.A. & McNaughton, S.J. 1992. The ecology of plants, large mammalian herbivores, and drought in Yellowstone National Park. *Ecology* 73, 2229–2241.

Fritts, S.H., Mack, C.M., Smith, D.W., et al. (2001) Outcomes of hard and soft releases of wolves in central Idaho and the Greater Yellowstone Area. *Large Mammal Restoration: Ecological and Sociological Challenges for the 21st Century.* (eds D.S. Maehr, R.F. Noss & J.L. Larkin), pp 125–147. Island Press, Washington, DC.

Fuller, T.K., Mech, L.D. & Cochrane, J.F. (2003) Wolf population dynamics. *Wolves: Behaviour, Ecology, and Conservation.* (eds L.D. Mech & L. Boitani), pp. 161–191. University of Chicago Press, Chicago.

Garrott, R.A., Bruggeman, J.E., Becker, M.S., Kalinowski, S.T. & White, P.J. (2007) Evaluating prey switching in wolf-ungulate systems. *Ecological Applications* 17(6), 1588–1597.

Garrott, R.A., Gude J.A., Bergman, E.J., Gower, C., White, P.J. & Hamlin, K.L. (2005) Generalizing wolf effects across the Greater Yellowstone area: A cautionary note. *Wildlife Society Bulletin* 33, 1245–1255.

Hebblewhite, M. & Smith, D.W. (in press) Wolf community ecology: Ecosystem effects of recovering wolves in Banff and Yellowstone National Parks. *The World of Wolves: New perspectives on Ecology, Behaviour and Policy.* (eds M. Musiani, L. Boitani & P.C. Paquet).

Hebblewhite, M., White, C.A., Neitvelt, C.G., McKenzie, J.A. et al. (2005) Human activity mediates a trophic cascade caused by wolves. *Ecology* 86, 2135–2144.

Houston, D. (1982) *The Northern Yellowstone Elk: Ecology and Management.* McMillan Publishing Co., New York.

Jhala, Y.V. & Giles. R.H. 1991 The status and conservation of the wolf in Gujarat and Rajasthan, India. *Conservation Biology* 5, 476–483.

Kaczensky, P., Hayes, R.D. & Promberger. C. (2005) Effect of raven *Corvus corax* scavenging on the kill rates of wolf *Canis lupus* packs. *Wildlife Biology* 11(2), 101–108.

Kauffman, M.J., Varley, N., Smith, D.W., Stahler, D.R., MacNulty, D.R. & Boyce, M.S. (2007) Landscape heterogeneity shapes predation in a newly restored predator–prey system. *Ecology Letters* 10, 1–11.

Larsen, E.J. & Ripple, W.J. (2003) Aspen age structure in the northern Yellowstone ecosystem: USA. *Forest Ecology and Management* 179, 469–482.

Leopold, A.S., Cain, S.A., Cottam, C.M., Gabrielson, I.N. & Kimball, T.L. (1963) *Wildlife Management in the National Parks. The Leopold Report*, Secretary of the Interior. Udall.

MacNulty, D.R. (2007) *Development, Senescence, and Cooperation in the Predatory Behaviour of a Social Carnivore,* Canis lupus. PhD thesis. University of Minnesota.

McLaren, B.E. & Peterson, R.O. (1994) Wolves, moose, and tree rings on Isle Royale. *Science* 266, 1555–1558.

Mech, L.D. (1970) *The Wolf: Ecology and Behaviour of an Endangered Species.* Doubleday Natural History Press, Garden City.

Mech, L.D., Smith, D.W., Murphy, K.M. & MacNulty, D.R. (2001) Winter severity and wolf predation on a formerly wolf-free elk herd. *Journal of Wildlife Management* 65, 998–1003.

Messier, F. (1995) Is there evidence for a cumulative effect of snow on moose and deer populations? *Journal of Animal Ecology* 64, 136.

National Park Service, (1990) *Wolves for Yellowstone?* Volumes I, II, III & IV: A report to the United States Congress, National Park Service: 1–15.

Oakleaf, J.K., Mack, C.M. & Murray, D.L. (2003) Effects of wolves on livestock calf survival and movements in central Idaho. *Journal of Wildlife Management* 67, 299–306

Phillips, M.K. & Smith, D.W. (1996) *The Wolves of Yellowstone.* Voyageur Press, Stillwater.

Pritchard, J.A. (1999) *Preserving Yellowstone's Natural Conditions: Science and the Perception of Nature.* University of Nebraska Press, Lincoln.

Ripple, W.J., Larsen, E.J., Renkin, R.A. & Smith, D.W. (2001) Trophic cascades among wolves, elk and aspen on Yellowstone National Park's northern range. *Biological Conservation* 102, 227–234.

Romme, W.H. & Despain, D.G. (1989) Historical perspective on the fires of 1988. *BioScience* 39, 695–699.

Ruth, T.K. (2004) Ghost of the Rockies: The Yellowstone cougar project. *Yellowstone Science* 12, 13–24.

Ruth, T.K., Smith, D.W., Haroldson, M.A. et al. (2003) Large-carnivore response to recreational big-game hunting along the Yellowstone National Park and

Absaroka-Beartooth Wilderness boundary. *Wildlife Society Bulletin* 31, 1150–1161.

Rutter, R.J. & Pimlott, D.H. (1968) *The World of the Wolf.* J.B. Lippincott Company, Philadelphia.

Sinclair, A.R.E., Mduma, S.A.R., Hopcraft, J.G.C., Fryxell, J.M., Hilborn, R. & Thirgood, S. (2007) Long-term ecosystem dynamics in the Serengeti: Lessons for conservation. *Conservation Biology* 21, 580–590.

Singer, F.J., Wang, G. & Hobbs, N. (2003) The role of ungulates and large predators on plants, community structure, and ecosystem processes in national parks. *Mammal Community Dynamics.* (eds C.J. Zabel & R.G. Anthony), pp 444–486. Cambridge University Press, Cambridge.

Singer, F.J., Zeigenfuss, L.C., Lubow, B. & Rock, M.J. (2002) Ecological evaluation of potential abundance of ungulates in U.S. National Parks: A case study. *Ecological Evaluation of the Abundance and Effects of Elk Herbivory in Rocky Mountain National Park.* (eds F.J. Singer & L.C. Zeigenfuss), pp 205–250. USGS-BRD, Fort Collins.

Smith, D.W. (2004) 2003 *Beaver Survey.* Internal Memorandum, Yellowstone National Park.

Smith, D.W. (2005) Ten years of Yellowstone wolves. *Yellowstone Science* 13, 7–42.

Smith, D.W. & Almberg, E. (2007) Wolf diseases in Yellowstone National Park. *Yellowstone Science* 15, 20–24.

Smith, D.W., Drummer, T.D., Murphy, K.M., Guernsey, D.S. & Evans, S.B. (2004) Winter prey selection and estimation of wolf kill rates in Yellowstone National Park, 1995–2000. *Journal of Wildlife Management* 68, 153–166.

Smith, D.W., Mech, L.D., Meagher, M. et al. 2000. Wolf-bison interactions in Yellowstone National Park. *Journal of Mammalogy* 81(4), 1128–1135.

Smith, D.W., Murphy, K.M. & Guernsey, D.S. (1999) Yellowstone Wolf Project: Annual Report 1998. National Park Service, YCR-NR-99-1. Yellowstone Center for Resources, Yellowstone National Park, Wyoming.

Smith, D.W., Peterson, R.O. & Houston, D. (2003) Yellowstone after wolves. *BioScience* 53, 330–340.

Smith, D.W., Stahler, D., Guernsey, D. & Bangs, E. (2006) Wolf restoration in Yellowstone National Park. *Wildlife in Shiretoko and Yellowstone National Parks: Lessons in Wildlife Conservation from Two World Heritage Sites.* (eds D.R. McCullough, K. Kaji & M. Yamanaka), pp. 242–254. Shiretoko Nature Foundation, Hokkaido.

Stahler, D.R., Heinrich, B. & Smith, D.W. (2002) Common ravens, *Corvus corax*, preferentially associate with gray wolves, *Canis lupus*, as a foraging strategy in winter. *Animal Behaviour* 64, 283–290.

Taper, M.L. & Gogan, P.J.P. (2002) The northern Yellowstone elk: Density dependence and climatic conditions. *Journal of Wildlife Management* 66(1), 106–122.

Turchi, G.M., Kennedy, P.L., Urban, D. & Hein, D. (1995) Bird species richness in relation to isolation of aspen habitats. *Wilson Bulletin* 107, 463–474.

US Fish and Wildlife Service (1994) *The Reintroduction of Gray Wolves to Yellowstone National Park and Central Idaho.* Final Environmental Impact Statement. Denver.

US Fish and Wildlife Service (1995–2006) Gray Wolf Recovery Weekly Progress Reports *1995–2006.* Helena, Montana or at USFWS website at US Fish and Wildlife Service, Nez Perce Tribe, National Park Service, Montana Fish, Wildlife & Parks, Idaho Fish and Game, and USDA Wildlife Services. 2006 and 2007. *Rocky Mountain Wolf Recovery 2005 and 2006 Interagency Annual Report.* (eds C.A. Sime & E.E. Bangs), USFWS, 585 Shepard Way, Helena.

US Fish and Wildlife Service, Nez Perce Tribe, National Park Service, Montana Fish, Wildlife & Parks, Idaho Fish and Game, and USDA Wildlife Services (2007) *Rocky Mountain Wolf Recovery 2006 Interagency Annual Report.* (eds C.A. Sime & E.E. Bangs). USFWS, Ecological Services, 585 Shepard Way, Helena.

Varley, J.D. & Brewster, W.G. (eds) (1992) *Wolves for Yellowstone*? A report to the United States Congress. Vol IV Research and Analysis. Mammoth Hot Springs, Yellowstone National Park, Wyoming.

Vucetich, J.A., Smith, D.W., Stahler, D.R. (2005) Influence of harvest, Climate, and wolf predation on Yellowstone elk, 1961–2004. *Oikos* 11, 259–270.

Vucetich, J.A., Peterson, R.O. & Waite, T.A. (2004) Raven scavenging favours group foraging in wolves. *Animal Behaviour* 67, 1117–1126.

Von Holdt, B.M., Stahler, D.R., Smith, D.W., Earl, D.A., Pollinger, J.P. & Wayne, R.K. (2007). The genealogy and genetic viability of reintroduced Yellowstone grey wolves. *Molecular Ecology* 17, 252–274.

Wagner, F.H. (2006) *Yellowstone's Destabilized Ecosystem: Elk Effects, Science, and Policy Conflict.* Oxford University Press, Oxford.

Weaver, J. (1978) *The Wolves of Yellowstone.* Natural Resources Report no. 14. US National Park Service, Washington, DC.

White, P.J. & Garrott, R.A. (2005) Northern Yellowstone elk after wolf restoration. *Wildlife Society Bulletin* 33, 942–955.

Wilmers, C.C., Crabtree, R.L., Smith, D.W., Murphy, K.M. & Getz, W.M. (2003) Trophic facilitation by introduced top predators: Grey wolf subsidies to scavengers in Yellowstone National Park. *Journal of Animal Ecology* 72, 909–916.

Wright, G.J., Peterson, R.O., Smith, D.W. & Lemkel, T.O. (2006) Selection of northern Yellowstone elk by gray wolves and hunters. *Journal of Wildlife Management* 70(4), 1070–1078.

6

Aspects and Implications of Bear Reintroduction

Joseph D. Clark[1]

[1]US Geological Survey, Southern Appalachian Field Laboratory, University of Tennessee

Summary

Bear reintroduction has been practised worldwide with varying degrees of success. Homing is a significant issue for American black bears, *Ursus americanus*, and winter-release techniques of females with cubs have been successfully used to improve settling rates and survival. Reintroduction success for all bear species appears to be positively correlated with translocation distance, and success is greater for subadults and females. Animals bred or held in captivity are usually poor candidates for reintroduction, but that may be the only option for some rare species. Habitat analyses are routinely performed, but patch size and configuration may also be important considerations for choosing future reintroduction sites for these wide-ranging species. Biological realities aside, socio-political impediments are more difficult to overcome because of real and perceived threats to human safety and property. Poor public acceptance and understanding were the most important reasons for some bear reintroduction failures, and conservation biologists need to develop methods for identifying areas where co-habitation suitability is high. Citizen-led approaches to develop acceptable restoration strategies may be useful for gaining public acceptance of large-carnivore reintroduction efforts, and public acceptance is where the greatest challenge lies.

Reintroduction of Top-Order Predators, 1st edition. Edited by M.W. Hayward and M.J. Somers.
 ISBN 978-1-4051-7680-4 (pb) and 978-1-4051-9273-6 (hb)

Introduction

Reintroduction is a well-established conservation practice but, more recently, interest in the reintroduction of bears and large carnivores has greatly increased. The re-establishment of large carnivores is an important conservation goal, as this group is recognized as being essential to the top-down regulation of ecosystems (Hilderbrand *et al.*, 1999, Terborgh *et al.*, 1999) and can serve as indicators of landscape-scale attributes such as connectivity and patch size (Carrol *et al.*, 2001). Reintroduction is an attempt to establish a species in an area that was once part of its historical range, where it has been extirpated or become extinct (IUCN, 1998), and has a population-recovery goal as its objective. Reintroduction should not be confused with translocation, which is usually implemented to eliminate human conflicts caused by individual animals. In response to a growing number of reintroduction programmes worldwide, the World Conservation Union formed the Reintroduction Specialist Group in 1988 which, subsequently, led to a strategic planning workshop which produced Reintroduction Guidelines (IUCN, 1998).

The distribution and numbers of many bear species have been dramatically reduced and fragmented because of habitat loss and overexploitation. In many areas around the world, however, habitats have recovered but may be isolated from extant bear populations. Bears may not be well adapted to recolonize such vacant habitat patches because they have poor dispersal abilities and low reproductive rates (Clark *et al.*, 2002). Consequently, reintroduction may be necessary to expedite the otherwise slow process of recolonizing human-altered environments. Bears unfortunately exhibit population and social characteristics that often are counter to what would be desired for reintroduction, including low genetic variability and a strong homing instinct (Clark *et al.*, 2002). Yet, bear reintroduction programmes have been among the most successful compared with those of other large carnivores. The goals for this chapter are to provide an overview of past and present bear reintroduction efforts worldwide, to summarize the findings and to offer guidance for future efforts to reintroduce bears and other large carnivores.

Historical aspects of bear reintroductions

Black bear reintroduction programmes can be characterized as belonging to 1 of 2 groups: large numbers of hard-released (releases without an acclimation period) male and female animals, or smaller numbers of soft-released (with an acclimation period) females. The most successful black bear reintroduction was a hard release of 254 American black bears of both sexes to Arkansas between 1958 and 1968 (Rogers, 1973). That bear population numbers approximately 3000 today, and more than 200 bears are killed by hunters each year (R. Eastridge, Arkansas Game and Fish Commission, USA; personal communication). Many other hard releases of black bears have occurred in North America with varying degrees of success (Clark *et al.*, 2002).

The first soft release took place from 1977 to 1984 in Pennsylvania (Alt, 1995). Female bears that were pregnant or had just given birth were radio-tracked to their winter dens in the source area, removed, and placed in den sites at the release area. The premise of this winter-den method is that the combination of hibernation, parturition and cub rearing would keep the adult females in the reintroduction area, thus increasing site fidelity. The winter-release technique has since been used in several other reintroduction programmes. For example, 23 adult females and 55 cubs were captured in winter dens and reintroduced in Louisiana from 2001 to 2006. First-year survival of reintroduced females was high (0.93) and only three females abandoned their cubs and left the release site (Benson & Chamberlain, 2007). The winter-den technique was used from 2000 to 2007 to translocate 55 females with 116 cubs from eastern Arkansas to Felsenthal National Wildlife Refuge in southern Arkansas (Wear *et al.*, 2005, Clark & Eastridge, 2006). Officials now believe that the number of bears at Felsenthal is sufficient to ensure population sustainability (Clark & Eastridge, 2006).

Brown bear, *Ursus arctos*, reintroductions generally have been less intensive than black bear reintroduction programmes, involving fewer individuals over a shorter time span. Captive bears were used for many early release programmes in Europe, but populations did not persist (Clark *et al.*, 2002). More recently, releases of wild bears that have occurred in Italy, Austria and France appear promising (Gerstl & Rauer, 1999; Clark *et al.*, 2002; Visaggi, 2007). In North America, the only brown bear reintroduction attempt occurred in the Cabinet Mountains in north-western Montana between 1990 and 1994 (Servheen *et al.*, 1995). Four animals were reintroduced, and there was genetic evidence that at least one of the bears survived and reproduced (Kasworm *et al.*, 2007).

To reinforce Andean bear, *Tremarctos ornatus*, populations in north-eastern Ecuador, seven bears were rehabilitated and released in 1995 (Castellanos, 2003, 2005). Rehabilitation consisted of keeping the animals in captivity for an extended period of time, supplying them with foods found in the wild and limiting contact with humans. Future plans are to reintroduce bears to more remote locations in Ecuador to try to avoid the conflicts with humans that have been observed thus far. Similar techniques were used to reintroduce three sun bears, *Helarctos malayanus*, in Indonesia (G. Fredriksson, University of Amsterdam, The Netherlands; personal communication).

Finally, officials in South Korea released four Asiatic black bear, *Ursus thibetanus*, cubs from a breeding facility in 2001 to stabilize a relic population near Mount Jiri (Han & Jung, 2006). Those cubs were released to study their behaviour and habitat use and were then recaptured and placed back in the captive facility. In 2004, six cubs from Russia were released at Mount Jiri. The cubs were reared in captivity but were trained in Russia for life in the wild. As of 2006, 20 cubs had been released, two of which died in snares, three were recaptured because of habituation to humans and one was lost. Plans are to release six more Russian bear cubs per year for 4 years.

Obstacles, solutions and challenges

Habitat

Central to the evaluation of habitat at the reintroduction site is the identification of the initial cause of population decline. Although it may be tempting to immediately initiate a reintroduction programme in response to an extinction crisis, careful consideration of the logistics, feasibility and efficacy of such action should come first. In China, for example, a workshop concluded that reintroduction of giant pandas, *Ailuropoda melanoleuca*, should not take place because the initial cause of the population decline had not been remedied (Reading *et al.*, 1998).

Clearly, little is gained by releasing animals in areas where habitat is unsuitable; thus, bear reintroductions have often been preceded by habitat evaluations (van Manen, 1990; Boyce & Waller, 2000; Hogg *et al.*, 2000). Habitat assessment tools, ranging from Habitat Suitability Index models to complex multivariate assessments, have been used to evaluate potential reintroduction sites for bears and other large carnivores (van Manen, 1990; Thatcher *et al.*, 2006). Food is probably the most critical single habitat component for bears, but security cover and denning habitat should be evaluated as well. For example, Hersey *et al.*, (2005) speculated that a lack of den trees due to timber harvesting in seasonally flooded forests in the Mississippi Alluvial Valley may limit the suitability of these bottomlands for American black bears. Such assessments can be helpful to identify total potential range so that long-term population goals can be set.

Tools to develop and apply metapopulation models to fragmented populations, such as patch occupancy models (Moilanen, 2004), may be helpful for comparing potential reintroduction sites to maximize the potential for range expansion. Such tools could be used to identify certain habitat fragments that could serve as lynchpins for surrounding patches if restocked with bears. For example, Clark *et al.*, (2006) used metapopulation parameters to identify patches most suitable for Florida black bear, *Ursus americanus floridanus*, reintroduction. Hanski (1994) suggested that carnivores may be good candidates to test whether metapopulation models can be applied to assess management actions such as habitat protection and reintroduction, and such approaches have the potential to greatly increase the efficiency of reintroduction programmes.

Homing

One of the obstacles to bear reintroduction, particularly for black bears, has been homing behaviour (Clark *et al.*, 2002). The winter-release method pioneered by Alt (1995) and later employed in the south-eastern USA has been successful in limiting homing behaviour and increasing survival rates and reintroduction success. Although Alt (1995) also translocated pregnant females, the use instead of females with neonates may limit immediate post-release movements as pregnant bears may select other den sites at the release area prior to parturition; bears with cubs rarely moved to a new den site (Eastridge & Clark, 2001). Natural den sites (e.g. caves and rock outcroppings) at the release area have been used with success, but it may be just as effective and more logistically feasible to use den boxes constructed of plywood and lined with straw. Den boxes placed on trees also have been successful (R. Eastridge, personal communication), resulting in more options for reintroduction in seasonally flooded areas. Studies in Louisiana, Arkansas and Tennessee clearly indicate that homing, dispersal and survival rates are improved with the winter den technique compared with hard releases (Eastridge & Clark, 2001; Wear *et al.*, 2005; Benson & Chamberlain, 2007). Another advantage is that population growth is maximized because the most productive population segment (adult females) are primarily used; thus, fewer animals are needed for population re-establishment. Also, there are opportunities for public involvement in the process, and reproductive data for viability analyses are easier to collect.

Bear behaviour

Bears have an extended reproductive cycle and the young reside with their mothers for several years for some bear species. During that time, they learn the subtleties of bear behaviour, including locating food, communication and use of space and other resources. Therefore, captive-raised bears will not have all the skills that wild-reared bears would have, and this puts them at a disadvantage. That may be one reason why the release of bear cubs has not been as successful as the release of young of some other carnivores, because more parental teaching is required for bears than for some other carnivore species. Also with bears, captive-rearing may make them more dependent on anthropogenic food sources or make them more exposed to humans after release. That can result in non-acceptance by the local human population and rejection of the entire reintroduction project. In Poland, for example, captive brown bears released in the 1940s killed at least two people; resentment and negative attitudes toward bear reintroduction by the public persisted there for many years (Buchalczyk, 1980). Unfortunately, there are many examples of the destruction or recapture of captive-reared bears in reintroduction projects.

Perhaps not surprisingly, early efforts to release captive American black bears met with poor success. For example, Stiver *et al.*, (1997) released captive black bears into Great Smoky Mountains National Park in Tennessee, which had been raised in a zoo-like facility where public viewing was permitted. The bears were released at ages ranging between 1.3 and 10 years. Of seven bears fitted with radio-collars, two were killed, one had to be returned to captivity because of nuisance activity and three others were suspected of being killed illegally.

Since the work of Stiver *et al.*, (1997), facilities in Tennessee and elsewhere in North America have been developed to rehabilitate orphaned cubs. Rehabilitation is a complex effort to prepare captive-born or hand-raised bears for release in the wild. At the facility in Tennessee, contacts between orphaned cubs and humans are kept to a minimum, and bears are fed foods commonly found in the wild. Clark *et al.*, (2002) reported on the fates of 11 rehabilitated bears released in Tennessee in 1998, ranging from 11 to 18 months of age. Survival was high, with estimates ranging from 0.90 to 1.00 for a 180-day period following release.

Nevertheless, rehabilitation is costly and labour intensive and may not be possible for potentially aggressive bear species. Because of the difficulties, expense and potential for negative encounters with the public, release of rehabilitated bears should be viewed as a last option.

Demographic considerations

One reason for the success of the historic bear reintroduction programme in Arkansas was a relatively large founder population, which included many adult females and excluded older males (Smith & Clark, 1994). However, Wear *et al.*, (2005) demonstrated how the exclusive use of adult females with cubs could result in successful population re-establishment with relatively few animals if survival and settling rates are high. The ratio of male to female reintroduced lions, *Panthera leo*, has been shown to affect rates of infanticide (Hayward *et al.*, 2007), and sexually selected infanticide may also occur in bears (Swenson *et al.*, 2001; McLellan, 2005). Thus, the sex ratio of reintroduced bears may be important as well.

Growth projections cannot be made if released bears are not monitored to determine dispersal, survival and reproductive rates. As a result, more bears may be stocked than needed or, conversely, the number released may be insufficient. Wear *et al.*, (2005) demonstrated how extinction probabilities of reintroduced bear populations could be greatly diminished and the time to population re-establishment greatly reduced with additional releases of bears. Also, it will be difficult to identify population processes that may limit growth (e.g. survival and recruitment) so that changes in protocols can be made. Therefore, population viability analyses should attempt to estimate and account for such variation (Saltz, 1996; White 2000; Eastridge & Clark, 2001). Large-scale disturbances such as fire, droughts and catastrophic storms are difficult to project but can have significant effects on population persistence and should be considered (Miller *et al.*, 1999). Also, target objectives for population establishment should be set. An acceptable extinction probability and a target time for population establishment should be determined, and a definition of what constitutes success or failure should be decided upon before any stockings occur.

Genetic considerations

The IUCN (International Union for the Conservation of Nature and Natural Resources, 1998) recommends using the same subspecies or suitable substitutes (Seddon & Soorae, 1999) whenever possible to capture the local genetic traits that may be necessary for survival. Otherwise, the dilution or loss of such genes could be permanent. For example, it remains unclear as to whether bears that exist in northern Louisiana today are descendents of native stock or of bears reintroduced from Minnesota (Pelton, 1991; Miller *et al.*, 1998; Warrilow *et al.*, 2001; Csiki *et al.*, 2003; Triant *et al.*, 2004). The legal ramifications of this are unclear as those bears are classified as *Ursus americanus luteolus*, now listed as Threatened under provisions of the US Endangered Species Act. Using modern techniques of molecular genetics, it is possible to compare the genes of extinct populations, even by use of museum samples, with potential source populations.

Bear populations on peninsular fringes of their range have been shown to have significantly reduced genetic variation compared to more centralized populations (Waits *et al.*, 1999), an important consideration when choosing a source. The long-term consequences of limited genetic diversity of founding populations are only just now being more fully understood for many historic reintroductions of other species such as pronghorn antelope (*Antilocapra americana*), wild turkey (*Meleagris gallopavo*) and elk (*Cervus elaphus*); (Stephen *et al.*, 2005; Latch *et al.*, 2006; Hicks *et al.*, 2007). Although the population consequences of inbreeding in bears have not been documented to the same extent as with some other carnivores (O'Brien *et al.*, 1985, 1990), morphological traits typically associated with inbreeding (e.g. cryptorchidism and missing tails) have been documented in small isolated populations of American black bears (Edwards, 2002).

Conversely, crossing artificial subspecific boundaries with source animals should not necessarily prevent reintroduction in critical management situations. Early mammalogists described and named large numbers of subspecies within most species of carnivores, often based on a small number of morphological characteristics from a small number of specimens (Miller *et al.*, 1999).

Hall & Kelson (1959) name 24 subspecies of grey wolves, *Canis lupus*, even though wolves enjoyed almost unrestricted gene flow across the North American continent. The morphological criteria used by Hall & Kelson (1959) are likely the result of minor clinal differences in neighbouring populations and probably do not merit subspecific status (Carbyn, 1987). This is probably true for bears also and has caused some unforeseen management problems for some reintroduction programmes. For example, it is not legally possible to translocate native American black bears from southern Arkansas to central Louisiana or Mississippi, because subspecific lines would be crossed involving a federally threatened species, even though the translocation distance might be only be a few dozen kilometres.

Human dimensions and bears

Humans have historically perceived large carnivores as killers of game and livestock, hazards for children and solitary travellers and threats to one's spiritual and physical wellbeing (Link & Crowley, 1994; Busch 1994 from Hardy-Short & Short, 2000). For those reasons, it was Aldo Leopold's view that carnivores represent the critical test of society's commitment to conservation (Meine, 1988). The socio-political impediments to carnivore reintroduction may be more difficult to overcome than the biological barriers, as poor public acceptance and understanding have been the most important reasons for some reintroduction failures (Reading & Kellert, 1993).

Conservation biologists and ecologists receive little training in the social sciences, often are not particularly interested in them (Kellert, 1985; Clark & Cragun, 1994), and tend to take a technical biological view of species recovery (Clark & Wallace, 1998). Yet, biologists have typically coordinated public input and have formulated public policy on large-carnivore reintroductions. That input has typically consisted of public meetings and information exchange. However, public meetings often are not useful for characterizing the attitudes of entire wildlife constituencies (Bath, 1998), but tend to provide a forum for the vocal extremes (Johnson *et al.*, 1993). Although increasing public knowledge has been shown to be effective in generating more positive attitudes toward wildlife (Kellert, 1985; Bath, 1989, 1991; Kleiman *et al.*, 1990), merely providing educational materials may not be sufficient to alter public misconceptions. This is rarely successful if beliefs are strongly held

(Chaiken & Stangor, 1987 from Reading & Kellert, 1993), because knowledge is only one of several factors influencing attitude (Kellert, 1994). Primm (1996) argued that government-led technical-rational solutions are not effective when the problems they were intended to solve are belief- and value-based. Changing long-held beliefs will not be easy, particularly for species that evoke as much emotion as do bears and other large carnivores. An alternate approach is to examine relationships between beliefs and attitudes (usually through surveys), and then to target information efforts toward those factors that are more directly linked to attitude (Bath, 1998). Thus, inventorying the social dimensions of species reintroduction is just as important as inventorying critical biological components such as habitat and prey base (J. Peine, personal communication).

As charismatic megafaunal species, it may be easier to gain support for bears and other carnivores because of their high public appeal compared with other species (Eckholm, 1978 and Westman, 1990 from Reading & Kellert, 1993). For example, most people identify with bears and have a positive view of them because they are aesthetically appealing, are intelligent, are of large size, have the capacity to stand erect and have an omnivorous diet (Kellert, 1994). In a national study of Americans, a significant majority was willing to set aside millions of hectares of national forest land for grizzly bear conservation, despite the potential loss of jobs and a reduction in timber harvests (Kellert, 1985). The North American attitude toward bears is highly positive, yet biologists may be far too conservative in acknowledging this public viewpoint toward bears and their population enhancement and recovery (Kellert, 1994).

Despite positive overall attitudes toward bears, attitudes toward bear reintroduction are more negative. These negative attitudes are partially associated with the perception that reintroduction will result in land-use restrictions. Rural, property-owning and resource-dependent groups tend to be more utilitarian and dominionistic in their values toward wildlife (Kellert, 1994), as fear of restrictions has played major roles in the opposition to black-footed ferret, *Mustela nigripes*, reintroduction (Reading & Kellert, 1993). Such restrictions could affect hunting, mineral extraction, grazing, logging and access to public lands, although historically, they rarely have. Other negative attitudes are linked to the potential danger to humans and the destruction of livestock and crops. In Europe, most opposition to brown bear reintroduction was from fear of livestock losses (P. Quenette, Office National de la Chasse et de la Faune Sauvage, France; personal communication). This is partly because the livestock-guarding tradition among herdsmen has been lost in the absence of large predators, and now that the predators have returned, herdsmen have been slow to readopt those husbandry practices. Similarly, proposed brown bear reintroductions in the western USA have been opposed mostly by ranchers. Thatcher *et al.*, (2006) used expert opinion techniques to include sociological variables in a model to identify Florida panther, *Puma concolor coryi*, reintroduction sites. Bowman *et al.*, (2004) used socio-economic criteria to estimate where support for American black bear reintroduction would be expected to be highest. Such tools could be useful for identifying areas of co-habitation suitability (J. Peine, personal communication).

Citizen surveys have traditionally been the most commonly used method to measure attitudes related to carnivore reintroduction (Hastings, 1986; Duda *et al.*, 1998; Williams *et al.*, 2002). However, there are sophisticated measurement techniques to evaluate social dimensions of ecosystem management programmes (Kellert & Clark 1991; Glesne & Peshkin, 1992; Clark, 1996), and conservationists need to solicit the help of social scientists and others early in the reintroduction process to take advantage of such tools. Public opinion is spatially and temporally dynamic and, to some extent, it can be shaped. Primm (1996) and Primm & Clark (1996) described a citizen-based process for policy-oriented learning (Sabatier & Jenkins-Smith, 1993), which is essentially a feedback process involving groups of belief-based "advocacy coalitions". The premise is that those beliefs, though difficult to change, can be altered on the basis of feedback, reflection and learning among the groups (Dryzek, 1990; Sabatier & Jenkins-Smith, 1993) which, over time, can effectively re-form public opinion. The concept is that citizens, working with experts and mediators, would develop technical solutions while resolving value conflicts among themselves. For example, in the US Fish and Wildlife Service's proposed plan to reintroduce grizzly bears into the Bitterroot Ecosystem in Montana and Idaho, a Citizens Management Committee was developed. This was the first time that management responsibility for recovery of a threatened or endangered species was legally transferred to a committee comprised of local citizens and agency representatives (Roy *et al.*, 2001). Although the US Fish and Wildlife Service reversed an earlier decision to go forward with the reintroduction (Doddridge, 2001; United States Fish and Wildlife Service, 2001), the project could be revived, thanks in part to the grass-roots support generated by the in-depth public policy process employed in the Bitterroot project.

Implications for other large carnivores

Top-carnivore population restoration is a worthwhile goal as carnivores have disproportionately large effects on ecosystems (Terborgh, 1988; Estes, 1996; Terborgh *et al.*, 1999), and have been eliminated at a disproportionately greater rate than species at other trophic levels (Miller *et al.*, 1999). Unfortunately, large carnivores seem to be disproportionately difficult to re-establish through translocation (Miller *et al.*, 1999).

One of the first questions that conservation biologists should address prior to the initiation of a reintroduction programme is whether or not the initial cause for the population decline has been identified and rectified. This may be important for populations of other declining large carnivore species as well. It is important to note that the artificial translocation of animals between isolated habitat fragments should not be viewed as an alternative to restoring geographically expansive natural landscapes or even functioning corridors. Ultimately, there may be very few remaining protected areas large enough to maintain ecological processes or viable populations of many large-carnivore species.

Homing by translocated bears has been problematic as has homing in leopards, *Panthera pardus*, lions, cougars and wolves (Linnell *et al.*, 1997). All those species have been shown to have a homing ability from >200 km, and there appears to a declining tendency to home for adult males, adult females and subadults across species lines (Linnell *et al.*, 1997). For example, male Florida panthers ranged widely following release, whereas females had small home ranges (Belden & McCown, 1996). Release success for pumas in New Mexico was highest for animals of between 12 and 27 months of age (Logan *et al.*, 1996). Holding facilities for translocated carnivores at the release site have been used to reduce homing behaviour (Linnell *et al.*, 1997), but this practice has not been particularly effective for bears (Eastridge & Clark, 2001). Finally, the use of pregnant females or females with neonates might help to limit homing in other large carnivores, as it appears to do so for black bears.

Molecular techniques should be used to help define more appropriate genetic subdivisions. Otherwise, the legal status of many threatened and endangered species, which are based on these early morphological characterizations, could hinder reintroduction programmes for some carnivores that could otherwise benefit. That is not to say that genetics considerations should be discounted, as inbreeding depression has been especially notable in large carnivores (O'Brien *et al.*, 1985; Roelke *et al.*, 1993). Rather, maximizing genetic diversity is probably the best strategy for most carnivore species (Miller *et al.*, 1999), and conservation biologists need more effective tools for characterizing the most important considerations for genetic management of wild populations.

The release of captive-raised bears has been problematic and generally is a poor option for other carnivores as well. Captive breeding for translocation is expensive and can erode the genetic basis for important morphological, physical and behavioural traits through artificial selection. Also, learned behavioural traits are easily lost. Preconditioning pens were developed to counteract that effect and were shown to increase survival and prey-catching skills in captive-bred black-footed ferrets (Biggins *et al.*, 1999). Captive-raised Florida panthers had less fear of humans and were more likely to be involved in nuisance activity (Belden & McCown, 1996).

The possibility that reintroduced animals could introduce disease to the release site should be carefully investigated. However, Griffith *et al.*, (1989) found that only 24% of reintroduction programmes utilized medical screening. The transmission of canine distemper from wild black-footed ferrets to a captive facility has been well documented (Williams *et al.*, 1988). Transmission from captive to wild individuals could also easily occur and lead to disaster.

Public buy-in will be essential to the successful reintroduction of carnivores because of the potential for reintroduced animals to cause property damage or personal injury. Ironically, the Arkansas bear reintroduction programme, the most successful in history, took place with no public involvement, whereas the Bitterroot project had excellent public input yet the reintroduction never took place. Nevertheless, the Bitterroot project stands as a model for public involvement in the decision-making process. Although deferring management of reintroduced grizzly bears and a non-essential experimental designation were criticized as being too lenient, it is doubtful that the programme would have achieved the public support it did without the management flexibility afforded by those measures (C. Schwartz, Montana State University; personal communication). Other carnivore reintroduction efforts should similarly consider taking such pragmatic steps to deal with the inevitable problems that occur post-reintroduction. Despite the success of the Arkansas bear reintroduction, forcing management programmes on the public seldom work in the long run.

Thankfully, reintroduction biology is becoming a recognized field of conservation biology (Seddon *et al.*, 2007). However, most reintroduction projects are poorly documented, and the published literature that exists is highly fragmented. Most reintroduction efforts are carried out solely as management actions with no scientific component to better understand what contributes to the success or failure of such efforts. Better use of the scientific method and greater collaboration among scientific disciplines needs to occur for future reintroduction projects, so that the information obtained can be better shared across taxonomic boundaries.

Acknowledgements

I thank Matt Hayward and Michael Somers for inviting me to present this manuscript at the Society for Conservation Biology Annual Meeting in Port Elizabeth, South Africa. I wish to acknowledge John Peine for sharing his perceptions on the sociological issues associated with large-carnivore reintroduction. I also want to thank Duro Huber and Chris Servheen, my co-authors on an earlier paper on bear reintroduction, for their thoughts on brown bear reintroduction in North America and Europe. Finally, I thank Jennifer Murrow and the anonymous reviewers for helpful comments on earlier drafts of this manuscript.

References

Alt, G.L. (1995) *Black Bear Population Establishment in Southwestern Pennsylvania.* Final Report for Job 06233, Pennsylvania Game Commission, Harrisburg, Pennsylvania.

Bath, A.J. (1989) The public and wolf reintroduction in Yellowstone National Park. *Society and Natural Resources* 2, 297–306.

Bath, A.J. (1991) Public attitudes in Wyoming, Montana and Idaho toward wolf restoration in Yellowstone National Park. *Transactions of the North American Wildlife and Natural Resources Conference* 56, 91–95.

Bath, A.J. (1998) The role of human dimensions in wildlife resource research in wildlife management. *Ursus* 10, 349–355.

Belden, R.C. & McCown, J.W. (1996) *Florida Panther Reintroduction Feasibility Study.* Final Report, Study no. 7507. Florida Game and Fresh Water Fish Commission, Tallahassee, Florida, USA.

Benson, J.F. & Chamberlain, M.J. (2007) Space use, survival, movements, and reproduction of reintroduced adult female Louisiana black bears. *Journal of Wildlife Management* 71, 2393–2403.

Biggins, D.E., Vargas, A., Godbey, J.L. & Anderson, S.H. (1999) Influence of prerelease experience in reintroduced black-footed ferrets (*Mustela nigripes*). *Biological Conservation* 89, 121–129.

Bowman, J.L., Leopold, B.D., Vilella F.J. & Gill, D.A. (2004) A spatially explicit model, derived from demographic variables, to predict attitudes toward black bear restoration. *Journal of Wildlife Management* 68, 223–232.

Boyce, M.S. & Waller, J. (2000) The application of resource selection function analysis to estimate the number of grizzly bears that could be supported by habitats in the Bitterroot ecosystem. *Grizzly Bear Recovery in the Bitterroot Ecosystem. Final Environmental Impact Statement.* pp. 231–241. US Department of the Interior Fish and Wildlife Service, Missoula.

Buchalczyk, T. (1980) The brown bear in Poland. *International Conference on Bear Research and Management* 4, 229–232.

Carbyn, L.N. (1987) Gray wolf and red wolf. *Wild Furbearer Management and Conservation in North America.* (eds M. Novak, J.A. Baker, M.E. Obbard & B. Malloch), pp. 359–376. Ontario Ministry of Natural Resources, Ontario.

Carroll, C., Noss, R.F., Shumaker, N.H. & Paquet, P.C. (2001) Is the return of the wolf, wolverine, and grizzly bear to Oregon and California biologically feasible? *Large Mammal Restoration.* (eds D.S. Maehr, R.F. Noss & J.L. Larkin), pp. 25–46. Island Press, Washington, DC.

Castellanos, A.X. (2003) Ecology of re-introduced Andean bears in the Maquipucuna Biological Reserve, Ecuador: Conservation implications. *Re-introduction News* 23, 32–34.

Castellanos, A.X. (2005) Reinforcement of Andean bear populations in the Alto Choco Reserve and neighboring areas, northern Ecuador. *Re-introduction News* 24, 12–13.

Clark, J.D. & Eastridge, R. (2006) Growth and sustainability of black bears at White River National Wildlife Refuge, Arkansas. *Journal of Wildlife Management* 70, 1094–1101.

Clark, J.D., Huber, D. & Servheen, C. (2002) Bear reintroduction: Lessons and challenges. *Ursus* 13, 335–345.

Clark, J.E., Pelton, M.R., Wear, B.J. & Ratajczak, D.R. (2002) Survival of orphaned black bears released in the Smoky Mountains. *Ursus* 13, 269–273.

Clark, J.E., van Manen, F.T. & Clark. J.D. (2006) *Patch Occupancy Models for Black Bears in the Coastal Plain and Interior Highlands of the Southeastern U.S.* Final Report, U.S.G.S. Southern Appalachian Research Branch, Knoxville, Tennessee.

Clark, T.W. (1996) Learning as a strategy for improving endangered species conservation. *Endangered Species Update* 13(1), 5–6, 22–24.

Clark, T.W. & Cragun, J.R. (1994) Organizational and managerial guidelines for endangered species restoration programs and recovery teams. *Restoration and Recovery of Endangered Species: Conceptual Issues, Planning, and Implementation.* (eds M.L. Bowles & C.J. Whelan), pp 9–33. Cambridge University Press, London.

Clark, T.W. & Wallace, R.L. (1998) Understanding the human factor in endangered species recovery: An introduction to human social process. *Endangered Species Update* 15 (1), 2–9.

Csiki, I., Lam, C., Key, A. et al. (2003) Genetic variation in black bears in Arkansas and Louisiana using microsatellite DNA markers. *Journal of Mammalogy* 84, 691–701.

Doddridge, J. (2001) Reevaluation of the record of decision for the Final Environmental Impact Statement and selection of alternative for grizzly bear recovery in the Bitterroot Ecosystem. *Federal Register* 66(121), 33623–33624.

Dryzek, J.S. (1990) *Discursive Democracy.* Cambridge University Press, New York.

Duda, M.D., Bissell, S.S. & Young, K.C. (1998) Large Predator Reintroduction. *Wildlife and the American Mind: Public Opinion on the Attitudes toward Fish and Wildlife Management.* (eds M.D. Duda, S.J. Bissell & K.C. Young), pp 169–231. Responsive Management, Harrisburg.

Eastridge, R. & Clark, J.D. (2001) Evaluation of 2 soft-release techniques to reintroduce black bears. *Wildlife Society Bulletin* 29, 1163–1174.

Edwards, A.S. (2002) *Ecology of the Black Bear* (Ursus americanus floridanus) *in Southwestern Alabama.* MSc thesis, University of Tennessee.

Estes, J.A. (1996) Predators and ecosystem management. *Wildlife Society Bulletin* 24, 390–396.

Gerstl, N.J. & Rauer, G. (1999) *10 Jahre Braunbär (Ein Projektbilanz: 1989–1999).* World Wildlife Fund, Österreich, Vienna.

Glesne C. & Peshkin, A. (1992) *Becoming Qualitative Researchers: An introduction.* Longman Publishing Group, White Plains.

Griffith, B., Scott, J.M., Carpenter, J.W. & Reed, C. (1989) Translocation as a species conservation tool: Status and strategy. *Science* 245, 477–480.

Hall, E.R. & Kelson, K.R. (1959) *The Mammals of North America. Volume 2.* Ronald Press Company, New York.

Han, S. & Jung, D.H. (2006) Asiatic black bear restoration on Mt. Jiri, South Korea. *Re-introduction News* 25, 35–37.

Hanski, I. (1994) A practical model of metapopulation dynamics. *Journal of Animal Ecology* 63, 151–162.

Hardy-Short, D.C. & Short, C.B. (2000) Science, economics and rhetoric: Environmental advocacy and the wolf reintroduction debate 1987–1999. *Wilderness Science in a time of Change Conference—Volume 2: Wilderness within the Context of Larger Systems* (ed S.F. McCool), pp 65–72. USDA Forest Service

Proceedings RMRS-P-15-Vol-2. Rocky Mountain Research Station, Fort Collins.

Hastings, B. (1986) *Wildlife-Related Perceptions of Visitors in Cades Cove, Great Smoky Mountains National Park*. PhD dissertation. University of Tennessee.

Hayward, M.W., Adendorff, J., O'Brien, J. et al. (2007) The reintroduction of large carnivores to the Eastern Cape, South Africa: An assessment. *Oryx* 41, 205–214.

Hersey, K., Edwards, A.E. & Clark, J.D. (2005) Assessing American black bear habitat in the Mobile-Tensaw Delta of southwestern Alabama. *Ursus* 16(2), 245–254.

Hicks, J.F., Rachlow, J.L., Rhodes, O.E. Jr., Williams, C.L. & Waits, L.P. (2007) Reintroduction and genetic structure: Rocky mountain elk in Yellowstone and the western states. *Journal of Mammalogy* 88, 129–138.

Hilderbrand, G.V., Hanley, T.A., Robbins, C.T. & Schwartz, C.C. (1999) Role of brown bears (*Ursus arctos*) in the flow of marine nitrogen into terrestrial ecosystems. *Oecologia* 121, 546–550.

Hogg, J., Weaver, N., Craighead, J. et al. (2000) Abundance and spatial distribution of grizzly bear food plants in the Salmon-Selway ecosystem: A preliminary analysis and report. *Grizzly Bear Recovery in the Bitterroot Ecosystem. Final Environmental Impact Statement*. pp. 247–270. US Department of the Interior Fish and Wildlife Service, Missoula.

IUCN (1998) *Guidelines for Re-introductions*. UCN/SSC Re-introduction Specialist Group, IUCN, Gland, Switzerland.

Johnson, K.N., Johnson, R.L., Edwards, D.K. & Wheaton, C.A. (1993) Public-participation in wildlife management—Opinions from public meetings and random surveys. *Wildlife Society Bulletin* 21, 218–225.

Kasworm, W.F., Proctor, M.F., Servheen, C. & Paetkau, D. (2007) Success of grizzly bear population augmentation in northwest Montana. *Journal of Wildlife Management* 71, 1261–1266.

Kellert, S.R. (1985) Social and perceptual factors in endangered species management. *Journal of Wildlife Management* 49, 528–536.

Kellert, S.R. (1994) Public attitudes toward bears and their conservation. *International Conference on Bear Research and Management* 9(1), 43–50.

Kellert, S.R. & Clark, T.W. (1991) The theory and application of a wildlife policy framework. *Public Policy Issues in Wildlife Management*. (eds W.R. Mangun & S.S. Nagel), pp. 17–36. Greenwood Press, New York.

Kleiman, D.G., Beck, B.B., Baker, A.J., Ballou, J.D., Dietz, L.A. & Dietz, J.M. (1990) The conservation program for the golden lion tamarin, *Leontopithecus rosailia*. *Endangered Species Update* 8(1), 82–85.

Latch, E.K., Applegate, R.D. & Rhodes, O.E. (2006) Genetic composition of wild turkeys in Kansas following decades of translocations. *Journal of Wildlife Management* 70, 1698–1703.

Link, M. & Crowley, K. (1994) *Following the Pack: The World of Wolf Research.* Voyager Press, Stillwater.

Linnell, J.D.C., Aanes, R., Swenson, J.E., Odden, J. & Smith, M.E. (1997) Translocation of carnivores as a method for managing problem animals: A review. *Biodiversity and Conservation* 6, 1245–1257.

Logan, K.A., Sweanor, L.L., Ruth, T.K. & Hornocker, M.G. (1996) *Cougars of the San Andres Mountains, New Mexico.* Final Report to New Mexico Department of Game and Fish. New Mexico Department of Game and Fish, Sante Fe.

McLellan, B.N. (2005) Sexually selected infanticide in grizzly bears: The effects of hunting on cub survival. *Ursus* 16(2), 141–156.

Meine, C. (1988) *Aldo Leopold: His life and work.* University of Wisconsin Press, Madison.

Miller, B., Ralls, K., Reading, R.P., Scott, J.M. & Estes, J. (1999) Biological and technical considerations of carnivore translocation: A review. *Animal Conservation* 2, 59–68.

Miller, D.A., Hallerman, E.M. & Vaughan, M.R. (1998) Genetic variation in black bear populations from Louisiana and Arkansas: Examining the potential influence of reintroductions from Minnesota. *Ursus* 10, 335–341.

Moilanen, A. (2004) SPOMSIM: Software for stochastic patch occupancy models of metapopulation dynamics. *Ecological Modelling* 179, 533–550.

O'Brien, S.J., Roelke, M.E., Marker, L. et al. (1985) Genetic basis for species vulnerability in the cheetah. *Science* 227, 1428–1434.

O'Brien, S.J., Roelke, M.E., Yuhki, N. et al. (1990) Genetic introgression within the Florida panther *Felis concolor coryi. National Geographic Research* 6, 485–494.

Pelton, M.R. (1991) Black bears in the Southeast: To list or not to list? *Eastern Workshop on Black Bear Research and Management* 10, 155–161.

Primm, S.A. (1996) A pragmatic approach to grizzly bear conservation. *Conservation Biology* 10, 1026–1035.

Primm, S.A. & Clark, T.W. (1996) Making sense of the policy process for carnivore conservation. *Conservation Biology* 10, 1036–1045.

Reading, R.P. & Kellert, S.R. (1993) Attitudes toward a proposed reintroduction of black-footed ferrets (*Mustela nigripes*). *Conservation Biology* 7, 569–580.

Reading, R.P., Mainka, S., Zhi L. & Milla, G. (1998) Giant panda re-introduction feasibility. *Re-introduction News* 15, 4–6.

Roelke, M.E., Martenson, J.S. & O'Brien, S.J. (1993) The consequences of demographic reduction and genetic depletion in the endangered Florida panther. *Current Biology* 3, 340–350.

Rogers, M.J. (1973) Movements and reproductive success of black bears introduced into Arkansas. *Proceedings of the Southeastern Association of Fish and Wildlife Agencies* 27, 307–308.

Roy, J., Servheen, C., Kaswork, W. & Waller, J. (2001) Restoration of grizzly bears to the Bitterroot Wilderness: The EIS approach. *Large Mammal Restoration*. (eds D.S. Maehr, R.F. Noss & J.L. Larkin), pp. 205–224. Island Press, Washington, DC.

Sabatier, P.A. & Jenkins-Smith, H.C. (eds) (1993). *Policy Change and Learning: An Advocacy Coalition Approach*. Westview Press, Boulder.

Saltz, D. (1996) Minimizing extinction probability due to demographic stochasticity in a reintroduced herd of Persian fallow deer *Dama dama mesopotamica*. *Biological Conservation* 75, 27–33.

Seddon, P.J. & Soorae, P.S. (1999) Guidelines for subspecific substitutions in wildlife restoration projects. *Conservation Biology* 13, 177–184.

Seddon, P.J., Armstrong, D.P. & Maloney R.F. (2007) Developing the science of reintroduction biology. *Conservation Biology* 21, 303–312.

Servheen, C., Kasworm, W.F. & Their, T.J. (1995) Transplanting grizzly bears *Ursus arctos horribilis* as a management tool—Results from the Cabinet Mountains, Montana, USA. *Biological Conservation* 71, 261–268.

Smith, K.G. & Clark, J.D. (1994) Black bears in Arkansas: Characteristics of a successful translocation. *Journal of Mammalogy* 75, 309–320.

Stephen, C.L., Whittaker, D.G., Gillis, D., Cox, L.L., Rhodes, O.E. Jr. & Wittaker, D.G. (2005) Genetic consequences of reintroductions: An example from Oregon prong horn antelope (*Antilocapra americana*). *Journal of Wildlife Management* 69, 1463–1474.

Stiver, W.H., Pelton, M.R. & Scott, C.D. (1997) Use of pen-reared black bears for augmentation or reintroductions. *International Conference on Bear Research and Management* 9(2), 145–150.

Swenson, J.E., Sandegren, F., Brunberg, S. & Segerström, P. (2001) Factors associated with loss of brown bear cubs in Sweden. *Ursus* 12, 69–80.

Terborgh, J. (1988) The big things that run the world—A sequel to E.O. Wilson. *Conservation Biology* 2, 402–403.

Terborgh, J., Estes, J.A., Paquet, P. et al. (1999) The role of top carnivores in regulating terrestrial ecosystems. *Continental Conservation: Scientific Foundation of Regional Reserve Networks*. (eds M.E. Soulé & J. Terborgh), pp. 39–64. Island Press, Washington, DC.

Thatcher, C., van Manen, F.T. & Clark. J.D. (2006) Habitat assessment to identify potential sites for Florida panther reintroduction in the Southeast. *Journal of Wildlife Management* 70, 752–763.

Triant, D.A., Pace, R.M. & Stine, M. (2004) Abundance, genetic diversity and conservation of Louisiana black bears (*Ursus americanus luteolus*) as detected through noninvasive sampling. *Conservation Genetics* 5, 647–659.

United States Fish and Wildlife Service (2001) Reevaluation of the record of decision for the final environmental impact statement and selection of alternative for grizzly bear recovery in the Bitterroot Ecosystem. *Federal Register* 66(121), 33623–33624.

van Manen, F.T. (1990) *A Feasibility Study for the Potential Reintroduction of Black Bears into the Big South Fork Area of Kentucky and Tennessee*. Tennessee Wildlife Resources Agency, Technical Report Number 91–3, Nashville.

Visaggi, B. (2007) The status of brown bears (*Ursus arctos arctos*) in the Italian Central Alps. *International Bear News* 16(3), 12–13.

Waits, L., Paetkau, D. & Strobeck, C. (1999) Genetics of the bears of the world. *Bears: Status, Survey and Conservation Action Plan*. (eds C. Servheen, S. Herrero & B. Peyton), pp. 25–32. IUCN, Gland, Switzerland.

Warrillow, J., Culver, M., Hallerman, E. & Vaughan, M. (2001) Subspecific affinity of black bears in the White River National Wildlife Refuge. *The Journal of Heredity* 92(3), 226–233.

Wear, B.J., Eastridge, R. & Clark, J.D. (2005) Factors affecting settling, survival, and viability of black bears reintroduced to Felsenthal National Wildlife Refuge, Arkansas. *Wildlife Society Bulletin* 33, 1363–1374.

White, G.C. (2000) Population Viability Analysis: Data requirements and essential analyses. *Research Technologies in Animal Ecology: Controversies and Consequences*. (eds L. Boitani & T.K. Fuller), pp. 289–331. Columbia University Press. New York.

Williams, E.S., Thorne, E.T., Appel, M.J.G. & Belitch, D.W. (1988) Canine distemper in black-footed ferrets (*Mustela nigripes*) from Wyoming. *Journal of Wildlife Diseases* 24, 387–398.

Williams, K.C., Ericsson, G. & Heberlein, T.A. (2002) A quantitative summary of attitudes toward wolves and their reintroduction. *Wildlife Society Bulletin* 30, 575–584.

7

Tiger Reintroduction in India: Conservation Tool or Costly Dream?

A.J.T. Johnsingh[1] *and M.D. Madhusudan*[1]

[1]Nature Conservation Foundation

Summary

The tiger (*Panthera tigris*), like many other large carnivores, has experienced serious declines in its global distribution and abundance. Reintroduction is one of a suite of important conservation tools developed to reverse such declines in a range of species across the globe. Most experience with large-carnivore reintroductions comes from North America, Europe and South Africa, where carnivore declines have ensued from their direct persecution by humans. Once the factors responsible for the original extirpation of a large carnivore have been removed, reintroduction has proved a viable conservation option given the backdrop of low human densities, extensive land availability and the commitment of adequate financial and socio-political support for the reintroduction project. In this chapter, we examine the role of reintroduction in the conservation of the tiger in India, where the species has been extirpated from many parts of its former range—not only through direct persecution, but also due to prey depletion and habitat loss. Given the complex socio-cultural, economic and political factors that drive habitat loss and prey depletion for the tiger, we review the feasibility of reintroduction as a conservation intervention. In the Indian setting, which is characterized by the persistence—even aggravation—of conservation threats to tigers, we argue that

Reintroduction of Top-Order Predators, 1st edition. Edited by M.W. Hayward and M.J. Somers.
 ISBN 978-1-4051-7680-4 (pb) and 978-1-4051-9273-6 (hb)

the prudent course of conservation action is to first invest in effective means of reducing threats to tigers and their habitats before exploring the option of tiger reintroduction.

Introduction

Over the past century, the world has witnessed an unprecedented increase in human impact on nature (Crutzen, 2002). Today, the planet's extensive and diverse plant and animal ecosystems, particularly in the tropics, vie for space with dense human populations in rapid socio-economic transition from subsistence-based to market-driven economies. One of the impacts of these transitions has been extensive wildlife habitat loss, leading to species declines. Among the groups affected, mammals face a severe extinction crisis, with nearly a quarter of extant species threatened with extinction (IUCN, 2007), and strong evidence suggesting that large-bodied mammals (body mass >2 kg) have seen the most extinctions at the hands of humans (Lyons *et al.*, 2004). By virtue of both their size and trophic position, large carnivores are an extremely vulnerable group among large mammals, showing declines both in population size and geographic range due to well-known reasons such as depletion of prey, hunting and direct persecution in conflicts with humans, as well as loss and alteration of habitat (Weber & Rabinowitz, 1996). In the past century, extinction has already taken a heavy toll on large carnivores worldwide. Four distinct subspecies of the tiger (*Panthera tigris*), the Balinese, Javan, Caspian and South China tigers, are already extinct, while populations of the remaining subspecies are in serious decline (Seidensticker *et al.*, 1999; Tilson *et al.*, 2004). In most parts of Europe, large predators like the brown bear (*Ursus arctos*), wolf (*Canis lupus*) and lynx (*Lynx* spp.) have been lost (Breitenmoser, 1998) and, even in Africa, lion (*Panthera leo*) and wild dog (*Lycaon pictus*) ranges have declined drastically (Woodroffe & Ginsberg, 1998).

Following global declines of wildlife over the past century, there have been renewed efforts to secure their future. Prominent among these efforts is the establishment of protected areas for wildlife, which today number 105,000 areas worldwide and cover 12.2% of the planet's land area (Chape *et al.*, 2005). While protected areas are mostly seen as cornerstones of efforts to protect remaining wildlife populations (e.g., Ranganathan *et al.*, 2008), often they also serve as sources for reintroductions. The American bison is a pioneering example of species reintroduction. By 1889, it had declined from an original population of 60 million to less than 900 animals in the United States. In 1907, a herd of 15 captive-bred bison from the Bronx Zoo was reintroduced to a newly established reserve in Oklahoma, and thereafter in other ranges of South Dakota, Nebraska and Montana (Kleiman, 1989). Today, following a series of reintroductions, the status of the American bison is clearly more secure, numbering more than 500,000 animals (Freese *et al.*, 2007). For large carnivores too, there are similarly encouraging examples. Perhaps one of the most successful is the reintroduction of 254 American black bears, *Ursus americanus*, from individuals captured in Minnesota and Manitoba to the Interior Highlands of Arkansas between 1958 and 1968, which have now increased to more than 2500 (Clark *et al.*, 2002, and this volume). Recent literature suggests that large-carnivore reintroductions are gaining in popularity across the world, for a variety of reasons ranging from aesthetic and cultural to functional (Mech, 1996; Breitenmoser, 1998; Miller *et al.*, 1999; Breitenmoser *et al.*, 2001; Ripple & Beschta, 2003; Robbins, 2004; Hunter *et al.*, 2007; Hayward *et al.*, 2007a,b; Gusset *et al.*, 2008).

Large carnivores in India have come under increasing threat over the past century. During this period, the Asian subspecies of the cheetah, *Acinonyx jubatus venaticus*, has gone extinct (Chavda, 1995), while the Asiatic lion, *Panthera leo persica*, occurs in a single population and the tiger is now confined only to a tiny fraction of its former habitat, with its status becoming increasingly precarious (Chavda, 2005; Jhala *et al.*, 2008). In India, large canids, the wolf (*C. lupus pallipes*) and the Asiatic wild dog (*Cuon alpinus)* as well as the nation's four species of bears, have seen major declines in distribution range and population sizes (Servheen *et al.*, 1999; Ginsberg & Macdonald, 1990). India has responded to these declines by enacting a strong preservationist law, the Wildlife (Protection) Act in 1972, creating more than 600 protected areas (covering 4.8 % of its land area). Although the protected areas are relatively small, they are important refuges for many threatened and endangered species, and provide the foundation of species conservation and recovery programmes such as Project Tiger.

While India has experimented with species reintroduction in the past, it has not been an important conservation theme, and only a handful of these attempts have involved large carnivores. However, in recent times, large-carnivore reintroduction is being given serious consideration, particularly in the case of the Asiatic lion (which survives as a single population in the Gir

National Park) and, more recently, for the tiger, which has suffered local extinctions across several sites in India (Anon, 2006; Johnsingh *et al.*, 2007; Jhala *et al.*, 2008).

Although large-carnivore declines have occurred worldwide, a significant fraction of large-carnivore reintroductions have been undertaken in North America, Western Europe and, more recently, southern Africa, with few attempts from other parts of the tropics. Although a wide array of large carnivores have been locally and regionally extirpated across Asia, a survey undertaken by Breitenmoser *et al.*, (2001) reported just one example of carnivore reintroduction from Asia out of 165 worldwide. In the West, large-carnivore extirpations have often been caused by direct persecution, and not from large-scale prey and habitat loss (Berger, 1998). In this context, large-carnivore reintroduction may be a viable conservation option because human densities are relatively lower, extensive land is still available, there is adequate financial and socio-political support and, most importantly, factors responsible for the original extirpation no longer prevail (see Macdonald, this volume). In stark contrast, most large-carnivore extirpations in India and in other parts of the densely populated tropics are associated with prey depletion and habitat loss, which are in turn driven by complex socio-cultural, economic and political factors (Tilson *et al.*, 2001). In countries with high human density, intense land hunger, widespread anthropogenic impact on wildlife and relatively poor socio-political, financial and governmental systems, is it feasible to undertake the complex technical and socio-political tasks associated with large-carnivore reintroduction?

In this chapter, we attempt to address this fundamental question by examining the case for reintroduction of the tiger in India. From a species that once numbered in the many tens of thousands across a wide range of terrestrial ecosystems in India, the tiger is now down to the last 1500 animals in the country (Jhala *et al.*, 2008). This is down from the widely quoted figure of 3000 tigers when its conservation status drew political attention and resulted in the institution of Project Tiger in 1973. Today, nearly all tiger populations are fragmented and have declined, with many former populations, including some within protected areas, having been completely extirpated. The complex suite of social factors responsible for the decline and eventual extirpations of these tiger populations continue to prevail (Government of India, 2005). Against this backdrop, we examine the potential of reintroduction as an additional measure to conserve the tiger in India.

Assessing the potential for tiger reintroduction in India

As a conservation endeavour, it is no surprise that successful reintroduction is subject to a range of biological factors (e.g., ecology, behaviour and genetics) and the complex ways in which they interact with a range of socio-economic, cultural, logistical and administrative factors. Clearly then, it is important to understand both species' traits and the real-world contexts when making decisions on the applicability and feasibility of any large-carnivore reintroduction. In this section, we discuss the intrinsic biological traits of tigers as relevant to reintroduction and the characteristics of the real-world in which any reintroduction must unfold, as well as some specific technical considerations of tiger reintroduction in India.

Intrinsic characteristics of species

The tiger is the largest terrestrial predator in Eurasia and occupies a wide range of habitats in the region (Karanth, 2001). There is limited genetic variation across the tiger's range (Luo *et al.*, 2004), and ongoing work in India suggests that there are relatively low levels of genetic variation, both within and between tiger populations (U. Ramakrishnan, Connecticut Agricultural Experiment Station, USA; personal communication.). One of the key determinants of tiger presence and abundance anywhere is the availability of large ungulates (Schaller, 1967; Karanth *et al.*, 2004). An adult tiger may annually consume 50 animals the size of a chital deer (*Axis axis*) (Chundawat *et al.*, 1999), with a breeding tigress consuming substantially more. Furthermore, tigers are reported to annually harvest their prey base at 8%–10%, which implies that each adult tiger needs a prey base of approximately 500 chital-sized animals for its survival (Sunquist, 1981; Karanth, 2001). Tiger abundance and density, therefore, are critically determined by the extent of habitat available to their principal prey as well as the densities at which these prey occur (Karanth *et al.*, 2004). Following from that, tigers have significantly smaller home ranges in sites with greater prey density, such as Nagarahole in southern India, as compared with areas of low prey density such as Siberia, where home ranges extend over hundreds of square kilometers (Karanth, 2001). Typically, resident males have home ranges that overlap those of several breeding females, with minimal overlap in home ranges within each sex (Sunquist, 1981; Smith *et al.*, 1987). Socially immature individuals, especially males, may range over large areas as transients before they are able to establish their own home ranges as breeding residents (Smith, 1993).

Adults are mostly solitary and come together for mating. Tigers are extremely fecund animals, with females giving birth on average to three cubs, which remain with the mother for 18–27 months (Smith & McDougal, 1991). However, 56% of young die within the first 2 years (Smith & McDougal, 1991). In many parts of its range, the tiger preys on domestic livestock and sometimes humans and, in response, it is subject to retaliatory killing (Madhusudan & Mishra, 2003). However, there is also evidence that tigers avoid areas disturbed by human activity (Karanth, 2001).

Provided that secure source populations are available, the high reproductive potential of tigers would appear to make reintroduction biologically feasible. However, other aspects of tiger biology also need to be taken into account before decisions are made. To establish a moderately sized tiger population, the following are needed: an adequate number of individuals to form a founding population and a healthy prey population, supported by sufficient habitat. If tigers are reintroduced in an area where the density of wild prey is low and there are large numbers of domestic livestock, reintroduced animals may rely on livestock as a food source. Furthermore, transient individuals with experience of dispersing and living in closer proximity to human populations may also fare better as candidates in reintroduction programmes than resident individuals.

Reintroduction and the real-world threats to tiger conservation

Tiger conservation in the Indian subcontinent faces a range of complex threats. First, direct poaching of tigers to supply high-value markets trading in tiger body-parts, particularly from Tibet, China and parts of South-East Asia, remains a serious threat to the species (Government of India, 2005). There have been 825 cases of tiger poaching over the past 14 years (WPSI, 2008).

Second, a suite of chronic extractive uses of natural resources threaten the tiger, its prey and their habitats. These regimes of natural resource use range from local hunting of tiger prey to meet traditional demands for wild meat (Madhusudan & Karanth, 2002) and grazing by millions of livestock which out-compete the herbivore prey of tigers even in important habitats

(Madhusudan, 2004), to the stealing of tiger kills (Johnsingh *et al.*, 2004) and the harvesting of large quantities of fuel wood (Shankar *et al.*, 1998) and a wide range of non-timber forest products (Shahabuddin & Prasad, 2004).

Third, the huge thrust on economic growth at all levels across India has eclipsed ecological concerns in the planning and implementation of development projects even in and around wildlife reserves. The unregulated local expansion of agriculture, together with chaotic development, continues to fragment existing habitats and populations. There is a lack of law or policy to address threats to tigers arising from poorly planned land use.

Fourth, in the pursuit of a coercive, law-enforcement-based approach to tiger conservation, there has been little effort to recognize or offset the human/livelihood costs of conservation, including loss of subsistence options and the threat of displacement, as well as material, monetary and human losses incurred in conflicts involving tigers, all of which are borne disproportionately by local communities. At the same time, the monetary/livelihood benefits of tiger conservation and revenues from non-consumptive use in wildlife reserves, such as tourism revenues, have rarely accrued to local people. In the face of continued economic losses and the absence of readily available measures to offset these losses, there is considerable local animosity to tigers and support for activities that undermine tiger conservation such as deliberate forest fires, hunting and poisoning wildlife and colluding with poachers/smugglers. Recent legislative measures under the Scheduled Tribes and Other Traditional Forest Dwellers (Recognition of Forest Rights) Act 2006 to correct some of these historical injustices have further complicated tiger-conservation efforts.

Finally, the extinction of tigers in India's premier Sariska Tiger Reserve has shown that there are serious systemic problems with the implementation of wildlife conservation in the subcontinent. Forest departments in India often function in an exclusionary authoritative manner without clear management objectives, without scientific systems of monitoring and with an intolerance of scrutiny by the public. Such conduct combined with corrupt motives reduces effectiveness of conservation measures. In the context of reintroduction, such systemic dysfunction is well illustrated by the lack of successful gharial, *Gavialis gangeticus*, conservation. This species is believed to have disappeared or declined in many north Indian rivers where it has been reintroduced since the 1980s. Likewise, little is known about the fate of one lion and two lionesses from Gir National park that were reintroduced into the 96-km^2 Chandaprabha Wildlife Sanctuary in 1957. Their number reportedly increased to 11 in 1965, but the population has since disappeared—although the cause is unknown owing to a lack of monitoring (Negi, 1965).

Although the examples above provide a synoptic account of the threats to tiger conservation, the drivers of threats are extremely varied across India's socio-cultural, political, economic and management contexts (Government of India, 2005). Yet, nowhere do any of these threats appear to have been comprehensively addressed to date. This leaves us pondering the sobering question of how useful tiger reintroduction would be as a conservation tool in India given that few of the direct causes of extirpation of tigers have been addressed.

Vital considerations for tiger reintroduction in India

Although it is debatable as to whether the causes of local tiger extirpation have been addressed across India, proposals are made frequently to reintroduce tigers (and many other species). To date, even for a high-profile species like the tiger, there are no species recovery plans that evaluate reintroduction as a conservation tool. We believe it is extremely important to carry out a careful review of the circumstances surrounding any reintroduction proposal. While most reintroduction proposals lack a rigorous methodology (Hein, 1997), methods are becoming available to guide the selection of potential reintroduction sites (Schadt *et al.*, 2002; Thatcher *et al.*, 2006).

It is first necessary to clearly articulate the objectives of the reintroduction (IUCN, 1998). For instance, tiger reintroductions could serve the purpose of establishing viable populations to avert extinctions, or to further tourism or even to perform the ecological function of regulating herbivore prey populations in an ecosystem (see Hayward, this volume). Unless these goals have been set *a priori*, it becomes impossible to assess the conservation outcome of a reintroduction project.

Second, it is essential to understand which among a suite of critical factors contributed to the extirpation of the tiger in the first place (see Macdonald, this volume). Simple though this may seem, it is often extremely difficult to do in the absence of baseline data. However, thorough surveys of recent local history are useful in evaluating whether direct threats (e.g., tiger poaching and retaliatory killings in conflicts), indirect threats (e.g., prey limitation, habitat loss or degradation) or stochastic factors (e.g., environmental and demographic factors) were responsible for the loss of a population.

Third, even before any reintroduction can be planned, it is vital to eliminate factors driving a population towards extinction (see Macdonald, this volume). This may involve action to eliminate (or at least to regulate to acceptable levels) poaching, tiger–human conflict and chronic anthropogenic resource use, as well as to foster an atmosphere eliminating bureaucratic and local antipathy to tiger conservation. If carried out sincerely, these tasks could well be one of the most difficult, time-consuming and expensive—but essential—preconditions to a planned tiger reintroduction.

Fourth, a whole range of technical considerations need to be taken into account. For example, reintroductions involving larger numbers of individuals are more likely to succeed than efforts with fewer individuals. It is therefore important to determine the number of animals that must be reintroduced. What would their age–sex composition be? Given the grave dangers associated with releasing captive-bred tigers into the wild and the difficulties of obtaining secure source populations to provide individuals for the reintroduction, where would animals be obtained from? What forms of pre-release management would be necessary?

Fifth, in the context of limited resources, the economics of competing conservation options of, say, habitat protection versus reintroduction must also be carefully examined before decisions are finally taken. Finally, it is necessary to acknowledge that any successful reintroduction programme involves the persistence of the established population. This may be assessed only with regular monitoring of the reintroduction programme against its stated goals.

Tiger reintroduction in India: brief review of potential sites

Although there are several sites in India where tiger reintroduction may be considered, we discuss, in this section, two places where the government is already seriously contemplating reintroduction—Sariska Tiger Reserve and Madhav National Park. Besides these two, we highlight three additional candidate sites and analyse their potential as well as the problems associated with each of them:

Sariska Tiger Reserve

The Sariska Tiger Reserve is a protected area of 880 km^2, which was designated as the 11th Tiger Reserve in the country in 1978–1979. The western most protected area in India with tigers, it is an isolated forest patch in the arid western Aravalli landscape, where summer temperatures can reach 47°C. The Reserve has three core areas, all of which are isolated and embedded in a buffer. Even the Core-I, notified as a National Park, has 11 villages with about 1800 people and 7000 livestock. Two state highways—Alwar–Thanagazhi–Jaipur and Sariska–Kalighati–Tehla—go through the Reserve and heavy traffic, particularly along the Alwar–Jaipur Highway, is responsible for the death of many animals including tigers. Large numbers of pilgrims visit two shrines in the area, and reaching the Pandupole shrine takes the pilgrims through the best wildlife area in the Reserve.

The extreme summer heat and the absence of secluded water bodies in Sariska, where tigers could cool themselves during the hot hours of the day, raise the question as to where would be the best source of tigers that are adapted to such extreme heat. Tigers from either Ranthambhore Tiger Reserve or Panna Tiger Reserve could be the most suitable candidates, but both of these Reserves suffer from the problem of a small population (<20 adult tigers).

The Kali valley (c. 100 km^2) of Sariska with abundant wild ungulates such as sambar (*Cervus unicolor*), chital and nilgai, *Boselaphus tragocamelus*, creates a deceptive picture that all is well with the Reserve, but anthropogenic pressures will need to be reduced in at least 200 km^2 around the areas of Kiraska, Haripura, Umri and Kankwari villages. The two state highways should be diverted and the pilgrim traffic along Sariska–Kalighati–Pandupole should be diverted to Bharthari–Kiraska–Pandupole. Generating popular and political support to the idea of resettling villages, realigning highways and regulating pilgrim traffic, all seem difficult but necessary tasks if a tiger population is to be successfully re-established here.

Madhav National Park

Madhav National Park, once a hunting preserve of the Maharaja of Gwalior, is in the north-western part of Madhya Pradesh, with a forest area of nearly 10,000 km^2. The last tiger was seen here in 1977, and the reasons for the decline of wildlife in the Park included rampant illicit felling, grazing and poaching soon after independence and merger of the state with the Indian Republic.

Reintroduction of tigers here would provide a genetic link between the existing populations in Panna and Ranthambhore Tiger Reserves. One major problem in this landscape would be that the forests, being deciduous, shed their leaves during early summer and there is almost no shady vegetation, except in the mixed and riparian areas, to provide thermal cover to the animals during the fierce summers. Chital, nilgai, wild pig (*Sus scrofa*), chinkara (*Gazella bennettii*) and chowsingha (*Tetracerus quadricornis*) are the wild ungulate prey reported from this area.

The area of Madhav National Park is 165 km^2. There is a proposal to add 190 km^2 to the existing national park. The entire area is surrounded by 122 villages, which put enormous pressures on the forests. The plan for linking the two forest blocks includes a 2-km-wide and 6-km-long corridor, which will involve relocation of a few villages (Anon, 2006). In terms of habitat suitability, this site would appear to be the least suitable.

Nandhour-Ladhya Conservation Reserve

The proposed Nandhour-Ladhya Conservation Reserve is between the Gola River in Uttarakhand (India) and the Sharada River which flows between India and Nepal. The forests here come under three forest divisions (Terai East, Champawat and Haldwani), totalling 1800 km^2, and the hilly northern part has nearly 1200 km^2 of intact tiger habitat, largely formed by the Haldwani and Champawat Forest Districts. An area totalling nearly 400 km^2, almost in the middle of this landscape, is without people and could be designated as the Nandhour Valley National Park after the scenic river that flows through the region. The hills have prey species such as sambar, chital, wild pig, common langur (*Semnopithecus entellus*), goral (*Naemorhedus goral*) and an occasional serow (*Capricornis* spp.). Other large carnivores are leopard, *Panthera pardus*, and sloth bear, *Melursus ursinus*. Available information shows that the Himalayan foothills are extremely productive for sambar, and a density as high as 25 sambar/km^2 has been reported from the Chilla Range of the nearby Rajaji National Park (Harihar *et al.*, 2007).

The major reason for the local extinction of tiger in this area was poaching of sambar and other ungulates by the local people who hunt with dogs (*Canis lupus familiaris*) and snares. Killing of tigers for skin and bones also may have happened here in the past. If strict protection is afforded, which is possible only with the support of local people, ungulate abundance can bounce back and in the absence of dholes, which also prey on species like chital and sambar and therefore can be a competitor to tiger in habitats like the Kanha and Nagarahole Tiger Reserves, a minimum population of 50 adult tigers could be supported here. Tigers for reintroduction could be obtained from the adjacent Corbett Tiger Reserve. At present, the connectivity with the Corbett Tiger Reserve is broken because of boulder mining in Gola River. In principle, tigers can disperse from the Corbett Tiger Reserve to the suggested Conservation Reserve through Naintital Forest District, but this is not happening—possibly because conditions such as prey availability are not suitable both in Nainital Forest District and in the Conservation Reserve. Connectivity with Nepal (Suklaphanta Tiger Reserve) along the Brahmadev corridor, east of Sharada River, is possible. However, connectivity with the adjacent Pilibhit Forest District (Uttar Pradesh) is broken because the intervening forest areas are degraded by developments (e.g. Sharada canal) and encroachments, and the forests are decimated by Indian as well as by Nepali wood cutters. The priority tasks here are the establishment of the Conservation Reserve and the National Park and the banning of boulder mining in the Gola River to re-establish connectivity with Corbett Tiger Reserve. With the assistance of the Nepal Government, the possibilities for linking the eastern part of Sukhlaphanta Reserve with the Conservation Reserve along the Brahmadev corridor should be expedited (Johnsingh *et al.*, 2004; Johnsingh, 2006).

Ganga-Yamuna Reserve

In order to enable readers to understand this potential reintroduction site, the hypothetical name of Ganga-Yamuna Reserve is given to the forests between the right bank of the Ganges and Yamuna (including the forests on the right bank) in north-western India. The area totals c. 2000 km^2 and is extremely productive for ungulates (with a density of 110 ungulates/km^2, Harihar *et al.*, 2007). This Reserve includes the western part of Rajaji National Park, Dehra Dun Forest District and Kalsi Forest District (all part of Uttarakhand), Shivalik Forest District (Uttar Pradesh), Kalesar Wildlife Sanctuary (Haryana) and Simbalbara Wildlife Sanctuary (Himachal Pradesh). Although this area can support a minimum population of c. 30 adult tigers, the present tiger situation is extremely critical here as a result of poaching of prey as well as tiger poaching and anthropogenic disturbances from Gujjar and other settlements as well as kill stealing by *bhabar* grass *Eulaliopsis binata* cutters in winter. The only source habitat to this Reserve is Chilla-Range and Corbett Tiger Reserve, but the corridor across the Ganges that has been planned since the 1980s is far from functional (Johnsingh *et al.*, 2004). Tigers for reintroduction could come from the Chilla Range, but the problems such as *bhabar* grass collection, gujjar resettlement and poaching need to be solved promptly.

Namdapha Tiger Reserve

Namdapha Tiger Reserve is named after the Namdapha River, which originates from Daphabum—the highest mountain peak (4598 m) in the Reserve. The area was declared a Wildlife Sanctuary in 1972 and as a c. 2000-km^2 Tiger Reserve and National Park in 1983. Because of its biogeographic location, with an altitude ranging from 250 m to 4500 m and copious rainfall, this Reserve is biologically extremely rich with more than 1000 plant species and 100 mammal species—of which at least 15 species (like clouded leopard (*Neofelis nebulosa*) and Malayan sun bear (*Helarctos malayanus*)) are of global conservation significance. Historically, the landscape where the Reserve is situated had abundant ungulate prey such as sambar, gaur (*Bos gaurus*), wild pig and barking deer, and should have supported a high density of tiger. However, no reliable information is available as an estimation of tiger population. Data based on pug marks put the Reserve's tiger population at 60 tigers—but this was totally unreliable (Datta *et al.,* 2008). Recent surveys, however, indicate a near extinction of tiger here, as 1900 trap nights did not yield a single tiger picture and not a single tiger sign was located during a 3-month field survey. Even prey density is extremely low (Datta *et al.*, 2008). Uncontrolled poaching of prey and tiger for several decades is the major reason for this depleted status. There is only one road (157 km) but, owing to the hilly terrain and heavy rains, it is not maintained and the functioning of the forest department is almost non-existent here. A protection force by the local Lisus who know the area very well and whose jungle skills are formidable may be the only way to bring back the prey abundance and the tiger. It would take more than a decade of very good protection to enable prey species to recover before any plan for the reintroduction of tigers could be thought about. Tigers for reintroduction could come either from Pakhe-Nameri Tiger Reserve or from Kaziranga Tiger Reserve.

Conclusion

An estimated 93% of the tiger's original global range is believed to have been lost in the past 150 years (Schaller, 2006). Today, tigers in the subcontinent are scattered across India, Nepal, Bhutan and Bangladesh. Where once they ranged widely across the Indian subcontinent, they now occupy only around 400,000 km^2 (Wikramanayake *et al.,* 1998). Breeding populations are now believed to be restricted to about 40,000 km^2, which is less than 1% of the tiger's historical range (Karanth, 2001). Based on these facts, it would seem that the tiger is an ideal candidate for conservation through reintroduction. However, these changes in tiger range and numbers have been mirrored by phenomenal increases in human population and rapid economic growth. The consequent loss of forest cover, increasing habitat degradation, decline of wild prey, escalating tiger–human conflicts, erosion of local support for conservation as well as systemic failures have contributed to the local and regional extirpation of tigers across India. The factors that were responsible for the downfall of the tiger still prevail over its historical range, making tiger reintroduction largely an unworkable proposition in India—a fact that has also been pointed out by Christie & Seidensticker (1999). For now, if we are serious about tiger conservation, there is no alternative but to invest in effectively protecting breeding populations from poaching and prey depletion, securing dispersal corridors to link breeding populations, and managing ubiquitous human presence and resource-use in tiger habitats in a more scientific and just manner.

References

Anon (2006) *Report of the High Level Committee Constituted to Review the Proposal for Reintroduction of Tigers in Madhav National Park, Shivpuri.* Submitted to Forest Department, Government of Madhya Pradesh, Bhopal.

Berger, J. (1998) Future prey: Some consequences of the loss and restoration of large carnivores. *Behavioral Ecology and Conservation Biology.* (ed. T.M. Caro), pp. 80–104. Oxford University Press, New York.

Breitenmoser, U. (1998) Large predators in the Alps: The fall and rise of man's competitors. *Biological Conservation* 83, 279–289.

Breitenmoser, U., Breitenmoser-Wursten, C., Carbyn, L.N. & Funk, S.M. (2001) Assessment of carnivore reintroductions. *Carnivore Conservation.* (eds J.L. Gittleman, S.M. Funk, D.W. MacDonald & R.K. Wayne), pp. 241–281. Cambridge University Press, Cambridge.

Chape, S., Harrison, J., Spalding, M. & Lysenko, I. (2005) Measuring the extent and effectiveness of protected areas as an indicator for meeting global biodiversity targets. *Philosophical Transactions of the Royal Society, London: Biological Sciences* 360, 443–455.

Chavda, D. (1995) *End of a trail: The cheetah in India,* Banyan Books, New Delhi.

Chavda, D. (2005) *The story of Asia's lions,* Marg Publications, Mumbai.

Christie, S. & Seidensticker, J. (1999) Is re-introduction of captive-bred tigers a feasible option for the future? *Riding the Tiger: Tiger Conservation in Human-Dominated Landscapes.* (eds J. Seidensticker, S. Christie & P. Jackson), pp. 207–209. Cambridge University Press, Cambridge.

Chundawat, R.S., Gogate, N., Johnsingh, A.J.T., Seidensticker, J., Christie, S. & Jackson, P. (1999) Tigers in Panna: Preliminary results from an Indian tropical dry forest. *Riding the Tiger: Tiger Conservation in Human-Dominated Landscapes.* (eds J. Seidensticker, S. Christie & P. Jackson), pp. 123–129. Cambridge University Press, London.

Clark, J.D., Huber, D. & Servheen, C. (2002) Bear reintroductions: Lessons and challenges. *Ursus* 13, 335–345.

Crutzen, P.J. (2002) Geology of mankind. *Nature* 415, 23.

Datta, A., Anand, M.O. & Naniwadekar, R. (2008) Empty forests: Large carnivore and prey abundance in Namdapha National Park, north-east India. *Biological Conservation* 141, 1429–1435.

Freese, C.H., Aune, K.E., Boyd, D.P. et al. (2007) Second chance for the plains bison. *Biological Conservation* 136, 175–184.

Ginsberg, J.R. & Macdonald, D.W. (1990) *Foxes, Wolves, Jackals, and Dogs: An Action Plan for the Conservation of Canids,* IUCN, Gland, Switzerland.

Government of India (2005) *Joining the Dots: Report of the Tiger Task Force.* Ministry of Environment and Forests, Government of India, New Delhi.

Gusset, M., Ryan, S.J., Hofmeyr, M. et al. (2008) Efforts going to the dogs? Evaluating attempts to re-introduce endangered wild dogs in South Africa. *Journal of Applied Ecology* 45, 100–108.

Harihar, A., Deepika, L.P., Ri, C., Pandav, B. & Goyal, S. (2007) Status of tiger and its prey species in Rajaji National Park. *Response of Tiger Population to Habitat, Wild Ungulate Prey and Human Disturbance in Rajaji National Park, Uttarahkand, India. Final Technical Report.* Wildlife Institute of India, Dehradun.

Hayward, M.W., Adendorff, J., O'Brien, J. et al. (2007a) Practical considerations for the reintroduction of large, terrestrial, mammalian predators based on reintroductions to South Africa's Eastern Cape Province. *The Open Conservation Biology Journal* 1, 1–11.

Hayward, M.W., Kerley, G.I.H., Adendorff, J. et al. (2007b) The reintroduction of large carnivores to the Eastern Cape, South Africa: An assessment. *Oryx* 41, 205–214.

Hein, E.W. (1997) Improving translocation programs. *Conservation Biology* 11, 1270.

Hunter, L.T.B., Pretorius, K., Carlisle, L.C. et al., (2007) Restoring lions *Panthera leo* to northern KwaZulu-Natal, South Africa: Short-term biological and technical success but equivocal long-term conservation. *Oryx* 41, 196–204.

IUCN (1998) *Guidelines for Reintroductions.* IUCN, Gland, Switzerland.

IUCN (2007) *Red List of Threatened Species.* Available: http://www.iucnredlist.org. Accessed 19 February, 2008.

Jhala, Y.V., Gopal, R. & Qureshi, Q. (2008) *Status of the Tigers, Co-predators, and Prey in India. TR 08/001.* National Tiger Conservation Authority, Government of India and Wildlife Institute of India, New Delhi and Dehradun.

Johnsingh, A.J.T. (2006) Status and conservation of the tiger in Uttaranchal, northern India. *Ambio* 35, 135–137.

Johnsingh, A.J.T., Goyal, S.P. & Qureshi, Q. (2007) Preparations for the reintroduction of Asiatic lion *Panthera leo persica* into Kuno Wildlife Sanctuary, Madhya Pradesh, India. *Oryx* 41, 93–96.

Johnsingh, A.J.T., Ramesh, K., Qureshi, Q., David, A., Goyal, S.P., Rawat, G.S., Rajapandian, K. & Prasad, S. (2004) *Conservation Status of Tiger and Associated Species in the Terai Arc Landscape, India,* RR-04/001, Wildlife Institute of India, Dehradun.

Karanth, K.U. (2001) *The Way of the Tiger: Natural History and Conservation of the Endangered Big Cat,* Voyageur Press, Stillwater, MN, USA.

Karanth, K.U., Nichols, J.D., Kumar, N.S., Link, W.A. & Hines, J.E. (2004) Tigers and their prey: Predicting carnivore densities from prey abundance. *Proceedings of the National Academy of Sciences of the United States of America* 101, 4854–4858.

Kleiman, D.G. (1989) Reintroduction of captive mammals for conservation. *BioScience* 39, 152–161.

Luo, S.J., Kim, J.H., Johnson, W.E. et al. (2004) Phylogeography and genetic ancestry of tigers (*Panthera tigris*). *PLoS Biology* 2, e442.

Lyons, S.K., Smith, F.A. & Brown, J.H. (2004) Of mice, mastodons and men: Human-mediated extinctions on four continents. *Evolutionary Ecology Research* 6, 339–358.

Madhusudan, M.D. (2004) Recovery of wild large herbivores following livestock decline in a tropical Indian wildlife reserve. *Journal of Applied Ecology* 41, 858–869.

Madhusudan, M.D. & Karanth, K.U. (2002) Local hunting and the conservation of large mammals in India. *Ambio* 31, 49–54.

Madhusudan, M.D. & Mishra, C. (2003) Why big, fierce animals are threatened: Conserving large mammals in densely populated landscapes. *Battles over Nature: Science and the Politics of Conservation.* (eds V. Saberwal & M. Rangarajan), pp. 31–55. Permanent Black, New Delhi.

Mech, L.D. (1996) A new era for carnivore conservation. *Wildlife Society Bulletin* 24, 397–401.

Miller, B., Ralls, K., Reading, R.P., Scott, J.M. & Estes, J. (1999) Biological and technical considerations of carnivore translocation: A review. *Animal Conservation* 2, 59–68.

Negi, S.S. (1965) Transplanting of Indian lions in Uttar Pradesh state. *Cheetal* 12, 98–101.

Ranganathan, J., Chan, K.M.A., Karanth, K.U. & Smith, J.L.D. (2008) Where can tigers persist in the future? A landscape-scale, density-based population model for the Indian subcontinent. *Biological Conservation* 141, 67–77.

Ripple, W.J. & Beschta, R.L. (2003) Wolf reintroduction, predation risk, and cottonwood recovery in Yellowstone National Park. *Forest Ecology and Management* 184, 299–313.

Robbins, J. (2004) Lessons from the wolf. *Scientific American* 290, 76–81.

Schadt, S., Revilla, E., Wiegand, T. et al. (2002) Assessing the suitability of central European landscapes for the reintroduction of Eurasian lynx. *Journal of Applied Ecology* 39, 189–203.

Schaller, G.B. (1967) *The Deer and the Tiger: A Study of Wildlife in India,* The University of Chicago Press, Chicago.

Schaller, G.B. (2006) Foreword. *Setting Priorities for the Conservation and Recovery of Wild Tigers: 2005–2015. A User's Guide.* (eds E. Dinerstein, C. Loucks, A. Heydlauff, et al.). Worldwide Fund for Nature, Wildlife Conservation Society, Smithsonian Institution and Save the Tiger Fund, Washington, DC and New York.

Seidensticker, J., Christie, S. & Jackson, P. (1999) *Riding the Tiger: Tiger Conservation in Human-Dominated Landscape.* (eds J. Seidensticker, S. Christie & P. Jackson). Cambridge University Press, Cambridge.

Servheen, C., Herrero, S. & Peyton, B. (1999) *Bears: Status Survey and Conservation Action Plan.* IUCN, Gland, Switzerland.

Shahabuddin, G. & Prasad, S. (2004) Assessing ecological sustainability of non-timber forest produce extraction: The Indian scenario. *Conservation and Society* 2, 235–250.

Shankar, U., Hegde, R. & Bawa, K.S. (1998) Extraction of non-timber forest products in the forests of Biligiri Rangan Hills, India. 6. Fuelwood pressure and management options. *Economic Botany* 52, 320–336.

Smith, J.L.D. (1993) The role of dispersal in structuring the Chitawan tiger population. *Behaviour* 124, 165–195.

Smith, J.L.D. & McDougal, C. (1991) The contribution of variance in lifetime reproduction to effective population size in tigers. *Conservation Biology* 5, 484–490.

Smith, J.L.D., McDougal, C., Sunquist, M.E., Tilson, R.L. & Seal, U.S. (1987) Female land tenure systems in tigers. *Tigers of the World: The Biology, Biopolitics, Management, and Conservation of an Endangered Species*, pp. 97–109. Noyes Publications, Park Ridge, New Jersey.

Sunquist, M.E. (1981) Social organization of tigers (*Panthera tigris*) in Royal Chitawan National Park, Nepal. *Smithsonian Contributions to Zoology* 336, 1–98.

Thatcher, C.A., Van Manen, F.T. & Clark, J.D. (2006) Identifying suitable sites for Florida panther reintroduction. *Journal of Wildlife Management* 70, 752–763.

Tilson, R., Defu, H., Muntifering, J. & Nyhus, P.J. (2004) Dramatic decline of wild South China tigers *Panthera tigris amoyensis*: Field survey of priority tiger reserves. *Oryx* 38, 40–47.

Tilson, R., Nyhus, P., Franklin, N., Sriyanto, Bastoni, Yunus, M. & Sumianto (2001) Tiger restoration in Asia: Ecological theory vs. sociological reality. *Large Mammal Restoration: Ecological and Sociological Challenges in the 21st Century.* (eds D.S. Maehr, R. Noss & J.L. Larkin). Island Press, Washington, DC.

Weber, W. & Rabinowitz, A. (1996) A global perspective on large carnivore conservation. *Conservation Biology* 10, 1046–1054.

Wikramanayake, E.D., Dinerstein, E., Robinson, J.G. et al. (1998) An ecology-based method for defining priorities for large mammal conservation: The tiger as case study. *Conservation Biology* 12, 865–878.

Woodroffe, R. & Ginsberg, J.R. (1998) Edge effects and the extinction of populations inside protected areas. *Science* 280, 2126–2128.

WPSI (2008) *WPSI's Tiger Poaching Statistics.* Wildlife Protection Society of India, New Delhi.

8

Snow Leopards: Is Reintroduction the Best Option?

Rodney M. Jackson[1] *and Som B. Ale*[2]

[1]Snow Leopard Conservancy
[2]Biological Sciences, University of Illinois

Summary

Reintroduction, including the translocation of problem animals, has been advocated as a means for re-establishing extirpated populations of large carnivores. Endangered throughout their range across 12 Central Asian countries, snow leopards, *Panthera uncia* (also classified as *Uncia uncia* Schreber, 1775) continue to decline due to poaching for their pelts and bones, killing by local herders in retaliation for livestock depredation and the widespread depletion of their natural prey base. On the other hand, the world's *ex situ* population continues to grow, raising the option of reintroducing captive-bred snow leopards into areas from which this species has been extirpated. Several important questions arise, however. Have wild snow leopard populations declined below some critical threshold level, meriting their reintroduction, or is it better to protect extant populations and allow natural range reoccupation to take its course? What is the most suitable stock for reintroduction, and what are the potential pitfalls and lessons that can we learn from reintroduction efforts involving other felids? This paper attempts to address these and related issues.

Reintroduction of Top-Order Predators, 1st edition. Edited by M.W. Hayward and M.J. Somers.
 ISBN 978-1-4051-7680-4 (pb) and 978-1-4051-9273-6 (hb)

Introduction

The history of intentional and accidental wildlife releases outside of their natural ranges to establish new food resources, for biological pest control or for aesthetic reasons dates back several centuries. By contrast, releasing a species within its natural range for restocking depleted populations, addressing human–wildlife conflict or meeting biodiversity conservation and restoration goals is relatively recent, especially for carnivores and felids in particular (Griffith *et al.*, 1989; Breitenmoser *et al.*, 2001; Hayward *et al.*, 2007). The first known effort targeting a felid involved the reintroduction of Eurasian lynx, *Lynx lynx*, to an area in Russia in 1941 (Festics, 1980, cited in Breitenmoser *et al.*, 2001). The rise of present-day reintroduction and translocation programmes may have been fuelled by the high-profile reintroductions of a few charismatic vertebrates in the 1970s and 1980s, such as the Arabian oryx (*Oryx leucoryx*) in Oman, golden lion tamarins (*Leontopithecus rosalia*) in Brazil, and Peregrine falcon (*Falco peregrinus*) in North America.

With range contraction (e.g. 173 species of mammals have lost >50% of their historic range areas in recent decades; Ceballos & Ehrlich, 2002) and species extinctions proceeding at unprecedented rates (Pimm & Lawton, 1998), reintroductions of species of economic and ecological value for conservation are gaining importance. The results of such efforts, however, are mixed (Griffith *et al.*, 1989; Breitenmoser *et al.*, 2001; Hayward *et al.*, 2007; Seddon *et al.*, 2007). For example, Breitenmoser *et al.* (2001) evaluated 165 carnivore reintroduction programmes, concluding that 42% were successful and 27% failed. The remaining 26% either had uncertain outcomes or, owing to a lack of information, could not be evaluated.

Perhaps the most successful carnivore reintroductions involve the lynx in Switzerland and other European countries, which began about 30 years ago (Breitenmoser & Baettig, 1992; Breitenmoser *et al.*, 2001; Linnell *et al.*, this volume); and the restoration of the grey wolf, *Canis lupus*, to the Yellowstone ecosystem in North America (Bangs *et al.*, 1998; Ripple & Beschta, 2003; Smith & Bangs, this volume). On the other hand, efforts at relocating Canadian lynx, *Lynx canadensis*, to sites in New York and Colorado from which the species has long been extirpated, have proven less effective, while reintroductions of European wildcat, *Felis sylvestris*, to several sites in Germany were adversely affected by high mortality, habitat modification and hybridization with domestic cats (Sunquist & Sunquist, 2002). Following the establishment of private game reserves in southern Africa, there has been a surge in lion (*Panthera leo*), leopard (*Panthera pardus*) and cheetah (*Acinonyx jubatus*) reintroductions, but the long-term conservation benefits have been questioned (Hunter *et al.*, 2007). The entire wild population of Asiatic lions, *P. leo persica*, is currently protected within a single national park, and recently Indian conservationists have been grappling with the urgency of translocating lions into new sites as a safeguard against an epizootic outbreak or catastrophic stochastic event (Johnsingh *et al.*, 2007, this volume).

Reintroductions and translocations are considered useful tools, enabling the recovery of endangered species or severely depleted populations (Griffith *et al.*, 1989; Wolf *et al.*, 1996; van Wieren, 2006). Reintroduction attempts to re-establish a target species within its historical range through the release of wild or captive-bred individuals, while translocation is defined as the act of re-stocking or supplementing an existing, usually near-extirpated population (IUCN, 1998; Breitenmoser *et al.*, 2001). At least at first glance, reintroduction appears to offer a viable means for reversing the downward trend in highly valued or flagship species, with conservation agencies supported by zoos, wildlife managers and donors capitalizing on such appeal—especially when these involve a top predator. There is a growing recognition of the important ecosystem service provided by predators whose loss may lead to unanticipated transformations in ecosystem function or representation (Berger *et al.*, 2001), as well as localized erosions in biodiversity (Terborgh *et al.*, 2001). For example, Berger (2007) advocated reintroductions for facilitating the persistence of species in peril and for restoring ecological functionality at the local landscape level within the Yellowstone ecosystem, an approach that is particularly applicable to wide-ranging, low-density carnivores.

Carnivore reintroductions and translocations tend to be risky, expensive and time-consuming due to the complex interaction of many biological, technical and socio-economic issues (Lindburg, 1992; IUCN, 1998; Miller *et al.*, 1999; Breitenmoser *et al.*, 2001). Knowledge of the species' genetics, disease, population demographics, dispersal pattern, movements and habitat requirements help determine which population cohort shows the highest survival rate, and whether this conforms with the most suitable genetic conservation unit for the particular release area (see Miller *et al.*, 1999 for details, and other chapters in this volume). Besides complying with local law and wildlife regulations, all reintroduction programmes need carefully defined and measurable goals and objectives (Rees, 2001). Any attempt must be supported by adequately trained and dedicated staff (including qualified veterinarians), equipment and the means for safely and efficiently transporting animals from capture to holding or release sites (Wemmer & Sunquist, 1988). Reintroduction (or translocation) programmes should always consist of an initial feasibility assessment, followed by a preparation phase, a release phase and a monitoring phase (IUCN, 1998; Miller *et al.*, 1999).

To our knowledge, there has been no formal attempt at reintroducing snow leopards, *Panthera uncia*, also classified as *Uncia uncia*. We know of two instances where villagers in Northern Pakistan released subadult snow leopards back into the wild after they had become inadvertently trapped within livestock enclosures. However, these do not represent a reintroduction or translocation, because the cats were released back into the same area without being held for an extended period or being housed outside of the area in which they were captured.

Few reviews deal exclusively with felids (e.g. Sunquist & Sunquist, 2002), but information on carnivore reintroduction in general is far more prolific (e.g. Linnell *et al.*, 1997, Miller *et al.*, 1999; Breitenmoser *et al.*, 2001). Because virtually no information exists on snow leopard reintroduction, we draw upon such literature for lessons learned in discussing the positive and negative aspects of reintroducing this species to areas from which it has either been extirpated or seriously depleted in number. We explore potential stocking sources and examine questions relating to the desirability and feasibility of snow leopard translocations resulting from human–wildlife conflict. Finally, we suggest that scarce financial resources may be better devoted to securing and maintaining habitat in order to allow for natural range reoccupation to occur under the metapopulation concept.

Snow leopards as candidates for reintroduction

Snow leopards, listed as endangered (IUCN, 2004), typically occur from elevations of 3000 m to more than 5000 m in the mountain ranges of Central Asia, although they may range as low as 900 m in Mongolia and Russia (Jackson, 1996; Schaller, 1998; McCarthy & Chapron, 2003). Snow leopard habitat is characterized by high aridity, wide daily and seasonal temperature fluctuations leading to a challenging climate with severe winters, low primary and secondary productivity, markedly rugged terrain and relatively sparse human habitation. The wild global population is roughly estimated at 4500–7500 animals occupying a vast, relatively fragmented range of 1.2–1.6 million km^2, which spans 12 countries (Afghanistan, Bhutan, China, India, Kyrgyzstan, Kazakhstan, Nepal, Mongolia, Pakistan, Russia, Tajikistan and Uzbekistan) (Figure 8.1). Solitary, secretive and sparsely distributed felids, such as snow leopards, are notoriously difficult to enumerate (Jackson *et al.*, 2006), so reliable information on the current status of snow leopards is lacking for significant portions of its extensive range. However, its numbers are declining in many areas, with the most recent extirpation having likely occurred in Inner Mongolia, China (Wang & Schaller, 1996).

By contrast, populations in the Himalayan region appear to be relatively secure, with apparent increases in parts of Nepal, India and Pakistan. The major threats are retributive killing from herders losing livestock to snow leopards, poaching for the animal's exquisite pelt and valuable bones (used in Chinese medicines and aphrodisiacs), an ever-diminishing prey base and habitat encroachment or competition from livestock (Jackson & Nowell, 1996; McCarthy & Chapron, 2003). As wild ungulates are hunted out, snow leopard can be expected to turn more to domestic stock, thereby causing local herders to turn against the cat—the start of the downward population spiral (Jackson & Fox, 1996).

While we acknowledge that snow leopards are not imminently threatened with extinction throughout their range (Fox, 1994; Nowell & Jackson, 1996), this cat evidently exhibits characteristics associated with extinction-prone species, including a sparse and fragmented distribution, declining population and a relatively high degree of vulnerability at the hand of humans. Unfortunately, definitive and critically needed information regarding the snow leopard's population size or metapopulation structure is lacking. Little is known about the cats' dispersal abilities, thus limiting our understanding of population parameters vital to assessing their real, as opposed to perceived, threats and extinction risk (Beier, 1993). We may presume that, as a large predator and habitat generalist, the snow leopard is capable of long-distance movements similar to those exhibited by the ecologically equivalent mountain lion, *Puma concolor* (e.g. Ruth *et al.*, 1998; Beier, 1995). While data specific to snow leopards are lacking, McCarthy *et al.* (2005) reported one instance in Mongolia of an adult radio-collared female travelling 30–40 km to cross a desert basin separating two isolated mountain ranges.

Recent field work supports the potential for non-invasive faecal sampling and the use of mitochondrial DNA genotyping for determining both snow leopard numbers and genetically derived dispersal patterns or movement rates from estimates of relatedness Schwartz *et al.* (2007). Rapid surveys using such

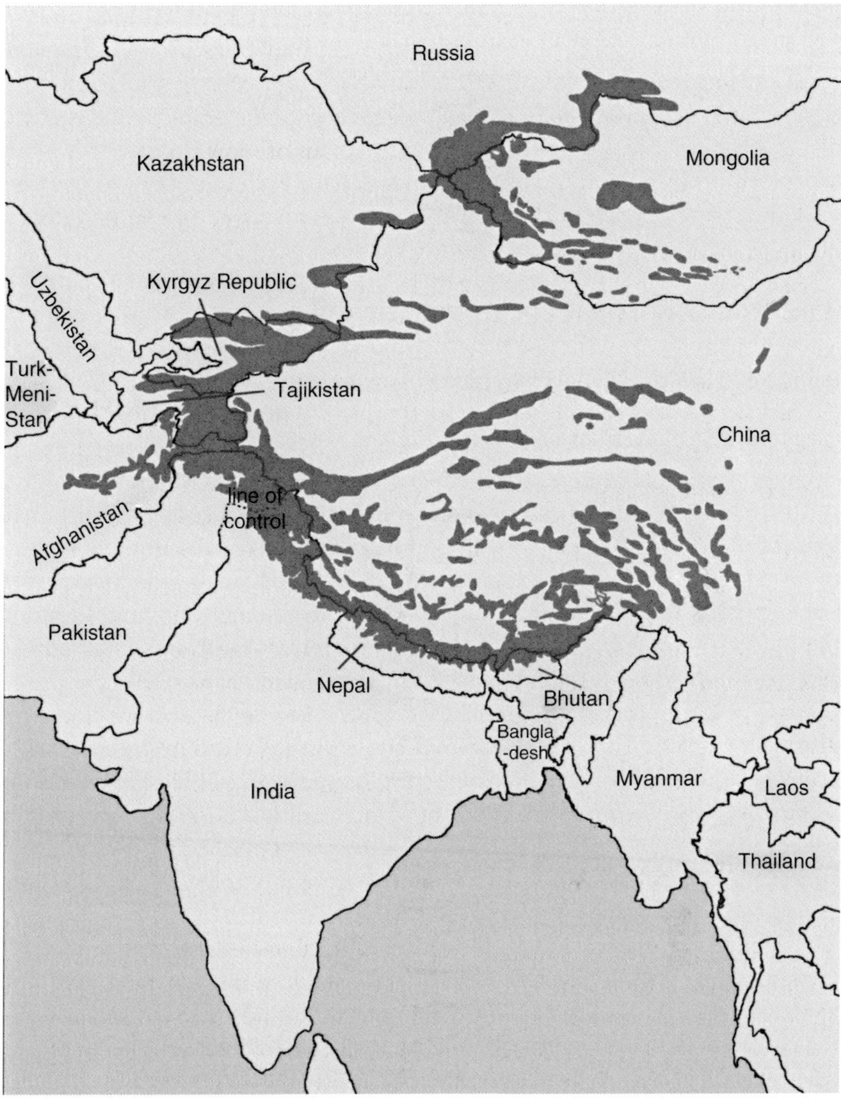

Figure 8.1 **Distribution of snow leopards in Central Asia (adapted from Fox, 1994).**

non-invasive techniques are urgently needed to assess current trends in poaching related to the rapidly growing demand for the bones of tiger *Panthera tigris* and other large felids, driven largely by China's emergence as an economic powerhouse. Certainly, if countries such as China continue the current demand for snow leopard pelts or bones, one can expect snow leopards to be extirpated from much more of their range. In this event, the need to reintroduce the species to selected areas will become more apparent and necessary.

The stocking source: captive- or wild-bred?

Reintroduction usually involves the release of captive-bred animals, although greater success may be achieved through wild-to-wild translocations (Griffith *et al.*, 1989; Wolf *et al.*, 1996; Seddon *et al.*, 2007). With excellent recruitment among the world's captive snow leopard population (e.g. Blomqvist, 2002), zoo managers or enthusiastic conservationists suggest using captive-raised leopards to replenish depleted wild populations. This optimistic view is contradicted by available evidence indicating that felids born or held in captivity are not necessarily good candidates for reintroduction or translocation (Sunquist & Sunquist, 2002). For example, captivity may decrease the innate ability of individuals to survive in the wild (Kleiman *et al.*, 1994), perhaps because of poor health conditions (Mathews *et al.*, 2005) or stress induced during release (Hartup *et al.*, 2005). Captive animals appear to lack necessary traits, such as fearfulness of humans (McPhee, 2003), predator recognition (Kleiman, 1989; Griffin *et al.*, 2000) or sufficient hunting skills (Scheepers & Venzke, 1995). Understanding and mitigating such factors is essential for ethical reasons as well as for achieving a successful outcome to any attempt at reintroduction using captive stock.

Although the science of reintroduction biology has only recently emerged (Seddon *et al.*, 2007), experience from recent decades offers some important guidelines (Breitenmoser *et al.*, 2001; Sunquist & Sunquist, 2002). For example, the best candidates for reintroduction are probably independent subadults in the dispersal phase of their lives. Behavioural competence is critical to the successful release of most captive-bred animals, and especially for socially complex animals. Snow leopards learn much of their survival behaviour from their mother or siblings during the maternal phase of life, a process that continues over extended periods among conspecific individuals sharing the same habitat. Social and environmentally learned traits are critical to their survival and ultimate reproductive success, and thus careful social preparation should constitute a key ingredient of any reintroduction effort. Like many other solitary carnivores, snow leopards must learn how to coexist and how to avoid potentially dangerous encounters with other males, particularly those sharing the same space. Captive-bred individuals usually have had little or no opportunity to acquire such behaviours, and they would thus be further handicapped if released into the wild.

An important challenge in reintroduction biology involves establishing the optimum number of individuals needed for a successful reintroduction programme. What do population ecology and genetics tell us in this regard? Reintroductions involving few founders are a cause of genetic inbreeding in the long term (see Frankham, this volume), and any programme that involves the release of genetically impoverished stock has a high risk of failure (Breitenmoser *et al.*, 2001; Seddon *et al.*, 2007). Ideally, we should aim to establish and maintain metapopulation of at least 250–500 breeding individuals (see Simberloff, 1988; Meffe & Carroll, 1994), clearly implying that landscape connectivity must exist for linking the reintroduced population with one or more nearby extant populations (although see Davies-Mostert *et al.*, this volume, for a description of the successful metapopulation approach of managing African wild dogs, *Lycaon pictus*, in South Africa). Fischer & Lindenmayer (2000) reviewed the literature covering two decades of animal relocations and suggested that source populations comprised of a large number ($n > 100$) of wild-caught individuals are needed for a successful carnivore reintroduction. For small- and medium-sized carnivores, a founder population of ca. 100 may be realistic, but for large and rare predators, like the snow leopard, finding even a dozen individuals for reintroduction presents a challenge. However, recent experience with the endangered Florida panther *P. concolor* suggests that even a few individuals may offer sufficient protection against demographic and genetic stochasticity as well as inbreeding depression (Land & Lacy, 2000 cited in Frankham *et al.*, 2004:124; Sunquist & Sunquist, 2002).

For a wild population to serve as a viable source, it must have sufficient annual recruitment and an assured supply of animals of dispersal age. While suitable habitat for relocation may exist, the removal of subadults from other sites could reduce population fitness if they are removed from the same metapopulation (Wemmer & Sunquist, 1988). How would one go about identifying and then capturing dispersing individuals for the relocation effort? Again, there is no easy answer. Reintroduction proponents would likely resort to captive-bred stock over wild-caught animals, an action that would simultaneously advance the conservation agenda of *ex situ* breeding institutions. Except in a few cases, like the Darjeeling Zoo in northern India, captive-bred animals are either not available, are poorly represented or suffer from disproportionately low breeding success within almost all institutions throughout the range of countries that the species normally inhabits. Therefore, the most logical sources are North American and European zoological institutions, which provided the founding stock for the Darjeeling collection. Potential constraints to transferring suitable candidates from Europe and North America to Asia include strict export and import regulations under the Convention on International Trade in Endangered Species of Wild Fauna and Flora (CITES), the costs of air-freighting live animals, questions relating to the mixing of genetic stock and the behavioural naivety of captive animals. Furthermore, there is a risk of viral infection: zoo-bred snow leopards may be infected with Feline Immunodeficiency Virus, which is highly unlikely to occur in the original Himalayan highlands (Lutz *et al.*, 1996).

High cost, logistical difficulties and a shortage of suitable habitat augur against reintroduction as a conservation strategy for most rare and endangered species held in captivity (Kleiman, 1989). Over two decades ago, Wemmer & Sunquist (1988) assessed the option of releasing captive-bred snow leopards, including need for a special breeding or release facility located within the snow leopard's remote habitat. They visualized a large *in situ* enclosure, preferably located in mountains with similar habitat and prey to the proposed release site(s), where cats could be encouraged to stalk and kill native prey species prior to release, rather than honing such hunting skills on domestic stock after being reintroduced. Wemmer & Sunquist (1988) suggested using wild-caught or young animals in preference to those with a lengthy captive life-history. These authors judged the snow leopard as being among the most challenging felid species to reintroduce into its native habitat, citing logistical problems in establishing the acclimating facility, along with the rigors and cost of monitoring the released individuals. They estimated the costs of constructing a suitable breeding facility at US$208,000 in addition to an annual maintenance cost of US$17,500—an estimate made in 1980, which would now be much higher.

Given the generally rugged terrain, paucity of roads and the scarcity of funding, snow leopard–range countries would all be severely constrained in meeting the standardized guidelines for reintroduction or translocation initiatives (IUCN, 1998; Miller *et al.*, 1999). Equally important, unless the underlying threats like poaching or prey-species depletion were mitigated, it is likely to amount to an exercise in futility.

This raises legitimate questions as to what is the best use of the limited funding available from within or outside the range countries for snow leopard conservation, and whether this should instead be allocated to actions that are more likely to guarantee success, such as training and capacity building, anti-poaching initiatives, habitat protection or facilitating land-use zoning and habitat improvements as a basis for encouraging natural recolonization. Most countries urgently require such resources for on-the-ground conservation work. Obviously, this approach assumes social and political willingness on the part of governments and conservationists to protect areas of sufficient size, to maintain and enhance their habitat quality, and to secure wild prey in sufficient number to minimize the predator's dependence upon domestic stock.

Would translocation help to resolve human–wildlife conflict and to re-populate depleted areas?

Given the apparent decline in the snow leopard population from key areas in China, the species' core distribution, as well as other areas under intense hunting pressure, would it not be appropriate to remove snow leopards from conflict situations for the purpose of augmenting depleted populations?

We begin by stressing that reintroduction projects should not target the welfare of individual animals, but rather that of entire populations or sub-populations. While some have advocated reintroduction as a humane means for dealing with orphaned animals, these reintroductions typically involve cubs or recently independent subadults—and their reintroduction may only intensify anti-predator feelings among the local people, likely leading to intensified retributive poisoning of snow leopards, which are perceived by local herders to be problem animals. With snow leopard habitat undergoing continued disturbance from agro-pastoral activities, conflict with local communities over livestock depredation is likely to grow (Jackson & Fox, 1996). The translocation of problem carnivores has been advocated as a remedial measure (Linnell *et al.*, 1997), but this appears problematic in areas where snow leopard interacts with subsistence pastoralists.

Although first-hand knowledge of snow leopard reintroduction or translocation is lacking, experience with other large felids suggests that translocation as a management tool for resolving human–animal conflict tends to be unsatisfactory (Miller *et al.*, 1999; Fischer & Lindenmayer, 2000; Sunquist & Sunquist, 2002). Relocated carnivores generally show poor survival, with varying tendencies for continuing their pattern of livestock depredation or returning to the original capture site (Linnell *et al.*, 1997). Some carnivores have successfully homed over 200-km or almost 500-km distances. For example, translocated puma, *P. concolor*, returned over a distance of more than 400 km, with females exhibiting stronger site fidelity than males (Ruth *et al.*, 1998). Even those individuals that do not return home may roam over greater distances, exposing themselves to greater threat and thereby reducing their likelihood of survival.

Livestock-depredating felids are thought to consist of inexperienced subadults or animals handicapped by old age or injury (Rabinowitz, 1986; Jackson & Nowell, 1996). With regard to snow leopards, circumstantial evidence suggests that depredators are either dispersing subadults or females with cubs, and are having a difficult time securing sufficient prey. Relocation of individuals with limited experience in hunting wild prey may simply transfer depredation and associated conflict from one site to another, since the particular individual's innate inclination for easy-to-kill livestock likely remains intact. Ultimately, such a translocation may only delay the cat's ultimate demise at the hands of an angry shepherd (Jackson & Fox, 1996).

In general, there has been very little follow-up of translocated animals, and evaluations of success have been fragmentary or lacking in scientific rigor (Miller *et al.,* 1999; Seddon *et al.*, 2007). Besides movement and habitat selection patterns, almost no data exist on damage levels following translocation efforts. Goodrich & Miquelle (2005) translocated four problem Amur tigers, *P. tigris altaica*, and although two of the tigers avoided further conflict with humans, these authors concluded that translocation of problem felids is only worthy of further consideration for large release areas with relatively low tiger densities and a low probability of encounters with people. "Soft" releases, involving use of on-site enclosures for enabling pre-release captivity aimed at facilitating acclimatization, may mitigate problems associated with restoration of widely roaming carnivores. Although snow leopards are solitary felids, they exhibit a complex system of social interaction through the deposition of signs (scrapes, scats, urine-spray and pugmarks) along their travel routes (Ahlborn & Jackson, 1988). Intraspecific conflict could possibly be reduced by distributing target snow leopard faeces prior to the actual introduction to maximize site fidelity while simultaneously reducing the tendency for homing behaviour. However, in areas where snow leopards are already resident, this would not obviate the possibility of adversely disrupting the local population's social organization, possibly resulting in the displacement of some residents from their home range (Linnell *et al.*, 1997).

The role of conservation in natural recolonization

Some of the issues mentioned in the preceding paragraphs would be minimized if snow leopards were to restore themselves naturally. Ale *et al.* (2007) monitored the natural recolonization of snow leopard to the Mount Everest area following an absence of several decades. Apparently, the species was extirpated prior to the establishment of Sagarmatha National Park in 1976. By the late 1980s, some evidence emerged of transient snow leopards visiting from the contiguous area in Tibet (China), and now included within the 35,000-km^2 Qomolangma Nature Reserve. Protective measures fostered the recovery of Himalayan tahr, *Hemitragus jemlahicus*, and musk deer, *Moschus chrysogaster*, the snow leopard's main prey along with domestic stock and smaller prey items. A minimum population of four snow leopards inhabits the core park area, which amounts to some 85 km^2 (Ale, 2007, S. Lovari *et al.*, Università di Siena, Italy; personal communication). While local people in one settlement lose almost 2% of their livestock to wild predators each year, they view the snow leopard as one of their mountain deities, and thus avoid hunting or killing it in retribution for taking livestock. Tahr are, at present, particularly unwary of snow leopards, although this can be expected to change as they develop suitable predator-avoidance behaviour. Improved livestock guarding and animal husbandry practices will probably be needed in the future, as perhaps will economic incentives should snow leopards increase predation pressures upon domestic stock.

The recovery of snow leopards to the Everest region may be taken as a prime example of natural reoccupation following in the footsteps of effective conservation measures, including extension of the area under protection to sustain a much larger, viable snow leopard population. Since enlargement under IUCN (International Union for the Conservation of Nature and Natural Resources) Category II Protected Area would be politically difficult because of pervasive human settlement within the watershed, the best alternative lies in creating corridors linking Everest's core habitat with other protected areas in Nepal, namely the Langtang National Park to the west and the

Khangchenjunga National Park to the east. The Qomolangma Nature Reserve (Tibet) and the Makalu-Barun Conservation Area (Nepal) could serve as "bridging" protected areas, since they encompass important habitat for snow leopards and other key species within the Eastern Himalaya (Wikramanayake *et al.*, 2001), the conservation of which is the main goal of the Sacred Himalayan Landscape initiative (Wikramanayake *et al.*, 2006). Provided suitable habitat exists within reasonable dispersal distance of a nearby population or that a permeable habitat corridor connects two more distant patches, we believe snow leopards are inherently capable of restoring depleted or extant populations. While research is needed to establish minimal dispersal distances, the maintenance of relatively intact landscape corridors with sufficient productive habitat to allow for movement and dispersal of relatively sedentary female or more mobile male snow leopards (Ruth *et al.*, 1998; Miller *et al.*, 1999) could constitute a viable, long-term conservation strategy for this sparsely distributed carnivore.

Clearly, captive-breeding and release programmes are merited in the case of serious endangerment but, at the time of writing, wild populations of snow leopard have not reached critically low levels nor has their habitat been irreversibly fragmented or reduced like that faced by the Bengal tiger, *P. tigris tigris* (Dinerstein *et al.*, 2007). Furthermore, given the scarcity of fiscal and human resources across snow leopard–range countries and the high cost of reintroduction, we suggest that valuable resources would be more productively used toward protecting their entire landscapes. Towards this goal, we urge a more pragmatic approach that would reduce human–wildlife conflict while investing in environmentally-friendly enterprises that would generate critically needed household income and encourage poverty-stricken communities to embrace wildlife conservation (Mishra *et al.*, 2003b). As a first step, such programmes must reduce livestock loss by predator-proofing night-time corrals or improving herding practices, while offering economic security through community-managed insurance mechanisms. A wide range of economic incentive projects specifically targeting the snow leopard and its prey have been launched over the past few decades, including handicraft production and sales in Mongolia and Kyrgyzstan and traditional home-stays in India and Tajikistan, along with other community-based nature tourism (see Jackson *et al.*, in press for details).

Nonetheless, under unavoidable situations such as an epidemic or other catastrophic event that may arise, biologists should be prepared to reintroduce or to translocate snow leopards (Wemmer & Sunquist, 1988). There is little doubt that large carnivores represent the most problematic of wildlife to restore because of the difficulty of reversing those human factors and landscape changes that were responsible for such extinction in the first place (Griffith *et al.*, 1989; Yalden, 1993; Breitenmoser *et al.*, 2001; Maehr, 2001). It makes sense to understand the reasons behind population declines so that important limiting factors may be removed or at least moderated. With subsistence agro-pastoralism, the dominant human activity across snow leopard range, conflict over livestock depredation is one of the most significant threats to the species (Nowell & Jackson, 1996; Mishra *et al.*, 2003b). The main factors implicated in such depredation by snow leopards are lax guarding, poorly constructed night-time pens, and insufficient wild prey forcing the cat to switch to alternative prey, i.e. livestock. Livestock-predation rates from snow leopards and other large predators range from around 2% to as much as 12% of livestock holdings each year, and this is clearly a significant economic burden for households with an approximate annual income of only US$200–400 (Jackson *et al.*, 1996; Mishra, 1997). Instances of surplus or multiple depredation that occur when a snow leopard enters a poorly constructed corral and kills numerous sheep or goats causes a few households to suffer disproportionate loss (Jackson & Wangchuk, 2004). In some cases, herders have sold the pelt or bones to help offset their economic loss (Thiele, 2003).

Bagchi *et al.* (2004) and Mishra *et al.* (2006) found higher livestock-depredation rates in areas with depleted wild prey. The snow leopard's principal prey are blue sheep (*Pseudois nayaur*), ibex (*Capra sibirica*) and Himalayan tahr, supplemented with small-sized prey like marmot (*Marmota* spp.), pika (*Ochotona* spp.), hare (*Lepus* spp.), small rodents and several game birds (Jackson, 1996; Schaller, 1998; McCarthy, 2000; Bagchi & Mishra, 2006; Ale, 2007). Annual prey requirements are estimated at 20 to 30 adult blue sheep, with radio-tracking data in Nepal indicating such a kill every 10 to 15 days (Jackson & Ahlborn, 1984; Jackson, 1996). With adequate and reliable prey, snow leopards should have smaller home ranges and wander over less territory, and fewer animals would therefore be exposed to the high mortality associated with reserve boundaries or unprotected habitat.

The importance of science-based planning

Biologists advocate the importance of refining the science of reintroduction biology (Seddon *et al.*, 2007), including setting criteria by which to assess success or failure. Breeding among first wild-born generations may be taken as one criterion and a breeding population with recruitment exceeding the adult death rate over a 3-year period as another (Sarrazin & Barbault, 1996). Other conservationists advocate establishment of a viable population of at least 500 individuals, but this is judged unrealistic because few extant populations of large carnivores exceed such a size (Nowell & Jackson, 1996). Other definitions, such as "the establishment of a self-sustaining population" are either too vague or problematic to readily apply; furthermore, none seem to address questions of metapopulation or subpopulation structure, which are judged important to montane felids, like snow leopards, that occupy fragmented habitat (Jackson & Fox, 1996).

Natural selection plays a minimal role in captive populations, so some questions remain unclear. For example, the small number of individuals within many *ex situ* populations and the inability of animals to choose their own breeding partners may be a serious concern. Will those traits that allow animals to successfully exploit specific environments in the wild remain intact in candidates released from the captive pool? Could lack of genetic variability lead to deterioration in the behavioural adaptability of the reintroduced population? In the wild, individuals with superior adaptive traits stand the greatest chance of long-term survival, reaching sexual maturity and passing genes to future generations.

Reintroduction biology as a scientific discipline is largely within the phase of inductive inference (Seddon *et al.,* 2007). Consequently, the focus has been on accessible and easily measured aspects, such as release techniques, rather than on underlying factors that are critical to the successful establishment and long-term persistence of a new population. The use of GIS and spatially-explicit modelling could help to identify potential core areas, corridors and the most appropriate sites for release, but may not alleviate the need for on-the-ground surveys to confirm prey number or density. The chances of a successful outcome would be greater if the programme were instilled with clear targets and a realistic goal supported by well-designed methodologies.

We emphasize the human dimension and socio-cultural aspects of reintroducing snow leopards, especially given the cat's reputation among pastoralists as a pest (Jackson & Wangchuk, 2001). Reintroduction success, especially of carnivores, will always be strongly dependent upon public support (Griffith *et al.*, 1989; Breitenmoser *et al.*, 2001). Indeed, Reading & Clark (1996) considered socio-political elements to be of higher priority than biological or technical considerations. Perhaps the highest profile example involves the release of wolves into the western United States, including the Yellowstone National Park, where they had been extirpated almost 70 years earlier (see Smith & Bangs, this volume). The lobby against the wolf-reintroduction programme was large and well organized. Ranchers and anti-environmental organizations all spoke out vociferously against a programme that is slowly being recognized as an ecological and conservation success (Bangs *et al.*, 1998). Similarly, Breitenmoser *et al.* (2001) reported that the return of lynx to the Swiss Alps was strongly supported by urban residents, compared to the rural community where strong opposition has persisted even 30 years after reintroduction.

A majority of herders in the Annapurna region, Nepal, considered total eradication of snow leopards as the only remedial measure worth considering (Oli *et al.*, 1994). Similar antagonism exists in other parts of the snow leopard's range (e.g. India), especially among pastoralists whose livelihoods are closely linked with livestock production, and in places where native prey is now scarce (Bagchi & Mishra, 2006). Clearly, prior to any predator translocation or augmentation, conservationists would have to address root causes for livestock depredation and to provide communities with incentives to coexist with predators (Jackson *et al.*, in press). Thus, the public should be sufficiently supportive to avoid direct conflict with reintroduced animals. In some areas, cultural resistance or public resentment may be sufficient to prevent reintroduction or translocation of snow leopards, even if sufficient habitat, prey or funds existed. A carefully targeted education programme could help avoid, and even prevent, such a situation from arising.

Conclusions

Reintroduction efforts are becoming more common as the number of animals at risk of extirpation grows. For example, the cumulative number of reintroductions involving captive-bred mammals increased from 39 in 1992 (Beck, 1994) to 69 in 1998 (Stanley-Price & Soorae, 2003) and then to 138 cases by 2005 (Seddon *et al.*, 2005). The majority of wildlife reintroductions (Griffith *et al.*, 1989; Wolf *et al.*, 1996), and those of large predators in particular

(Wemmer & Sunquist, 1988; Mills, 1991), failed to establish viable populations—only 10% were judged a success (Schaller, 1996). Few of the numerous lion reintroduction efforts in South Africa show potential for harbouring significant populations or for connecting other isolated lion populations (Hunter *et al.*, 2007), but this may reflect a landscape increasingly fragmented by humans. Elsewhere, mortality rates for large cats may reach 50%–70%, depending upon the age and social status of the animals being reintroduced (Sunquist & Sunquist, 2002). Under circumstances in which site fidelity is strong, the reintroduced or translocated animals competing for space with an existing population would be at great disadvantage, judging by the numerous examples of felids being killed by other resident animals (Sunquist & Sunquist, 2002). Finally, carnivore reintroductions are extremely lengthy, costly and complex (IUCN, 1998).

In the light of these considerations, we view proposals for reintroducing captive- or wild-bred snow leopards as premature, unduly burdened with uncertainty, and less cost-effective than well-directed conventional conservation initiatives aimed at increasing existing populations and maintaining essential corridor connectivity between protected areas or separated core populations. These constitute critical prerequisites for enabling the natural reoccupation of depleted sites by snow leopard under the classic metapopulation "source and sink" concept (Pulliam & Danielson, 1991; Beier, 1995; Sweanor *et al.*, 2000). Managing human–wildlife issues and protecting large prey and sufficient habitat are judged a far more effective and holistic conservation approach than waiting to reintroduce or translocate snow leopards from one site to another. The total snow leopard population size is uncertain but, despite localized extirpations, the species still persists over a large area. It has not reached the critically low level of free-ranging felids like the Bengal tiger (suffering a 40% loss in range, Dinerstein *et al.*, 2007), the Asiatic lion (comprising around 300 individuals within a single 2000-km^2 protected area; Johnsingh *et al.*, 2007) or the Iberian lynx, *Lynx pardinus*, (with fewer than 150 left in the wild). By supporting *in situ* conservation action and, particularly, economic or other incentive programmes that involve local communities from the planning phase through to implementation and monitoring, there should be little need for a snow leopard reintroduction effort—at least under the present scenario, with the current state of our knowledge on reintroduction science in general, and on the state of the snow leopard population and our understanding of its biology in particular.

References

Ahlborn, G. & Jackson, R. (1988) Marking in free-ranging snow leopards in west Nepal: A preliminary assessment. *Proceedings of the 5th International Snow Leopard Symposium. International Snow Leopard Trust.* (ed. H. Freeman), pp. 25–49. International Snow Leopard Trust, Seattle.

Ale, S.B. (2007) *Ecology of the Snow Leopard and the Himalayan Tahr in Sagarmatha (Mt. Everest) National Park, Nepal.* PhD thesis, University of Illinois-Chicago, Illinois.

Ale, S.B., Yonzon, P. & Thapa, K. (2007) Recovery of snow leopard *Uncia uncia* in Sagarmatha (Mount Everest) National Park, Nepal. *Oryx* 41, 89–92.

Bagchi, S. & Mishra, C. (2006) Living with large carnivores: Predation on livestock by the snow leopard (*Uncia uncia*). *Journal of Zoology* 268, 217–224.

Bagchi, S., Mishra, C. & Bhatnagar, Y.V. (2004) Conflicts between traditional pastoralism and conservation of Himalayan ibex (*Capra sibirica*) in the Trans-Himalayan mountains. *Animal Conservation* 7, 121–128.

Bangs, E.E., Fritts, S.H., Fontaine, J.A. et al. (1998) Status of gray wolf restoration in Montana, Idaho, and Wyoming. *Wildlife Society Bulletin* 26, 785–798.

Beck, B.B. (1994) Reintroduction of captive-born animals. *Creative Conservation: Interactive Management of Wild and Captive Animals.* (eds P.J.S. Olney, G.M. Mace & A.T.C. Feistner), pp. 265–286. Chapman & Hall, London.

Beier, P. (1993) Determining minimum habitat areas and habitat corridors for cougars. *Conservation Biology* 7, 94–108.

Beier, P. (1995) Dispersal of juvenile cougars in fragmented habitat. *Journal of Wildlife Management* 59, 228–237.

Berger, J. (2007) Carnivore repatriation and Holarctic prey: Narrowing the deficit in ecological effectiveness. *Conservation Biology* 21, 1105–1116.

Berger, J., Stacey, P.B., Bellis, L. & Johnson, M.P. (2001) A mammalian predator–prey imbalance: Grizzly bear and wolf extinction affect avian neotropical migrants. *Ecological Applications* 11, 947–960.

Blomqvist, L. (2002) The global snow leopard population in captivity in 2001. *International Pedigree Book for Snow Leopards* 8, 21–24.

Breitenmoser, U. & Baettig, M. (1992) Wiederansiedlung und Ausbreitung des Luchses *Lynx lynx* im Schweizer Jura. *Revue Suisse Zool* 99, 163–176.

Breitenmoser, U., Breitenmoser-Wursten, C., Carbyn, L.N. & Funk, S.M. (2001) Assessment of carnivore reintroductions. *Carnivore Conservation.* (eds J.L. Gittleman, S.M. Funk, D. Macdonald & R.K. Wayne), pp. 241–281. Cambridge University Press, Cambridge.

Ceballos, G. & Ehrlich, P.R. (2002) Mammal population losses and the extinction crisis. *Science* 296, 904–907.

Dinerstein, E., Loucks, C., Wikramanayake, E.D. et al. (2007) The fate of wild tigers. *BioScience* 57, 508–514.

Frankham, R., Ballou, J.D. & Briscoe, D.A. (2004) *A Primer of Conservation Genetics.* Cambridge University Press, Cambridge.

Fischer, J. & Lindenmayer, D.B. (2000) An assessment of the published results of animal relocations. *Biological Conservation* 96, 1–11.

Fox, J.L. (1994) Snow leopard conservation in the wild—A comprehensive perspective on a low density and highly fragmented population. *Proceedings of the Seventh International Snow Leopard Symposium.* (eds J.L. Fox & D. Jizeng), pp. 3–15. International Snow Leopard Trust, Seattle.

Goodrich, J.M. & Miquelle, M.G. (2005) Translocation of problem Amur tigers (*Panthera trigris altaica*) to alleviate tiger-human conflicts *Oryx* 39, 454–457.

Griffin, A.S., Blumstein, D.T. & Evans, C. (2000) Training captive-bred or translocated animals to avoid predators. *Conservation Biology* 14, 1317–1326.

Griffith, B., Scott, J.M., Carpenter, J.W. & Reed, C. (1989) Translocation as a species conservation tool: Status and strategy. *Science* 245, 477–480.

Hartup, B.K., Olsen, G.H. & Czekala, N.M. (2005) Fecal corticoid monitoring in Whooping Cranes (*Grus american*a) undergoing reintroduction. *Zoo Biology* 24, 15–28.

Hayward, M.W., Adendorff, J., O'Brien, J. et al. (2007) The reintroduction of large carnivores to the Eastern Cape, South Africa: An assessment. *Oryx* 41, 205–214.

Hunter, L.T.B., Pretorius, K., Carlisle, L.C. et al. (2007) Restoring lions *Panthera leo* to northern KwaZulu-Natal, South Africa: Short-term biological and technical success but equivocal long-term conservation. *Oryx* 41, 196–204.

IUCN (1998) *Guidelines for Reintroductions.* IUCN/SSC Re-introduction Specialist Group, IUCN, Gland, Switzerland.

IUCN (2004) *2004 Red List of Threatened Species.* IUCN, Gland, Switzerland.

Jackson, P. & Nowell, K. (1996) Problems and possible solutions in management of felid predators. *Journal of Wildlife Research* 1, 304–314.

Jackson, R. (1996) *Home Range, Movements and Habitat Use of Snow Leopard* (Uncia uncia) *in Nepal.* PhD dissertation, University of London.

Jackson, R. & Ahlborn, G. (1984) Preliminary habitat suitability model for snow leopard *Panthera uncia. International Pedigree Book of Snow Leopards* 4, 43–52.

Jackson, R. & Fox, J.L. (1996) Snow leopard conservation: Accomplishments and research priorities. *Proceedings of the 8th International Snow Leopard Symposium.* (eds R. Jackson & A. Ahmad), pp. 128–145. International Snow Leopard Trust, Seattle.

Jackson, R. & Wangchuk, R. (2001) Linking snow leopard conservation and people-wildlife conflict resolution: Grassroots measures to protect the endangered snow leopard from herder retribution. *Endangered Species Update* 18, 138–141.

Jackson, R. & Wangchuk, R. (2004) A community-based approach to mitigating livestock depredation by snow leopards. *Human Dimensions of Wildlife* 9, 307–315.

Jackson, R.M., Ahlborn, G., Gurung, M. & Ale, S. (1996) Reducing livestock depredation losses in the Nepalese Himalaya. *Proceedings of the 17th Vertebrate Pest Conference.* (eds R.M. Timm & A.C. Crabb), pp. 241–247. University of California, Davis.

Jackson, R.M., Mishra, C., McCarthy, T. & Ale, S. (in press) Snow leopards, conservation and conflict. *Biology and Conservation of Wild Felids.* (eds D.W. Macdonald & A.J. Loveridge). Oxford Press, Oxford.

Johnsingh, A.J.T., Goyal S.P. & Qureshi, Q. (2007) Preparations for the reintroduction of the Asiatic lion *Panthera leo persica* into Kuno Wildlife Sanctuary, Madhya Pradesh, India. *Oryx* 41, 93–96.

Kleiman, D.G. (1989) Reintroduction of captive mammals for conservation. *BioScience* 39, 152–161.

Kleiman, D.G., Stanley Price, M.R. & Beck, B.B. (1994) Criteria for reintroductions. *Creative Conservation: Interactive Management of Wild and Captive Animals.* (eds P.J.S. Olney, G.M. Mace & A.T.C. Feistner), pp. 287–303. Chapman and Hall, New York.

Land, D.E. & Lacy, R.C. (2000) Introgression level achieved through Florida panther genetic restoration. *Endangered Species Update* 17, 99–103.

Lindburg, D.G. (1992) Are wildlife reintroductions worth the cost? *Zoo Biology* 11, 1–2.

Linnell, J.D.C., Aanes, R. Swenson, J.E. Odden, J. & Smith, M.E. (1997) Translocation of carnivores as a method for managing problem animals: A review. *Biodiversity and Conservation* 6, 1245–1257.

Lutz, H., Hofmann-Lehmann, R., Fehr, D. et al. (1996) Liberation into the wild of wild felines—Danger of the release of virus infections. *Schweiz Arch Tierheilkd* 138, 579–585.

Maehr, D.S. (2001) Large mammal restoration. *Large Mammal Restoration: Ecological and Sociological Challenges in the 21st Century.* (eds D.S. Maehr, R.F., Noss & J.L. Larkin), pp. 345–354. Island Press, Washington, DC.

Mathews, F., Orros, M., McLaren, G., Gelling, M. & Foster. R. (2005) Keeping fit on the ark: Assessing the suitability of captive-bred animals for release. *Biological Conservation* 121, 569–577.

McCarthy, T.M. (2000) *Ecology and Conservation of Snow Leopards, Gobi Brown Bears, and Wild Bactrian Camels in Mongolia.* PhD dissertation, University of Massachusetts, Amherst.

McCarthy, T.M. & Chapron, G. (eds.) (2003) *Snow Leopard Survival Strategy.* International Snow Leopard Trust and Snow Leopard Network, Seattle.

McCarthy, T.M., Fuller, T.K. & Munkhtsog, B. (2005) Movements and activities of snow leopards in Southwestern Mongolia. *Biological Conservation* 124, 527–537.

McPhee, M.E. (2003) Generations in captivity increases behavioural variance: Considerations for captive breeding and reintroduction programmes. *Biological Conservation* 115, 71–77.

Meffe, G.K. & Carroll, C.R. (1994) *Principles of Conservation Biology.* Sinauer Associates, Sunderland.

Miller, B., Ralls, K., Reading, R.P. Scott, J.M. & Estes, J. (1999) Biological and technical considerations of carnivore translocation: A review. *Animal Conservation* 2, 59–68.

Mills, M.G.L. (1991) Conservation management of large carnivores in Africa. *Koedoe* 34, 81–90.

Mishra, C. (1997) Livestock depredation by large carnivores in the Indian trans-Himalaya: Conflict perceptions and conservation prospects. *Environmental Conservation* 24, 338–343.

Mishra, C., Allen, P., McCarthy, T., Madhusudan, M.D., Bayarjargal, A. & Prins, H. H.T. (2003b) The role of incentive programs in conserving the snow leopard *Uncia uncia. Conservation Biology*, 17, 1512–1523.

Mishra, C., Madhusudan, M.D. & Datta, A. (2006) Mammals of the high altitudes of western Arunachal Pradesh, eastern Himalaya: An assessment of threats and conservation needs. *Oryx* 40, 1–7.

Nowell, K. & Jackson, P. (1996) *Wild Cats: Status, Survey and Conservation Action Plan.* IUCN/Species Survival Commission Cat Specialist Group, Gland, Switzerland.

Oli, M.K., Taylor, I.R. & Rogers, M.E. (1994) Snow Leopard (*Panthera uncia*) Predation of livestock: An assessment of local perceptions in the Annapurna Conservation Area, Nepal. *Biological Conservation* 68, 63–68.

Pimm, S.L. & Lawton J.H. (1998) Planning for biodiversity. *Science* 279, 2068–2069.

Pulliam, H.R. & Danielson, B.J. (1991) Sources, sinks, and habitat selection: A landscape perspective on population dynamics. *American Naturalist* 137(supplement): S50–66.

Rabinowitz, A.R. (1986) Jaguar predation on domestic livestock in Belize. *Wildlife Society Bulletin* 14, 170–174.

Reading, R.P. & Clark, T.W. (1996) Carnivore reintroductions: An interdisciplinary examination. *Carnivore Behavior, Ecology and Evolution, Volume II.* (ed. J.L. Gittleman), pp. 296–336. Cornell University Press, Ithaca.

Rees, P.A. (2001) Is there a legal obligation to reintroduce animal species into their former habitats? *Oryx* 35, 216–223.

Ripple, W.J. & Beschta, R.L. (2003) Wolf reintroduction, predation risk, and cottonwood recovery in Yellowstone National Park. *Forest Ecology and Management* 184, 299–313.

Ruth, T.K., Logan, K.A., Sweanor, L.L., Hornocker, M.G. & Temple, L.J. (1998) Evaluating Cougar Translocation in New Mexico. *Journal of Wildlife Management* 62: 1264–1275.

Sarrazin, F. & Barbault, R. (1996) Reintroduction: Challenges and lessons for basic ecology. *Trends in Ecology and Evolution* 11, 474–478.

Schaller, G.B. (1996) Introduction: Carnivores and conservation biology. *Carnivore Behavior, Ecology and Evolution, Volume II.* (ed. J.L. Gittleman), pp. 1–10. Cornell University Press, Ithaca,

Schaller, G.B. (1998) *Wildlife of the Tibetan steppe.* Chicago University Press, Chicago.

Scheepers, J.L. & Venzke, K.A.E. (1995) Attempts to reintroduce African wild dogs *Lycaon pictus* into Etosha National Park, Namibia. *South African Journal of Wildlife Research* 25, 138–140.

Schwartz, M.K., Luikart G. & Waples, R.S. (2007) Genetic monitoring as a promising tool for conservation and management. *Trends in Ecology and Evolution* 22, 25–33.

Seddon, P.J., Armstrong, D.P. & Maloney, R.F. (2007) Developing the science of reintroduction biology. *Conservation Biology* 21, 303–312.

Seddon, P.J., Soorae, P.S. & Launay, F. (2005) Taxonomic bias in reintroduction projects. *Animal Conservation* 8, 51–58.

Simberloff, D. (1988) The contribution of population and community biology to conservation science. *Annual Review of Ecology and Systematics* 19, 473–511.

Stanley Price, M.R. & Soorae P.S. (2003) Reintroductions: Whence and whither? *International Zoo Yearbook* 38, 61–75.

Sunquist, M. & Sunquist, F. (2002) *Wild Cats of the World.* University of Chicago Press, Chicago.

Sweanor, L.L., Logan, K.A. & Hornocker, M.G. (2000) Cougar dispersal, metapopulation dynamics and conservation. *Conservation Biology* 14, 798–808.

Terborgh, J., Lopez, L., Nunez, P. et al. (2001) Ecological meltdown in predator-free forest fragments. *Science* 294, 1923–1925.

Thiele, S. (2003) *Fading Footprints: The Killing and Trade of Snow Leopards.* Traffic International, Cambridge.

van Wieren, S.E. (2006) Populations: Re-introductions. *Restoration Ecology: The New Frontier*. (eds J. van Andel & J. Aronson), pp. 82–92. Blackwell Publishing, Malden.

Wang, X. & Schaller, G.B. (1996) Status of large mammals in western Inner Mongolia, China. Journal of East China Normal University, *Natural Science* (Special Issue of Zoology) 12, 93–104.

Wemmer, C. & Sunquist, M.E. (1988) Felid reintroductions: Economic and energetic considerations. *Proceedings of the 5th International Snow Leopard Symposium.* (ed H. Freeman), pp. 193–205. International Snow Leopard Trust, Seattle.

Wikramanayake, E., Carpenter, C., Strand, H. & McKnight, M. (2001). *Ecoregion-Based Conservation in the Eastern Himalaya: Identifying Important Areas for Biodiversity Conservation.* World Wildlife Fund and International Centre for Integrated Mountain Development (ICIMOD), Kathmandu.

Wikramanayake, E., Moktan, V., Aziz, T., Khaling, S., Khan, A. A. & Tshering, D. (2006) *The WWF Snow Leopard Action Strategy for the Himalayan Region.* World Wildlife Fund, Bhutan.

Wolf, C.M., Griffith, B., Reed, C. & Temple S.A. (1996) Avian and mammalian translocations: Update and reanalysis of 1987 survey data. *Conservation Biology* 10, 1142–1154.

Yalden, D.W. (1993) The problems of reintroducing carnivores. *Symposia of the Zoological Society of London* 65, 289–306.

9

The Suitability of the Jaguar (*Panthera onca*) for Reintroduction

Marcella J. Kelly[1] *and Scott Silver*[2]

[1]Department of Fisheries and Wildlife, Virginia Tech
[2]Queens Zoo, Wildlife Conservation Society

Summary

As the largest and most iconic felid in tropical America, jaguars, *Panthera onca*, and jaguar conservation have received a good deal of attention by the public and conservationists alike. Jaguars are widely distributed throughout Central and South America, and exist within a wide variety of habitats and conservation contexts. Therefore it is somewhat surprising that, to date, no true jaguar reintroduction studies have been undertaken. While there have been a few incidents of jaguar releases (usually relocations of wild-born animals), even these have lacked pre- and post-release observations or data collection. Currently, there are few, if any, circumstances in which jaguar reintroductions would be feasible or desirable (i.e. where suitable habitat exists, but where threats and resident jaguar populations are absent). However, high rates of habitat conversion as a consequence of human development and the resultant isolation of local populations increase the likelihood that such circumstances may arise in the near future. To that end, current studies of jaguar population biology, ecology and behaviour, as well as models of successful carnivore reintroduction project organization and design will prove invaluable assets to any jaguar reintroduction projects. Such models can and

Reintroduction of Top-Order Predators, 1st edition. Edited by M.W. Hayward and M.J. Somers.
 ISBN 978-1-4051-7680-4 (pb) and 978-1-4051-9273-6 (hb)

should be incorporated in undertaking jaguar reintroduction projects should they become necessary.

Introduction

Large carnivores are fundamental elements in ecosystems (Morrison *et al.*, 2007), known to shape behaviour, distribution and abundance of their prey (Berger *et al.*, 2001a; Terborgh *et al.*, 2001; Sinclair *et al.*, 2003). Additionally, they influence ecosystems well beyond single-species interactions through trophic cascade effects (Crooks & Soule, 1999; Berger *et al.*, 2001b; Cote *et al.*, 2004; Morrison *et al.*, 2007). For example, Terborgh *et al.* (2001; 2006) found higher densities of herbivore prey species and lower densities of saplings in "jaguar, *Panthera onca*–free" sites than in sites with a full complement of neotropical predators, demonstrating that the absence of top predators can have an impact on vegetation structure and diversity. Large carnivores, however, are highly vulnerable to extirpation by humans, and intact top-predator faunas are becoming increasingly rare (Morrison *et al.*, 2007).

The jaguar has been singled out as a flagship, umbrella and landscape species whose conservation is thought to assist in the preservation of its entire community (Noss, 1990; Terborgh, 1992; Terborgh *et al.*, 1999; Gittleman *et al.*, 2001; Sanderson *et al.*, 2002b; Coppolillo *et al.*, 2004). As a flagship species, jaguars garner attention as charismatic megafauna, capturing the imagination of the general public across their range. As an umbrella species, they have broad ramifications for conservation of biodiversity and ecosystem protection because these cats often live in tropical areas where biodiversity is high. Protecting jaguars with their large home ranges, therefore, is thought to ensure protection of vast amounts of biodiversity under their "umbrella" (Noss, 1990; Gittleman *et al.*, 2001). As a landscape species, jaguars are wide-ranging and live in an ecologically and jurisdictionally complex landscape (Sanderson *et al.*, 2002a; Coppolillo *et al.*, 2004). Their requirements in time and space make them particularly vulnerable to human alteration and use of wild landscapes (Sanderson *et al.*, 2002a). Achieving effective jaguar conservation, therefore, requires addressing threats facing large swaths of critical habitats, assuring presence of adequate prey species and addressing impacts of the local communities that are ultimately responsible for the landscape heterogeneity.

As the largest felid in the Western Hemisphere, jaguars are an important icon of wildness throughout much of Central and South America. Yet the jaguar remains the least studied of all "great" cats (Valdez, 2000) and has been extirpated from more than 50% of its historic range (Sanderson *et al.*, 2002b). The situation is worse in Mexico and Central America, where jaguar populations exist in only 33% of their former range, and 75% of the populations that do exist are reduced in number (Swank & Teer, 1989; Sanderson *et al.*, 2002a; Marieb, 2005). Despite its internationally protected status, the jaguar's range continues to decrease (Fuller & Swift, 1985; Seymour, 1989; Sanderson *et al.*, 2002a; Marieb, 2005; IUCN, 2006). As current trends continue, jaguar reintroductions may become inevitable to restore extirpated populations and rebuild intact ecosystems.

While a few jaguar translocations have occurred, to date, no true jaguar reintroductions have taken place. This leaves us to compare the potential for jaguars to be reintroduced based on lessons learned from reintroductions of other species. It is widely accepted that reintroductions, especially carnivore reintroductions, have a poor success rate (Yalden, 1993; Reading & Clark, 1996; Breitenmoser *et al.*, 2001; Armstrong & Seddon, 2007). However, the potential for success has increased recently due to numerous advancements, including the establishment of the IUCN (International Union for the Conservation of Nature and Natural Resources) Reintroduction Specialist Group (Stanley Price & Soorae, 2003), better reporting beginning in the 1990s, especially substantial increases in peer-reviewed publications, and the rise of restoration ecology (van Wieren, 2006) and reintroduction biology (Armstrong & Seddon, 2007). In addition to the helpful reintroduction guidelines provided by the IUCN Reintroduction Specialist Group, Reading and Clark (1996) also describe an interdisciplinary approach to improve the success rate of carnivore reintroductions. They define three aspects that should be considered in any carnivore reintroduction programme: (1) biological/ecological and technical aspects; (2) valuational (human dimensional) aspects; and (3) organizational aspects. Below, we examine the potential for jaguar reintroduction using the Reading and Clark (1996) framework.

Biological, ecological and technical aspects

Important considerations for jaguar reintroductions are: habitat requirements (space and available prey), behaviour, demography, physiology, genetics and also knowledge of effective release protocols.

Jaguar ecology and natural history

While jaguars have long been icons of wildness, beauty and mystery, little is known of the daily existence of these solitary felids. Information on space use comes from only a handful of telemetry studies in limited habitats, and describes jaguar home-range size as 10–40 km^2 in Belize (Rabinowitz & Nottingham, 1986), and 52–176 km^2 in the Brazilian Pantanal (Soisalo & Cavalcanti, 2006). Clearly, for a release site to hold a viable population of jaguars, it will have to be large (Frankham, this volume). Recently, a number of studies have used remote camera trapping to estimate jaguar abundance and population density within currently protected areas. For example, jaguar densities are high in Belize, ranging from ~6–11 jaguars per 100 km^2 for rainforest habitats (Silver *et al.*, 2004; Miller & Miller, 2005), while the Bolivian Chaco has lower densities from ~2–5 jaguars per 100 km^2 (Maffei *et al.*, 2004). Maffei *et al.*, (in press) present a useful review of density estimates across the jaguar's range. This may serve to determine the number of cats that a reintroduction site of a particular size could potentially hold, and thereby provide some basis for estimating minimum area size requirements for reintroduction sites necessary to support a viable reintroduced population. For example, using 500 animals as the effective population size necessary to maintain the adaptive potential of a species (Frankel & Soule, 1981), then area requirements would range from 4545–25,000 km^2 for jaguar densities of between two and 11 animals per 100 km^2, respectively. Alternatively, preferred prey abundance might prove to be a better method of estimating carrying capacity than area requirements (Hayward *et al.*, 2007b).

Reintroduction sites must contain adequate prey populations. Given that the jaguar's distribution extends from northern Sonora Mexico, through Central America and down to northern Argentina (Sanderson *et al.*, 2002a), it is not surprising that this range encompasses a wide variety of habitats. These include xeric, arid scrublands, swampy grasslands, montane forests, lowland tropical rainforests, dry deciduous forests, tropical pine forests and mangrove swamps (Sunquist & Sunquist, 2002). Consequently, jaguars have highly variable prey requirements across their range (e.g. Rabinowitz & Nottingham, 1986; Emmons, 1987; Crawshaw, 1995; Aranda & Sanchez-Cordero, 1996; Taber *et al.*, 1997; Troëng, 2000; Garla *et al.*, 2001; Novack *et al.*, 2005; Weckel *et al.*, 2006; Azevedo & Murray, 2007). Jaguars are considered to be opportunistic predators, and they have been found to eat tapir (*Tapirus* spp.), caiman (*Caiman* spp.), armadillo (*Dasypus novemcinctus.*), peccary (*Tayassu pecari* and *Dicotlyes* spp.), and even coatimundi (*Nasua nasua*), skunk (*Mephitis* spp.), turtle eggs and cattle (*Bos taurus*). In some areas, they subsist on large prey (>20 kg); in other regions, they primarily eat medium sized prey (10–20 kg). Although they will eat small prey in marginal habitats, their physical characteristics suggest they have evolved to prey on large vertebrates (Carbone *et al.*, 1999).

While there are some exceptions, jaguar diets tend to reflect the relative abundance of various prey species in an area (Sunquist & Sunquist, 2002). Data can be used from previous diet studies to determine the likely prey composition of an area. Reintroduction sites will need to be surveyed for adequate prey prior to jaguar release, but estimating the carrying capacity of jaguar in a given habitat based upon prey abundance can be problematic. While there is little information on how much wild cats eat, Emmons (1987) estimated that jaguars consume 34–43 g/kg of body weight per day. For a 34-kg jaguar, this translates into 1.2–1.5 kg per day, which is similar to what zoos feed captive jaguars (Emmons, 1987). Space requirements from telemetry studies, combined with prey data from diet studies, can provide guidelines to examine potential reintroduction sites for adequate space and prey. Comparison of density estimates across habitat types (Maffei *et al.*, in press) illustrates the relationship between prey abundance in these habitats and area requirements for supporting a minimum viable population.

The jaguar's wide distribution and variable prey indicates a high degree of behavioural and ecological flexibility that may make jaguars more amenable to reintroduction than more specialized species. In addition, as the competitively dominant carnivore across their range, they may be more resilient than more specialized carnivores to the reintroduction process because they are free from competitive persecution from other predators, as suggested for other top predators (Hayward *et al.*, 2007a,b). In contrast, jaguars at the edge of their distribution in Mexico have a narrower food niche than pumas, and appear more restricted to larger prey such as white-tailed deer, *Odocoileus virginianus*, and peccary (Nuñez *et al.*, 2000) and are easily disturbed by human presence (Dugleby *et al.*, 2001), possibly making them more difficult candidates for reintroductions.

Territoriality must be considered in designing a jaguar reintroduction programme. There is evidence from telemetry and camera trapping that male and female jaguar home ranges overlap substantially, both within and between the sexes (Harmsen, 2006; Soisalo & Cavalcanti, 2006). To date, however, social interactions such as home-range tenure and degree of territoriality have not been determined. In addition, for wild jaguars, we still know almost nothing about breeding behaviour, inter-birth intervals, litter sizes, life expectancies and ages of first and last reproduction (but see Quigley & Crawshaw [2002] for some data from the Pantanal). Some of this information may be obtained from zoo populations, with the caveat that captive animals may not accurately reflect demographic rates for wild jaguars. Similarly, there is little information on jaguar physiological requirements, but jaguars are strongly associated with watercourses and streams, and they rarely occur above 1200 m in elevation (Sunquist & Sunquist, 2002).

Genetic concerns should always be considered in reintroduction programmes (Frankham, this volume). Recent genetic analyses by Eizirik *et al.*, (2001) and Ruiz-Garcia *et al.*, (2006) found that the traditional classification of jaguars into several subspecies could not be proven by genetic analysis. Thus, the original eight subspecies should not be used as management units for this species. Their results showed only that the Central and northern South American sequences were older and more basal in comparison to the two southern South American clusters, and that the Amazon River was defined as the only true barrier to jaguar dispersal, which still may be a crossable barrier. Compared to pumas, *Puma concolor* (Culver *et al.*, 2000; Walker *et al.*, 2000), jaguars have significantly higher levels of genetic diversity and, compared with leopards, which are ecologically similar and phylogentically closer, jaguars have comparable expected heterozygosity (Spong *et al.*, 2000). This suggests greater flexibility when introducing jaguars from any given area. Jaguars do not appear to be suffering from low genetic diversity, and only two genetic population clusters appear to be important. Therefore, we suggest that there are currently no identified genetic impediments to reintroductions, but that founder animals should originate from a population cluster that is consistent with the proposed reintroduction site.

Further genetic research on wild jaguars is still needed, however, as many DNA samples used in past studies were obtained from zoos or museums. It would be ideal to collect DNA at a finer geographical scale in order to investigate the current genetic status of these wild cats more precisely.

Finally, the technical aspects of potential jaguar reintroductions will depend on information from previous studies on other species. In general, past studies on carnivores have shown that soft releases appear more effective than hard releases (Hayward *et al.*, 2007a,b). Releasing wild-caught carnivores, or a mix of wild-caught and captive animals, appears to be a more successful strategy than using only captive animals as founders (Breitenmoser *et al.*, 2001). Carnivore reintroduction projects with fewer than 20 animals released suffer from a higher risk of failure (Breitenmoser *et al.*, 2001; van Wieren, 2006), but Armstrong and Seddon (2007) caution that comparative analyses across species may give misleading information regarding release group size and establishment success.

Valuation and human dimensions

Human perception of carnivores is an important influence on the success or failure of carnivore reintroduction programmes (Reading & Clark, 1996). Local support is crucial and therefore local values and attitudes must be assessed prior to any reintroduction. Effective public-relations campaigns are required to educate the public and to develop public support for carnivore reintroduction (Reading & Kellert, 1993). Human attitudes towards carnivores are highly variable, but some trends exist. Rural people tend to express strong dominionistic and utilitarian values and are likely to favour exploitation and subjugation of wildlife (Kellert *et al.*, 1996; Reading & Clark, 1996). People with more formal education and higher incomes tend to display naturalistic values with strong interest in outdoor recreation and support for wildlife conservation. Younger people and females tend to demonstrate moralistic and humanistic values and have great affection for individual animals, opposing consumptive uses (Reading & Clark, 1996).

While their widespread distribution means that they coexist in many different ethno-cultural contexts, the attitudes towards jaguars in the human communities closest to them are variable and often poorly understood (Conforti & Azevedo, 2003; Zimmerman *et al.*, 2005). Human–jaguar conflict is ubiquitous throughout the jaguar's distribution, even if the relative effects vary from region to region. The sources of conflict include direct competition for space and food, conversion and fragmentation of jaguar habitat, overhunting of jaguar prey, livestock depredation, direct killing/poisoning of jaguars and, finally, human perceptions of large predators. By and large throughout their range, the perceptions of jaguar by people who coexist with them are rooted in the context of either fear or a sense of competition born from livestock depredation.

Jaguars are reported to kill livestock in places where they occur in close contact (Schaller & Crawshaw, 1980; Mondolfi & Hoogesteijn, 1986; Rabinowitz, 1986b; Hoogesteijn *et al.*, 1993; Mazzolli *et al.*, 2002; Conforti &

Azevedo, 2003; Polisar *et al.*, 2003; Zimmerman *et al.*, 2005; Michalski *et al.*, 2006; Palmeira *et al.*, 2008). In the Venezuelan Llanos, cattle constituted up to 56% of total prey consumed by jaguar (Hoogesteijn *et al.*, 1993). In Brazil, most local livestock owners surrounding Iguacu National Park had positive perceptions of jaguars (Conforti & Azevedo, 2003). Perception did not depend on whether residents had experienced depredation, yet still, 36.5% did not favour the presence of jaguars in the Park (Conforti & Azevedo, 2003). In the Pantanal, attitudes towards jaguar were mixed and difficult to predict but appeared more closely related to respondents' age and relative wealth than to jaguar-related benefits through tourism or costs through cattle predation (Zimmerman *et al.*, 2005).

In the Venezuelan Llanos, high depredation rates and shooting of livestock-killing jaguars are commonplace, often maiming cats and potentially creating future marauding jaguars (Hoogesteijn *et al.*, 1993). Cultural attitudes such as "machismo" elevate jaguar-killers to local heroes in their communities in Venezuela (Hoogesteijn *et al.*, 1993) while, in Northern Belize, attitudes of dominion and domination over wildlife drive Mennonite ranching communities to kill large numbers of jaguars as an interpretation of God's design (personal observation).

There is no question that jaguars can become cattle-killers and, after this occurs, it is difficult to alter this behaviour (Rabinowitz, 1986b). However, several studies give excellent suggestions for modifying ranching practices and thereby minimizing this risk (Hoogesteijn *et al.*, 1993; Polisar *et al.*, 2003; Azevedo & Murray, 2007). Changing ranching practices surrounding a reintroduction site will undoubtedly be necessary and will require a large educational and technical campaign before reintroduction.

In addition to conflict over livestock, humans tend to fear jaguars. In Brazil, 52% of interview respondents viewed jaguars as a risk to human life (Conforti & Azevedo, 2003), yet there is very little evidence for unprovoked attacks by jaguars on humans. This is in stark contrast to tigers, lions and leopards which have a long history of attacking and killing humans (Guggisberg, 1975). Educational campaigns could allay these fears about jaguars and make reintroduction programmes easier.

The fact that jaguars project powerful cultural and symbolic values across their range means that it may be easier to garner support for such a charismatic species compared to lesser known species (Westman, 1990). However, as noted above, it is obvious that human valuation of jaguars is very complex. Reintroduction of jaguars will require assessment of the local communities' values, recognition of the type of values held and, if they are anti-reintroduction, will require public educational campaigns to address concerns and alter values. Change in values is slow, especially in established communities or social groups (Williams, 1979), but is not impossible. Reading and Clark (1996) describe how change in values can be accomplished. This value shift may be the largest stumbling block to potential jaguar reintroductions in the future.

Organizational aspects

Just as the extensive range of the jaguar finds a high level of variability in the habitats and human cultural contexts in which they are found, the political and support capacity for potential reintroductions will also be highly variable. In countries with limited governmental capacities, the burden of resource and technical support for a reintroduction may come from non-governmental organizations (NGOs) and/or academic institutions.

To prevent failure being caused by an individual or organization lacking necessary expertise, the organizations responsible for reintroductions should be well matched to their tasks (Clark & Westrum, 1989; Clark *et al.*, 1989.). Since reintroduction science is in its infancy, reintroductions should be treated as carefully designed experiments, allowing us to learn from experience (Falk *et al.*, 1996; van Wieren, 2006). This generally points to including an academic institution with strong biology or wildlife sciences programmes (including carnivore ecology) as a key player in reintroductions. While academic institutions (and some governmental organizations [GOs] and NGOs) have scientific qualifications and can identify and train good students to research, design and implement scientific reintroduction studies, they are rigid in their academic requirements and timelines. Therefore, including an academic institution will require 1–2 years for study design and scientific training (usually for graduate students). This should not be an impediment considering the time it will take to garner public support through education and outreach prior to a carnivore reintroduction programme. For example, the red wolf, *Canis rufus*, reintroduction to Alligator River Wildlife Refuge in North Carolina, USA, began in 1987, 3 years after the reintroduction site was located. In those 3 years, the US Fish and Wildlife Service completed an intensive effort in contacting, educating and listening to concerns of local residents in order to facilitate local acceptance (Banks, 1988; Phillips & Parker, 1988; More & Smith, 1991).

While academic institutions can direct the science of reintroductions, biologists often do not have the skills or necessary expertise to address the concerns of surrounding communities or local governments. This task may be better suited either to researchers in human dimensions or to appropriate GOs and NGOs. For jaguar reintroduction programmes, especially in developing nations, this task will more likely fall on the shoulders of NGOs. As an example, the Wildlife Conservation Society, the Belize Zoo and the Belize Audubon Society have educational programmes for school children to teach jaguar ecology and conservation. Such organizations are already well placed to engage with the public should jaguar reintroductions be considered.

Government agencies (e.g. Departments of Forestry, Natural Resources, Environment, etc.) will also be involved in any potential jaguar reintroduction programme. Government agencies tend to be characterized by bureaucracy with rigid hierarchies and fixed rules and regulations, while NGOs tend to have a more flexible organization with a risk-embracing style (Reading & Clark, 1996; Slotow & Hunter, this volume). These styles can clash, resulting in conflict, communication breakdowns and delays. Therefore, it will be necessary to form a multidisciplinary jaguar reintroduction team, with members that are aware of the internal structures of their own, and the other, organizations involved. There will undoubtedly be numerous stakeholders (e.g. black-footed ferret recovery efforts included more than 20 organizations [Clark & Harvey, 1988]), but efficiency can be enhanced with a team of well-trained professionals who possess problem-solving experience and the ability to work with an interdisciplinary team (Reading & Clark, 1996).

Any potential reintroduction will have to start with a reintroduction feasibility study. At this stage, stakeholders will be identified and experts contacted. The minimum required personnel and stakeholders for a jaguar reintroduction programme are similar to other carnivore introductions, but a high priority should be placed on pre-and post-release monitoring of jaguar, since there has been no reintroduction research undertaken for this species. Often socio-political considerations are more concerned with the removal of problem jaguars from sensitive areas and are less concerned with adding to our knowledge base concerning the impacts and components of reintroduction protocols. It is incumbent upon conservation biologists to resist reintroductions/translocation projects if their design does not adequately commit resources of time and funding for improving our understanding of jaguar reintroductions. Furthermore, while methodological rigor should be of paramount importance in future jaguar introductions, unfocused monitoring is an inefficient use of conservation funding (Armstrong & Seddon, 2007). Monitoring should be designed to address questions *a priori* and should be driven by scientific questions, not vice versa—in other words, the research should not be driven by monitoring (Armstrong & Seddon, 2007). Numerous questions in reintroduction biology remain unanswered (Armstrong & Seddon, 2007), and a more strategic approach integrating biological aspects, human dimensional aspects and stakeholder organizational aspects, will allow us to advance the field and gain maximum knowledge from any single reintroduction programme.

Jaguar translocation history

To date, there have been no formal translocation programmes involving reintroducing jaguars into previously inhabited, but currently uninhabited areas. This is primarily due to a lack of suitable sites with available prey. Most previously inhabited sites have been converted to other uses, and other more "intact" sites lack adequate prey. In contrast, there have been numerous instances of translocating "problem" jaguars (ones that kill livestock) to other areas already occupied by jaguars. These attempts have been either opportunistic and/or clandestine translocations (personal observation) or have been formal translocation programmes (Hoogesteijn *et al.*, 2002). In general, translocations of problem jaguars have not been successful. For example, a male problem jaguar in Argentina was shot and killed by local people within 1 week of release (Crawshaw, 1995) and, in Belize, a translocated, cattle-killing, female immediately began to prey on cattle in her new location until she was hunted and killed (Rabinowitz, 1986a). For most other opportunistic or programmatic translocations, there is little to no information on success or failure from such operations because few have been undertaken with monitoring before or after release: the survival of the individuals released and their impacts on the resident populations have not been documented.

Translocation/reintroduction potential

Compared with cervids and bovids, cats are generally more difficult to reintroduce because they live at low densities, require large areas with a full complement of prey species and usually need to spend time perfecting hunting and killing behaviour, often via learning from an adult (Sunquist & Sunquist, 2002). In addition, territoriality and site fidelity are often strong for felids, putting animals reintroduced into an established population at a disadvantage.

Despite these difficulties and despite the lack of a documented history of reintroductions or translocations, the jaguar has potential for becoming a candidate for reintroduction. The jaguar's ecological profile is such that its habitat continues to shrink and fragment across its range, and the current declining status and nature of the human–jaguar conflict all increase the likelihood of reintroductions playing a future role in jaguar conservation. Current jaguar distribution maps suggest an increasing risk of populations becoming genetically isolated throughout their range (Marieb, 2005). This continued range reduction also makes it increasingly likely that local extinctions will be caused by a combination of anthropogenic and stochastic events. In some areas, future jaguar management could be on the metapopulation scale, where releases of individuals to re-establish populations or to increase genetic variation of established isolated small populations are potential options (see Davies-Mostert *et al.*, this volume, for an example of such metapopulation management with African wild dogs *Lycaon pictus*).

Areas without jaguars usually lack prey or protection from poaching and, therefore, few of these could actually support them. Suitable areas for future reintroduction will need to restore sufficient prey populations and eradicate or reduce poaching if reintroduction programmes are to be successful. There also may be potential for reintroduction to areas outside established reserves. For example, large private reserves that focus on tourism (e.g. in the Brazilian Pantanal) and that have previously lost their jaguar population due to hunting or past land-use practices, may provide opportunities for reintroduction once causes of jaguar decline have ceased or been reversed. The incorporation of ecotourism with reintroduction programmes has proven to be economically beneficial in Africa (Lindsey *et al.*, this volume) and could serve as a model for jaguar reintroductions.

Currently, there is no shortage of individuals for reintroduction/translocation. Problem or orphaned jaguar are routinely brought into captivity, and zoological parks and wildlife rehabilitation centres within Central and South America try to accommodate local drop-offs resulting from accidents and anti-depredation efforts. Government-funded zoological parks are often required to accept animals in need of placement as a result of illegal hunting or depredation control and, as a result, often have more captive jaguar than they can reasonably maintain in captivity. Therefore, depending upon the criteria for candidates, reintroducing a minimum of 20 jaguars at a site (as suggested earlier to increase success rates), could be feasible.

Conclusion

Based on recent jaguar abundance surveys (Maffei *et al.*, in press), several protected areas currently support key jaguar populations. Large areas in the Brazilian Pantanal, the Bolivian Chaco, La Selva Maya of Central America and the Amazon, are strongholds for jaguar populations. However, as habitat fragmentation and the resultant genetic isolation continue, the potential for reintroduction and translocation to re-establish populations, or to bolster current populations, increases.

Any reintroduction will need to begin with a feasibility study. We suggest forming a multidisciplinary jaguar reintroduction team to conduct this feasibility study. The responsibilities of such a team would include, but are not limited to:

- Identifying suitable empty habitat, including area requirements and prey availability, for a jaguar population;
- Identifying the reasons for the absence of jaguars from an area;
- Identifying why natural recolonization has not taken place;
- Assessing the level of protection of the suitable area;
- Identifying potential stakeholders, organizations and institutions involved in the potential reintroduction programme;
- Assessing attitudes towards jaguars in adjacent human communities;
- Identifying potential funding sources for a reintroduction programme, including the potential for long-term commitment for pre- and post-release monitoring.

We probably do not know enough about jaguar ecology to predict the response of jaguars to reintroduction and to predict the success of a reintroduction programme (cf. Africa's predators in Hayward, this volume). We will have to be guided by lessons learned from other felid translocations/reintroductions (e.g. concerning release methodology, suitable sex/age class candidates, etc.) as these are likely to be applicable also to jaguars. A strategic approach that includes biological/ecological knowledge of the species, addresses human attitudes and concerns and includes multiple stakeholder individuals or organizations is more likely to be successful than an opportunistic, *ad hoc* approach towards jaguar reintroduction. In short, a successful reintroduction or translocation of a jaguar population is likely to be contingent on the proper combination of suitable habitat, socio-cultural tolerance by local and national communities and the resources in time, money and expertise to carry out such a project responsibly. To date, this "perfect storm" of circumstances has not occurred but, should all these factors fall into place, reintroduction of this most majestic of the New World felids may, in fact, be possible and worthwhile.

References

Aranda, M. & Sanchez-Cordero, V. (1996) Prey spectra of jaguar (*Panthera onca*) and puma (*Puma concolor*) in tropical forests of Mexico. *Studies of Neotropical Fauna and Environment* 31, 65–67.

Armstrong, D.P. & Seddon, P.J. (2007) Directions in reintroduction biology. *Trends in Ecology and Evolution* 23, 20–25.

Azevedo, F.C.C. & Murray, D.L. (2007) Evaluation of potential factors predisposing livestock to predation by Jaguars. *The Journal of Wildlife Management* 71, 2379–2386.

Banks, V. (1988) The red wolf gets a second chance to live by its wits. *Smithsonian* 18, 100–107.

Berger, J., Stacey, P.B., Bellis, L. & Johnson, M.P. (2001a) A mammalian predator-prey imbalance: Grizzly bear and wolf extinction affect avian neotropical migrants. *Ecological Applications* 11, 947–960.

Berger, J., Swenson, J.E. & Persson, I.L. (2001b) Recolonizing carnivores and naive prey: Conservation lessons from Pleistocene extinctions. *Science* 291, 1036–1039.

Breitenmoser, U., Breitenmoser-Würsten, C., Carbyn, L.N. & Funk. S. M. (2001) Assessment of carnivore reintroductions. *Carnivore Conservation.* (eds J.L. Gittleman, S.M. Funk, D. Macdonald & R.K. Wayne), pp. 240–281. Cambridge University Press, Cambridge.

Carbone, C., Mace, G.M., Roberts, S.C. & Macdonald, D.W. (1999) Energetic constraints on the diet of terrestrial carnivores. *Nature* 402, 286–288.

Clark, T.W. & Harvey, A.H. (1988) Implementing endangered species recovery policy: Learning as we go? *Endangered Species Update* 5, 35–42.

Clark, T.W. & Westrum, R. (1989) High-performance teams in wildlife conservation: A species reintroduction and recovery example. *Environmental Management* 12, 663–670.

Clark, T.W., Crete, R. & Cada, J. (1989) Designing and managing successful endangered species recovery programs. *Environmental Management* 13, 159–170.

Conforti, V.A. & de Azevedo, F.C.C. (2003) Local perceptions of jaguar (*Panthera onca*) and pumas (*Puma concolor*) in the Iguacu National Park area, south Brazil. *Biological Conservation* 111, 215–221.

Coppolillo, P., Gomez, H., Maisels, F. & Wallace, R. (2004) Selection criteria for suites of landscape species as a basis for site-based conservation. *Biological Conservation* 115, 419–430.

Cote, S.D., Rooney, T.P. Trembleay, J.P. Dussault, C. & Waller, D.M. (2004) Ecological impacts of deer overabundance. *Annual Review of Ecology, Evolution, and Systematics* 35, 113–147.

Crawshaw, P.G. Jr. (1995) *Comparative Feeding Ecology of Ocelot* (Felis pardalis) *and Jaguar* (Panthera onca) *in a Protected Subtropical Forest in Brazil and Argentina.* PhD dissertation, University of Florida.

Crooks, K.R. & Soule, M.E. (1999) Mesopredator release and avifaunal extinctions in a fragmented system, *Nature* 400, 563–566.

Culver, M., Johnson, W.E., Pecon-Slattery, J. & O'Brien S.J. (2000) Genomic ancestry of the American puma (*Puma concolor*). *The Journal of Heredity* 91, 186–197.

Eizirik, E., Kim, J.H., Menotti-Raymond, M., Crawshaw, P. Jr, & O'Brien, S.J. (2001) Phylogeography, population history and conservation genetics of jaguars (*Panthera onca*, Mammalia, Felidae). *Molecular Ecology* 10, 65–79.

Emmons, L.H. (1987) Comparative feeding ecology of felids in a neotropical rainforest. *Behavioral Ecology and Sociobiology* 20, 271–283.

Falk, D.A., Millar, C.I. & Olwell, M. (eds) (1996) *Restoring Diversity: Strategies for Reintroduction of Endangered Plants.* Island Press, Washington, DC.

Frankel, O. & Soule, M. (1981) *Conservation and Evolution* Cambridge University Press, Cambridge.

Fuller, K.S. & Swift, B. (1985) *Latin American Wildlife Trade Laws, 2nd edition.* TRAFFIC (USA) World Wildlife Fund, Washington, DC.

Garla, R.C., Setz, E.Z.F. & Gobbi, N. (2001) Jaguar (*Panthera onca*) food habits in Atlantic rain forest of southeastern Brazil. *Biotropica* 33, 691–696.

Gittleman, J.L., Funk, S.M., MacDonald, D. & Wayne, R.K. (2001) Why "carnivore conservation"? *Carnivore Conservation* (eds J.L. Gittleman, S.M. Funk, D. MacDonald & R.K. Wayne), pp. 1–7. Cambridge University Press, Cambridge.

Guggisberg, C.A.W. (1975) *Wild Cats of the World.* Taplinger Publishing, New York.

Harmsen, B.J. (2006) *The Use of Camera Traps for Estimating Abundance and Studying the Ecology of Jaguars* (Panthera onca). PhD thesis, University of Southampton.

Hayward, M.W., Adendorff J., O'Brien, J. et al. (2007a) Practical considerations for the reintroduction of large, terrestrial, mammalian predators based on reintroductions to South Africa's Eastern Cape Province. *The Open Conservation Biology Journal* 1, 1–11.

Hayward, M.W., O'Brien, J. & Kerley, G.I.H. (2007b) Carrying capacity of large African predators: Predictions and tests. *Biological Conservation* 139, 219–229.

Hoogesteijn, R., Boede, E.O. & Mondolfi, E. (2002) Observaciones de la depredación de bovinos por jaguares en Venezuela y los programas gubernamentales de control. *El Jaguar en el Nuevo Milenio*. (eds R.A. Mendellin, C. Equihua, C.L.B. Chetkiewicz, et al.), pp. 183–197. Fundo de Cultura Económica, Mexico City.

Hoogesteijn, R., Hoogesteijn, A. & Mondolfi, E. (1993) Jaguar predation and conservation: Cattle mortality caused by felines on three ranches in the Venzuelan Llanos. *Symposia of the Zoological Society of London* 65, 391–407.

IUCN (2006). 2006 *IUCN Red List of Threatened Species*. Available: <www.iucnredlist.org>. Accessed 10 November 2007.

Kellert, S.R., Black, M., Reid Rush, C. & Bath, A.J. (1996) Human culture and large carnivore conservation in North America. *Conservation Biology* 10, 977–990.

Maffei, L., Cuéllar, E. & Noss, A. (2004) One thousand jaguars (*Panthera onca*) in Bolivia's Chaco? Camera trapping in the Kaa-Iya National Park. *Journal of Zoology, London* 262, 295–304.

Maffei, L., Noss, A.J., Silver, S. & Kelly M.J. (in press) Abundance/density case study: Jaguars in South and Central America. *Camera Traps in Animal Ecology* (ed A. O'Connell). Springer-Verlag.

Marieb, K. (2005) *Jaguar in the New Millennium Dataset Update: The State of the Jaguar in 2005.* Wildlife Conservation Society, New York.

Mazzolli, M., Graipel, M.E. & Dunstone, N. (2002) Mountain lion depredation in southern Brazil. *Biological conservation* 105, 43–51.

Michalski, F., Boulhosa, R.L.P., Faria, A. & Peres, C.A. (2006). Human-wildlife conflicts in a fragmented Amazonian forest landscape: Determinants of large felid depredation on livestock. *Animal Conservation* 9, 179–188.

Miller, C.M. & Miller, B. (2005) *Jaguar density in La Selva Maya*. Unpublished report. Wildlife Conservation Society, Gallon Jug, Belize.

Mondolfi, E. & Hoogesteijn, R. (1986) Notes on the biology and status of the jaguar in Venezuela. *Cats of the World: Biology, Conservation and Management.* (eds S. D. Miller & D.D. Everett), pp. 85–123. National Wildlife Federation and Ceasar Kleberg Wildlife Research Institute, Washington, DC.

More, D.E. III. & Smith, R. (1991) The red wolf as a model for carnivore reintroductions. *Beyond Captive Breeding: Re-introducing Endangered Mammals to the Wild.* (ed. J.H.W. Gipps), pp. 263–278. Clarendon Press, Oxford.

Morrison, J.C., Secrest, W. Dinerstein, E., Wilcove, D.S. & Lamoreux, J.F. (2007) Persistence of large mammal faunas as indicator of global human impacts. *Journal of Mammalogy* 88, 1363–1380.

Noss, R.F. (1990) Indicators for monitoring biodiversity: A hierarchical approach. *Conservation Biology* 4, 355–364.

Novack, A.J., Main, M.B., Sunquist, M.E. & Labisky, R.F. (2005) Foraging ecology of jaguar (*Panthera onca*) and puma (*Puma concolor*) in hunted and non-hunted sites within the Maya Biosphere Reserve, Guatemala. *Journal of Zoology, London* 267, 167–178.

Núñez, R., Miller, B. & Lindzey, F. (2000) Food habits of jaguars and pumas in Jalisco, Mexico. *Journal of Zoology, London* 252, 373–379.

Palmeira, F.B.L., Crawshaw, P.G. Jr., Haddad, C.M., Ferraz, K.M.P.M.B., Verdade, L.M. (2008) Cattle depredation by puma (*Puma concolor*) and jaguar (*Panthera onca*) in central-western Brazil. *Biological Conservation* 141, 118–125.

Phillips, M.K. & Parker, W.T. (1988) Red wolf recovery: A progress report. *Conservation Biology* 2, 139–141.

Polisar, J., Matix, I., Scognamillo, D., Farrell, L., Sunquist, M.E. & Eisenberg, J.F. (2003) Jaguars, pumas, their prey base, and cattle ranching: Ecological interpretations of a management problem. *Biological Conservation* 109, 297–310.

Quigley, H.B. & Crawshaw, P.G. Jr. (2002) Reproduction, growth, and dispersal of jaguar in the Pantanal region of Brazil. *Jaguars in the New Millennium. A Status Assessment, Priority Detection, and Recommendations for the Conservation of Jaguars in the Americas.* (eds R.A. Medellin, C. Chetkiewicz, P. Crawshaw, Jr. et al.). Univ. Nacional Autonoma de Mexico/Wildlife Conservation Society. Mexico City.

Rabinowitz, A.R. (1986a) *Jaguar*. Random House, New York.

Rabinowitz, A.R. (1986b) Jaguar predation on domestic livestock in Belize. *Wildlife Society Bulletin* 14(2), 170–174.

Rabinowitz, A.R. & Nottingham, B.G. (1986) Ecology and behaviour of the Jaguar (*Panthera onca*) in Belize, Central America. *Journal of Zoology, London* 210, 149–159.

Reading, R.P. & Clark, T.W. (1996) Carnivore reintroduction: An interdisciplinary examination. *Carnivore Behavior, Ecology, and Evolution (vol. 2).* (ed. J.L. Gittleman), pp. 296–336. Cornell University Press, Ithaca.

Reading, R.P. & Kellert, S.R. (1993) Attitudes toward a proposed reintroduction of black-footed ferrets (*Mustela nigripes*). *Conservation Biology* 7, 569–580.

Ruiz-Garcia, M., Payan, E., Murillo, A. & Alvarez, D. (2006) DNA microsatellite characterization of the jaguar (*Panthera onca*) in Colombia. *Genes and Genetic Systems* 81, 115–127.

Sanderson, E.W., Redford, K.H., Chetkiewicz, C.L.B. et al. (2002a) Planning to save a species: The jaguar as a model. *Conservation Biology*, 16, 58–72.

Sanderson, E.W., Redford, K.H., Vedder, A., Ward, S.E. & Coppolillo, P.B. (2002b) A conceptual model for conservation planning based on landscape species requirements. *Landscape and Urban Planning* 58, 41–56.

Seymour, K.L. (1989) *Panthera onca. Mammalian Species* 340, 1–9.

Schaller, G.B. & Crawshaw, P.G. Jr. (1980) Movement patterns of the jaguar. *Biotropica* 12, 161–168.

Silver, S.C., Ostro, L.E.T. Marsh, L.K. et al. (2004) The use of camera traps for estimating jaguar *Panthera onca* abundance and density using capture/recapture analysis. *Oryx* 38, 148–154.

Sinclair; A.R.E., Mduma, S. & Brashares, J. (2003) Patterns of predation in a diverse predator-prey system. *Nature* 425, 288–290.

Soisalo, M.K. & Cavalcanti, S.M.C. (2006) Estimating the density of a jaguar population in the Brazilian Pantanal using camera-traps and capture-recapture sampling in combination with GPS radio-telemetry. *Biological Conservation* 129, 487–496.

Spong, G., Johansson, M. & Bjoerklund, M. (2000) High genetic variation in leopards indicates large and long-term stable population size. *Molecular Ecology* 9, 1773–1782.

Stanley Price, M.R. & Soorae, P.S. (2003) Reintroductions: Whence and whither? *The International Zoo Yearbook* 38, 61–75.

Sunquist, M.E. & Sunquist, F. (2002) *Wild Cats of the World*. University of Chicago Press, Chicago.

Swank, W.G. & Teer, J.G. (1989) Status of the jaguar—1987. *Oryx* 23, 14–21.

Taber, A.B., Novaro, A.J., Neris, N. & Coleman, F.H. (1997) The food habits of sympatric jaguar and puma in the Paraguayan Chaco. *Biotropica* 29, 204–213.

Terborgh, J. (1992) Maintenance of diversity in tropical forests. *Biotropica* 24, 283–292.

Terborgh, J., Estes, J., Paquet, P. et al. (1999) The role of top carnivores in regulating terrestrial ecosystems. *Continental Conservation: Scientific Foundations of Regional Reserve Networks*. (eds M.E. Soulé & J. Terborgh), pp. 39–64. Island Press, Washington, DC.

Terborgh, J., Feeley, K., Silman, M., Nunez, P. & Balukjian, B. (2006) Vegetation dynamics of predator-free land-bridge islands. *Journal of Ecology* 94, 253–263.

Terborgh, J., Lopez, L., Nunes, V.P. et al. (2001) Ecological meltdown in predator-free forest fragments. *Science* 294, 1923–26.

Troëng, S. (2000) Predation of green (*Chelonia mydas*) and letherback (*Cermochelys coriacea*) turtles by jaguars (*Panthera onca*) at Tortuga National Park, Costa Rica. *Chelonian Conservation and Biology* 3, 751–753.

Valdez, R. (2000) Jaguar. *Ecology and Management of Large Mammals in North America*. (eds S. Demarais & P.R. Krausman), pp. 378–388. Prentice Hall, New Jersey.

van Wieren, S.E. (2006) Populations: Re-introduction. *Restoration Ecology: The New Frontier*. (eds J. van Andel & J. Aronson), pp. 82–92. Blackwell Publishing, Malden.

Walker, C.W., Harveston, L.A., Pittman, M.T., Tewes, M.E. & Honeycutt, R.L. (2000) Microsatellite variation in two populations of mountain lions (*Puma concolor*) in Texas. *The Southwestern Naturalist* 45, 196–203.

Weckel, M., Giuliano, W. & Silver, S. (2006) Jaguar (*Panthera onca*) feeding ecology: Distribution of predator and prey through time and space. *Journal of Zoology, London* 270, 25–30.

Westman, W.E. (1990) Managing for biodiversity: Unresolved science and policy question. *Bioscience* 40, 26–33.

Williams, R.M., Jr. (1979) Change and stability in values and value systems: A sociological perspective. *Understanding Human Values: Individual and Societal.* (ed. M. Rokeach), pp. 15–46. The Free Press, New York.

Yalden, D.W. (1993) The problems of reintroducing carnivores. *Symposia of the Zoological Society of London* 65, 289–306.

Zimmerman, A., Walpole, M.J. & Leader-Williams. N. (2005) Cattle ranchers' attitudes to conflicts with jaguars in the Pantanal of Brazil. *Oryx* 39, 406–412.

10

The Status and Conservation of Leopards and Other Large Carnivores in the Congo Basin, and the Potential Role of Reintroduction

Philipp Henschel[1]

[1]Wildlife Conservation Society—Gabon Program

Summary

The Congo Basin contains the world's second largest expanse of tropical rainforest, and yet also within the catchment lies an extensive, geographically isolated forest–savannah mosaic. While the forests in this region have long been considered an important stronghold for leopards, *Panthera pardus*, the apex predator in this habitat, the forest–savannah mosaic also once harboured important populations of lions, *Panthera leo*, African wild dogs, *Lycaon pictus*, and spotted hyaenas, *Crocuta crocuta*. Uncontrolled hunting by man, however, has led to a dramatic decrease in ungulate populations, especially in the more accessible open habitats. Today, lions and African wild dogs are almost certainly regionally extinct, while spotted hyaenas have been reduced to one small and isolated population in the Republic of Congo. In remote forest regions, wildlife populations have remained less severely affected, but in densely populated areas where demand for wild game is high, intensive commercial hunting has led to a widespread disappearance of leopards, even from within protected areas. Conservation efforts directed towards leopards and

Reintroduction of Top-Order Predators, 1st edition. Edited by M.W. Hayward and M.J. Somers.
 ISBN 978-1-4051-7680-4 (pb) and 978-1-4051-9273-6 (hb)

spotted hyaenas should promote rigorous protection of remaining populations and their prey to prevent any further range loss. Owing to the present geographical isolation of their former range within this region, however, any effort to re-establish lions or African wild dogs would inevitably need to involve reintroduction. Most suitable habitat is currently without protection and wild prey is scarce, so potential reintroductions would need to be preceded by the creation of sufficiently large protected areas and their restocking with prey, provided that government and local support for such a proposal could be acquired and guaranteed for the long term.

Introduction

The Congo Basin: Habitat and fauna

The rainforest of the Congo Basin represents the world's second-largest expanse of dense humid tropical forest, surpassed in size only by the Amazon. Climatic changes have dictated the extent of this forest throughout its geological history, leading to its fragmentation in arid phases and, during 80%–90% of the past 800,000 years, the African rainforest was less extensive and more fragmented than at present (Maley, 2001). During the last glacial maximum (~18,000 BP), hyper-arid conditions caused the retraction of the forest to a series of refuges, which were mainly riparian or mountain forests, and palynological data suggest that the remainder of the Congo Basin was covered by a forest–savannah mosaic dominated by open, grass-rich vegetation (Dupont *et al.*, 2000; Maley, 2001). The discovery of 7000-year-old molars of a black rhinoceros, *Diceros bicornis*, a species not recorded in this region in historical times, in a rock shelter in southern Congo (van Neer & Lanfranchi, 1985), suggests that a more diverse savannah fauna existed during this period than at present. Other larger savannah taxa might have likewise disappeared from this region during the last hyper-humid phase between approximately 9000 and 4000 BP, which was characterized by maximum forest extension and an extreme reduction of open habitat (Maley, 2001).

Today, within the Congo Basin, there remains a single important expanse of natural open habitat, which has been classified as a distinct terrestrial ecoregion and termed the Western Congolian forest–savannah mosaic (Olson *et al.*, 2001). It stretches north and south from the lower reaches of the Congo River (Figure 10.1). Its northern part, in Gabon and the Republic of Congo

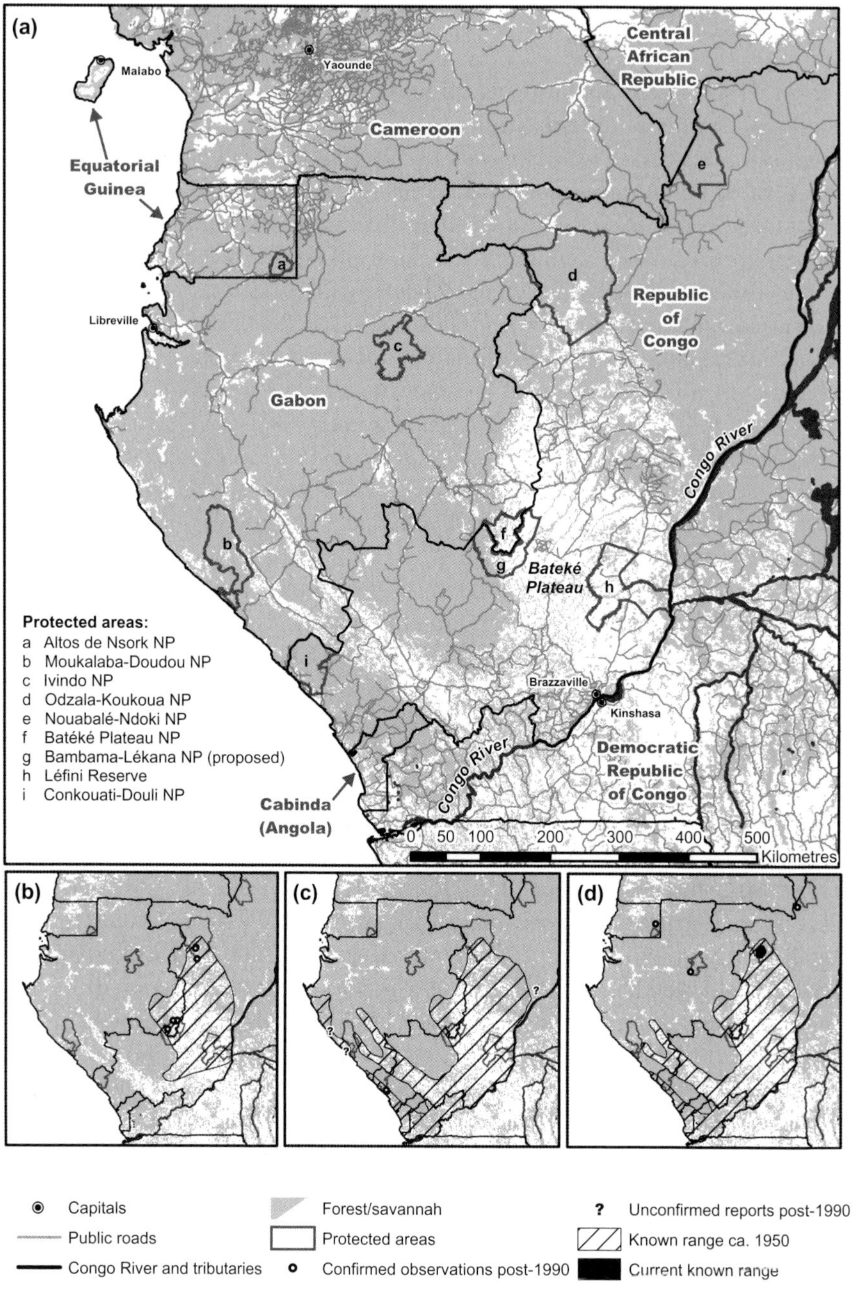

Figure 10.1 **The distribution of open habitat in the western proportion of the Congo Basin (a) and the historical range, recent records and current known range of the larger savannah carnivores (b) lion; (c) African wild dog; and (d) spotted hyaena. Only protected areas mentioned in the context of savannah carnivores are shown.**

(hereafter, termed "Congo"), is isolated from the southern part in the Democratic Republic of Congo (DRC) and Angola by the Congo River. It is separated from the Northern Congolian forest–savannah mosaic of Cameroon and the Central African Republic (CAR) by a wide band of contiguous rainforest. It is not known when the Western Congolian forest–savannah mosaic became isolated from the surrounding grasslands, but the presence of southern reedbuck, *Redunca arundinum*, in this region has led to the early assumption that the most recent connection existed towards the south, and not towards the Northern Congolian forest–savannah mosaic, which harbours the Bohor reedbuck, *Redunca redunca*, (Malbrant & Maclatchy, 1947). This assumption has recently been corroborated by two genetic studies on the biogeography of lion and bushbuck, *Tragelaphus scriptus*, which confirmed that samples for the two species collected in Gabon and Congo shared the same haplotypes as populations from south of the Congo River, and were more genetically distinct from populations in the Northern Congolian forest–savannah mosaic (Barnett *et al.*, 2006; Moodley & Bruford, 2007).

The isolated northern part of the Western Congolian forest–savannah mosaic consists of roughly 200,000 km^2 of open grasslands, interspersed with wooded savannah and dense gallery forest along the deeper river valleys. In colonial times, it harboured a range of species that are characteristic of the African savannah, including lion, African wild dog, spotted hyaena, defassa waterbuck (*Kobus ellipsiprymnus defassa*), southern reedbuck, bushbuck and common duiker (*Sylvicapra grimmia*) (Malbrant & Maclatchy, 1949). Larger Alcelaphinae, Antilopinae and Hippotraginae grazers, however, were never recorded in this landscape, and neither was the cheetah, *Acinonyx jubatus* (Malbrant & Maclatchy, 1949). The larger fauna in this landscape was instead comprised of several species that are characteristic of the rainforest, such as forest elephant (*Loxodonta cyclotis*), forest buffalo (*Syncerus caffer nanus*), yellow-backed duiker (*Cephalophus silvicultor*) and red river hog (*Potamochoerus porcus*), which were all widely distributed across the Western forest–savannah mosaic (Malbrant & Maclatchy, 1949). While several forest species, such as forest buffalo and red river hog, actually reach their highest densities in this mosaic of habitats (Tutin *et al.*, 1997), there are only isolated observations of savannah species from within the contiguous forest (Malbrant & Maclatchy, 1949; Juste & Castrovejo, 1992; Henschel & Ray, 2003; Henschel, 2006), underlining the unsuitability of this habitat for savannah species. The only large carnivore that appears equally adapted to both the contiguous forest and the Western forest–savannah mosaic is the leopard, and the species has been subject to a number of studies in the Congo Basin over the past decades. The savannah carnivores in this region have received little scientific attention to date.

Large carnivores in the Congo Basin: historical distribution, recent decline and current status

Leopards—historical distribution and numbers

As a habitat generalist, the leopard occurs in all major vegetation types found within the Congo Basin, including lowland and mountain forest, logged secondary forest, the open habitat of the Western Congolian forest–savannah mosaic and even inundated forests and swamp systems (Hunter *et al.*, in press). Consequently, it seems safe to assume that leopards once had a continuous distribution across the Congo Basin and, in the two most recent Africa-wide status surveys on the species, this region was considered a stronghold for the species in Africa (Myers, 1976; Martin & de Meulenaer, 1988). This assumption was based on the vast amount of unaltered and seemingly prey-rich forest habitat still available to leopards and their role as the apex predator therein, which was suspected to result in extremely high leopard population densities in this habitat. Although the Congo Basin represented only 12% of the leopard's range in Africa at the time of the latest status survey, it was estimated in 1988 that this region harboured an approximate 40% of Africa's leopards (Martin & de Meulenaer, 1988). Leopard population density had never been determined in rainforest habitat, however, and several authorities in the field criticised these estimates, arguing that the biomass of potential prey is generally lower in forests compared to savannah, which should result in correspondingly lower leopard densities in this biome (Jackson, 1989; Bailey, 1993).

Leopards—recent decline

The figures published by Martin & de Meulenaer (1988) are still quoted today, and remain the chief source of information for African governments proposing to open or raise harvest quotas for trophy hunting of leopards. However, evidence is mounting that leopards have already disappeared from a number of forest sites on the fringes of the Congo Basin (e.g. Angelici *et al.*, 1998; Andama, 2000; Maisels *et al.*, 2001). While the reasons for these local extinctions are not fully understood, they occurred in two of the most densely populated regions of Central Africa, the Cross River region between Cameroon and Nigeria, and the Albertine Rift Mountains (Burgess *et al.*, 2007).

Across the Congo Basin, "bushmeat" constitutes the primary source of animal protein for the majority of the rural population, and the bulk of the species captured by hunters in these rural areas consists of medium-sized ungulates, such as forest duikers and red river hogs (Wilkie & Carpenter, 1999). Interestingly, a first study on leopard feeding habits in a forest reserve in DRC revealed that leopard prey was likewise dominated by medium-sized ungulates (Hart *et al.*, 1996). These results were corroborated in subsequent studies on leopard feeding habits from protected areas throughout the Congo Basin (Ososky, 1998; Ray & Sunquist, 2001; Henschel *et al.*, 2005), and correspond well with data on leopard prey preferences from across their range (Hayward *et al.*, 2006a). In densely populated areas and urban markets across the Congo Basin, however, rodents have recently gained importance as food items, and this is seen as a sign that duikers and other larger-bodied species have become depleted in nearby forests (Wilkie & Carpenter, 1999).

That populations of big cats may decline as a direct consequence of exploitation competition with human hunters, has already been suggested for felids in the neotropics (Jorgenson & Redford, 1993) and also for leopards in the Congo Basin (Hart *et al.*, 1996; Ray, 2001). Since leopard population density is known to be positively correlated with the biomass of their preferred prey across their range in eastern and southern Africa (Marker & Dickman, 2005; Hayward *et al.*, 2007), the same principles are likely to apply for leopards in the Congo Basin rainforest. It therefore appears logical that the bushmeat harvest and consumption across the Congo Basin—estimated to be in excess of 1 million metric tons per annum (Wilkie & Carpenter, 1999)—has had a marked effect on leopard populations, and it is possible that the local extinctions of leopards in parts of the Cross River region and the Albertine Rift may be a result of this intensified competition for prey with human hunters.

Leopards—a new dataset from Gabon

To investigate the exact manner in which the bushmeat harvest affects leopard populations in the Congo Basin, hunting intensity, leopard population density and diet, and the abundance of preferred leopard prey was recently determined in four rainforest sites in central Gabon. The sites were located at varying distances from settlements (range 6–24 km, measured from the centre of the site), and two of them were inside a protected area and two were village hunting zones (Henschel, PhD thesis, in preparation). The results revealed a clear pattern: hunting was most intense near settlements, and signs of hunting were only rarely detected beyond 12 km from settlements. No leopards were photographed at one commercially hunted study site, and population densities at the remaining sites varied between 2.7 and 12.1 leopards/100 km^2. Leopard density increased significantly with distance from settlements. While no leopard scats were found at the commercially hunted site, mean leopard prey weight varied between 19.8 and 31.6 kg at the remaining sites, and both mean prey weight and the ungulate to rodent ratio in leopard diet increased with distance from settlements. Several larger species were not detected at the commercially hunted site and, across sites, the abundance of ungulates increased with distance from settlements (Henschel, PhD thesis, in preparation). These data suggest that there is a strong correlation between commercial bushmeat hunting near settlements and the local disappearance of leopards (Henschel, PhD thesis, in preparation).

Across the Congo Basin, roads, major rivers and, occasionally, railway lines represent points of market access which facilitate the commercialization of local bushmeat hunting. Access to transportation is a crucial step leading to unsustainable levels of hunting (Wilkie & Carpenter, 1999). Consequently, the distance from public roads was a strong predictor of forest elephant and duiker abundance, human presence and levels of poaching (Laurance *et al.*, 2006a; Blake *et al.*, 2007). Similarly, variation in the proportion of area occupied (PAO) by leopards across the four study sites in central Gabon was best explained by the distance from roadside settlements, when occupancy modelling was used to analyse camera trap data; the most likely model indicated that PAO increased with distance from settlements, and reached 1.0 at ~20 km from settlements (Henschel, PhD thesis, in preparation).

The same patterns are likely to apply across the Congo Basin, but reliable data on leopard occurrence from this region are too sparse to allow regional priority-setting exercises similar to those conducted for jaguars (Sanderson *et al.*, 2002) and tigers (Wikramanayake *et al.*, 1998), or to construct more sophisticated spatially explicit habitat models (e.g. Schadt *et al.*, 2002). Besides a larger set of reliable leopard presence/absence data from sites across the Congo Basin, a realistic leopard population model for this region would need to incorporate data on habitat type and quality, its connectivity and productivity, forms of land use, and infrastructure and human population density. However, since the PAO by leopards in central Gabon was best explained by the distance from public roads and settlements (Henschel, PhD thesis, in preparation), it seems reasonable to construct a simple geographic population model to predict leopard occurrence based on the distribution of these features.

Accurate geographic datasets containing both public and logging roads and settlements were available for the western proportion of the Congo Basin (provided by Global Forest Watch World Resources Institute, Washington, DC, United States). Based on leopard data from Gabon, all suitable leopard habitat within the Congo Basin was divided into three different strata. The first stratum comprised areas that were unlikely to support any resident leopards, and was defined by a buffer of 10 km around roadside settlements and of 5 km around settlements with no road and market access, and thus no commercial hunting. Secondly, an intermediate stratum was defined that extended 5 km beyond the first "leopard-free" stratum and probably still experiences a degree of hunting but is likely to support leopards at reduced densities. Thirdly, a remote stratum was defined at a minimum distance of 15 km from roadside settlements or 10 km from settlements with no road access, which represents core leopard areas that receive little hunting pressure. All geographic data were imported into an ESRI ArcGIS 9.1 software package (Redlands, California, United States), and strata were mapped with the "Buffer Wizard" extension, whereby isolated core areas of less than 50 km^2 were excluded. While this simple stratification model cannot be expected to reliably predict leopard occurrence across the Congo Basin, it can draw attention to areas where leopards are seemingly extirpated or where there could be large populations that might merit focused conservation effort.

The model results were supplemented by any available information on leopard occurrence from field surveys in potential leopard habitat, almost all of which were conducted in the larger protected areas across the region. Leopards or other carnivores were among the researched species at only a few sites, and information on the occurrence of leopards comes mainly from general wildlife surveys. These surveys generally rely on the detection of spoor for terrestrial species, as direct observations are rare in rainforest habitat. Inside protected areas in Gabon and CAR, signs of leopard are usually encountered on a daily basis and, even in hunted areas, the presence of leopards in a given area becomes relatively unlikely if no evidence is encountered during several weeks of fieldwork (Henschel & Ray, 2003). Survey results were utilized only where the survey methods were appropriate to detect signs of leopard, and sites with no surveys or an inappropriate survey protocol were categorized as "data deficient". Accurate geographic coverage of roads, settlements and data from wildlife inventories were not available for large parts of both DRC and CAR, and therefore data on the status of leopards are presented only for the western proportion of the Congo Basin (Table 10.1; Figure 10.2).

Leopards—current status

In Gabon and Congo, leopards are still widely distributed and were detected in all but one (Mwagné National Park in Gabon) of the larger protected areas that were surveyed in these two countries (Table 10.1; Figure 10.2). Survey effort was extremely low at this site and local hunters reported the species as present (Maisels *et al.*, 2004). In Equatorial Guinea, leopards appear largely absent across the country and were only confirmed for the Monte Mitra Forest inside Monte Alén National Park (Nchanji *et al.*, 2005), where the species survives in an isolated population (Table 10.1; Figure 10.2). In the rainforests of southern Cameroon, leopards still have a wide distribution in the east, where they occur in all protected areas. In the more densely populated southwestern part of the country, leopards have almost completely disappeared, and isolated populations can only be found in Campo Ma'an National Park, on the border with Equatorial Guinea (Matthews & Matthews, 2006), and possibly in Korup National Park in the Cross River region (Table 10.1; Figure 10.2). Although signs of leopard were never detected in the Korup area despite extensive fieldwork (e.g. Forboseh *et al.*, 2007; Astaras *et al.*, 2008), local hunters report the species as present, and leopard tracks were recently confirmed across the border in the southern section of Nigerian Cross River National Park (Okon, 2005). For southern Nigeria, this represents the only recent record for the species' presence, and leopards can be regarded as virtually extinct there (Angelici *et al.*, 1998).

The leopard population model predicted leopards to be absent in only two of the 32 protected areas with available survey data, and no leopards were detected during field surveys at these sites (Table 10.1). Signs of leopard presence were equally not detected at an additional seven protected areas that contained core leopard areas according to model predictions (Table 10.1; Figure 10.2),

Table 10.1 **Larger protected areas in the western proportion of the Congo Basin, with their current classification, IUCN (International Union for the Conservation of Nature and Natural Resources) protected area category, size and location, and data on the presence/absence of leopards at the site. Presence/absence of leopards at any given site was predicted using a geographic population model based on field data from Gabon (Henschel, PhD thesis, in preparation), and supplemented with field survey data from the respective protected area. Numbers in the first column refer to protected area locations shown in Figure 10.2.**

Id	Name	IUCN PA category[a]	Total area (km^2)	Country	Model prediction about leopard presence	Leopard status at site indicated by surveys	Source (personal communication or reference)
1	Cross River NP	II	3650	Nigeria	Present	Confirmed present	Okon, 2005
2	Korup NP	II	1300	Cameroon	Present	Not detected	C. Astaras
3	Mont Cameroun FR	None	650	Cameroon	Absent	Not detected	Forboseh et al., 2007
4	Takamanda FR	None	600	Cameroon	Present	Not detected	Sunderland-Groves & Maisels, 2003
5	Banyang-Mbo WS	IV	700	Cameroon	Present	Not detected	Willcox, 2002
6	Douala Edéa Reserve	IV	1700	Cameroon	Present	Not detected	Ngandjui & Blanc, 2000
7	Ebo Forest	None (II)	1400	Cameroon	Present	Not detected	B. Morgan
8	Campo Ma'an NP	II	2600	Cameroon	Present	Confirmed present	Matthews & Matthews, 2006

Continued

Table 10.1 ***Continued***

Id	Name	IUCN PA category[a]	Total area (km^2)	Country	Model prediction about leopard presence	Leopard status at site indicated by surveys	Source (personal communication or reference)
9	Mpem et Djim NP	II	1050	Cameroon	Present	No data	
10	Mbam et Djerem NP	II	4300	Cameroon	Present	Confirmed present	Maisels *et al.*, 2000
11	Dja Reserve	IV	5900	Cameroon	Present	Confirmed present	Williamson & Usongo, 1995
12	Boumba Bek-Nki	None (II)	5600	Cameroon	Present	Confirmed present	Madzou & Ebanega, 2006
13	Lobéké NP	II	2150	Cameroon	Present	Confirmed present	Ekobo, 1998
14	Dzanga-Sangha NP and reserve	II + IV	1250 + 3100	CAR	Present	Confirmed present	Ray & Sunquist, 2001
15	Nouabalé-Ndoki NP	II	4100	Congo	Present	Confirmed present	Ososky, 1998
16	Odzala-Kokoua NP	II	13600	Congo	Present	Confirmed present	Henschel, 2008
17	Bambama-Lékana	None (II)	3900	Congo	Present	Confirmed present	Aust *et al.*, 2005

18	Léfini Reserve	IV	6650	Congo	Present	Confirmed present	Mathot *et al.*, 2006
19	Conkouati-Douli NP	II	5050	Congo	Present	Confirmed present	H. VanLeeuwe
20	Moukalaba-Doudou NP	II	4450	Gabon	Present	Confirmed present	Boddicker, 2006
21	Loango NP	II	1550	Gabon	Present	Confirmed present	Boddicker, 2006
22	Birougou NP	II	700	Gabon	Present	Confirmed present	Aba'a Nseme & Bezangoye Ndoukoue, 2007
23	Batéké Plateau NP	II	2050	Gabon	Present	Confirmed present	Bout, 2006
24	Waka NP	II	1050	Gabon	Present	Confirmed present	Abitsi, 2006
25	Lopé NP	II	4950	Gabon	Present	Confirmed present	Henschel *et al.*, 2005
26	Wonga-Wongué Reserve	IV	4950	Gabon	Present	No data	
27	Pongara NP	II	850	Gabon	Present	Confirmed present	Latour, 2006
28	Ivindo NP	II	3000	Gabon	Present	Confirmed present	Henschel, PhD thesis, in preparation

Continued

Table 10.1 ***Continued***

Id	Name	IUCN PA category[a]	Total area (km^2)	Country	Model prediction about leopard presence	Leopard status at site indicated by surveys	Source (personal communication or reference)
29	Mwagné NP	II	1150	Gabon	Present	Not detected	Maisels *et al.*, 2004
30	Monts de Cristal NP	II	1200	Gabon	Present	Confirmed present	Aba'a Nseme, 2006
31	Minkébé NP	II	7550	Gabon	Present	Confirmed present	W.W.F. Minkébé, unpublished data
32	Altos de Nsork NP	II	400	Equatorial Guinea	Present	Not detected	Larison *et al.*, 1999
33	Estuario del Muni Reserve	IV	700	Equatorial Guinea	Absent	No data	
34	Monte Alén NP	II	2000	Equatorial Guinea	Present	Confirmed present	Nchanji *et al.*, 2005
35	Rio Campo Reserve	IV	350	Equatorial Guinea	Absent	Not detected	Larison *et al.*, 1999

[a]IUCN categories listed in parentheses are the levels that will be assigned once the areas are upgraded; these sites have been proposed as national parks. IUCN categories: (II) National Park; (IV) Habitat/Species Management Area.

CAR, Central African Republic; Congo, Republic of Congo; FR, forest reserve; IUCN, International Union for the Conservation of Nature and Natural Resources; NP, national park; PA, protected area, WS, wildlife sanctuary.

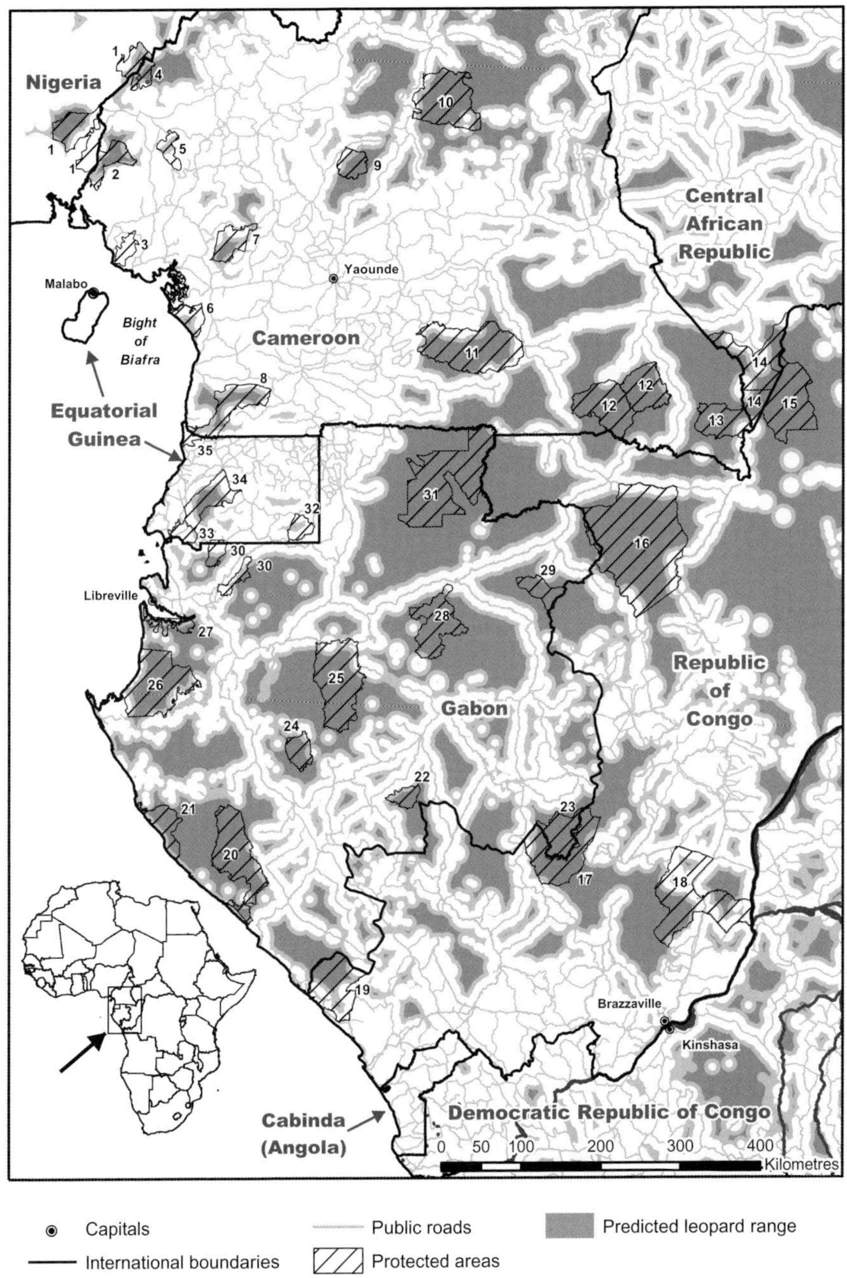

Figure 10.2 **Predicted distribution of leopard in the western proportion of the Congo Basin (arrow in insert). Numbers refer to protected areas listed in Table 10.1.**

suggesting either that the model was inappropriate or too optimistic, or that leopards do in fact occur at these sites and were simply not detected in surveys. Interestingly, all protected areas that had no confirmed records of leopard presence were smaller than 2000 km^2, and most of these were situated in south-western Cameroon or Equatorial Guinea whereas, in Gabon, leopards were recorded in almost all sites irrespective of their size (Table 10.1). In Gabon, leopards occur widely even outside protected areas, and populations in the smaller parks and reserves form part of larger, contiguous populations. In south-western Cameroon and Equatorial Guinea (Figure 10.2), however, the species' range has contracted to small, isolated populations, and this might already have led to local extinctions in the smaller forest reserves.

Large savannah carnivores—historical distribution

Historically, lions, African wild dogs and spotted hyaenas probably occupied all suitable open habitat within the northern part of the Western Congolian forest–savannah mosaic, yet missionaries documented the local disappearance of lions from the coastal savannahs of today's Congo and Cabinda as early as 1750). Likewise, du Chaillu (1861) did not encounter lions when he explored the grasslands behind the coast of today's Gabon, where he recorded only leopards, African wild dogs and spotted hyaenas. Further inland, however, in the extensive grasslands north of the Congo River, explorers and ethnologists alike still described lions as locally common around 1900 (e.g. Guiral, 1889; Dusseljé, 1910).

The first comprehensive study on the fauna in this part of Africa was conducted almost 50 years later, by naturalists Malbrant & Maclatchy (1949), and their contribution remains the only attempt so far to map the distribution of the larger carnivores in this region. By the time of their study, lions had disappeared from the savannahs of southern Congo around Brazzaville (Figure 10.1b), whereas African wild dogs and spotted hyaenas had suffered no apparent range loss and were still widely distributed (Figure 10.1c,d). Lions appeared most abundant in the Léfini Reserve and Odzala-Kokoua National Park (Figure 10.1a), while African wild dogs and spotted hyaenas were described as locally common in many localities, including the coastal savannahs (Malbrant & Maclatchy, 1949), along which African wild dogs in particular had penetrated deeply into Gabon (Figure 10.1c).

Large savannah carnivores—recent decline

The dramatic range loss that occurred over the following decades is very poorly documented, but seems to be tied to a massive reduction in wild prey and an increased persecution of the carnivores themselves. Pastoralism was never extensively practised by the inhabitants of either forest–savannah mosaic, and the wild game that constituted the major source of animal protein was traditionally killed in well-organized net-hunts (Dusseljé, 1910). Larger species like forest buffalo and forest elephants were reportedly not very vulnerable to this form of hunting (Dusseljé, 1910). Hunting with guns gradually replaced the traditional net-hunting, however, and the larger species soon disappeared from densely populated landscapes (Malbrant & Maclatchy, 1949). This trend continued, and today the forest buffalo is largely absent from southern and central Congo and south-eastern Gabon, and the largest remaining population in either forest–savannah mosaic is thought to occur in the remote Odzala-Kokoua National Park in northern Congo (East, 1999). Similarly, waterbuck and southern reedbuck have lost much of their former range, and both species might be extinct in Congo, whereas their range in Gabon is restricted to the band of savannah extending south from Moukalaba-Doudou National Park on the coast (East, 1999). The extreme scarcity of wild prey has also led to an increase in human–carnivore conflict, particularly in the surroundings of newly established cattle ranches (Malbrant & Maclatchy, 1949). It is these cattle ranches which precipitated the initiation of programmes that relied on professional hunters (e.g. de Baleine, 1987), as well as on poisoning, to eradicate large carnivores (Henschel, 2006). No official records are available stating the number of large carnivores killed in these programmes, but accounts by villagers document that lions were still present in the region of the Léfini Reserve around 1960 (Sautter, 1960), and that entire prides were poisoned by ranch owners in neighbouring Gabon in the 1970s (Henschel, 2006).

Large savannah carnivores—current status

By 1990, it was believed that lions had disappeared from Léfini and that the only population in Congo survived in a hunting reserve that is today incorporated into the Odzala-Kokoua National Park (Dowsett, 1995). In 1994, two male lions were shot in this reserve after they attacked and killed a worker at the reserve's headquarters. These two individuals were considered to be "two of Congo's last lions" (Dowsett, 1995). Following this incident, very few substantiated records of lion presence were obtained at this site, and most occurred within a few months after the killing (Dowsett & Dowsett-Lemaire, 1997). A comprehensive large-carnivore survey at the site in 2007 did not produce any signs of lion presence (Henschel, 2008). In neighbouring Gabon, one male lion accompanied by a female was shot north of the Batéké Plateau National Park in 1995 (Figure 10.1b), and one female was observed in the same area 1 year later (Henschel, 2006). Two lion surveys in this part of Gabon in 2001 and 2003, respectively, did not produce any evidence of lion presence (Henschel, 2006); however, one set of felid tracks identified as lion was detected by a team conducting wildlife monitoring inside the Batéké Plateau National Park in 2004 (Bout, 2006). This single set of tracks remains the sole convincing evidence of lion presence found within the Congo Basin in more than one decade, and it therefore seems reasonable to assume that lions are effectively extinct in this northern part of the Western Congolian forest–savannah mosaic.

The data on African wild dogs are extremely scarce. While the species was listed as extinct in this region in the most recent status survey (Sillero-Zubiri *et al.*, 2004), it was acknowledged in a prior status survey that there are still occasional rumours of their presence in coastal Gabon (Woodroffe *et al.*, 1997). The rumours and occasional unconfirmed sightings persist in one region west of Moukalaba-Doudou National Park in Gabon (L. White, Wildlife Conservation Society; personal communication), and similar reports originate from one area in north-eastern Congo (Figure 10.1c). The last confirmed sighting dates back to 1991, when one individual was observed in a savannah south of Conkouati-Douli National Park in coastal Congo (Dowsett & Dowsett-Lemaire, 1991). While it cannot be ruled out that a few individuals persist in one of the aforementioned areas, there is no recent field evidence suggesting the presence of a resident population of African wild dogs anywhere within this northern part of the Western Congolian forest–savannah mosaic.

Spotted hyaenas also experienced an extreme collapse of their former range within the Congo Basin but, until recently, two resident populations persisted in Congo—one on the coast in Conkouati-Douli National Park and one in the north in Odzala-Kokoua National Park (Mills & Hofer, 1998). While no additional signs of hyaena presence were found in Conkouati-Douli National

Park in the past decade (H. van Leeuwe, Wildlife Conservation Society; personal communication), the species was still locally abundant in the savannah sector of Odzala-Kokoua National Park in 2007 (Henschel, 2008). Furthermore, in recent years, several individual spotted hyaenas have been recorded at different localities within the Congo Basin, deep inside rainforest habitat (Juste & Castroviejo, 1992; Henschel & Ray, 2003; F. Maisels, Edinburgh University, UK; personal communication) and at distances of between 200 and 420 km from the nearest known hyaena population in Odzala-Kokoua National Park (Figure 10.1d). In all cases, these were single individuals that were either found dead (Juste & Castroviejo, 1992; F. Maisels, Edinburgh University, UK; personal communication), or were recorded only once in an area (Henschel & Ray, 2003). The available information suggests that there is currently just one resident population of spotted hyaenas in this northern part of the Western Congolian forest–savannah mosaic, which occupies the savannah sector of Odzala-Kokoua National Park. The observations of individuals recorded at other sites in recent years might represent unsuccessful dispersal events from the Odzala population.

Is there a need for reintroduction?

Leopards

The current status of leopards in the rainforests of central and north-eastern Gabon, northern Congo and south-eastern Cameroon can be regarded as secure. In this sparsely settled region, leopards occur in contiguous populations (Figure 10.2) and large, remote protected areas, such as Minkébé National Park in Gabon and Odzala-Koukoua National Park in Congo, can potentially secure the long-term survival of leopards. In the human-dominated landscapes of Equatorial Guinea, south-western Cameroon and southern Nigeria, however, leopards are absent from most protected areas (Table 10.1; Figure 10.2). There are in fact indicators that in some parts of these so-called Biafran forests (Figure 10.2), leopards had already disappeared several decades ago. Hunter interviews at two forest sites in south-western Cameroon revealed that, at these sites, leopards had not been documented for more than 30 years (Maisels *et al.*, 2001; Willcox, 2002), and this discovery raised concern that the absence of the apex predator of the system might have already led to a localized increase in herbivores and, therewith, associated changes in forest dynamics and composition at these sites (Willcox & Nambu, 2007).

However, evidence of change has been emerging in recent years. The discoveries of remnant populations of highly endangered primate species (e.g. Morgan *et al.*, 2003), and the growing recognition of the Biafran forests as a biodiversity hotspot (Oates *et al.*, 2004) and a centre of endemism (Bergl *et al.*, 2007), has reinvigorated plans to enlarge the protected area network and to increase the protection status at a number of sites (Morgan & Sunderland-Groves, 2006; Bergl *et al.*, 2007; Forboseh *et al.*, 2007). Leopards, as the dominant predator of this forest, should ultimately be restored to re-establish their ecological functionality, which is considered to be one of the central arguments for the restoration of large carnivores (Berger, 2007). However, reintroductions of large carnivores are extremely lengthy, costly and complex processes (IUCN, 1998) and should be avoided if it appears possible to protect and encourage the remnants of an existing population (Yalden, 1993).

The joint results from the geographic population model and wildlife surveys suggest that in the Biafran forest region leopards still persist in at least three protected areas: the southern section of the Cross River National Park in Nigeria, Campo Ma'an National Park in Cameroon and Monte Alén National Park in Equatorial Guinea (Table 10.1; Figure 10.2). For the conservation of leopards in these forests, it should be an absolute priority to strengthen these three populations and to avert their local extinction. Any such effort should begin with systematic presence/absence surveys in these national parks, in order to map the current occurrence of leopards across the landscapes and to investigate the factors that determine whether they are present. This would allow the identification of core populations and the formulation of strategies for their protection. If properly managed, these parks could harbour 90–120 leopards, based on their size and a population density estimate of 4.6 leopards/100 km^2 obtained at a protected area in Gabon (Henschel, PhD thesis, in preparation).

Closed populations of this size can be expected to suffer from genetic deterioration through inbreeding, and several migrants per generation would need to be translocated between reserves to compensate for these effects (Frankham, this volume). This requirement would need to be incorporated into any strategy designed to secure the long-term survival of leopards in these parks. However, costly approaches involving periodic translocations to mimic natural dispersal, which have been used for large carnivores elsewhere (e.g. Gusset, this volume), do not seem feasible in the Congo Basin. The major obstacles are poor infrastructure in most protected areas and the lack of expertise needed for large-carnivore reintroductions; most protected areas possess no functional road network and, to date, not a single large carnivore has ever been captured alive and radio-collared anywhere in the Congo Basin.

A more suitable approach would be to design a leopard conservation landscape around the remnant populations of the Biafran forest using cost–distance models, which have found prior use in the management of metapopulations of other species of large cats in human-dominated landscapes (e.g. Wikramanayake *et al.*, 2004). Through rigorous protection of potential dispersal corridors, the populations in Campo Ma'an and Monte Alén could probably be reconnected to populations in northern Gabon, and the Cross River National Park population could potentially expand into the Korup National Park and adjoining forest reserves. Setting aside all financial and logistical constraints, reintroductions of individual leopards into any of these sites would exclusively promote the persistence of one single species. The establishment and maintenance of wildlife corridors between individual protected areas, however, would encourage dispersal for a whole suite of larger mammals.

Spotted hyaenas

The status of the spotted hyaena in the isolated northern part of the Western Congolian forest–savannah mosaic is critical, with just one resident population remaining in the savannah sector of the Odzala-Kokoua National Park. The loss of this population would represent the local extinction of the species from its former range in Gabon and Congo and, owing to the geographical isolation of the Western Congolian forest–savannah mosaic, the chances for natural recolonization would be minimal. As for the leopard, it should be a priority to secure the conservation of this last, isolated population to avoid the need for reintroduction to restore the species in this region.

Spotted hyaenas have been completely protected under Congolese law since 1983 (IUCN, 1989) but, to date, there have been no detailed scientific studies on the species in Congo, and no focused attempt to secure its survival there. Nonetheless, spotted hyaenas persist in a small population in the savannah sector of the remote Odzala-Kokoua National Park, but not much is known about the current status of this population. Odzala-Kokoua National

Park is the largest protected area in Congo since its extension in 2001, when the park size increased from 2800 km^2 to 13,600 km^2 (Aveling & Froment, 2001). However, open habitat suitable for spotted hyaenas can only be found on the southern tip of the park and, in the course of the park extension in 2001, the extent of savannah habitat under protection increased only slightly from 750 km^2 to just above 1000 km^2, despite the existence of an additional 1500 km^2 of uninhabited, open habitat just south of the park. Owing to uncontrolled hunting and the resulting scarcity of prey, these unprotected savannahs are currently not occupied by spotted hyaenas. Even inside the park, hyaenas were most common in the remoter savannah areas, and signs of hyaena and potential prey were largely absent towards the southern limit of the park where signs of hunters were frequent (Henschel, 2008). The size of this spotted hyaena population could not be determined during an initial large-carnivore survey in 2007, but subsequent survey results suggest that the species currently occupies an area of approximately 500 km^2 (Henschel, 2008). Estimates of hyaena population density are also not available for the Western Congolian forest–savannah mosaic, which hampers our ability to predict the number of individuals that this area might support. Furthermore, biomass estimates for preferred prey species of spotted hyaenas are also unavailable for these savannahs, and such estimates might otherwise have been used to predict the carrying capacity for hyaenas in this area (Hayward, this volume).

The small size of the area currently occupied by the species and the complete isolation of this population make it inevitable that inbreeding and loss of genetic diversity has occurred (Frankham, this volume). Consequently, a study should be conducted to assess the genetic diversity of this population and to investigate the need for population supplementation to enhance the genetic diversity.

Irrespective of whether or not an introduction of unrelated individuals into the population of Odzala-Kokoua National Park is deemed necessary, the range and size of this population should be increased. This could be achieved by promoting more rigorous protection of the savannahs towards the southern limit of the park and by including the 1500 km^2 of open habitat into the park limits that are currently without protection and do not support any resident hyaenas. Another prospect might be the establishment of a second population of spotted hyaenas in the centre of their former range, the Batéké Plateau (Figure 10.1a). The Batéké Plateau National Park in Gabon and the proposed Bambama-Lékana National Park across the border in Congo will together protect almost 6000 km^2 of intact grasslands but, owing to uncontrolled hunting preceding the recent establishment of the Gabonese park, and ongoing hunting on the Congolese side, potential prey is only patchily distributed and numbers are low (Bout, 2006). However, the continued protection of these parks will ultimately lead to an increase in ungulate populations, and the restoration of a hyaena population in this landscape would serve two conservation goals simultaneously. Large-bodied and/or social carnivores that are capable of killing comparatively large prey, and reach high population densities, can be expected to have the greatest impact on ecosystem function (Woodroffe & Ginsberg, 2005). The restoration of spotted hyaenas in these parks would be an important step towards the restoration of ecological functionality in this landscape, and the establishment of a well-protected population of spotted hyaenas would significantly increase the prospects for the long-term survival of this species in this region.

The distance between the current population in Odzala-Kokoua National Park and the Batéké Plateau is 250 km. The records of spotted hyaenas in forest sites across this region in recent years (e.g. Juste & Castroviejo, 1992), however, suggest that individuals travel even farther in their search for suitable habitat. While dispersal is usually male-biased in spotted hyaenas (Boydston *et al.*, 2005), clan fission and dispersal by females has also been observed when the carrying capacity of the natal home range is reached and when food availability is therefore low (Holekamp *et al.*, 1993). Corridors should be identified and protected to encourage dispersal, and strategically located stepping-stones could be used to increase dispersal success (Wikramanayake *et al.*, 2004). Ultimately, Léfini Reserve could be connected to the Batéké Plateau/Bambama-Lékana National Parks, although its proximity to Brazzaville and the immense demand, originating from the capital, for wild meat has made the protection of this site very challenging in the past.

Lions and African wild dogs

The current situations for lions and African wild dogs in the Congo Basin have certain similarities. Despite persistent rumours about their presence in some areas and occasional unconfirmed reports about sightings of their sign, no material evidence of their presence has been produced for more than a decade, and it seems reasonable to assume that both species are virtually extinct in this northern part of the Western Congolian forest–savannah mosaic. The nearest known populations for both species are in northern Cameroon (Chardonnet, 2002; Sillero-Zubiri *et al.*, 2004) and are separated from the Western Congolian forest–savannah mosaic by a 1000-km wide continuous rainforest belt. Natural reinvasions are therefore highly unlikely, and any effort to re-establish either species would inevitably involve the introduction of captive or wild individuals from outside this region.

Given the high cost and complexity of large reintroduction programmes (IUCN, 1998), a number of factors have to be considered thoroughly when deciding whether or not the reintroduction of a large carnivore should be attempted. These include:

1 The justification for the reintroduction—will it mark a significant contribution to the survival of a species or the functionality of an ecosystem? (IUCN, 1998; Berger, 2007);
2 Biological/technical aspects, such as the availability of protected habitat, prey and a suitable release stock (IUCN, 1998);
3 Organizational aspects, such as the availability of adequate human and financial resources for the reintroduction (Yalden, 1993);
4 Valuational aspects, such as the local perception of wildlife in general, and attitudes towards the reintroduction of a specific large carnivore in particular (Reading & Clark, 1996).

The above factors should all be addressed in an initial feasibility assessment that should precede any well-planned reintroduction programme (IUCN, 1998); however, the reintroduction of a large-carnivore species has never been attempted or even considered in this region, and many of the questions revolving around the feasibility of such a task simply cannot be addressed at this stage. Nonetheless, there appear to be two central factors of disproportionate importance when considering the reintroduction of either lions or African wild dogs into this region: the availability of protected habitat and community attitudes towards the species.

Availability of protected habitat

In the open landscape of this forest–savannah mosaic, prey is scarce outside protected areas as a result of uncontrolled bushmeat hunting, and this can be considered the main cause underlying the initial decline of large carnivores in this region. The contributors to this book contend that the most important factor regarding the success of large-carnivore restorations is whether the agents of the initial decline have been removed (Macdonald, this volume). In a region where bushmeat constitutes the primary source of animal protein for the majority of the rural population, the survival of large carnivores and their prey can most likely only be ascertained through the designation and rigorous protection of sufficiently large protected areas.

The last sightings of African wild dogs occurred in the coastal savannahs in Congo and Gabon (Figure 10.1c), which are also the last refuge for waterbuck and southern reedbuck in this region (East, 1999). Both species of ungulates are in the body-mass range of preferred prey species for wild dogs (Hayward *et al.*, 2006b), and their presence along the coast might have facilitated the persistence of wild dogs in this area. The coastal region, however, is characterized by a dense human population, and there are no protected areas that contain substantial expanses of open habitat, nor is there uninhabited land available which would permit the creation of new ones (Figure 10.1a). The only large expanse of uninhabited and unfragmented open habitat that remains in the Western forest–savannah mosaic is the Batéké Plateau, but prey availability is low and both waterbuck and southern reedbuck no longer occur even inside the protected areas in this landscape (Bout, 2006; Mathot *et al.*, 2006). While prey populations could be increased by protecting these parks and ungulate species could be reintroduced, the size of the current and proposed protected areas will most likely be too small to support a viable, self-sustaining population of African wild dogs. Wild dogs generally occur at low densities even in the absence of larger competitors, and the species is reportedly very vulnerable to anthropogenic mortality (Woodroffe *et al.*, 1997), which can be high even inside protected areas (Rasmussen, 1997). Mortality along reserve borders has a greater effect on population persistence in smaller parks and reserves (Woodroffe & Ginsberg, 1998), and African wild dogs are considered to require protected areas in excess of 10,000 km^2 to maintain viable populations (Woodroffe & Ginsberg, 1999).

Lions, however, are capable of reaching high population densities when preferred prey is abundant, and have good chances of persistence even in comparatively small parks and reserves (Woodroffe & Ginsberg, 2005). As the dominant predator, their numbers in protected areas are determined chiefly by the available biomass of their preferred prey, and a monitoring of ungulate biomass in the protected areas of this landscape could be used to predict carrying capacity for lions at these sites (Hayward, this volume). Furthermore, this technique could help to decide when and if a lion reintroduction would most likely lead to the establishment of viable population.

Attitudes towards carnivores

Any reintroduction of large carnivores needs the consensus of the local human population (Moore, 1992), as a lack of acceptance often leads to the killing of reintroduced individuals (e.g. Breitenmoser *et al.*, 2001). While, in general, reintroduced animals might be relatively safe from direct persecution inside protected areas, large carnivores are wide-ranging, and human-induced mortality on reserve borders has been shown to lead to the extinction of local populations of large carnivores (Woodroffe & Ginsberg, 1998). Lions, in particular, have long been feared by the local population inhabiting the Western forest–savannah mosaic (Guiral, 1889; Dusseljé, 1910; Malbrant & Maclatchy, 1949; Sautter, 1960), but virtually nothing is known about people's attitudes towards spotted hyaenas and African wild dogs.

If the attitudes of the local population towards lions were to remain unchanged, any attempt to reintroduce them into this northern part of the Western Congolian forest–savannah mosaic would inevitably fail. A possible incentive to further the acceptance of lions in the local population might the contribution of revenues from wildlife tourism to local communities. For the Gabonese government, a major impetus for establishing new national parks was the prospect of developing a viable ecotourism industry (Laurance *et al.*, 2006b). Creating the possibility for tourists to observe western lowland gorillas *Gorilla g. gorilla* and lions in one national park has the potential to allow for an increase in ecotourism in areas where the economic incentives to communities are well understood and accepted.

Acknowledgements

I am most grateful to the editors for inviting me to the conference and for giving me the opportunity to contribute this chapter to their book. Travel costs to the conference were kindly covered by the Society for Conservation Biology, and all my own survey work in Gabon and Congo was funded by the Great Cats Program of the Wildlife Conservation Society. I am greatly indebted to numerous colleagues who provided reports and unpublished data on the occurrence of leopards and other large carnivores across the Congo Basin, and I am particularly thankful to Boo Maisels and Bethan Morgan in this respect. The manuscript was greatly improved by comments from three anonymous reviewers and Matt Hayward, and I want to thank Matt for his continuous help and patience with this chapter.

References

Aba'a Nseme, R. (2006) *Abondance relative des grands mammifères et des activités humaines au Parc National des Monts de Cristal et sa périphérie, Gabon*. Wildlife Conservation Society, Gabon Program, Libreville.

Aba'a Nseme, R. & Bezangoye Ndoukoue, A. (2007) *Estimation de la densité, de l'abondance et de la distribution relative des grands mammifères et l'impact des activités anthropiques au Parc National des Monts Birougou et ses environs*. Wildlife Conservation Society, Gabon Program, Libreville.

Abitsi, G. (2006) *Inventaires de reconnaissance des grands mammifères et de l'impact des activités anthropiques, Parc National de Waka, Gabon*. Wildlife Conservation Society, Gabon Program, Libreville.

Andama, E. (2000) *The Status and Distribution of Carnivores in Bwindi Impenetrable Forest National Park, South-western Uganda*. MSc thesis, Makerere University, Kampala.

Angelici, F.M., Akani, G.C. & Luiselli, L. (1998) The leopard *Panthera pardus* in southeastern Nigeria: Status, ecological correlates of occurrence and conservation implications. *Italian Journal of Zoology* 65, 307–310.

Astaras, C., Mühlenberg, M. & Waltert, M. (2008) Note on drill (*Mandrillus leucophaeus*) ecology and conservation status in Korup National Park, southwest Cameroon. *American Journal of Primatology* 70, 306–310.

Aust, P. & Inkamba Nkulu, C. (2005) *A Survey of the Status of Lions* (Panthera leo) *on the Batéké Plateau, Republic of Congo*. Wildlife Conservation Society, Congo Program, Brazzaville.

Aveling, C. & Froment, J.M. (2001) L'extension du Parc National d'Odzala, une opportunité de développement. *Canopée* 20, 13–14.

Bailey, T.N. (1993) *The African Leopard: Ecology and Behaviour of a Solitary Felid*. Columbia University Press, New York.

Barnett, R., Yamaguchi, N., Barnes, I. & Cooper, A. (2006) The origin, current diversity and future conservation of the modern lion (*Panthera leo*). *Proceedings of the Royal Society of London, Series B: Biological Sciences* 273, 2119–2125.

Berger, J. (2007) Carnivore repatriation and holarctic prey: Narrowing the deficit in ecological effectiveness. *Conservation Biology* 21, 1105–1116.

Bergl, R.A., Oates, J.F. & Fotso, R. (2007) Distribution and protected area coverage of endemic taxa in West Africa's Biafran forests and highlands. *Biological Conservation* 134, 195–208.

Blake, S., Strindberg, S., Boudjan, P. et al. (2007) Forest elephant crisis in the Congo Basin. *PLoS Biology* 5, 945–953.

Boddicker, M. (2006) Large mammals encountered in the Gamba Complex of protected areas, Gabon. *Gamba, Gabon: Biodiversity of an Equatorial African Rainforest.* (eds A. Alonso, M.E. Lee, P. Campbell, O.S.G Pauwels. & F. Dallmeier), pp. 417–423. Bulletin of the Biological Society of Washington, No. 12.

Bout, N. (2006) *Parc National des Plateaux Batéké, Gabon: Suivi écologique des grand mammifères et de l'impact humain.* Wildlife Conservation Society, Gabon Program, Libreville.

Boydston, E.E., Kapheim, K.M., van Horn, R.C., Smale, L. & Holekamp, K.E. (2005) Sexually dimorphic patterns of space use throughout ontogeny in the spotted hyaena (*Crocuta crocuta*). *Journal of Zoology* 267, 271–281.

Breitenmoser, U., Breitenmoser-Würsten, C., Carbyn, L.N. & Funk, S.M. (2001) Assessment of carnivore reintroductions. *Carnivore Conservation.* (eds J.L. Gittleman, S.M. Funk, D.W. Macdonald & R.K. Wayne), pp. 241–281. Cambridge University Press, Cambridge.

Burgess, N.D., Balmford, A., Cordeiro, N.J. et al. (2007) Correlations among species distributions, human density and human infrastructure across the high biodiversity tropical mountains of Africa. *Biological Conservation* 134, 164–177.

Chardonnet, P. (2002) *Conservation of the African Lion: Contribution to a Status Survey.* International Foundation for the Conservation of Wildlife, France, and Conservation Force, USA.

de Baleine, P. (1987) *Les veillées de chasse d'Henri Guizard.* Flammarion, Paris.

Dowsett, R.J. (1995) The strange case of two of Congo's last lions. *CAT News* 22, 9–10.

Dowsett, R.J. & Dowsett-Lemaire, F. (1991) *Flore et Faune du Bassin du Kouilou (Congo) et leur exploitation.* Tauraco Research Report No. 4, Liège, Belgium.

Dowsett, R.J. & Dowsett-Lemaire, F. (1997) *Flore et Faune du Parc National d'Odzala.* Tauraco Research Report No. 6, Liège, Belgium.

Du Chaillu, P.B. (1861) *Explorations and Adventures in Equatorial Africa.* John Murray, London.

Dupont, L.M., Jahns, S., Marret, F. & Ning, S. (2000) Vegetation change in equatorial West Africa: Time-slices for the last 150 ka. *Palaeogeography, Palaeoclimatology, Palaeoecology* 155, 95–122.

Dusseljé, E. (1910) *Les Tégués de l'Alima, Congo français.* Imprimerie de Cauwer, Anvers, Belgium.

East, R. (1999) *African Antelope Database 1998.* IUCN, Gland, Switzerland.

Ekobo, A. (1998) *Large Mammals and Vegetation Surveys in the Boumba-Bek and Nki Project Area*. WWF, Cameroon Programme, Yaoundé.

Forboseh, P.F., Eno-Nku, M. & Sunderland, T.C.H. (2007) Priority setting for conservation in south-west Cameroon based on large mammal surveys. *Oryx* 41, 255–262.

Guiral, L. (1889) *Le Congo Français: Du Gabon à Brazzaville*. Plon, Paris.

Güssfeldt, P., Falkenstein, J. & Pechuël-Loesche, E. (1882) *Die Loango-Expedition 1873–1876*. Verlag von Paul Frohberg, Leipzig.

Hart, J.A., Katembo, M. & Punga, K. (1996) Diet, prey selection and ecological relations of leopard and golden cat in the Ituri Forest, Zaire. *African Journal of Ecology* 34, 364–379.

Hayward, M.W., Henschel, P, O'Brien, J., Hofmeyr, M., Balme, G. & Kerley, G.I.H. (2006a) Prey preferences of the leopard (*Panthera pardus*). *Journal of Zoology, London* 270, 298–313.

Hayward, M.W., O'Brien, J., Hofmeyr, M. & Kerley, G.I.H. (2006b) Prey preferences of the African wild dog *Lycaon pictus*: Ecological requirements for their conservation. *Journal of Mammalogy* 87, 1122–1131.

Hayward, M.W., O'Brien, J. & Kerley, G.I.H. (2007) Carrying capacity of large African predators: Predictions and tests. *Biological Conservation* 139, 219–229.

Henschel, P. (2006) The lion in Gabon: Historical records and notes on current status. *CAT News* 44, 10–13.

Henschel, P. (2008) *Survey on the Status of Large Carnivores in the Savanna Sector of Odzala-Kokoua National Park, Republic of Congo*. Wildlife Conservation Society, Great Cats Program, New York.

Henschel, P. (in preparation) *The Conservation Biology of the Leopard* Panthera pardus *in Gabon: Status, Threats and Strategies for Conservation*. PhD thesis, University of Göttingen, Göttingen.

Henschel, P. & Ray, J.C. (2003) *Leopards in African Rainforests: Survey and Monitoring Techniques*. Wildlife Conservation Society, Global Carnivore Program, New York.

Henschel, P., Abernethy, K.A. & White, L.J.T. (2005) Leopard food habits in the Lopé National Park, Gabon, Central Africa. *African Journal of Ecology* 43, 21–28.

Holekamp, K.E., Ogutu, J.O., Dublin, H.T., Frank, L.G. & Smale, L. (1993) Fission of a spotted hyaena clan—Consequences of prolonged female absenteeism and causes of female emigration. *Ethology* 93, 285–299.

Hunter, L., Henschel, P. & Ray, J.C. (in press) Leopard *Panthera pardus. The Mammals of Africa, Vol. 4 Carnivora.* (eds J. Kingdon & T. Butynski). Academic Press, New York.

IUCN (1989) *La conservation des ecosystèmes forestiers du Congo. Basé sur le travail de Philippe Hecketsweiler*. IUCN, Gland, Switzerland.

IUCN (1998) *IUCN Guidelines for Re-introductions*. IUCN, Gland, Switzerland.

Jackson, P. (1989) *The Status of the Leopard in Sub-Saharan Africa: A Review by Leopard Specialists*. Unpublished report of the Cat Specialist Group, IUCN, Gland, Switzerland.

Jorgenson, J.P. & Redford, K.H. (1993) Humans and big cats as predators in the neotropics. *Symposia of the Zoological Society of London* 65, 367–390.

Juste, J. & Castroviejo, J. (1992) Unusual record of the spotted hyaena (*Crocuta crocuta*) in Rio Muni, Equatorial-Guinea. *International Journal of Mammalian Biology* 57, 380–381.

Larison, B., Smith, T.B., Girman, D., Stauffer, D., Mila, B., Drewes, R.C., et al. (1999) *Biotic Surveys of Bioko and Rio Muni, Equatorial Guinea*. Unpublished report to the Biodiversity Support Program, Center for Tropical Research, San Francisco State University, San Francisco.

Latour, S. (2006) *Recensement d'éléphants et de grands singes dans la région du Parc National de Pongara, Gabon*. Wildlife Conservation Society, Gabon Program, Libreville.

Laurance, W.F., Alonso, A., Lee, M. & Campbell, P. (2006b) Challenges for forest conservation in Gabon, Central Africa. *Futures* 38, 454–470.

Laurance, W.F., Croes, B.M., Tchignoumba, L., Lahm, S.A., Alonso, A., Lee, M.E., et al. (2006a) Impacts of roads and hunting on Central African rainforest mammals. *Conservation Biology* 20, 1251–1261.

Madzou, Y.C. & Ebanega, M.O. (2006) Wild game and its use in the tropical environment, Cameroon—The forest in search of a balance between exploitation for survival and conservation in the Northern region of Boumba-Bek (South East Cameroon). *Nature & Faune* 21, 18–33.

Maisels, F., Ella Akou, M., Douckaga, M. & Moundounga, A. (2004) *Mwagne National Park, Gabon: Large mammals and Human Impact.* Trip report, Nov-Dec 2004. Wildlife Conservation Society, Gabon Program, Libreville.

Maisels, F., Fotso, R.C. & Hoyle, D. (2000) *Mbam Djerem National Park: Conservation Status, Large Mammals and Human Impact.* Wildlife Conservation Society, Cameroon Program, Yaoundé.

Maisels, F., Keming, E., Kemei, M & Toh, C. (2001) The extirpation of large mammals and implications for mountain forest conservation: The case of the Kilum-Ijum Forest, Northwest Province, Cameroon. *Oryx* 35, 322–331.

Malbrant, R. & Maclatchy, A. (1947) Affinités australes de la faune du Congo Français et du Gabon. *Mammalia* 11, 129–138.

Malbrant, R. & Maclatchy, A. (1949) *Faune de l'Equateur Africain Français, Tome II, Mammifères.* Paul Lechevalier, Paris.

Maley, J. (2001) The impact of arid phases on the African rainforest through geological history. *African Rainforest Ecology and Conservation—An Interdisciplinary Perspective.* (eds W. Weber, L. White, A. Vedder & L. Naughton-Treves), pp. 344–354. Yale University Press, New Haven.

Marker, L.L. & Dickman, A.J. (2005) Factors affecting leopard (*Panthera pardus*) spatial ecology, with particular reference to Namibian farmlands. *South African Journal of Wildlife Research* 35, 105–115.

Martin, R.B. & de Meulenaer, T. (1988) *Survey of the Status of the Leopard* Panthera pardus *in Sub-Saharan Africa*. CITES Secretariat, Lausanne.

Mathot, L., Ikoli, F. & Missilou, B.R. (2006) *Rapport annuel de monitoring de la faune du Projet Lésio-Louna, 2006*. Projet Lésio-Louna, Fondation John Aspinall, Brazzaville.

Matthews, A. & Matthews, A. (2006) Inventory of large and medium-sized mammals in south-western Cameroon. *Mammalia* 70, 276–287.

Mills, M.G.L. & Hofer, H. (1998) *Hyaenas. Status Survey and Conservation Action Plan*. IUCN/SSC Hyaena Specialist Group. IUCN Gland, Switzerland.

Moodley, Y. & Bruford, M.W. (2007) Molecular Biogeography: Towards an integrated framework for conserving Pan-African biodiversity. *PLoS One*, 2, e454.

Moore, D. (1992) Re-establishing large predators. *Re-introduction News* 4, 6.

Morgan, B.J. & Sunderland-Groves, J. (2006) The Cross-Sanaga gorillas: The northernmost gorilla populations. *Gorilla Journal* 32, 16–18.

Morgan, B.J., Wild, C. & Ekobo, A. (2003) Newly discovered gorilla population in the Ebo Forest, Littoral Province, Cameroon. *International Journal of Primatology* 24, 1129–1137.

Myers, N. (1976) *The Leopard* Panthera pardus *in Africa*. IUCN Monograph No. 5. Morges.

Nchanji, A.N., Ngua Ayecaba, G. & Esono Esono, P. (2005) An assessment of the large mammals of the Monte Mitra forest, Monte Alén National Park. *A Biodiversity Assessment of the Monte Mitra Forest, Monte Alén National Park, Equatorial Guinea* (ed T.C.H. Sunderland), pp. 20–31. Smithsonian Institution, Washington, DC.

Ngandjui, G. & Blanc, C.P. (2000) Biogéographie et biodiversité: Aires protégées et conservation des mammifères au Cameroun. *Biogeographica* 76, 63–77.

Oates, J.F., Bergl, R.A. & Linder, J.M. (2004) *Africa's Gulf of Guinea Forests: Biodiversity Patterns and Conservation Priorities*. Advances in Applied Biodiversity Science No. 6. Conservation International, Washington, DC.

Okon, D. (2005) *Report on Old Ekuri Reconnaissance Survey of Red Colobus*. Wildlife Conservation Society, Calabar, Nigeria.

Olson, D.M., Dinerstein, E., Wikramanayake, E.D., Burgess, N.D., Powell, G.V.N., Underwood, E.C., et al. (2001) Terrestrial ecoregions of the worlds: A new map of life on earth. *Bioscience* 51, 933–938.

Ososky, J.J. (1998) *Diet of Leopards and Golden Cats in Ndoki Park, Republic of Congo*. MSc thesis, Northern Illinois University.

Rasmussen, G. (1997) *Conservation Status of the Painted Hunting Dog* Lycaon pictus *in Zimbabwe*. Department of National Parks & Wildlife Management, Zimbabwe.

Ray, J.C. (2001) Carnivore biogeography and conservation in the African forest: A community perspective. *African Rainforest Ecology and Conservation—An Interdisciplinary Perspective.* (eds W. Weber, L. White, A. Vedder & L. Naughton-Treves), pp. 214–232. Yale University Press, New Haven.

Ray, J.C. & Sunquist, M.E. (2001) Trophic relations in a community of African forest carnivores. *Oecologica*, 127, 397–408.

Reading, R.P. & Clark, T.W. (1996) Carnivore reintroductions: An interdisciplinary examination. *Carnivore Behavior, Ecology and Evolution, Volume II* (ed J.L. Gittleman), pp. 296–336.Cornell University Press, New York.

Sanderson, E.W., Redford, K.H., Chetkiewicz, C.L.B., Medellin, R.A., Rabinowitz, A. R., Robinson, J.G. & Taber, A.B. (2002) Planning to save a species: The jaguar as a model. *Conservation Biology*, 16, 58–72.

Sautter, G. (1960) Le plateau congolais de Mbé. *Cahiers d'Etudes Africaines*, 1(2), 5–48.

Schadt, S., Revilla, E., Wiegand, T. et al. (2002) Assessing the suitability of central European landscapes for the reintroduction of Eurasian lynx. *Journal of Applied Ecology*, 39, 189–203.

Sillero-Zubiri, C., Hoffmann, M. & Macdonald D.W. (eds) (2004) *Canids: Foxes, Wolves, Jackals and Dogs. Status Survey and Conservation Action Plan.* IUCN/SSC Canid Specialist Group. IUCN, Gland, Switzerland.

Sunderland-Groves, J. & Maisels, F. (2003) Large mammals of Takamanda Forest Reserve, Cameroon. *Takamanda: The Biodiversity of an African Rainforest* (eds J.A. Comiskey, T.C.H. Sunderland & J.L. Sunderland-Groves), pp. 111–127. Smithsonian Institution, Washington, DC.

Tutin, C.E.G., White, L.J.T. & Mackanga-Missandzou, A. (1997) The use by rainforest mammals of natural forest fragments in an Equatorial African savanna. *Conservation Biology* 11, 1190–1203.

van Neer, W. & Lanfranchi, R. (1985) Etude de la faune découverte dans l'abri tshitolien de Ntadi Yomba (République Populaire du Congo). *Anthropologie* 89, 351–364.

Wikramanayake, E.D., Dinerstein, E., Robinson, J.G. et al. (1998) An ecology-based method for defining priorities for large mammal conservation: The tiger as case study. *Conservation Biology* 12, 865–878.

Wikramanayake, E.D., McKnight, M., Dinerstein, E., Joshi, A., Gurung, B. & Smith, D. (2004) Designing a conservation landscape for tigers in human-dominated environments. *Conservation Biology* 18, 839–844.

Wilkie, D.S. & Carpenter, J.F. (1999) Bushmeat hunting in the Congo Basin: An assessment of impacts and options for mitigation. *Biodiversity and Conservation* 8, 927–955.

Willcox, A.S. (2002) *The Extirpated Ark: The Status of Hunting in the Banyang-Mbo Wildlife Sanctuary of Southwest Cameroon.* MSc thesis, Durrell Institute of Conservation and Ecology, Canterbury.

Willcox, A.S. & Nambu, D.M. (2007) Wildlife hunting practices and bushmeat dynamics of the Banyangi and Mbo people of Southwestern Cameroon. *Biological Conservation* 134, 251–261.

Williamson, L. & Usongo, L. (1995) *Survey of Primate Populations and large mammal inventory, Reserve de faune du Dja, Cameroun*. Project ECOFAC, Composante Cameroun, AGRECO-CTFT, Yaoundé, Cameroon.

Woodroffe, R. & Ginsberg, J.R. (1998) Edge effects and the extinction of populations inside protected areas. *Science* 280, 2126–2128.

Woodroffe, R. & Ginsberg, J.R. (1999) Conserving the African wild dog *Lycaon pictus*. I. Diagnosing and treating causes of decline. *Oryx* 33, 132–142.

Woodroffe, R. & Ginsberg, J.R. (2005) King of the beasts? Evidence for guild redundancy among large mammalian carnivores. *Large Carnivores and the Conservation of Biodiversity.* (eds J.C. Ray, K.H. Redford, R.S. Steneck & J. Berger), pp. 154–175. Island Press, Washington, DC.

Woodroffe, R., Ginsberg, J.R. & Macdonald, D.W. (1997) *The African Wild Dog—Status Survey and Conservation Action Plan*. IUCN Canid specialist Group. IUCN Gland, Switzerland.

Yalden, D.W. (1993) The problems of reintroducing carnivores. *Symposia of the Zoological Society of London* 65, 289–306.

11

Reintroducing the Dingo: Can Australia's Conservation Wastelands be Restored?

Chris R. Dickman[1], *Alistair S. Glen*[2] *and Mike Letnic*[1]

[1]Institute of Wildlife Research, School of Biological Sciences, University of Sydney
[2]Western Australian Department of Environment and Conservation, and Invasive Animals CRC, Dwellingup Research Centre

Summary

Introduced to Australia around 4000 years ago, the dingo, *Canis lupus dingo*, now occupies large areas of the mainland and is the continent's top predator. Owing to its destructive attacks on livestock, especially sheep, it is maintained at zero or very low densities in semi-arid rangeland habitats, where sheep grazing is the dominant land use. These vast areas have been greatly degraded and suffer from eroded soils, impoverished native vegetation communities and unprecedented levels of extinction of native mammals and other vertebrates. They are Australia's conservation wastelands. Using the 325,000 km^2 rangeland environment in the Western Division of New South Wales as a case study, we propose that reintroduction of the dingo would have positive effects on the diversity of small and medium-sized native vertebrates by suppressing populations of their major predators, the introduced red fox, *Vulpes vulpes*, and feral cat, *Felis catus*. Using a rank-scoring scheme to determine their sus-

Reintroduction of Top-Order Predators, 1st edition. Edited by M.W. Hayward and M.J. Somers.
 ISBN 978-1-4051-7680-4 (pb) and 978-1-4051-9273-6 (hb)

ceptibility to fox and cat predation, we estimate that 70 out of 80 species of vertebrates listed as threatened at the state level would benefit from the mesopredator suppression effect if dingoes were reintroduced. Other benefits potentially include reduced populations of introduced pest species, maintenance of native vegetation and the restoration of ecological interactions and ecosystem services performed by native species. We suggest four steps that could make dingo reintroduction practicable—quantifying the biodiversity benefits of reintroduction, exploring novel methods of protecting sheep flocks and farm incomes, engaging the community, and changing legislation—and conclude that dingo reintroduction would be a cost-effective means of restoring Australia's conservation wastelands.

Introduction

Large mammals often fare poorly in the presence of humans. Recent analyses suggest that human activity was the primary cause of extinction of megafauna in Australia and the Americas in the late Pleistocene (Burney & Flannery, 2005; Martin, 2005; but see also Wroe *et al.*, 2004, 2006), and there is little doubt that deleterious impacts are continuing (Johnson, 2006). Owing to loss or fragmentation of their habitat, over-hunting for bushmeat or the harvest of body parts, direct persecution or combinations of these and other threats (Baillie *et al.*, 2004), many species are sliding towards oblivion. Large carnivores, in particular, are likely to face persecution owing to their attacks on humans and especially on livestock, although intrinsic biological traits also are important predictors of their extinction risk (Cardillo *et al.*, 2004). Persecution often causes the local or regional demise of carnivores; if the original population is small, species extinction can result (Paddle, 2000).

Removing large predators from a system may increase livestock productivity, but it can also have other unintended and often negative consequences. For example, smaller predators often benefit from the removal of a top predator because of reduced competition or intraguild predation and then, in turn, exert greater predatory effects on the smaller prey that they usually favour (Soulé *et al.*, 1988; Crooks & Soulé, 1999). Removal of a top predator can also alter the balance of advantages within communities of smaller species of predators via indirect amensal and commensal pathways (Glen & Dickman, 2005, 2008). Perhaps not surprisingly, populations of large herbivores expand if top predators are removed; this can lead to negative effects on vegetation

(Ray *et al.*, 2005) and even to community-level trophic cascades that extensively redistribute plant biomass and the composition of plant species (Polis *et al.*, 2000; Schmitz *et al.*, 2000). Where present, top predators may dampen variability in community structure and species composition and hence assist in buffering communities against the effects of climate change (Wilmers & Getz, 2005). Other, diverse, effects of top predators have been explored in model communities and are theoretically relatively well known (Morin, 1999; Sinclair *et al.*, 2000; Glen & Dickman, 2005). Recent developments that incorporate variations in the behaviour and density of interactants suggest that we will be able to predict the effects of top predators with increasing precision in future (Garrott *et al.*, 2007; Hayward, this volume).

To reverse the negative effects of predator loss, several attempts have been made to reintroduce species of felids, canids, ursids and other taxa to parts of their former ranges. Research in Yellowstone National Park, USA, provides an excellent example of the diverse system-level effects that can occur when a top predator is restored (see Smith *et al.*, this volume). The grey wolf, *Canis lupus*, was reintroduced to Yellowstone in 1995 and 1996 after an absence of some seven decades. As wolves became established, populations of elk (*Cervus elaphus*) predictably declined, and most individuals moved to habitats where wolf activity was low (Fortin *et al.*, 2005; Forester *et al.*, 2007). In the absence of wolves, elk probably suppressed recruitment of aspen (*Populus tremuloides*), cottonwoods (*Populus angustifolia* and *Populus trichocarpa*) and willows (*Salix boothii* and *Salix geyeriana*); their recent reduction following the reintroduction of wolves appears to be allowing these trees to regenerate (Beschta, 2003; Beyer *et al.*, 2007; Ripple & Beschta, 2007a). Because other species such as beavers, *Castor canadensis*, were probably out-competed by elk during the period of elk ascendancy, the reintroduction of wolves will likely benefit them via indirect commensal effects (Wolf *et al.*, 2007). Observations of a smaller carnivore, the coyote (*Canis latrans*), confirm that some individuals are killed by wolves, and that coyote density is suppressed in the presence of wolves by interference competition (Berger & Gese, 2007). Coyotes gain increased access to food where wolves are present by scavenging the remains of wolf-kills (Switalski, 2003), but this is not sufficient to offset the directly depressive effects of interference at the population level.

The reintroduction of wolves to Yellowstone was highly contentious (see Smith *et al.*, this volume). On the one hand, the grey wolf was listed as a threatened species under the US Endangered Species Act and once ranged widely throughout the Yellowstone region. On the other hand, however, it was despised by ranchers who feared for the safety of their flocks (Bangs *et al.*, 1998). Despite the controversy, there appears little doubt that wolves are now ranging widely in Yellowstone and driving interactions at the landscape scale that maintain and enhance biodiversity. Broadly positive environmental effects have also been reported following the arrival of wolves in Isle Royale National Park in Lake Superior (McLaren & Peterson, 1994) and Banff National Park, Canada (Hebblewhite *et al.*, 2005), and in studies of other species of top predators elsewhere (e.g. Krebs *et al.*, 2001; Soulé *et al.*, 2003; Sergio *et al.*, 2006; Ripple & Beschta, 2007b). As the benefits of returning predators to their former ranges are realized, some researchers are advocating more radical translocations that would shift large mammals between continents to restore the ecological effects of now-extinct megafauna. The proposed release of lions (*Panthera leo*), cheetahs (*Acinonyx jubatus*) and large herbivores from the Old World to Canada and the USA—Pleistocene re-wilding (Donlan *et al.*, 2005)—has attracted much debate (Caro, 2007).

In Australia, controversial calls are being made to reintroduce a close relative of the grey wolf—the dingo, *C. lupus dingo*—to rangeland environments from which it is currently excluded. This species was introduced to Australia around 4000 years ago and now occupies all continental habitats. It is present on many offshore islands, but has not been introduced to Tasmania (Corbett, 1995). Along with human hunting, the dingo is often held responsible for the demise on the mainland of the thylacine (*Thylacinus cynocephalus*), Tasmanian devil (*Sarcophilus harrisii*) and native-hen (*Gallinura mortierii*) (Johnson & Wroe, 2003). However, with the more recent introduction of the red fox (*Vulpes vulpes*) and domestic cat (*Felis catus*) to Australia, the dingo is being seen increasingly as a means of suppressing the numbers of both species of smaller predators, and thus of reducing the predatory pressures experienced by many small native species of vertebrates (O'Neill, 2002; Dickman *et al.*, 2006; Glen *et al.*, 2007; Johnson *et al.*, 2007). This is the mesopredator suppression concept of Crooks & Soulé (1999). Both the fox and the cat are considered to be serious threats to populations of many threatened species (Dickman, 1996; Saunders & McLeod, 2007), and both have been listed as key threatening processes under the Commonwealth's *Environment Protection and Biodiversity Conservation Act 1999.* Although foxes can be controlled by poison baiting in some areas (e.g. in the Western Shield programme; Armstrong, 2004), broad-scale baiting programmes are ineffective if blanket coverage is not achieved (Gentle *et al.*, 2007); eradication is prohibitively expensive (e.g. Saunders *et al.*, 2006). No methods for the broad-scale control of feral cats are known. Hence, dingoes are being seen increasingly as a potentially cost-effective means of suppressing fox and cat populations in the longer term.

In this chapter, we discuss the case for reintroducing the dingo to rangeland environments in Australia. We first comment briefly on relevant aspects of dingo biology and management, and then summarize the available evidence that it suppresses populations of foxes and cats. We use the extensively degraded sheep rangelands of western New South Wales—part of Australia's broader conservation wastelands in semi-arid regions where sheep are grazed (Caughley *et al.*, 1987; Grigg, 1988)—as a case study of how reintroduction of the dingo could benefit native fauna, and finally we suggest practical steps that could be taken to implement a reintroduction programme.

Dingo biology and management

Attaining a mass of up to 24 kg, the dingo is a robust canid capable of tackling prey ranging in size from grasshoppers to swamp buffalo, *Bubalus bubalis*, although prey of about its own size seem to be favoured. Solitary animals may hunt rabbits, *Oryctolagus cuniculus*, rodents and even large lizards but, in productive areas, packs work cooperatively to hunt and kill larger prey such as feral pigs, *Sus scrofa*, cattle and kangaroos (Thomson, 1992a,b). Carrion is also eaten, and may be an important food source during drought (Corbett & Newsome, 1987). Home ranges vary from about 20 km^2 in productive forested country to more than 100 km^2 in arid environments, with the ranges of individual pack members showing substantial overlap (McIlroy *et al.*, 1986; Thomson & Marsack, 1992). In arid areas, dingoes appear to have strongly depressive effects on the densities of both emus, *Dromaius novaehollandiae*, and red kangaroos, *Macropus rufus* (Caughley *et al.*, 1980; Pople *et al.*, 2000), and may have similar effects on pest species such as feral pigs and goats (*Capra hircus*) elsewhere (Fleming *et al.*, 2001).

Dingoes are a major pest in pastoral areas, with the most serious impact on sheep, then cattle and goats. The annual depredation rate varies greatly but may exceed 30% for sheep (Thomson, 1984); dingoes can also kill up to 30% of calves each year, although losses of adult cattle are much less (Allen & Gonzalez, 1998). Costs to land holders may go beyond those caused by stock losses, owing to increased veterinary costs for injured animals, loss of genetic stock, missed opportunity costs arising from diversion of labour and capital to predator control, and reduced land values (Fleming *et al.*, 2001).

Emotional trauma for land holders is an additional cost (Cathles, 2001). To reduce their depredatory impacts, dingoes are listed as pests in several states in Australia and are mandated for destruction under state legislation. Control techniques include trapping, shooting, poisoning and fencing (Allen & Fleming, 2004). The best known fence, the so-called "dog fence" or "barrier fence", runs for 5614 km from south-eastern Queensland to Fowlers Bay in South Australia, and keeps dingoes from entering the "inside country" of western New South Wales and southern South Australia (Breckwoldt, 1988). The fence is maintained continuously, with professional "doggers" engaged to track down dingoes that breech the barrier and evade detection (Wilson, 2001). Pure dingoes are becoming scarce, in part because of efforts to eradicate them, but also because of hybridization in many areas with feral dogs, *C. lupus familiaris* (Corbett, 2001). Hybrids can be very difficult to recognize in the field, and in this chapter we use the term "dingo" to cover both pure and hybrid individuals.

Effects of dingoes on foxes and cats

There is a growing body of evidence suggesting that dingoes exert strong ecological effects on foxes and feral cats, with consequent benefits for biodiversity. Firstly, dingoes kill cats and foxes (e.g. Marsack & Campbell, 1990; Paltridge, 2002). While few studies have examined the effect of dingoes on fox populations, bounty records and field studies suggest that there is an inverse relationship between the abundance of dingoes and foxes (Newsome *et al.*, 2001; Letnic, 2007; Figure 11.1). Cat populations also appear to be lower in the presence of dingoes (Pettigrew, 1993; Burrows *et al.*, 2003).

Secondly, dingoes may have behaviourally mediated effects. Changes in the behaviour of animals, brought about by the threat of predation, can be as ecologically significant as changes in their abundance (Schmitz *et al.*, 1997). Thus, fear of dingoes may alter the activity patterns of cats and foxes, with flow-on effects for native prey. Through territorial scent marking, for example, dingoes may exclude smaller predators from contested resources such as nest mounds of the endangered malleefowl, *Leipoa ocellata* (O'Neill, 2002). It is also possible that the territorial behaviour of dingoes excludes foxes and cats from larger areas, as has been observed for various species of carnivores in North America (e.g. Harrison *et al.*, 1989).

Dingoes may also compete with cats and foxes for limited resources such as food. Rabbits, for example, are an important prey resource for dingoes,

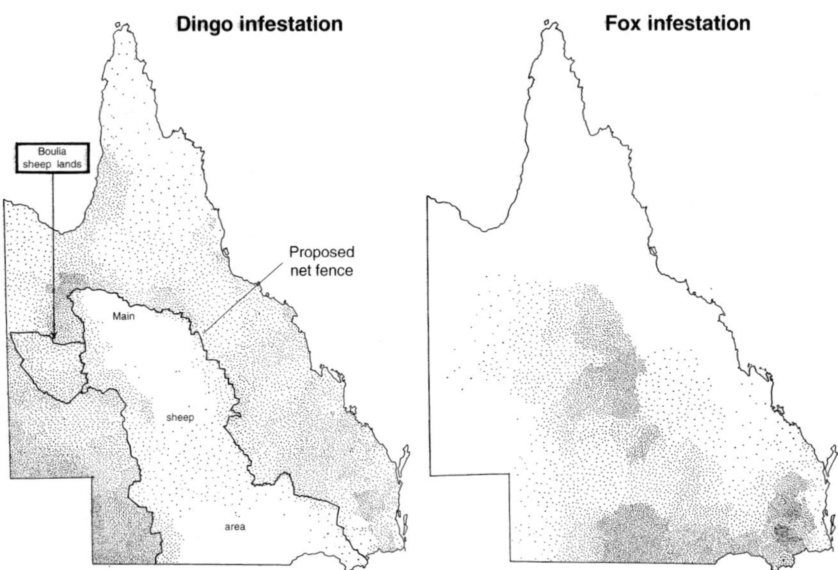

Figure 11.1 **Bounty returns for dingoes and foxes in Queensland for the 1951–1952 financial year. Each dot represents five scalps. The data suggest that foxes were less abundant in areas where dingoes were present, and that they were numerous in the main sheep area where dingoes were controlled. Extracted from Anon (1952).**

foxes and cats in many areas. Dietary overlap between sympatric dingoes, foxes and cats is high (Triggs *et al.,* 1984; Mitchell & Banks, 2005; Glen *et al.,* 2006; Glen & Dickman, 2008), and dingoes can also monopolize access to carcasses, thus limiting the availability of carrion to foxes and cats (Corbett, 1995).

Regional-scale surveys suggest that medium-sized marsupials such as the bilby, *Macrotis lagotis*, are more likely to occur in areas with dingoes than without them (Southgate *et al.,* 2007). Continental-scale studies using historical and contemporary distribution records have also found positive relationships between dingo abundance and the persistence of marsupials and native rodents (Smith & Quin, 1996; Johnson *et al.*, 2007). These studies suggest that dingoes may serve as "nature's keeper" by reducing the abundance of cats and foxes on vast geographical scales. Hence, maintaining populations of dingoes is likely to ameliorate the impact of fox and cat predation on native fauna.

Case study—western New South Wales

Background and rationale

Lying inland of the Great Dividing Range, the western region of New South Wales comprises gently undulating aeolian plains and alluvial flats less than 200 m above sea level, with occasional hills and outcrops rising to 500 m or more. For convenience, we define our area of study here to be the administrative region known as the Western Division. This vast area (325,000 km^2) is bounded in the west by the border with South Australia, in the north by the border with Queensland, in the south by the Murray River, and in the east by a more convoluted boundary that lies just west of the 375-mm rainfall isohyet (Figure 11.2). Aridity increases towards the western boundary, with 226 mm of rain falling on average each year in the north-west and 263 mm in the south-west (Bureau of Meteorology, 1988). The region is prone to long-term droughts and also to wildfires at intervals of 10–15 years (Luke & McArthur, 1978). The dominant vegetation is shrub woodland; spinifex (*Triodia* spp.) and Mitchell (*Astrebla* spp.) grasslands occur patchily, while tree clearing has resulted in large areas of improved pasture throughout (Pressey *et al.,* 2004). Livestock were moved into the Western Division as from the 1840s; sheep grazing now occupies the vast majority of the region, but dry-land and irrigated cropping are increasing (Crabb, 2004). Up to 91% of the Western Division has eroded soil and degraded native vegetation, and large areas are at risk of becoming salinized in future (Crabb, 2004). Under the *Western Lands Act 1901*, the Western Lands Commissioner is the statutory owner of the Western Division, and more than 95% of the land area is leased for pastoral enterprises (Pickard, 1988).

We have focused on western New South Wales for several reasons. Firstly, dingoes have been very scarce in this region since 1930 owing to the erection of the dog fence, the operation of a bounty scheme and the continuing imperative to protect livestock (Glen & Short, 2000). Dingoes once ranged widely throughout the region and could, in theory, be reintroduced.

Secondly, western New South Wales has been surveyed extensively and the status of its vertebrate fauna is well known (e.g. Denny, 1992; Dickman *et al.,* 1993, 2002; Sadlier & Pressey, 1994; Smith *et al.,* 1994; Ayers *et al.,* 1996; Lunney *et al.,* 2000; Ellis *et al.,* 2007). Some 38% of the native terrestrial mammals that were present at the time of European settlement are now

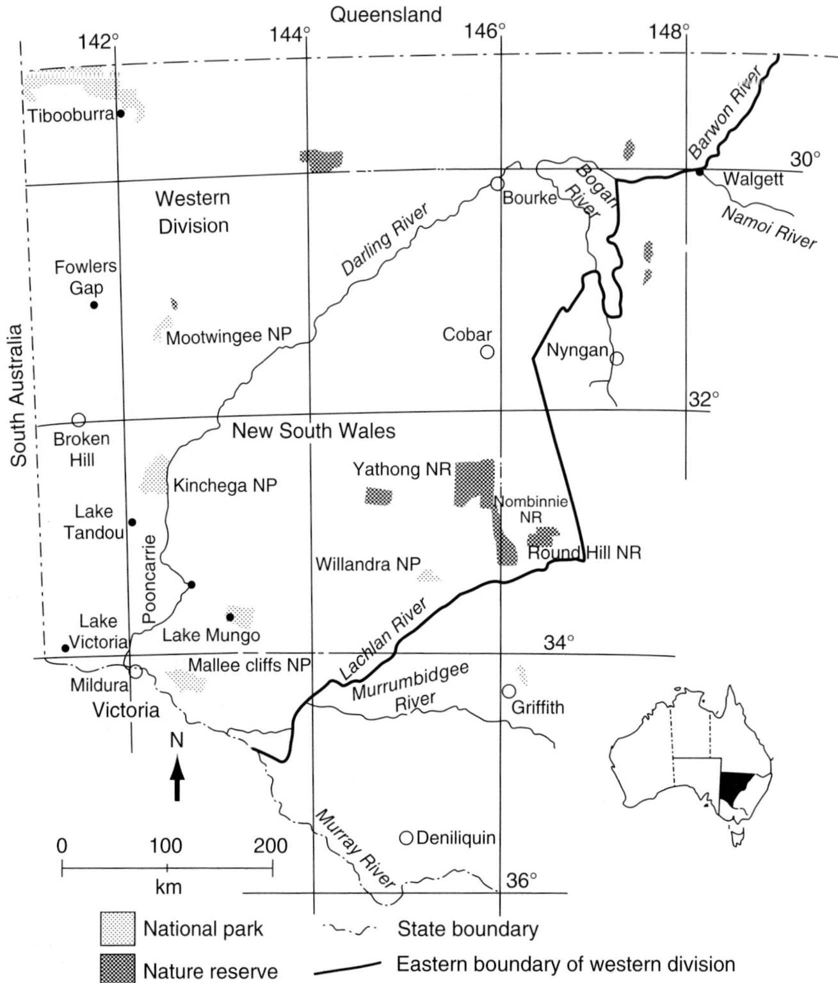

Figure 11.2 **The Western Division of New South Wales, showing major towns, rivers, National Parks and Nature Reserves.**

regionally extinct, and 16 out of 32 (excluding Chiroptera) that persist are listed as vulnerable or endangered under the New South Wales *Threatened Species Conservation Act 1995*. Losses of native mammals are much less in areas to the east of the Western Division, and are reduced also in some rangeland areas beyond the state boundaries where dingoes still occur (Dickman *et al.*, 1993). At least 11 species of birds have been reduced to vagrant status or have disappeared entirely from the Western Division, and 41 of the 300 currently resident species are listed as threatened (Smith *et al.*, 1994). Reptiles have fared better, with no known extinctions, but 23 of the recorded 112 species are nonetheless listed as vulnerable or endangered (Sadlier & Pressey, 1994). This conservation wasteland is therefore in dire need of restoration efforts.

Thirdly, foxes and cats, operating in concert with the pervasive changes wrought by the pastoral industry, have been blamed for the extinctions and range reductions of many of the original native species (Dickman *et al.*, 1993; Letnic, 2000, 2007; Lunney, 2001; Fisher *et al.*, 2003). If these diagnoses are correct, reintroduction of the dingo could potentially benefit extant but threatened species. Conditions could also be ameliorated, via the dingo's suppressive effects on the two smaller species of predators, for the reintroduction of other species that are regionally, but not nationally, extinct.

Which species would benefit from reintroducing the dingo?

Assuming that dingoes would suppress populations of foxes and cats after their reintroduction, native vertebrate species currently vulnerable to predation from the smaller predators could be expected to derive most benefit, and we consider these species here. We suggest, in passing, that pest species such as feral pigs and goats may decline in the presence of dingoes, that populations of large and currently common native mammals such as red and grey kangaroos would likely also decline, and that perennial native shrubs and trees would regenerate. However, we do not focus on these issues further, as they have been explored by Kerle *et al.* (2007) and Letnic (2007) among others.

To identify native vertebrates at most risk of predation from foxes and cats, we first catalogued all vertebrate species that are listed as vulnerable and endangered under the *Threatened Species Conservation Act 1995* and that occur in the Western Division. We then scored the relative density of foxes and cats in the localities where the threatened species occur in the Western Division using the generalized maps of Wilson *et al.* (1992), and defined five sets of independent biological attributes of these species that could increase or reduce their vulnerability to fox and cat predation. Each attribute was scored from 0 to 3, with 0 indicating no or negligible susceptibility to the predator and 3 indicating high susceptibility. Following Dickman (1996), and also after inspection of the attribute scores (Tables 11.1 and 11.2), we

Table 11.1 **Susceptibility of threatened vertebrate species in the Western Division of New South Wales to predation from feral cats, *Felis catus*.**

Species[a]	Factors contributing to susceptibility of native species[b]						
	Cat density	Body weight	Habitat	Behaviour	Mobility	Fecundity	Overall risk[c]
Mammals—vulnerable							
Dasyurus maculatus	1	0	2	2	1	1	N
Ningaui yvonneae	1–2	3	2	3	0	1	H
Phascogale tapoatafa	3	3	2	1	1	1	H
Sminthopsis macroura	1	3	3	3	0	0–1	H
Phascolarctos cinereus	1–2	0	2	1	1	2	N
Leggadina forresti	1	3	3	3	1	1	H
Pseudomys hermannsburgensis	1–2	3	2	3	1	0–1	H
Rattus villosissimus	1	3	2	3	2	0	H
Mammals—endangered							
Antechinomys laniger	3	3	3	3	0	0–1	H
Lasiorhinus latifrons	1	0	2	2	2	3	N
Cercartetus concinnus	2	3	2	3	2	0	H
Petrogale penicillata	1	0	0	2	2	2	N
Petrogale xanthopus	1	0	0	2	2	2	N
Notomys fuscus	1	3	2	3	2	0–1	H
Pseudomys bolami	1	3	2	3	1	0–1	H
Pseudomys glaucus	1	3	2	3	1	0–1	H
Birds—vulnerable							
Anseranus semipalmata	1	0	0	0	2	1	N
Oxyura australis	1–2	1	0	1	1	1	N
Stictonetta naevosa	1	0	0	1	2	0–1	N

Botaurus poiciloptilus	1	0	0	0–1	1	1	N
Lophoictinia isura	1	1	2	0	0	1–2	N
Hamirostra melanosternon	1	0	3	0	0	2	N
Falco hypoleucos	1	1	3	0	0	1–2	N
Grus rubicunda	1–2	0	0	0	1–2	2	N
Limosa limosa	1	1	0	1	1–2	1	N
Calyptorhynchus banksii	1–2	0	2–3	1	1	2–3	N
Calyptorhynchus lathami	2–3	0	1–2	0–1	2	2–3	N
Cacatua leadbeateri	1–2	1	2–3	1	1–2	1	L
Glossopsitta porphyrocephala	1	3	2	1	2	1	L
Polytelis swainsonii	2–3	3	2	1–2	1	1	H
Neophema pulchella	2–3	3	3	2	2	1	H
Neophema splendida	1	3	3	2	2	1	H
Ninox connivens	1	1	1–2	1	1	1–2	N
Tyto capensis	1–2	1	2–3	2–3	1	1	H
Tyto novaehollandiae	1	0	2	1	1	1–2	N
Amytornis striatus	1	3	2	2	1	2	L
Hylacola cauta	1–2	3	2	2	1	1	L
Pyrrholaemus brunneus	1	3	2	2	1	1	L
Chthonicola sagittata	1	3	2–3	2	1	1	H
Melithreptus gularis	1	3	2	1	1–2	2	L
Grantiella picta	2	3	2	1	1–2	1–2	L
Certhionyx variegatus	1	3	3	1	1–2	1–2	H
Drymodes brunneopygia	1,3	3	2	2	1–2	2–3	H
Pomatostomus halli	2	3	2–3	1	2	1–2	H
Cinclosoma castanotus	1–2	3	2	2	1	2	L
Pachycephala inornata	1	3	2	1–2	1	1	L
Stagonopleura guttata	1–2	3	2–3	2	1–2	1	H

Continued

Table 11.1 **Continued**

	Factors contributing to susceptibility of native species[b]						
Species[a]	**Cat density**	**Body weight**	**Habitat**	**Behaviour**	**Mobility**	**Fecundity**	**Overall risk[c]**
Birds—endangered							
Leipoa ocellata	2–3	0	2–3	2	1	0	N
Ardeotis australis	1	0	3	2–3	1–2	2	N
Pedionomus torquatus	2	3	3	2	1	1	H
Rostratula benghalensis	1	2	1	1–2	2–3	1	N
Burhinus grallarius	2	2	3	3	1–2	2	H
Phaps histrionica	1	2	2–3	1–2	2	2	L
Polytelis anthopeplus	1	3	2–3	1–2	1–2	1	H
Amytornis barbatus	1	3	2–3	2	2	2	H
Manorina melanotis	1	3	2	1–2	2	1	L
Pachycephala rufogularis	1	3	2–3	1–2	1	1–2	H
Reptiles—vulnerable							
Emydura macquarii	1	0	1	0–1	1	0	N
Antaresia stimsoni	1	0	1–2	2	1	0	N
Aspidites ramsayi	1–2	0	2–3	2	1	0	N
Brachyurophis fasciolata	1–2	2	2–3	2	1	1–2	L
Demansia torquata	1	2–3	2–3	1	1	1	H
Hoplocephalus bitorquatus	1	1–2	2	1	1	1	N
Ctenotus brooksi	1	3	2–3	1	1	1	H
Lerista xanthura	1	3	3	1–2	1	2	H
Tiliqua multifasciata	1	1	2–3	2	1	0–1	L
Tiliqua occipitalis	1–2	1	2	2	1	0–1	N
Diplodactylus stenodactylus	1	3	2–3	2	1	2	H
Strophurus elderi	1	3	2–3	2	1	2	H

Reptiles—endangered							
Echiopsis curta	1,3	1	2	1–2	1	0–1	L
Pseudonaja modesta	1	2	2	1–2	1	0–1	N
Ramphotyphlops endoterus	1	3	3	2	1	1	H
Aprasia inaurita	1	3	2–3	1–2	1	2	H
Delma australis	1	3	2–3	2	1	2	H
Anomalopus mackayi	1	3	3	1–2	1	1	H
Ctenotus pantherinus	1	2–3	2–3	2	1	1	H
Cyclodomorphus melanops	1	2–3	2–3	1–2	1	1–2	H
Cyclodomorphus venustus	1	2–3	3	1–2	1	1–2	H
Ctenophorus decresii	1	2	3	2	1	1	L
Diplodactylus conspicillatus	1–2	3	2–3	2	1	2	H

[a]Threatened species listed on schedules of the New South Wales *Threatened Species Conservation Act 1995* were accessed 12 December 2007. Listed species such as the swift parrot (*Lathamus discolor*) that are vagrants in the Western Division were excluded.

[b]Cat density is ranked from 0 (cats absent) to 3 (high density) in localities where the threatened species occur using the cat-density map of Wilson *et al.*, (1992) and distributional records of the threatened species from Dickman *et al.*, 1993, 2002; Sadlier & Pressey, 1994; Smith *et al.*, 1994; Ayers *et al.*, 1996; Lunney *et al.*, 2000; and Ellis *et al.*, 2007). For most species, the major part of the distribution (≥75%) coincided with a particular density of cats, and these species were thus given the appropriate score. Some species had distributions that overlapped relatively large areas with different cat densities (>25% of the overall distribution), and these species are shown by a hyphen to indicate the range of cat-density scores encompassed. If a species' distribution fell into two areas of very different cat density, the scores are separated by a comma. Body weight scores ranged from 0 (for mammals >2000 g, birds >1000 g and reptiles >500 g) to 3 (for mammals <220 g, birds <200 g and reptiles <10 g). Habitat scores ranged from 0 for species that use very dense ground-level vegetation or habitats that are physically difficult for cats to access, to 3 for open vegetation where cover is sparse or absent. Behaviour scores ranged from 0 for species that are diurnal; aquatic, arboreal, fossorial or volant; and have known anti-predator behaviour to 3 for species that are nocturnal; scansorial or terrestrial; and have no known anti-predator behaviours. Mobility scores ranged from 0 for species showing no coloniality, site fidelity, or seasonal tendency to congregate to 3 for species that are colonial, sedentary and aggregate seasonally for feeding, reproduction or hibernation. Fecundity scores ranged from 0 for species producing ≥10 young per female per year to 3 for species producing <1 young per female per year.

[c]Overall risk: N, no risk or negligible risk to cat predation; L, low risk; H, high risk.

Table 11.2 **Susceptibility of threatened vertebrate species in the Western Division of New South Wales to predation from red foxes, *Vulpes vulpes*.**

	Factors contributing to susceptibility of native species[b]						
Species[a]	**Fox density**	**Body weight**	**Habitat**	**Behaviour**	**Mobility**	**Fecundity**	**Overall risk[c]**
Mammals—vulnerable							
Dasyurus maculatus	1–2	2–3	2	2	1	1	L
Ningaui yvonneae	2	2	2	3	0	1	N
Phascogale tapoatafa	2	3	2	1	1	1	L
Sminthopsis macroura	1–2	2	3	3	0	0–1	H
Phascolarctos cinereus	1–2	2–3	2	1	1	2	L
Leggadina forresti	2	2	3	3	1	1	H
Pseudomys hermannsburgensis	1–2	2	2	3	1	0–1	L
Rattus villosissimus	1–2	3	2	3	2	0	H
Mammals—endangered							
Antechinomys laniger	2	2	3	3	0	0–1	H
Lasiorhinus latifrons	2	0–1	2	3	2	3	L
Cercartetus concinnus	2	2	2	3	2	0	N
Petrogale penicillata	2	2	1	2	2	2	H*
Petrogale xanthopus	2–3	2	1	2	2	2	H*
Notomys fuscus	1	2–3	2	3	2	0–1	H
Pseudomys bolami	2	2	2	3	1	0–1	L
Pseudomys glaucus	2	2	2	3	1	0–1	L

Birds—vulnerable							
Anseranus semipalmata	1–2	2	1	1	2	1	N
Oxyura australis	1–2	3	0	2	1	1	N
Stictonetta naevosa	1–2	3	1	2	2	0–1	L
Botaurus poiciloptilus	2	3	1	1–2	1	1	L
Lophoictinia isura	1–2	3	2	0	0	1–2	N
Hamirostra melanosternon	1,3	3	3	0	0	2	N
Falco hypoleucos	1–2	3	3	0	0	1–2	N
Grus rubicunda	1	1	1	0–1	1–2	2	N
Limosa limosa	1	3	1	2	1–2	1	L
Calyptorhynchus banksii	1–2	3	2–3	1	1	2–3	H
Calyptorhynchus lathami	1	3	1–2	0–1	2	2–3	L
Cacatua leadbeateri	1–2	3	2–3	1	1–2	1	H
Glossopsitta porphyrocephala	2	3	2	1	2	1	L
Polytelis swainsonii	1–2	3	2	1–2	1	1	L
Neophema pulchella	2	3	3	2	2	1	H
Neophema splendida	2	3	3	2	2	1	H
Ninox connivens	1	3	1–2	1	1	1–2	N*
Tyto capensis	1	3	2–3	2–3	1	1	H
Tyto novaehollandiae	1–2	3	2	1	1	1–2	N*
Amytornis striatus	1	2	2	2	1	2	N
Hylacola cauta	1–2	2	2	2	1	1	N
Pyrrholaemus brunneus	2	2	2	2	1	1	N
Chthonicola sagittata	2	2	2–3	2	1	1	L
Melithreptus gularis	1	3	2	1	1–2	2	L
Grantiella picta	1–2	3	2	1	1–2	1–2	L
Certhionyx variegatus	1–2	3	3	1	1–2	1–2	H
Drymodes brunneopygia	1	2–3	2	2	1–2	2–3	L
Pomatostomus halli	1,3	3	2–3	1	2	1–2	H

Continued

Table 11.2 ***Continued***

	Factors contributing to susceptibility of native species[b]						
Species[a]	**Fox density**	**Body weight**	**Habitat**	**Behaviour**	**Mobility**	**Fecundity**	**Overall risk[c]**
Cinclosoma castanotus	1–2	3	2	2	1	2	L
Pachycephala inornata	1–2	3	2	1–2	1	1	L
Stagonopleura guttata	1–2	2	2–3	2	1–2	1	L
Birds—endangered							
Leipoa ocellata	2	3	2–3	2	1	0	H
Ardeotis australis	1	1	3	2–3	1–2	2	H
Pedionomus torquatus	2	3	3	2	1	1	H
Rostratula benghalensis	2	3	1	2–3	2–3	1	H
Burhinus grallarius	1–2	3	3	3	1–2	2	H
Phaps histrionica	1	3	2–3	1–2	2	2	H
Polytelis anthopeplus	2	3	2–3	1–2	1–2	1	H
Amytornis barbatus	1	2	2–3	2	2	2	L
Manorina melanotis	2	3	2	1–2	2	1	L
Pachycephala rufogularis	2	3	2–3	1–2	1	1–2	H
Reptiles—vulnerable							
Emydura macquarii	2–3	3	2	1–2	1	0	H
Antaresia stimsoni	1–2	2–3	2	2	1	0	N
Aspidites ramsayi	1	0–1	2–3	2	1	0	N
Brachyurophis fasciolata	1–2	3	2–3	3	1	1–2	H
Demansia torquata	1	3	2–3	1	1	1	H
Hoplocephalus bitorquatus	1–2	3	2	1	1	1	L

Ctenotus brooksi	1	2	2–3	1	1	1	L
Lerista xanthura	1–2	2	3	2–3	1	2	H
Tiliqua multifasciata	1	3	2–3	2	1	0–1	H
Tiliqua occipitalis	2	3	2	2	1	0–1	L
Diplodactylus stenodactylus	1	2	2–3	2	1	2	L
Strophurus elderi	1,3	2	2–3	2	1	2	H
Reptiles—endangered							
Echiopsis curta	2	3	2	1–2	1	0–1	L
Pseudonaja modesta	1–2	3	2	1–2	1	0–1	L
Ramphotyphlops endoterus	1	2	3	3	1	1	H
Aprasia inaurita	2	2	2–3	2–3	1	2	H
Delma australis	1–2	2	2–3	2–3	1	2	H
Anomalopus mackayi	1	2	3	2–3	1	1	H
Ctenotus pantherinus	1	2–3	2–3	2	1	1	H
Cyclodomorphus melanops	2	2–3	2–3	1–2	1	1–2	H
Cyclodomorphus venustus	1	2–3	3	1–2	1	1–2	H
Ctenophorus decresii	1	3	3	2	1	1	H
Diplodactylus conspicillatus	1	2	2–3	2	1	2	L

[a]Threatened species are listed as in Table 11.1.

[b]Fox density is ranked from 0 (foxes absent) to 3 (high density) in localities where the threatened species occur using the fox density map of Wilson et al. (1992). Distributional records of the threatened species, and scoring under this category, are as given in Table 11.1. Body weight scores ranged from 0 (for mammals >25,000 g, birds >25,000 g and reptiles >10,000 g) to 3 (for mammals 35–5,500 g, birds 10–9,900 g and reptiles 10–2,500 g). Habitat scores ranged from 0 for species that use very dense ground-level vegetation or habitats that are physically difficult for foxes to access, to 3 for open vegetation where cover is sparse or absent. Behaviour scores ranged from 0 for species that are diurnal; arboreal or volant; and have known anti-predator behaviour to 3 for species that are nocturnal; fossorial, scansorial, semi-aquatic or terrestrial; and have no known anti-predator behaviours. Mobility and Fecundity scores were awarded as in noted in Table 11.1.

[c]Overall risk: N, no risk or negligible risk to cat predation; L, low risk; H, high risk. **Post hoc* risk assessment: see text.

considered predator density and the attributes body weight, habitat use and behaviour to be most likely to predispose native fauna to predator risk, and we used these to assign overall risk values for each of the threatened species on our list. Predator density was expected to be important as higher densities should increase the per capita encounter rate of prey with the predators. Inclusion of body weight follows recognition that predators often take prey within preferred size ranges (Burbidge & McKenzie, 1989; Hayward *et al.*, 2006), while the habitat attribute recognizes that prey should be at more or less risk of predation depending on the complexity of the physical environment and the ability of predators to gain access to it (Dickman, 1992). Behavioural attributes such as the temporal activity of prey, use of terrestrial, below- or above-ground environments and possession of specific anti-predator behaviours were also expected to be important predictors of the vulnerability of prey to predators.

We considered species to be at no risk if they received one or more scores of zero in any of these four categories, at low risk if they received one score of 3 and non-zero scores in all remaining categories, and at high risk if they were awarded two or more scores of 3 for any of the four categories. Risk was defined as the likelihood of predator impact at the level of prey populations. The attributes mobility and fecundity were also scored, but were generally less variable and thus had less power to distinguish susceptibility among species than the other attributes; we used them to help identify species at low risk only. Several species were awarded a range of scores if they met all the specified criteria or if there was uncertainty about where they should be placed. In those cases where there was uncertainty about placement, we adopted the precautionary principle and used the higher score when assigning risk. The rationale and detailed methodology of this approach have been elaborated by Dickman (1996), with examples of its application given by Newsome *et al.*, (1997) and Mahon (2001).

In total, 80 species of vertebrates listed as threatened in the schedules of the *Threatened Species Conservation Act 1995* are resident in the Western Division; 16 species are mammals, 41 are birds and 23 are reptiles. Few threatened amphibians occur in the region, and were not considered further. The rank-scoring system identified 11 of the 16 species of mammals (69%) as being at high risk of cat predation, and 25 species of birds (61%) and 17 species of reptiles (74%) as being at low to high risk (Table 11.1). Vulnerable and endangered mammals were at equal risk of cat predation, whereas risks appeared greater for endangered than vulnerable birds (70% versus 58%, respectively) and for endangered than vulnerable reptiles (91% versus 58%, respectively). Our assessments of risk accorded with those of other workers for the few native species that have been studied (see Dickman, 1996 for summary), suggesting that the scoring system is robust.

Native vertebrates appeared likely to be even more susceptible to predation by the red fox. Fourteen of the 16 species of mammals (88%) were identified as being at low or high risk, as were 30 of the 41 species of birds (73%) and 21 of 23 species of reptiles (91%) (Table 11.2). Except for the western pygmy-possum, *Cercartetus concinnus*, all endangered species of vertebrates were identified as being at some risk of fox predation. The increase in the number of native species susceptible to fox predation arises from the generally higher density of foxes in the Western Division (Wilson *et al.*, 1992), the ability of foxes to tackle larger-bodied prey, and their abilities to dig animals from their burrows and to hunt in shallow water for riparian prey (e.g. Macquarie tortoise, *Emydura macquarii*). In reviewing species' susceptibility to fox predation, we carried out *post hoc* amendments of risk assessment for four species (Table 11.2). Thus, the rock-wallabies, *Petrogale penicillata* and *Petrogale xanthopus*, were considered to be at high risk of fox predation in view of experimental evidence that ecologically similar species are strongly depressed in the presence of the predator (Kinnear *et al.*, 2002). Conversely, we considered the owls *Ninox connivens* and *Tyto novaehollandiae* to be at no risk of fox predation, rather than low risk, owing to their above-ground roosting habits. Other birds, such as the honeyeaters *Grantiella picta* and *Melithreptus gularis*, also spend most of their time foraging and roosting above ground, but were still considered to be at low risk of fox predation if they use low shrubs or come to the ground occasionally (Ford *et al.*, 2001).

In combination, the two species of predators appear likely to pose some degree of risk to all threatened species of native mammals in the Western Division, 33 of the 41 listed species of birds, and 21 of the 23 listed species of reptiles (Tables 11.1 and 11.2). Only some species of owls, raptors, waterfowl and large snakes may be secure from the predator threat. If populations of foxes and cats were effectively suppressed by the reintroduction of the dingo, up to 70 threatened native species therefore could be expected to benefit. The most positive effects could be expected for species with high scores in several attribute categories or with large parts of their ranges in western New South Wales. In addition, up to 21 species that have become locally extinct in western New South Wales could be successfully reintroduced if fox and cat activity were suppressed (Dickman *et al.*, 1993; Smith *et al.*, 1994); five species have already become established in predator-free conditions at Scotia Reserve in the state's south-west (Finlayson *et al.*, 2008). Conversely, four or five large-bodied species that still persist in the Western Division, such as the southern hairy-nosed wombat, *Lasiorhinus latifrons*, may be eaten by dingoes if this canid were reintroduced. However, all of these large-bodied species occurred sympatrically with dingoes prior to European settlement, and it is unlikely that any impact of dingoes on them would exceed that of foxes and cats under present conditions.

We conclude that the reintroduction of the dingo to the conservation wastelands of western New South Wales would have positive effects for most of the threatened vertebrates that currently occur there, and would improve conditions for restoring many others that have become locally extinct.

Reintroducing the dingo

Whatever its merits from the perspective of biodiversity conservation, any proposal to reintroduce dingoes to western New South Wales would face not just opposition, but also a firestorm of controversy (see Coman & Jones, 2007 for comments about proposals to reintroduce dingoes to parts of Victoria). This is entirely understandable: reintroduced dingoes would attack livestock and cause considerable hardship for pastoralists, and they are generally hated with a passion in country areas of Australia. It is also mandatory for land holders in western New South Wales to kill wild dogs (including dingoes) on their property under both the *Wild Dog Destruction Act 1921* and under the pest-control provisions of the *Rural Lands Protection Act 1998* (Davis, 2001). In the face of such challenges, how might a dingo reintroduction proceed in the Western Division? We suggest below a series of steps that should be taken.

Step 1: Quantify benefits to biodiversity

Although we have identified some 70 extant but threatened species of vertebrates that should benefit from the reintroduction of dingoes, experimental studies are needed to measure the magnitude of their responses. These studies should monitor the responses of other components of the system not considered here, such as populations of invertebrates and plants, as well as ecological processes and ecosystem services. In the first instance, experiments could be run most easily in national parks, such as Sturt National Park in the north-western corner of New South Wales, and on privately owned conservation reserves. Research by Graeme Finlayson and colleagues at Scotia Reserve, which is owned and run by the Australian Wildlife Conservancy, provides an excellent example of the ecosystem benefits that can be expected when foxes and cats are removed (Vieira *et al.*, 2007; Finlayson *et al.*, 2008). Such benefits need to be demonstrable and substantial if calls for dingo reintroduction are to proceed further.

Step 2: Protect flocks and farm incomes

Livestock herds are run successfully in many parts of the world in the presence of top-order predators. Several methods are employed to make this possible but, with a few exceptions (e.g. O'Neill, 2002), these approaches have yet to be explored in Australia's rangelands. Such methods include the placement of guard animals among flocks (e.g. Braithwait, 1996; Green & Woodruff, 1999), deployment of frightening devices (e.g. VerCauteren *et al.*, 2003), aversive conditioning (e.g. Burns, 1983), and even translocation of "rogue" individuals (Bradley *et al.*, 2005). Use of guard animals is the most widely used of these stock-protection methods, with alpacas or livestock guarding–dogs such as the maremma or Anatolian shepherd appearing to be cost-effective in the Australian environment (Jenkins, 2003), even in areas where flocks are dispersed. In addition to stock protection, compensation schemes have been set up in the United States to shift the financial burden of stock losses from producers to those who support predator reintroductions. The Defenders of Wildlife, set up in 1947 and funded by private donations, provides an excellent example of how such programmes work (Wagner *et al.*, 1997). As sheep and goats are more susceptible to dingo attack than cattle, consideration should also be given to moving towards cattle-based enterprises. Although switching involves initial capital and other costs, productivity may increase in the longer term (Fleming *et al.*, 2001). Finally, compelling arguments have been raised to commercialize native herbivores, especially kangaroos, and thus to shift the view under which these animals are regarded as pests to one where they can be made use of as resources (Grigg, 1988, 2002; Pickard, 1988; Archer, 2002). Detailed analyses by Grigg (2002) confirm the cost-effectiveness of such a move.

Step 3: Engage the community

Steps 1 and 2 will be feasible only if both the proponents of dingo reintroduction and the statutory authorities involved in reintroduction programmes are engaged at all times with land holders in western New South Wales. Without incorporation of community attitudes and concerns, any broad-scale attempt to reintroduce dingoes would face disruption and would almost certainly fail. Who should drive the engagement process? If dingoes were listed as a threatened species in New South Wales (at least two submissions have been made to list the dingo as a vulnerable species under the *Threatened Species Conservation Act 1995*; Dickman & Lunney, 2001), community involvement would become part of the recovery planning process undertaken as a statutory responsibility by the New South Wales Department of Environment and Climate Change. If dingoes remain unlisted, engagement would need to be undertaken by non-government groups such as dingo conservation associations or private conservation organizations. There would also need to be active collaboration with the research community.

Step 4: Change legislation

As land holders are obligated to kill dingoes on their properties under the *Wild Dog Destruction Act 1921* and the *Rural Lands Protection Act 1998*, legislative amendments or repeals will be necessary. In the case of the latter Act, at least, the Minister for Agriculture has the power to specify areas over which dingo control must take place and areas that may be exempt; thus, with ministerial approval, it should be possible to demarcate areas such as Sturt National Park where dingo reintroductions could legally take place. The consequences of listing the dingo as a vulnerable species under the *Threatened Species Conservation Act 1995* would set up an intriguing legislative conundrum about whether to kill or to conserve.

Conclusions

Recent studies in the United States suggest that government-subsidized control of predators there has failed to prevent a long-term decline in the sheep industry (Berger, 2006). It is likely that a similar situation prevails in the sheep rangelands of Australia, where historical over-grazing and the imposition of inappropriate farming practices have driven shifts from productive land to wasteland over vast areas (Grigg, 1988, 2002). In addition to exploring the benefits of reintroducing dingoes to these areas, we therefore advocate tallying the costs of not doing so. Here, we have emphasized the costs of losing more native species if current land management continues in the rangelands. However, if we do insist on continuing "business as usual", we must factor in the catastrophic costs in future of the loss of ecological processes and ecosystem function owing to more over-grazing, the further spread of noxious weeds, the continuing overuse of poisons to reduce impacts of pests, and ongoing loss and salinization of the soil that remains. If returning dingoes to the system can help to alleviate these costs, then we cannot afford to delay reintroductions any longer.

Acknowledgements

We thank Matt Hayward for the invitation to prepare this chapter, and Carol McKechnie, Gus Bernardi, Matt Hayward and two referees for critical comments. C.R. Dickman receives project funding from the Australian Research Council, A.S. Glen is supported by an Invasive Animals CRC Postdoctoral Fellowship, and M. Letnic is supported by an Australian Research Council Postdoctoral Fellowship.

References

Allen, L.R. & Fleming, P.J.S. (2004) Review of canid management in Australia for the protection of livestock and wildlife—Potential application to coyote management. *Sheep and Goat Research Journal* 19, 97–104.

Allen, L.R. & Gonzalez, T. (1998) Baiting reduces dingo numbers, changes age structures yet often increases calf losses. *Australian Vertebrate Pest Control Conference* 11, 421–428.

Anon (1952) Annual report on the operations of "The Stock Routes and Rural Lands Protection Acts, 1944–1951" for the year 1951–52. *Queensland Parliamentary Papers* 1951–1952.

Archer, M. (2002) Confronting crises in conservation: A talk on the wild side. *A Zoological Revolution: Using Native Fauna to Assist in its own Survival.* (eds D. Lunney

& C.R. Dickman), pp. 12–52. Royal Zoological Society of New South Wales, Sydney, and Australian Museum, Sydney.

Armstrong, R. (2004) Baiting operations: Western Shield review—February 2003. *Conservation Science Western Australia* 5, 31–50.

Ayers, D., Nash, S. & Baggett, K. (1996) *Threatened Species of Western New South Wales.* NSW National Parks and Wildlife Service, Sydney.

Baillie, J.E.M., Hilton-Taylor, C. & Stuart, S.N. (eds) (2004) *2004 IUCN Red List of Threatened Species: A Global Assessment.* IUCN, Gland, Switzerland.

Bangs, E.E., Fritts, S.H., Fontaine, J. et al. (1998) Status of gray wolf restoration in Montana, Idaho, and Wyoming. *Wildlife Society Bulletin* 26, 785–798.

Berger, K.M. (2006) Carnivore-livestock conflicts: Effects of subsidized predator control and economic correlates on the sheep industry. *Conservation Biology* 20, 751–761.

Berger, K.M. & Gese, E.M. (2007) Does interference competition with wolves limit the distribution and abundance of coyotes? *Journal of Animal Ecology* 76, 1075–1085.

Beschta, R.L. (2003) Cottonwoods, elk, and wolves in the Lamar Valley of Yellowstone National Park. *Ecological Applications* 13, 1295–1309.

Beyer, H.L., Merrill, E.H., Varley, N. & Boyce, M.S. (2007) Willow on Yellowstone's northern range: Evidence for a trophic cascade? *Ecological Applications* 17, 1563–1571.

Bradley, E.H., Pletscher, D.H., Bangs, E.E. et al. (2005) Evaluating wolf translocation as a nonlethal method to reduce livestock conflicts in the northwestern United States. *Conservation Biology* 19, 1498–1508.

Braithwait, J. (1996) *Using Guard Animals to Protect Livestock.* Conservation Commission of the State of Missouri, Jefferson City.

Breckwoldt, R. (1988) *A Very Elegant Animal: The Dingo.* Angus and Robertson, Sydney.

Burbidge, A.A. & McKenzie, N.L. (1989) Patterns in the modern decline of Western Australia's vertebrate fauna: Causes and conservation implications. *Biological Conservation* 50, 143–198.

Bureau of Meteorology, (1988) *Climatic Averages Australia.* Australian Government Publishing Service, Canberra.

Burney, D.A. & Flannery, T.F. (2005) Fifty millennia of catastrophic extinctions after human contact. *Trends in Ecology and Evolution* 20, 395–401.

Burns, R.J. (1983) Coyote predation aversion with lithium chloride: Management implications and comments. *Wildlife Society Bulletin* 11, 128–132.

Burrows, N.D., Algar, D., Robinson, A.D., Sinagra, J., Ward, B. & Liddelow, G. (2003) Controlling introduced predators in the Gibson Desert of Western Australia. *Journal of Arid Environments* 55, 691–713.

Cardillo, M., Purvis, A., Sechrest, W., Gittleman, J.L., Bielby, J. & Mace, G.M. (2004) Human population density and extinction risk in the world's carnivores. *PLoS Biology* 2, 909–914.

Caro, T. (2007) The Pleistocene re-wilding gambit. *Trends in Ecology and Evolution* 22, 281–283.

Cathles, H. (2001) A landholder perspective. *A Symposium on the Dingo*. (eds C.R. Dickman & D. Lunney), pp. 75–83. Royal Zoological Society of New South Wales, Sydney.

Caughley, G., Grigg, G.C., Caughley, J. & Hill, G.J.E. (1980) Does dingo predation control the densities of kangaroos and emus? *Australian Wildlife Research* 7, 1–12.

Caughley, G., Shepherd, N. & Short, J. (eds) (1987) *Kangaroos: Their Ecology and Management in the Sheep Rangelands of Australia*. Cambridge University Press, Cambridge.

Coman, B.J. & Jones, E. (2007) The loaded dog. *Quadrant* 51(11), 10–15.

Corbett, L. (1995) *The Dingo in Australia and Asia.* University of New South Wales Press, Sydney.

Corbett, L. (2001) The conservation status of the dingo *Canis lupus dingo* in Australia, with particular reference to New South Wales: Threats to pure dingoes and potential solutions. *A Symposium on the Dingo.* (eds C.R. Dickman & D. Lunney), pp. 10–19. Royal Zoological Society of New South Wales, Sydney.

Corbett, L.K. & Newsome, A.E. (1987) The feeding ecology of the dingo. III. Dietary relationships with widely fluctuating prey populations in arid Australia: An hypothesis of alternation of predation. *Oecologia* 74, 215–227.

Crabb, P. (2004) The Darling Basin: Coping with the pressures of change? *The Darling*. (eds R. Breckwoldt, R. Boden & J. Andrew), pp. 408–433. Murray-Darling Basin Commission, Canberra.

Crooks, K.R. & Soulé, M.E. (1999) Mesopredator release and avifaunal extinctions in a fragmented system. *Nature* 400, 563–566.

Davis, E. (2001) Legislative issues relating to control of dingoes and other wild dogs in New South Wales. I. Approaches to future management. *A Symposium on the Dingo.* (eds C. R. Dickman & D. Lunney), pp. 39–41. Royal Zoological Society of New South Wales, Sydney.

Denny, M. (1992) *Historical and Ecological Study of the Effects of European Settlement on Inland NSW.* Nature Conservation Council of New South Wales, Sydney.

Dickman, C.R. (1992) Predation and habitat shift in the house mouse, *Mus domesticus. Ecology* 73, 313–322.

Dickman, C.R. (1996) *Overview of the Impacts of Feral Cats on Australian Native Fauna*. Australian Nature Conservation Agency, Canberra.

Dickman, C.R. & Lunney, D. (2001) Last howl of the dingo: The legislative, ecological and practical issues arising from the kill-or-conserve dilemma. *A Symposium on the Dingo.* (eds C. R. Dickman & D. Lunney), pp. 95–107. Royal Zoological Society of New South Wales, Sydney.

Dickman, C.R., Glen, A.S., Mackey, B., Holden, C. & Soulé, M.E. (2006) Review of the Dingo Trophic Regulation Workshop, National Wine Centre, Adelaide, Australia, 13–14 October 2005. *Ecological Management and Restoration* 7, 162–163.

Dickman, C.R., Pressey, R.L., Lim, L. & Parnaby, H.E. (1993) Mammals of particular conservation concern in the Western Division of New South Wales. *Biological Conservation* 65, 219–248.

Dickman, C.R., Whish, G.L. & Pressey, R.L. (2002) Mammals of particular conservation concern in the Western Division of New South Wales: Distributions, habitats and threats. *New South Wales National Parks and Wildlife Service Occasional Paper* 22, 1–60.

Donlan, J., Greene, H.W., Berger, J. et al. (2005) Re-wilding North America. *Nature* 436, 913–914.

Ellis, M., Drielsma, M., Mazzer, L. & Baigent, E. (2007) Clearing, grazing and reservation: Assessing regional impacts of vegetation management on the fauna of south western New South Wales. *Animals of Arid Australia: Out on their Own?* (eds C. R. Dickman, D. Lunney & S. Burgin), pp. 102–131. Royal Zoological Society of New South Wales, Sydney.

Finlayson, G.R., Vieira, E.M., Priddel, D, Wheeler, R. & Dickman, C.R. (2008) Multiscale patterns of habitat use by re-introduced mammals: A case study using medium-sized marsupials. *Biological Conservation* 141, 320–331.

Fisher, D.O., Blomberg, S.O. & Owens, I.P.F. (2003) Extrinsic vs intrinsic factors in the decline and extinction of Australian marsupials. *Proceedings of the Royal Society of London, B* 270, 1801–1808.

Fleming, P., Corbett, L., Harden, R. & Thomson, P. (2001) *Managing the Impacts of Dingoes and other Wild Dogs.* Bureau of Rural Sciences, Canberra.

Ford, H.A., Barrett, G.W., Saunders, D.A. & Recher, H.F. (2001) Why have birds in the woodlands of southern Australia declined? *Biological Conservation* 97, 71–88.

Forester, J.D., Ives, A.R., Turner, M.G. et al. (2007) State-space models link elk movement patterns to landscape characteristics in Yellowstone National Park. *Ecological Monographs* 77, 285–299.

Fortin, D., Beyer, H.L., Boyce, M.S., Smith, D.W., Duchesne, T. & Mao, J.S. (2005) Wolves influence elk movements: Behaviour shapes a trophic cascade in Yellowstone National Park. *Ecology* 86, 1320–1330.

Garrott, R.A., Bruggeman, J.E., Becker, M.S., Kalinowski, S.T. & White, J.P. (2007) Evaluating prey switching in wolf-ungulate systems. *Ecological Applications* 17, 1588–1597.

Gentle, M.N., Saunders, G.R. & Dickman, C.R. (2007) Poisoning for production: How effective is fox baiting in south-eastern Australia? *Mammal Review* 37, 177–190.

Glen, A.S. & Dickman, C.R. (2005) Complex interactions among mammalian carnivores in Australia, and their implications for wildlife management. *Biological Reviews* 80, 387–401.

Glen, A.S. & Dickman, C.R. (2008) Niche overlap between marsupial and eutherian carnivores: Does competition threaten the endangered spotted-tailed quoll? *Journal of Applied Ecology* 45, 700–707.

Glen, A.S. & Short, J. (2000) The control of dingoes in New South Wales in the period 1883–1930 and its likely impact on their distribution and abundance. *Australian Zoologist* 31, 432–442.

Glen, A.S., Dickman, C.R., Soulé, M.E. & Mackey, B.G. (2007) Evaluating the role of the dingo as a trophic regulator in Australian ecosystems. *Austral Ecology* 32, 492–501.

Glen, A.S., Fay, A.R. & Dickman, C.R. (2006) Diets of sympatric red foxes *Vulpes vulpes* and wild dogs *Canis lupus* in the Northern Rivers district, New South Wales. *Australian Mammalogy* 28, 101–104.

Green, J.S. & Woodruff, R.A. (1999) Livestock guarding dogs: Protecting sheep from predators. *USDA Agriculture Information Bulletin* 588, 1–32.

Grigg, G. (1988) Kangaroo harvesting and the conservation of the sheep rangelands. *Australian Zoologist* 24, 124–128.

Grigg, G. (2002) Conservation benefit from harvesting kangaroos: Status report at the start of a new millennium. A paper to stimulate discussion and research. *A Zoological Revolution: Using Native Fauna to Assist in its own Survival.* (eds D. Lunney & C.R. Dickman), pp. 53–76. Royal Zoological Society of New South Wales, Sydney, and Australian Museum, Sydney.

Harrison, D.J., Bissonette, J.A. & Sherburne, J.A. (1989) Spatial relationships between coyotes and red foxes in eastern Maine, USA. *Journal of Wildlife Management* 53, 181–185.

Hayward, M.W., Henschel, P., O'Brien, J. et al. (2006) Prey preferences of the leopard (*Panthera pardus*). *Journal of Zoology, London* 270, 298–313.

Hebblewhite, M., White, C.A., Nietvelt, C.G. et al. (2005) Human activity mediates a trophic cascade caused by wolves. *Ecology* 86, 2135–2144.

Jenkins, D.J. (2003) *Guard Animals for Livestock Protection: Existing and Potential Use in Australia.* NSW Agriculture, Orange.

Johnson, C. (2006) *Australia's Mammal Extinctions: A 50,000 Year History.* Cambridge University Press, Cambridge.

Johnson, C.N. & Wroe, S. (2003) Causes of extinction of vertebrates during the Holocene of mainland Australia: Arrival of the dingo, or human impact? *The Holocene* 13, 941–948.

Johnson, C.N., Isaac, J.L. & Fisher, D.O. (2007) Rarity of a top predator triggers continent-wide collapse of mammal prey: Dingoes and marsupials in Australia. *Proceedings of the Royal Society of London, B* 274, 341–346.

Kerle, J.A., Fleming, M.R. & Foulkes, J.N. (2007) Managing biodiversity in arid Australia: A landscape view. *Animals of Arid Australia: Out on their Own?* (eds C.R. Dickman, D. Lunney & S. Burgin), pp. 42–64. Royal Zoological Society of New South Wales, Sydney.

Kinnear, J.E., Sumner, N.R. & Onus, M.L. (2002) The red fox in Australia—An exotic predator turned biocontrol agent. *Biological Conservation* 108, 335–359.

Krebs, C.J., Boutin, S. & Boonstra, R. (eds) (2001) *Ecosystem Dynamics of the Boreal Forest: The Kluane Project.* Oxford University Press, New York.

Letnic, M. (2000) Dispossession, degradation and extinction: Environmental history in arid Australia. *Biodiversity and Conservation* 9, 295–308.

Letnic, M. (2007) The impacts of pastoralism on the fauna of arid Australia. *Animals of Arid Australia: Out on their Own?* (eds C.R. Dickman, D. Lunney & S. Burgin), pp. 65–75. Royal Zoological Society of New South Wales, Sydney.

Luke, R.H. & McArthur, A.G. (1978) *Bushfires in Australia.* Australian Government Publishing Service, Canberra.

Lunney, D. (2001) Causes of the extinction of native mammals of the Western Division of New South Wales: An ecological interpretation of the nineteenth century historical record. *The Rangeland Journal* 23, 44–70.

Lunney, D., Curtin, A.L., Ayers, D. et al. (2000). The threatened and non-threatened native vertebrate fauna of New South Wales: Status and ecological attributes. *New South Wales National Parks and Wildlife Service Environmental and Heritage Monograph* Series No. 4, 1–134.

Mahon, P.S. (2001) *Threat Abatement Plan for Predation by the Red Fox* (Vulpes vulpes). New South Wales National Parks and Wildlife Service, Sydney.

Marsack, P. & Campbell, G. (1990) Feeding behaviour and diet of dingoes in the Nullarbor region, Western Australia. *Australian Wildlife Research* 17, 349–357.

Martin, P.S. (2005) *Twilight of the Mammoths: Ice Age Extinctions and the Rewilding of America.* University of California Press, Berkeley.

McIlroy, J.C., Cooper, R.J., Gifford, E.J., Green, B.F. & Newgrain, K.W. (1986) The effect on wild dogs, *Canis f. familiaris*, of 1080-poisoning campaigns in Kosciusko National Park, N.S.W. *Australian Wildlife Research* 13, 535–544.

McLaren, B.E. & Peterson, R.O. (1994) Wolves, moose and tree rings on Isle Royale. *Science* 266, 1555–1558.

Mitchell, B.D. & Banks, P.B. (2005) Do wild dogs exclude foxes? Evidence for competition from dietary and spatial overlaps. *Austral Ecology* 30, 581–591.

Morin, P.J. (1999) *Community Ecology.* Blackwell Science, Oxford.

Newsome, A.E., Catling, P.C., Cooke, B.D. & Smyth, R. (2001) Two ecological universes separated by the dingo fence in semi-arid Australia: Interactions between landscapes, herbivory and carnivory, with and without dingoes. *The Rangeland Journal* 23, 71–98.

Newsome, A.E., Pech, R., Smyth, R., Banks, P. & Dickman, C.R. (1997) *Potential Impacts on Australian Native Fauna of Rabbit Calicivirus Disease*. Environment Australia, Canberra.

O'Neill, A. (2002) *Living with the Dingo*. Envirobook, Annandale, Sydney.

Paddle, R. (2000) *The Last Tasmanian Tiger: The History and Extinction of the Thylacine.* Cambridge University Press, Cambridge.

Paltridge, R. (2002) The diets of cats, foxes and dingoes in relation to prey availability in the Tanami Desert, Northern Territory. *Wildlife Research* 29, 389–403.

Pettigrew, J.D. (1993) A burst of feral cats in the Diamantina: A lesson for the management of pest species? *Cat Management Workshop Proceedings.* (eds G. Siepen & C. Owens), pp. 25–32. Queensland Department of Environment and Heritage, Brisbane.

Pickard, J. (1988) Kangaroos on western lands leases: The Western Lands Commission view. *Australian Zoologist* 24, 151–153.

Polis, G.A., Sears, A.L.W., Huxel, G.R., Strong, D.R. & Maron, J. (2000) When is a trophic cascade a trophic cascade? *Trends in Ecology and Evolution* 15, 473–475.

Pople, A.R., Grigg, G.C., Cairns, S.C., Beard, L.A. & Alexander, P. (2000) Trends in numbers of kangaroos and emus on either side of the South Australian dingo fence: Evidence for predator regulation. *Wildlife Research* 27, 269–276.

Pressey, B., Whish, G. & Wall, S. (2004) Conservation of terrestrial environments in the Darling River Basin. *The Darling.* (eds R. Breckwoldt, R. Boden & J. Andrew), pp. 373–405. Murray-Darling Basin Commission, Canberra.

Ray, J.C., Redford, K.H., Steneck, R.S. & Berger, J. (editors). (2005) *Large Carnivores and the Conservation of Biodiversity*. Island Press, Washington, DC.

Ripple, W.J. & Beschta, R.L. (2007a) Restoring Yellowstone's aspen with wolves. *Biological Conservation* 138, 514–519.

Ripple, W.J. & Beschta, R.L. (2007b) Hardwood tree decline following large carnivore loss on the Great Plains, USA. *Frontiers in Ecology and the Environment* 5, 241–246.

Sadlier, R. A. & Pressey, R.L. (1994) Reptiles and amphibians of particular conservation concern in the Western Division of New South Wales: A preliminary review. *Biological Conservation* 69, 41–54.

Saunders, G. & McLeod, L. (2007) *Improving Fox Management Strategies in Australia.* Bureau of Rural Sciences, Canberra.

Saunders, G., Lane, C., Harris, S. & Dickman, C.R. (2006) *Foxes in Tasmania: A Report of an Incursion by an Invasive Species.* Invasive Animals Cooperative Research Centre, Canberra.

Schmitz, O.J., Beckerman, A.P. & O'Brien, K.M. (1997) Behaviorally mediated trophic cascades: Effects of predation risk on food web interactions. *Ecology* 78, 1388–1399.

Schmitz, O.J., Hambäck, P.A. & Beckerman, A.P. (2000) Trophic cascades in terrestrial systems: A review of the effects of carnivore removals on plants. *American Naturalist* 155, 141–153.

Sergio, F., Newton, I., Marchesi, L. & Pedrini, P. (2006) Ecologically justified charisma: Preservation of top predators delivers biodiversity conservation. *Journal of Applied Ecology* 43, 1049–1055.

Sinclair, A.R.E., Krebs, C.J., Fryxell, J.M. et al. (2000) Testing hypotheses of trophic level interactions: A boreal forest ecosystem. *Oikos* 89, 313–328.

Smith, A.P. & Quin, D.G. (1996) Patterns and causes of extinction and decline in Australian conilurine rodents. *Biological Conservation* 77, 243–267.

Smith, P.J., Pressey, R.L. & Smith, J.E. (1994) Birds of particular conservation concern in the Western Division of New South Wales. *Biological Conservation* 69, 315–338.

Soulé, M.E., Bolger, D.T., Alberts, A.C. et al. (1988) Reconstructed dynamics of rapid extinctions of chaparral-requiring birds in urban habitat islands. *Conservation Biology* 2, 75–92.

Soulé, M.E., Estes, J.A., Berger, J. & Martinez del Rio, C.M. (2003) Ecological effectiveness: Conservation goals for interactive species. *Conservation Biology* 17, 1238–1250.

Southgate, R., Paltridge, R., Masters, P. & Carthew, S. (2007) Bilby distribution and fire: A test of alternative models of habitat suitability in the Tanami Desert, Australia. *Ecography* 30, 759–776.

Switalski, T.A. (2003) Coyote foraging ecology and vigilance in response to gray wolf reintroduction in Yellowstone National Park. *Canadian Journal of Zoology* 81, 985–993.

Thomson, P.C. (1984) Dingoes and sheep in pastoral areas. *Journal of Agriculture, Western Australia* 25, 27–31.

Thomson, P.C. (1992a) The behavioural ecology of dingoes in north-western Australia. III. Hunting and feeding behaviour, and diet. *Wildlife Research* 19, 531–541.

Thomson, P.C. (1992b) The behavioural ecology of dingoes in north-western Australia. IV. Social and spatial organisation, and movements. *Wildlife Research* 19, 543–563.

Thomson, P.C. & Marsack, P.R. (1992) Aerial baiting of dingoes in arid pastoral areas with reference to rabies control. *Wildlife Rabies Contingency Planning in Australia.* (eds P. O'Brien & G. Berry), pp. 125–134. Australian Government Publishing Service, Canberra.

Triggs, B., Brunner, H. & Cullen, J.M. (1984) The food of fox, dog and cat in Croajingalong National Park, south-eastern Victoria. *Australian Wildlife Research* 11, 491–499.

VerCauteren, K.C., LaVelle, M.J. & Moyles, S. (2003) Coyote-activated frightening devices for reducing sheep predation on open range. *Proceedings of the 10th Wildlife Damage Management Conference.* (eds K. A. Fagerstone & G. W. Witmer), pp. 146–151.Wildlife Damage Management Working Group of the Wildlife Society, Fort Collins.

Vieira, E.M, Finlayson, G.R. & Dickman, C.R. (2007) Habitat use and density of numbats (*Myrmecobius fasciatus*) reintroduced in an area of mallee vegetation, New South Wales. *Australian Mammalogy* 29, 17–24.

Wagner, K.K., Schmidt, R.H. & Conover, M.R. (1997) Compensation programs for wildlife damage in North America. *Wildlife Society Bulletin* 25, 312–319.

Wilmers, C.C. & Getz, W.M. (2005) Gray wolves as climate change buffers in Yellowstone. *PLoS Biology* 3, 571–576.

Wilson, G., Dexter, N., O'Brien, P. & Bomford, M. (1992) *Pest Animals in Australia: A Survey of Introduced Wild Mammals*. Kenthurst Press, Sydney.

Wilson, N. (2001) *A Dogger's Life*. Aussie Outback Publishing, Junortoun, Victoria.

Wolf, E. C., Cooper, D.J. & Hobbs, N.T. (2007) Hydrologic regime and herbivory stabilize an alternative state in Yellowstone National Park. *Ecological Applications* 17, 1572–1587.

Wroe, S., Field, J., Fullagar, R. & Jermiin, L.S. (2004) Megafaunal extinction in the late Quaternary and the global overkill hypothesis. *Alcheringa* 28, 291–331.

Wroe, S., Field, J. & Grayson, D.K. (2006) Megafaunal extinction: Climate, humans and assumptions. *Trends in Ecology and Evolution* 21, 61–62.

12

The Role of Social Behaviour in Carnivore Reintroductions

Michael J. Somers[1] *and Markus Gusset*[2]

[1]Centre for Wildlife Management, Centre for Invasion Biology, University of Pretoria
[2]Wildlife Conservation Research Unit, Department of Zoology, University of Oxford

Summary

Reintroductions are becoming increasingly important in conservation management, particularly for large carnivores. Despite an increase in our understanding of carnivore social behaviour, wildlife managers often disregard this knowledge when reintroducing animals—largely owing to behavioural ecology and reintroduction biology rarely being unified in the literature or in graduate conservation management programmes. Here, we combine these two disciplines and outline the importance of considering aspects of social behaviour when reintroducing large carnivores. We identify two time periods of particular relevance: the time in temporary captivity before release and the period immediately after release. Prior to release, group composition of the animals to be released is important to promote social compatibility. After release, Allee effects arising from difficulty in finding suitable mates emerge as one of the most important constraints in some large-carnivore reintroduction programmes. In our view, incorporating considerations of social behaviour in conservation management would increase the efficiency and effectiveness of costly (carnivore) reintroduction programmes.

Reintroduction of Top-Order Predators, 1st edition. Edited by M.W. Hayward and M.J. Somers.
 ISBN 978-1-4051-7680-4 (pb) and 978-1-4051-9273-6 (hb)

Introduction

Reintroductions are becoming increasingly important in conservation management, particularly for large carnivores (Reading & Clark, 1996; Breitenmoser *et al.*, 2001; Hayward & Somers, this volume). There has also been a series of recent works on bridging the gap between behavioural research and conservation management (Caro & Durant, 1995; Curio, 1996; Clemmons & Buchholz, 1997; Caro, 1998, 1999, 2007; Martin, 1998; Sutherland, 1998; Anthony & Blumstein, 2000; Gosling & Sutherland, 2000; Festa-Bianchet & Apollonio, 2003; Blumstein & Fernández-Juricic, 2004; Linklater, 2004; Buchholz, 2007; Angeloni *et al.*, 2008). Although the ultimate aims of conservation biology and behavioural ecology are converging, as proponents of both disciplines share the common interest of conserving wildlife (Martin, 1998), the end products do not show this yet (Angeloni *et al.*, 2008). Despite an increase in our understanding of social behaviour, wildlife managers often disregard this knowledge when reintroducing animals. The difference in perspective and approach persists as a mismatch between conservation needs and research practice in behavioural ecology (Caro, 2007). This mismatch perhaps stems from behavioural ecologists having historically focused on basic research, and on ultimate rather than proximate questions, while conservation biologists have focused mostly on applied questions (Linklater, 2004).

Reintroductions have generally proved to be problematic and prone to failure for a multitude of biological and non-biological reasons (i.e. technical, organizational, valuational and even legal) (Fischer & Lindenmayer, 2000). Considering these challenges, would a better understanding of the role of social behaviour promote reintroduction success? This question has received surprisingly little attention to date (but see Kleiman, 1989). Here, we discuss some of the aspects that are of particular importance when reintroducing large carnivores from a social behaviour perspective.

State of knowledge

We conducted a literature search using a database comprising 14,071 papers published on carnivores between 1972 and 2008 (available from http://www.carnivoreconservation.org). We used the search string ("social behaviour" or "social behavior") and ("reintroduction" or "re-introduction" or "translocation"). We received one result only (Schröpfer & Rohde, 1997), indicating that carnivore behavioural ecology and reintroduction biology have rarely been unified in the literature. Similarly, social behaviour often does not feature prominently in graduate conservation management programmes (van Heezik & Seddon, 2005). However, there has been considerable progress in our understanding of carnivore social behaviour over the past four decades. In addition, reintroduction efforts are being increasingly monitored and evaluated (e.g. Hayward *et al.*, 2007b; Gusset *et al.*, 2008a). We thus set out to identify stages of relevance to improve reintroduction programmes for large carnivores with knowledge from social behaviour.

Stages of relevance

The success of any reintroduction attempt depends on two factors, namely establishing and maintaining a population in the release area (Gusset, this volume). For social species, this suggests that founder group composition is likely to determine establishment success, whereas persistence is likely to depend on the formation of new groups to maintain the population's reproductive capacity. Accordingly, we have identified two time periods of particular importance for applying aspects of social behaviour to large-carnivore reintroductions: the time in temporary captivity before release and the period immediately after release.

Pre-release stage

Maintaining animals in a pre-release enclosure for a period of time has been shown to increase reintroduction success in various species (Fischer & Lindenmayer, 2000). This is termed a "soft release". For carnivores in general, the underlying rationale is to familiarize the animals with the release area and to break homing tendencies (Linnell *et al.*, 1997; Miller *et al.*, 1999). There are numerous examples of translocated carnivores returning to the site of capture (Linnell *et al.*, 1997), a problem related to post-release ranging behaviour (see below) that could be partly overcome by keeping animals in a temporary holding facility before release. This was successfully applied when reintroducing felids (Hunter, 1999), including lions, *Panthera leo* (Hunter *et al.*, 2007;

Trinkel *et al.*, 2008; Slotow & Hunter, this volume); canids (Moehrenschlager & Somers, 2004), including grey wolves, *Canis lupus* (Fritts *et al.*, 1997; Bradley *et al.*, 2005; Smith & Bangs, this volume) and African wild dogs, *Lycaon pictus* (Gusset *et al.*, 2006, 2008a; Davies-Mostert *et al.*, this volume); and other social large carnivores (Hayward *et al.*, 2007a).

Additional benefits of keeping social animals together before release may be social integration of animals into new groups (Kleiman, 1989) and reduction of stress (Texeira *et al.*, 2007). For wild dogs, Gusset *et al.* (2006, 2008a) showed that packs kept in a temporary holding facility for bonding before release were more likely to remain intact when set free and had higher individual post-release survival rates. The same seems to be true for reintroduced wolves, as ensuring social integration prevented pack break-ups after release and increased site fidelity (Fritts *et al.*, 1997; Bradley *et al.*, 2005). Similarly, lions established enduring social relationships before release, which ultimately facilitated the formation of cohesive social groups (Hayward *et al.*, 2007a; Hunter *et al.*, 2007; Trinkel *et al.*, 2008) (Table 12.1).

Table 12.1 **The importance of social integration and management measures to promote social compatibility before release in large-carnivore reintroductions.**

Species	Social integration and management measures
Importance of social integration	
African wild dog	Packs more likely to remain intact when set free and higher individual post-release survival rates[a,b]
Grey wolf	Preventing pack break-ups after release and increased site fidelity[c,d]
Lion	Establishing enduring social relationships and ultimately facilitating the formation of cohesive social groups[e,f,g]
Management measures to promote social compatibility	
African wild dog	Manipulation of social relationships (e.g. through temporary or permanent separation of individuals[a]) based on behavioural observations

[a]Gusset *et al.*, 2006; [b]Gusset *et al.*, 2008a; [c]Fritts *et al.*, 1997; [d]Bradley *et al.*, 2005; [e]Hayward *et al.*, 2007b; [f]Hunter *et al.*, 2007; [g]Trinkel *et al.*, 2008.

If there is a lack of cohesion in a group before release, possibly as a result of its artificial creation, the animals are unlikely to become successful breeders after release and may display intensified post-release ranging behaviour. Creating the opportunity to exercise mate selection before release could increase the likelihood that successful reproductive units will form (Kleiman, 1989). Behavioural observations on social interactions are a suitable means to determine individual preferences manifested in the form of group compatibility, which allows the composition of socially integrated groups for release via artificial selection. For example, management manipulation of social relationships (e.g. through temporary or permanent separation of individuals) was successfully applied to promote bonding in wild dogs (Gusset *et al.*, 2006) and other canids (Moehrenschlager & Somers, 2004) (Table 12.1). Another form of manipulating social relationships is assisted replacement of resident male coalitions in reintroduced lions (Trinkel *et al.*, 2008; Slotow & Hunter, this volume).

Supplying suitable free-ranging animals for reintroduction that mirror natural group composition may be difficult (e.g. Gusset *et al.*, 2006; Slotow & Hunter, this volume), thus posing the challenge of using suboptimally composed groups and also captive-bred animals. At times, there may be no option but to reintroduce animals bred or raised in captivity (Christie, this volume). Reintroductions using captive-bred carnivores are significantly less likely to succeed than those using wild-caught individuals (Jule *et al.*, 2008); yet origin did not affect post-release survival rates of wild dogs in this study. Interestingly, wide-ranging carnivores are particularly prone to stress in captivity (more stereotypic pacing and higher infant mortality) (Clubb & Mason, 2003), which may exacerbate the problem of reintroducing wide-ranging carnivores (e.g. Vickery & Mason, 2003; see below). This may necessitate innovative approaches to preparing captive animals destined for reintroduction (e.g. through pre-release training; Kleiman, 1989), such as conditioning wolves to avoid humans (Badridze, 1999; also see Marnewick *et al.*, this volume). Considering cultural transmission of socially learned behaviour in reintroduction efforts may be essential (Ryan, 2006). For example, as a result of their lacking survival skills (particularly hunting and anti-predatory skills), wild dogs bred or raised in captivity are preferably used for release when they are bonded with wild-caught animals in a pre-release enclosure first (Gusset *et al.*, 2006).

Post-release stage

Wide-ranging carnivores are particularly prone to anthropogenic edge effects at the outside boundaries of protected areas (Woodroffe & Ginsberg, 1998). This can have important implications for the establishment of reintroduced carnivores in terms of mortalities inflicted by post-release ranging behaviour (e.g. Woodroffe *et al.*, 2007; Gusset *et al.*, 2008b). Ranging behaviour was successfully restricted by perimeter fencing in reintroduced lions (Hunter, 1999; Hunter *et al.*, 2007; Slotow & Hunter, this volume), wild dogs (Gusset *et al.*, 2008a; Davies-Mostert *et al.*, this volume) and other social large carnivores (Hayward *et al.*, 2007a). Therefore, ranging behaviour appears to be an important factor to consider in carnivore reintroductions both pre- and post-release (Linnell *et al.*, 1997; Woodroffe & Ginsberg, 1998; Clubb & Mason, 2003). It seems that wide-ranging carnivores, such as wolves and wild dogs, are indeed particularly difficult to reintroduce successfully (Moehrenschlager & Somers, 2004).

If the suitability of a patch of habitat is elevated by conspecific presence, further individuals will settle preferentially in an occupied patch, irrespective of whether an alternative patch of equal quality exists (Dobson & Poole, 1998). From a reintroduction perspective, conspecific attraction as an important factor influencing habitat selection could be useful as a conservation tool that can be employed to encourage preferential recolonization of a given area and to restrict post-release ranging behaviour. For example, the lack of conspecific cues outside the release area possibly increased site fidelity in reintroduced wolves (Fritts *et al.*, 1997). Providing conspecific cues by acoustic stimulation through playbacks was demonstrated to attract wild dogs to the calling station (Robbins & McCreery, 2003). Conversely, such cues could possibly be used to discourage animals from recolonizing an undesired area.

The importance of facilitating conspecific interactions for the persistence of (typically small) re-established populations is illustrated by the occurrence of Allee effects (Deredec & Courchamp, 2007). An Allee effect is defined as a reduction in individual fitness with decreasing size of the aggregation unit considered (e.g. population or social group; Stephens *et al.*, 1999). Difficulty in finding suitable mates at low density probably is the most commonly cited mechanism of the Allee effect (Courchamp *et al.*, 1999; Stephens & Sutherland, 1999). For example, a reintroduced wild dog population studied over a period of 25 years increased only after it was artificially augmented to a critical minimum number of four packs, which simultaneously produced enough unrelated dispersers for successful pack formation events to occur (Somers *et al.*, 2008). Furthermore, a mate-finding Allee effect at low pack number was inferred to account for the initially slow expansion of reintroduced populations of wolves (Hurford *et al.*, 2006) and wild dogs (Gusset *et al.*, unpublished data) (Table 12.2). Interestingly, Hurford *et al.* (2006) found reintroduced wolves spread faster when pair-bonded before dispersal, reiterating the importance of social integration (see above).

As an Allee effect can be generated by a shortage of interactions among conspecifics at low density, the degree of sociality of a species might reflect the degree of severity of the Allee effect to which it is subject. Allee effects can thus have particularly serious impacts on the population dynamics of obligate

Table 12.2 **Observed Allee effects (i.e. a reduction in individual fitness with decreasing size of the aggregation unit considered) and management measures to mitigate Allee effects in large-carnivore reintroductions.**

Species	Allee effects and management measures
Observed Allee effects	
African wild dog	Allee effect arising from difficulty in finding suitable mates at low pack number[a]
Grey wolf	Allee effect arising from difficulty in finding suitable mates at low pack number[b]
African wild dog	Allee effect arising from difficulty in exercising cooperative activities (e.g. cooperative hunting[c]) at small pack size
Management measures to mitigate Allee effects	
African wild dog	Mate-finding Allee effect mitigated by artificially augmenting a population to a critical minimum number of packs[d]
African wild dog	Allee effect at the pack level mitigated by artificially augmenting a pack to a critical minimum number of individuals[e]

[a]Gusset *et al.*, unpublished data; [b]Hurford *et al.*, 2006; [c]Rasmussen *et al.*, 2008; [d]Somers *et al.*, 2008; [e]Graf *et al.*, 2006.

co-operators, which may rely on a minimum group size for survival and reproduction (Courchamp *et al.*, 1999; Stephens & Sutherland, 1999). For wild dog packs to exceed this potential critical threshold and to capitalize on the benefits provided by a larger size (e.g. in terms of cooperative hunting; Rasmussen *et al.*, 2008), Graf *et al.* (2006) demonstrated that packs destined for reintroduction can be artificially augmented before release (Table 12.2).

Conclusions

In any reintroduction attempt involving social species, founder group composition is likely to determine establishment success, whereas persistence is likely to depend on the formation of new groups to maintain the population's reproductive capacity. The outcome of both these stages can be influenced by aspects of the target species' social behaviour, which was confirmed by an evaluation of both short- and long-term reintroduction successes in wild dogs (Gusset, this volume). Monitoring and managing social behaviour both pre- and post-release is thus well worth the effort from a management perspective.

The study by Graf *et al.* (2006) on testing group augmentation theory within a wild dog reintroduction framework provides an example for how theoretical behavioural ecology and practical reintroduction biology can be mutually beneficial. Measures of behavioural ecology can provide information about how release areas differ in quality, and can identify critical resources in theses areas as well as documenting how re-established species contribute to ecosystem functioning (Lindell, 2008). For example, the ecological effectiveness of reintroduced wolves became evident after triggering a behaviourally mediated trophic cascade (Berger & Smith, 2005; Smith & Bangs, this volume). Therefore, in our view, incorporating considerations of social behaviour in conservation management would increase the efficiency and effectiveness of costly (carnivore) reintroduction programmes.

Acknowledgements

We are grateful to two anonymous referees for helpful comments on this chapter.

References

Angeloni, L., Schlaepfer, M.A., Lawler, J.J. & Crooks, K.R. (2008) A reassessment of the interface between conservation and behaviour. *Animal Behaviour* 75, 731–737.

Anthony, L.L. & Blumstein, D.T. (2000) Integrating behaviour into wildlife conservation: The multiple ways that behaviour can reduce N_e. *Biological Conservation* 95, 303–315.

Badridze, J. (1999) Preparing captive-raised wolves for re-introduction, Georgia, Commonwealth of Independent States (C.I.S.). *Re-introduction News* 18, 5–6.

Berger, J. & Smith, D.W. (2005) Restoring functionality in Yellowstone with recovering carnivores: Gains and uncertainties. *Large Carnivores and the Conservation of Biodiversity*. (eds J.C. Ray, K.H. Redford, R.S. Steneck & J. Berger), pp. 100–109. Island Press, Washington.

Blumstein, D.T. & Fernández-Juricic, E. (2004) The emergence of conservation behavior. *Conservation Biology* 18, 1175–1177.

Bradley, E.H., Pletscher, D.H., Bangs, E.E. et al. (2005) Evaluating wolf translocation as a nonlethal method to reduce livestock conflicts in the northwestern United States. *Conservation Biology* 19, 1498–1508.

Breitenmoser, U., Breitenmoser-Würsten, C., Carbyn, L.N. & Funk, S.M. (2001) Assessment of carnivore reintroductions. *Carnivore Conservation*. (eds J.L. Gittleman, S.M. Funk, D. Macdonald & R.K. Wayne), pp. 241–281. Cambridge University Press, Cambridge.

Buchholz, R. (2007) Behavioural biology: An effective and relevant conservation tool. *Trends in Ecology and Evolution* 22, 401–407.

Caro, T. (ed.) (1998) *Behavioral Ecology and Conservation Biology*. Oxford University Press, Oxford.

Caro, T. (1999) The behaviour-conservation interface. *Trends in Ecology and Evolution* 14, 366–369.

Caro, T. (2007) Behavior and conservation: A bridge too far? *Trends in Ecology and Evolution* 22, 394–400.

Caro, T.M. & Durant, S.M. (1995) The importance of behavioral ecology for conservation biology: Examples from Serengeti carnivores. *Serengeti II: Dynamics, Management, and Conservation of an Ecosystem*. (eds A.R.E. Sinclair & P. Arcese), pp. 451–472. University of Chicago Press, Chicago.

Clemmons, J.R. & Buchholz, R. (eds) (1997) *Behavioral Approaches to Conservation in the Wild*. Cambridge University Press, Cambridge.

Clubb, R. & Mason, G. (2003) Captivity effects on wide-ranging carnivores. *Nature* 425, 473–474.

Courchamp, F., Clutton-Brock, T. & Grenfell, B. (1999) Inverse density dependence and the Allee effect. *Trends in Ecology and Evolution* 14, 405–410.

Curio, E. (1996) Conservation needs ethology. *Trends in Ecology and Evolution* 11, 260–263.

Deredec, A. & Courchamp, F. (2007) Importance of the Allee effect for reintroductions. *Écoscience* 14, 440–451.

Dobson, A. & Poole, J. (1998) Conspecific aggregation and conservation biology. *Behavioral Ecology and Conservation Biology*. (ed. T. Caro), pp. 193–208. Oxford University Press, Oxford.

Festa-Bianchet, M. & Apollonio, M. (eds) (2003) *Animal Behavior and Wildlife Conservation*. Island Press, Washington.

Fischer, J. & Lindenmayer, D.B. (2000) An assessment of the published results of animal relocations. *Biological Conservation* 96, 1–11.

Fritts, S.H., Bangs, E.E., Fontaine, J.A. et al. (1997) Planning and implementing a reintroduction of wolves to Yellowstone National Park and central Idaho. *Restoration Ecology* 5, 7–27.

Gosling, L.M. & Sutherland, W.J. (eds) (2000) *Behaviour and Conservation*. Cambridge University Press, Cambridge.

Graf, J.A., Gusset, M., Reid, C., Janse van Rensburg, S., Slotow, R. & Somers, M.J. (2006) Evolutionary ecology meets wildlife management: Artificial group augmentation in the re-introduction of endangered African wild dogs (*Lycaon pictus*). *Animal Conservation* 9, 398–403.

Gusset, M., Maddock, A.H., Gunther, G.J. et al. (2008b) Conflicting human interests over the re-introduction of endangered wild dogs in South Africa. *Biodiversity and Conservation* 17, 83–101.

Gusset, M., Ryan, S.J., Hofmeyr, M. et al. (2008a) Efforts going to the dogs? Evaluating attempts to re-introduce endangered wild dogs in South Africa. *Journal of Applied Ecology* 45, 100–108.

Gusset, M., Slotow, R. & Somers, M.J. (2006) Divided we fail: The importance of social integration for the re-introduction of endangered African wild dogs (*Lycaon pictus*). *Journal of Zoology, London* 270, 502–511.

Hayward, M.W., Adendorff, J., O'Brien, J. et al. (2007a) Practical considerations for the reintroduction of large, terrestrial, mammalian predators based on reintroductions to South Africa's Eastern Cape Province. *The Open Conservation Biology Journal* 1, 1–11.

Hayward, M.W., Adendorff, J., O'Brien, J. et al. (2007b) The reintroduction of large carnivores to the Eastern Cape, South Africa: An assessment. *Oryx* 41, 205–214.

Hunter, L. (1999) Large felid restoration: Lessons from the Phinda Resource Reserve, South Africa, 1992–1999. *Re-introduction News* 18, 9–11.

Hunter, L.T.B., Pretorius, K., Carlisle, L.C. et al. (2007) Restoring lions *Panthera leo* to northern KwaZulu-Natal, South Africa: Short-term biological and technical success but equivocal long-term conservation. *Oryx* 41, 196–204.

Hurford, A., Hebblewhite, M. & Lewis, M.A. (2006) A spatially explicit model for an Allee effect: Why wolves recolonize so slowly in Greater Yellowstone. *Theoretical Population Biology* 70, 244–254.

Jule, K.R., Leaver, L.A. & Lea, S.E.G. (2008) The effects of captive experience on reintroduction survival in carnivores: A review and analysis. *Biological Conservation* 141, 355–363.

Kleiman, D.G. (1989) Reintroduction of captive mammals for conservation: Guidelines for reintroducing endangered species into the wild. *BioScience* 39, 152–161.

Lindell, C.A. (2008) The value of animal behavior in evaluations of restoration success. *Restoration Ecology* 16, 197–203.

Linklater, W.L. (2004) Wanted for conservation research: Behavioral ecologists with a broader perspective. *BioScience* 54, 352–360.

Linnell, J.D.C., Aanes, R., Swenson, J.E., Odden, J. & Smith, M.E. (1997) Translocation of carnivores as a method for managing problem animals: A review. *Biodiversity and Conservation* 6, 1245–1257.

Martin, K. (1998) The role of animal behavior studies in wildlife science and management. *Wildlife Society Bulletin* 26, 911–920.

Miller, B., Ralls, K., Reading, R.P., Scott, J.M. & Estes, J. (1999) Biological and technical considerations of carnivore translocation: A review. *Animal Conservation* 2, 59–68.

Moehrenschlager, A. & Somers, M.J. (2004) Canid reintroductions and metapopulation management. *Canids: Foxes, Wolves, Jackals and Dogs: Status Survey and Conservation Action Plan*. (eds C. Sillero-Zubiri, M. Hoffmann & D.W. Macdonald), pp. 289–297. IUCN, Gland, Switzerland.

Rasmussen, G.S.A., Gusset, M., Courchamp, F. & Macdonald, D.W. (2008) Achilles' heel of sociality revealed by energetic poverty trap in cursorial hunters. *American Naturalist* 172, 508–518.

Reading, R.P. & Clark, T.W. (1996) Carnivore reintroductions: An interdisciplinary examination. *Carnivore Behavior, Ecology, and Evolution*. (ed. J.L. Gittleman), pp. 296–336. Cornell University Press, Ithaca.

Robbins, R.L. & McCreery, E.K. (2003) Acoustic stimulation as a tool in African wild dog conservation. *Biological Conservation* 111, 263–267.

Ryan, S.J. (2006) The role of culture in conservation planning for small or endangered populations. *Conservation Biology* 20, 1321–1324.

Schröpfer, R. & Rohde, A. (1997) The integration of a young female in a male pack of European wolves *Canis lupus* L. *Zeitschrift für Säugetierkunde* 62 (Suppl. II), 209–213.

Somers, M.J., Graf, J.A., Szykman, M., Slotow, R. & Gusset, M. (2008) Dynamics of a small re-introduced population of wild dogs over 25 years: Allee effects and the implications of sociality for endangered species' recovery. *Oecologia* 158, 239–247.

Stephens, P.A. & Sutherland, W.J. (1999) Consequences of the Allee effect for behaviour, ecology and conservation. *Trends in Ecology and Evolution* 14, 401–405.

Stephens, P.A., Sutherland, W.J. & Freckleton, R.P. (1999) What is the Allee effect? *Oikos* 87, 185–190.

Sutherland, W.J. (1998) The importance of behavioural studies in conservation biology. *Animal Behaviour* 56, 801–809.

Teixeira, C.P., De Azevedo, C.S., Mendl, M., Cipreste, C.F. & Young, R.J. (2007) Revisiting translocation and reintroduction programmes: The importance of considering stress. *Animal Behaviour* 73, 1–13.

Trinkel, M., Ferguson, N., Reid, A. et al. (2008) Translocating lions into an inbred lion population in the Hluhluwe-iMfolozi Park, South Africa. *Animal Conservation* 11, 138–143.

van Heezik, Y. & Seddon, P.J. (2005) Structure and content of graduate wildlife management and conservation biology programs: An international perspective. *Conservation Biology* 19, 7–14.

Vickery, S.S. & Mason, G.J. (2003) Behavioral persistence in captive bears: Implications for reintroduction. *Ursus* 14, 35–43.

Woodroffe, R. & Ginsberg, J.R. (1998) Edge effects and the extinction of populations inside protected areas. *Science* 280, 2126–2128.

Woodroffe, R., Davies-Mostert, H., Ginsberg, J. et al. (2007) Rates and causes of mortality in endangered African wild dogs *Lycaon pictus*: Lessons for management and monitoring. *Oryx* 41, 215–223.

13

Survival of Cheetahs Relocated from Ranchland to Fenced Protected Areas in South Africa

Kelly Marnewick[1]*, Matt W. Hayward*[2]*, Deon Cilliers*[3] *and Michael J. Somers*[4]

[1]Centre for Wildlife Management, University of Pretoria, and De Wildt Wild Cheetah Project, De Wildt Cheetah and Wildlife Trust
[2]Mammal Research Institute, Polish Academy of Science
[3]De Wildt Wild Cheetah Project, De Wildt Cheetah and Wildlife Trust
[4]Centre for Wildlife Management, Centre for Invasion Biology, University of Pretoria

Summary

In South Africa, wildlife can be privately owned and utilized for economic gain, with the consequent formation of thousands of wildlife ranches that are stocked with wildlife for the main purpose of hunting and live sale. When predators prey on antelope, the economic value attached to wildlife results in conflict. The cheetah, *Acinonyx jubatus*, is protected by legislation in South Africa, and cheetahs have consequently been illegally shot and trapped in an attempt to reduce losses. A compensation–relocation programme for "problem" cheetahs was therefore initiated in South Africa by landowners,

Reintroduction of Top-Order Predators, 1st edition. Edited by M.W. Hayward and M.J. Somers.
 ISBN 978-1-4051-7680-4 (pb) and 978-1-4051-9273-6 (hb)

conservation officials and biologists; this programme allowed landowners to legally capture "damage-causing" cheetahs on their property for relocation into fenced protected areas. Trapped cheetahs were temporarily placed in a specially designed holding facility to habituate them to humans to facilitate monitoring and future viewing for ecotourism. Cheetahs were released into approved reserves using a soft-release method and were subsequently monitored. A total of 29 reserves and 189 cheetahs (92 adults: 59 males and 33 females, plus 94 cubs born on the reserves) were included in the survival analyses using the Kaplan-Meier (product limit) estimator with staggered entry. The mean annual survivorship for all cheetahs, including cubs born in this study, was 82.8%. The final survivorship value for all adult cheetahs was 0.23 and for cubs was 0.04. Cubs had significantly higher survival on reserves where other competing predators were absent. The median survival time was 38 months for adult males and more than 53 months for adult females, which is higher than the corresponding 17 months for adult males and 8 months for adult females on Namibian ranchland.

Introduction

The land-use system in South Africa is unique in Africa in that land and wildlife can be privately owned and utilized for commercial purposes (Benson, 1991; Lindsey *et al.*, this volume). This has resulted in more than 10,000,000 ha of land being fenced to form more than 5000 wildlife ranches that are stocked with various wildlife species for the main purpose of sport hunting (Eloff, 2002). Wildlife is therefore consumptively utilized for economic gain by landowners, which provides concomitant habitat conservation (Hayward, 2005). Lions (*Panthera leo*) and spotted hyaenas (*Crocuta crocuta*) have been extirpated from most ranchlands in South Africa, but leopards (*Panthera pardus*), cheetahs (*Acinonyx jubatus*) and brown hyaenas (*Hyaena brunnea*) still persist (Wilson, 2006). In the Thabazimbi district, the mean ranch size is 1800 ha and the ranches are enclosed in game fencing, which is not predator proof (Wilson, 2006), allowing predators to move either under or over the fences. Large predators can only be legally reintroduced onto a property when, among other considerations, predator-proof fencing has been erected. This means that only larger properties are able to sustain confined large predators like lions and spotted hyaenas, and thus the average wildlife ranch will not be able to benefit from their value as trophy animals. Additionally, lions pose a threat to ranch staff, who work mostly on foot and unarmed, so their presence is not desired. For these reasons, only leopards, cheetahs and brown hyaenas persist on ranchland in South Africa.

In some areas, cheetahs may fare better outside than inside conservation areas, owing to the lack of intraguild competition (Laurenson, 1995). Additionally, prey species on wildlife ranches are often maintained at artificially high densities (van der Waal & Dekker, 2000), by means of supplementary feeding and water provisioning, which further improves conditions for cheetahs in these areas. While ecological conditions may theoretically favour cheetahs outside reserves, conflict with landowners frequently occurs owing to the perceived threat of cheetahs to ungulate populations and domestic stock (Marker, 2002; Wilson, 2006). This is exacerbated when ranchers stock expensive rare or endangered antelope or rare colour variations, e.g. black impala (*Aepyceros melampus*) or white blesbok (*Damaliscus pygargus phillipsi*) (KM, unpublished data). This often results in landowners illegally shooting, trapping and removing cheetahs from their land (KM, unpublished data).

There is a booming non-consumptive, photographic ecotourism market in South Africa, which has resulted in many privately owned reserves being established. In order to attract tourists, these reserves are reintroducing a diverse range of species from antelope to the Big Five (lion, leopard, elephant [*Loxodonta africana*], African buffalo [*Syncerus caffer*] and white [*Ceratotherium simum*], or black [*Diceros bicornis*], rhinoceros). Such reserves find great economic benefit from the presence of cheetahs on their property (Lindsey *et al.*, this volume).

In 2000, a group of landowners from the Thabazimbi district in the western part of South Africa's Limpopo province (Figure 13.1) approached the De Wildt Cheetah and Wildlife Trust looking for solutions to the conflict between landowners and cheetahs. As a result, the National Cheetah Management Program (now known as the National Cheetah Conservation Forum of South Africa) was formed and included most role-players in South Africa who had an interest in cheetahs, from landowners to conservation officials and researchers. Several issues were discussed around the conflict, and a compensation–relocation programme was initiated as one of the short-term methods of reducing conflict while ensuring cheetah survival.

The compensation–relocation programme made legal provision for landowners, who were experiencing problems with cheetah predation, to trap them live rather than using lethal control methods. The landowner would then be compensated by a pre-determined amount (currently ZAR10,000—

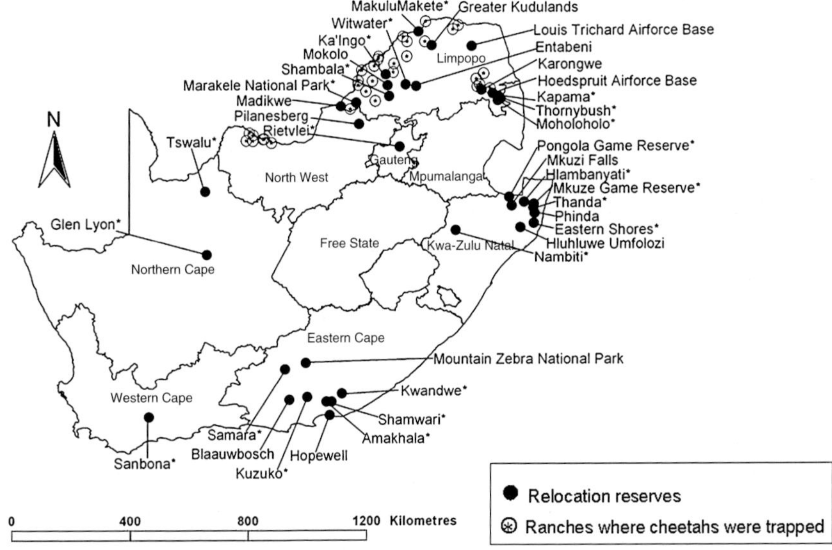

Figure 13.1 **Locations where cheetahs were trapped, as well as relocation reserves in South Africa. Reserves marked with an asterisk were included in the analyses. Other reserves were omitted either because no data were supplied or because relocations began after the start of data analysis.**

approximately US$1500) per cheetah. The cheetah would then be relocated to a conservation reserve in South Africa where cheetahs were required for ecotourism purposes. The relocation venue would then pay a minimum donation (currently ZAR15,000—approximately US$2200) for the cheetah. The ZAR5000 (approximately US$700) excess would be used to cover any incidental and holding costs for the cheetahs.

In order to prevent some of the problems that are common to relocations, the cheetahs are relocated only into fenced protected areas. This ensures that they are not able to return to the site of capture (Hunter, 1998) or to become problem animals in the relocation area as occurs in many relocation programmes (Linnell *et al.,* 1997). Additionally, all releases were soft releases, which further increase the chances of success (Hunter, 1998; Moehrenschlager & Somers, 2004).

Finally, this compensation–relocation programme is not seen as a long-term solution to conflict, but rather as a short-term method of buying some time while other mitigation measures, such as education, improved livestock husbandry practices, research and non-lethal damage prevention are implemented. While in some cases landowners trapped cheetahs specifically for the financial benefit of compensation, in other cases cheetahs that would otherwise have been killed were made available for relocation owing to the financial gain. It is not possible to quantify how many cheetahs would have been killed or would not have been trapped if compensation was not offered.

Trapping cheetahs on ranchland is not easy—it is time consuming and labour intensive. It requires investigation into a good trapping site, chopping down trees to build a boma, obtaining and daily feeding a goat if live bait is used, maintenance of the trap and trap time lost in capturing non-target animals. Even then, there is still no guarantee that the cheetah will be caught. In a study on ranchland in the Thabazimbi district, it took approximately 1,500 trap nights to trap five cheetahs (Marnewick & Cilliers, 2006). Thus, many ranchers feel that it is not worth the effort setting traps and maintaining them if they are not going to receive any benefit from trapping the cheetah; they feel that shooting is cheaper and quicker, with immediate results and some sense of satisfaction. In contrast to this, other ranchers are happy to leave cheetahs on their ranches because they know that they can obtain help if they feel that the cheetahs can no longer be tolerated. The above demonstrates that there are several issues of concern in this compensation–relocation programme pertaining to conservation principles and long-term sustainability. Nonetheless, from the human perspective, this has encouraged cooperation from landowners, who often feel conflicted with and marginalized by predator conservationists and governmental authorities.

Previously, several attempts have been made to relocate cheetahs from ranchlands to reserves. In Zimbabwe, cheetahs were successfully relocated from ranches to Matusadona National Park (Purchase & Vhurumuku, 2006). A similar relocation project in Suikerbosrand Nature Reserve in South Africa (Pettifer, 1981) was less successful. Here, eight adult cheetahs were released onto the 13,400-ha reserve over a period of 15 months. The population had grown to approximately 24 individuals after 2 years, and the prey population became depleted owing to overpopulation of cheetahs (Hayward *et al.*, 2007c), and the prey then had to be supplemented. The rapid increase of the cheetah population was attributed to the absence of other large, competing predators.

Cheetahs were also relocated from Namibian ranchlands to Pilanesberg and Madikwe Game Reserves in South Africa (Hofmeyr & van Dyk, 1998).

At Pilanesberg, seven cheetahs were reintroduced in 1981/1982 from the De Wildt Cheetah Breeding Centre, but most of these were later removed to protect antelope populations. A further 16 cheetahs were introduced from Namibia in 1995/1996, after which the population remained stable at 17 individuals (Hofmeyr & van Dyk, 1998) before rising to 20 by 2001 (van Dyk & Slotow, 2003). Nineteen cheetahs were reintroduced to Madikwe from 1994. However, only four reintroduced individuals still survived in 1998 (Hofmeyr & van Dyk, 1998).

Cheetahs that were relocated from Namibia to the Zambezi National Park in Zambia (Anon, 1995) all died after release, owing to snaring and conflict with other cheetahs. Cheetahs were reintroduced into Phinda in 1992 (Hunter, 1998) and into several other reserves in the Eastern Cape of South Africa since 2000 (Hayward *et al.*, 2007b), many of which are included in this study.

Methods

Trapping

Perceptions of the landowner are often stronger than reality and can strongly influence attitudes towards predation (Mech, 1981). Negative attitudes towards large predators are normally motivated by fear of economic loss (Kellert, 1985; Marker, 2002) as opposed to actual losses. Therefore, as it was not possible to quantify actual losses on every ranch, in situations where the landowner could not be convinced otherwise, cheetahs that were perceived to be causing damage were trapped on cattle and wildlife ranches in Limpopo and the North West Province (Figure 13.1.). Cheetahs were trapped by landowners, conservation officials and field staff of the members of the National Cheetah Conservation Forum of South Africa. Where landowners were trapping independently, it was impossible to attempt to convince them to leave the cheetahs on the property.

Double-door, box trap cages were mostly used (Marnewick & Cilliers, 2006). De Wildt occasionally received cheetahs that had been trapped by landowners using undesirable methods that led to the cheetahs being injured. If these injuries were considered severe enough to prevent relocation of the cheetah, then the cheetah was placed in a reputable captive-breeding centre (e.g. De Wildt Cheetah Breeding Centre, Cango Wildlife Ranch or Hoedspruit Centre for Endangered Species). Such injuries included broken jaws, loss of limbs or part of limbs and, in some cases, broken bones that did not recover well after veterinary care. Some cheetahs were released and survived after pinning and plating of bones, blindness in one eye, or after surgery on lacerations caused by snares and dogs during capture. However, the eventual hunting success seems to be dependent on the specific injury and the degree of recovery of the cheetah.

Trapped cheetahs were then transported in a crate to one of three holding facilities located in the Limpopo province. De Wildt Shingwedzi near Bela-Bela is now the main holding facility as it is specifically designed to hold wild cheetahs, is separate from any captive cheetahs and has staff experienced in managing wild cheetahs. The cheetahs were usually not immobilized or sedated for transportation, but were simply moved from the capture cage into the crate. Immobilization was used only if it was not possible to remove the cheetah from the capture cage.

Holding

The holding facility was specifically designed to hold wild cheetahs (Figure 13.2). As the cheetahs were not habituated to humans, the facility was intentionally small in size, with the limited amount of space preventing injuries when the cheetahs tried to flee from human presence during holding. Unable to build up enough speed in the small camps, the cheetahs could not hurt themselves by running into fences. To habituate the cheetahs to human activities and vehicles for both viewing and monitoring purposes, the holding facility was situated near a major road on the ranch. While in captivity, the cheetahs were fed daily and became accustomed to humans. This practice contrasts with plans for the Amur leopard (Christie, this volume), because the economic value of the cheetahs drives their conservation at the reintroduction sites, whereas the leopards will be at risk from human poaching at their reintroduction sites.

Cheetahs were held here for approximately 3–4 months, with the time dependent on the availability of relocation venues, how habituated the cheetahs became and any injuries that needed attention.

Prior to relocation to a suitable reserve, the cheetahs were immobilized and fitted with a radio telemetry collar and a microchip implant. Measurements and bio-samples were taken and a general health check was carried out by qualified veterinarians. If females were released onto reserves with males, they

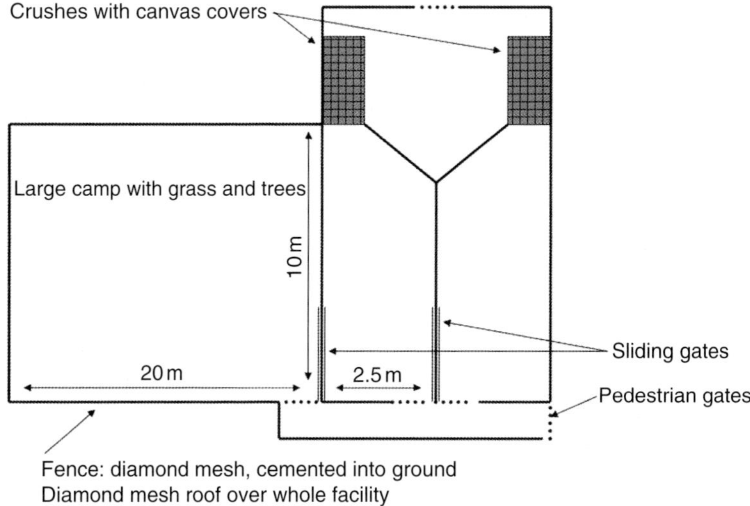

Figure 13.2 **Schematic aerial view of the temporary holding facility for wild cheetahs.**

were sometimes contracepted for the first year using Suprelorin (Peptech Animal Health, Sydney, Australia; Bertschinger *et al.*, 2002; Bertschinger *et al.*, 2006) to prevent unwanted growth of the cheetah population in confined reserves. Such unwanted growth is the biggest problem faced in managing many reintroduced predators once the agents of their decline have been removed (Hayward *et al.*, 2007c).

Males received as individuals were bonded artificially to form coalitions as this is believed to be more suitable for relocation purposes (Hunter, 1998). Males were first put in adjoining camps (Figure 13.2) to allow them to become accustomed to each other. Once they were observed lying next to each other, either side of the fence, and showing no obvious signs of aggression, the sliding gate between the two camps was opened. They were further monitored and, if there was no fighting over food, the bonding was considered successful. Once the cheetahs were habituated to the presence of humans and vehicles, and the male groups formed, the sliding gate was opened into the larger camp (400 m^2), where they remained until relocated to a reserve.

The cheetahs were again transported in crates without drugs to the relocation reserve, where they were released into a suitably fenced holding boma of approximately 1 ha in size. If males and females were to be released on the same reserve, they were held in separate but adjoining bomas in order to become accustomed to each other through the fence. If possible, the female was released first to allow her time to settle into a range before the males were released.

The cheetahs were monitored several times per day (ideally for several minutes at a time) to further habituate the cheetahs to humans and vehicles. Tourist game drives were taken past the boma to allow the cheetahs to habituate to the game-viewing vehicles. If the relocation reserve wanted to view their cheetahs on foot after release, it was recommended that reserve staff spend time with the cheetahs in the boma on foot to ensure that they were fully habituated before release. Many reserves obtained very relaxed cheetahs by allowing a staff member to spend several hours at a time in the boma working on a lap top or reading a book out loud to accustom the cheetahs to human voices.

Although wild cheetahs pose little threat to adult humans, staff were urged to always carry a stick whilst on foot in the boma and were told to never sit down on the ground and to always respect the comfort zone of the cheetah. While it may be irregular to habituate other large carnivores to humans on foot, cheetahs are unique in that they can be safely approached and observed. Additionally, it is necessary to have the cheetahs habituated for effective monitoring as, on many reserves, it is not possible to obtain visuals from a vehicle if the cat has moved off the road. Habituated cheetahs are also easer to manage in case of injury or escape. The first release of wild cheetahs onto a reserve in this project was done without habituating the cheetahs and, after release, it was not possible to obtain visuals of the cheetahs. Additionally, one of the reasons that reserves introduce cheetahs is for tourism. Cheetahs can make excellent viewing animals, but need to be habituated to humans if walking safaris are to be offered.

The frequency of feeding was gradually decreased from daily to weekly (as is usual in wild cheetahs). It was recommended to the managers that, when feeding, a whistle should be blown prior to the cheetahs being fed. This resulted in the cheetah being conditioned to the sight of a human *and* the sound of a whistle equating to food being given. Human presence, without the whistle being blown, did not result in food for the cheetah. This practice desensitized the cheetah to human presence by beneficial association. It also conditioned them to only expect food when both stimuli (human and whistle) were present (S. McKay, personal communication[1]). The whistle can also be useful after release for management reasons, such as recapture after escape or darting to administer veterinary care (Hayward *et al.*, 2007a). If a cheetah heard a whistle, it would be inclined to look for a human being in order to complete the conditioned behaviour sequence and thus receive food.

Relocation venues needed to comply with certain criteria before being considered for releases. Such criteria included an ecological management plan, and this required proof that the reserve could support the cheetahs for a minimum of 2 years without supplementing the prey population. A model was used to quantify the sustainability of the prey population by including the following in the ecological management plan: stocking rates of the reserve, as well as consumption rates of cheetahs, preferred prey availability and prey growth rates (J.W. Kruger, Limpopo Department of Environment and Tourism, RSA unpublished data). The precision of this model may not be satisfactory (as reserves as small as 1500 ha have been included), so predicting the carrying capacity of a reserve based on the biomass of preferred prey should provide more robust estimates of the sustainability of a reintroduced cheetah population (Hayward *et al.*, 2007c). The reserve must be fenced according to specifications and a monitoring programme must be in place. Additionally, the relevant permits and permissions must be obtained from government, and a memorandum of understanding must be signed which includes agreements to monitoring, confirmation that the cheetahs remain wild and are not held in small camps, and confirmation that they will not be sold or hunted. Only two reserves had cheetahs from previous introductions and one reserve was omitted from the analyses owing to lack of feedback from managers. Dominant competitors (lions and/or spotted hyaenas) were present on 13 of the 23 reserves included in the data analyses.

Release

The cheetahs were held in bomas for at least 3 months before they were released onto the reserve. If males and females were to be released, females were released first to give them the opportunity to settle into the range before the males were released. During the release, cheetahs were lured out of the boma by dragging an antelope carcass or hind-quarter on a piece of rope until the cheetah was far enough away to allow the gate to be closed without frightening the cheetah. Although it is feasible to open the gate and let the cheetahs leave at their own accord, we lured the cats out to reduce the risk of other animals entering the open boma and possibly injuring or killing the confined cheetahs.

After release, the cheetahs were closely monitored using telemetry for the first few weeks until reserve staff were satisfied that the cheetahs had settled in and were hunting effectively. If they were not hunting, supplementary feeding was considered. This was seldom necessary and only occurred if the cheetah had not eaten for a period of approximately 7 days; the timing varied according to the individual cheetah and how well it retained condition. If supplementary feeding took place, only a small amount of food (e.g. a hind-quarter) was fed in order to maintain condition and energy levels, but to leave the cat hungry. It was recommended that monitoring should continue on a daily basis after release.

Data collection

Basic data on release and death dates (accurate to the nearest month) for the Kaplan-Meier analyses were collected from relocation reserve managers; this provided information for 29 reserves and 186 cheetahs for a complete 5-year period (Figure 13.1). Many reserves offered this information for all their cheetahs, including those that had been relocated privately between reserves and not through the compensation–relocation programme—and these were also included in the analyses. Information collected included month of release and month of death or censoring if applicable. For cubs born on reserves, managers were asked to report the month in which the cubs were born and how many cubs there were, and also to note the months in which cubs were seen to have died or gone missing. Females were generally carefully monitored, and managers were able to give data on cubs from a young age (normally still in the den).

Data analyses

Because the cheetahs were not all reintroduced at the same time, but rather over a period of several years, survivorship was measured using the Kaplan-Meier estimator (product limit estimator) with staggered entry (Pollock *et al.*, 1989). This allows for the staggered entry of animals and compares survival functions using the log rank test (χ^2). The Kaplan-Meier estimator also allows for inclusion of data from censored animals (e.g. those who escaped and could not be found or whose fates were unknown). Log rank tests were used to compare the overall survival curves obtained from the Kaplan-Meier analyses (Pollock *et al.*, 1989). The Z-test was used to compare survivorship values at the end of the 6-year study period. Median survival times were estimated as the smallest survival time for which the survivorship function was less than or equal to 0.5 (i.e. the value on the x-axis where the y-axis value is equal to 0.5).

Results

Capture of cheetahs

From 2000 until the end of 2006, 136 cheetahs were received through the compensation–relocation programme; of these, 20 individuals were retained in captivity as they were either too young (unweaned cubs) to be released or were injured (e.g. badly broken limbs, broken jaws, etc.) and deemed unfit for release. Methods are currently being developed to rehabilitate young cheetahs to ensure that they seldom end up in captivity (KM, unpublished data).

Cheetah and reserve data

Sufficient data for the Kaplan-Meier analyses were obtained for 186 cheetahs, of which 92 were adults (59 males and 33 females) and 94 were cubs born on reserves. Owing to inaccurate information or to a lack of response from the reserves, 35 cheetahs were omitted from the analyses. These cheetahs were relocated in the same manner as all the other cheetahs in the study, and it is not likely that the managers' non-response to requests for data could bias survival of cheetahs. The fate of most of these cheetahs is known, and some of the omitted cheetahs are on reserves where monitoring is excellent—we were just not able to obtain accurate information for analyses.

The cubs were born from 23 females, of which two had two litters each. Litter size ranged from two to seven cubs per litter (mean = 4.5 ± 1.87). The litter sizes could have been underestimated in some cases as some cubs could have died before emerging from the lair. However, because most of these relocated cheetahs were thoroughly habituated to humans on foot, monitoring staff were often able to observe cubs from a very young age. In the Serengeti, the litter size ranged between one and six cubs (mean = 3.5 ± 1.87) (Laurenson, 1995).

The relocations from which data were collected took place from September 2000 to September 2007. The relocation reserves ranged in size from 1500 ha to 70,000 ha, with a mean reserve size of approximately 36,000 ha.

Cost of relocations

While the principal aim of the relocation programme is for it to be financially self-sustaining (with funds paid out and paid into the compensation fund), this is not the case. For a normal relocation, where the cheetah is not injured or ill and does not require any additional veterinary attention, the cost is roughly ZAR18,250 (approximately US$2700). These costs include the cost of food, collars, general veterinary care, permits, staff salaries and transportation. Excluded are the fixed costs of building and maintaining the holding facilities, fencing the protected areas and any costs incurred at the relocation venue. The ZAR5000 deficit from the relocation venue donation contributes to these expenses, making the actual cost approximately ZAR13,250 (approximately US$1900). These costs soar when the cheetah requires surgery, or when the cheetah is received at a young age, is held for extended periods and needs to go through a re-wilding programme. The costs of the actual capture are also not included: capture cages, labour, bait animals and their food, health care, etc.

Survival of relocated cheetahs

Survivorship was determined for each sex, age group and year and for cheetahs with and without the presence of other large predators (Table 13.1; Figure 13.3A and 13.3B). Cheetahs survived significantly longer at sites where other competing predators (lions and/or spotted hyaenas) were not present than at

Table 13.1 **Kaplan-Meier survivorship estimates with variance and median survival time in months for various age and sex classes of relocated cheetahs and years of relocation. Annual survivorship is the percentage chance that a reintroduced animal will survive for 1 year. Cubs are those that were born on reserves as a result of relocated cheetahs.**

Group	Sample size, *n*	Survivorship for 5-year study period	Variance	Median survival time (months)	Annual survivorship, %
All adults	92	0.23	0.001	28	84.6
Females	33	0.45	0.005	>53 (50% survivorship not reached)	89.0
Males	59	0.19	0.001	38	83.8
All individuals (males, females and cubs)	168	0.14	0.000	38	82.8
With competitors	106	0.25	0.001	39	85.0
Without competitors	62	0.26	0.001	41	85.2
All cubs	94	0.04	0.000	16	80.8
With competitors	57	0.04	0.000	16	80.8
Without competitors	37	0.76	0.006	>36 (50% survivorship not reached)	95.2
All females	65	0.12	0.000	8	82.4
With competitors	44	0.40	0.004	54	88.0
Without competitors	21	0.64	0.011	>41 (50% survivorship not reached)	92.8
All males	103	0.12	0.000	37	82.4
With competitors	62	0.19	0.001	36	83.8
Without competitors	41	0.27	0.002	40	85.4
Year 2001		1	0.000	50% survivorship not reached	n/a
Year 2002		0.85	0.004	50% survivorship not reached	n/a
Year 2003		0.48	0.004	11	n/a
Year 2004		0.64	0.003	50% survivorship not reached	n/a
Year 2005		0.87	0.002	50% survivorship not reached	n/a
Year 2006		0.79	0.002	50% survivorship not reached	n/a

n/a, invalid assessment.

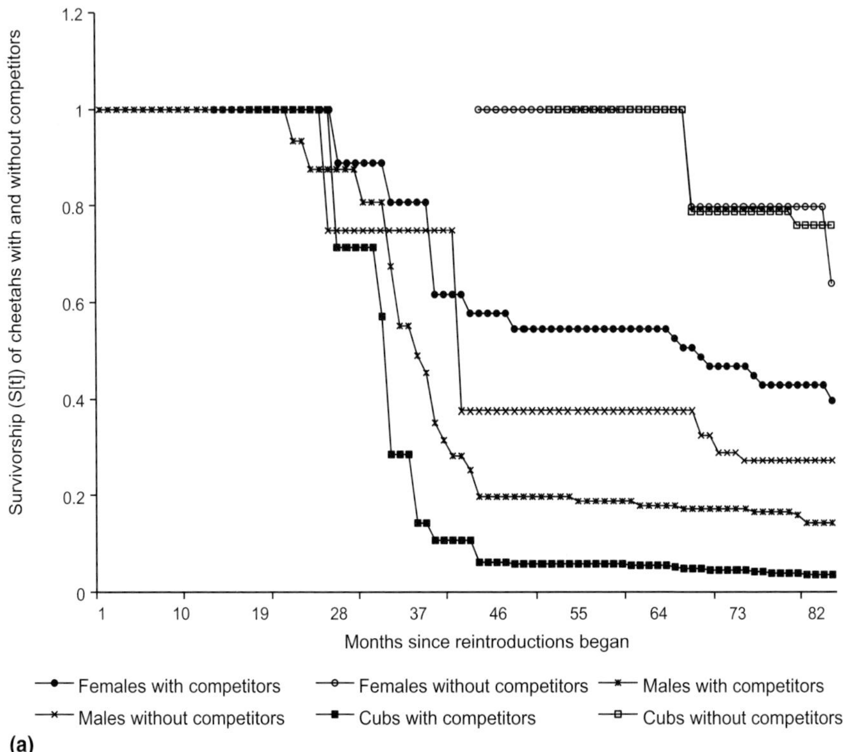

Figure 13.3 **Kaplain-Meier survivorship of cheetahs on relocation reserves (a) with and without other competing predators and (b) for different years.**

sites where they were sympatric (Table 13.2). There was a significantly higher final survivorship value for adults when compared to cubs, and adult female cheetahs survived significantly longer than males (Table 13.2).

The mean annual survivorship for all cheetahs, including cubs born in this study, was 0.14 for the complete 5-year period of the study, and a cheetah in the reintroduced population had an 82.8% chance of surviving for 1 year. Only adult cheetahs were reintroduced, and the final survivorship value for all adult cheetahs was 0.23 (95% CI = 0.1707–0.2869). This means that any adult cheetah released as part of the relocation programme has a 23% chance of surviving for 5 years or an 84.6% chance of surviving for 1 year.

A highly significant difference in cheetah survivorship existed between the different complete years ($Z = -21.47$; df = 5, $p < 0.001$). Survivorship was

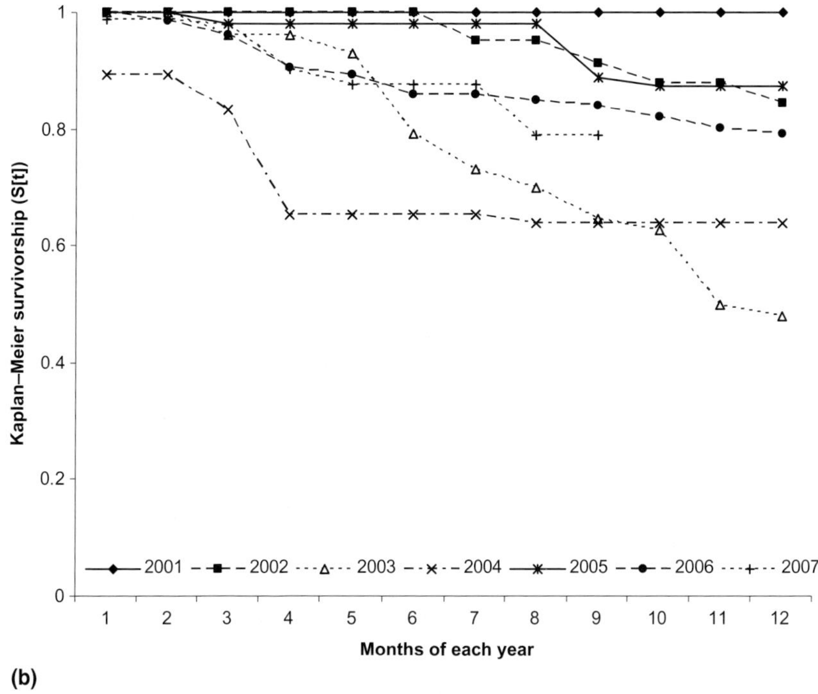

Figure 13.3 ***Continued***

lowest during 2003, owing to eight cheetahs being placed on a reserve where six of them were killed by lions. During the same year, three cheetahs escaped from another reserve and died, and four other cheetahs were not monitored and were classified as censored according to the Kaplan-Meier method (censored animals are those who escaped and could not be found, or whose fates were unknown).

The first cubs from reintroduced parents were born in February 2002. The final survivorship value for cubs was 0.04 (95% CI = 0.0327–0.0570), which meant that cubs born from relocated cheetahs have a 4% chance of surviving for 5 years or an 80.8% chance of surviving for 1 year. However, the final survivorship value for cubs on reserves where competing predators were absent was 0.76 (95% CI = 0.6034–0.9148), compared to a final survivorship value of 0.04 (95% CI = 0.0228–0.0474) when competitors were present. This highly significant difference ($Z = 9.09$; $df = 1$; $p < 0.01$) highlights the impact of dominant competitors on cub survivorship, with an annual survivorship

Table 13.2 **Comparison of the survival of reintroduced cheetahs analysed by age, sex, presence of dominant competitors and year of reintroduction.**

	Z-test results				Log rank test results		
Category	**Z statistic**	**Z squared**	**Degrees of freedom, df**	**Probability**	**Chi-square**	**Degrees of freedom, df**	**Probability**
Years	−21.47	460.78	5	<0.001			
Adults versus cubs	6.02	36.20	1	<0.001	164.8362	83	<0.001
Males versus females	−0.19	0.04	1	0.849	113.1246	83	>0.10
Females with versus without competitors	−1.99	3.95	1	0.047	110.7239	70	<0.001
Males with versus without competitors	−1.45	2.10	1	0.147	218.1531	83	<0.001
Cubs with versus without competitors	9.09	82.56	1	<0.001	134.1494	67	<0.001
All cheetahs with versus without competitors	−0.11	0.01	1	0.912	268.6893	83	<0.001

for cubs without competitors of 95.2% and with competitors of 80.8%. Importantly, cub survivorship is not as important as adult survivorship in long-term population persistence (Crooks *et al.,* 1998), and all of the reintroduced populations still persisted 7 years after the reintroduction programme began. In one population, all but one of the cheetahs were killed by lions, and management decided not to introduce additional cheetahs from ranchlands as they expected that the cheetahs would meet the same fate. The lions here were captive bred—which may have contributed to the problem. However, cheetahs have subsequently been introduced into the study area from other reserves where lions did occur, and these cheetahs are reportedly doing well.

Cheetah cub survival increases dramatically with increase in the age of the cubs. Here, cheetah cubs were not able to be accurately divided into age groups, which could result in the survival values being overestimated. In studies elsewhere, it was found that estimating cub survival after emergence can inflate survival by up to 300% and estimating survival 2 weeks after emergence can overestimate survival by another 150%. (S. Durant, Zoological Society of London, UK; personal communication). Ideally, cub survival should be analysed in age-specific analyses such as mixed linear models (Durant *et al.,* 2004). However, such models do not take into consideration the staggered entry of the reintroductions.

Comparison of survivorship between cheetah populations

The mean annual juvenile survival in the Serengeti was estimated at 0.10 (Kelly & Durant, 2000). This was far lower than that for cubs from reintroduced parents where other competitors were present on the reserve (80.8% annual survivorship; Table 13.1), which is surprising given that cub survival is so low in the Serengeti (Laurenson, 1994). However, Laurenson (1994) did count cubs in the den and monitored them intensively thereafter, which could account for the differences noted between the two studies.

The median survival time for adult males in our study was 38 months and for adult females was more than 53 months (50% survivorship had not yet been achieved for adult females; Table 13.1). On Namibian ranchlands, the median survival for marked adult males was approximately 17 months and for females was 8 months (Marker *et al.,* 2003). (The median survival time of Namibian cheetahs was obtained from Figure 8 in the source by estimating the shortest survival time for which the survivorship function was less than or equal to 0.5—i.e. the value on the *x*-axis where the *y*-axis value is equal to 0.5—as we have used here). On Namibian ranchland, competition with other large carnivores is minimal, whereas persecution from landowners is the main threat (Marker-Krause *et al.*, 1996).

The lowest median survival time (8 months) was for the total female group (including adults and cubs and in reserves both with and without competitors), which is the same as that recorded on Namibian ranchland for adult females. The highest median survival time (54 months) was for the same group of females but on reserves with competitors present; however, females on reserves without competitors had not yet reached a 50% survivorship after 41 months. Adult females generally had the highest survivorship value (S[t] = 0.45; 95% CI = 0.3105–0.5894). All females had higher survivorship values than all males, but this was not significantly different ($Z = -0.19$; df = 1; $p = 0.849$). There was also no significant difference between survival values of females and males in Namibia, although females also had higher survivorship (Marker *et al.*, 2003). In the Serengeti, adult females had mean annual survival of 0.8516 (Durant *et al.*, 2004), which is comparable to the female survival of 0.8960 obtained in this study. Serengeti males had a mean annual survival of 0.6837 (Durant *et al.*, 2004), which is lower than the adult male survival of 0.83 obtained in this study.

Comparison of survival of cheetahs in different study areas is difficult and has some inherent problems including monitoring methods and intensity, age group classifications of cheetahs and different methods of data analyses.

General discussion

Our data show that cub survival on reserves where other large predators were present was lower than adult survivorship. This supports Laurenson's (1995) assertion that cub mortality in the Serengeti limits recruitment and that it may also limit recruitment in reintroduced populations where other large carnivores are present. Some authors have suggested that cub survivorship is not as important as adult survivorship for population persistence, however (Crooks *et al.*, 1998). This reinforces Mills' (2005) view that high levels of cub mortality and intraguild predation are natural elements of cheetah population dynamics.

Reintroduced cheetahs originated from ranchland areas where other competing predators (lions and spotted hyaenas) were not present. It is possible that these females were naive to the dangers of competing predators and were thus not able to effectively protect their cubs. Additionally, cheetahs are thought to avoid competition by seeking out areas of "competition refuge" that have low lion and spotted hyaena densities (Durant, 1998), which is more difficult in small, more densely vegetated and fenced protected areas like those studied here. Kelly & Durant (2000) predicted that cheetah populations would go extinct within 50 years when lion abundance was average or high but that cheetah populations could persist at low lion densities. At first glance, such a prediction appears to cause confusion as to how such an interaction evolved. However, the heterogeneity of African ecosystems would originally have supported diverse herbivore communities that would have favoured lions when their preferred prey were present, and cheetahs when their smaller preferred prey weight range was dominant (Hayward *et al.*, 2007c). This becomes problematic for cheetah conservation today because many reserves are small or homogeneous, such that they lack refuges, or are stocked at artificially high densities to support tourist-attracting species, like lions.

A sudden decrease in cheetah survival was apparent between 20 and 40 months after reintroduction for all groups of cheetahs (Figure 13.3A), suggesting that this is a critical time in which cheetahs need to adapt to their environment in order to survive. This also supports the findings of Marker *et al.* (2003) that time spent in captivity does not affect survival. If it did, the cheetahs would be expected to die soon after release as most had been in captivity for several months by this stage.

In South Africa (this study), Namibia and the Serengeti, female cheetahs have higher survival rates than males, although this was not always significant. Caro (1994) attributed this lower male survival to intra-male aggression. Cheetahs have been killed by other cheetahs in this reintroduction programme when a coalition of males killed three cheetahs on one reserve (Hayward *et al.*, 2007b). A coalition of three males is reported to have killed several cheetahs on Madikwe Game Reserve in the North West Province (M. Hofmeyr, South African National Parks; personal communication). However, most ($n = 10$) of the cheetahs killed by predators in this study were killed by lions (Table 13.3).

Several alternative methods can be used to define a successful reintroduction, but most of these definitions do not apply in small isolated populations of large predators, as in this study (Hayward *et al.*, 2007b). This reintroduction programme is still young and no long-term success can be claimed as yet. However, in the short term, we can use the same definition as for the

Table 13.3 **Causes of post-release death in relocated cheetahs broken down into age and sex categories.**

	Male		Female		
Cause of death	**Subadult**	**Adult**	**Subadult**	**Adult**	**Total**
Natural	0	2	3	1	6
Predators	0	5	2	4	11
Unknown	0	1	0	1	2
Escape/missing	0	5	0	2	7
Disease	2	2	0	0	4
Other	1	1	1	0	3
Total	3	16	6	8	33
	19		14		

evaluation of success of predator reintroduction into confined reserves in the Eastern Cape of South Africa: a reintroduction is considered successful when a 3-year breeding population exists in which recruitment exceeds the adult death rate (Hayward *et al.*, 2007b). Consequently, with the exception of the cheetah population that was reduced to one individual, all reintroductions described here are considered successful, at least in the short term, with females breeding and a general increase in the number of cheetahs in confined reserves. The real measure of success will be the long-term survival of these reintroduced populations.

The challenge now is to manage these small isolated populations under one metapopulation management plan (Davies-Mostert *et al.* this volume). This will require the cooperation of all reserve owners and managers and nature conservation authorities (see Slotow & Hunter, this volume). Alternatively, where several smaller reserves are clustered together, the possibility of dropping fences and managing the area as a single unit will further increase the long-term viability of reintroduced cheetah populations without excessive management (Hayward *et al.*, 2007b). Larger areas may also remove some of the pressure on cheetahs as a result of the presence of lions and spotted hyaenas. Long-term permanent management, however, will be required for the conservation of cheetahs in fenced protected areas (Hayward *et al.*, 2007a). A national cheetah DNA database for cheetahs in fenced conservation areas needs to be developed and maintained; this database will form the basis of a studbook which will allow reserve managers to intelligently swap cheetahs between reserves to ensure maintenance of genetic diversity (Hayward *et al.*, 2007c). Incorporation of pelage patterns (Kelly, 2001) in the studbook would minimize the need for intrusive management interventions aimed at simply identifying individuals requiring translocation (Hayward *et al.*, 2007c). A studbook and organized metapopulation management plan are of vital importance to ensure long-term viability of this fragmented cheetah population in South Africa. This would require cooperation from all the reserves and would mean that this studbook should be consulted before any cheetahs are moved between reserves (e.g. Slotow & Hunter, this volume).

While the relocation of cheetahs is successful, relocation should not be seen as a solution to conflict on ranchlands. There is a large difference between adult cheetah survival on reserves without lions and adult cheetah survival on Namibian ranchland—with lower survival on ranchlands. Namibian ranchlands generally have no large predators present, so survival rates would be expected to be comparable to those on reserves without large predators, but this is not the case. This shows how detrimental persecution can be to the survival of cheetahs outside protected areas. Additionally, the removal of adult cheetahs has been shown to be more detrimental to the survival of the population than the removal of cubs (Crooks *et al.*, 1998). Cheetahs removed from ranchland are mostly adults (this study; Marker *et al.*, 2003) and often males which are trapped at scent-marking posts (McVittie, 1979; Marker, 2002; Wilson, 2006). The effect of these removals on the source population on ranchlands must also be considered and weighed up against the benefits of the reintroductions and the likelihood of the captured individual surviving human persecution on the ranchland.

In this study, relocated cheetahs had a higher median survival time than cheetahs on Namibian ranchlands. No survival data are available for South African ranchlands, so a direct comparison is not possible. This difference in survival could suggest that ranchlands are not ideal conservation areas for cheetahs, as has been suggested by Laurenson (1995) and Kelly & Durant (2000). This also highlights the impact that human conflict can have on cheetah survival outside conservation areas. However, it must be considered that relocated cheetahs are given every possible opportunity to survive, including inoculations and veterinary care for injuries. Cheetahs on ranchlands have to contend with persecution, illegal hunting, illegal capture and trade (Marnewick *et al.*, 2007), road accidents and disease.

Acknowledgements

We would like to thank all the reserve mangers and staff who willingly and enthusiastically provided data for this study. Thanks are also expressed to all members of the National Cheetah Conservation Forum of South Africa Relocation Committee who shared expertise and advised on the placement of cheetahs and to Ann van Dyk who provided excellent husbandry advice on holding wild cheetahs in captivity. The Columbus Zoo and Aquarium provided support for the De Wildt Wild Cheetah Project. Luke Hunter and Sarah Durant gave valuable comment on earlier versions of this manuscript. Ken Pollock kindly cleared up some last-minute statistical questions.

Notes

1 Shannon McKay, Animal Behaviour Consultant, e-mail: chairperson@animal-behaviour.org.za.

References

Anon (1995) Conservation of Namibia's cheetahs. *Cat News* 23, 17–19.

Benson, D.E. (1991) Values and management of wildlife and recreation on private land in South Africa. *Wildlife Society Bulletin* 19(4), 497–510.

Bertschinger, H.J., Jago, M., Nöthling, J.O. & Human, A. (2006) Repeated use of the GnRH analogue deslorelin to down-regulate reproduction in male cheetahs (*Acinonyx jubatus*). *Theriogenology* 66, 1762–1767.

Bertschinger, H.J., Trigg, T.E., Jöchle, W. & Human, A. (2002) Induction of contraception in some African wild carnivores by down regulation of LH and FSH secretion using the GnRH analogue deslorelin. *Reproduction Supplement* 60, 41–52.

Caro, T.M. (1994) *Cheetahs of the Serengeti Plains: Group Living in an Asocial Species.* University of Chicago Press, Chicago.

Crooks, K., Sanjayan, M.A. & Doak, D. (1998) New insights on cheetah conservation through demographic modelling. *Conservation Biology* 12(4), 889–895.

Durant, S.M. (1998) Competition refuges and co-existence: An example from Serengeti carnivores. *Journal of Animal Ecology* 67, 370–386.

Durant, S.M., Kelly, M. & Caro, T.M. (2004) Factors affecting life and death in Serengeti cheetahs: Environment, age, and sociality. *Behavioural Ecology* 15(1), 11–22.

Eloff, T. (2002) The economic realities of the game industry in South Africa. *Sustainable Utilization—Conservation in Practice.* (eds H. Ebedes, B. Reilly, W. Van Hoven & B. Penzhorn), pp. 78–86. South African Game Ranchers Organisation, Pretoria.

Hayward, M.W. (2005) Lessons from South Africa. *Nature Australia* 28, 80.

Hayward, M.W., Adendorff, J., O'Brien, J. et al. (2007a) Practical considerations for the reintroduction of large, terrestrial, mammalian predators based on reintroductions to South Africa's Eastern Cape Province. *The Open Conservation Biology Journal* 1, 1–11.

Hayward, M.W., Adendorff, J., O'Brien, J. et al. (2007b) The re-introduction of large carnivores to the Eastern Cape, South Africa: An assessment. *Oryx* 41(2), 205–213.

Hayward, M.W., O'Brien J. & Kerley G.I.H. (2007c) Carrying capacity of large African predators: Predictions and tests. *Biological Conservation* 139, 219–29.

Hofmeyr, M. & van Dyk, G. (1998) Cheetah introductions to two north-west parks: Case studies from Pilanesburg National Park and Madikwe Game Reserve. *Cheetahs as Game Ranch Animals.* (ed. B.L. Penzhorn), pp. 60–71. Wildlife Group of the South African Veterinary Association, Onderstepoort.

Hunter, L.T.B. (1998) Early post-release movements and behaviour of reintroduced cheetahs and lions, and technical considerations in large carnivore restoration. *Cheetahs as Game Ranch Animals.* (ed. B.L. Penzhorn), pp. 72–82. Wildlife Group of the South African Veterinary Association, Onderstepoort.

Kellert, S.R. (1985) Social and perceptual factors in endangered species management. *Journal of Wildlife Management* 49, 528–536.

Kelly, M.J. (2001) Computer-aided photograph matching in studies using individual identification: An example from Serengeti cheetahs. *Journal of Mammalogy* 82(2), 440–449.

Kelly, M.J. & Durant, S.M. (2000) Viability of the Serengeti cheetah population. *Conservation Biology* 14, 786–797.

Laurenson, M.K. (1994) High juvenile mortality in cheetahs (*Acinonyx jubatus*) and its consequence for maternal care. *Journal of Zoology* 234, 387–408.

Laurenson, M.K. (1995) Implications of high offspring mortality for cheetah population dynamics. *Serengeti II: Dynamics, Management and Conservation of an Ecosystem.* (eds A.R.E. Sinclair & P. Arcese), pp. 385–399. The University of Chicago Press, Chicago.

Linnell, J.D., Aanes, R., Swenson, J.E., Odden, J. & Smith, M.E. (1997) Translocation of carnivores as a method for managing problem animals: A review. *Biodiversity and Conservation* 6, 1245–1257.

Marker, L.L. (2002) *Aspects of Cheetah* Acinonyx jubatus *Biology, Ecology and Conservation Strategies on Namibian farmlands.* PhD thesis, University of Oxford.

Marker, L.L., Dickman, A.J., Jeo, R.M., Mills, M.G.L. & Macdonald, D.W. (2003) Demography of the Namibian cheetah, *Acinonyx jubatus jubatus. Biological Conservation* 114, 413–425.

Marker-Krause, L., Krause, D., Barnett, D. & Hurlbut, S. (1996) *Cheetah Survival on Namibian Farmlands.* Cheetahs Conservation Fund, Windhoek.

Marnewick, K. & Cilliers, D. (2006) Range use of two coalitions of male cheetahs *Acinonyx jubatus* in the Thabazimbi district of the Limpopo province, South Africa. *South African Journal of Wildlife Research* 36(2): 147–151.

Marnewick, K., Beckhelling, A., Cilliers, D. et al. (2007) The status of the cheetah in South Africa. *Cat News Special Edition: The Status and Conservation Needs of the Cheetah in Southern Africa.* (eds C. Breitenmoser & S. Durant), pp. 22–31, IUCN Cat Specialist Group, Gland, Switzerland.

McVittie, R. (1979) Changes in the social behaviour of South West African cheetah. *Madoqua* 11(3), 171–184.

Mech, L.D. (1981) *The Wolf: Ecology and Behaviour of an Endangered Species.* Doubleday, New York.

Mills M. G. L. (2005) Large carnivores and biodiversity in African savanna ecosystems. *Large Carnivores and the Conservation of Biodiversity.* (eds J.C. Ray, K.H. Redford, R.S. Steneck & J. Berger), pp. 208–229. Island Press, Washington.

Moehrenschlager, A. & Somers, M.J. (2004) Canid reintroductions and metapopulation management. *Canids: Foxes, Wolves, Jackals and Dogs. Status Survey and Conservation Action Plan.* (eds C. Sillero-Zubiri, M. Hoffman. &. D.W.Macdonald), pp. 289–298. IUCN/SSC Canid Specialist Group, Gland, Switzerland.

Pettifer, H.L. (1981) Aspects of the ecology of cheetahs (*Acinonyx jubatus*) on the Suikerbosrand Nature Reserve. *Worldwide Furbearer Conference Proceedings.* (eds J.A. Chapman & D. Pursely), pp. 1121–1142, Vol. 2. Virginia.

Pollock, K.H., Winterstein, S.R. Bunck, C.M. & Curtis, P.D. (1989) Survival analyses in telemetry studies: The staggered entry design. *Journal of Wildlife Management* 53, 7–15.

Purchase, G.K. & Vhurumuku, G. (2006) *Evaluation of a Wild-Wild Translocation of Cheetah* (Acinonyx jubatus) *from Private Land to Matusadona National Park, Zimbabwe (1994–2005).* Report to the Zambezi Society, Bulawayo. Available: http://www.zamsoc.org. Accessed: 14 October 2008.

Van Der Waal, C. & Dekker, B. (2000) Game ranching in the Northern Province of South Africa. *South African Journal of Wildlife Research* 30(4), 151–156.

Van Dyk, G. & Slotow, R. (2003) The effects of fences and lions on the ecology of African wild dogs reintroduced to Pilanesberg National Park, South Africa. *African Zoology* 38, 79–94.

Wilson, K.A. (2006) *Status and Distribution of the Cheetah outside Formal Conservation Areas in the Thabazimbi district, Limpopo province.* MSc (Wildlife Management) dissertation, University of Pretoria.

14

A Framework for Evaluating Reintroduction Success in Carnivores: Lessons from African Wild Dogs

Markus Gusset[1]

[1]Wildlife Conservation Research Unit, Department of Zoology, University of Oxford

Summary

To provide a framework for assessing reintroduction success in carnivores, I evaluated one of the most extensive endangered species reintroduction efforts to date, namely the establishment of an actively managed metapopulation of African wild dogs, *Lycaon pictus*, in South Africa. This intensive management approach involves the reintroduction of wild dogs into suitable conservation areas and periodic translocations among them. Analyses of individual survival, breeding success and population viability suggested that the crucial factor influencing wild dog reintroduction success is dispersal behaviour (natural or artificial) and the resulting formation (natural or artificial) of new packs, given the dependency of wild dogs to living in cohesive social groups for successful reproduction. This case study provides several lessons for reintroduction biologists. (1) It illustrates the virtue of defining criteria with which to gauge reintroduction success. (2) It outlines two potential modelling approaches for assessing short- and long-term reintroduction success. (3) It highlights how reintroduction success may be related to unanticipated factors. (4) It proposes future avenues for investigation specifically targeted

Reintroduction of Top-Order Predators, 1st edition. Edited by M.W. Hayward and M.J. Somers.
 ISBN 978-1-4051-7680-4 (pb) and 978-1-4051-9273-6 (hb)

at improving reintroduction success. (5) Perhaps most importantly, this study demonstrates the importance of monitoring and evaluation in reintroduction programmes.

Definitions and determinants of reintroduction success

Reintroductions are a commonly used and potentially powerful tool for ecological restoration and endangered species recovery (Macdonald *et al.*, 2002; van Wieren, 2006). There may even be legal obligations to re-establish a species within its historical range following extirpation or extinction (Rees, 2001). Interestingly, however, there is no general agreement on what constitutes a successful reintroduction. Although the principal aim of any reintroduction attempt is to establish a self-sustaining population that requires minimal long-term management (IUCN, 1998), this may not be a pragmatic criterion for success (Hayward *et al.*, 2007a,b). Instead, we could consider a reintroduction as comprising a sequence of three objectives (Seddon, 1999): survival of the release generation; breeding by the release generation and their offspring; and persistence of the re-established population, perhaps assessed through population viability modelling (Sarrazin & Barbault, 1996). Evaluations of reintroduction success, a designated key aspect of any reintroduction programme (IUCN, 1998), should thus have both a short- and long-term component (Figure 14.1), with time frames depending on the target species' life history traits.

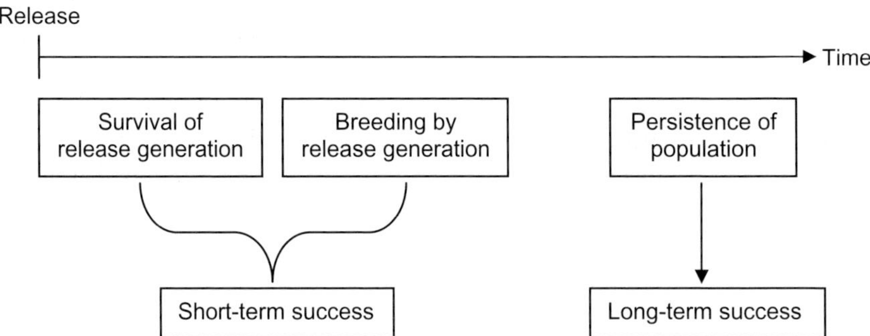

Figure 14.1 **Short- and long-term criteria for evaluating reintroduction success.**

Previous evaluations of reintroduction success suggested that characteristics of the released animals, aspects of the release sites and circumstances of the release events are the best indicators for meeting the respective success criteria (Griffith *et al.*, 1989; Kleiman, 1989; Beck *et al.*, 1994; Kleiman *et al.*, 1994; Wolf *et al.*, 1996, 1998; Reading *et al.*, 1997; Fischer & Lindenmayer, 2000). Despite a taxonomic bias towards reintroducing carnivores (Seddon *et al.*, 2005), carnivore reintroductions have been qualitatively reviewed only (Reading & Clark, 1996; Breitenmoser *et al.*, 2001). Decisive predictors of reintroduction success did not emerge from these two reviews, demonstrating the need for evaluating success within and across taxa.

Evaluating reintroduction success: a case study

To provide a framework for assessing reintroduction success in carnivores, I evaluated one of the most extensive endangered species reintroduction efforts to date, namely the establishment of an actively managed metapopulation of African wild dogs, *Lycaon pictus*, in South Africa (see Davies-Mostert *et al.*, this volume). In an effort to restore wild dog numbers in increasingly fragmented landscapes and to complement the single viable population in South Africa occurring in Kruger National Park, a plan was launched to manage separate subpopulations of wild dogs in several small, geographically isolated conservation areas as a single metapopulation (Mills *et al.*, 1998). This intensive management approach involves the reintroduction of wild dogs into suitable conservation areas, and periodic translocations among them to mimic natural dispersal and maintain gene flow (also see Frankham, this volume).

Similar to carnivore reintroductions worldwide (Yalden, 1993; Reading & Clark, 1996; Linnell *et al.*, 1997; Miller *et al.*, 1999; Breitenmoser *et al.*, 2001; Hayward & Somers, this volume), reintroducing wild dogs in South Africa is a controversial issue. Wild dogs can act as an umbrella and flagship species for conservation and can provide financial benefits through ecotourism. At the same time, however, wild dogs can come into conflict with humans keeping livestock and economically valuable game species (also see Lindsey *et al.*, this volume). There have been numerous attempts to reintroduce wild dogs in Africa during the past 30 years, many of which have met with limited success owing to various, often unknown, causes (see Table 1 in Gusset *et al.*, 2006b). Reintroduction was thus not considered a high priority in wild dog conservation (Woodroffe & Ginsberg, 1997, 1999; Woodroffe *et al.*, 2004).

Nevertheless, particularly with the implementation of the metapopulation management plan, wild dogs have been successfully reintroduced into various sites in South Africa (Moehrenschlager & Somers, 2004; Davies-Mostert *et al.*, this volume).

The initial target size of nine packs for the metapopulation (Mills *et al.*, 1998) was achieved in just half of the allotted 10 years (Lindsey *et al.*, 2005; Davies-Mostert *et al.*, this volume). However, despite the high costs associated with continuing wild dog reintroductions and translocations (Lindsey *et al.*, 2005), factors that have led to this success remain elusive. Therefore, the South African wild dog metapopulation management plan provided an opportunity to evaluate both short- and long-term reintroduction success (*sensu* Seddon, 1999) within an endangered species over time and across locations from a multi-disciplinary perspective (Gusset, 2006). Analyses of individual survival, breeding success and population viability were used to assess reintroduction success against the criteria defined in Figure 14.1.

Evaluating short-term reintroduction success

Known-fate modelling in program MARK was used to estimate the survival of reintroduced wild dogs and their offspring, and to model covariate effects relative to survival (Gusset *et al.*, 2008b). Using different reintroduction attempts as natural quasi experiments, explicit *a priori* hypotheses on indicators of reintroduction success were tested. Data were collected by post-release monitoring from 12 reintroduction sites and 18 release events, resulting in a total of 256 individual records (127 released wild dogs, which produced 129 pups).

Reintroduced wild dogs and their offspring had high short-term survival rates (Figure 14.2), with offspring produced at all release sites included in this analysis within 2 years after release (for release sites, see Davies-Mostert *et al.*, this volume). Information-theoretic inference revealed that wild dog reintroductions should be attempted with socially integrated animals that are released into securely fenced areas, unless measures are implemented to mitigate human-related mortalities outside protected areas.

Evaluating long-term reintroduction success

An individual-based, pattern-oriented model of wild dog population and pack dynamics was developed (Gusset *et al.*, unpublished data). This custom built

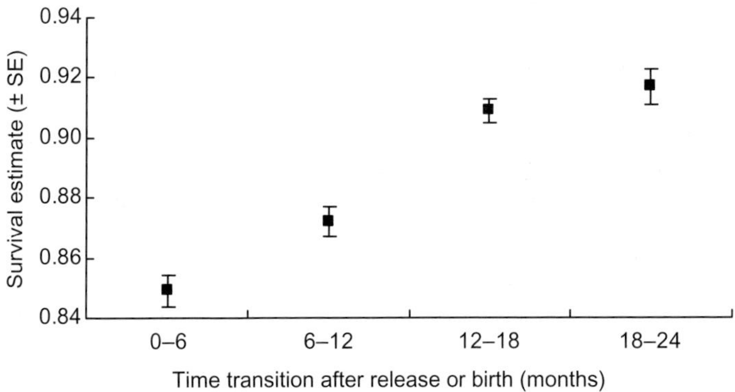

Figure 14.2 **Survival estimates for reintroduced wild dogs and their offspring over four time transitions after release or birth.**

model appeared to capture the essential characteristics of a reintroduced wild dog population monitored over a 25-year period (Somers *et al.*, 2008) and to be relatively robust to parameter uncertainty, suggesting that it was valid enough for addressing management problems. Local sensitivity analysis showed that the most sensitive parameter relevant for management was dispersal mortality.

A small reintroduced wild dog population consisting of one to four packs had a good chance of long-term persistence (i.e. a long intrinsic mean time to extinction) under logistically realistic release and intervention protocols, provided that the population was periodically supplemented with additional packs (Figure 14.3). The model revealed that floating disperser groups buffer a population's reproductive capacity from a loss of breeding individuals and that the formation of new packs was limited by a shortage of suitable unrelated mates at low pack numbers (i.e. a mate-finding Allee effect).

Conclusions of case study

According to the criteria defined in Figure 14.1, the evaluated wild dog reintroductions can be considered successful. The consensual outcome of the two models presented above suggests that the crucial factor influencing wild dog reintroduction success is dispersal behaviour (natural or artificial) and the resulting formation (natural or artificial) of new packs, given the

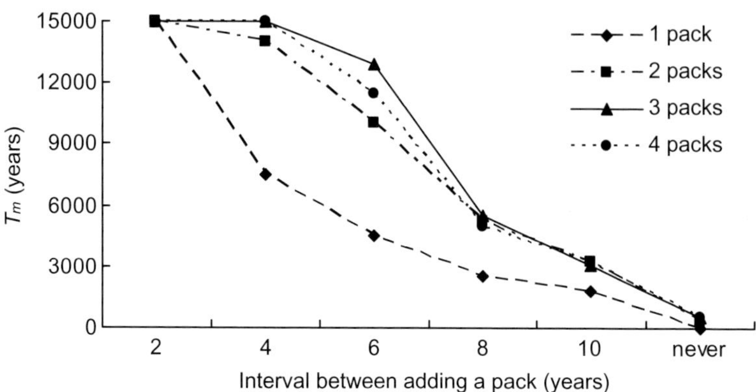

Figure 14.3 **Intrinsic mean time to extinction (T_m) of a small reintroduced wild dog population under different initial conditions and supplementation regimes (pack size = 6; no harvesting).**

dependency of wild dogs to living in cohesive social groups for successful reproduction (also see Graf *et al.*, 2006; Gusset *et al.*, 2006a,b; Gusset *et al.*, 2008a,b; Somers *et al.*, 2008). This process can evidently be constrained by human-related mortality of dispersers, a mate-finding Allee effect that hampers pack formation and a lack of social integration in artificially composed packs (Figure 14.4). Investigating and facilitating dispersal behaviour of wild dogs outside protected areas, unravelling the intricate process of pack formation in wild dogs and improving human conservation behaviour towards wild dogs should thus form the focus of future conservation management and research activities.

This case study provides several lessons for reintroduction biologists.

1 It illustrates the virtue of defining criteria with which to gauge reintroduction success.
2 It outlines two potential modelling approaches for assessing short- and long-term reintroduction success.
3 It highlights how reintroduction success may be related to unanticipated factors (cf. Mills *et al.*, 1998).
4 It proposes future avenues for investigation specifically targeted at improving reintroduction success.

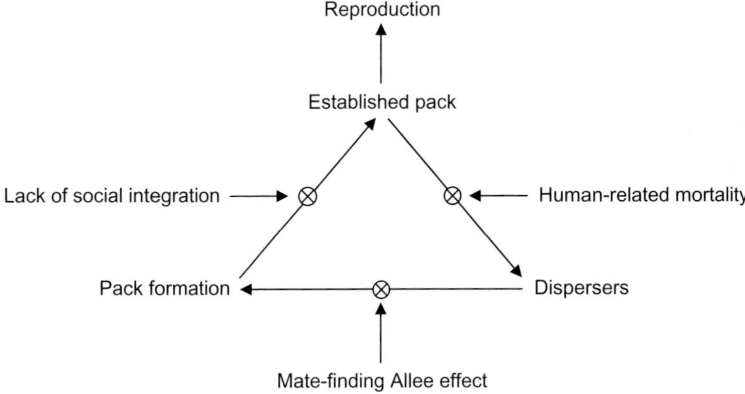

Figure 14.4 **Schematic illustration of how wild dog reintroductions can be constrained by behavioural factors (including human behaviour).**

5 Perhaps most importantly, this study demonstrates the importance of monitoring and evaluation in reintroduction programmes.

This case study may provide guidelines for how a rigorous assessment of reintroduction success can be undertaken with the appropriate level of focused pre- and post-release data collection. The outlined process could serve as a generic approach to evaluating other (carnivore) reintroductions against set measurable objectives. I will next elaborate on some of the implications, all which are interrelated, of these conclusions for reintroduction biology.

Implications for reintroduction biology

In reintroduction attempts, it would be ideal to release a group of animals that will survive, breed and thereby establish a self-sustaining population with a high probability of long-term persistence—all without post-release interventions. However, this is not always feasible (Seddon, 1999); human-induced fragmentation of the landscape often leaves nothing but small patches of suitable habitat, which can sustain only a limited number of animals and, to a large extent, this fragmentation prevents natural dispersal among patches. It might thus be unrealistic to expect survival and persistence without periodic interventions, thereby creating actively managed metapopulations (Moehrenschlager & Somers, 2004; Akçakaya *et al.*, 2007). If this conservation strategy is to be considered an important wildlife management tool, we would be well advised to ensure that best practices are applied.

A particularly neglected aspect in endangered species recovery is that a species' decline is often brought about by adverse effects that are mediated by behaviour (Curio, 1996; Sutherland, 1998; Caro, 1999; Buchholz, 2007). Except for the potential effects of captivity on behaviour (Jule *et al.*, 2008; Christie, this volume), behavioural considerations do not feature prominently in reviews of reintroductions (Griffith *et al.*, 1989; Beck *et al.*, 1994; Kleiman *et al.*, 1994; Wolf *et al.*, 1996, 1998; Reading *et al.*, 1997; Fischer & Lindenmayer, 2000; Macdonald *et al.*, 2002; van Wieren, 2006; but see Kleiman, 1989; Somers & Gusset, this volume). Without paying attention to behavioural details (e.g. pre-release socialization in the case study above), well-intentioned recovery programmes may waste valuable funds and even have detrimental effects on the population under recovery. Unfortunately, the practicalities of incorporating behavioural considerations into decision-making often remain unclear, and conservation practitioners continue to have difficulties recognizing how behavioural knowledge can help tackle real-world conservation challenges. The same applies to considering animal-welfare issues (e.g. effects of stress) in reintroduction attempts (Shepherdson, 1994; Teixeira *et al.*, 2007; Marnewick *et al.*, this volume). I thus call for increased integration between the fields of animal behaviour and reintroduction biology.

Past failures demonstrate that the science of reintroduction biology is still in its infancy (Stanley Price & Soorae, 2003; Seddon *et al.*, 2007; Armstrong & Seddon, 2008), which prompts us to learn from earlier experiences. Reintroduction success has not increased over time (Fischer & Lindenmayer, 2000), and many reintroduction attempts are heavily based upon subjective beliefs (Hein, 1997), as conservation efforts in general are not always based upon a critical appraisal of the available evidence (Pullin *et al.*, 2004; Pullin & Knight, 2005). The absence of rigorous evaluation has been identified as a major obstacle in promoting conservation biology as a scientific discipline (Kleiman *et al.*, 2000; Stem *et al.*, 2005; Ferraro & Pattanayak, 2006). The emerging field of evidence-based conservation holds promise for predicting those management actions that are likely to be most effective in achieving conservation goals (Pullin & Knight, 2001, 2003; Sutherland *et al.*, 2004).

Reintroduction programmes may, however, succeed despite the absence of rigorous hypothesis testing, experimental design, monitoring or adequate documentation. The number of animals may increase with little understanding of the mechanisms involved, so there may be no scientific basis on which to make adjustments when problems arise. Similarly, it is possible for a programme to reach its goals, but to do so inefficiently or with negative secondary effects (Kleiman *et al.*, 2000). Failure to objectively evaluate programmes could lead to the acceptance of practices that may be suboptimal, and unevaluated practices may be adopted simply because they have been used in the past (Sutherland *et al.*, 2004). A greater shift to evidence-based conservation would allow for actively demonstrating the effectiveness of conservation efforts and would help to ensure that the results of research can have an impact upon practice (Pullin & Stewart, 2006). The production of comprehensive evaluations can justify management actions by citing scientific evidence to increase transparency and credibility, especially if these actions are controversial (e.g. fencing in the case study above), as is often the case in carnivore reintroductions. Furthermore, such systematic reviews can help evaluate the relative effectiveness of different reintroduction strategies, thus maximizing the efficiency of limited conservation funding.

In conclusion, reintroductions, in general, and carnivore reintroductions, in particular, are extremely lengthy, costly and complex processes (IUCN, 1998), necessitating proper multi-disciplinary evaluation to underpin management recommendations with scientific evidence. Evaluating conservation efforts, however, is generally hampered by a lack of monitoring and documentation (Nichols & Williams, 2006). Specifically required are data on the behaviour and dynamics of reintroduced populations, which allow for building models to assess short- and long-term reintroduction success against defined criteria (Seddon, 1999), as advocated in the case study above. I thus encourage long-term monitoring of reintroduced animals and the effects of management practices, and I also advocate assessment of the level of intervention necessary to achieve population establishment and persistence. Pre- and post-release monitoring should be directed specifically towards addressing questions framed during the reintroduction planning stages. I also prompt the authorities in charge to disseminate their findings (including failures), and I suggest integrating guidelines and mechanisms for regular evaluations into reintroduction programmes. Without monitoring and evaluation, the possibility of adaptive management is severely limited.

Outlook

Reintroductions are not only used for endangered species recovery (as in the case study above), but can also be an integral component of ecological restoration (Macdonald *et al.*, 2002; van Wieren, 2006). Here, one goal can be the re-establishment of top predators in ecosystems from which they have been lost (Hayward & Somers, this volume). Therefore, the next challenge is to predict the response of carnivores to reintroductions (Hayward, this volume) and to assess the effects of reintroduced carnivores on ecosystem functioning (e.g. Smith & Bangs, this volume). A priority should be on evaluating functional densities at which top predators need to be restored, in order to reverse ecological as well as biological extinction.

Acknowledgements

Volker Grimm, Oliver Jakoby, Michael Müller and Sadie Ryan provided invaluable help in implementing the two models. I thank the editors for inviting me to the conference and to write this chapter. The Society for Conservation Biology generously provided financial support to attend the conference. I am grateful to two anonymous referees for helpful comments on this chapter.

References

Akçakaya, H.R., Mills, G. & Doncaster, C.P. (2007) The role of metapopulations in conservation. *Key Topics in Conservation Biology*. (eds D. Macdonald & K. Service), pp. 64–84. Blackwell Publishing, Oxford.

Armstrong, D.B. & Seddon, P.J. (2008) Directions in reintroduction biology. *Trends in Ecology and Evolution* 23, 20–25.

Beck, B.B., Rapaport, L.G., Stanley Price, M.R. & Wilson, A.C. (1994) Reintroduction of captive-born animals. *Creative Conservation: Interactive Management of Wild and Captive Animals*. (eds P.J.S. Olney, G.M. Mace & A.T.C. Feistner), pp. 265–286. Chapman and Hall, London.

Breitenmoser, U., Breitenmoser-Würsten, C., Carbyn, L.N. & Funk, S.M. (2001) Assessment of carnivore reintroductions. *Carnivore conservation*. (eds J.L. Gittleman, S.M. Funk, D. Macdonald & R.K. Wayne), pp. 241–281. Cambridge University Press, Cambridge.

Buchholz, R. (2007) Behavioural biology: An effective and relevant conservation tool. *Trends in Ecology and Evolution* 22, 401–407.

Caro, T. (1999) The behaviour–conservation interface. *Trends in Ecology and Evolution* 14, 366–369.

Curio, E. (1996) Conservation needs ethology. *Trends in Ecology and Evolution* 11, 260–263.

Ferraro, P.J. & Pattanayak, S.K. (2006) Money for nothing? A call for empirical evaluation of biodiversity conservation investments. *PLoS Biology* 4, 482–488.

Fischer, J. & Lindenmayer, D.B. (2000) An assessment of the published results of animal relocations. *Biological Conservation* 96, 1–11.

Graf, J.A., Gusset, M., Reid, C., Janse van Rensburg, S., Slotow, R. & Somers, M.J. (2006) Evolutionary ecology meets wildlife management: Artificial group augmentation in the re-introduction of endangered African wild dogs (*Lycaon pictus*). *Animal Conservation* 9, 398–403.

Griffith, B., Scott, J.M., Carpenter, J.W. & Reed, C. (1989) Translocation as a species conservation tool: Status and strategy. *Science* 245, 477–480.

Gusset, M. (2006) *The Re-introduction of Endangered African Wild Dogs* (Lycaon pictus)*—A Multi-Disciplinary Evaluation.* PhD thesis, University of KwaZulu-Natal.

Gusset, M., Graf, J.A. & Somers, M.J. (2006a) The re-introduction of endangered wild dogs into Hluhluwe-iMfolozi Park, South Africa: An update on the first 25 years. *Re-introduction News* 25, 31–33.

Gusset, M., Maddock, A.H., Gunther, G.J. et al. (2008a) Conflicting human interests over the re-introduction of endangered wild dogs in South Africa. *Biodiversity and Conservation* 17, 83–101.

Gusset, M., Ryan, S.J., Hofmeyr, M. et al. (2008b) Efforts going to the dogs? Evaluating attempts to re-introduce endangered wild dogs in South Africa. *Journal of Applied Ecology* 45, 100–108.

Gusset, M., Slotow, R. & Somers, M.J. (2006b) Divided we fail: The importance of social integration for the re-introduction of endangered African wild dogs (*Lycaon pictus*). *Journal of Zoology, London* 270, 502–511.

Hayward, M.W., Adendorff, J., O'Brien, J. et al. (2007a) Practical considerations for the reintroduction of large, terrestrial, mammalian predators based on reintroductions to South Africa's Eastern Cape Province. *The Open Conservation Biology Journal* 1, 1–11.

Hayward, M.W., Adendorff, J., O'Brien, J. et al. (2007b) The reintroduction of large carnivores to the Eastern Cape, South Africa: An assessment. *Oryx* 41, 205–214.

Hein, E.W. (1997) Improving translocation programs. *Conservation Biology* 11, 1270–1271.

IUCN (1998) *IUCN Guidelines for Re-introductions*. IUCN, Gland, Switzerland.

Jule, K.R., Leaver, L.A. & Lea, S.E.G. (2008) The effects of captive experience on reintroduction survival in carnivores: A review and analysis. *Biological Conservation* 141, 355–363.

Kleiman, D.G. (1989) Reintroduction of captive mammals for conservation: Guidelines for reintroducing endangered species into the wild. *BioScience* 39, 152–161.

Kleiman, D.G., Reading, R.P., Miller, B.J. et al. (2000) Improving the evaluation of conservation programs. *Conservation Biology* 14, 356–365.

Kleiman, D.G., Stanley Price, M.R. & Beck, B.B. (1994) Criteria for reintroductions. *Creative Conservation: Interactive Management of Wild and Captive Animals.* (eds P.J.S. Olney, G.M. Mace & A.T.C. Feistner), pp. 287–303. Chapman and Hall, London.

Lindsey, P.A., Alexander, R., Du Toit, J.T. & Mills, M.G.L. (2005) The cost efficiency of wild dog conservation in South Africa. *Conservation Biology* 19, 1205–1214.

Linnell, J.D.C., Aanes, R., Swenson, J.E., Odden, J. & Smith, M.E. (1997) Translocation of carnivores as a method for managing problem animals: A review. *Biodiversity and Conservation* 6, 1245–1257.

Macdonald, D.W., Moorhouse, T.P., Enck, J.W. & Tattersall, F.H. (2002) Mammals. *Handbook of Ecological Restoration: Principles of Restoration.* (eds M.R. Perrow & A.J. Davy), pp. 389–408. Cambridge University Press, Cambridge.

Miller, B., Ralls, K., Reading, R.P., Scott, J.M. & Estes, J. (1999) Biological and technical considerations of carnivore translocation: A review. *Animal Conservation* 2, 59–68.

Mills, M.G.L., Ellis, S., Woodroffe, R. et al. (eds) (1998) *Population and Habitat Viability Assessment for the African Wild Dog* (Lycaon pictus) *in Southern Africa.* Final workshop report. IUCN/SSC Conservation Breeding Specialist Group, Apple Valley.

Moehrenschlager, A. & Somers, M.J. (2004) Canid reintroductions and metapopulation management. *Canids: Foxes, Wolves, Jackals and Dogs: Status Survey and Conservation Action Plan.* (eds C. Sillero-Zubiri, M. Hoffmann & D.W. Macdonald), pp. 289–297. IUCN, Gland, Switzerland.

Nichols, J.D. & Williams, B.K. (2006) Monitoring for conservation. *Trends in Ecology and Evolution* 21, 668–673.

Pullin, A.S. & Knight, T.M. (2001) Effectiveness in conservation practice: Pointers from medicine and public health. *Conservation Biology* 15, 50–54.

Pullin, A.S. & Knight, T.M. (2003) Support for decision making in conservation practice: An evidence-based approach. *Journal for Nature Conservation* 11, 83–90.

Pullin, A.S. & Knight, T.M. (2005) Assessing conservation management's evidence base: A survey of management-plan compilers in the United Kingdom and Australia. *Conservation Biology* 19, 1989–1996.

Pullin, A.S. & Stewart, G.B. (2006) Guidelines for systematic review in conservation and environmental management. *Conservation Biology* 20, 1647–1656.

Pullin, A.S., Knight, T.M., Stone, D.A. & Charman, K. (2004) Do conservation managers use scientific evidence to support their decision-making? *Biological Conservation* 119, 245–252.

Reading, R.P. & Clark, T.W. (1996) Carnivore reintroductions: An interdisciplinary examination. *Carnivore Behavior, Ecology, and Evolution.* (ed. J.L. Gittleman), pp. 296–336. Cornell University Press, Ithaca.

Reading, R.P., Clark, T.W. & Griffith, B. (1997) The influence of valuational and organizational considerations on the success of rare species translocations. *Biological Conservation* 79, 217–225.

Rees, P.A. (2001) Is there a legal obligation to reintroduce animal species into their former habitats? *Oryx* 35, 216–223.

Sarrazin, F. & Barbault, R. (1996). Reintroductions: Challenges and lessons for basic ecology. *Trends in Ecology and Evolution* 11, 474–478.

Seddon, P.J. (1999) Persistence without intervention: Assessing success in wildlife reintroductions. *Trends in Ecology and Evolution* 14, 503.

Seddon, P.J., Armstrong, D.P. & Maloney, R.F. (2007) Developing the science of reintroduction biology. *Conservation Biology* 21, 303–312.

Seddon, P.J., Soorae, P.S. & Launay, F. (2005) Taxonomic bias in reintroduction projects. *Animal Conservation* 8, 51–58.

Shepherdson, D. (1994) The role of environmental enrichment in the captive breeding and re-introduction of endangered species. *Creative Conservation: Interactive Management of Wild and Captive Animals.* (eds P.J.S. Olney, G.M. Mace & A.T.C. Feistner), pp. 167–177. Chapman and Hall, London.

Somers, M.J., Graf, J.A., Szykman, M., Slotow, R. & Gusset, M. (2008) Dynamics of a small re-introduced population of wild dogs over 25 years: Allee effects and the implications of sociality for endangered species' recovery. *Oecologia* 158, 239–247.

Stanley Price, M.R. & Soorae, P.S. (2003) Reintroductions: Whence and whither? *International Zoo Yearbook* 38, 61–75.

Stem, C., Margoluis, R., Salafsky, N. & Brown, M. (2005) Monitoring and evaluation in conservation: A review of trends and approaches. *Conservation Biology* 19, 295–309.

Sutherland, W.J. (1998) The importance of behavioural studies in conservation biology. *Animal Behaviour* 56, 801–809.

Sutherland, W.J., Pullin, A.S., Dolman, P.M. & Knight, T.M. (2004) The need for evidence-based conservation. *Trends in Ecology and Evolution* 19, 305–308.

Teixeira, C.P., De Azevedo, C.S., Mendl, M., Cipreste, C.F. & Young, R.J. (2007) Revisiting translocation and reintroduction programmes: The importance of considering stress. *Animal Behaviour* 73, 1–13.

van Wieren, S.E. (2006) Populations: Re-introductions. *Restoration Ecology: The New Frontier*. (eds J. van Andel & J. Aronson), pp. 82–92. Blackwell Publishing, Malden.

Wolf, C.M., Garland Jr., T. & Griffith, B. (1998) Predictors of avian and mammalian translocation success: Reanalysis with phylogenetically independent contrasts. *Biological Conservation* 86, 243–255.

Wolf, C.M., Griffith, B., Reed, C. & Temple, S.A. (1996) Avian and mammalian translocations: Update and reanalysis of 1987 survey data. *Conservation Biology* 10, 1142–1154.

Woodroffe, R. & Ginsberg, J.R. (1997) The role of captive breeding and reintroduction in wild dog conservation. *The African Wild Dog: Status Survey and Conservation Action Plan*. (eds R. Woodroffe, J. Ginsberg & D. Macdonald), pp. 100–111. IUCN, Gland, Switzerland.

Woodroffe, R. & Ginsberg, J.R. (1999) Conserving the African wild dog *Lycaon pictus*. II. Is there a role for reintroduction? *Oryx* 33, 143–151.

Woodroffe, R., McNutt, J.W. & Mills, M.G.L. (2004) African wild dog *Lycaon pictus* (Temminck, 1820). *Canids: Foxes, Wolves, Jackals and Dogs: Status Survey and Conservation Action Plan*. (eds C. Sillero-Zubiri, M. Hoffmann & D.W. Macdonald), pp. 174–183. IUCN, Gland, Switzerland.

Yalden, D.W. (1993) The problems of reintroducing carnivores. *Symposia of the Zoological Society of London* 65, 289–306.

15

A Synthesis of Early Indicators of the Drivers of Predator Conservation on Private Lands in South Africa

Peter A. Lindsey[1], *Stephanie S. Romañach*[2] *and Harriet T. Davies-Mostert*[3]

[1]Mammal Research Institute, University of Pretoria
[2]Tropical Resource Ecology Programme, University of Zimbabwe
[3]Carnivore Conservation Group, Endangered Wildlife Trust, and Wildlife Conservation Research Unit (WildCRU), Oxford University

Summary

Legislative changes granting user rights to landowners over wildlife occurring on their land have resulted in a large-scale land-use shift from livestock farming to game ranching in southern Africa. These changes have resulted in significant benefits for wildlife conservation in general, but had more questionable outcomes for predator conservation. While predators have been widely reintroduced onto private game reserves, persecution of free-ranging predators on game ranchland is commonplace. Prospects for conserving predators are poor where land uses involve livestock or the consumptive utilization of wildlife (particularly where high proportions of ungulate populations are utilized annually). Conversely, effective predator conservation is most likely where the financial costs associated with having predators are low, and where the financial and ecological benefits associated with conserving

Reintroduction of Top-Order Predators, 1st edition. Edited by M.W. Hayward and M.J. Somers.
 ISBN 978-1-4051-7680-4 (pb) and 978-1-4051-9273-6 (hb)

them are high. These conditions are commonly met in conservancies where multiple landowners remove internal game fencing to create larger wildlife areas. On conservancies, the most viable land uses are typically ecotourism or low off-take trophy hunting. Under these conditions, predators are key draw cards for tourists and hunters, the financial costs associated with predators are low, and predators play an important ecological role by controlling prey populations. Efforts to promote the conservation status of predators on private land in southern Africa should focus on encouraging the formation of conservancies to increase the area available for predator reintroductions and to provide more areas where natural recolonization by large predators is tolerated. Encouragingly, there are several financial and ecological incentives for landowners to form conservancies, with the effect that a trend towards conservancy formation is likely and that prospects for predator conservation on private land in southern Africa may improve.

Historical distribution of large predators in South Africa

South Africa is home to a diverse array of large (>20 kg) predator species, including lion (*Panthera leo*), leopard (*Panthera pardus*), cheetah (*Acinonyx jubatus*), spotted hyaena (*Crocuta crocuta*), brown hyaena (*Hyaena brunnea*) and African wild dog (*Lycaon pictus*). Historically, these species were widely distributed throughout South Africa (Skinner & Smithers, 1990). However, with the arrival of European settlers, over-hunting for sport had a severe impact on predators, and later through persecution by farmers protecting their livestock (Stuart *et al.*, 1985). It is probable that predator populations were also severely affected by reductions in the abundance of prey species. During the 19th and 20th centuries, ungulate populations in South Africa were decimated by outbreaks of bovine pleuropneumonia and rinderpest (in 1850 and 1896, respectively) and by overhunting (Bond *et al.*, 2004). Colonial administrations responded to declining wildlife populations by establishing protectionist policies that prevented landowners from utilizing wildlife areas (Bond *et al.*, 2004). The effect of these policies was to make wildlife a burden for landowners, with no financial value. Under these conditions, wildlife populations continued to wane owing to a mixture of benign neglect, over-hunting, persecution and competition with livestock. By the 1980s, large predators, with the exception of leopards and brown hyaenas, were generally limited to large protected areas and isolated pockets in the extreme north of the country (Skinner & Smithers, 1990).

Changes in legislation governing wildlife on private land

During the 1960s and 1970s, legislative changes occurred in several southern African countries, granting varying degrees of user rights over wildlife to landowners. These changes (occurring in Zimbabwe in 1960 and 1975, Namibia in 1967, and South Africa at varying times by province) had the effect of enabling landowners to derive financial benefits from wildlife occurring on their land through hunting and trade in live wild animals (Bond *et al.*, 2004). These legislative changes resulted in a wholesale shift from traditional livestock farming to game ranching across large areas of southern Africa. In Zimbabwe, an estimated 27,000 km^2 of private land was used for wildlife production by 1999 (Bond *et al.*, 2004). In Namibia, up to 25% of private land is used for wildlife production (Krug, 2001). In South Africa, there are an estimated 5000 game ranches and a further 4000 mixed livestock/game ranches, covering an area of approximately 159,000 km^2 (Falkena, 2003). Smaller game-ranching industries are also developing in Botswana and Zambia (Lindsey *et al.*, 2007b).

The shift to game ranching resulted in major benefits for wildlife conservation. A huge market for live wild animals developed and reintroductions of wild ungulates occurred on a large scale. In Zimbabwe, wildlife populations on private land quadrupled during 1984–2000 (Bond *et al.*, 2004). In Namibia, wildlife populations on private land increased in numbers and diversity by 70% and 44%, respectively, during 1967–1995 (Barnes & de Jager, 1996). In South Africa, an estimated 1.7 million wild animals occur on game ranches (Flack, 2003). Reintroductions by game ranchers resulted in the recovery of endangered species such as bontebok (*Damaliscus pygargus*), mountain zebra (*Equus zebra*) and white rhinoceros (*Ceratotherium simum*), and major population increases in many other species (Flack, 2003).

The potential for conserving predators on game ranchland

The shift to game ranching has resulted in improved prospects for conserving predators on private land. As livestock were replaced with wild ungulates, prey populations increased and the primary reason for the persecution of predators—conflict over livestock—was removed over large areas. The huge areas used for game ranching in South Africa (corresponding to nearly eight times the size of Kruger National Park) mean that there is potentially significant scope for improving the conservation status of predators outside of formally protected areas. If one were to assume that all land used for game ranching in South Africa was potentially suitable for large predators, the following population sizes could be supported (given densities equal to those observed in Kruger National Park, Mills & Funston, 2003): 15,900 lions, 5565 leopards, 1431 cheetahs, 22,101 spotted hyaenas and 2226 wild dogs (brown hyaenas do not occur in Kruger National Park). While achieving such population sizes on game ranchland is clearly not realistic, these projections do serve to highlight the fact that, if predators were successfully re-established on a fraction of available game ranchland, the conservation benefits would be significant. The potential for conservation gains is particularly high for competitively inferior species, such as wild dogs and cheetahs, which occur at low densities in protected areas, partly due to competition with lions and spotted hyaenas (Mills & Gorman, 1997; Durant, 2000).

The conservation of predators on game ranchland in practice

Predators have benefited from the shift to game ranching, primarily through an increasing trend for owners of private game reserves to reintroduce them to boost their ecotourism operations (Hayward *et al.*, 2007; Hunter *et al.*, 2007). Large predators are among the most popular species with tourists and are thus crucial for the viability of ecotourism enterprises (Lindsey *et al.*, 2007a,b). Lions have been reintroduced into 27 reserves in South Africa, including 22 private game reserves, expanding the geographic range of the species by at least 5000 km^2 (L. Hunter, personal communication). Cheetahs have been reintroduced into more than 70 reserves in South Africa, including a large number of private game reserves (K. Marnewick, personal communication). Wild dogs have been reintroduced into at least 14 reserves in South Africa, including nine private game reserves, expanding the geographic range of the species by more than 4650 km^2 (Gusset *et al.*, 2008). These reintroductions are particularly important in the context of South Africa which, by African standards, is poorly endowed with protected areas of sufficient size to hold viable populations of large predators. However, aside from the reintroductions mentioned above, free-ranging predators occurring on private land appear not to have benefited particularly from the shift to game ranching.

Current population status of large predators in South Africa

Large predators can be grouped into three categories regarding their conservation status in South Africa:

1 The smaller and/or more secretive species (including leopard, caracal [*Caracal caracal*], brown hyaena and jackal species [*Canis* spp.]) are fairly well distributed throughout South Africa, occurring widely outside of protected areas (Friedmann *et al.*, 2002) (Figure 15.1). Owing to the paucity of detailed information on the current or historic conservation status of these species, assessing the impact of the shift to game ranching on their conservation status is difficult.
2 Larger species that occur at low densities inside protected areas and in some areas outside of reserves, including cheetahs and wild dogs (Lindsey *et al.*, 2004; Marnewick *et al.*, 2005). The South African wild dog population numbers 300–350 individuals, with approximately 120 individuals occurring in Kruger National park, 155 individuals occurring in small reserves comprising an actively managed metapopulation (Davies-Mostert *et al.*, this volume), and approximately 75 individuals occurring outside of protected areas on private land close to source populations in Limpopo Province, KwaZulu-Natal Province and southern Zimbabwe (Lindsey *et al.*, 2004). Cheetahs occur more widely outside of protected areas and are believed to be increasing in number in response to the shift from livestock farming to game ranching (Marnewick *et al.*, 2005, 2007). There are at least

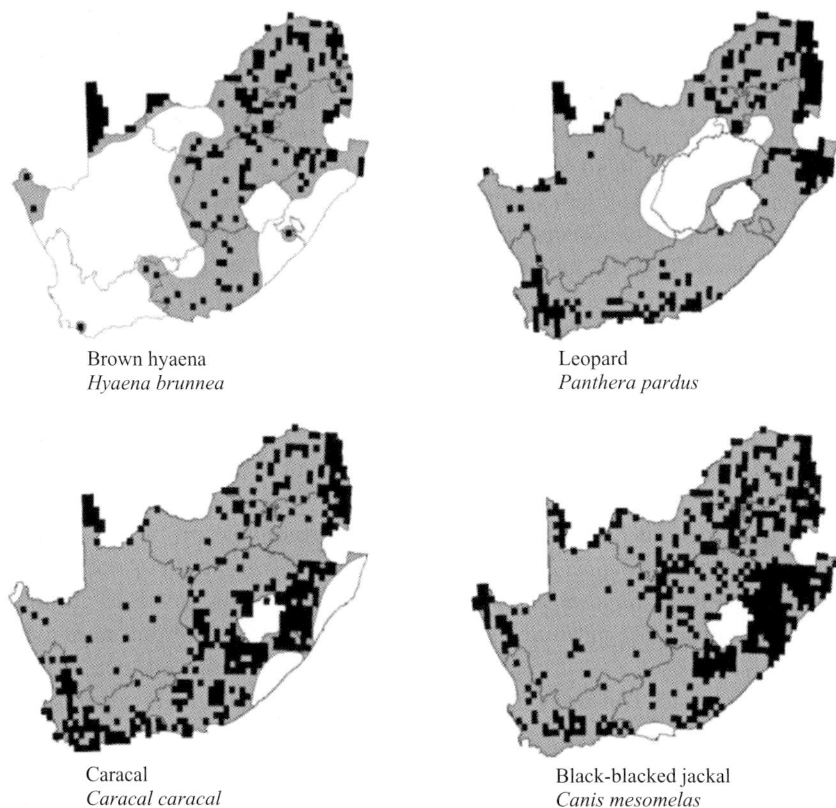

Figure 15.1 **The distribution of smaller and/or more secretive predator species in South Africa (taken from Friedmann *et al.*, 2002). Grey shading represents extent of occurrence and black areas represent area of occupancy.**

800 free-ranging cheetahs in South Africa, most of which occur on private land in the north of the country (Friedmann *et al.*, 2002; Marnewick *et al.*, 2005) (Figure 15.2).

3 Lions and spotted hyaenas occur at relatively high densities inside protected areas, but are virtually absent outside of reserves (Friedmann *et al.*, 2002). Significant populations of both lions and spotted hyaenas occur in Kruger National Park, Kgalagadi Transfrontier Park, Hluhluwe-iMfolozi Park, Madikwe Game Reserve and other protected areas.

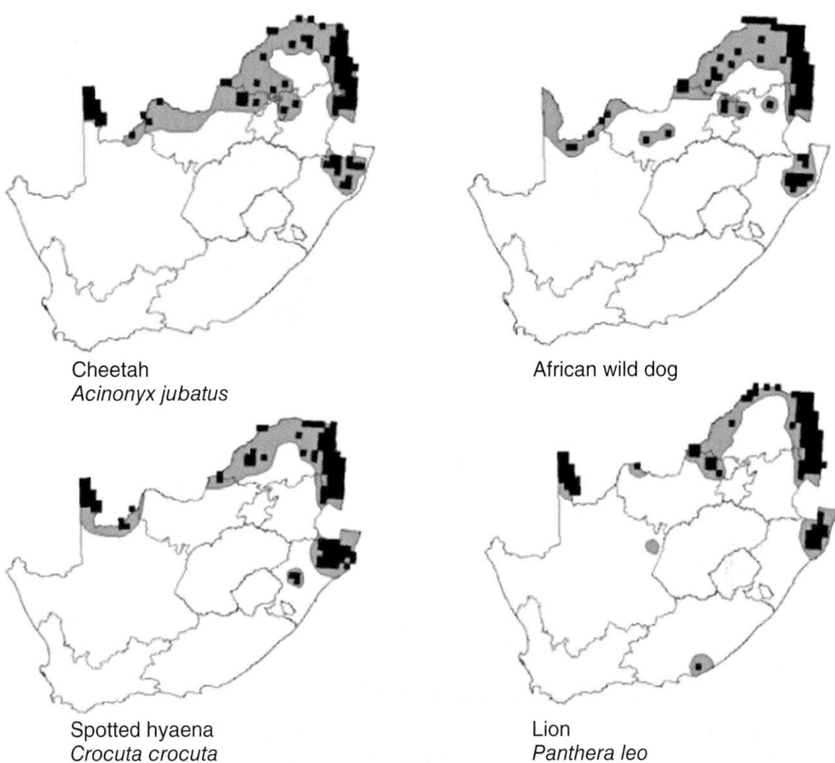

Figure 15.2 **The distribution of lions, cheetahs, spotted hyaenas and wild dogs in South Africa (taken from Friedmann *et al.*, 2002). Grey shading represents extent of occurrence and black areas represent area of occupancy.**

Factors limiting the conservation status of predators on game ranches

Several key factors continue to limit expansion in the population size and distribution of large predators on game ranches: (1) questionable quota-setting and illegal hunting; (2) illegal capture and live sale of predators; and (3) persecution by landowners.

Questionable quota-setting and illegal hunting

Threats from questionable quota-setting and illegal hunting are perhaps most serious for leopards, which is the predator most commonly hunted in South Africa (Lindsey *et al.*, 2007b). Game ranchers tend to be more tolerant of leopards than other large predator species owing to their value as hunting trophies (Lindsey *et al.*, 2005a). However, the impact of trophy hunting on leopard populations in South Africa is poorly understood and, despite a dearth of information on their population status, the Convention on International Trade in Endangered Species of Wild Fauna and Flora (CITES) quota for this species was recently increased from 75 to 150 individuals per year (Daly *et al.*, 2005). At present, there is no scientific basis for determining a sustainable hunting quota for leopards in South Africa, or for denoting areas to which quotas should be allocated, with the effect that current off-takes may have detrimental effects on leopard populations (Daly *et al.*, 2005).

Illegal capture and live sale of predators

The threat from the illegal capture and live sale of predators is most significant for cheetahs, which are commonly captured illegally and sold to captive-breeding programmes in South Africa or abroad and to "canned hunting" outfits (where cheetahs are hunted in small enclosures) in Namibia where cheetah hunting is legal (Marnewick *et al.*, 2005, 2007).

Persecution by landowners

Ongoing persecution of large predators is probably the most important reason for the failure of large predators to benefit more from the shift to game ranching (Lindsey *et al.*, 2005a). Game ranchers typically persecute predators to protect wild ungulates that could be hunted as trophies or captured and sold live. Wild ungulates are valuable and so predation can impart significant financial costs on landowners. Greater kudu (*Tragelaphus strepsiceros*), nyala (*Tragelaphus angasi*) and sable antelope (*Hippotragus niger*), for example, are sold for approximately US$300, US$1000 and US$10,000, respectively, during live-game auctions (Damm, 2005). Correspondingly, Marker *et al.* (2003)

actually found that cheetahs were more commonly persecuted by Namibian game ranchers than by livestock farmers. Similarly, Lindsey *et al.* (2005b) estimated that a single pack of wild dogs can impose costs of US$14,000–78,000 per year to landowners, if one assumes that every animal killed results in the loss of potential revenues from live sales. Other reasons for the persecution of predators on game ranches include the following (Lindsey *et al.*, 2005a): the feeling that the game ranch is too small (a reason usually given for disliking lions and wild dogs); because they have no value (wild dogs); because they waste food (cheetahs); because they pose a threat to human life (lions); because they chase wildlife and make it more skittish (wild dogs); and because they chase game into fences (wild dogs).

In addition to the ongoing threats facing predators, the shift to game ranching has resulted in a number of broader conservation problems, which are listed in Box 1.

Correlates of landowner attitudes towards predators

The tolerance of game ranchers for predators varies markedly with land use (Lindsey *et al.*, 2005a; Romañach *et al.*, 2007). Attitudes are typically negative where livestock is retained and where wildlife is used consumptively, through hunting or live capture and sale (Lindsey *et al.*, 2005a). In these circumstances, game ranchers perceive that predators kill animals that could be hunted or sold by the landowner. Attitudes are particularly negative where land use relies on high proportional off-takes of ungulate populations, such as where recreational hunting or hunting for meat (usually by local hunters) is practised. Revenues per animal hunted are relatively low for meat hunting and so large numbers of animals are cropped to generate profits. Conversely, game-rancher attitudes tend to be positive where ecotourism is the primary land use, or on properties that are kept by wealthy and often absentee landowners primarily for their aesthetic value (Lindsey *et al.*, 2005a) (Figure 15.3).

Attitudes also tend to be negative where individual game ranches are small and/or separated from their neighbours by game fencing (Lindsey *et al.*, 2005a). Although usually relatively permeable to predators (unless specifically designed to contain them), game fencing is significant for predator conservation by influencing land-use options. The presence of perimeter game fencing around game ranches of the size typical of South Africa (10.7–14.1 km^2, Bothma, 2002) precludes reintroductions of large, charismatic species and

Box 1. **Conservation problems associated with the game-ranching industry**

The shift to game ranching has not been uniformly positive for wildlife conservation. In South Africa, Namibia and Botswana, landowners are required by law to contain wildlife (as a fugitive resource) with game fencing to earn the right to utilize it (Bond *et al.*, 2004). The effect of this legislation has been the division of vast areas of game ranchland into small fenced pockets curtailing natural movement of wildlife. While fencing is sometimes an important tool to enable reintroductions and containment of relatively small areas surrounded by communities that are intolerant of predators (Gusset *et al.*, 2008), the division of adjacent blocks of wildlife habitat by fencing has had negative conservation impacts by influencing land use and reducing ecological resilience. The high value of wild animals as hunting trophies has promoted several practices that are undesirable from a conservation perspective (Lindsey *et al.*, 2006). To maximize potential returns from consumptive utilization, game ranches are sometimes overstocked, resulting in ecological degradation comparable to that resulting from overstocking with livestock (Bond *et al.*, 2004).

To increase the diversity of hunting trophies, exotic species have been widely introduced onto game ranches, including potentially invasive species like European wild boar, *Sus scrofa*, and indigenous African species that have been introduced beyond their natural geographic range (Lindsey *et al.*, 2006). Some game ranchers manipulate the breeding of ungulate species to offer prized aberrant varieties, such as white or black springbok (*Antidorcas marsupialis*) and, in some cases, closely related species are crossbred to create "new" species for sale as hunting trophies (e.g. "red wildebeest"; Hamman *et al.*, 2003). The small size of most South African game ranches and the ubiquity of game fencing mean that most wildlife populations on ranches are small, resulting in a risk of inbreeding and loss of genetic diversity (Frankham, this volume). Finally, there have been some problems involving ongoing persecution of predators and the development of a large "canned hunting" industry involving predators on private land in South Africa (Lindsey *et al.*, 2006).

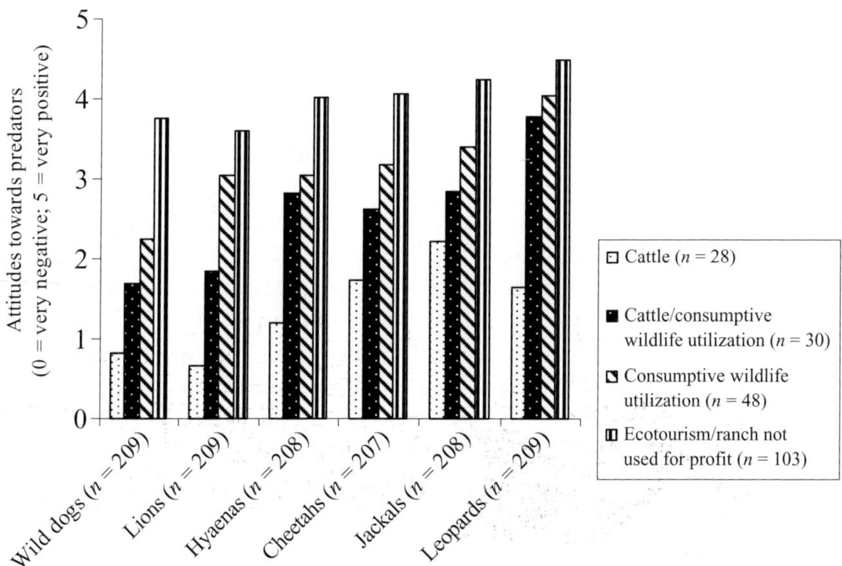

Figure 15.3 **Relationship between land use and game-rancher attitudes towards predators (taken from Lindsey *et al.*, 2005a).**

thus reduces the viability of ecotourism as a land use. Landowners with small, game-fenced properties typically rely on consumptive options, such as recreational and/or trophy hunting, and live capture and sale, which are not conducive to predator conservation (Lindsey *et al.*, 2005a). Game-rancher attitudes are more positive towards predators where neighbouring landowners have removed internal game fencing to create larger pooled wildlife areas or conservancies (Lindsey *et al.*, 2005a) (Figure 15.4). Finally, older game ranchers and those whose families have occupied a piece of land for generations are less positive towards predators than younger game ranchers and city-based or foreign investors (Lindsey *et al.*, 2005a).

How can we improve tolerance of landowners towards predators?

Effective law enforcement to control the persecution of predators by landowners in remote game-ranching areas is not realistic. The best prospects for

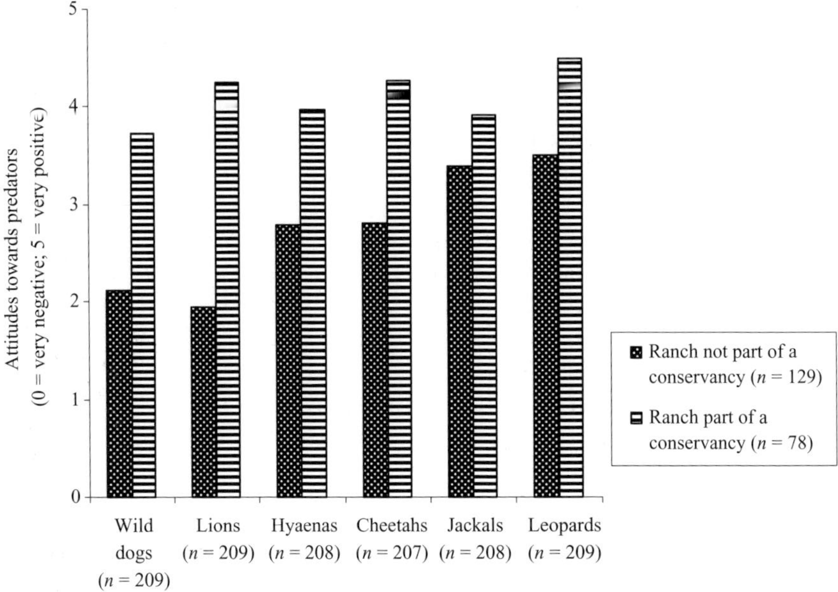

Figure 15.4 **Influence of whether or not properties belong to a conservancy on game-rancher attitudes towards predators (taken from Lindsey *et al.,* 2005a).**

conserving predators come through promoting conditions under which landowners are tolerant of or even desire the presence of predators on their land. Game-rancher attitudes tend to be most positive towards predators where there are clear financial and ecological benefits associated with having predators and where the costs of predation are low (Lindsey *et al.,* 2005a).

Large predators are extremely popular among tourists, and significant potential exists for deriving financial returns from selling trips to see them (Lindsey *et al.,* 2005b, 2007b; Davies-Mostert *et al.,* this volume). The potential gains from trips to see a wild dog pack with pups at a den site, for example, is estimated to exceed the annual costs associated with predation by the pack under most game-ranching scenarios (Lindsey *et al.,* 2005b). Similar potential is likely to exist for other large predator species. Raising awareness of the tourism options involving predators, and encouraging landowners to exploit this potential, represent one means of improving the prospects for predator conservation.

Similarly, raising awareness of the ecological benefits associated with having predators is important. Predators can limit the densities of some non-migratory prey species and thus potentially buffer the impact of droughts on prey populations (Mills & Funston, 2003; Sinclair *et al.*, 2003). Predators often select weak or sick prey, effectively keeping prey populations healthy. Wild dogs, for example, exhibit clear selection for the weakest sectors of prey populations throughout the year (Pole *et al.*, 2004). Large predators may also reduce the abundance of mesopredators such as jackals which are a perceived nuisance and are often blamed for spreading diseases such as rabies. Reducing the financial costs associated with conserving predators represents an additional means of promoting landowner tolerance. Reducing the costs of predation is most realistically achieved by promoting land uses that do not rely on human off-take of significant proportions of prey populations. Conservancies provide conditions that are particularly conducive to predator conservation, in which the costs of predation tend to be relatively low, and both the financial and ecological benefits associated with having predators are high.

Promoting conservancy formation to further predator conservation

Conservancies are more conducive to predator conservation than single ranches for two reasons:

1 Conservancy members are typically bound by a constitution and/or cooperative management agreements that limit the behaviour of individual landowners. These agreements, combined with peer pressure from neighbours sharing the wildlife resource, would likely dissuade game ranchers from independently killing predators.
2 The pooling of land in conservancies enables landowners to reintroduce large charismatic species (such as buffalo [*Syncerus caffer*], elephant [*Loxodonta africana*], black rhinoceros [*Diceros bicornis*] and white rhinoceros), which in turn increases the viability of ecotourism and low off-take, high-revenue trophy hunting. With a shift from the high off-take recreational hunting that is typical of fenced game ranches to ecotourism and low off-take trophy hunting, the financial costs associated with predation would decline. Predators would actually become financial assets for ecotourism and/or trophy hunting operations in conservancies and, in many cases, are

reintroduced for these purposes. As human off-take of prey population declines with the shift in land use to ecotourism and low off-take trophy hunting, the ecological value of large predators in terms of regulating prey populations would increase. Wild dogs are perhaps the predator species that could benefit most from conservancy formation (Box 2). Though conservancy owners would likely reintroduce lions and spotted hyaenas, which are key predators and competitors for wild dogs, persecution by humans (the key cause for disappearance of wild dogs outside of protected areas) is likely to cease within conservancies. Savé Valley Conservancy in Zimbabwe is one of the best known conservancies in southern Africa, and clearly highlights the potential benefits of conservancies for predator conservation (Box 3).

There are several strong financial and ecological reasons for game ranchers to form conservancies and, thus, there is reason to be optimistic that increasing numbers of them will be formed in future:

1 Land-use options are wider in conservancies, including high-end ecotourism and trophy hunting, both of which are potentially more profitable than the recreational hunting that is typical of fenced game ranches (Falkena, 2003).

Box 2. **The potential importance of conservancies for predator conservation: Wild dogs as a case study**

Wild dogs have been the victims of human misconceptions for decades and continue to suffer from negative attitudes (Fanshawe *et al.*, 1991; Lindsey *et al.*, 2005a). Wild dogs are the least popular large predator species among southern African game ranchers, who perceive them to impart major financial costs through predation, with no compensatory value, owing to the ban imposed on hunting wild dogs (Lindsey *et al.*, 2005a). Wild dogs are widely persecuted by game ranchers in South Africa and, as a result, have a very limited distribution outside of protected areas (Lindsey *et al.*, 2004). Lindsey *et al.* (2005b) showed that the theoretical willingness of tourists to pay to view wild dogs at a den is sufficiently high that potential revenues are adequate to off-set the costs of predation by wild dogs. More recently, Davies-Mostert *et al.* (this volume) have demonstrated the willingness of tourists to pay to see wild dogs at Venetia Limpopo Nature Reserve in South Africa through the sale of wild dog–viewing trips. However, wild dogs are vulnerable to disturbance during the denning period, which represents something of a bottleneck for survival of the species outside of protected areas (Romañach & Lindsey, 2008).

For most of the year, wild dogs use a home range of approximately 545 km^2, but during the denning season, a 3-month period when they have pups at a den, wild dogs use much smaller home ranges (80–120 km^2) (Gorman *et al.*, 1992; Pole, 2000; Creel & Creel, 2002). During that period, predation by wild dogs is focused and may cause localized reductions in prey populations on the game ranch hosting the denning pack and on their immediate neighbours (Romañach & Lindsey, 2008). These impacts are likely to be significantly greater if game ranches are isolated from their neighbours by perimeter game fencing, which is typically permeable to wild dogs but not to their prey. Wild dogs tend to use game fencing as a tool during hunting, and this enables them to catch larger (and economically more valuable) prey, such as greater kudu and waterbuck (*Kobus ellipsiprymnus*), more often than they would under "normal" conditions (van Dyk & Slotow, 2003; Rhodes & Rhodes, 2004). If wild dogs did cause localized reductions in prey densities during denning, the presence of game fencing would prevent the recovery of prey populations through natural influx following the wild dogs' departure from the den site. For these reasons, wild dogs are extremely vulnerable to persecution when they den on game ranchland. In conservancies, the chances of survival are higher. Ecotourism is more commonly an important land use in conservancies, for which wild dogs are an asset to landowners. In addition, the removal of internal game fencing during the formation of conservancies is likely to reduce the average number (and thus the financial value) of animals killed by wild dogs, and permits more rapid natural recovery of prey populations following the wild dogs' departure.

Box 3. **Predator conservation within conservancies: Savé Valley Conservancy as a case study**

Savé Valley Conservancy (3450 km^2) in Zimbabwe was formed in 1991 when 18 game ranchers agreed to create a large cooperatively managed wildlife area (Lindsey *et al.*, 2008). During the early years of the conservancy, 3950 individuals of 14 species were reintroduced, including 553 elephants and 426 buffaloes (Lindsey *et al.*, 2008). Land use within Savé Valley Conservancy is focused on high-revenue trophy hunting and, prior to the political upheavals in Zimbabwe, ecotourism. Predator populations in Savé Valley Conservancy have recovered naturally over time. Following the livestock-ranching years, lions and wild dogs had been eradicated, and cheetahs and spotted hyaenas were greatly reduced in number. Lions recolonized the area during the late 1990s, and the population is now increasing rapidly (Davidson & Romañach, 2007). Wild dogs recolonized the area during the early 1990s and increased in number to reach one of the highest recorded densities for this species (196 individuals in 10 packs in 2004 at 5.7 individuals per 100 km^2) (Pole, 2004; Romañach & Lindsey, 2008). The conservancy also has a large leopard population, a recovering spotted hyaena population, and small populations of cheetahs and brown hyaenas (Lindsey *et al.*, 2008).

Landowner attitudes towards predators are generally positive because they are considered to be crucial for ecotourism and trophy hunting; lions, leopards and cheetahs are hunted as trophies (Lindsey *et al.*, 2005a). The minority of landowners with negative perceptions of particular predator species (typically wild dogs; Lindsey *et al.*, 2005a) are generally tolerant of them because their land uses do not rely on off-takes of significant proportions of prey populations, and they thus do not compete directly with predators. Off-takes from trophy hunting within Savé Valley Conservancy are proportionally low (2%–5% of male populations), and predators are crucial for controlling populations of prey species.

2. Both ecotourists and foreign trophy hunters appreciate a "wilderness" feel to wildlife areas and dislike game fencing and so are more likely to be attracted to conservancies (Lindsey *et al.*, 2006, 2007a).
3. The economies of scale that are associated with conservancies reduce management costs. Pooled land units can support the costly infrastructure required for high-end ecotourism; for example, fewer water points and less per capita fence maintenance are needed (du Toit, 2004, Lindsey *et al.*, 2008).
4. Larger areas support greater habitat diversity and can thus sustainably support a wider variety of species than small game ranches.
5. Conservancies tend to be more resilient to natural disasters, such as fire, disease or drought. For example, the removal of internal game fencing enables ungulates to make use of patchy primary productivity resulting from sporadic rainfall (Lindsey *et al.*, 2008).
6. Larger wildlife populations that can be conserved in conservancies compared to isolated game ranches are less susceptible to inbreeding and demographic stochasticity (Frankham, this volume) and thus require less management intervention. That said, some form of metapopulation management would likely be required in all but the larger conservancies that are capable of holding viable populations of predators.

Reasons for optimism for the future of predators on game ranches in southern Africa

Future land-use trends on game ranches in southern Africa may result in improved prospects for predator conservation on private land. For the reasons cited in this chapter, we believe that an increasing number of new conservancies may be created, and that existing conservancies may be expanded to incorporate additional game ranches, creating a greater number of—and larger—zones of predator tolerance. The numbers of tourists visiting South Africa are increasing steadily with the effect that ecotourism is likely to become an increasingly viable form of land use (Figure 15.5). In addition, the creation of transfrontier conservation areas is likely to create new hubs for ecotourism in areas where that form of land use was previously unviable. For example, with the formation of the Shashe-Limpopo Transfrontier Conservation Area in northern South Africa (crossing into southern Botswana and Zimbabwe),

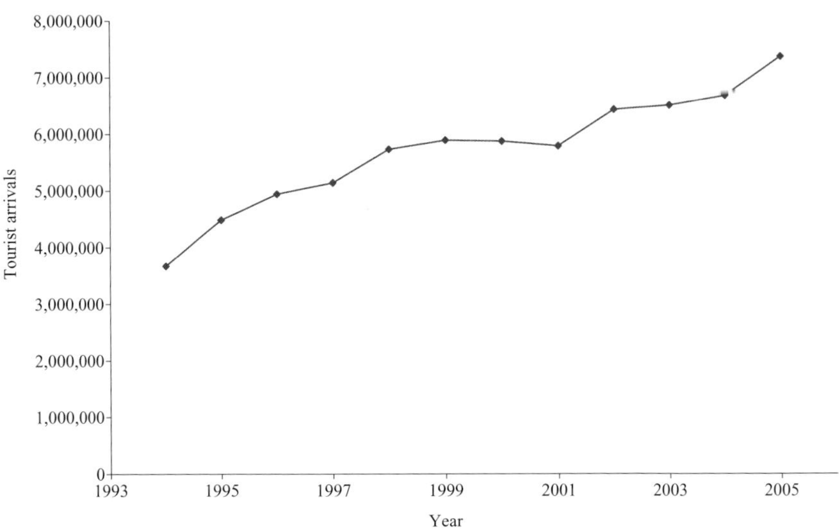

Figure 15.5 **Tourist arrivals to South Africa (derived from http://www.southafrica.net, July 2007).**

ecotourism is likely to become a more viable land use for landowners in the Limpopo Valley (an area currently characterized by high off-take consumptive wildlife use and intolerance of predators; Lindsey *et al.*, 2005a). At the same time, the market for live wild animals in South Africa appears to be diminishing. During 2005, both the volume of wild animals captured and sold, and the average prices paid, declined—trends that are likely to continue (Damm, 2005; Figure 15.6).

During the rapid expansion phase of the game-ranching industry, there was a huge and growing market for live wildlife to re-stock newly formed game ranches. However, the demand for live wildlife is slowing as the rate of conversion from livestock farms to game ranches slows (with most suitable land already having been converted), and the supply of live wild animals from the game ranches formed during the past few years is increasing. The effect of these changes is likely to reduce competition between predators and landowners, and to reduce the financial costs associated with conserving predators on game ranchland.

Finally, game ranching represents a popular form of investment for foreign and city-based investors (Falkena, 2003). In many cases, foreign investors do

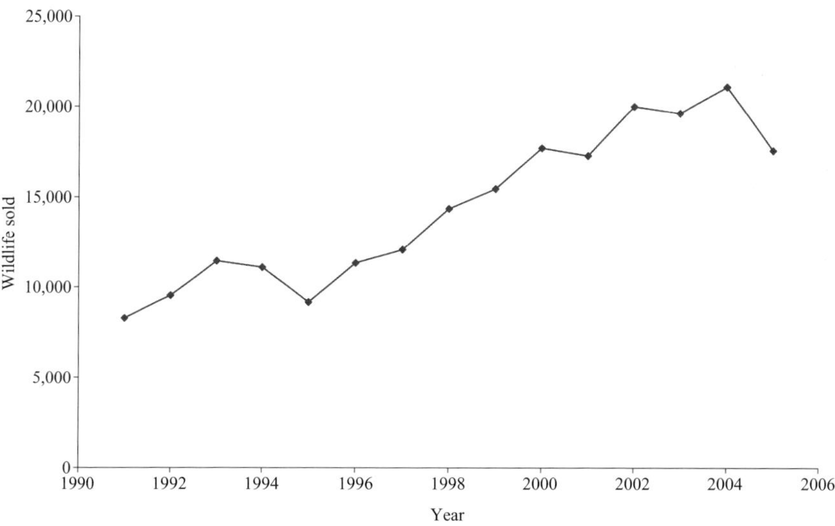

Figure 15.6 **Number of wildlife sold at live-game auctions in South Africa (Damm, 2005).**

not rely on game ranches for their income and often purchase properties for their aesthetic and conservation value (Lindsey *et al.,* 2005a). Such investors do not typically harbour the same prejudices towards predators as those borne by people whose families have occupied a particular farm for generations. In addition, a younger generation of game ranchers is gradually replacing older landowners and, as a result, traditional prejudices towards predators will probably fade (Lindsey *et al.,* 2005a).

Incentives for predator conservation where landowners do not have user rights over wildlife

Southern African nations are unusual in the extent to which they have granted user rights over wildlife to landowners (Cirelli, 2002). In most African countries, ownership of wildlife is retained by the state, and landowners have severe restrictions regarding the extent to which they can utilize wildlife. Under those circumstances, wildlife does not have the same financial value to landowners as in southern Africa. Superficially, this might be seen as a good thing for predator conservation because conflict with landowners over wild prey is unlikely to exist. However, realistically the effect of these policies has been to result in increased reliance on livestock as a land use, and neglect of wildlife populations, or even active persecution of wildlife to prevent competition with livestock for grazing. As wildlife populations decline, the potential for conflict between predators and humans over livestock is likely to increase, further intensifying the extent to which predators are persecuted. Kenya provides a graphic illustration of this phenomenon. Wildlife is owned by the state, and landowners are not permitted to derive revenues from wildlife through consumptive utilization (Cirelli, 2002; Lindsey *et al.*, 2007b). These policies have resulted in steep declines in wildlife populations occurring outside of protected areas in Kenya, including predator declines (Western *et al.*, 2006; Georgiadis *et al.*, 2007).

Ownership of wildlife is also retained by the state in many countries outside of Africa, and notably in the USA. While the USA has achieved considerable conservation success with this model, conservation gains would be achieved by granting user rights over wildlife to landowners. Wildlife-based land uses have not proliferated to nearly the same extent on private land in the USA as in southern Africa, largely because the right to utilize wildlife on private land is typically dependent on hunting licenses being purchased from the state (with the exception of some exotic species). In some states, "ranching for wildlife" programmes have been developed, where saleable hunting tags are allocated to landowners and some flexibility is granted to ranchers to determine seasons and harvest limits (Grewell, 2001). These programmes have had some success at improving wildlife habitat on private land and at increasing wildlife populations (Leal & Grewell, 1999; Grewell, 2001). However, if ranchers were granted full user rights over non-endangered wildlife species occurring on their property, a similar shift to game ranching as observed in southern Africa would likely occur and, under these circumstances, it is likely that landowners would actively reintroduce key wildlife species. A shift to game ranching would be particularly likely (and valuable) in ranching areas neighbouring protected domains, such as Yellowstone National Park. Such a shift in land use would effectively increase the size of the state-protected area network. An increase in game ranching would likely be particularly positive for predators by reducing conflict over livestock and by shifting land use towards ecotourism, for which large predators, such as grey wolves (*Canis lupus*), would be significant draw cards.

Conclusions

The shift to game ranching in southern Africa has had major benefits for wildlife conservation generally, but more mixed outcomes for predator conservation, owing primarily to ongoing persecution by landowners. Current trends in predator populations outside of protected areas are poorly understood, and predator ecology and conservation outside of protected domains is a priority for future research. Despite this dearth of information, it is clear that the prospects for predator conservation are brightest where the financial costs associated with their presence are low, and where the financial and ecological benefits associated with conserving them are high. These conditions are most easily met in conservancies. Efforts to promote predator conservation should thus focus on developing incentives to promote the formation of conservancies, perhaps by lobbying for tax incentives for game ranchers who remove game fencing that separates their land from that of their neighbours. Outside southern Africa, granting user rights over wildlife to landowners could stimulate similar conservation gains on private land as observed in southern Africa, especially if lessons learnt regarding the determinants for tolerance of predators were heeded.

References

Barnes, J.I. & de Jager, J.L.V. (1996) Economic and financial incentives for wildlife use on private land in Namibia and the implications for policy. *South African Journal of Wildlife Research* 26, 37–46.

Bond, I., Child, B., de la Harpe, D., Jones, B., Barnes, J. & Anderson, H. (2004) Private land contribution to conservation in South Africa. *Parks in Transition.* (ed. B. Child), pp. 29–61. Earthscan, London.

Bothma, J.P. (2002) Some economics of game ranching. *Proceedings of a Symposium on Game Ranch Planning and Management, Onderstepoort, South Africa, 1–2 November, 2002.* (ed. B. Penzhorn), pp. 23–40, Wildlife Group of South African Veterinary Association, Onderstepoort.

Cirelli, M.T. (2002) *Legal Trends in Wildlife Management.* Food and Agriculture Organisation report, Rome.

Creel, S. & Creel, N.M. (2002) *The African Wild Dog: Behavior, Ecology and Conservation.* Princeton University Press, Princeton.

Daly, B., Power, J., Camacho, G. et al. (2005) *Leopard* (Panthera pardus) *PHVA Workshop Report.* Conservation Breeding Specialist Group (SSC/IUCN)/CBSG South Africa/Endangered Wildlife Trust, Johannesburg.

Damm, G. (2005) Game sale statistics for South Africa in 2004. *African Indaba* 3, 16–18.

Davidson, Z. & Romañach, S. (2007) *Estimations of Lion and Hyena Density in the Savé Valley Conservancy Using Two Different Census Techniques: Spoor Transects and Call-up Stations.* Savé Valley Conservancy report, Zimbabwe.

du Toit, R. (2004) *Review of Wildlife Issues Associated with the Land Reform Programme in Zimbabwe.* World Wide Fund for Nature—Southern African Regional Programme Office, Working Paper No. 10 (Available: http://www.zimconservation.com/PDFs/WWF_Review.pdf. Accessed: 15 October 2008

Durant, S. (2000) Predator avoidance, breeding experience and reproductive success in endangered cheetahs, *Acinonyx jubatus. Animal Behaviour* 60, 121–130.

Falkena, H. (2003) *Game Ranch Profitability in South Africa.* The S.A. Financial Sector Forum, Rivonia.

Fanshawe, J., Frame, L. & Ginsberg, J.R. (1991) The wild dog: Africa's vanishing carnivore. *Oryx* 25, 137–146.

Flack, P. H. (2003) Consumptive tourism—A useful conservation tool. *Vision, Business, Ecotourism and the Environment.* (ed. D. Butchart), pp. 155–157. Endangered Wildlife Trust, Johannesburg.

Friedmann, Y., Daly, B., Keith, M., Peddemors, V., Chimimba, C. & Byers, O. (2002) *Conservation Assessment and Management Plan for the Mammals of South Africa.* Conservation Africa/Endangered Wildlife Trust. Conservation Breeding Specialist Group (SSC/IUCN), Apple Valley.

Georgiadis, N., Ihwagi, F., Olwero, J. & Romañach, S. (2007) Savanna herbivore dynamics in a livestock-dominated landscape: II. Conservation and management implications of predator restoration. *Biological Conservation* 137, 473–483.

Gorman, M., Mills, M. & French, J. (1992) Satellite tracking of the African wild dog *Lycaon pictus. Wildlife Telemetry: Remote Monitoring and Tracking of Animals.* (eds E. Priede & S. Swift), pp. 219–228. Ellis Horwood, London.

Grewell, J.B. (2001) *Turning Wildlife into an Asset: A Guide for State Policy Makers.* Available: http://www.perc.org/perc.php?id=122. Accessed 15 October 2008.

Gusset, M., Maddock, A., Gunther, G. et al. (2008) Conflicting human interests over the re-introduction of wild dogs in South Africa. *Biodiversity and Conservation* 17, 83–101.

Gusset, M., Ryan, S.J., Hofmeyr, M. et al. (2008) Efforts going to the dogs? Evaluating attempts to re-introduce endangered wild dogs in South Africa. *Journal of Applied Ecology* 45, 100–108.

Hamman, K., Vrahimis, S. & Blom, H. (2003) Can current trends in the game industry be reconciled with nature conservation? *African Indaba Yearbook* 1(5), 3.

Hayward, M.W., Adendorff, J., O'Brien, J. et al. (2007) The reintroduction of large carnivores to the Eastern Cape, South Africa: An assessment. *Oryx* 41, 205–214.

Hunter, L., Pistorius, K., Carlisle, M. et al. (2007) Restoring lions *Panthera leo* to northern KwaZulu-Natal, South Africa: Short-term biological and technical success but equivocal long-term conservation. *Oryx* 41, 196–204.

Krug, W. (2001) *Private Supply of Protected Land in Southern Africa: A Review of Markets, Approaches, Barriers and Issues.* Workshop Paper World Bank/OECD International Workshop on Market Creation for Biodiversity Products and Services, Paris.

Leal, D. & Grewell, B. 1999. *Hunting for Habitat: A Practical Guide to State-Landowner Partnerships.* Available: http://www.perc.org/articles/article119.php. Accessed 15 October 2008.

Lindsey, P.A., Alexander, R., Frank, L. & Romañach, S. (2006) The potential of trophy hunting to create incentives for wildlife conservation in Africa where alternative wildlife-based land uses may not be viable. *Animal Conservation* 9(3), 283–298.

Lindsey, P.A., Alexander, R., Mills, M.G.L., Woodroffe, R. & Romañach, S. (2007a) Wildlife viewing preferences of visitors to protected areas in South Africa: Implications for the role of ecotourism in conservation. *Journal of Ecotourism* 6(1), 19–33.

Lindsey, P.A., du Toit, J. & Mills, M.G.L. (2004) The distribution and population status of African wild dogs *Lycaon pictus* outside protected areas in South Africa. *South African Journal of Wildlife Research* 34(2), 143–151.

Lindsey, P.A., du Toit, J. & Mills, M.G.L. (2005a) Attitudes of ranchers towards African wild dogs *Lycaon pictus*: Conservation implications for wild dogs on private land. *Biological Conservation* 125, 113–121.

Lindsey, P.A., du Toit, J., Mills, M. & Alexander, R. (2005b) The potential contribution of ecotourism to wild dog *Lycaon pictus* conservation. *Biological Conservation* 123, 339–348.

Lindsey, P.A., du Toit, R., Pole, A. & Romañach, S. (2008) Savé Valley Conservancy: A large scale African experiment in cooperative wildlife management. *Evolution and Innovation in Wildlife Conservation from Parks and Game Ranches to Transfrontier Conservation areas.* (eds B. Child, H. Suich & A. Spenceley). Earthscan and SASUSG (IUCN), London.

Lindsey, P.A., Roulet, P. & Romañach, S. (2007b) Economic and conservation significance of the trophy hunting industry in sub-Saharan Africa. *Biological Conservation* 134, 455–469.

Marker, L., Mills, M.G.L. & Macdonald, D. (2003) Factors influencing perceptions of conflict and tolerance toward cheetahs on Namibian farmlands. *Conservation Biology* 17 1290–1298.

Marnewick, K., Beckhelling, A., Cilliers, D. et al. (2005) *The Status of the Cheetah in South Africa.* Cheetah Conservation Project report. De Wildt Cheetah Breeding Centre, Pretoria.

Marnewick, K., Beckhelling, A., Cilliers, D. et al. (2007) The status of the cheetah in South Africa. *Cat News, Special Issue* 3, 22–31.

Mills, M.G.L. & Funston, P. (2003) Large carnivores and savannah heterogeneity. *The Kruger Experience.* (eds J. du Toit, K. Rogers & H. Biggs), pp. 370–388. Island Press, Washington, DC.

Mills, M.G.L. & Gorman, M. (1997) Factors affecting the density and distribution of wild dogs in the Kruger National Park. *Conservation Biology* 11(6), 1397–1406.

Pole, A. (2000) *The Behaviour and Ecology of African Wild Dogs* Lycaon pictus *in an Environment with Reduced Competitor Density.* PhD thesis, University of Aberdeen, Aberdeen.

Pole, A., Gordon, I., Martyn, L., Gorman, L. & MacAskill, M. (2004) Prey selection by African wild dogs (*Lycaon pictus*) in southern Zimbabwe. *Journal of Zoology, London* 262, 207–215.

Rhodes, R. & Rhodes, G. (2004) Prey selection and use of natural and man-made barriers by African wild dogs while hunting. *South African Journal of Wildlife Research* 34, 135–142.

Romañach, S. & Lindsey, P. (2008) Conservation implications of prey responses to wild dogs *Lycaon pictus* during the denning season on game ranches. *Animal Conservation* 11(2), 111–117.

Romañach, S., Woodroffe, R. & Lindsey, P. (2007) Determinants of peoples' attitudes towards predators in a livestock dominated landscape. *Oryx* 41(2), 185–195.

Sinclair, A., Mduma, S. & Brashares, J. (2003) Patterns of predation in a diverse predator-prey system. *Nature* 425, 288–290.

Skinner, J. & Smithers, R. (1990) *The Mammals of the Southern African Subregion.* University of Pretoria, Pretoria.

Stuart, C., Macdonald, A. & Mills, M.G.L. (1985) History, current status and conservation of large mammalian predators in Cape Province, Republic of South Africa. *Biological Conservation* 31, 7–19.

van Dyk, G. & Slotow, R. (2003) The effects of fences and lions on the ecology of African wild dogs reintroduced into Pilanesberg National Park, South Africa. *African Zoology* 38, 79–94.

Western, D., Russell, S. & Mutu, K. (2006) *The Status of Wildlife in Kenya's Protected and Non-protected Areas.* A paper commissioned by Kenya's wildlife policy review team presented at the first stakeholders symposium of the wildlife policy and legislation review, 27–28 September 2006.

16

Moving Beyond the Descriptive: Predicting the Responses of Top-Order Predators to Reintroduction

Matt W. Hayward[1]

[1]Mammal Research Institute, Polish Academy of Science

Summary

The reintroduction of large carnivores to South Africa has yielded important information on methods to successfully reintroduce top-order predators. These programmes also identified major information deficiencies that have limited the ability of conservation managers to make successful and satisfactory management decisions. The first question involved identification of the species—and their numbers—that reintroduced predators would prey upon and the predators' potential impact on prey populations. To solve this, literature reviews were conducted to ascertain the preferred prey of Africa's large-predator guild using Jacobs' electivity index. These analyses were then used to predict the diets of lions, *Panthera leo*, at novel sites, and these predictions were tested using independent data from four sites over several years throughout southern Africa. Three of these test sites involved recently reintroduced lion populations. Lion diet was accurately predicted in nine of 13 tests and explained 62% of the variation in the data. In each case, the rank of prey taken was accurate.

The second problem identified by conservation managers of South Africa's Eastern Cape was an inadequate knowledge of the number of predators that

Reintroduction of Top-Order Predators, 1st edition. Edited by M.W. Hayward and M.J. Somers.
 ISBN 978-1-4051-7680-4 (pb) and 978-1-4051-9273-6 (hb)

their area could sustain (i.e. a reserve's carrying capacity). The known relationships between predator density and that of their prey were refined to create new equations using the biomass of significantly preferred prey or of prey in the preferred prey-weight range of each of Africa's large-predator guild. Predictions made from these new equations were successfully tested on sites where conservation managers or scientists had evidence that predators had exceeded carrying capacity. These methods can be used on all adequately studied predators. The ability to predict the diet and carrying capacity of predators at reintroduction sites will substantially improve success rates by ensuring that an adequate prey base is present to support the reintroduced stock and by highlighting to conservation managers when management actions should be considered to avoid overpopulation.

Reintroduction of top-order predators to the Eastern Cape

There has been a massive increase in the area of land reserved as conservation estate in South Africa's Eastern Cape Province since 1994 (Hayward *et al.*, 2007c). This increase in conservation estate has led to a burgeoning ecotourism industry that employs 4.5 times more staff and pays them 4.8 times more than the previous pastoralism land-use of the area (Langholtz & Kerley, 2006) and yields similarly greater profits per hectare (Sims-Castley *et al.*, 2004). As part of their creation, these conservation areas have reintroduced large numbers of wildlife, including top-order predators. In the Eastern Cape, there have been at least 29 reintroduction programmes of seven carnivore species to 11 conservation areas (Hayward *et al.*, 2007c), and this has doubled the number of African reintroductions previously reported (Breitenmoser *et al.*, 2001).

Lion, *Panthera leo*, reintroductions began in earnest in 2000 and have been so successful that, by 2005, more than 50 occurred in the province (Hayward *et al.*, 2007c). African wild dogs, *Lycaon pictus*, were reintroduced in 2002, and several successful breeding attempts at the two sites have increased the population to 25 from the 12 founders (Hayward *et al.*, 2007c). Spotted hyaenas, *Crocuta crocuta*, have only been returned to the province since 2003; however, several cubs have been successfully raised, and it is possible that 18 individuals existed in 2007 (J. Adendorff, SAN Parks; personal communication) from the 11 reintroduced (Hayward *et al.*, 2007c). Cheetah, *Acinonyx jubatus*, reintroduction has had varying success, with intraguild predation and infanticide limiting the population increase such that 41 survived in 2005 from 36 reintroduced (Hayward *et al.*, 2007c). Cheetahs at sites without lions and spotted hyaenas increased substantially; for example, the Samara cheetah population has increased from three individuals in 2002 to 18 in 2007. Leopard (*Panthera pardus*), serval (*Leptailurus serval*) and brown hyaena (*Hyaena brunnea*) have also been reintroduced; however, their cryptic nature has limited the amount of monitoring that has occurred (but see Hayward *et al.*, 2007a for information on the monitoring of a leopard reintroduced to Addo Elephant National Park, South Africa).

Overall, these reintroductions were evaluated as being successful according to criteria applicable 5 years after the initiation of the programmes; that is, a 3-year breeding programme where births exceed deaths (Hayward *et al.*, 2007c). This success is likely to be attributable to a combination of ecological and sociological factors. The agents of the original demise—human persecution (Skead, 1987)—have been removed and sufficient preferred prey exists to sustain each predator. All sites are fully fenced, which reduces human–wildlife conflicts, and this has been shown to be a critical factor in African wild dog reintroductions (Gusset *et al.*, 2008). All sites derive a substantial amount of money from wildlife tourism (Langholtz & Kerley, 2006) and charismatic megafauna, including top-order predators, are key elements of that (Lindsey *et al.*, this volume). Thus, there is an economic incentive to ensure that top-order predators persist at these sites at sufficient densities to ensure observation by tourists (Hayward *et al.*, 2007b). Reintroducing subordinate predators (wild dogs, cheetahs) prior to dominant ones (lions, hyaenas) is also considered important as it allowed them to find refuge habitat to avoid competitive interactions (Hayward *et al.*, 2007b).

Information deficiencies of conservation managers

Despite these successes, information deficiencies have limited the ability of conservation managers to adequately perform their roles (Hayward *et al.*, 2007b). The first question concerned identification of the species—and their numbers—that reintroduced predators would prey upon.

The second question related to the number of reintroduced predators that a reserve could sustain, which is essentially an estimate of carrying capacity.

This concern arose because managers had previously guessed at the carrying capacity of their site, yet had observed either population declines in prey species or behaviours of the predators that they interpreted as indicative of overpopulation (e.g. restriction to peripheral areas of a reserve along fences)(Hayward & Hayward, 2007). Lions have been the major concern, and several individuals have been relocated to restock new reserves and thereby to resolve overabundance issues (Hayward *et al.*, 2007c). Concern has also been raised at the overabundance of spotted hyaena in South Africa's Addo Elephant National Park's Main Camp section, where the population is now estimated at 18 individuals (J. Adendorff, SAN Parks; personal communication).

Given the problems identified by conservation managers in the Eastern Cape, this research was designed to identify the species—and the number of individuals—that top-order predators eat and to predict the carrying capacity of the reserves in question. The initial task involved identifying the preferred prey of Africa's large predators, and the application of these results allowed predictions of diet and carrying capacity to be made. These predictions could subsequently be tested with actual data collected in the field.

Prey preferences of Africa's top-order predators

Predators and their prey are in a continuing evolutionary arms race. Predators have evolved morphological and behavioural features that increase their chances of successfully killing and consuming prey, and prey have evolved similar features to avoid such mortality. This evolutionary arms race has led to individual predator species being adapted to prey on specific species. This is a key tenet of optimal foraging theory (Pyke *et al.*, 1977; Krebs, 1978).

One method of determining the optimal prey of a predator is to identify those species that it preferentially kills and those that it avoids. Preferential predation means killing a species more frequently than expected based on its relative abundance, while avoidance occurs when a species is preyed upon less frequently than expected. *Preference* may be a misnomer, however, as preferential predation reflects the ease with which prey is captured (Schaller, 1972). Nonetheless, decisions relating to preference made at one phase of predatory behaviour (e.g. to hunt or not) are reinforced at later stages (e.g. hunt success) (Creel & Creel, 2002), suggesting that conscious thought is involved to cause the preference.

Optimal foraging, however, may also mask the detection of prey preferences or reduce the degree of preference/avoidance. For example, lions have not evolved to subsist on small prey; however, if a mouse poked its head up beneath a lion's paw, then it is likely to be killed and consumed (Ravnsborg *et al.*, 2004). Similarly, African wild dogs have evolved to prey on large vertebrates (Carbone *et al.*, 1999); however, certain populations can persist for periods on suboptimally sized prey where larger, more optimal prey are scarce (Woodroffe *et al.*, 2007). Thus, there needs to be considerable evidence for preferential predation of a particular prey species if it is to be detected.

Methods of determining prey preferences

There are numerous electivity indices which have various strengths and weaknesses, but each essentially compares the proportion that a species comprises of the total prey community with the proportion that is killed by a predator (Krebs, 1989). We used Jacobs' derivation of Ivlev's index (Jacobs, 1974):

$$D = \frac{r_i - p_i}{r_i + p_i - 2r_i p_i} \qquad (1)$$

where r_i is the proportion of kills of species i and p_i is the proportional abundance of that species in the community of prey, to determine the prey preferences of lions, leopards, cheetahs, African wild dogs and spotted hyaenas. Jacobs' index minimizes many of the problems associated with electivity indices.

Searches of the literature were conducted for studies that documented the diets of each predator and also coupled those diets with estimates of prey abundance (either actual or relative). A Jacobs' index value was calculated for each prey species at each site, and then these values were tested for significant preference or avoidance using a Student's t-test (for normal data) or sign test against means of zero (Hayward & Kerley, 2005).

As well as determining the prey species that were significantly preferred by a predator, we determined the preferred prey-weight range of a predator. This weight range was calculated as the most preferred body masses identifiable from a distance-weighted least-squares regression fit of Jacobs' index values against prey body mass. Three-quarters of the adult female body mass of each prey species was used to account for juveniles and young killed by predators, following Schaller (1972). The ideal weight of prey was taken to be the mode of this regression fit, and the mean mass of significantly preferred prey was also calculated to compare with this. Finally, the ratio between predator body mass (three-quarters of the adult female body mass) and that of their significantly preferred prey was calculated.

The value of investigating foraging ecology from a species' perspective (i.e. across numerous populations) in this manner is that it is not biased by the results from one area, population or available prey community as at least five samples are needed for a significant preference or avoidance (Hayward *et al.*, 2006a). Furthermore, these methods are not biased by predation by particular sexes, age classes or group sizes as the data arise from hunting by entire populations of each species (Hayward *et al.*, 2006a). Similarly, methods used to ascertain the diet ranged from faecal studies to incidental observations to continuous following, thus ensuring that the biases of one method were compensated for by those of another. The inclusion of studies with a relatively small sample size is justified based on the highly significant relationship between results that include small samples and those with more than 100 kill records (Hayward *et al.*, 2006a). Furthermore, such low sample-size studies are unusual and, for results to differ significantly from 0 (non-selection), there must be concordance in preference or avoidance in at least five studies.

Prey preferences of Africa's top-order predators

Lions

Jacobs' index scores for 22,684 kills of 42 prey species derived from 32 studies from 11 countries over 48 locations or time periods revealed that lions significantly prefer blue wildebeest, Cape buffalo, gemsbok, giraffe and plain's zebra (Table 16.1) (Hayward & Kerley, 2005). Their preferred prey-weight range is 190–550 kg (Figure 16.1a); however, there is a linear relationship between prey body mass and preference when the megaherbivores (>600 kg) are excluded.

Megaherbivores appear to avoid top-down population limitation, but this may be a consequence of centuries of selective hunting of lions with modern weaponry, which has reduced pride size. Large prides may have been more adept at hunting megaherbivores, as currently occurs with the large prides in Botswana (Joubert, 2006). Lion pride size in many places throughout Africa is still limited by poaching (Bauer *et al.*, 2003; Bauer & de Iongh, 2005). Lions

Table 16.1 **Preferred prey characteristics of Africa's large-predator guild summarized from previous publications. All body mass estimates were derived from published records of three-quarters of the adult female body mass (in kg), and those used for each predator are presented.**

Predator (three-quarters of adult female body mass; kg)	Preferred prey species	Mean mass of preferred prey species	Ideal prey body mass	Preferred prey-weight range	Ratio of predator to preferred prey body mass
African wild dog (19)	Kudu (*Tragelaphus strepsiceros*) Thomson's gazelle (*Gazella thomsoni*) Impala (*Aepyceros melampus*) Bushbuck (*Tragelaphus scriptus*)	51	24 and 132	16–32 and 120–140	1:7.8
Cheetah (30)	Blesbok (*Damaliscus dorcas phillipsi*) Impala Thomson's gazelle Grant's gazelle (*Gazella granti*) Springbok (*Antidorcas marsupialis*)	27	36	20–60	1:0.9
Leopard (29)	Impala Bushbuck Common duiker (*Sylvicapra grimmia*)	23	25	10–40	1:0.8
Lion (80)	Blue wildebeest (*Connochaetes taurinus*) Buffalo (*Syncerus caffer*) Gemsbok (*Oryx gazelle*) Giraffe (*Giraffa camelopardalis*) Plain's zebra (*Equus burchellii*)	290	350	190–550	1:3.6
Spotted hyena (60)	Nil	n/a	102	56–182	1:1.7[a]

[a]Based on most preferred-prey species as no species was significantly preferred.

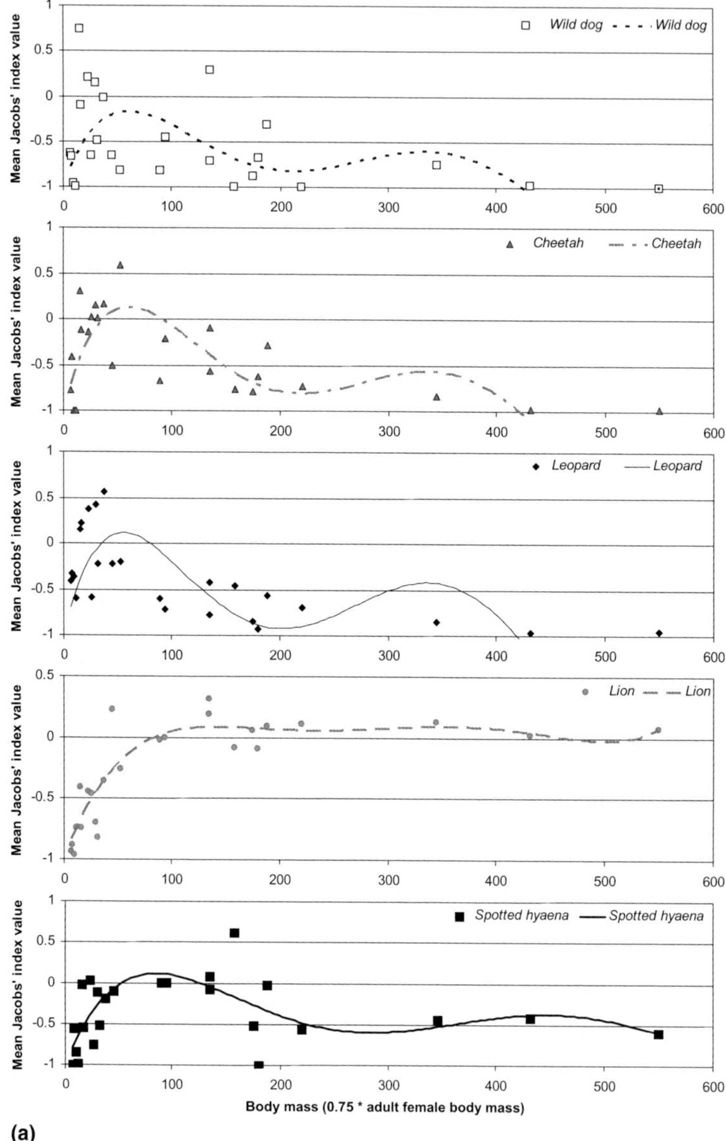

Figure 16.1 **The relationship between prey preference (Jacobs' index) and prey body size for all members of Africa's large-predator guild based on a distance-weighted least-squares regression. (a) Includes all available prey species. (b) Includes only prey of less than 200 kg.**

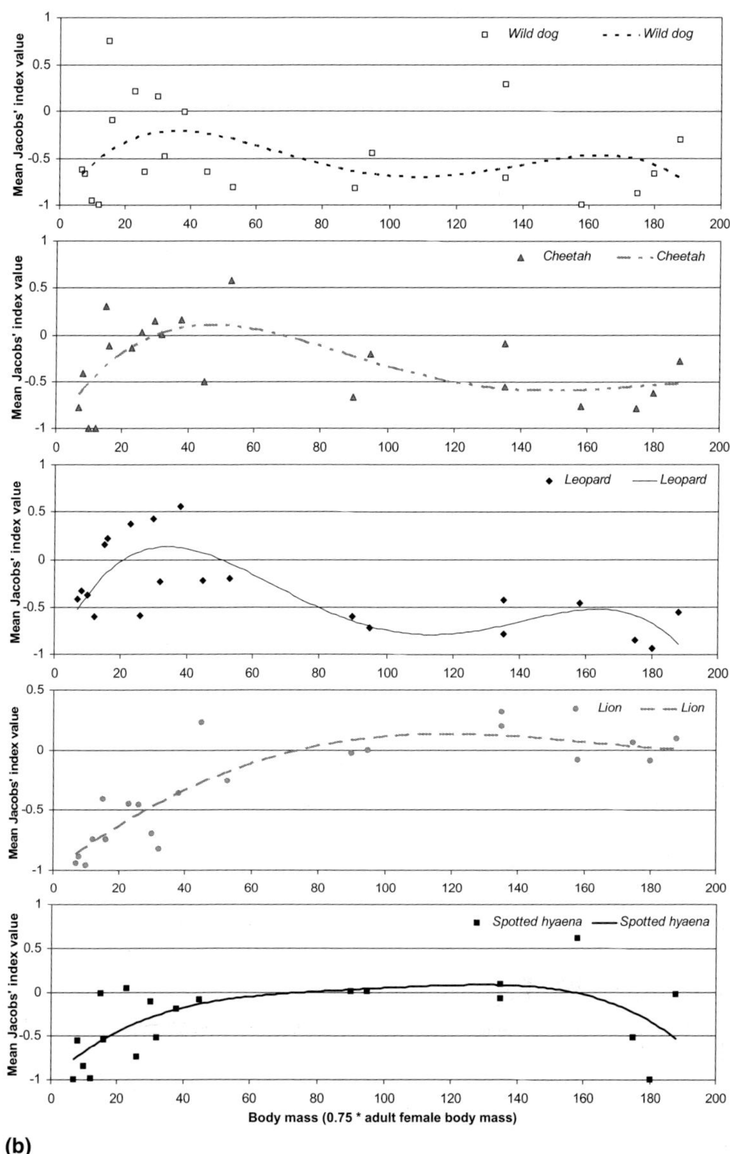

Figure 16.1 ***Continued***

therefore occupy the upper end of the African predator niche where they are free from competition from all but hyaenas (Hayward, 2006). Prey species outside the preferred weight range are generally avoided. Eland and waterbuck may become significantly preferred with a larger sample size; however, owing to their rarity in most environments, roan and kudu appear to avoid preferential predation (Hayward *et al.*, 2007d).

Leopard

Jacobs' index scores for 8643 kills of 111 prey species derived from 33 studies from 13 countries over 41 sites or time periods revealed that leopards prefer prey weighing between 10 and 40 kg (Figure 16.1b), and significantly prefer impala, bushbuck and common duiker (Table 16.1) (Hayward *et al.*, 2006a). The mean body mass of significantly preferred leopard prey is 23 kg. Species outside the preferred weight range are generally avoided. The solitary hunting strategy of the leopard limits it to hunting prey smaller than itself (Table 16.1).

The highly adaptable predatory nature of the leopard means that it can persist on prey as small as rock hyrax (*Procavia capensis*), on domestic livestock and on prey as large as adult male eland (see references in Hayward *et al.*, 2006a). Leopard populations that persist on prey outside the preferred weight range tend to be at either end of the morphological spectrum (e.g. excessively small as in the Cape leopards), which is attributed to character displacement (Hayward *et al.*, 2006a).

Cheetah

Jacobs' index scores for 3909 kills of 58 prey species derived from 23 studies from six countries over 48 locations or periods revealed that cheetah prefer to kill the most abundant prey present at a site within a body mass range of 23 to 56 kg (Table 16.1; Figure 16.1b). This preference affords minimal injury risk while hunting (Hayward *et al.*, 2006b). Blesbok, impala, Thomson's and Grant's gazelles and springbok are significantly preferred, and these species are slightly smaller than cheetahs (Table 16.1). Species outside the preferred weight range are generally avoided. Morphological adaptations limit the cheetah to capturing medium-sized prey that can be subdued with minimal injury risk. This, coincidentally, means that prey can be consumed rapidly before kleptoparasites arrive; however, cheetahs do not prey on larger prey in denser habitats, suggesting that kleptoparasitism avoidance is not an important issue in their selection of prey (Hayward *et al.*, 2006b).

African wild dog

Jacobs' index scores were calculated from 4874 kills of 45 prey species in 18 studies from five of the 14 African wild dog–range countries over 24 locations or periods. These revealed that they significantly prefer kudu, Thomson's gazelle, impala and bushbuck (Hayward *et al.*, 2006c). Wild dogs significantly prefer prey within a bimodal body mass range of 16–32 kg and 120–140 kg (Table 16.1; Figure 16.1), which follows optimal pack sizes based on energetic costs and benefits (Creel & Creel, 2002; Hayward *et al.*, 2006c). Species outside the preferred weight range are generally avoided. Essentially, larger packs target larger prey to satisfy their greater combined energy requirements. This illustrates the importance of group hunting for wild dogs and is reflected in the fact that they prefer to prey on species much larger than themselves (Table 16.1).

Spotted hyaena

Jacobs' index scores were calculated from 3478 kills of 30 prey species in 15 studies, which assumed that hyaenas were predominately predatory, from six countries over 21 locations or periods. These revealed that spotted hyaenas do not significantly prefer any prey species and that only three species are significantly avoided (Hayward, 2006). This finding may have been driven, however, by some studies misidentifying scavenged food as hunted prey. The most preferred prey-weight range for spotted hyaenas is from 56 to 182 kg (Table 16.1; Figure 16.1a). Spotted hyaenas have a very similar diet to that of lions, with 68.8% overlap (Hayward, 2006). The lack of significant preference is due to the ability of spotted hyaenas to scavenge, to hunt small prey solitarily and to hunt large prey in groups. The flexible and unselective nature of predation by spotted hyaenas means that the most abundant large prey at a site is likely to be locally preferred.

Predicting the diet of top-order predators

Having identified the range of species that Africa's top-order predators prefer to prey on, it is a relatively simple task to predict what they will actually prey on at a given site. To achieve this, we simply solved Equation 1 for r and then converted this proportion to a whole number by multiplying by the number of kills observed at test sites, according to the formula:

$$R_i = \frac{D_i p_i + p_i}{1 - D_i + 2D_i p_i} \times \sum K \qquad (2)$$

where R_i is the predicted number of kills of species i when a total of ΣK kills are observed at a test site, D_i represents the Jacobs' index value of species i calculated from our earlier prey preference studies, and p_i represents the proportional abundance of prey species i at a site (Hayward *et al.*, 2007d). Multiplication by ΣK was used to allow direct comparison between the predicted and observed number of kills, although this does not result in the total predicted number of kills equalling the observed number of kills. In a management situation, where the total number of kills at a site is unknown, this could be replaced by 100 to give the percentage of all kills made up of species i or to give estimates of the number of kills that a lion population, for example, will make.

We tested our predictions of lion diet using data from South Africa's Addo Elephant National Park (Addo), Shamwari Game Reserve (Shamwari) and Madikwe Game Reserve (Madikwe), and published accounts from Makalali Game Reserve (Makalali) and Zimbabwe's Hwange National Park (Hwange) (Hayward *et al.*, 2007d). None of these sites were used in the original determinations of Jacobs' prey preference value (D). The number of kills actually observed by lion researchers, using continuous following or intensive incidental sightings, were compared with the predicted number of kills of that species at each site over several years using the log-likelihood goodness-of-fit (G) test (Zar, 1996). We used linear regression to measure the accuracy of our predictions, where a significant gradient indicated a relationship between the predicted and observed number of kills at a site and the r^2 value illustrated the effect size.

Lion diet was precisely predicted in nine out of 13 tests, and the order of prey species (from most to least preferred) was always accurately predicted (Figure 16.2) (Hayward *et al.*, 2007d). The relationship between predicted and observed number of kills explained 64.5% of the variance in the data. This is satisfactory given the fact that opportunistic predation on species that would not be expected, based on mean Jacobs' index values, is carried out—and this is a sound optimal foraging strategy when such species can be ingested with minimal search and handling time (Hayward *et al.*, 2007d).

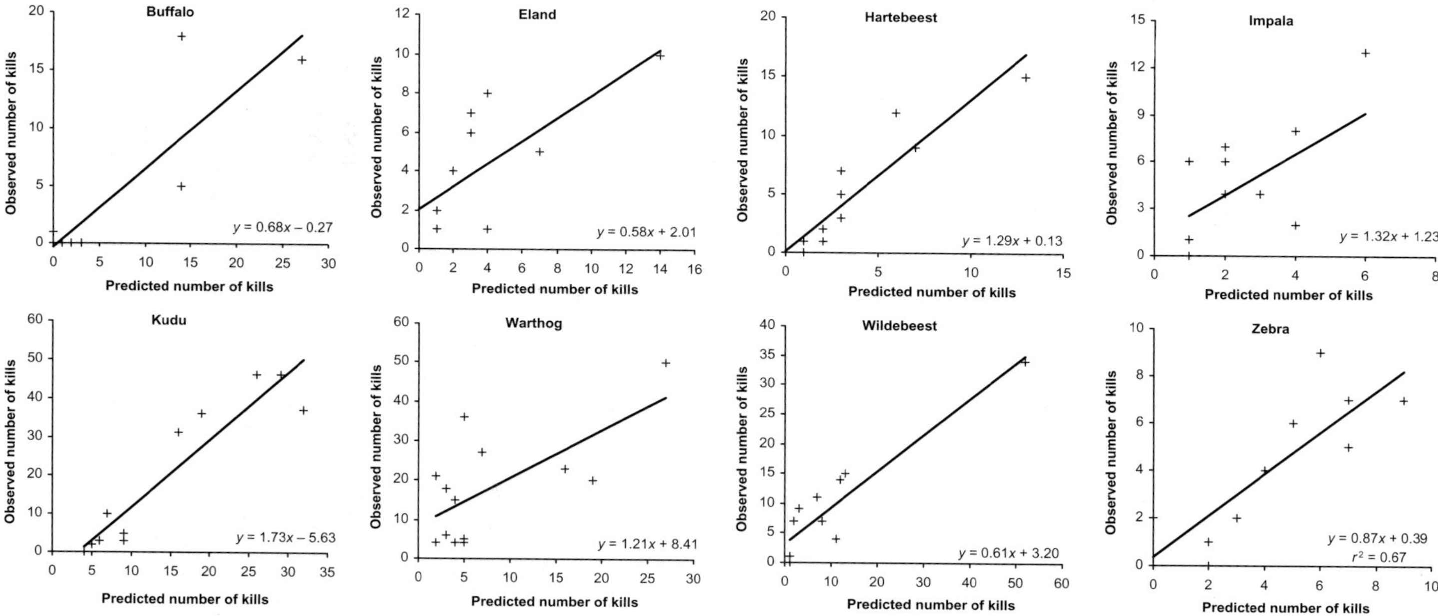

Figure 16.2 **Linear regressions of the predicted and observed number of kills of buffalo ($r^2 = 0.8$), eland ($r^2 = 0.4$), hartebeest ($r^2 = 0.9$), impala ($r^2 = 0.3$), kudu ($r^2 = 0.9$), warthog ($r^2 = 0.4$), wildebeest ($r^2 = 0.9$) and zebra ($r^2 = 0.7$) at all study sites.**

The four imprecise tests were largely caused by poor predictions of two of the 32 species assessed (warthog and kudu) and occurred at sites where lion diet was accurately predicted in other years (Figure 16.2). Warthog are below the preferred weight range of lion prey; however, the numbers of warthog kills were under-predicted in our tests. The most likely explanation for this suboptimal predation is that warthog were preyed upon by lion populations that had exceeded their ecological carrying capacity, as may occur in small, fenced populations when a new cohort of cubs gains independence or in open populations where migratory herds move away (Viljoen, 1993; Hayward *et al.*, 2007d). Alternatively, inaccurate counts of burrowing warthog may be the cause of this suboptimal predation (Hayward *et al.*, 2007d).

Kudu generally escape preferential predation by their rarity in the environment (Hayward & Kerley, 2005); however, they are the most abundant ungulate in the Thicket Biome of South Africa's Eastern Cape Province, where Addo and Shamwari are located. Consequently, preferentially hunting them becomes an optimal strategy (Hayward *et al.*, 2007d).

Thus, there are ecological reasons that readily explain the inaccuracies of the model's predictions. These inaccuracies may alternatively be due to altered hunting success in enclosed reserves, as several predators have been shown to alter their diet by using fences as part of their hunting strategy (van Dyk & Slotow, 2003).

Evidence of the ability to predict the diet of a top-order predator is presented solely for lions because there were several lion studies that had sufficient data with which to test these predictions. Nonetheless, the same techniques should work for all other large predators that have been satisfactorily studied; however, we know of no available information to test the predictions for other members of the guild.

Predicting the carrying capacity of top-order predators

In natural ecosystems, carnivore densities generally reflect the abundance of their prey. Karl van Orsdol and colleagues (1985) illustrated this relationship in their seminal work on lions. Since then, similar relationships between predator density and that of their prey have been found for cheetah (Laurenson, 1995), leopard (Stander *et al.*, 1997), tiger, *Panthera tigris*, (Karanth *et al.*, 2004) and wolf, *Canis lupus* (Peterson *et al.*, 1998 in Fuller & Sievert, 2001), and across carnivorans (Carbone & Gittleman, 2002).

Ultimately, these predator–prey relationships in Africa relate to rainfall and soil nutrients (East, 1984).

While this research substantially improved our understanding of predator–prey interactions, the research on prey preferences afforded a chance to investigate those relationships more closely. Originally, lion density was linked to the biomass of all available prey species (van Orsdol *et al.*, 1985); however, it is likely that preferred prey or preferred prey-weight range (Table 16.1) would offer a stronger relationship. Cheetah density was related to the biomass of prey weighing between 15 and 60 kg, along with a negative relationship with lion density (Laurenson, 1995); however, the preferred prey-weight range of cheetahs is 20–60 kg (Table 16.1), which may alter this relationship. Likewise, leopard density exhibited a strong relationship with the biomass of prey weighing between 15 and 60 kg (Stander *et al.*, 1997); however, this weight range is much greater than the preferred prey-weight range of leopard (10–40 kg; Table 16.1).

Prey-preference information with data from up to 24 sites in eastern and southern Africa was used to refine these predator–prey relationships, which were derived from a larger sample size than similar previous studies and, in each case, explained more of the variation in the data (Figure 16.3; Hayward *et al.*, 2007e). These new equations (Table 16.2) were then used to predict carnivore carrying capacity at 10 sites in South Africa where reintroductions were planned or had occurred and where wildlife census data were available. These test sites were not used in deriving the predictive equations. Wildlife managers or scientists had evidence that overpopulation of large carnivores may have occurred at some of these sites, and these were used as tests of our predictions.

Eight lions were reintroduced to Madjuma Lion Reserve in 1996, and the blue wildebeest population immediately plummeted, ultimately leading to the removal of the lions (Power, 2002). We predicted a carrying capacity of two lions at Madjuma (Figure 16.4; Hayward *et al.*, 2007e).

Lions were reintroduced to Pilanesberg National Park in 1993 and exceeded 50 individuals in 1998 (Tambling & du Toit, 2005). By 2002, excessive lion predation had caused declines in blue wildebeest (45%), eland (76%), waterbuck (67%) and kudu (65%) (Tambling & du Toit, 2005). We predicted a carrying capacity of 50 lions in Pilanesberg in 1997, based on available prey, and population declines began as soon as this was exceeded (Figure 16.4; Hayward *et al.*, 2007e). Clearly, the decline of prey in Pilanesberg has further decreased the national park's predator carrying capacity.

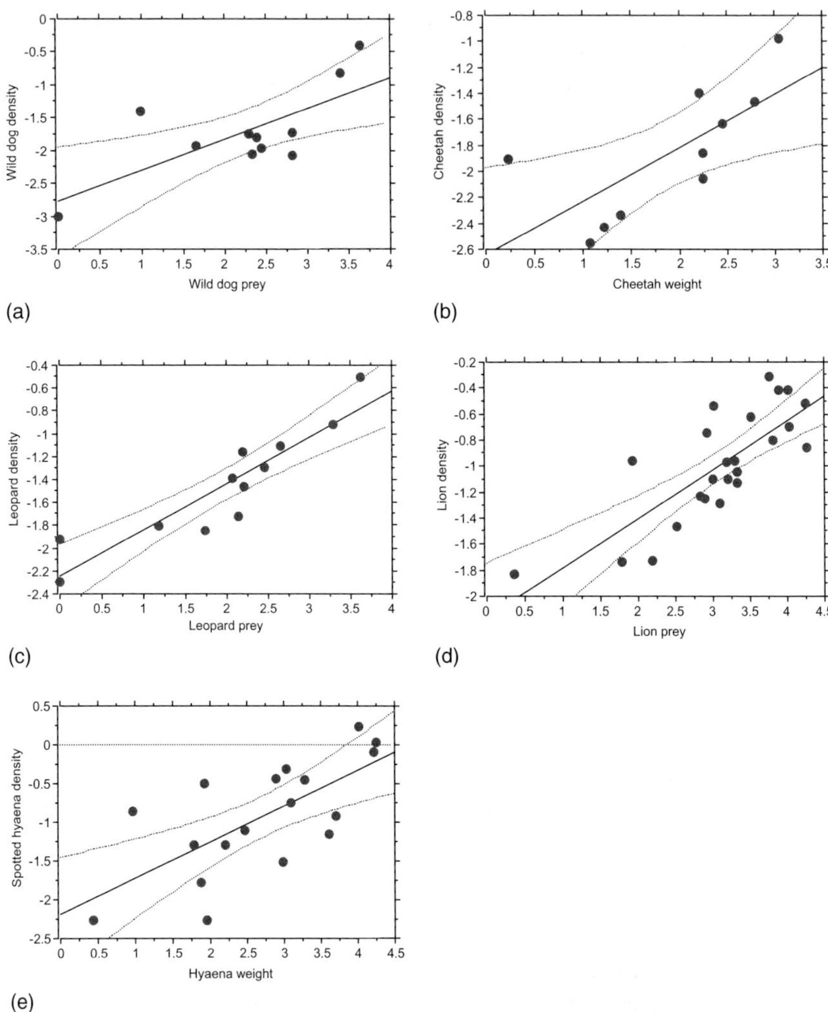

Figure 16.3 **Linear relationships between the log of the biomass of preferred prey or preferred prey-weight range (depending upon the strongest relationship) and the log of the biomass of each member of Africa's large-predator guild. Confidence intervals are also shown. (a) African wild dog, (b) cheetah, (c) leopard, (d) lion and (e) spotted hyaena. Regression statistics are shown in Table 16.2.**

Table 16.2 **Regression statistics for relationships between predator density and the biomass of their preferred prey, preferred prey-weight range or competitors. Only statistics for the strongest relationship are presented, as these should provide the most accurate estimates of the carrying capacity of a site.**

Predator	**Relationship (x)**	**Equation**	**Effect size (r^2)**	**Degrees of freedom (df)**	**Probability**
African wild dog	Preferred prey	$y = -2.780 + 0.470x$	0.523	10	0.012
Cheetah	Weight range (23–56 kg)	$y = -2.641 + 0.411x$	0.519	9	0.019
Leopard	Preferred prey	$y = -2.248 + 0.405x$	0.833	11	<0.001
Lion	Preferred prey	$y = -2.158 + 0.377x$	0.626	23	<0.001
Spotted hyaena	Weight range (56–182 kg)	$y = -2.195 + 0.467x$	0.487	17	0.001

Lions were reintroduced to Phinda Resource Reserve in 1992 (Hunter *et al.*, 2006) and, between 1996 and 1998, managers removed 30 individuals owing to declines in the wildebeest population (Hunter, 1998). The 13 lion at Phinda in 1995 were four below the predicted carrying capacity, suggesting that lion were not solely responsible for the wildebeest decline; however, our data support the management intervention (Hayward *et al.*, 2007e).

Phinda also reintroduced cheetah at this time and, by 1995, there were 21 individuals (Hunter, 1998). Despite a precipitous decline in common reedbuck, *Redunca arundinum*, managers did not intervene because of a high cheetah mortality rate at the time (Hunter, 1998). This decline in reedbuck abundance may have been due to cheetah overpopulation, as we predicted that the Phinda cheetah population exceeded carrying capacity by 14 (Hayward *et al.*, 2007c).

The six other sites where reintroductions of predators had only recently occurred or were planned provided additional support for the predictions. Shamwari Game Reserve managers had independently become concerned about lion over-abundance, such that they contracepted one lioness and

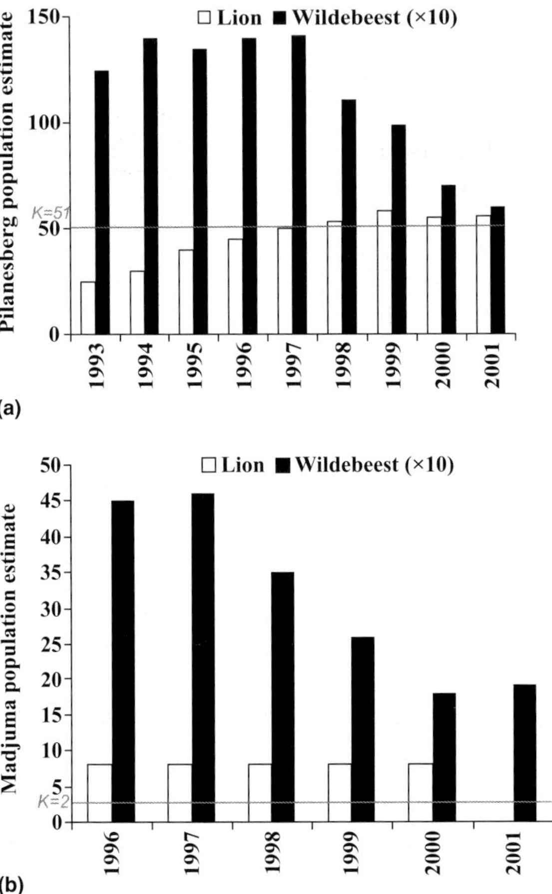

Figure 16.4 **Comparison between the predicted carrying capacity of lion at (a) Pilanesberg National Park and (b) Madjuma Game Reserve, and the response of blue wildebeest—a preferred prey species of the lion. The predicted carrying capacity (*K*) is shown as grey lines. A negative correlation was noted between lion and wildebeest population sizes at Pilanesberg (Spearman's $r = -0.65$; $n = 9$, $p = 0.057$), but no relationship existed at Madjuma because the lion population was contracepted. Permission to use this figure was provided by Elsevier Ltd.**

sold another (Hayward *et al.*, 2007e), and our predictions supported this management intervention (Hayward *et al.*, 2007e). Similarly, managers of Addo have contractual requirements to reintroduce predators to private concessions within the park. They delayed this until mid-2007 because of insufficient prey densities, and our predictions suggest a very low carrying capacity in these concessions with the current wildlife densities (Hayward *et al.*, 2007e).

The carrying capacity predictions also make ecological sense. Small, enclosed reserves are often stocked at artificially high levels and are sustained by heavy management regimes. These sites were predicted to support the highest densities of predators. The lowest densities were predicted at newly restocked sites or those in arid areas that naturally support low wildlife densities (Hayward *et al.*, 2007e).

The tests of our carrying capacity predictions were accurate in three out of four tests, and the fourth was ambiguous. The predictions also received support from conservation managers and made ecological sense. Consequently, the equations presented in Table 16.2 should be valuable tools for conservation managers throughout sub-Saharan Africa. It is likely that similar relationships exist for other predators. Predictions of carrying capacity based on other equations that did not use preferred prey or preferred prey-weight range (Laurenson, 1995; Gros *et al.*, 1996; Stander *et al.*, 1997; Carbone & Gittleman, 2002) invariably were excessively large for the test populations (Hayward *et al.*, 2007e).

Implications for top-order predator reintroduction

Areas where top-order predators persist are largely natural islands in a sea of altered landscapes where detrimental interactions with humans are highly likely (Woodroffe & Ginsberg, 1998; Hayward *et al.*, 2007e). Thus, there are few sites remaining on Earth where human impact is sufficiently low to allow wildlife to exist unencumbered by any management activity. Even in some of the largest conservation areas, genetic management of large carnivores is likely to be necessary to avoid inbreeding problems (Frankham, this volume). Hence, knowledge of predator carrying capacity and potential impacts on herbivores is imperative.

Knowledge of the prey preferences of predators provides some significant advances in the ability of conservation managers to predict the responses of top-order predators and their prey to environmental fluctuations. These fluctuations may arise simply through the reintroduction process or may be natural climatic variations, such as droughts, or even global, human-induced climate change.

This research may also offer ways to manage predator numbers to benefit the more highly threatened subordinate predators. By increasing the abundance of the preferred prey of subordinate competitors, at the expense of the preferred prey of dominant competitors, the carrying capacity of subordinate competitors is likely to increase (Hayward *et al.*, 2007e). The concern is that the abundance of dominant competitors will remain unchanged as they subsist on smaller, suboptimal prey. African wild dogs have been reported persisting on small, suboptimal prey in Kenya (Woodroffe *et al.*, 2007), so this is possible. Given that predators exceeding 21.5 kg in weight are considered to have evolved as obligate predators of large vertebrates (Carbone *et al.*, 1999), which is entirely supported by the prey preference results for African predators, it would seem that populations that survive on suboptimal prey are unlikely to do so for long. If anything, such suboptimal predation may be an early indicator that a predator population is at risk of extinction (Hayward *et al.*, 2007e). Consequently, although dominant competitors may switch to smaller prey, it is unlikely that such suboptimal predation could persist in the long term. The success of this management option will be determined by whether subordinate predators are resilient enough to cope with increased competitive interactions before a new equilibrium with dominant competitors is reached.

Another management benefit offered by this research is the opportunity to predict the impact of predation on threatened prey species, and potentially to manage this threat. The roan population in South Africa's Kruger National Park has declined to virtual extinction, and this was linked to increased predation that arose when boreholes created in the roan's semi-arid refuge habitats allowed the plain's zebra and blue wildebeest to invade (Harrington *et al.*, 1999). Zebra and wildebeest are the preferred prey of lions, which followed them in to the area. Roan are within the preferred weight range of lions, but generally avoid preferential predation owing to the inherent rarity of lion-sized prey, and therefore of lions themselves, in the environments where roan live. With this rarity removed in Kruger, however, the roan then became targeted by lions (Hayward *et al.*, 2007d). This could have been predicted with knowledge of prey preference ecology. Indeed, the risk of predation to any small population of prey species can now be assessed and predicted, potentially allowing managers to alter the relative abundance of one prey species to provide a buffer for a rarer prey species (Hayward *et al.*, 2007e).

This research also highlighted questions about what constitutes habitat for large, generalist predators. Our prey preference values were derived from studies throughout the distributional range of the lion (Hayward & Kerley, 2005), but none came from South Africa's Thicket Biome. We tested the predictions of lion diet at sites with unique or highly disturbed vegetation (especially the former agricultural lands of Addo and Shamwari), and they proved precise (see section on predicting the diet of top-order predators). We concluded that, for lions and probably other top-order predators, vegetation communities are less important than available prey for survival and conservation (Hayward *et al.*, 2007c). This is supported by our carrying capacity estimates (Hayward *et al.*, 2007d). Consequently, essential habitat for top-order predators comprises an adequate supply of preferred prey or prey with body masses within their preferred prey-weight range, or habitat that can support this prey. In the absence of sufficient numbers of suitably sized prey, predators are unlikely to be able to exist at a particular site (Karanth *et al.*, 2004).

The ability to predict the diet and carrying capacity of Africa's top-order predators has arisen because they are exceedingly well studied. The basic natural history (diet, population sizes, etc.) of numerous other species of top-order predator is also very well known (e.g. there are more than 100 published studies of the diet of wolves *C. lupus* from throughout the Holarctic; unpublished data). Other species are less well studied, and these require detailed research in order that their natural history can be satisfactorily understood, and to allow prediction of their responses to reintroduction and environmental stochasticity.

It is possible that small reserves may eventually attain some equilibrium between predator and prey abundance. This concept is attractive because it allays the need for conservation management interference. It is also a risky strategy to leave the wildlife in small, enclosed reserves to attain their natural balance, given the lack of spatial or temporal refuges that would protect prey populations from hyper-predation, as their populations are likely to decline earlier than those of their predators. In small, enclosed reserves, this could lead to a complete extinction of certain prey species before the equilibrium is reached. The same concept applies to the recent debate on whether to resume culling elephant, *Loxodonta africana*, populations in southern Africa where delays in management could lead to detrimental impacts on biodiversity (Owen-Smith *et al.*, 2006).

Finally, throughout sub-Saharan Africa, ungulate populations are in decline (Ogutu & Owen-Smith, 2003; Estes *et al.*, 2006). Given the strong relationships with prey population sizes, this is likely to lead to declines in predator numbers via bottom-up limitation. As predator populations are already small, owing to their location at the apex of food chains, this will place them under increased pressure as new threats associated with the small-population paradigm come into play (Caughley, 1994).

Acknowledgements

Graham Kerley of the Nelson Mandela Metropolitan University provided funding, friendship, assistance and support, and was an ideal collaborator while this research was being undertaken. Gina Hayward conducted field work in Addo Elephant National Park while this work was being written up. The Society for Conservation Biology kindly provided a travel grant to attend the 21st Annual Meeting in Port Elizabeth, and additional support was received from the European Union Marie Curie Actions BIORES Transfer of Knowledge Project. This manuscript was improved by excellent reviews from Chris Carbone and Matt Gommper, and discussions with Paul Funston.

References

Bauer, H. & de Iongh, H.H. (2005) Lion (*Panthera leo*) home ranges and livestock conflicts in Waza National Park, Cameroon. *African Journal of Ecology* 43, 208–214.

Bauer, H., de Iongh, H.H. & Di Silvestre, I. (2003) Lion (*Panthera leo*) social behaviour in the west and central African savannah belt. *Mammalian Biology* 68, 239–243.

Breitenmoser, U., Breitenmoser-Wursten, C., Carbyn, L.N. & Funk, S.M. (2001) Assessment of carnivore reintroductions. *Carnivore Conservation.* (eds J.L. Gittleman, S.M. Funk, D.W. Macdonald & R.K. Wayne), pp. 241–280. Cambridge University Press and the Zoological Society of London, Cambridge.

Carbone, C. & Gittleman, J.L. (2002) A common rule for the scaling of carnivore density. *Science* 295, 2273–2276.

Carbone, C., Mace, G.M., Roberts, S.C. & Macdonald, D.W. (1999) Energetic constraints on the diet of terrestrial carnivores. *Nature* 402, 286–288.

Caughley, G. (1994) Directions in conservation biology. *Journal of Animal Ecology* 63, 215–244.

Creel, S. & Creel, N.M. (2002) *The African Wild Dog: Behavior, Ecology, and Conservation.* Princeton University Press, Princeton.

East, R. (1984) Rainfall, soil nutrient status and biomass of large African savanna mammals. *African Journal of Ecology* 22, 245–270.

Estes, R.D., Atwood, J.L. & Estes, A.B. (2006) Downward trends in Ngorongoro Crater ungulate populations 1986–2005: Conservation concerns and the need for ecological research. *Biological Conservation* 131, 106–120.

Fuller, T.K. & Sievert, P.R. (2001) Carnivore demography and the consequences of changes in prey availability. *Carnivore Conservation.* (eds J.L. Gittleman, S.M. Funk, D.W. Macdonald & R.K. Wayne), pp. 163–178. Cambridge University Press and the Zoological Society of London, Cambridge.

Gros, P.M., Kelly, M.J. & Caro, T.M. (1996) Estimating carnivore densities for conservation purposes: Indirect methods compared to baseline demographic data. *Oikos* 77, 197–206.

Gusset, M., Ryan, S.J., Hofmeyr, M. et al. (2008) Efforts going to the dogs? Evaluating attempts to re-introduce endangered wild dogs in South Africa. *Journal of Applied Ecology* 45: 100–108. DOI: 10.1111/j.1365–2664.2007.01357.x.

Harrington, R., Owen-Smith, N., Viljoen, P. C., Biggs, H. C., Mason, D.R. & Funston, P.J. (1999) Establishing the causes of the roan antelope decline in the Kruger National Park, South Africa. *Biological Conservation* 90, 69–78.

Hayward, M.W. (2006) Prey preferences of the spotted hyaena *Crocuta crocuta* and evidence of dietary competition with lion *Panthera leo*. *Journal of Zoology, London* 270, 606–614 DOI: 10.1111/j.1469–7998.2006.00184.x.

Hayward, M.W. & Hayward, G.J. (2007) Activity patterns of reintroduced lion *Panthera leo* and spotted hyaena *Crocuta crocuta* in Addo Elephant National Park, South Africa. *African Journal of Ecology,* 45, 135–141. DOI: 10.1111/j.1365–2028.2006.00686.x.

Hayward, M.W. & Kerley, G.I.H. (2005) Prey preferences of the lion (*Panthera leo*). *Journal of Zoology, London* 267, 309–322. DOI:10.1017/S0952836905007508.

Hayward, M.W., Adendorff, J., Moolman, L. C., Hayward, G.J. & Kerley, G.I.H. (2007a) The successful reintroduction of leopard *Panthera pardus* to the Addo Elephant National Park. *African Journal of Ecology* 45, 103–104.

Hayward, M.W., Adendorff, J., O'Brien, J. et al. (2007b) Practical considerations for the reintroduction of large, terrestrial, mammalian predators based on reintroductions to South Africa's Eastern Cape Province. *The Open Conservation Biology Journal* 1, 1–11. DOI: 10.2174/1874–8392/07.

Hayward, M.W., Adendorff, J., O'Brien, J. et al. (2007c) The reintroduction of large predators to the Eastern Cape Province, South Africa: An assessment. *Oryx* 42, 205–214.

Hayward, M.W., Henschel, P., O'Brien, J., Hofmeyr, M., Balme, G. & Kerley, G.I.H. (2006a) Prey preferences of the leopard (*Panthera pardus*). *Journal of Zoology, London* 270, 298–313. DOI:10.1111/j.1469–7998.2006.00139.x.

Hayward, M.W., Hofmeyr, M., O'Brien, J. & Kerley, G.I.H. (2006b) Prey preferences of the cheetah *Acinonyx jubatus*: Morphological limitations or the need to capture rapidly consumable prey before kleptoparasites arrive? *Journal of Zoology, London* 270, 615–627. DOI: 10.1111/j.1469–7998.2006.00184.x.

Hayward, M.W., Hofmeyr, M., O'Brien, J. & Kerley, G.I.H. (2007d) Testing predictions of the prey of the lion (*Panthera leo*) derived from modelled prey preferences. *Journal of Wildlife Management* 71, 1567–1575.

Hayward, M.W., O'Brien, J., Hofmeyr, M. & Kerley, G.I.H. (2006c) Prey preferences of the African wild dog *Lycaon pictus*: Ecological requirements for their conservation. *Journal of Mammalogy* 87, 1122–1131.

Hayward, M.W., O'Brien, J. & Kerley, G.I.H. (2007e) Carrying capacity of large African predators: Predictions and tests. *Biological Conservation* 139, 219–229.

Hunter, L.T.B. (1998) *The Behavioural Ecology of Reintroduced Lions and Cheetahs in the Phinda Resource Reserve, KwaZulu-Natal, South Africa.* PhD thesis, University of Pretoria.

Hunter, L.T.B., Pretorius, K., Carlisle, L.C. et al. (2006) Restoring lions *Panthera leo* to northern KwaZulu-Natal, South Africa: Short-term biological and technical success but equivocal long-term conservation. *Oryx* 41, 196–204.

Jacobs, J. (1974) Quantitative measurement of food selection—A modification of the forage ratio and Ivlev's electivity index. *Oecologia* 14, 413–417.

Joubert, D. (2006) Hunting behaviour of lions (*Panthera leo*) on elephants (*Loxodonta africana*) in the Chobe National Park, Botswana. *African Journal of Ecology* 44, 279–281.

Karanth, K.U., Nichols, J.D., Kumar, N.S., Link, W.A. & Hines, J.E. (2004) Tigers and their prey: Predicting carnivore densities from prey abundance. *Proceedings of the National Academy of Science, USA,* 101, 4854–4858.

Krebs, C.J. (1989) *Ecological Methodology.* Harper Collins Inc., New York.

Krebs, J.R. (1978) Optimal foraging: Decision rules for predators. *Behavioural Ecology: An Evolutionary Approach.* (eds J.R. Krebs & N.B. Davies), pp. 23–63. Blackwell Scientific Publications, Oxford.

Langholtz, J.A. & Kerley, G.I.H. (2006) *Combining Conservation and Development on Private Lands: An Assessment of Ecotourism-Based Private Game Reserves in the Eastern Cape.* Centre for African Conservation Ecology, Nelson Mandela Metropolitan University, Port Elizabeth, South Africa.

Laurenson, M.K. (1995) Implications of high offspring mortality for cheetah population dynamics. *Serengeti II: Dynamics, Management and Conservation of an Ecosystem.* (eds A.R.E. Sinclair & P. Arcese), pp. 385–399. University of Chicago Press, Chicago.

Ogutu, J.O. & Owen-Smith, N. (2003) ENSO, rainfall and temperature influences on extreme population declines among African savanna ungulates. *Ecology Letters* 6, 412–419.

Owen-Smith, N., Kerley, G.I.H., Page, B., Slotow, R. & van Aarde, R.J. (2006) A scientific perspective on the management of elephants in the Kruger National Park and elsewhere. *South African Journal of Science* 102, 389–394.

Power, R.J. (2002) Prey selection of lions *Panthera leo* in a small, enclosed reserve. *Koedoe* 45, 67–75.

Pyke, G.H., Pulliam, H.R. & Charnov, E.L. (1977) Optimal foraging: A selective review of theory and tests. *Quarterly Review of Biology* 52, 137–154.

Ravnsborg, R.S.L., Hayward, M.W. & Kerley, G.I.H. (2004) *Assessing the Diet of Wild Lions (Panthera leo) in the Addo Elephant National Park.* Department of Zoology, University of Port Elizabeth, Port Elizabeth.

Schaller, G.B. (1972) *The Serengeti Lion.* University of Chicago Press, Chicago.

Sims-Castley, R., Kerley, G.I.H. & Geach, B. (2004) *A Questionnaire-Based Assessment of the Socio-Economic Significance of Ecotourism-Based Private Game Reserves in the Eastern Cape.* Terrestrial Ecology Research Unit, University of Port Elizabeth, Port Elizabeth.

Skead, C.J. (1987) *Historical Mammal Incidence in the Cape Province. Volume 2: The Eastern Half of the Cape Province, including the Ciskei, Transkei and East Griqualand.* Chief Directorate Nature and Environmental Conservation of the Provincial Administration of the Cape of Good Hope, South Africa., Cape Town.

Stander, P.E., Haden, P.J., Kaqece & Ghau. (1997) The ecology of asociality in Namibian leopards. *Journal of Zoology, London* 242, 343–364.

Tambling, C.J. & du Toit, J.T. (2005) Modelling wildebeest population dynamics: Implications of predation and harvesting in a closed system. *Journal of Applied Ecology* 42, 431–441.

van Dyk, G. & Slotow, R. (2003) The effects of fences and lions on the ecology of African wild dogs reintroduced to Pilanesberg National Park, South Africa. *African Zoology* 38, 79–94.

van Orsdol, K.G., Hanby, J.P. & Bygott, J.D. (1985) Ecological correlates of lion social organisation (*Panthera leo*). *Journal of Zoology, London* 206, 97–112.

Viljoen, P.C. (1993) The effects of changes in prey availability on lion predation in a large natural ecosystem in northern Botswana. *Symposia of the Zoological Society of London* 65, 193–213.

Woodroffe, R. & Ginsberg, J.R. (1998) Edge effects and the extinction of populations inside protected areas. *Science* 280, 2126–2128.

Woodroffe, R., Lindsey, P.A., Romanach, S.S. & ole Ranah, S.M.K. (2007) African wild dogs (*Lycaon pictus*) can subsist on small prey: Implications for conservation. *Journal of Mammalogy* 88, 181–193.

Zar, J.H. (1996) *Biostatistical Analysis.* Prentice-Hall, Englewood Cliffs, New Jersey.

17

Genetic Considerations in Reintroduction Programmes for Top-Order, Terrestrial Predators

Richard Frankham[1]

[1]Department of Biological Sciences, Macquarie University

Summary

Genetic considerations are important both to the initial success of reintroduction programmes and to their long-term viability. Genetic contributions to initial success will be maximized by choosing founders with low inbreeding coefficients and high genetic diversity that are well adapted to the reintroduction environment. Inbreeding and loss of genetic diversity are unavoidable in all closed populations and so reduce the long-term viability of reintroduction programmes. The severity of their impacts in isolated populations is inversely related to the effective population size (N_e) and increases with the number of generations. For example, the reintroduced population of lions, *Panthera leo*, in the Eastern Cape, South Africa, has a carrying capacity (K) of only 10–15 animals and will reach an inbreeding coefficient of at least 60% after five generations (without immigrants), equivalent to five generations of full-sib mating. Such a population will have reduced reproduction and survival rates and a substantially elevated extinction risk, owing to inbreeding. In the long term, most closed reintroduced populations of large terrestrial predators are expected to go extinct for genetic reasons, typically in combination with other threatening factors. To avoid such genetic deterioration, unrelated migrants

Reintroduction of Top-Order Predators, 1st edition. Edited by M.W. Hayward and M.J. Somers.
 ISBN 978-1-4051-7680-4 (pb) and 978-1-4051-9273-6 (hb)

need to be introduced at regular intervals. To avoid outbreeding depression, the immigrants must be from the same species and evolutionary significant unit and have the same karyotype. If they are taken from within the former continuous range of the species and from a similar environment, the risks of outbreeding depression should be very low.

Introduction

My role is to consider genetic factors affecting the success of animal reintroductions for large terrestrial predators. Genetic factors (primarily inbreeding and loss of genetic diversity) impinge upon both the initial success of reintroductions and upon their long-term viability (Moritz, 1999; Frankham *et al.*, 2002). As detailed below, inbreeding leads to reductions in reproduction and survival (inbreeding depression). Loss of genetic diversity reduces the ability of populations to evolve in response to environmental change. As inbreeding in small populations typically has the most immediate impact on populations, this chapter concentrates primarily on inbreeding. However, the two factors are closely related in random-mating populations (see below).

Initial phase

The primary issues in the initial phase are the impacts of genetic factors on the reproduction and survival rates of the reintroduced population and its ability to evolve to cope with this habitat. Consequently, populations chosen for reintroductions should be as well adapted as possible to the reintroduction site, with high genetic diversity and low inbreeding levels—e.g. animals from one or more nearby sites with similar habitats would be suitable. Conversely, long-term captive populations typically show poor adaptation to wild environments (reviewed by Frankham, 2008).

Where well-adapted populations have low genetic diversity, it is desirable to cross different populations to generate a reintroduced population with high genetic diversity. If the reintroduction environment is different to that for any existing population, as might occur for a species that has been extinct in the wild and has existed only in captivity for many generations, the only option is to ensure high genetic diversity so that the population has the potential to genetically adapt to the reintroduction site.

Recommendations for the number of founders are typically 20–30 individuals that successfully breed. This represents a loss of 1.7%–2.5% of initial genetic diversity if variation in family sizes is random (Poisson) (Frankham *et al.*, 2002). If smaller numbers of founders are used initially, then additional unrelated founders should be introduced later.

Long-term viability

Many deterministic (habitat loss, over exploitation, introduced species and pollution) and stochastic (demographic, environmental and genetic stochasticity, plus catastrophes) factors impinge upon extinction risk. The genetic issues affecting long term viability and extinction risk are (reviewed by Moritz, 1999; Frankham *et al.*, 2002; Frankham, 2005):

1. Inbreeding depression,
2. Loss of genetic diversity,
3. Mutation accumulation,
4. Genetic adaptation to captivity,
5. Outbreeding depression.

The fourth issue—genetic adaptation to captivity—has been addressed above and will not be considered further. The first three issues are all associated with small population size, but the impacts of mutation accumulation appear much smaller over the time frames of importance in conservation than the other factors (reviewed by Frankham, 2005), so will not be considered further. I will defer treatment of outbreeding depression to later in the chapter, where it will be considered in the context of what can be done to remedy problems caused by inbreeding and loss of genetic diversity.

Inbreeding and loss of genetic diversity are unavoidable in closed populations (Frankham *et al.*, 2002). The relationships between population size, loss of genetic diversity and inbreeding in closed random-mating populations are described by the following equation:

$$H_t/H_0 = (1-1/[2N_e])^t = 1-F \qquad (1)$$

where H_t is heterozygosity (Hardy-Weinberg expected heterozygosity) at generation t; H_0 is the initial heterozygosity; N_e is the genetically effective population size; and F is the inbreeding coefficient.

There are three points to note from Equation 1. First, since the middle term in the equation is approximately $e^{-t/2Ne}$, it predicts an exponential decay of genetic diversity over generations, and this occurs at a faster rate in smaller than in larger populations (Figure 17.1). Second, the inbreeding coefficient equals the proportionate loss of genetic diversity. Third, the rate of decay in genetic diversity and the increase in inbreeding both depend upon the genetically effective population size, rather than the actual or census size.

The effective size is typically much smaller than the number of potentially breeding adults in populations, owing to fluctuations in population size, high variation in family sizes (greater than Poisson variation) and unequal sex ratios (Frankham *et al.*, 2002; Allendorf & Luikart, 2006). N_e is typically an order of magnitude lower than census population sizes across a broad range of major taxa (Frankham, 1995a).

Inbreeding has long been known to reduce reproduction and survival in naturally outbreeding species (inbreeding depression). Darwin (1876) provided compelling evidence on this, based on comparisons of the progeny of self- and cross-fertilization in 57 species of plants. Self-fertilization reduced seed production by an average of 41% and height by 13%. Not all species showed inbreeding depression for all characters studied, but virtually all showed it for most reproductive fitness characters. Subsequently, similar conclusions were found to apply for laboratory and domestic animals and plants (Charlesworth & Charlesworth, 1987; Falconer & Mackay, 1996; Lynch & Walsh, 1998). Inbreeding has deleterious consequences on all aspects of reproduction and survival, including sperm production, mating ability, female

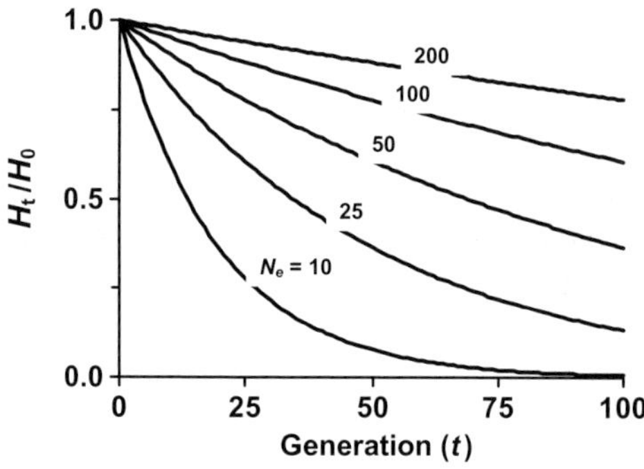

Figure 17.1 **Predicted decline in genetic diversity over generations in populations with different effective sizes (from Frankham *et al.*, 2002, after Foose, 1986).**

fecundity, juvenile survival, mothering ability, age at sexual maturity and adult survival in animals, and in related components in plants (Ralls & Ballou, 1983; Crnokrak & Roff, 1999; Keller & Waller, 2002; Frankham *et al.*, 2002; Frankham, 2005).

Inbreeding depression has been found in essentially all naturally outbreeding diploid eukaryotic taxa that have been thoroughly studied, and the magnitudes of effects are similar across major taxa (Ralls *et al.*, 1988; Crnokrak & Roff, 1999; Hedrick & Kalinowski, 2000). Inbreeding depression has been reported in at least 16 species of terrestrial predators (Table 17.1), including grey wolves in captivity and in the wild (Laikre & Ryman, 1991; Vilà *et al.*, 2003; Liberg *et al.*, 2005), Mexican wolves in captivity and in the wild (Fredrickson & Hedrick, 2002; Hedrick & Fredrickson, 2008), Florida panther in the wild (Pimm *et al.*, 2006) and lions in the wild (Packer *et al.*, 1991; Packer & Pusey, 1993). Non-significant inbreeding depression has been reported in some species, including red wolves in captivity (Kalinowski *et al.*, 1999) and the dwarf mongoose (*Helogale parvula*) in the wild (Keane *et al.*, 1996). However, these studies have been small and had low statistical power (Kalinowski & Hedrick, 1999), and they usually show trends in the direction of inbreeding depression, as is evident in the dwarf mongoose study (Keane *et al.*, 1996). Lacy (1997) concluded that no species of mammal that has been adequately studied has been shown to be unaffected by inbreeding. Genetic rescue following outcrossing has been documented in grey wolves, Mexican wolves and Florida panthers (Vilà *et al.*, 2003; Pimm *et al.*, 2006; Hedrick & Fredrickson, 2008), as well as in other wild populations and many experimental laboratory studies (Frankham, 2005). Notably, captive carnivores do not differ in inbreeding depression from other major vertebrates (Laikre, 1999; Wilcken, 2002).

Inbreeding has been shown to cause extinctions, both in captivity (Frankham, 1995b; Reed *et al.*, 2003; Frankham, 2005) and in the wild (Newman & Pilson, 1997; Saccheri *et al.*, 1998; Vilas *et al.*, 2006). For example, inbreeding in *Drosophila* increased extinction risk in benign captive conditions no matter whether it was due to full-sib mating or due to unavoidable inbreeding in random-mating populations with effective sizes of 10 or 20 individuals (Figure 17.2; Reed *et al.*, 2003). Whilst extinctions did not begin until inbreeding coefficients of about 40% were reached, the apparent lag does not imply that small amounts of inbreeding are not deleterious; rather, the apparent lag is due to the requirement for offspring numbers per pair to decline from more than100 to less than two (replacement) before extinction

Table 17.1 **Reports of inbreeding depression in predators.**

Species	Captive/wild	Reference
Arctic fox, *Vulpes lagopus*	Captive	Laikre, 1999
Brown bear, *Ursus arctos*	Captive	Laikre *et al.*, 1996
Cheetah, *Acinonyx jubatus*	Captive	Hedrick, 1987
Dog, *Canis lupus familiaris*	Captive	Laikre, 1999
Florida panther, *Puma concolor coryi*[a]	Wild	Pimm *et al.*, 2006
Grey wolf, *Canis lupus*[a]	Captive and wild	Laikre & Ryman, 1991; Vilà *et al.*, 2003; Liberg *et al.*, 2005
Lion, *Panthera leo*	Wild	Laikre, 1999
Lynx, *Lynx lynx*	Captive	Laikre, 1999
Mexican wolf, *Canis lupus baileyi*[a]	Captive and wild	Hedrick & Fredrickson, 2008
Mink, *Mustela* spp.	Captive	Laikre, 1999
Persian leopard *Panthera pardus saxicolor*	Captive	Laikre, 1999
Red panda *Ailurus fulgens*	Captive	Laikre, 1999
Tiger, *Panthera tigris*	Captive	Laikre, 1999
Clouded leopard, *Neofelis nebulosa*	Captive	Wilcken, 2002
Sand cat, *Felis margarita*	Captive	Wilcken, 2002
Red wolf, *Canis rufus*	Captive	Wilcken, 2002

[a]Species in which outcrossing has led to genetic rescue.

occurs. All the surviving populations in this study had reduced reproductive fitness, compared to their base population. Similar relationships between inbreeding and extinction under full-sib mating have been reported for many other species, including mice (*Mus musculus*), guinea pigs (*Cavia porcellus*), chickens (*Gallus gallus*), Japanese quails (*Coturnix japonica*) and turkeys (*Meleagris gallopavo*) (Frankham, 1995b; Frankham, 1998).

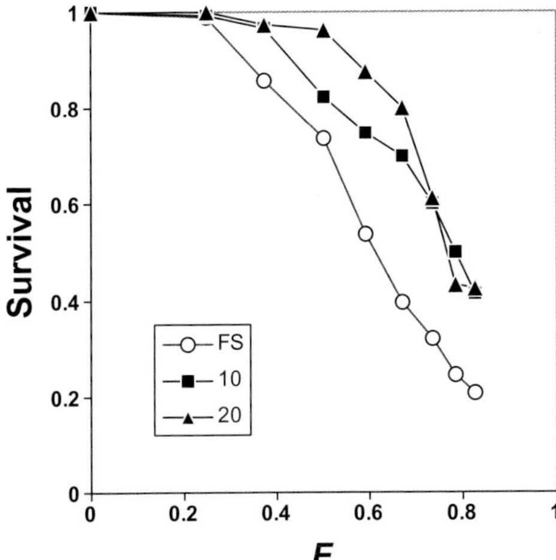

Figure 17.2 **Relation between inbreeding and extinction in fruit fly populations. Proportion of populations surviving at different levels of inbreeding for populations maintained with full-sib mating (FS) or with effective population sizes of 10 or 20 and maintained with random mating (from Reed *et al.*, 2003).**

Extinctions in the wild due to genetic factors have been reported in butterflies and two species of plants (Newman & Pilson, 1997; Saccheri *et al.*, 1998; Vilas *et al.*, 2006). Furthermore, computer projections for 30 species of animals show that median times to extinction are reduced by 30%–40% owing to inbreeding depression, compared to otherwise identical models without inbreeding depression (O'Grady *et al.*, 2006). Whilst the impacts vary somewhat across species (Figure 17.3), almost all naturally outbreeding animal species have their projected times to extinction shortened by inbreeding depression. Based upon analyses of the effects of inbreeding on litter size in the small wild Swedish grey wolf population, Liberg *et al.* (2005) predicted that the population would reach a zero population growth (lambda) at F = 0.48. This is similar to the point where *Drosophila* data show elevated extinction risk from inbreeding (Figure 17.2), even though not all aspects of the life cycle have been evaluated for effects of inbreeding in the wolf population.

Many reintroduced populations are being placed in habitat with low carrying capacities (Hayward *et al.*, 2007a). For example, some populations are being placed into areas with carrying capacities of 10–15 individuals or less

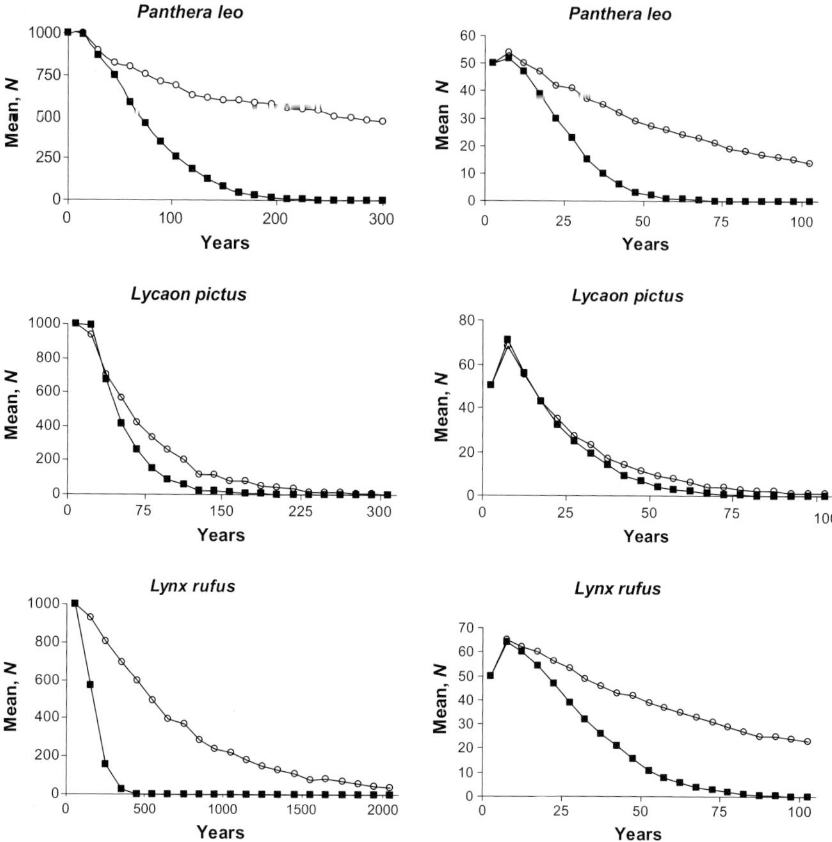

Figure 17.3 **Stochastic computer projections without inbreeding depression (open circles) and with inbreeding depression (closed squares) for African lions, African wild dogs and bobcats, for populations begun with either 1000 individuals (left-hand side) or 50 individuals (right-hand side). All known or suspected threatening factors are included in the simulations and each has 1000 replicates (from the study by O'Grady *et al.*, 2006).**

in the Eastern Cape region of South Africa (see below). These populations will rapidly become highly inbred, with consequent reduction in fecundity and survival and elevated extinction risks. Other natural populations exist in large reserves, such as Kruger National Park, where their carrying capacities are several hundred individuals. Below, I consider a range of case studies for large terrestrial African predators by determining the accumulation of the inbreeding coefficients using Equation 1. To do this, the carrying capacities supplied by Matthew Hayward (personal communication), based on Hayward *et al.* (2007b) have to be converted into effective population sizes. For a broad range of taxa, the ratio between effective population size and average census size has been found to be approximately 0.1 (Frankham, 1995a), so this value has been used in my calculations. While many populations will have average sizes of less than carrying capacity, I will very conservatively assume that all populations have average sizes at carrying capacity. The small populations that I consider are closed reintroduced ones, while the larger ones are natural populations of varying sizes that are often not closed, but are assumed to be closed for illustrative purposes to extend the range of population sizes.

Case studies for large terrestrial predators in Africa

Lions reintroduced into the Eastern Cape

The carrying capacity for this reintroduced lion population is only ~10–15 individuals (Hayward *et al.*, 2007a). N_e in this population will be only 1–1.5, assuming that $N_e/N = 0.1$. If we are very conservative and assume that $N_e = 3$ then, after five generations, the inbreeding coefficient will be $F = 0.60$, equivalent to the inbreeding generated by approximately five generations of brother–sister mating. At this level of inbreeding, the extinction risk from genetic factors will be elevated. After 10 generations, $F = 0.84$, which is equivalent to approximately eight generations of full-sib mating, and the extinction risk from genetic factors is expected to be greatly elevated.

Carrying capacities for reintroduced cheetah and African wild dog, *Lycaon pictus*, populations in the Eastern Cape are lower, leading to situations for these species that are even worse than for the lions.

Ngorongoro lions

The Ngorongoro crater has a carrying capacity for lions of ~50 individuals, yielding an effective population size of approximately five individuals. This is not a reintroduced population, but a small natural one. Assuming that this population is closed to immigrants, in five generations it is predicted to reach

$F = 0.41$, equivalent to more than two generations of full-sib mating. At this level of inbreeding, we expect the extinction risk from inbreeding to be moderately elevated. In 10 generations, the predicted F is 0.65, equivalent to more than four generations of full-sib mating. At this point, the extinction risk from inbreeding depression is expected to be substantially increased.

Cheetahs in Kruger National Park

Kruger National Park has a carrying capacity for cheetahs of ~200 individuals, implying that $N_e \sim 20$. If this population is closed to immigration then, within five generations, if would have $F = 0.12$, equivalent to all individuals having resulted from matings between half-sibs. After 10 generations, the population inbreeding would be approaching that of a full-sib mating ($F = 0.22$; full-sib mating $F = 0.25$). Given that there are game lodges around Kruger National Park, the assumption of a closed population is highly questionable. However, if these game park cheetahs were recently derived from the Kruger populations, then they would not be unrelated immigrants. Details of the gene flow in this region are required to determine its future genetic fate.

African wild dogs in Kruger National Park

The carrying capacity for African wild dogs in Kruger National Park is ~400 individuals. If this natural population is closed, it will have $N_e \sim 40$ and inbreeding coefficients after five, 10 and 20 generations of 0.06, 0.12 and 0.22, respectively. The latter case is approaching the inbreeding level of full-sib matings. Again, the assumption of a closed population for Kruger National Park is questionable. The size of this unit may extend well beyond the Park boundaries and its effective size may be larger.

Management intervention required to avoid adverse long-term genetic problems

From the case studies, it is clear that reintroduced populations will suffer adverse genetic effects that will increase their extinction risk, with the effects being most immediate in the smallest populations and least in the largest populations. This indicates that most reintroduced populations are not viable in the long term for genetic reasons, let alone all the other threatening factors they face. To minimize the genetic problems, it is essential that the reintroduced populations be augmented with unrelated individuals from other populations (Moritz, 1999; Frankham *et al.*, 2002). There is extensive evidence from studies in laboratory and domestic animals and plants that augmentation improves fitness of small inbred populations (Frankham *et al.*, 2002).

Sadly, very few examples of augmentation into fragmented natural or translocated populations have been described (Frankham *et al.*, 2002). In wild populations in natural habitats, augmentation has improved the fitness of Florida panthers, greater prairie chickens (*Tympanuchus cupido*), Swedish adders (*Vipera berus*), desert topminnow fish (*Poeciliopsis lucida*) and scarlet gilia (*Ipomopsis aggregata* and *Silene alba*) plants (Heschel & Paige, 1995; Westemeier *et al.*, 1998; Madsen *et al.*, 1999, 2004; Richards, 2000; Pimm *et al.*, 2006). The recent efforts in South Africa are particularly notable, with augmentation having been done in fragmented populations of African wild dogs, lions, African elephants (*Loxodonta africana*) and black rhinoceroses (*Diceros bicornis*) (G. Kerley, Nelson Mandela Metropolitan University, South Africa; personal communication; R. Slotow, personal communication). The African wild dog conservation management plan for South Africa is a particularly well-designed programme (Davies-Mostert *et al.*, this volume).

Risk of outbreeding depression

The decision to augment populations involves a cost/benefit calculation between the risk and cost of inbreeding depression and the risk and cost of outbreeding depression (Moritz, 1999). Outbreeding depression is a reduction in reproductive fitness owing to crossing individuals from different populations (Frankham *et al.*, 2002). The risk of fitness reduction with inbreeding is very high, as essentially all well-studied naturally outbreeding eukaryotic diploid (or higher ploidy) species show inbreeding depression (see above). Conversely, outbreeding depression occurs in some crosses between populations within species (see Endler, 1977; Moritz, 1999; Frankham *et al.*, 2002; Edmands, 2007; McClelland & Naish, 2007). We are currently engaged in a comprehensive review and analysis of outbreeding depression, including the development of theory to predict its extent. In this review, we have reached conclusions that disagree strongly with those of Edmands (2007), and we consider that her views are coloured by working on populations that have been isolated for up to 13 million years (Edmands *et al.*, 2005). Many of the populations she studied would almost certainly be considered different species in other major taxa. In brief, our conclusions (which apply across all major taxa of animals and plants, including terrestrial predators) are as follows.

1 There are two major factors causing outbreeding depression—adaptation to different environments and fixation of different chromosomal types (Moritz, 1999; Coyne & Orr, 2004; Gravilets, 2004).
2 Outbreeding depression owing to adaptation to different environments is expected to increase with selective differences, genetic diversity, effective population size and number of generations.
3 Full speciation typically takes around 1 million years (Coyne & Orr, 2004).
4 It has proven difficult to produce outbreeding depression in laboratory studies, with no significant reproductive isolation being evident in up to 170 generations in invertebrates and in 500 generations for yeast populations kept in the same environment (Rice & Hostert, 1993; Florin & Ödeen, 2002; Coyne & Orr, 2004; Dettman *et al.*, 2007). Furthermore, there is anecdotal evidence from *Drosophila* laboratory stocks that reproductive isolation is not evident even after 1000 generations in similar conditions. Wild populations of stickleback fish (*Gasterosteus* spp.) in the same environment, but isolated for about 3000 generations, do not show outbreeding depression (Rundle *et al.*, 2000).
5 Modest levels of reproductive isolation have been produced in some laboratory studies with invertebrates and with yeast populations maintained under different environmental conditions (Rice & Hostert, 1993; Florin & Ödeen, 2002; Dettman *et al.*, 2007). Wild fish populations that inhabited different environments for about 3000 generations showed considerable outbreeding depression (Rundle *et al.*, 2000).
6 Even crosses between different species have been found to be about as likely to be beneficial as deleterious (Arnold, 1997).
7 Based upon a large meta-analysis, crosses between fish populations within species have ranged from beneficial to deleterious in particular species, but the overall trend is towards them being beneficial in parental wild environments (McClelland & Naish, 2007).
8 The risk of outbreeding depression for populations that were previously connected and where the environments are similar is very low, unless

population sizes are very large and the number of generations is very large (several hundred or more).

Thus, for most situations involving large terrestrial predators whose populations have been isolated following European colonization, the risk of outbreeding depression will be low. However, it is critical that the taxonomy be thoroughly resolved before any augmentation is done, as many groups have cryptic species (Frankham *et al.*, 2002). For example, even African elephants have recently had their taxonomy revised (Roca *et al.*, 2001; Eggert *et al.*, 2002). Furthermore, the populations should have their chromosomes examined if this has not already been done. It is also advisable that augmentation initially be done on an experimental basis where its impacts can be monitored and evaluated.

Augmentation regimes

In fragmented idealized populations, one immigrant per generation is sufficient to prevent them from differentiating, irrespective of population size (Wright, 1969). In practice, populations do not fit the assumption of the idealized population (Falconer & Mackay, 1996), so up to 10 immigrants per generation have been recommended (Lacy, 1987; Mills & Allendorf, 1996; Vucetich & Waite, 2000). Note that these practical recommendations do not assume that all migrants successfully breed. The immigrants need to be unrelated to the population they enter and ideally should be adapted to the environment of this population. Provided they are unrelated, they can be from another inbred population (Spielman & Frankham, 1992). It is desirable, but not critical, that immigrants be added to populations each generation, and augmentation needs to be more frequent for small than for large populations.

Conclusions

Most reintroduced populations are small and will suffer serious genetic problems from inbreeding depression within relatively few generations unless regular programmes of augmentation from other populations are instituted and continued.

References

Allendorf, F.W. & Luikart, G. (2006) *Conservation and the Genetics of Populations.* Blackwell, Malden.

Arnold, M.L. (1997) *Natural Hybridization and Evolution.* Oxford University Press, New York.

Charlesworth, D., & Charlesworth, B (1987) Inbreeding depression and its evolutionary consequences. *Annual Review of Ecology and Systematics* 18, 237–268.

Coyne, J.A. & Orr, H.A. (2004) *Speciation.* Sinauer, Sunderland.

Crnokrak, P. & Roff, D.A. (1999) Inbreeding depression in the wild. *Heredity* 83, 260–270.

Darwin, C. (1876) *The Effects of Cross and Self Fertilisation in the Vegetable Kingdom.* John Murray, London.

Dettman, J.R., Sirjusingh, C., Kohn, L.M. & Anderson, J.B. (2007) Incipient speciation by divergent adaptation and antagonistic epistasis in yeast. *Nature* 447, 585–588.

Edmands, S. (2007) Between a rock and a hard place: Evaluating the relative risks of inbreeding and outbreeding depression for conservation and management. *Molecular Ecology* 16, 463–475.

Edmands, S., Feaman, H.V., Harrison, J.S. & Timmerman, C.C. (2005) Genetic consequences of many generations of hybridization between divergent copepod populations. *Journal of Heredity* 96, 114–123.

Eggert, L.S., Rasner, C.A. & Woodruff, D.S. (2002) The evolution and phylogeography of the African elephant inferred from mitochondrial DNA sequence and nuclear microsatellite markers. *Proceedings of the Royal Society London B* 269, 1993–2006.

Endler, J.A. (1977) *Genetic Variation, Speciation and Clines.* Princeton University Press, Princeton.

Falconer, D.S. & Mackay, T.F.C. (1996) *Introduction to Quantitative Genetics.* Longman, Harlow, UK.

Florin, A.B. & Ödeen, A. (2002) Laboratory environments are not conducive for allopatric speciation. *Journal of Evolutionary Biology* 15, 10–19.

Foose, T.J. (1986) Riders of the last ark: The role of captive breeding in conservation strategies. *The Last Extinction.* (eds L. Kaufman & K. Mallory), pp. 141–165. MIT Press, Cambridge.

Frankham, R. (1995a) Effective population size/adult population size ratios in wildlife: A review. *Genetical Research* 66, 95–107.

Frankham, R. (1995b) Inbreeding and extinction: A threshold effect. *Conservation Biology* 9, 792–799.

Frankham, R. (1998) Inbreeding and extinction: Island populations. *Conservation Biology* 12, 665–675.

Frankham, R. (2005) Genetics and extinction. *Biological Conservation* 126, 131–140.

Frankham, R. (2008) Genetic adaptation to captivity in species conservation programs. *Molecular Ecology* 17, 325–333.

Frankham, R., Ballou, J.D. & Briscoe, D.A. (2002) *Introduction to Conservation Genetics*. Cambridge University Press, Cambridge.

Fredrickson, R. & Hedrick, P. (2002) Body size in endangered Mexican wolves: Effects of inbreeding and cross-lineage matings. *Animal Conservation* 5, 39–43.

Gravilets, S. (2004) *Fitness Landscapes and the Origin of Species*. Princeton University Press, Princeton.

Hayward, M.W., Adendorff, J., O'Brien, J., *et al.* (2007a) The reintroduction of large, terrestrial, mammalian predators to the Eastern Cape, South Africa. *Oryx* 41, 205–214.

Hayward, M.W., O'Brien, J. & Kerley, G.I.H. (2007b) Carrying capacity of large African predators: Predictions and tests. *Biological Conservation* 139, 219–229.

Hedrick, P.W. (1987) Genetic bottlenecks. *Science* 237, 963.

Hedrick, P.W. & Fredrickson, R.J. (2008) Captive breeding and the reintroduction of Mexican and red wolves. *Molecular Ecology* 17, 344–350.

Hedrick, P.W. & Kalinowski, S.T. (2000) Inbreeding depression in conservation biology. *Annual Review of Ecology and Systematics* 31, 139–162.

Heschel, M.S. & Paige, K.N. (1995) Inbreeding depression, environmental stress, and population size variation in scarlet gilia (*Ipomopsis aggregata*). *Conservation Biology* 9, 126–133.

Kalinowski, S.T. & Hedrick, P.W. (1999) Detecting inbreeding depression is difficult in captive endangered species. *Animal Conservation* 2, 131–136.

Kalinowski, S.T., Hedrick, P.W. & Miller, P.S. (1999) No inbreeding depression observed in Mexican and red wolf captive programs. *Conservation Biology* 13, 1371–1377.

Keane, B., Creel, S.R. & Waser, P.M. (1996) No evidence of inbreeding avoidance or inbreeding depression in a social carnivore. *Behavioral Ecology* 7, 480–489.

Keller, L.F. & Waller, D.M. (2002) Inbreeding effects in wild populations. *Trends in Ecology and Evolution* 17, 230–241.

Lacy, R.C. (1987) Loss of genetic diversity from managed populations: Interacting effects of drift, mutation, immigration, selection, and population subdivision. *Conservation Biology* 1, 143–158.

Lacy, R.C. (1997) Importance of genetic variation to the viability of mammalian populations. *Journal of Mammalogy* 78, 320–335.

Laikre, L. (1999) Conservation genetics of Nordic carnivores: Lessons from zoos. *Hereditas* 130, 203–216.

Laikre, L., & Ryman, N. (1991) Inbreeding depression in a captive wolf (*Canis lupus*) population. *Conservation Biology* 5, 33–40.

Laikre, L., Andren, R. Larsson, H.O. & Ryman, N. (1996) Inbreeding depression in brown bear, *Ursus arctos. Biological Conservation* 76, 69–72.

Liberg, O., Andrén, H., Pedersen, H.C., *et al.* (2005) Severe inbreeding depression in a wild wolf (*Canis lupus*) population. *Biology Letters* 1, 17–20.

Lynch, M. & Walsh, B. (1998) *Genetics and Analysis of Quantitative Traits.* Sinauer, Sunderland.

Madsen, T., Shine, R. Olsson, M. & Wittzell, H. (1999) Restoration of an inbred adder population. *Nature* 402, 34–35.

Madsen, T., Ujvari, B. & Olsson, M. (2004) Novel genes continue to enhance population growth in adders (*Vipera berus*). *Biological Conservation* 120, 145–147.

McClelland, E.K. & Naish, K.A. (2007) What is the fitness outcome of crossing unrelated fish populations? A meta-analysis and an evaluation of future research directions. *Conservation Genetics* 8, 397–416.

Mills, L.S. & Allendorf, F.W. (1996) The one-migrant-per-generation rule in conservation and management. *Conservation Biology* 10, 1509–1518.

Moritz, C. (1999) Conservation units and translocations: Strategies for conserving evolutionary processes. *Hereditas* 130, 217–228.

Newman, D. & Pilson, D. (1997) Increased probability of extinction due to decreased genetic effective population size: Experimental populations of *Clarkia pulchella. Evolution* 51, 354–362.

O'Grady, J.J., Brook, B.W., Reed, D.H., Ballou, J.D., Tonkyn, D.W. & Frankham, R. (2006) Realistic levels of inbreeding depression strongly affect extinction risk in wild populations. *Biological Conservation* 133, 42–51.

Packer, C. & Pusey, A.E. (1993) Dispersal, kinship, and inbreeding in African lions. *The Natural History of Inbreeding and Outbreeding: Theoretical and Empirical Perspectives.* (ed. N.W. Thornhill), pp. 375–391. University of Chicago Press, Chicago.

Packer, C., Pusey, A.E., Rowley, H., Gilbert, D.A., Martenson, J. & O'Brien. S.J. (1991) Case study of a population bottleneck: Lions of the Ngorongoro crater. *Conservation Biology* 5, 219–230.

Pimm, S.L., Dollar, L. & Bass, O.L.J. (2006) The genetic rescue of the Florida panther. *Animal Conservation* 9, 115–122.

Ralls, K. & Ballou, J. (1983) Extinction: Lessons from zoos. *Genetics and Conservation: A Reference for Managing Wild Animal and Plant Populations.* (eds C.M. Schonewald-Cox, S.M. Chambers, B. MacBryde, & L. Thomas), pp. 164–184. Benjamin/Cummings, Menlo Park.

Ralls, K., Ballou, J.D. & Templeton, A. (1988) Estimates of lethal equivalents and the cost of inbreeding in mammals. *Conservation Biology* 2, 185–193.

Reed, D.H., Lowe, E. Briscoe, D.A. & Frankham, R. (2003) Inbreeding and extinction: Effects of rate of inbreeding. *Conservation Genetics* 4, 405–410.

Rice, W.R. & Hostert, E.E. (1993) Laboratory experiments on speciation: What have we learned in 40 years? *Evolution* 47, 1637–1653.

Richards, C.M. (2000) Inbreeding depression and genetic rescue in a plant metapopulation. *American Naturalist* 155, 383–394.

Roca, A.L., Georgiadis, N. Pecon-Slattery, J. & O'Brien, S.J. (2001) Genetic evidence for two species of elephants in Africa. *Science* 293, 1473–1477.

Rundle, H.D., Nagel, L. Wenrick Boughman, J. & Schluter, D. (2000) Natural selection and parallel speciation in sympatric stickleback. *Science* 287, 306–308.

Saccheri, I., Kuussaari, M., Kankare, M., Vikman, P., Fortelius, W. & Hanski, I. (1998) Inbreeding and extinction in a butterfly metapopulation. *Nature* 392, 491–494.

Spielman, D. & Frankham, R. (1992) Modeling problems in conservation genetics using captive *Drosophila* populations: Improvement in reproductive fitness due to immigration of one individual into small partially inbred populations. *Zoo Biology* 11, 343–351.

Vilà, C., Sundqvist, A.K., Flagstad, Ö. *et al.* (2003) Rescue of a severely bottlenecked wolf (*Canis lupus*) population by a single immigrant. *Proceedings of the Royal Society of London B: Biological Sciences* 270, 91–97.

Vilas, C., Miguel, E.S., Amaro, R. & Garcia, C. (2006) Relative contribution of inbreeding depression and eroded adaptive diversity to extinction risk in small populations of shore campion. *Conservation Biology* 20, 229–238.

Vucetich, J.A. & Waite, T.A. (2000) Is one migrant per generation sufficient for the genetic management of fluctuating populations? *Animal Conservation* 3, 261–266.

Westemeier, R.L., Brawn, J.D. Simpson, S.A. *et al.* (1998) Tracking the long-term decline and recovery of an isolated population. *Science* 282, 1695–1698.

Wilcken, J. (2002) *The cost of Inbreeding Revisited.* MSc thesis, Macquarie University, Sydney.

Wright, S. (1969) *Evolution and the Genetics of Populations. 2. The Theory of Gene Frequencies.* University of Chicago Press, Chicago.

18

Breeding Far Eastern Leopards for Reintroduction: The Zoo Programme Perspective

Sarah Christie[1]

[1]Zoological Society of London

Summary

The Amur leopard, *Panthera pardus orientalis*, is one of only two large/medium cats for which a reintroduction from zoo stocks is currently judged a necessary conservation action by experts such as the IUCN/SSC (International Union for the Conservation of Nature and Natural Resources/Species Survival Commission) Cat Specialist Group (the other one being the Iberian lynx, *Lynx pardinus*). In addition to the customary planning to address the problems associated with the release of translocated large predators at a given location, it is also necessary to establish appropriate breeding and release-management strategies for the relevant zoo population. In both these arenas, the socio-political issues are far more problematic than the biological ones. This chapter examines the biological and socio-political problems associated with producing Amur leopards suitable for reintroduction from the stocks present in the world's zoos, and also considers some relevant aspects of site selection, breeding and release strategy, and enclosure design. It places the reintroduction breeding strategy within the context of overall generation of conservation support for Amur leopards from the world's zoos, but does not attempt to give an account of all factors involved in production of the Amur leopard

Reintroduction of Top-Order Predators, 1st edition. Edited by M.W. Hayward and M.J. Somers.
 ISBN 978-1-4051-7680-4 (pb) and 978-1-4051-9273-6 (hb)

reintroduction plan, which is currently neither complete nor officially approved.

Introduction

The Amur or Far Eastern leopard, *Panthera pardus orientalis*, is arguably the world's most endangered big cat, with only 25–34 animals remaining in the wild (Pikunov *et al.*, 2007) in south-west Primorye in the Russian Far East (Figure 18.1). The vast majority of its current range lies in Russia, although individuals do range over the border into neighbouring China and there are still sporadic, unverified reports from North Korea. The population has been recognized as a distinct subspecies (Miththapala *et al.*, 1996; Uphyrkina *et al.*, 2002) and deserves protection as a unique genetic contribution to the species and to the region. As a top-order predator, it is also a significant indicator of ecosystem health and integrity (Ray, 2005). Its current range lies in a region of importance to Russia's economic development and also of considerable biological significance in terms of both biodiversity richness and endemism; 31% of Russia's endangered species are found there and half of these are unique to the region. The area is bounded by China, North Korea and the Sea of Japan on three sides and by human-dominated areas of Russia on the fourth. Potential for expansion exists only over the border with China, and only if wildlife- and habitat-protection laws there are effectively enforced.

The extant population of Far Eastern leopards is at risk from a multitude of threats, including illegal killing of leopards and their prey, habitat loss due to fires and infrastructure development, disturbance and poacher access from road construction through leopard habitat, a decline in the effectiveness of protected area management in south-west Primorye and the potential ill effects of small population size such as inbreeding depression, disease or demographic imbalance. Genetic analyses (Uphyrkhina *et al.*, 2002) indicate a loss of genetic diversity, but as yet there is no evidence of a consequent loss of fitness such as a decline in fertility or cub survival.

A range of conservation actions have been put in place by relevant non-governmental organizations working with the Russian authorities. The Amur Leopard and Tiger Alliance (ALTA, see www.amur-leopard.org) has a comprehensive, but under-resourced, programme to address poaching and habitat

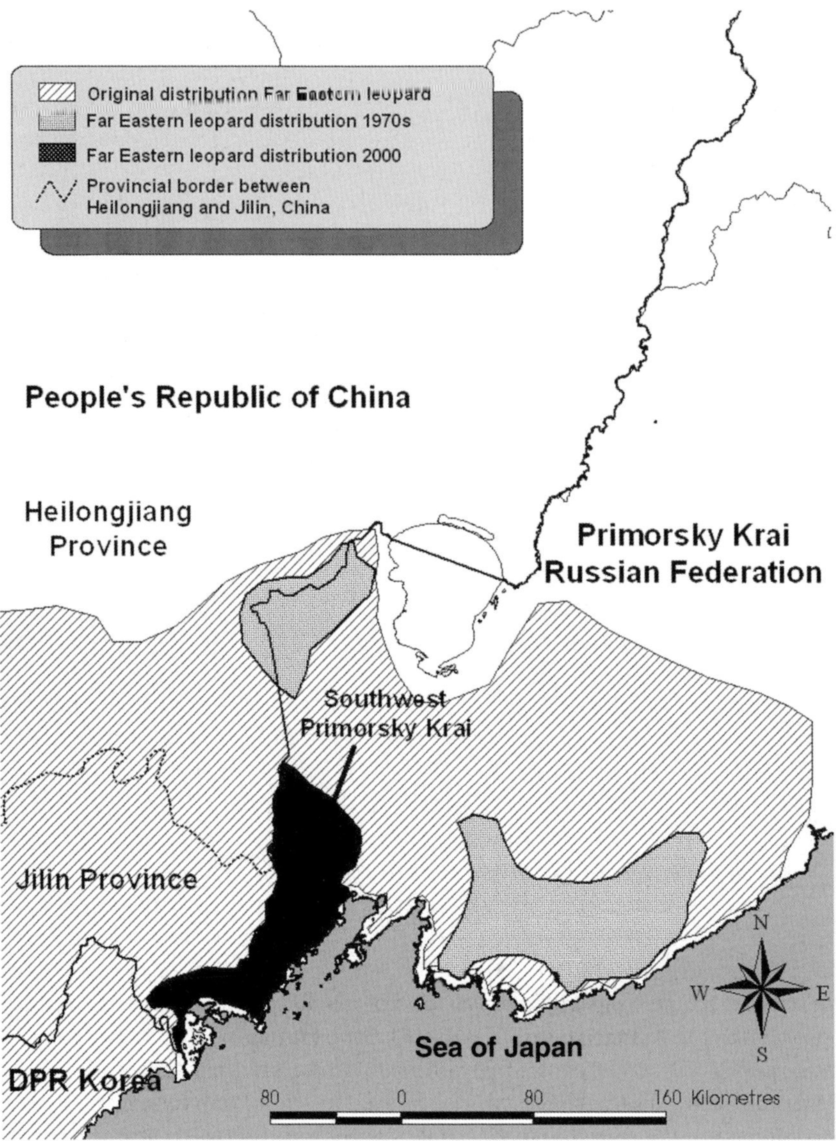

Figure 18.1 **Amur leopard current and historical range in south-west Primorye, Russia. Source: WCS/Tigris Foundation.**

loss as a result of human-induced fires and wildlife–human conflicts, to monitor leopard numbers, to evaluate wildlife disease status in the region and to improve local understanding of, and attitudes towards, the leopards. The key implementing agencies in ALTA are the Wildlife Conservation Society (WCS) and the Phoenix Fund, with other partners involved in Russia to a lesser degree (Moscow Zoo, the Zoological Society of London [ZSL], the International Fund for Animal Welfare, the Tigris Foundation and Wildlife Vets International) or providing relevant funding (ZSL, the Tigris Foundation, AMUR, 21st Century Tiger, David Shepherd Wildlife Foundation, Wildlife Alliance and Helsinki and Minnesota zoos). The other key agency is the World Wide Fund for Nature (WWF Russia), which has an Amur leopard programme covering anti-poaching, public education and the establishment of necessary protected areas, and is a partner in WCS's ecological monitoring. ALTA and WWF Russia coordinate leopard-conservation activities on the ground and are also working together on reintroduction planning.

To safeguard against the potential loss of Far Eastern leopards in the wild, experts have concluded that it is highly desirable that a second wild population be established in the near future (WCS, 2001). This view is supported by the IUCN/SSC Cat Specialist Group. Achieving this second population would not reduce the need to protect the original population in south-west Primorye, but would provide an opportunity to increase the numbers and genetic representation of this subspecies and would also increase the probability of survival in the wild if one or some combination of the many threats in south-west Primorye should force that population to extinction.

A reintroduction plan for this leopard is currently being prepared by a group of Russian and international scientists and conservationists for submission to the Russian government, and discussion on the subject with government authorities in Moscow has begun, facilitated by WWF Russia. I stress at this point that nothing will happen on the ground until the necessary political support and substantial funding have been obtained. This chapter is not intended to outline the entire plan, as it is not yet completed let alone authorized. Instead, I deal with the biological and political factors associated with managing the zoo population to produce cats suitable for release and with related factors, such as selection of release site and design of the proposed breeding and release centre.

Source of stock for release

In general, it is widely considered preferable to use wild-caught, translocated individuals for reintroduction projects rather than captive-bred stock. For carnivores, Jule *et al.* (2008) have recently reviewed information on the difference in success rates, which confirms this. Factors affecting success include lack of experience in hunting, lack of experience in exploring and utilizing home range, lack of human- and other predator-avoidance behaviours and vulnerability to disease.

As Jule *et al.* (2008) note, it would be of interest to further analyse the effects of each of these factors. While some projects have provided captive-bred carnivores with experience with live prey, there have been few efforts to ensure that captive-bred individuals slated for release do not become accustomed to humans—a much more problematic characteristic than lack of hunting experience. Release programmes for social species may have the option of pairing a captive-born individual with a mate accustomed to life in the wild in order to facilitate the learning process—at least in circumstances where there are such animals available (i.e. supplementations of existing wild populations or ongoing reintroductions in which some animals have already become established). This would not be possible for the Amur leopard, which is not social and would be released into an area with no existing leopards, making the learning period prior to release at dispersal age even more important.

The wild population of Amur leopards, at about 35 individuals, is far too small to withstand removal of sufficient animals to establish a new population. It is also genetically depauperate in comparison to the zoo population (Uphyrkhina *et al.*, 2002). Leopards for release would therefore be sourced from the managed conservation breeding programmes in the world's zoos, and pre-release breeding and management protocols are being designed to mitigate all the above factors as far as possible (see below).

The zoo population

The zoo population of this taxon is held almost exclusively in North America, Europe and Russia and has, since 1998, been managed to produce maximum conservation support for its wild conspecifics in terms of fund-raising, public awareness, generation of useful data and skills, and maintenance of a genetic "lifeboat" (see Christie, in press, for a fuller account of the conservation support roles of zoo animals, which extend well beyond reintroduction). The European/Russian zoo breeding programme (EEP—European Endangered species Programme) for Amur leopards is coordinated jointly by myself at ZSL and Tanya Arzhanova at Moscow Zoo, and the North American/Canadian programme (PMP—Population Management Program) is coordinated by Diana Weinhardt at Minnesota Zoo. ZSL has established a centralized service for EEP participant zoos and anyone else wishing to support the ALTA Amur leopard-conservation programme; a website at www.amurleopard.org and a regular email service provide supporters with news, pictures and reports from anti-poaching, outreach, camera-trapping, fire-fighting and veterinary projects run by WCS, Phoenix, ZSL and the Tigris Foundation, and ZSL acts as a collection point for funds raised. The PMP has played a similar role, gathering funds from participants and forwarding them to ZSL. Overall, zoos have provided a significant proportion of the funds so far spent on the conservation of this leopard in the wild.

Numbers and genetics

In early 2008, there were ~130 leopards in the EEP and ~97 in the PMP. There are a few additional leopards in zoos in Japan, Korea and China, but these are inaccessible to the conservation breeding programme and/or of inappropriate genetic makeup to be useful. The EEP population currently retains 88.9% of wild-gene diversity, which is just below the generally accepted desirable level of 90%. The PMP population contains no genetic lines that are not also present in the EEP population. Little can be done to improve gene diversity retention other than to breed from as many optimal pairings as possible on both sides of the Atlantic—and perhaps, if the necessary artificial reproductive techniques (ART) develop sufficiently and if the wild population proves to contain significant diversity not present in the captive stock, to use semen collected from wild male leopards to fertilize oocytes from the captive population.

To date, there have been very few instances of using ART to bring about genetically useful matings with real conservation implications from pairings that could not have mated naturally if given the chance, in felids or in any other group. However, the Berlin Institute of Zoo Biology and Wildlife

Research is now able to store feline sperm, ovarian tissue and early embryos produced by IVF and is researching application of these techniques to exotic cats with particular emphasis on the Amur leopard. If they are successful, their work *could* bring real conservation benefits. It could enable breeding from zoo cats that have died since their gametes were harvested and hence extend the life of the captive gene pool; it could transfer genetic material from the wild to the captive population without removing any leopards from the wild; and it could also enable careful planning of breeding for release. Embryos of appropriate genetic makeup and sexes could be stored and implanted as necessary into one or two females held in the *in situ* breeding centres, which would eliminate the need for long-distance transfers of pairs for breeding and would also ensure a balanced sex ratio in cubs produced for release, something that cannot be assured by any other means. However, these methods are both expensive and experimental; there is still a very long way to go in this arena, and current plans remain based on natural mating.

Breeding strategy in the Amur leopard EEP and the Founder 2 problem

As if this leopard did not already have sufficient difficulties, the managed zoo population in both the American and European regions includes a considerable contribution of genes from one founder—Founder 2—who was not an Amur leopard. (NB: Founder 89 has also been shown to have non-Amur leopard genes; however, his genetic contribution to the captive population is tiny in comparison and is not of sufficient significance to merit special attention in the genetic management strategy.) Founder 2 is long dead, but molecular genetics on samples from his descendants (Uphyrkhina *et al.*, 2002) indicates that he was probably of the geographically adjacent *japonensis* subspecies from northern China. If this is so, he was simply from the other end of what was quite recently a cline (see Frankham, this volume, for genetic management strategies). Taxonomists favouring a morphological approach (who suggest his appearance is very different—see Figure 18.2) consider him more likely to be *pernigra* from the Himalayas. In the end though, this debate is purely academic. Taking a pragmatic approach, whatever his origin, his genes are so widespread within the zoo population, and the remaining wild population is so small and genetically impoverished that, as for the

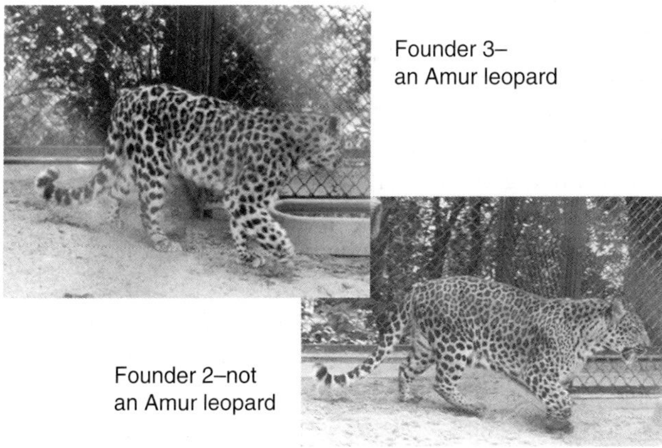

Figure 18.2 **Founder 2 (not an Amur leopard) and his life-long mate Founder 3 (an Amur leopard) at Frankfurt Zoo in the 1970s). No copyright known.**

Prezwalski's horse population and its domestic horse genes (Bowling *et al.*, 2003), there is no realistic option other than to retain his genes in the zoo and reintroduced population.

The debate over Founder 2 might be thought relatively inconsequential in biological terms, especially given the documented success in improving Florida panther, *Puma concolor*, viability using Texas puma genes (Pimm *et al.*, 2006). However, relevant events clearly demonstrate that socio-political factors can often override biological ones in decision-making processes. Initially, in the mid-1990s, representatives of European and Russian zoos were strongly opposed to retaining representation of Founder 2, largely on philosophical grounds, and strenuous efforts were made to breed the few available pure-bred leopards exclusively to each other. These pure-bred cats had all come from Pyongyang zoo in North Korea during the 1980s and 1990s, and were variously reported as wild caught or captive bred without any substantiating material. Genetic investigations by Uphyrkhina *et al.*, (2002) concluded that they were closely related to the wild population in Russia and were also sufficiently related to one another to be the result of three generations of brother–sister pairings (O.V. Uphyrkhina, Institute of Biology and Soils, Far East Branch of Russian Academy of Sciences, Vladivostok, Russia; personal communication). Breeding attempts within this group largely failed to produce healthy offspring and for the past 5 years these cats, where still alive and in breeding condition, have instead been paired with leopards containing low levels of Founder 2.

It was clear in 1998, and was further underlined at a meeting in Vladivostok, "Workshop on Conservation of the Far Eastern Leopard 2001" (WCS, 2001)—despite arguments that evolution might be expected to act on any undesirable genes present—that leopards with high levels of Founder 2 genes would not be acceptable to many scientists and conservationists for release. Hence, rather than simply treating Founder 2 as another founder on the grounds of his probable nearby geographical origin (according to molecular genetics), as the PMP has done, EEP strategy has been to manage breeding so as to minimize his contribution as far as possible while still maintaining acceptable overall levels of genetic diversity. The usual method of selecting cats for breeding on the basis of their mean kinship ranking (simply put, the level of unrelatedness to the rest of the population) has been balanced with consideration of their Founder 2 content, so that a cat with a high mean kinship rank but with more than 25% Founder 2 content might not get a breeding position while one with a lower mean kinship rank but only 12.5% Founder 2 is certain to do so. All leopards with more than 41% Founder 2 (simply a convenient cut-off point in the distribution of percentages) have been excluded from breeding since 1999 and, in recent years, those with more than 30% have also been mostly excluded as numbers of animals with lower levels have risen.

This policy has resulted in an overall decrease in the prevalence of Founder 2 genes and an increase in the number of leopards with low percentages of them. It is unfortunate that it was not possible to adopt this approach earlier, as several pure-bred leopards died without surviving offspring before the new policy was agreed. As of early 2008, 20% of the total EEP population (13 male and 13 female leopards) contained a Founder 2 contribution of 20% or less, as did 4% (two male and two female leopards) of the PMP population. Breeding from animals of between 20% and 30% Founder 2 will continue to some extent in order to conserve a wide gene pool in the population overall, but it is the pool of young leopards carrying a Founder 2 contribution of less than 20% that would provide the necessary breeding pairs for production of cubs for release in the Russian Far East.

The PMP programme has recently recognized the political realities of breeding for possible reintroduction—i.e. that whatever the real biological consequences may be, many relevant scientists remain fundamentally opposed to Founder 2's inclusion—and has adopted the EEP approach of minimizing his contribution. Two young leopards with low Founder 2 content are being identified for shipment from Europe to Minnesota to assist in reducing overall Founder 2 levels in the PMP.

Melanism is present in the population, thanks partly to the enthusiasm with which its initial appearance was greeted by some participating zoos, which actively sought out and bred from these cats to the extent of importing them to Canada from Europe for the purpose. There are no records of the melanism gene in the wild population of Amur leopards, but it is not possible to attribute the gene in the zoo population exclusively to Founder 2 because all leopards with a genetic contribution from him also contain genes from his life-long mate, Founder 3. While the melanism gene could conceivably—given the snowy winters in the region—exert an impact on survival in the wild, being a recessive gene it would be likely to be expressed in only one cub per litter at most and to be rapidly selected against in the wild if it did increase mortality rates. The fact is, however, that when expressed it is *visible* and so, like the fox colour gene in the Prezwalski horse, is likely to attract intense hostility from those who are philosophically opposed to the inclusion of Founder 2 genes in the first place. Once again, socio-political factors outweighed biological ones in the management decision process and melanistic cats are now excluded from the breeding pool—although not all possible melanism gene *carriers* are excluded, as to do that would effectively cripple the programme. Invisible genes (e.g. those affecting physiological processes such as temperature control) might have a more significant impact on survival in the wild. As we cannot detect them, however, the only possible strategy to mitigate their possible effects is to minimize Founder 2's overall contributions.

The matter of birth seasonality is an interesting one in this context. This is a factor that could compromise survival and could be affected by genes from another geographical location. It is also one which we can detect in zoo leopards. There are few data on birth seasonality from Amur leopards, but Amur tigers (*Panthera tigris altaica*) in the wild do not show a pronounced peak in birthing during the spring—in fact, most births are in late summer or autumn, with births reported in nearly every month of the year (Kerley *et al.*, 2003). This could be considered surprising given the severe winters in the region. Captive Amur tigers, with a dataset of well over 4000 births, do show a significant birth peak in April–June, with 45% of births occurring in those months (Traylor-Holzer, 2003), though births do occur throughout the year. Additionally, in two pure-bred Amur leopards in Prague Zoo, the quality of semen collected varied with season, with better-quality ejaculate obtained in spring and early summer than in December (K. Jewgenow, Institut für Zoo- und Wildtierforschung, Berlin, Germany; personal communication).

With this in mind, along with the need to allay as far as possible the fears of those objecting to Founder 2's genes, birth seasonality in the Amur leopard EEP with and without Founder 2 was investigated in 2001. Figure 18.3a shows the distribution of litters born to wild-caught pairs with and without Founder 2; there is a 2-month difference in average birth date between the two groups. Figure 18.3b compares birth distribution in leopards with low, medium and high Founder 2 content; the difference between the low and medium Founder 2 groups is statistically significant ($\chi^2 > 20.12$, df = 11, $p < 0.05$ for each), indicating that Founder 2's genes do affect the birth season in this population.

However, the subsequent analysis of the whole population's birth distribution shown in Figure 18.3c clearly indicates that, overall, there is a peak in spring. As field scientists currently do not believe that this leopard is a seasonal breeder in the wild, they will presumably be less concerned about this factor in leopards for release than about melanism; but in any case, it seems that provided Founder 2 levels remain below 20%, there is unlikely to be an effect on birth seasonality.

Some genetic lines in the zoo population have experienced high levels of inbreeding in the past, although management strategy over the past 10 years has ensured that current inbreeding coefficients are below 0.1. Past problems have been due partly to a shortage of founders, but also to a lack of active management prior to the mid-1990s, particularly in the pure-bred (and inbred) lines originating in Pyongyang zoo. At present, the EEP is collecting and collating data on any possibly inheritable defects, which have included deformed leg bones, cryptorchidism and "manx" tails, and ensuring that any affected animals are not included in the breeding pool. The bulk of the population is free from such problems. A veterinary team has been assembled by the EEP's veterinary advisor, John Lewis, to investigate specific factors where necessary, and a protocol for data collection has been circulated to participating zoos.

It is worth noting that in one instance of a possibly inherited defect—cryptorchidism—in a pure-bred cat, the strength of feeling among EEP participants about purity was such that attempts to breed from the animal in question continued despite clear veterinary advice pointing out that the problem is often associated with other damaging genes. As this leopard has

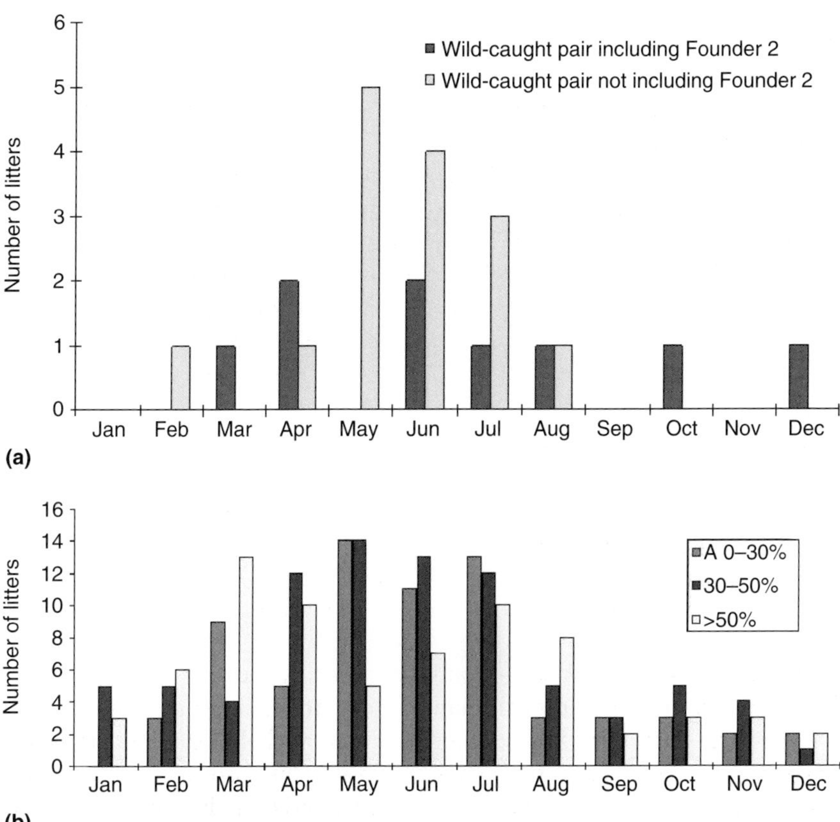

Figure 18.3 **Birth seasonality in the Amur leopard EEP with and without Founder 2, between 1960 and 2000, was investigated in 2001. (a) Birth seasonality in pairs of wild-caught Amur leopards not including Founder 2, contrasted with births to Founder 2 and his life-long mate Founder 3. (b) Differences in birth distribution between leopards with low, medium and high Founder 2 content (shown in key). (c) Birth seasonality in the whole population between 1960 and 2000. During this period, 445 cubs were born in 217 litters throughout Europe. Source: ZSL.**

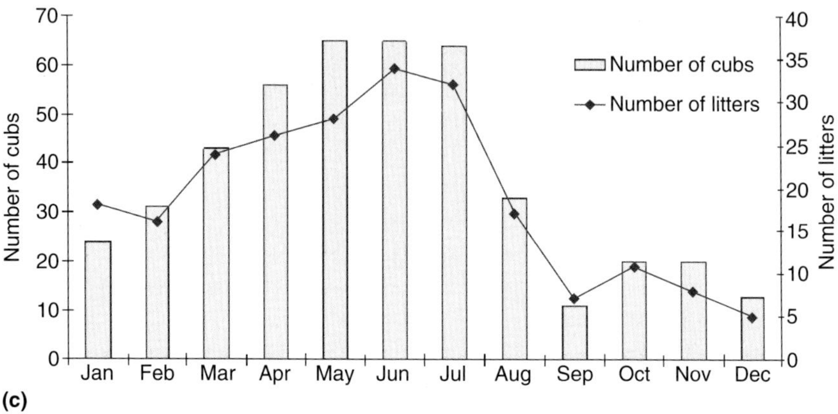

Figure 18.3 ***Continued***

also failed to show normal mating behaviour, ART has been used as well as natural mating attempts. However, no pregnancy has yet resulted.

Preparations in the field

Release-site selection

There is general consensus among stakeholders that the first effort should focus on establishing a second population rather than on supplementing the existing wild one given the potential veterinary, behavioural and genetic risks of adding captive-bred cats to the wild population and the lack of any evidence of loss of fitness resulting from small population size in the wild as yet. The release site for this second population should have the following characteristics.

- Be within the historical range of the Amur leopard (Figure 18.1);
- Be sufficiently separated from the current range to ensure no possibility of genetic mixing with the existing population;
- Be as far away as possible from human habitation in order to minimize chances of conflicts;
- Contain a high prey base of appropriate species;

- Contain cliffs and rocky areas to facilitate the leopard's use of refuges on release;
- Contain adequate infrastructure (roads, electricity and water supply) for management and monitoring activities;
- Be within a well-managed area with sufficient protection.

Additional criteria, including those related to the attitudes and reactions of local residents and other stakeholder groups, do of course need to be met before a reintroduction can proceed (see IUCN, 1998); here we are considering only criteria relating to site selection.

Lazovsky Zapovednik (zapovedniks are IUCN Category 1 protected areas) is located within the historical range and at the same latitude as the existing population (see Figure 18.4). Its physical characteristics also resemble the current range in that it is situated on the coast, which tends to create slightly

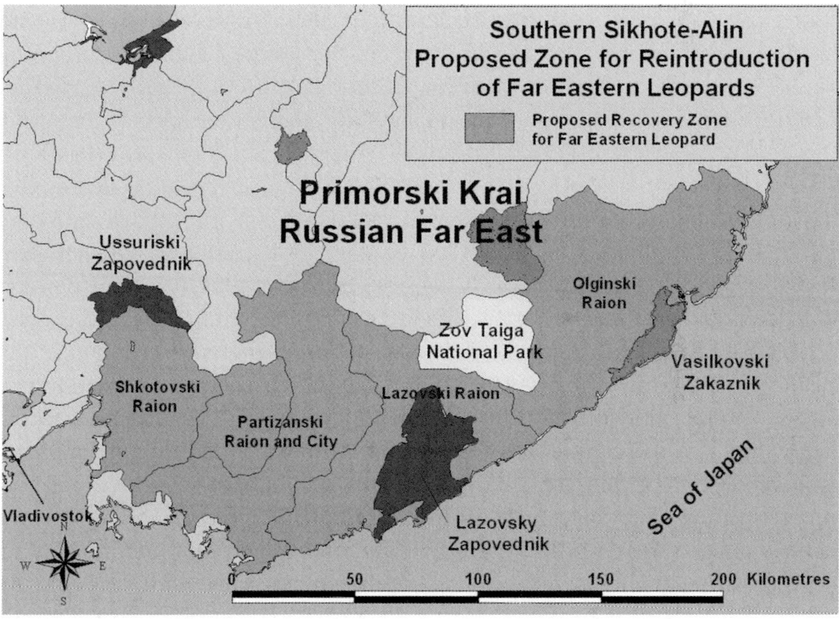

Figure 18.4 **South-west Primorye showing current leopard range and protected areas including Lazovsky Zapovednik.**

warmer weather conditions, it contains similar cliffs and rocky areas, and the habitat types are also similar. Sika deer (*Cervus nippon*) occur at the relatively high density of 8.6 head/km^2, but species within the leopard's preferred prey-weight range (Hayward *et al.*, 2007b) are less abundant (A.I. Myslenkov, Federal State Department, Lazovsky State Nature Reserve, Lazo, Primorsky Krai, Russia; personal communication). This is due partly to effective protection work carried out by the reserve staff with support from Phoenix Fund, but also to the fact that at the time the leopard became extinct in south Sikhote Alin, sika deer could legally be hunted there, while they are now fully protected. In the leopard's current range, it remains possible to legally hunt sika deer.

Tigers would present a risk to a small, reintroduced founder population of Amur leopards, in that intraguild predation (Palomares & Caro, 1999) has been demonstrated in the region (V. Aramiliev, Pacific Institute of Geography, Far East Branch of Russian Academy of Sciences, Vladivostok, Russia; personal communication). Lazovsky contains tigers, as do all other potential release sites. Their presence is unavoidable and all that can be done is to take mitigating action, e.g. providing leopards for release with aversion training in relation to tigers and/or ensuring that site topography favours separation between the two as far as is possible. Spatial separation appears to exist in south-west Primorye, where tigers and leopards currently coexist (D. Miquelle [WCS] & A.A. Murzin [Pacific Institute of Geography, Far East Branch of Russian Academy of Sciences, Vladivostok] unpublished data), and is the basis for including "cliffs and rocky areas" which are assumed to provide refuge for leopards. Red deer, which are generally a preferred prey item for tigers but are too large for leopards, are present in Lazovsky but at low density (0.4 head/km^2, A. Myslenkov, personal communication), so the sika deer population there may be targeted by both tigers and leopards. As red deer are almost unknown in south-west Primorye, clearly it is possible for the two big cats to coexist with sika deer as the primary prey item. Leopards take more small prey such as badgers and raccoon dogs than do tigers, so prey selection will not overlap completely.

Other factors

Other significant factors that must be addressed early in the planning process include: disease status of wildlife in general in the release area and of zoo leopards that may be used for breeding stock, local and political support for such a plan, and potential funding sources.

Acceptance of a reintroduction programme by local communities will clearly be critical to success, and social research to assess attitudes of local people is in the pipeline. While Phoenix Fund and ZSL staff have carried out studies in existing leopard range and Phoenix and WWF Russia have had considerable success in influencing attitudes towards tigers and leopards among children in south-west Primorye, work in the proposed release area is yet to begin, and Durham University is seeking funding for a 3-year study designed to assess local attitudes as a first step.

Steps must be taken to ensure that released cats do not harbour pathogens likely to adversely affect wildlife in the area and that they are not themselves vulnerable to pathogens already present in the environment. Towards this end, since 2006 ZSL and the Primorskii State Agricultural Academy, in partnership with WCS, have been implementing a 3-year programme focused on increasing wildlife health-monitoring capacity in the region, as well as collecting baseline data on wildlife diseases in the area and disease status in zoo leopards genetically suitable for production of cubs for release. Wildlife vets and students in the region participate in workshops that include lectures and hands-on training sessions, taught by international experts, with training programmes held in a local rehabilitation centre (Utyos) in Khabarovski Krai and in Moscow and Novosibirsk zoos. Training sessions in the zoos have served the additional function of collecting samples from Amur leopards for disease analysis, as these are the only two zoos in Russia holding cats genetically suitable for reintroduction.

Other suitable stock in European and American zoos is also being sampled as part of the disease testing programme, with additional specialist investigations such as MHC (major histocompatibility complex) testing and expert analysis of heart murmurs being coordinated by John Lewis. Meanwhile, samples are being collected in and around the proposed release area from tigers, wild ungulates, small carnivores, and domestic ungulates and carnivores. In Ussurisk, a laboratory belonging to the Academy is being renovated and outfitted to enable in-country sample analysis in the long term, although samples are at present being analysed in UK and European laboratories as well.

The draft reintroduction plan has so far been the subject of one governmental meeting in Moscow, facilitated by WWF Russia, and comments made have influenced subsequent work. When the plan is complete and officially approved, it will then be possible to approach potential funding sources. However, finding sufficient support for such a major effort represents one of the great challenges of the reintroduction effort.

Breeding and release strategy

If this reintroduction is to succeed, it is clear that the design of the breeding and release centre, and the management of the leopards within it, must focus strongly on overcoming the difficulties imposed by the captive origin of the cats. In addition, a "soft" rather than "hard" release strategy should be used—i.e. the breeding enclosure should be located at the point of release. Three necessary behaviours should, if possible, be acquired prior to release: hunting and killing of live natural prey, avoidance of humans and avoidance of tigers. (The leopards will of course also need to learn exploratory behaviour within the home range, but this is not a factor that can be addressed in the breeding enclosure other than by placing it within the release habitat.)

This section of the reintroduction plan is not yet complete, and there appear to be no models. While various projects have experimented with hard- and soft-release sites and with varying levels of experience of hunting for zoo-bred cats before release, there appear to have been no serious efforts to date to avoid contact with humans and instil human-avoidance behaviours, let alone avoidance of larger predators, in such cats. Avoiding contact with humans involves a complete reversal of accepted zoo enclosure-design principles which, as well as ensuring a good viewing experience for the public, tend to focus strongly on ensuring that the animals can be observed, moved around, given treatments and captured by staff with maximum ease for the keepers and with minimum stress for the animals.

The outline presented here is therefore experimental, is still under discussion, and is in no way intended to provide a final or complete account of intended protocols.

Breeding-centre design

The breeding centre will need to include a short-term holding facility, a veterinary examination room, storage for equipment and supplies, and staff housing, offices and meeting facilities, as well as several breeding enclosures.

The breeding enclosures would be located at a considerable distance from the rest of the centre to ensure that the animals in the enclosures could not smell, see or hear the humans present there. This stands in stark contrast to the reintroduction of African top-order predators that are intended for ecotourism purposes (Marnewick *et al.*, this volume). Feeding live prey to the release candidates from birth is a highly desirable tactic and, if this strategy is to be used, thought will also need to be given to provision of breeding facilities for prey items, e.g. deer and rabbits. This approach, although likely to attract criticism from animal-welfare agencies, would have the significant benefit of ensuring that released animals are able to identify and kill appropriate prey species. Nonetheless, relevant Ethics Committees would need to carefully consider the costs and benefits. Provision of a couple of "leopard display enclosures"—located at the main part of the centre, well out of sight, sound and smell of the breeding enclosures—might also be desirable, as the project would be bound to attract interest, and good public relations will be of paramount importance, yet people must be kept away from leopards intended for release. One of the display enclosures might perhaps contain a tiger, and it is conceivable that a tiger housed there could be useful in aversion training for release stock.

The centre, and particularly the breeding enclosure(s), would be located within the release site to allow a "soft" rather than "hard" release. Pairs of physically and behaviourally healthy zoo leopards of suitable genetic makeup, which had proven themselves to be successful breeders and rearers of cubs in zoo conditions, would be transferred to the facility for breeding purposes and returned to their home zoos when sufficient offspring from their genetic line had become established in the wild. Cubs would be born and reared with as little interference from humans as possible, with routine monitoring done long-range by video. The male would be removed as soon as pregnancy was confirmed. When the cubs were old enough to begin to learn to hunt, live prey would be supplied in the enclosure—basic hunting behaviour is instinctive in cats, and it is assumed that if cubs were given the opportunity to learn from experience while young, they would develop sufficient hunting skills to form a basis for a life in the wild.

When the cubs reached dispersal age, the mother would be removed, the cubs given a veterinary check-up and fitted with adult-sized radio collars, and the gates opened so that they could move out into the surrounding forest but still return to a known area for shelter and, if necessary, supplementary feeding.

More than one breeding and release enclosure should be established within reach of the centre, and consideration should be given to setting up one or more additional enclosures at a different location within the overall release area. Given that releases will need to be continued over a period of years, if leopards settle into home ranges near the release point there could be potential for aggressive encounters if further animals—particularly of the same sex—were released at the same site. The other components of the centre need not be duplicated to achieve this, but the holding facility at the centre should be designed to hold sufficient adult leopards to serve several breeding enclosures.

Design of breeding enclosures

It is imperative that leopards destined for release grow up without familiarity with humans and learn to fear humans as much as possible. The leopard breeding enclosure(s) associated with the centre should therefore be situated within reach of transport, water supply and electrical power, but out of sight, sound and smell of the other buildings necessary for the operation of the centre and of all associated human activities.

Breeding enclosures should be as large as can be achieved with available funds and should be in a wooded area so that the leopards have plenty of cover; they should not be visible to a casual observer unless at the edges of the enclosure. Enclosures should take advantage of natural features in the landscape and, if at all possible, should include rocky areas, a natural stream for water, and natural shelter areas such as caves, overhangs or fallen/hollow trees. If natural shelter is not available in the area, it will need to be constructed from natural materials, i.e. trees and rocks. As few man-made items as possible should be present, and capture of leopards for radio collaring or final medical assessments would be performed by darting from vehicles, not by the normal zoo methods of simply shutting the animal into its night den for darting or accustoming it to sleeping in the intended transport crate. Monitoring of the cats would be carried out via video cameras scattered around the enclosures and linked to viewing screens in the staff areas.

Enclosures could be shaped in a rough figure of eight with the central connection containing a leopard-proof closable gate. This design would allow the leopards to be separated if necessary, or to be shut into one end to facilitate catching them or while live prey, if used, is released in the other end. The figure-of-eight shape would also allow for live prey to be chased around without being cornered, which would help the leopards improve hunting skills. Chasing deer along the fences would be to some extent inevitable, but it is at least possible to avoid corners. Leopards can climb, and their enclosures in zoos have traditionally been roofed, although larger modern facilities have departed from this model. Serious escape attempts are unlikely in a large densely wooded enclosure with plenty of food, but nevertheless the fence would need to be high, perhaps 5 m, with a substantial overhang. Use of hotwire is also desirable both to discourage escape and in the hope of conditioning leopards against approaching man-made structures. Although a wild-caught African leopard is known to have scaled a 3-m high electric fence in order to escape from a boma (Hayward *et al.*, 2007a), that animal had a far stronger motivation for crossing the fence than leopards in these enclosures would have. Large gates into each half, and dirt roads within, would permit vehicle access for captures of leopards and release of live deer, if used.

Management of leopards

Leopards selected for breeding would undergo a final set of health tests before shipment from their home zoos, and would arrive in spring to allow plenty of time for acclimatization before the onset of winter. They would initially go into the holding facility for a quarantine and acclimatization period before transfer to the breeding enclosure.

All cats in the enclosure would be radio-collared at all times, to assist in locating them within the enclosure and with recapture should there be an escape. Expandable collars allowing for growth are available for young cats. Live prey, if used, would be introduced into the enclosure regularly via vehicles or through specially constructed gates, with the leopards shut into the opposite part of the enclosure each time to keep them as unaware as possible of the association between humans and food supply.

Monitoring via video cameras would help to establish that the female was pregnant and, once this was achieved, the male would be removed to the holding facility or perhaps a display enclosure. The cubs would be captured, collared and given a veterinary check-up as soon as they began to show independence from their mother. The mother would be removed at some point prior to the cubs reaching dispersal age, at which time they would again be captured, fitted with an adult-sized radio collar and given a final health check.

All gates would then be opened and perhaps also the fence breached in a few places, the supply of live food stopped and, if necessary, bait used to tempt the young leopards out. The cats would be monitored as they dispersed, but supplemental food would still be provided, probably for several months.

Breeding leopards would be held in the centre until they had contributed sufficient cubs and would then be returned to their home zoo and replaced by other cats of different genetic lines. It is expected that the process of establishing a stable population would take at least 10 years.

Next steps

It is intended that the plan will be completed and submitted to the Russian authorities during 2008, after which final discussions on the work will take place and the plan will be amended accordingly. Health evaluations of zoo leopards will also continue during this period and should be completed in 2009. As and when official endorsement is forthcoming, it will be possible to seek funding, which will be the next big hurdle for the project.

In the meantime, all involved will continue their efforts to protect the existing wild leopards, and the European and American conservation breeding programmes in zoos will continue to be managed so as to produce the maximum possible conservation support for their wild relations, as well as experienced young breeding pairs suitable for *in situ* breeding for release.

Acknowledgements

The reintroduction plan, and hence this chapter, is dependent on the dedicated work of many individuals including Dale Miquelle (WCS), Alexy Kostyria (Insitute of Biology and Soils, Far Eastern Branch of the Russian Academy of Sciences), Vladimir Aramilev (Institute for Sustainable Use of Natural Resources), Dimitri Pikunov (Institute of Geography, Far Eastern Branch of the Russian Academy of Sciences), Yuri Darman (WWF Russia), Tanya Arzhanova (Moscow Zoo), Michiel Hotte (ZSL and Tigris Foundation) and John Lewis (Wildlife Vets International). Useful comments on the chapter itself were kindly provided by Matt Hayward, John Lewis, Ron Tilson, Dale Miquelle, Michiel Hötte, Josh Ginsberg and Richard Reading. Thanks are also due to all those who have provided and/or continue to provide support for activities relevant to reintroduction planning; WCS, WWF Russia, Phoenix, ZSL, Tigris Foundation, AMUR, the UK government's Darwin Initiative, the Trust for Mutual Understanding, Wildlife Vets International, Twycross Zoo Conservation Fund and Lucie Bergers Fund.

References

Bowling, A.T., Zimmerman, W., Ryder, O. et al. (2003) Genetic variation in Prezwalski's horses, with special focus on the last wild-caught mare 231 Orlitza III. *Cytogenetics and Genome Research* 101, 226–2344.

Christie, S. (in press) Why keep tigers in zoos? *Tigers of the World: The Science, Politics and Conservation of* Panthera tigris. (eds R. Tilson & P. Nyhus). Andrews Press.

Hayward, M.W., Adendorff, J., Moolman, L.C., Hayward, G.J. & Kerley, G.I.H. (2007a) The successful reintroduction of leopard *Panthera pardus* to the Addo Elephant National Park. *African Journal of Ecology* 45, 103–104.

Hayward, M.W., Henschel, P., O'Brien, J., Hofmeyr, M. Balme, G. & Kerley, G.I.H. (2006) Prey preferences of the leopard (*Panthera pardus*). *Journal of Zoology, London* 270, 298–313.

Hayward, M.W., O'Brien, J. & Kerley, G.I.H. (2007b) Carrying capacity of large African predators: Predictions and tests. *Biological Conservation* 139, 219–229.

IUCN (1998) *IUCN Guidelines for Reintroduction.* IUCN/SSC Reintroduction Specialist Group, IUCN. Gland, Switzerland.

Jule, K.R., Leaver, L.A., Lea, S.E.G. (2008) The effects of captive experience in reintroduction survival in carnivores: A review and analysis. *Biological Conservation* 141, 355–363.

Kerley, L.L., Goodrich, J.M. Miquelle, D.G. et al. (2003) Reproductive parameters of wild female Amur (Siberian) tigers (*Panthera tigris altaica*). *Journal of Mammalogy* 84, 288–298.

Miththapala S., Seidensticker, J. & O'Brien, S.J. (1996) Phylogeographic subspecies recognition in leopards (*Panthera pardus*): Molecular genetic variation. *Conservation Biology* 10, 1115–11321.

Palomares, F. & Caro, T.M. 1999. Interspecific killing among mammalian carnivores. *The American Naturalist* 153, 492–508.

Pikunov, D.G., Seryodkin, I.V., Aramilev, V.V., Nikolaev, I.G. & Murzin, A.A. (2007) *Numbers of Far Eastern Leopards* (Panthera pardus orientalis) *and Amur tigers* (Panthera tigris altaica) *in the Southwest Region of Primorski Krai, Russia, in 2007.* Final report.

Pimm, S.L., Dollar, L. & Bass Jr, O.L. (2006) The genetic rescue of the Florida panther *Animal Conservation* 9, 115–122.

Ray, J.C. (2005) Large carnivorous animals as tools for conserving biodiversity: Assumptions and uncertainties. *Large Carnivores and the Conservation of Biodiversity.* (eds J.C. Ray, K.H. Redford, R.S. Steneck & J. Berger), pp. 34–56. Island Press, Washington, DC.

Traylor-Holzer, K. (2003) *Using Computer Simulation to Assess Management Strategies for Retention of Genetic Variation in Captive Tiger Populations.* PhD thesis, University of Minnesota.

Uphyrkhina, O., Miquelle, D.G., Quigley, H. & O'Brien S.J. (2002) Conservation Genetics of the Far Eastern Leopard (*Panthera pardus orientalis*). *Journal of Heredity* 93, 303–311.

WCS (2001) *Report on a Workshop for the Conservation of the Far Eastern Leopard in the Wild, 11–14 May 2001.* Vladivostok, Russia, organized by the Wildlife Conservation Society and the State Ministry of Natural Resources, Russian Federation. Sponsored by The US Fish & Wildlife Service and the IUCN Cat Specialist Group.

19

Lessons Learnt and Plans Laid: Seven Awkward Questions for the Future of Reintroductions

David W. Macdonald[1]

[1]Wildlife Conservation Research Unit, Department of Zoology, University of Oxford

Summary

Reintroduction is a rapidly growing science which, if carried out properly, has the potential to be a valuable component of the conservationist's toolkit. However, many pitfalls exist that can result in failure of a reintroduction and can potentially waste valuable and limited resources. Issues that have emerged from the preceding chapters of this book and other studies are outlined below.

Introduction

The IUCN (International Union for the Conservation of Nature and Natural Resources) Red List of Threatened Species currently lists 276 carnivores; six of which are listed as Critically Endangered, 33 as Endangered and 40 as Vulnerable (IUCN, 2007). With almost 30% of carnivore species facing a high to extremely high risk of extinction in the wild (IUCN, 1994, 2007), reintroductions are potentially an all-too-necessary tool in conservation biology (Griffith *et al.*, 1989; Seddon, 1999; Fischer & Lindenmayer, 2000; Seddon, *et*

Reintroduction of Top-Order Predators, 1st edition. Edited by M.W. Hayward and M.J. Somers.
 ISBN 978-1-4051-7680-4 (pb) and 978-1-4051-9273-6 (hb)

al., 2007). Re-establishment of large carnivores is considered important insofar as they play a role in top-down regulation of ecosystems (Hilderbrand *et al.*, 1999; Terborgh *et al.*, 1999) and, anyway, some people value them. Against this background, successful reintroductions, in particular of carnivores (Yalden, 1993; Reading & Clark, 1996; Breitenmoser *et al.*, 2001; Armstrong & Seddon, 2007) are, perhaps surprisingly, few and a disappointingly large proportion of attempted reintroductions fail to fulfil their aspirations (Beck *et al.*, 1994; Wolf *et al.*, 1996; Fischer & Lindenmayer, 2000).

This is not a new issue. All sorts of people have been moving animals around for centuries, often under the shifting banner of what constitutes conservation and in 1988, the IUCN/SSC, alerted to a mounting enthusiasm for reintroductions, established the Reintroduction Specialist Group to develop reintroduction guidelines for practitioners and provide a means of disseminating information on reintroduction projects worldwide (IUCN, 1998). The guidelines sought to provide direct, practical assistance to those planning, approving or carrying out reintroductions so that reintroductions would be both justifiable and likely to succeed; they have been widely adopted as the international standard for carrying out species reintroductions for conservation (McLean, 2003).

On a wider canvass, I expect restoration to be a major thrust of conservation activities in the coming decades, so it is timely to evaluate lessons learnt about reintroduction—potentially an important element in the restoration tool-kit. The principal aim of reintroduction is "to establish a viable, free-ranging population in the wild, of a species, subspecies or race, which has become globally or locally extinct, or extirpated, in the wild. It should be reintroduced within the species' former natural habitat and range and should require minimal long-term management" (IUCN, 1998) (although most large carnivores will require some level of management action [e.g. Frankham, this volume]). This aim clearly can have appeal, for both the (sometimes-linked) purposes of fostering ecosystems that function "naturally" and of satisfying those with an interest in their composition. To achieve an overview of experience in tackling this aim for top-order carnivores, there is no better compendium than the preceding chapters of this book, to which I have been invited to provide this post-script. From the 18 vantage points they provide, what general view of carnivore reintroductions emerges? Reading them with this question in mind, seven awkward issues emerged. I have phrased these below as questions that might be considered in future, and have drawn on both carnivore and non-carnivore examples to elaborate them.

Look before you leap—is reintroduction the right answer?

An understandable desire when faced with a wildlife problem is to do something, but a top priority is to ensure that it is the right thing. When is reintroduction the right thing to do, and how, in general terms, should it be done? Bearing in mind that reintroduction is likely to involve many complications and that delivery of the desired benefits will generally be at high costs (in diverse currencies, sometimes including animal welfare), the general qualifying condition for a reintroduction is compelling evidence that it will make a significant contribution to conservation of the species in the wild or to the functionality of the ecosystem into which the animals are reintroduced (IUCN, 1998; Berger, 2007).

The IUCN guidelines answer the general question of which objectives may justify reintroduction. They may include "to enhance the long-term survival of a species; to re-establish a keystone species (in the ecological or cultural sense) in an ecosystem; to maintain and/or restore natural biodiversity; to provide long-term economic benefits to the local and/or national economy; to promote conservation awareness, or a combination of these". Furthermore, the IUCN (1998) is clear that these objectives can, potentially, be achieved by moving animals into an area under four sets of circumstances:

1. Reintroduction of a species into an area where it is no longer found, but which once formed part of its historical range;
2. Translocation of wild animals into an existing population;
3. Reinforcement or supplementation of existing populations through addition of (not necessarily wild) individuals;
4. Conservation introduction of a species into an area beyond its recorded distribution, but within a suitable eco-geographic region and habitat. Conservation introduction is deemed acceptable only when no suitable sites for restoration remain within a species' historical range.

Conservation invariably affects not only the target species, but also the associated ecosystem, environment, land-use and human communities. Therefore, any intervention should be based on a comprehensive evaluation of likely consequences for all constituencies and, in this context, obvious prerequisites to advancing down the road to reintroduction include whether the initial threat that led to the original demise of the species has either been removed or abated, and the availability of (1) suitable habitat/prey, (2) genetically suitable stock, (3) sufficient human and financial resources and (4) enthusiasm amongst local communities (Yalden, 1993; Reading & Clark, 1996; IUCN, 1998).

Set down so matter-of-factly, these prerequisites might seem alluringly straightforward, but the 18 preceding chapters in this book generally illustrate a more daunting reality. Two cases, with which I have personal experience, illustrate the challenging intricacy of, respectively, processes and principles.

The first example illustrates the principle that moving animals around inevitably requires dealing with regulation and bureaucracy, and that is likely to be protracted. Although not a top-order carnivore, the possibility of reintroducing the Eurasian beaver, *Castor fiber*, to Britain might plausibly meet all of the aforementioned worthy objectives of reintroduction (Macdonald *et al.*, 2000a, 2002b). Until recently classified as Vulnerable, the beaver's status has now improved to Near Threatened owing to successful hunting bans and reintroduction programmes across Europe (Gippoliti, 2002). In the UK, the process began in the early 1990s with a feasibility study which established that reintroducing the beaver into the UK could have advantages, not only for the beaver's conservation but also for ecosystem functioning, recreating opportunities lost for other species, together with potential community benefits and seemingly manageable risk (Macdonald *et al.*, 1995). This triggered focused reports on the history of the beaver in Scotland (Kitchener & Conroy, 1997), potential costs of reintroduction (Tattersall & Macdonald, 1995), a review of available habitat (Webb, *et al.*, 1997), site suitability assessment (Macdonald *et al.*, 2000a), interactions of fisheries (Collen, 1997), potential impacts on hydrology (Gurnell, 1997), various simulation studies (South *et al.*, 2000, 2001, 2002) and likely stimulation of ecotourism (Campbell *et al.*, 2007), amongst others.

Meanwhile, a formal public consultation, and associated parliamentary consideration, led Scotland's relevant statutory agency, Scottish Natural Heritage, to conclude that reintroduction of the beaver into Scotland was generally widely accepted and was feasible provided that habitat creation was undertaken. These issues are still under consideration by the statutory agencies of other countries within the UK. In May 2008, a licence was granted for a trial reintroduction (http://www.scotland.gov.uk). There are many reasons why one might expect decision-making about the reintroduction of the beaver to be less problematic than that for a top-order carnivore, but many people have been industriously occupied in this process for well over a decade and the first, experimental, release of beavers is only now imminent.

The second example illustrates the fact that matters of principle may interact with those of process. At first sight, confirmation that for the candidate species the original problem has abated, or that the optimal habitat is available, might seem black or white. That the reality may involve many shades of grey is illustrated, challengingly, by the case of the Scottish wildcat, *Felis sylvestris grampia*, which has been the top-order felid in Britain since the eradication of lynx, *Lynx lynx*.

Scottish wildcats are perilously rare (as few as 400 may remain) due to a long history of habitat loss, a more recent history of persecution and the insidious risk of cross-breeding with and disease transmission from the domestic cat *Felis catus* (Stahl & Artois, 1991; Macdonald *et al.*, 2004; Macdonald *et al.*, in press). The domestic cat is genetically very close to the wildcat, from which it is descended (Driscoll *et al.*, 2007), and the niceties of distinguishing one from the other (e.g. Daniels *et al.*, 1998; Kitchener *et al.*, 2005) provide a painful example of several general problems afflicting carnivore reintroductions. These include deciding upon the right genetic stock (e.g. Florida panthers, Onorata *et al.*, in press), the risk of genetic extinction of "pure" populations (Suminski, 1962; Kitchener, 1995; Rhymer & Simberloff, 1996; Beaumont *et al.*, 2001), and the legal ramifications of taxonomic uncertainty, especially at subspecific levels (Macdonald *et al.*, 2004). Although plans are advancing to abate the cross-breeding threat (through responsible cat ownership e.g. Kilshaw, *et al.*, 2008), it will be a prolonged and imperfect under-taking, partly because the best wildcat habitat is also generally the most challenged in terms of feral cats. It may therefore be desirable, in parallel, to release wildcats (perhaps including captive-bred individuals) to remote Highland regions where the habitat is poor (insofar as having only a low carrying capacity for wildcats) but more optimal (insofar as having few feral cats or people, and greater feasibility for conservation management).

This would be an intervention hovering between reintroduction and reinforcement. Our team is currently investigating the scope of this option, considering, for example, the need for afforestation (to enhance the prey base) and the likely impact of wildcats on other conservation priorities such as black grouse, *Tetrao tetrix britannicus* (to minimize the risks of unintended consequences). Dickman *et al.*, (this volume) illustrate powerfully the community-level consequences (in this instance intended) of reintroducing to New South Wales, Australia, the dingo, *Canis lupus dingo* (another instance where the taxonomic nomenclature has legal and ideological, ramifications for conservation). In this case, part of the objective is that restored dingoes would limit numbers of invasive red foxes, *Vulpes vulpes*, and feral cats through mesopredator suppression, thereby alleviating their impact on native prey. Of course, dingoes themselves, like foxes, reached Australia thanks to the agency of people, highlighting just one of the many fine judgments involved in deciding which incomers are welcome (Macdonald *et al.*, 2007b).

The case studies in this book, and my two foregoing examples, emphasize that generic guidelines are more easily drafted than followed. Nonetheless, prudence dictates that a reintroduction (or any of the other three similar interventions defined above) should begin with an evidenced-based review (known, in medical circles, as a Cochrane review; see Dickersin & Manheimer, 1998), minimizing the risk of unintended consequences through the biological equivalent of what economists call a Full Life Cycle analysis—in short, following through every linkage, whether within or between disciplines or sectoral interests. Next, a field trial, preferably experimental in design, during which ideally actions are reversible, is desirable. Finally, it is self-evident that the participation, or at least tolerance or regulation, of all the affected constituencies is essential, and this inevitably means being reconciled to a long haul and mountainous bureaucracy that is supportable only by significant funding (Macdonald *et al.*, 2002a,b).

Should reintroduction be the last resort?

There is a hierarchy of conservation interventions, because it is logically appropriate for some steps to precede others, and because considerations of urgency, value, time and money also result in some steps taking priority over others. In general, reintroduction may rank rather low, partly because it is often a last resort which would be better forestalled by earlier interventions, and partly because it is likely to be expensive and risky.

Ideally, if a small population still exists in the wild, one step before reintroduction would be reinforcement (defined above), exemplified by attempts to ameliorate inbreeding depression in the Mexican wolf *Canis lupus baileyi* (Hedrick *et al.*, 1997; Kalinowski *et al.*, 1999). Although, in principle, reinforcement (aka augmentation) is a tool to increase the genetic diversity of a wild population and lower the risk of inbreeding (Amos & Balmford, 2001), increase the number of available mates or to increase overall population size as protection against stochastic events, the reality is that few successful examples have been described (Frankham, *et al.*, 2002).

Indeed, generally imperfect outcomes indicate a diversity of reasons for careful preparation such as the undesirability of mixing genetically distinct lineages (Rhymer & Simberloff, 1996), which may have disastrous consequences. For example, the translocation of Tatra mountain ibex, *Capra ibex ibex*, from Sinai and Turkey into a population in Czechoslovakia resulted in outbreeding depression with offspring inheriting an inappropriate calving date and thus giving birth in mid-winter, losing their young, and precipitating the extinction of the recipient population (Greig, 1979). In addition, there is the risk of introduction of new recessive genes (detrimental at some future bottleneck) into a gene pool that may already have purged many deleterious genes (Almos & Balmford, 2001) or introduction of diseases, e.g. the introduction and spread of a pathogenic mite into the European honey bee, *Apis mellifera*, colonies by stock originally introduced from Asia to Europe (Paxton, 1992; Williams, 1995). Predation risk should also be assessed, e.g. 21 translocations of the black-faced impala, *Aepyceros melampus petersi*, established that for a successful reintroduction, a minimum number of 15 individuals should be reintroduced to withstand the effects of cheetah predation (Matson *et al.*, 2004).

Although reintroduction and reinforcement have the appeal of action and speed, there can be wisdom in restraint. First, if the aforementioned IUCN qualifying conditions are not met, the costs may be heavily stacked against the benefits, and this is why Johnsingh & Madhu (this volume) argue against reintroductions of the tiger, *Panthera tigris*. Furthermore, irrespective of the qualifying conditions, the budget may be inadequate to undertake the task properly, or the species biology may render it an unpromising candidate, as Henschel (this volume) argues for leopards, *Panthera pardus*. Similarly, Stanley Price & Gordon (1989) argue that the late maturity (13–15 years) and long inter-birth interval (6–7 years) of orangutans, *Pongo* spp., necessitate an impractically large introduction to be viable (although the large number of orangutans in rehabilitation centres generates a heart-rending, if possibly fruitless, desire for their reintroduction). In short, in the ideal world conservationists might prefer to prioritize the protection and enhancement of existing populations as an alternative to reintroduction; however, the world is often not ideal.

Faced with a choice between natural recolonization and reintroduction, the conservationist's priority is doubtless generally to nurture natural processes of restoration. That said, this choice may often be rather abstract and, as most conservation problems were caused by human actions in the first place, being too dismissive of human intervention to solve them may sometimes smack of misplaced Puritanism. As is so often the case in conservation, and against a backcloth of helpful general guidelines, the practical reality necessitates case-by-case judgments. These should pay attention to both local environmental and human dimensions, and particularly to the species' natural history (Macdonald *et al.*, 2002a,b). Wolves, *Canis lupus*, for example, being marathon dispersers, might best be helped to reach a new destination by habitat restoration to restore linkage (Poulle *et al.*, 1997; Linnell, 2004).

Re-inventing the wheel: are the IUCN guidelines sufficient?

The IUCN/SSC Reintroduction Specialist Group guidelines were officially approved by the IUCN Council in 1995 and published in 1998, crystallizing ideas that had been widely debated during at least the previous decade. Yet, in 2008 many of the chapters in this book can point to reintroductions that have failed. Have the guidelines been inadequate? Despite the detailed framework they provide, and the strong emphasis on pre-release feasibility studies, have circumstances somehow changed to bring forward an unforeseen generation of problems? For example, climate change may result in species ranges contracting or expanding, which will have implications for the future of reintroductions, (e.g. Arctic fox, *Alopex lagopus*, Linnell *et al.*, 2005 and see McCarty, 2001).

Scouring the chapters of this book reveals that the many failures that the authors have unearthed can be attributed not to deficiencies in the guidelines, but to not following them. Linnell *et al.*, (this volume) criticizes reintroductions of Eurasian lynx which ignored the genetics of released individuals and did not coordinate releases with metapopulation dynamics in mind (Akçakaya *et al.*, 2007). A similar absence of joined-up thinking is criticized by Slotow and Hunter (this volume) with regard to African lions, *Panthera leo*, where the ready success of individual reintroductions is illusory insofar as there is little evidence that they collectively contribute to the species' conservation. Breitenmoser *et al.*, (2001) make the point that not only is it important to adhere to the guidelines, but also to coordinate efforts to deliver a larger conservation goal.

The 18 chapters in this book represent a compendious search for successes and failures in the literature on carnivore reintroductions, and an over-arching review of them all reveals a recurring list of 20 problems unearthed by these authors (Table 19.1). In every case, these were problems foreseen by the existing guidelines, and in many cases were thus probably avoidable (e.g. low founder numbers, poor adaptive behaviour, lack of feasibility studies, lack of biological data, poor coordination etc.). Of course, emphasis and detail need to be fine tuned as science advances (the role of animal welfare science is one with potential to grow [Moorhouse *et al.*, 2007]) and new considerations may emerge (e.g. impacts of climate change). The authors of the 18 chapters were invited to rank the considerations that they personally felt were most important in evaluating a reintroduction—a profile of their consensus is given in Figure 19.1. These authors report that many lessons were learnt, but they also refer to cases where the recurrence of lessons not learnt raises the fear that some projects, doubtless through understandable eagerness and frustration, rush ahead more hopefully than thoughtfully. Insofar as generalities provide the framework for detailed case-by-case planning, the IUCN guidelines provide that framework, but greater professionalism appears to be needed in applying them.

Have you taken stock of the bigger picture?

Sciences, both natural and social, advance, but conservation combines science and policy, and thus involves politics—which necessitates not only evidence but also judgment. The practice and politics of biodiversity conservation have evolved at dizzying speed since its modern emergence in the 1950s. Behavioural ecology, population genetics and metapopulation dynamics are amongst the fields that have revolutionized natural science; concepts of valuation have been imported from economics. In the policy arena, there has been a radical shift from a separationist emphasis on protected areas, to an integrationist emphasis on the merging of biodiversity conservation, human livelihoods and development (Macdonald *et al.*, 2007a). The demolition of former silos, and the linkage of people, places and nature, raises a new agenda for 21st century conservation and my guess is that one major strand of this will involve restoration. Restoration goes beyond holding the line for threatened wildlife, and seeks to regain lost ground. Reintroduction is a major component of the restoration toolkit. It also makes particularly clear that much of conservation

Table 19.1 **Problems identified with reintroductions and potential solutions in the IUCN Guidelines.**

Problems identified	IUCN guidelines
• Lack of national-level coordination. • Failure to coordinate reintroductions to produce a metapopulation. • Lack of attention paid to genetic origins of reintroduced stock. • Genetic isolation. • Insufficient number of individuals released, leading to loss of genetic variability. • Lack of shyness towards humans. • Inability to hunt natural prey leading to loss of live stock and/or starvation. • Inability to avoid predation by sympatric carnivores. • Lack of social behaviour resulting in poor pack/pride formation post-release. • Potentially detrimental welfare implications.	• Multidisciplinary, coordinated approach. • Individuals should be of the same subspecies or race as those extirpated. • Molecular genetic studies should be undertaken; a study of genetic variation within and between populations of this and related taxa can also be helpful. • The build-up of the released population should be modelled under various sets of conditions, in order to specify the optimal number and composition of individuals to be released per year and the number of years necessary to promote establishment of a viable population. • Individuals should be given the opportunity to acquire the necessary information to enable survival in the wild, through training in their captive environment. • A captive-bred individual's probability of survival should approximate that of a wild counterpart. • Care should be taken to ensure that potentially dangerous captive-bred animals (such as large carnivores or primates) are not so confident in the presence of humans that they might be a danger to local inhabitants and/or their livestock. • The welfare of animals for release is of paramount concern through all these stages.

• Lack of pre-release feasibility study. • Lack of ecological knowledge. • Failure to anticipate the effects of the reintroduced species on other species. • Reintroduction of species into areas with insufficient carrying capacity. • Failure to reduce existing threats sufficiently. • Lack of coordinating reintroduction efforts. • Lack of data on dispersal distances.	• Feasibility study. • Detailed studies should be made of the status and biology of wild populations to determine critical needs. • Understanding the effect the reintroduced species will have on the ecosystem is important. • Population and habitat viability analysis should be used to identify significant environmental and population variables. • Thorough research is needed into previous reintroductions of the same or similar species. • Reintroductions should only take place where the habitat and landscape requirements of the species are satisfied. • The area should have sufficient carrying capacity to sustain growth of the reintroduced population and to support a viable (self-sustaining) population in the long run. • Identification and elimination, or reduction to a sufficient level, of previous causes of decline. • Evaluation of cost-effectiveness and success of reintroduction techniques.
• Lack of post-release monitoring.	• Design of pre- and post-release monitoring programme. • Post-release monitoring is required of all (or sample of) individuals, including demographic, ecological and behavioural studies of released stock, study of processes of long-term adaptation by individuals and the population, collection and investigation of mortalities. • Interventions (e.g. supplemental feeding; veterinary; aid; horticultural aid) when necessary. • Decisions for revision, rescheduling or discontinuation of programme where necessary.
• Illegal or unofficial releases. • Poor public acceptance understanding.	• Full permission and involvement of all relevant government agencies of the recipient or host country required. • Continuing public relations activities, including education and mass media coverage. • The programme should be fully understood, accepted and supported by local communities. • Socio-economic studies should be made to asses the impacts, costs and benefits of the reintroduction programme to local human populations.

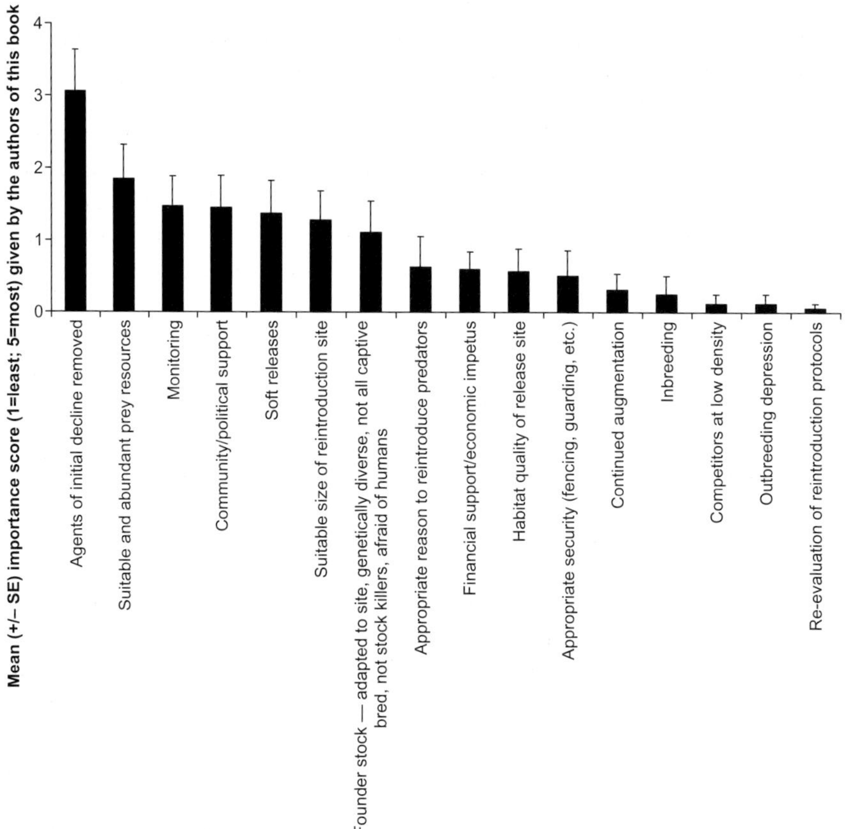

Figure 19.1 **Important considerations for reintroductions—a biologist's view.**

involves a sort of consumer choice: society can choose what it wishes to restore, and indeed, to reintroduce. Deciding to reintroduce a top-order carnivore is a particularly exacting decision. Different people, for example at different stages of development, have widely diverging expectations and tolerance of nature conservation (Sayer, 1995) and may favour different choices. There are also some interesting parallels between thinking about reintroduction and alien species (in both cases, animals that may be welcomed by some people but not others) (Macdonald *et al.*, 2007b).

It may be a simplistic dichotomy, but the future of conservation might be partitioned between stopping the rot and repairing the damage. The history of conservation biology has largely been in the former area, identifying causes of population decline and the means to lessen their impact, and intervening to maintain population viability and minimize extinction risk (e.g. Caughley, 1994). Restoration ecology turns to reversing habitat loss and reversing population decline—at an extreme from a zero base, which is where reintroduction may be indispensable (Young, 2000). The over-arching goal is to restore complex and functional ecosystems, with a keen eye to sustainability, and thus encompassing technical, historical, political, social, cultural and aesthetic aspects (Higgs, 1997). Thus, restoration ecology is commonly defined as "the process of assisting the recovery of an ecosystem that has been degraded, damaged, or destroyed" (SERI, 2004).

Ehrenfeld (2000) identified three approaches to restoration ecology, each with its relevance to top-order carnivores. First is a focus on keystone, endangered or charismatic species or species assemblages (criticized if it is blinkered with respect to downstream consequences for landscape or ecosystem interactions). Second is a focus on ecosystem functions such as material and energy flows (which can lead to fretting over the definition of an ecosystem) (Harris & van Diggelen, 2005). The third approach is to restore ecosystem services (e.g. protection of watersheds, maintaining water quality, soil maintenance and climate regulation; see Primack, 1993). For example, the Society for Ecological Restoration International advocates restoring ecosystems to mitigate and adapt to the effects of global climate change: "Ecological restoration offers hope in two key areas: by reconnecting fragmented ecosystems allowing animals and plants to migrate in response to such change; and, by capturing carbon through the restoration of forests, peat-forming wetlands, and other ecosystems that act as carbon sinks" (SERI, 2007).

A conceptual conundrum that permeates discussion of restoration is naturalness. In brief, while it might seem easy to aspire to restoring naturalness, is it less easy to identify naturalness in terms of, for example, whether its definition includes human activities and the scale at which it operates. The quest for a natural benchmark is crucially afflicted by the shifting baseline: do we aspire to recreate ecosystems as they were pre- the Industrial, Agricultural, Stone or even Pleistocene ages (Macdonald *et al.*, 2007a, see also Katz, 1992; Elliot, 1997; Harris & van Diggelen, 2005; Donlan *et al.*, 2006; Hayward, in press).

As an aside, waxing too lyrical about naturalness might be imprudent for those interested in restoring top-order carnivores insofar as the natural state of peoples' attitudes to these animals has generally been deep enmity (a state which Kruuk [2002] argues is still our innate predisposition). Indeed, seeing the victims of man-eating lions in Tanzania (Baldus, 2004) or tigers in the Sundurbans (Sanyal, 1987) makes it chillingly obvious why humanity's evolutionary perspective of top-order carnivores might be in the same category as venomous snakes and spiders. In the context of these carnivores, valuing their restoration is surely a post-modern Enlightenment rather than an evolutionarily natural state of affairs! Insofar as recreating conditions that are truly pristine (in the problematic sense of being devoid of any human influence) is patently fantasy, and ever more so as humanity's footprint becomes heavier, the pragmatic reality is probably that restoration is more about creating a new future than recreating the past. A similar thought is captured in Choi's (2004) term, "futuristic restoration". It is necessary to accommodate the dynamics of change in "restoration" planning, as illustrated by the observation made by Harris *et al.* (2006) that climate change may mean that the former location of an ecosystem may soon be an entirely inappropriate place to recreate it.

An exciting initiative with which my team is involved is the proposal to restore the Highland ecosystem at the Alladale Wilderness Reserve (http://www.alladale.com) in northern Scotland, which includes as a long-term aim the reintroduction, albeit within a fenced reserve, of top-order carnivores such as wolves, lynx and bears, *Ursus arctos*. This project illustrates perfectly both the aforementioned dilemmas, and the issue of future-proofing. First, considering the poorly understood interaction of climate change, human land-use change and over-hunting, exactly which of the ecosystems that have prevailed in the area during the past 1000 or so years should we make our benchmark for restoration? Second, how large a (fenced) area is needed to make viable the level of population processes amongst reintroduced species for them to "count" as a conservation gain (on a spatial, and perhaps ideological, scale ranging from zoo cage, through park to wilderness)? And third, whichever of the previous phases of Alladale's environment we might prefer to recreate, what will be appropriate there in the light of climate change and in the context of the foreseeable socio-economic future? There is a risk of conservationists being too precious about the past, so it may be more fruitful, as Harris *et al.*, (2006) suggest, to worry more about the future function (ecological integrity) of a site, bringing forward what we can of the desirable past while striving to ensure resilience to future change.

Different contexts dictate different endpoints for restoration, and the relevant vocabulary includes a hierarchy of "concepts". The "wilderness concept" involves self-regulation by nature and intervention by humans is minimal; the "arcadian concept" is based on the long tradition of human interference with nature such as ancient agricultural techniques; and the "functional concept" is heavily anthropogenic, considering nature as something for human use e.g. forestry and fishery (see Harris & van Diggelen, 2005).

The modern reality that conservation has no choice but to be integrated with human livelihoods everywhere, and with development in poorer countries (Adams & Hulme, 1998), is anticipated by the IUCN Guideline (1998) requirement that a prerequisite for reintroduction is identification and elimination of previous threats such as poaching, competition with livestock and habitat loss. Removing these threats can be at the price of annoying stakeholders, for example by restricting access to resources (e.g. Fiallo & Jacobsen, 1995; Nepal & Weber, 1995) or when damage is caused to livestock or crops (e.g. Parry & Campbell, 1992; Heinen, 1993). These conflicts with top-order carnivores are much discussed in Macdonald & Sillero-Zubiri (2002, 2004), Macdonald *et al.*, (2006) and Macdonald & Loveridge (in press) and in specific case studies such as Wang & Macdonald (2006). Thus we see a shift from exclusive protected areas to community-based conservation such as integrated conservation and development projects (e.g. project CAMPFIRE in Africa—Lewis *et al.*, 1990; Pecks, 1993), which link controlled exploitation of wildlife resources in protected areas to the curtailment of human encroachment therein (Kiss, 1990). Programmes such as integrated conservation and development projects often involve buffer zones, which provide variable levels of protection from human activity while at the same time enabling multiple-use by people (although there is worry that in terms of governance, finance and the growing human footprint, there are constraints on the delivery of this philosophy (Barrett & Arcese, 1995; Spinnage, 1996, 1998; Neumann, 1997).

Breaking down the silos broadens the stage on which cost–benefit analyses are conducted (Sarker *et al.*, 2006; Wilson *et al.*, 2006). The spatial distribution of benefits (economic value of ecosystem services—Daily, 1997; Millenium Ecosystem Assessment, 2005) and costs (equal or greater levels of biodiversity—Ando *et al.*, 1998; Polasky *et al.*, 2001; Ferraro, 2003; Stewart & Possingham, 2005) can, in principle, be compared to the distribution of biodiversity, allowing areas of value for both biodiversity and people to be located, and areas of conflict or trade-off, where net economic benefits of ecosystem conservation are low but biodiversity values are high (and vice versa) to be identified (Naidoo & Ricketts, 2006). In addition, such analyses can, in principle, target the greatest benefits per unit cost; this is obviously a worthy aim but the practical difficulty of quantifying the relevant values, far less monetizing the costs and benefits, risks spurious precision.

A question of scale: what size is worth it?

On what scale should top-order carnivores be reintroduced? This is an obvious question that might be phrased in terms of viability, cost-effectiveness and various yardsticks of worthwhileness (including perceptions of naturalness). The answers will doubtless be less obvious, other than the unhelpful generality of the bigger the scale the better. Slotow & Hunter (this volume) suggest that the answer should be phrased within national policy, and other chapters in this book record reintroductions at scales varying from large protected areas such as Yellowstone National Park (wolves) to small private game ranches (cheetah, *Acinonyx jubatus*) and highly managed metapopulations (African wild dog, *Lycaon pictus*). Expansive schemes, such as that involving Yellowstone's wolves, can function with minimal intervention and are relatively immune from conflicts beyond their borders (Smith & Bangs, this volume). However, Yellowstone was already a National Park waiting for the wolves to return—in contrast, some other carnivores have little of their historical habitat remaining (Johnsingh & Madhusingh, this volume). Clark & Frankham (this volume) conclude that very few protected areas are large enough for the reintroduction of viable populations of lost carnivores, and presumably the short-list of unprotected areas where protection, restoration and reintroduction are feasible is even shorter.

Relevant factors include (1) availability of potentially suitable habitat; (2) its connectivity and (3) carrying capacity, thus determining (4) its reproductive and dispersal potential and inbreeding risks, and (5) threats beyond its border. Each set of authors in this book has experiences that focus their attention on different elements of this list, emphasizing the need for each case to be considered separately. Frankham (this volume) emphasizes the importance of a sufficient number of founders to minimize the risks of losing genetic diversity (Moritz, 1999; Frankham *et al.*, 2002), and suggests a rule of thumb of 20–30 successfully breeding individuals. Hayward (this volume) focuses on assessing carrying capacity using prey-preference data, and Frankham (this volume) points out the need to ensure that a suitable effective population size (N_e) is reintroduced to lower the risk of inbreeding depression (N_e is typically an order of magnitude lower than census population sizes). Linnell *et al.*, (this volume) argues that reintroductions of Eurasian lynx have been into sites that are either too small or too isolated—or both. Davies-Mostert *et al.*, (this volume) attempted to circumvent both shortcomings by implementing a "managed metapopulation", but conclude from the experience that this was essentially a holding measure while long-lasting solutions such as habitat restoration and linkage through wildlife corridors are established.

One such example of a potentially long-lasting solution is the growing importance of transfrontier parks across Africa in an attempt to manage the large herds of migratory herbivores and their predators. The Kgalagadi Transfrontier Park (38,000 km^2) was the first such park to be officially established in 1999 across the South Africa–Botswana border, and is co-managed as a single ecosystem unit by SANParks and the Department of Wildlife and National Parks of Botswana (Braak, 2003). Another example is the current development of the Mesoamerican Biological Corridor, which aims to establish an internationally managed system of connected protected areas between Mexico and Columbia, for the benefit of both biodiversity and local and regional economies (López & Jiménez, 2007). Linnell *et al.*, (this volume) also take inspiration from this model for Eurasian lynx, and it could be widely extended. Even in smaller countries, such as the United Kingdom, which is dominated by a mosaic of fragmented habitats, there is scope to move conservation efforts from a local scale to a wider, national scale. Macdonald *et al.*, (2000b) put forward the idea that in the UK, large-scale habitat enhancement to benefit both biodiversity and address issues of climate change, is possible through small changes in government policy and through the use of existing funding sources such as the EU Life Fund and new sources with industry involvement. Indeed, they suggested radical options such as the creation of large fenced wilderness areas to which top-order carnivores might be reintroduced, much in the manner now proposed at Alladale (see above).

These issues put reintroductions into strategic context, within a bigger picture of metapopulations and their management, and potentially as a step in transition to conservation networks, including transfrontier ones (e.g. Marino *et al.*, in press).

Metapopulation—at what point does management become metaphor?

Conceptually, a metapopulation is a set of local populations that are all subject to extinction and persist at the metapopulation level through recolonization (Levins, 1969; Gilpin & Hanski, 1991), but few systems in nature actually conform to this definition (Harrison, 1991; Harrison & Taylor, 1997). For carnivores, the functioning of such metapopulations is perturbed by persecution and illegal hunting, or inhospitality of intervening habitats in fragmented landscapes. Easterbee *et al.*, (1991) suspected that the Scottish wildcat could not easily cross the urbanized and industrial belt that runs across central Scotland and was therefore restricted to the highlands to the north despite the availability of suitable habitat to the south. These risks apply to any organism, but are acute for carnivores because of their relatively large home ranges, low numbers and direct persecution by humans (Noss *et al.*, 1996; Woodroffe & Ginsberg, 1998). Davies-Mostert *et al.*, (this volume) describe the concept of a managed metapopulation as a metaphor for a conservation technique rather than management of a real metapopulation.

At least in the case of the African wild dog, the constellation of reintroduced populations have no natural opportunity for dispersal, and the level of intervention is very great. Gusset (this volume) develops this theme, listing options that may be available when reintroducing large carnivores into less-than-optimal-sized habitat. As always, there is a spectrum of naturalness, or intensity of intervention. Gusset cites a continuum that embraces small populations of relocated cheetahs contained in fenced areas with coordinated management, where several smaller reserves are clustered together, puncturing the fences and coalescing the fragments into a single management unit. In all these variants, it would be mistaken to think that the essential principles are particular to reintroduced populations. Rather, the challenge is to apply the general principles of population biology (demographic stochasticity, inbreeding depression, etc.) within the particular constraints within which a reintroduction is enacted. The concept of a managed metapopulation, based on the metaphor (*sensu* Davies-Mostert *et al.*, this volume) of emulating the functioning of a real metapopulation is illustrated by the case of the Ethiopian wolf, *Canis simensis*, mostly restricted to the Bale Mountains of Ethiopia with fewer than 500 individuals left. Sillero-Zubiri & Macdonald (1997) concluded that the Ethiopian wolf was not a suitable candidate for reintroduction because it failed to meet several of 13 key reintroduction criteria (Kleiman *et al.*, 1994): the original causes of decline had not been removed, there was a lack of suitable or available habitat, the impact of a reintroduction on existing wild populations could not be established and there was insufficient local support and resources. However, a genetic study (Gottelli *et al.*, 1994) indicated that management (translocation) to substitute for dispersal might be required to prevent loss of genetic variability in the smaller populations (see Randall *et al.*, 2007).

What are the societal gaps and how good is the crystal ball?

Unsurprisingly, the IUCN (1998) states that a thorough assessment of attitudes of local people to the proposed project should be carried out and that it be fully understood, accepted and supported by local communities. Furthermore, it states that "Socio-economic studies should be made to assess impacts, costs and benefits of the reintroduction programme to local human populations". When considering reintroducing top-order carnivores to a neighbourhood, it would seem a minimal courtesy to ask prospective neighbours whether they mind (considering that the incomers might well eat either them or their stock).

More generally, and with the human dimension recognized as essential to modern conservation, a generation of conservation biologists, questing for the best outcomes from community involvement, has been brought up to seek expertise from social science. Regardless of whether this has yet lived up to expectation, the authors of this book nonetheless provide a rich harvest of examples of the folly of earlier neglect of societal issues. For example:

- Failure to anticipate poor public acceptance and understanding, and the lack of education campaigns to influence these or surveys of local attitudes and local community involvement to monitor them (e.g. Bowman *et al.*, 2004; Clark, this volume);
- Failure to mitigate conflict, such as taking steps to reduce livestock depredation (provision of guard dogs or fences e.g. Dickman *et al.*, this volume), or through financial compensation (Loveridge *et al.*, 2007);

- Lack of cooperation amongst involved constituencies, such as through development of conservancies or economic or financial incentives (e.g. Lindsey *et al.*, this volume) is also a significant issue, as is failure to ameliorate antagonism towards dangerous carnivores by both correcting unjustified perceptions, and also by behavioural "training" or other means of reducing risk (e.g. Christie, this volume; Clark, this volume);
- Finally, lack of appropriate financial structures to offset the economic burden of consequences of the reintroduction, for example by fostering ecotourism or sustainable use of wildlife (Neumann, 1997; Al-Kharousi, 2006; Jackson & Ale, this volume).

Macdonald *et al.*. (2002b) emphasized the importance of considering not merely the attitude of communities towards reintroduction, but also their capacity to cope with the challenges and opportunities.

Of course, it is easy to be wise in hindsight, and even the most successful reintroductions can be damaged by unforeseen events. The reintroduction of the Arabian Oryx, *Oryx leucoryx*, into Oman is rightly hailed as a benchmark success (Stanley Price, 1989). However, much good has been undone by poaching for private collections (by 2005, 94 out of 400 individuals remained, of which only four were female, Spalton *et al.*, 1999). The Arabian Oryx Sanctuary is inhabited and protected by the Harasiis tribe (ca. 3000 individuals), who are largely dependent on its resources, including wildlife. With the success of the oryx came competition for grazing with domestic goat (*Capra hircus domestica*) and camel (*Camelus dromedarius*), and competition between the lineages of the Harasiis tribe over access to employment and special benefits, and between the Harasiis and rival tribes (Chatty, 1998). The current decline of oryx and the growing economic needs of local people might be tackled by developing a framework for legal trade of the Arabian Oryx, perhaps decreasing the oryx price in illegal markets (Al-Kharousi, 2006). These turns of events were not foreseen when, three decades earlier, the programme began, and very probably opacity of the crystal ball will remain an inevitable threat to all reintroduction projects. The practical lesson is that reintroduction schemes must have structures to devise and implement adaptive management as the need, inevitably, arises. Furthermore, even when the original goals have been achieved, there is a need for continuing vigilance in order to minimize the impact of unforeseen developments.

What is the missing science, and why?

No farmer would jump into a new livestock enterprise without being expert in the behaviour and husbandry of the new species. So too, it would be unprofessional to attempt such radical intervention as reintroduction of a wild species without excellent knowledge of its behavioural ecology in the wild, and likely requirements for its successful reintroduction. To take a non-carnivore example, water voles (*Arvicola terrestris*) have been widely eradicated from Britain by the invasive American mink, *Neovision vison*, and habitat loss in the face of agriculture. Restoration proposals included captive breeding and reintroduction of water voles. Critical first questions were to discover how to remove the mink (Bonesi *et al.*, 2007) and how to restore the habitat (Moorhouse *et al.*, 2007). Field experimentation, comparing the survival of captive-bred water voles in recreated habitat strips of different dimensions, revealed that post-establishment survival rates and population densities of captive-bred, released water voles were positively correlated with vegetation abundance, suggesting that large quantities of vegetation not only promote a higher likelihood of an individual becoming established on site, but also higher survival rates, owing to increased levels of cover for established individuals, leading to higher population densities. The same principle of doing the scientific home-work thoroughly is variously illustrated through the emphasis made by Hayward *et al.* (this volume) on knowing about diet and carrying capacity. Similarly, Johnsingh & Madhusingh (this volume) emphasize the importance of home range size and social interactions, and Clark (this volume) considers reproductive biology and, in the context of bears, dispersal or ranging behaviour.

Using a carnivore example, the value of experimentation and pre- and post-release monitoring is illustrated by the case of the European mink, *Mustela lutreola*, widely displaced from its extensive eastern European range by invasive American mink (Sidorovich *et al.*, 1999). Maran *et al.*, (in press) examined the impact of biological and pre-release factors on survival of individuals released (following exhaustive community consultations) into an island sanctuary (Macdonald *et al.*, 2002a,b,c). Survival was significantly higher in individuals held in larger, more natural enclosures and with less human contact than in animals from smaller standard breeding enclosures with more human contact. In addition, yearling survival was higher than adult survival—likely because they had limited adaptations to captivity compared to adults. The study also found that the highest mortality occurred in the first 1–1.5 months after release while individuals established home ranges and adapted to the wild, indicating that, for the European mink, this period is critical and could be targeted for support to aid survival. In particular, female mink had a higher mortality rate than males, suggesting that a higher proportion of females should be released to account for this difference.

Frankham (this volume) outlines genetic considerations, including the risks of inbreeding depression (high post-release mortality results in the founder group being smaller than the number of individuals released [Castro *et al.*, 2004]) and outbreeding depression if the reintroduced individuals do not have the right adaptive qualities. Pre-empting these problems requires knowledge of the genetic diversity of wild populations and of those in captive breeding programmes. A general recommendation is that a population in captivity should attempt to preserve at least 0.9 of the average heterozygosity of the founders for 200 years (Soulé *et al.*, 1986). The likely loss of genetic variation in a reintroduced population will be affected by its mating system (Parker & Waite, 1997): the fewer the breeders, the lower the effective population size (N_e), and thus, eventually, the lower the genetic variability (Castro *et al.*, 2004).

Armed with the correct data, modelling can underpin plans, for example determining the minimum founder size (e.g. Davies-Mostert *et al.*, this volume) or potential expansion (e.g. Linnell *et al.*, this volume), and to evaluate determinants of failure or success (Bertolero *et al.*, 2007). Modelling is also a tool for adaptive management as a reintroduction takes root. Following three failed reintroductions of the endangered New Zealand bird, the hihi (*Notiomystis cincta*), Armstrong *et al.*, (2007) initiated an 8-year series of management manipulations on a reintroduced hihi population, on Mokoia Island, in order to assess the effects of supplementary feeding and mite control on survival. A population model, developed to predict persistence under different management regimes, was updated on an annual basis to guide adaptive management (it turned out that provision of sugar water during the breeding season and mite control were important).

The cases mentioned above highlight the importance of not only understanding a species' ecological needs and biology, but also the importance of evidence-based conservation (e.g. pre-release experiments, post-release monitoring, modelling and adaptive management) in the successful re-establishment of a species. Valuable lessons applicable to carnivore reintroductions can also be learnt from experiences with different taxa. Taking one taxon which includes several top-order carnivores, Macdonald & Sillero-Zubiri (2004) discuss the generic question of whether enough is already known to underpin conservation interventions, or whether show-stopping scientific gaps remain. The authors of the previous 18 chapters identify two categories of science deficit in the failures to which they draw attention: first, instances where research had not produced the needed scientific facts, and second, instances where the facts existed but had not been thoroughly considered. There can be excuses for the former, but not for the latter.

What is the role of animal welfare?

I think a significant opportunity exists in the better integration of conservation biology and animal welfare science, and McLaren *et al.*, (2007) show that techniques are developing to deliver this. The relevance of welfare to reintroduction programmes is manifold, ranging from the preparation of the released individuals to their impacts on other species while under human management (in terms of duty of care, there are parallels here to the interesting questions of scale raised above regarding where to draw the boundaries along the continuum between zoo and wilderness). Reintroductions can be significantly more successful when using wild rather than captive animals (Wolf *et al.*, 1996; Seddon *et al.*, 2007; Jule *et al.*, 2008), yet this option is not always available because some species already exist in small, isolated populations, unable to withstand the loss of even a single individual. Thus there may be significant pressures for reintroductions to use captive-bred individuals, of which many, particularly amongst carnivores, may not be good candidates for reintroduction or translocation (Sunquist & Sunquist, 2002). They may lack necessary hunting skills, perhaps resulting in livestock kills, injury or starvation (Childes, 1988; Scheepers & Venzke, 1995; Rabin, 2003), fear of humans (McPhee, 2003) and predator recognition (Kleiman, 1989; Griffin *et al.*, 2000).

Returning to the recurrent theme of this essay, each case needs individual consideration. For example, Christie (this volume) outlines three behaviours essential for successful reintroductions of the Amur leopard, *Panthera pardus orientalis*—and these behaviours should be demonstrated pre-release: shyness of humans, ability to hunt live prey and aversion to other predators, particularly tigers. Some unhelpful behaviour associated with captivity can be lessened through appropriate pre-release management. Clark (this volume) describes how survival rates in black bears, *Ursus americanus*, increase when they are released in winter at suitable den sites and using soft-release techniques (where the animal is maintained in pre-release enclosures for some time to adapt to their surroundings), whereas Somers & Gusset (this volume) stress the importance of keeping social animals together before release to assist social integration and hence to improve the chance of success—and also to reduce stress. (See also the impact of pre-release experience, mentioned above, on the success of released European mink [Macdonald *et al.*, 2002c].) In other cases, suitable genetic management may help ameliorate the phenotypic changes that can occur in captivity (Snyder *et al.*, 1996) and may have deleterious effects on fitness in the wild (Mason *et al.*, 1967; Fleming & Gross, 1993), including inbreeding (Fleming, 1994).

Clearly, these welfare issues are important, not just operationally to improve the chances of a reintroduction's success but also ethically, and are not easily resolved. For instance, the welfare of a reintroduced carnivore may depend on its ability to hunt (e.g. Christie, this volume), but one cannot dodge the hard choice that this necessitates placing prey in an enclosure with a predator from which they cannot escape. While the undoubted redness of Nature's tooth and claw is beyond the reach of human ethics, interactions brought about while reintroduced individuals are under human care are clearly not (and there is an interesting continuum between the two). Animals kept in captivity may have poorer health (Mathews *et al.*, 2005) than their wild counterparts, with consequences for their survival upon release (Kleiman *et al.*, 1994) or with associated increased stress levels during the release process (Hartup *et al.*, 2005) which can, in turn, lead to the onset of disease owing to lowered immuno-competence (Viggers *et al.*, 1993). Moorhouse *et al.* (2007) use a powerful technique, leukocyte coping capacity (LCC), to reveal how factors associated with captive conditions may lead to the suppression of an individual's immune system and hence its ability to fight infection when released. They examined the impact of housing conditions (laboratory-caged versus outdoor enclosures), handling and radio-collaring on stress levels in captive-bred water voles being prepared for a reintroduction programme. Weight loss and LCC were used to infer relative stress. LCC measures the response of circulating leukocytes to a bacterial-type challenge.

Stress reduces this response, possibly leaving the animal more susceptible to opportunistic infection. Lowered LCC scores indicate immunosuppression and, together with body weight losses, can be indicators of stress in mammals (see Moorhouse *et al.*, 2007). Housing conditions had a significant impact, with laboratory-caged individuals displaying greater weight loss, dehydration and reduced ability to combat infection than those housed in outdoor enclosures. Additionally, both groups showed reduced LCC scores and therefore inferred elevated levels of stress as time passed in captivity, indicating that other elements of the procedure, such as repeated handling, and anaesthesia, may have also caused stress to both groups (from which the authors concluded that minimizing the time for which animals were held prior to release could be advantageous in this respect).

Reintroductions obviously affect the recipient community. Wild populations are susceptible to diseases carried by reintroduced stock (Hess, 1996). Therefore a two-pronged attack is needed: first, screening to minimize any potential effects of disease on both captive and wild populations (Snyder *et al.*, 1996; Leighton 2002) and second, to determine factors that affect the resistance of captive individuals to disease (Moorhouse *et al.*, in press). Reintroduced carnivores may also suffer from competition with other predators; Marnewick *et al.*, (this volume) point out that lions at a release site may kill reintroduced cheetahs. Sunquist & Sunquist (2002) emphasize the risk of interspecific competition between reintroduced individuals and the existing residents.

Does the generalization adequately describe the particular?

Like most spheres of conservation, reintroduction is an inescapably interdisciplinary subject and one for which the interface between conservation and development is increasingly apparent (Macdonald *et al.*, 2007a). This intricate web of factors means that there are always likely to be several alternative rational ways of conducting any reintroduction programme, and there will be tough choices to be made between them. They should be made transparently, and with the evidence recorded. Similarly, despite the unquestionable wisdom of the IUCN's over-arching guidelines, within that framework no one formula can accommodate the detail of all reintroductions. Rather, the lesson of the previous 18 chapters is that each case needs individual fine-tuning, particularly in the context of local socio-economic circumstances. Lindsey *et al.* (this volume) highlight the importance of user rights given to landowners in Africa, which has conferred an economic value upon wildlife and promoted a shift to game ranching and hence predator reintroductions. This system is suited to some African countries which have a well-developed tourism and hunting market but may not be transferable to some other regions. A different financial mechanism is described by Marnewick *et al.* (this volume) who illustrate the use of compensation programmes by the example of encouraging landowners to live-trap problem cheetahs rather than killing them. Obviously, the solution of live-trapping leads to the problem of translocation, as discussed for cheetahs in Namibia by Marker *et al.* (in press).

Of course, to say that all cases must be tackled on their own merits is not to say that each must start from scratch. On the contrary, it is essential that the envelope of possibilities is shaped by previous lessons learnt. Linnell *et al.* (this volume) emphasize for the Eurasian lynx the numerous lessons offered by past problems (poor management, genetic and physical isolation of released populations, etc.), which can be readily applied to other species. Similarly, post-release monitoring was all too often neglected in the early days (Seddon *et al.*, 2007), and should now be regarded as essential. Monitoring provides the basis for adaptive management and, should things go wrong, at least increases the chances that lessons can be learnt for the future (e.g. Armstrong *et al.*, 2007). Amongst top-order carnivores, it is inevitably the case that the reintroduced animals have the likelihood of damaging some human livelihoods and even, albeit at an extreme, threatening human lives. These heightened stakes make it essential that reintroductions are thoroughly monitored, and that contingency plans are adapted as circumstances are thereby revealed.

Summary

What conclusions can be drawn from the wealth of information provided by the preceding 18 chapters? That reintroductions are complex and costly is nothing new, but together the chapters in this book have suggested to me that at least seven, often overlapping, awkward questions could usefully be addressed when considering whether, and how, to undertake the reintroduction (or translocation) of top-order carnivores.

- First, and above all, is reintroduction the right solution to the problem? This show-stopping question provokes a cascade of others: what are the costs and benefits of the reintroduction and of alternative options, and are the financial and human resources available to deliver the planned outcomes?

- Second, has the bigger picture been properly evaluated? Science and society are changing, and simply rebuilding the past may be neither possible nor prudent. Putting aside nostalgia, reintroductions should be planned to create a new future more than to restore an old past.
- Third, there is the question of scale, and the associated issue of naturalness. On what scale is it worthwhile to conduct a reintroduction if it is to be a priority for biodiversity conservation?
- Fourth, has society the capacity to cope with the challenges of reintroduction and to take up the benefits? While the verdict is out on community-based conservation as a panacea, there is no doubt that the human dimension is an inextricable element of 21st century conservation. Human affairs, however, are complicated and hard to predict, so in laying plans for a reintroduction the conservationist generally peers into a crystal ball that is far from clear. This makes it essential to have adaptable contingency plans.
- Fifth, what is the missing science and why? It is a mantra of conservation biology that policies should be based on evidence, yet all too often reintroductions have disregarded the evidence. Such sloppiness is not acceptable in modern conservation. Trickier is the case where there are genuine gaps in knowledge, and the general rule is that the necessary research should be done before the reintroduction, rather than its omission lamented afterwards. In practice, a sensible compromise is for projects to be phased, each phase including an experimental component to maximize the lessons learnt en route.
- Sixth, what is the role of animal welfare? Although an unhelpful, indeed destructive, 20th century dichotomy was exaggerated between those interested in individual animals and those whose priority was their populations (an emergent property of the individuals), I think there is practical and philosophical advantage to be gained by conservation better embracing the breadth of this spectrum. In that reintroductions involve the intensive, intrusive management of both the animals to be introduced and the community that receives them, in a manner closely akin to agricultural husbandry, there are clear issues of the duty of care. At the least, it is obvious that animal welfare science can contribute to the success of a reintroduction, and on a wider canvass there would be merit in thinking harder about the welfare and ethical corollaries at each stage of the reintroduction process.
- Seventh, an English idiom draws attention to the difficulty appreciating generalizations when swamped with detail—the inability to see the wood

for the trees. In this case, the IUCN (1998) reintroduction guidelines provide the wood (i.e. the bigger picture). However, it seems to me that this idiom works equally in reverse, so that important detail of the trees may be missed if the view of the wood is too superficial. In the context of reintroductions, the question is whether the generalizations adequately prescribe the particular? To judge by the 18 excellent chapters in this book, the answer is no. Rather, each case of reintroduction must be evaluated and planned on its own merits and taking account of its own circumstances.

I expect restoration ecology to be a major thrust of conservation in the coming decades, and the lessons learnt from this book will help to ensure that reintroductions (and translocations) are a useful component of the toolkit for repairing damaged ecosystems and building a resilient environment for the future.

Acknowledgements

I am deeply grateful to Kerry Kilshaw, without whose expert help I could not have prepared this chapter in time, and to Matt Hayward for assembling the data for Figure 19.1.

References

Adams, W.M. & Hulme, D. (1998) *Conservation and Communities: Changing Narratives, Policies and Practices in African Conservation*. Community Conservation in Africa Working Paper, University of Manchester, Manchester.

Akçakaya, H.R., Mills, G. & Doncaster, C.P. (2007) The role of metapopulations in conservation. *Key Topics in Conservation Biology*. (eds D.W. Macdonald & K. Service), pp. 64–84. Blackwell Publishing, London.

Al-Kharousi, Y.H. (2006) Poaching of re-introduced Arabian oryx in Oman, will accession to CITES help? *Re-introduction NEWS* 25, 23–25.

Amos, W. & Balmford, A. (2001) When does conservation genetics matter? *Heredity* 87, 257–265.

Ando, A., Camm, J., Polasky, S. & Solow, A. (1998) Species distributions, land values, and efficient conservation. *Science* 279, 2126–2128.

Armstrong, D., Castro, I. & Griffiths, R. (2007) Using adaptive management to determine requirements of re-introduced populations, the case of the New Zealand hihi. *Journal of Applied Ecology* 44, 953–962.

Armstrong, D.P. & Seddon, P.J. (2007) Directions in reintroduction biology. *Trends in Ecology and Evolution* 23, 20–25.

Baldus, R.D. (2004) *Lion Conservation in Tanzania Leads to Serious Human–Lion Conflicts with a Case Study of a Man-Eating Lion Killing 35 People.* GTZ Wildlife Programme in Tanzania, Wildlife Division, Dar Es Salaam.

Barrett, C. & Arcese, P. (1995) Are integrated conservation-development projects (ICDPs) sustainable? On the conservation of large mammals in sub-Saharan Africa. *World Development* 23, 1073–1084.

Beaumont, M., Barratt, E.M., Gottelli, D. et al. (2001) Genetic diversity and introgression in the Scottish wildcat. *Molecular Ecology* 10, 319–336.

Beck, B.B., Rapaport, L.G., Stanley Price, M.R. & Wilson, A.C. (1994) Reintroduction of captive-born animals. *Creative Conservation: Interactive Management of Wild and Captive Animals.* (eds P.J.S. Olney, G.M. Mace & A.T.C. Feistner), pp. 265–286. Chapman and Hall, London.

Berger, J. (2007) Carnivore repatriation and Holarctic prey: Narrowing the deficit in ecological effectiveness. *Conservation Biology* 21, 1105–1116.

Bertolero, A., Oro, D. & Besnard, A. (2007) Assessing the efficacy of reintroduction programmes by modelling adult survival: The example of Hermann's tortoise. *Animal Conservation* 10, 360–368.

Bonesi, L., Rushton, S.P., Macdonald, D.W. (2007) Trapping for mink control and water vole survival: Identifying key criteria using a spatially explicit individual based model. *Biological Conservation* 136, 636–650.

Bowman, J.L., Leopold, B.D., Vilella, F.J. & Gill, D.A. (2004) A spatially explicit model, derived from demographic variables, to predict attitudes toward black bear restoration. *Journal of Wildlife Management* 68, 223–232.

Braak, L. (2003) Transboundary protected areas: Motivations, expectations, challenges from an African perspective. *Workshop: Transboundary Protected Areas: Guiding TBPA Approaches and Processes in East Africa.* 24–28 February 2003. Mweka.

Breitenmoser, U., Breitenmoser-Wursten, C., Carbyn, L.N. & Funk, S.M. (2001) Assessment of carnivore reintroductions. *Carnivore Conservation.* (eds J.L. Gittleman, S.M. Funk, D.W. Macdonald & R.K. Wayne), pp. 241–280. Cambridge University Press and the Zoological Society of London, Cambridge.

Campbell, R., Dutton, A. & Hughes, J. (2007) *Economic Impacts of the Beaver.* Wildlife Conservation Research Unit, Oxford.

Castro, I., Mason, K.M., Armstrong, D.P. & Lambert, D.M. (2004) Effect of extra-pair paternity on effective population size in a reintroduced population of the endangered hihi, and potential for behavioural management. *Conservation Genetics* 5, 381–393.

Caughley, G. (1994) Directions in conservation biology. *Journal of Animal Ecology* 63, 215–244.

Chatty, D. (1998) Enclosures and exclusions: Wildlife conservation schemes and pastoral tribes in the Middle East. *Forced Migration Review* 27–30.

Childes, S.L. (1988) The past history, present status and distribution of the hunting dog *Lycaon pictus* in Zimbabwe. *Biological Conservation* 44, 301–316.

Choi, Y.D. (2004) Theories for ecological restoration in changing environment, toward "futuristic" restoration. *Ecological Research* 19, 75–81.

Collen, P. (1997) *Review of the Potential Impact of Reintroducing European Beaver* Castor fiber L. *on the Ecology and Movement of Native Fish, and the Likely Implications for Current Angling Practices in Scotland.* Review No. 86. Scottish Natural Heritage, Perth.

Daily, G.C. (1997) *Nature's Services: Societal Dependence on Natural Ecosystems.* Island Press, Washington, DC.

Daniels, M.J., Balharry, D., Hirst, D., Aspinall, R.J. & Kitchener, A.C. (1998) Morphological and pelage characteristics of wild living cats in Scotland: Implications for defining the "wildcat". *Journal of Zoology, London* 244, 231–247.

Dickersin, K. & Manheimer, E. (1998) The Cochrane Collaboration: Evaluation of health care and services using systematic reviews of the results of randomized clinical trials. *Clinical Obstetrics and Gynecology* 41, 315–331.

Donlan, C.J., Berger, J., Bock, C.E. et al. (2006) Pleistocene Rewilding: An optimistic agenda for twenty-first century conservation. *The American Naturalist* 168, 660–681.

Driscoll, C.A., Menotti-Raymond, M., Roca, A.L. et al. (2007) The Near Eastern Origin of Cat Domestication. *Science* 317, 519–523.

Easterbee, N., Hepburn, L.V. & Jefferies, D.J. (1991) *Survey of the Status and Distribution of the Wildcat in Scotland, 1983–1987.* Nature Conservancy Council for Scotland, Edinburgh.

Ehrenfeld, J.G. (2000) Evaluating wetlands within an urban context. *Ecological Engineering* 15, 253–265.

Elliot, R. (1997) *Faking Nature, the Ethics of Environmental Restoration.* Routledge, London.

Ferraro, P.J. (2003) Assigning priority to environmental policy interventions in a heterogeneous world. *Journal of Policy Analysis and Management* 22, 27–43.

Fiallo, E.A. & Jacobsen, S.K. (1995) Local communities and protected areas: Attitudes of rural residents toward conservation and Machalilla National Park, Ecuador. *Environmental Conservation* 22, 3, 241–249.

Fischer, J. & Lindenmayer, D.B. (2000) An assessment of the published results of animal relocations. *Biological Conservation* 96, 1–11.

Fleming, I.A. (1994) Captive breeding and the conservation of wild salmon populations, *Conservation Biology* 8, 886–888.

Fleming, I.A. & Gross, M.T. (1993) Breeding success of hatchery and wild coho salmon (*Oncorhynchus kisutch*) in competition. Ecological Applications 3, 230–245.

Frankham, R., Ballou, J.D. & Briscoe D.A. (2002) *Introduction to Conservation Genetics*. Cambridge University Press, Cambridge.

Gilpin, M.E. & Hanski, I. (1991) *Metapopulation Dynamics: Empirical and Theoretical Investigations*. Linnaean Society of London and Academic Press, London.

Gippoliti, S. (2002) *Castor Fiber. 2007 IUCN Red List of Threatened Species*. Available: www.iucnredlist.org. Accessed 02 June 2008.

Gottelli, D., Sillero-Zubiri, C., Applebaum, G.D. et al. (1994) Molecular genetics of the most endangered canid: The Ethiopian wolf *Canis simensis. Molecular Ecology* 3, 301–312.

Greig, J.C. (1979) Principles of genetic conservation in relation to wildlife management in Southern Africa. *South African Wildlife Research* 9, 57–78.

Griffin, A.S., Blumstein, D.T. & Evans, C. (2000) Training captive-bred or translocated animals to avoid predators. *Conservation Biology* 14, 1317–1326.

Griffith, B., Scott, J.M., Carpenter, J.W. & Reed, C. (1989) Translocation as a species conservation tool: Status and strategy. *Science* 245, 477–480.

Gurnell A. (1997) *Analysis of the Effects of Beaver Dam-Building Activities on Local Hydrology*. SNH Review 85.

Harris, J.A. & van Diggelen, R. (2005) Ecological restoration as a project for global society. *Restoration Ecology, The New Frontier*. (eds J. van Andel & J. Aronson), pp. 3–16. Blackwell Publishing, London.

Harris, J.A., Hobbs, R.J., Higgs, E. & Aronson, J. (2006) Ecological restoration and global climate change. *Restoration Ecology* 14 (2), 170–176.

Harrison, S. (1991) Local extinctions in a metapopulation context: An empirical evaluation. *Metapopulation Dynamics: Empirical and Theoretical Investigations*. (eds M.E. Gilpin & I.A. Hanski), pp. 73–88. Academic Press, London.

Harrison, S. & Taylor, A.D. (1997). Empirical evidence for metapopulations dynamics. *Metapopulation Biology: Ecology, Genetics and Evolution*. (eds I.A. Hanski & M.E. Gilpin), pp. 27–42. Academic Press, London.

Hartup, B.K., Olsen, G.H. & Czekala, N.M. (2005) Fecal corticoid monitoring in whooping cranes (*Grus americana*) undergoing reintroduction. *Zoo Biology* 24, 15–28.

Hayward, M.W. (in press) Conservation management for the past, present and future. *Biodiversity and Conservation*. DOI 10.1007/s10531–008–9436-y.

Hedrick, P.W., Miller, P.S., Geffen, E. & Wayne, R. (1997) Genetic evaluation of three captive Mexican wolf lineages. *Zoological Biology* 16, 47–69.

Heinen, J.T. (1993) Park–people relations in Kosi Tappu Wildlife Reserve, Nepal: A socio-economic analysis. *Environmental Conservation* 20, 1, 25–34.

Hess, G. (1996) Disease in metapopulation models: Implications for conservation. *Ecology* 77, 1617–1632.

Higgs, E.S. (1997) What good is ecological restoration? *Conservation Biology* 11, 338–348.

Hilderbrand, G.V., Hanley, T.A., Robbins, C.T. & Schwartz, C.C. (1999) Role of brown bears (*Ursus arctos*) in the flow of marine nitrogen into terrestrial ecosystems. *Oecologia* 121, 546–550.

IUCN (1994) *IUCN Red List Categories.* Prepared by the IUCN Species Survival Commission. IUCN, Gland, Switzerland.

IUCN (1998) *Guidelines for Re-introductions.* Prepared by the IUCN SSC Re-introduction Specialist Group. IUCN, Gland, Switzerland and Cambridge, UK. 10 pp.

IUCN (2007) *2007 IUCN Red List of Threatened Species.* Available: www.iucnredlist.org. Accessed 2 June 2008.

Jule, K.R., Leaver, L.A. & Lea, E.G.L. (2008) The effects of captive experience on reintroduction survival in carnivores: A review and analysis. *Biological Conservation* 141, 355–363.

Kalinowski, S.T., Hedrick, P.W. & Miller, P.S. (1999) No inbreeding depression observed in Mexican and red wolf captive breeding program. *Conservation Biology* 13, 1371–1377.

Katz, E. (1992) The big lie, human restoration of nature. Research in Philosophy and Technology 12, 231–241.

Kilshaw, K., Macdonald, D.W. & Kitchener, A. (2008) *Feral Cat Management in the Cairngorms; Scoping Study.* Report to Scottish Natural Heritage, No. 22371.

Kiss, A. (1990) *Living with Wildlife: Wildlife Resource Management with Local Participation in Africa.* World Bank Technical Paper Number 130. Washington, DC.

Kitchener, A.C. (1995) *The Wildcat.* The Mammal Society, London.

Kitchener, A.C. & Conroy, J. (1997) The history of the Eurasian Beaver *Castor fiber* in Scotland. *Mammal Review* 27, 95–108.

Kitchener, A.C., Yamaguchi, N., Ward, J.M. & Macdonald, D.W. (2005) A diagnosis for the Scottish wildcat (*Felis silvestris*): A tool for conservation action for a critically-endangered felid. *Animal Conservation* 8, 223–237.

Kleiman, D.G. (1989) Reintroduction of captive mammals for conservation: Guidelines for reintroducing endangered species into the wild. *BioScience* 39, 152–161.

Kleiman, D.G., Stanley Price, M.R. & Beck, B.B. (1994) Criteria for reintroductions. *Creative Conservation: Interactive Management of Wild and Captive Animals.* (eds P.J.S. Olney, G.M. Mace & A.T.C. Feistner), pp. 287–303. Chapman and Hall, London.

Kruuk, H. (2002) *Hunter and Hunted: Relationship between Carnivores and People.* Cambridge University Press, Cambridge.

Leighton, F.A. (2002) Health risk assessment of the translocation of wild animals. *Revue Scientifique et Technique de l'Office Internationale des Epizooties* 21, 187–195.

Levins, R.A. (1969) Some demographic and genetic consequences of environmental heterogeneity for biological control. *Bulletin of the Entomological Society of America* 15, 237–240.

Lewis, D., Kaweche, G.B. & Mwenya, A. (1990) Wildlife conservation outside protected areas—Lessons from an experiment in Zambia. *Conservation Biology* 4, 171–180.

Linnell, J.D.C. (2004) *Wolves Returning to Germany: Opportunity and Challenge,* Feature Article Series 4. Large Carnivore Initiative for Europe.

Linnell, J.D.C., Landa, A., Andersen, R., Strand, O., Eide, N., van Dijk, J. & May, R.M. (2005) Captive breeding, population supplementation and reintroduction as tools to conserve endangered Arctic fox populations in Norway: Detailed proposal and progress 2001–2004. *Oppdragsmelding* 825, 1–22.

López, A. & Jiménez, A. (2007) Environmental conflict and cooperation: The Mesoamerican biological corridor as a mechanism for transborder environmental cooperation. *Latin America Assessment.* A product of the Environment and Conflict Prevention Initiative of the of the UNEP's Division of Early Warning and Assessment December 2007, 54 pp.

Loveridge, A.J., Reynolds, J.C. & Milner-Gulland, E.J. (2007) Is sport hunting part of conservation? *Key Topics in Conservation Biology.* (eds D.W. Macdonald & K. Service), pp. 224–240. Blackwell Publishing, London.

Macdonald, D.W. & Loveridge, A.J. (eds) (in press) *Biology and Conservation of Wild Felids.* Oxford University Press, Oxford.

Macdonald, D.W. & Sillero-Zubiri, C. (2002) Large carnivores and conflict: Lion conservation in context. *Lion Conservation Research Workshop 2: Modelling Conflict.* (eds A.J. Loveridge, A. Lynam & D.W. Macdonald), pp. 1–8. Oxford: Wildlife Conservation Research Unit, Oxford.

Macdonald, D.W. & Sillero-Zubiri, C. (eds) (2004) *The Biology and Conservation of Wild Canids.* Oxford University Press, Oxford.

Macdonald, D.W., Collins, N.M. & Wrangham, R. (2007a) Principles, practice and priorities: The quest for "alignment". *Key Topics in Conservation Biology.* (eds D.W. Macdonald & K. Service), pp. 273–292. Blackwell Publishing, Oxford.

Macdonald, D.W., Daniels, M.J., Driscoll, C., Kitchener, A. & Yamaguchi, N. (2004) *The Scottish Wildcat: Analyses for Conservation and an Action Plan.* Wildlife Conservation Research Unit, University of Oxford, Oxford.

Macdonald, D.W., King, C.M. & Strachan, R. (2007b) Introduced species and the line between biodiversity conservation and naturalistic eugenics. *Key Topics in*

Conservation Biology. (eds D.W. Macdonald & K. Service), pp. 187–206. Blackwell Publishing, Oxford.

Macdonald, D.W., Mace, G.M. & Rushton, S.P. (2000b) British mammals: Is there a radical future? *Priorities for the Conservation of Mammalian Diversity: Has the Panda Had its Day*? (eds A. Entwistle & N. Dunstone), pp. 175–205. Cambridge University Press, Cambridge.

Macdonald, D.W., Moorhouse, T.P. & Enck, J.W. (2002a) The ecological context: A species population perspective. *Handbook of Ecological Restoration*. (eds M.R. Perrow & A.J. Davy), pp. 47–65.Cambridge University Press, Cambridge.

Macdonald, D.W., Moorhouse, T.P., Enck, J.W. & Tattersall, F.H. (2002b) Mammals. *Handbook of Ecological Restoration*. (eds M.R. Perrow & A.J. Davy), pp. 389–408. Cambridge University Press, Cambridge.

Macdonald, D.W., Sidorovich, V.E., Maran, T. & Kruuk, H. (2002c) *European mink*, Mustela lutreola: *Analyses for Conservation*. WildCRU and Darwin Initiative, Oxford.

Macdonald, D.W., Sillero-Zubiri, C., Wang, S.W. & Wilson, D.C. (2006) Lions and conflict: Lessons from a wider context. *Lion Conservation Research Workshop 3 and 4: From Conflict to Socioecology*. (eds A.J. Loveridge, A. Lynam & D.W. Macdonald), pp. 1–16. Wildlife Conservation Research Unit, Oxford.

Macdonald, D.W., Tattersall, F.H., Brown, E.D. & Balharry, D. (1995) Reintroducing the European beaver to Britain: Nostalgic meddling or restoring biodiversity? *Mammal Review* 25, 161–200.

Macdonald, D.W., Tattersall, F.H., Rushton, S.P, South, A.B, Rao, S., Maitland, P. & Strachan, R. (2000a) Reintroducing the beaver (*Castor fiber*) to Scotland: A protocol for identifying and assessing suitable release sites. *Animal Conservation* 3, 125–133.

Macdonald, D.W., Yamaguchi, N., Kitchener, A.C., Daniels, M., Kilshaw, K. & Driscoll, C. (in press) Reversing cryptic extinction: The history, present and future of the Scottish wildcat. *The Biology and Conservation of Wild Felids*. (eds D.W. Macdonald & A.J. Loveridge). Oxford University Press, Oxford.

Maran, T., Põdra, M., Põlma, M. & Macdonald, D.W. (in press) The survival of captive born animals in restoration programmes—Case study of the endangered European mink *Mustela lutreola*. *Journal of Animal Ecology*.

Marino, J., Lucherini, M., Villalba, L., Bennett, M., Cossíos, D., Iriarte, A., Perovic, P. & Sillero-Zubiri, C. (in press) Highland cats: Ecology and conservation of the rare and elusive Andean cat. *The Biology and Conservation of Wild Felids*. (eds D.W. Macdonald & A.J. Loveridge). Oxford University Press. Oxford.

Marker, L., Dickman, A.J., Mills, M.G.L. & Macdonald, D.W. (in press) Cheetahs and ranchers in Namibia—A case study. *The Biology and Conservation of Wild Felids*. (eds D.W. Macdonald & A.J. Loveridge). Oxford University Press, Oxford.

Mason, J.W., Bryndilson, O.M. & Degursz, P.E. (1967) Comparative survival of wild and domestic strains of brook trout in streams. *Transactions of the North American Fisheries Society* 96, 313–319.

Mathews, F., Orros, M., McLaren, G., Gelling, M. & Foster, R. (2005) Keeping fit on the ark: Assessing the suitability of captive-bred animals for release. *Biological Conservation* 121, 569–577.

Matson, T.K., Goldizen, A.W. & Jarman, P.J. (2004) Factors affecting the success of translocations of the black-faced impala in Namibia. *Biological Conservation*, 116, 359–365.

McCarty, J.P. (2001) Ecological consequences of recent climate change. *Conservation Biology* 15, 320–331.

McLaren, G.W., Bonacic, C. & Rowan, A. (2007) Animal welfare and conservation: Measuring stress in the wild. *Key Topics in Conservation biology*. (eds D.W. Macdonald & K. Service), pp. 120–134. Blackwell Publishing, Oxford.

McLean, I.F.G. (2003) *A Policy for Conservation Translocations of Species in Britain*. Joint Nature Conservation Committee on behalf of The Countryside Council for Wales, English Nature and Scottish Natural Heritage, Peterborough.

McPhee, M.E. (2003) Generations in captivity increases behavioural variance: Considerations for captive breeding and reintroduction programmes. *Biological Conservation* 115, 71–77.

Millenium Ecosystem Assessment (2005) *Ecosystems and Human Well-Being: Synthesis*. Island Press, Washington, DC.

Moorhouse, T.P., Gelling, M. & Macdonald, D.W. (in press) Promoting survival in wildlife reintroductions: Evidence from a replicated reintroduction experiment. *Journal of Animal Ecology*.

Moorhouse, T.P., Gelling, M., McLaren, G.W., Mian, R. & Macdonald, D.W. (2007) Physiological consequences of captive conditions in water voles (*Arvicola terrestris*). *Journal of Zoology, London* 271, 19–26.

Moritz, C. (1999) Conservation units and translocations: Strategies for conserving evolutionary processes. *Hereditas* 130, 217–228.

Naidoo, R. & Ricketts, T.H. (2006) Mapping the economic costs and benefits of conservation. *PLoS Biology* 4 (11), e360.

Nepal, S.K. & Weber, K.E. (1995) Prospects for co-existence: Wildlife and local people. *Ambio* 24, 238–245.

Neumann, R. (1997) Primitive ideas: Protected area buffer zones and the politics of land in Africa. *Development and Change* 28 (3), 559–582.

Noss, R.F., Quigley, H.B., Hornocker, M.G., Merrill, T. & Paquet, P.C. (1996) Conservation biology and carnivore conservation in the Rocky Mountains. *Conservation Biology* 10, 949–963.

Onorato, D., Belden, C., Cunningham, M., Land, D., McBride, R. & Roelke, M. (in press) Florida panther (*Puma concolor coryi*)—Historical findings and future obstacles to population persistence assessed via a long-term study. *The Biology and Conservation of Wild Felids.* (eds D.W. Macdonald & A.J. Loveridge). Oxford University Press, Oxford.

Parker, P.G. & Waite, T.A. (1997) Mating systems, effective population size and conservation of natural populations. *Behavioural Approaches in Conservation in the Wild.* (eds. J.R. Clemmens & R. Buchhotz), pp. 243–261. Cambridge University Press, London.

Parry, D. & Campbell, B. (1992) Attitudes of rural communities to animal wildlife and its utilization in Chobe Enclave and Mababe Depression, Botswana. *Environmental Conservation* 19, 245–252.

Paxton, R. (1992) The mite marches on; *Varroa jacobsoni* found in the UK. *Bee World* 73, 94–99.

Pecks, J.E. (1993) *From Royal Game to Popular Heritage—Wildlife Policy and Resource Tenure under Colonial and Independent Rule in Zimbabe.* Paper presented to the 36th annual meeting of the Africa Studies Centre, December 4–7 1993, Boston.

Polasky, S., Camm, J.D. & Garber-Yonts, B. (2001) Selecting biological reserves cost-effectively: An application to terrestrial vertebrate conservation in Oregon. *Landscape Economy* 77, 68–78.

Poulle, M.L., Lequette, B. & Carles, L. (1997) Significance of ungulates in the diet of recently settled wolves in the Mercantour mountains (southeastern France). *Revue d'Ecologie: Terre et la Vie* 52, 357–368.

Primack, R.B. (1993) The value of biological diversity, Indirect economic values. *Essentials of Conservation Biology*, pp. 216–236. Sinauer Associates, Sunderland.

Rabin, L.A. (2003) Maintaining behavioural diversity in captivity for conservation: Natural behaviour management, *Animal Welfare* 12, 85–94.

Randall, D.A., Pollinger, J.P., Wayne, R., Tallents, L.A., Johnson, P. & Macdonald, D.W. (2007) Inbreeding is reduced by female-biased dispersal and mating behavior in Ethiopian wolves. *Behavioural Ecology*. Published online.

Reading, P.R. & Clark, T.W. (1996) Carnivore introductions: An interdisciplinary Examination. *Carnivore Behavior, Ecology and Evolution.* (eds J.L. Gittleman, S.M. Funk, D.W. Macdonald & R.K. Wayne), pp. 296–336. Cornell University Press, Ithaca and London.

Rhymer, J.M. & Simberloff, D. (1996) Extinction by hybridization and introgression. *Annual Review of Ecology and Systematics* 27, 83–109.

Sanyal, P. (1987) Managing the man-eaters in the Sundarbans Tiger Reserve of India—A case study. *Tigers of the World: The Biology, Biopolitics, Management and Conservation of an Endangered Species.* (eds R.L. Tilson & U.S. Seal), pp. 416–425. Noyes Publications, New Jersey.

Sarkar, S., Pressey, R.L., Faith, D.P. et al. (2006) Biodiversity conservation planning tools: Present status and challenges for the future, *Annual Review of Environment and Resources* 31, 123–159.

Sayer, J.A. (1995) Science and International Nature Conservation. *CIFOR Occasional Paper* 4, 1–16.

Scheepers, J.L. & Venzke, K.A.E. (1995) Attempts to reintroduce African wild dogs Lycaon pictus into Etosha National Park, Namibia. *South African Journal of Wildlife Research* 25, 138–140.

Seddon, P.J. (1999) Persistence without intervention: Assessing success in wildlife reintroductions. *Trends in Ecology and Evolution* 14, 503–503.

Seddon, P.J., Armstrong, D.P. & Maloney, R.F. (2007) Developing the science of reintroduction biology. *Conservation Biology* 21, 303–312.

SERI (Society for Ecological Restoration International) (2004) *The SER International Primer on Ecological Restoration*. Society for Ecological Restoration International, Tucson. Available: www.ser.org. Accessed 13 October 2008.

SERI (Society for Ecological Restoration International) (2007) Ecological restoration, a global strategy for mitigating climate change. *ScienceDaily*. Available: http://www.sciencedaily.com/releases/2007/08/070817165031.htm. Accessed 16 October 2008.

Sidorovich, V.E., Kruuk, H. & Macdonald, D.W. (1999) Body size, and interactions between European and American mink (*Mustela lutreola* and *M. vison*) in Eastern Europe. *Journal of Zoology, London* 248, 521–527.

Sillero-Zubiri, C. & Macdonald, D.W. (eds) (1997) *The Ethiopian Wolf, Status Survey and Conservation Action Plan*. IUCN, Gland, Switzerland.

Snyder, N.F.R., Derrickson, S.R., Beissinger, S.R., Wiley, J.W., Smith, T.B., Toone, W.D. & Miller, B. (1996) Limitations of captive breeding in endangered species recovery. *Conservation Biology* 10, 338–348.

Soulé, M.E., Gilpin, M., Conway, W. & Foose, T. (1986) The millennium ark: How long a voyage, how many staterooms, how many passengers? *Zoo Biology* 5, 101–113.

South, A.B., Rushton, S.P., Kenward, R.E. & Macdonald, D.W. (2002) Modelling vertebrate dispersal and demography in real landscapes: How does uncertainty regarding dispersal behaviour influence predictions of spatial population dynamics? *Dispersal Ecology* (eds J.M. Bullock, R.E. Kenward & R.S. Hails), pp. 327–349. Blackwell Publishing, Oxford.

South, A.B., Rushton, S.P. & Macdonald, D.W. (2000) Simulating the proposed reintroduction of the European beaver (*Castor fiber*) to Scotland. *Biological Conservation* 93 103–116.

South, A.B., Rushton, S.P., Macdonald, D.W. & Fuller, R. (2001) Reintroduction of the European beaver (*Castor fiber*) to Norfolk, UK: A preliminary modelling analysis. *Journal of Zoology, London* 254, 473–479.

Spalton, J.A., Lawrence, M.W. & Brend, S.A. (1999) Arabian oryx reintroduction in Oman, successes and setbacks. *Oryx* 33, 168–175.

Spinnage, C. (1996) The rule of law and African game—A review of some recent trends and concerns. *Oryx* 30, 178–186.

Spinnage, C. (1998) Social change and conservation misrepresentation in Africa. *Oryx* 32, 265–276.

Stahl, P. & Artois, M. (1991) *Status and Conservation of the Wildcat in Europe and Around the Mediterranean Rim.* Council of Europe, Strasbourg.

Stanley Price, M. (1989) *Animal Reintroductions, the Arabian oryx in Oman.* Cambridge University Press, Cambridge.

Stanley Price, M. & Gordon, I. (1989) How to go wild. *New Scientist* 1688,

Stewart, R. & Possingham, H. (2005) Efficiency, costs and trade-offs in marine reserve system design. *Environmental Modeling and Assessment* 10, 203–213.

Suminski, P. (1962) Research in the native form of the wildcat (*Felis silvestris* Schreber) on the background of its geographical distribution. *Folia Forestalia Polenica* 8, 1–81.

Sunquist, M. & Sunquist, F. (2002) *Wild Cats of the World.* University of Chicago Press, Chicago.

Tattersall, F.H. & Macdonald, D.W. (1995) *A Review of the Direct and Indirect Costs of Re-introducing the European Beaver* (Castor fiber) *to Scotland.* Report, Contract No. SNH/110/95 IBB. WildCRU, Oxford.

Terborgh, J., Estes, J.A., Paquet, P., Ralls, K., Boyd-Heger, D., Miller, B.J. & Noss, R. F. (1999) The role of top carnivores in regulating terrestrial ecosystems. *Continental Conservation: Scientific Foundation of Regional Reserve Networks.* (eds M.E. Soulé & J. Terborgh), pp. 39–64. Island Press, Washington, DC.

Viggers, K.L., Lindenmayer, D.B. & Spratt, D.M. (1993) The importance of disease in reintroduction programmes. *Wildlife Research* 20, 697–698.

Wang, S.W. & Macdonald, D.W. (2006) Livestock predation by carnivores in Jigme Singye Wangchuck National Park, Bhutan. *Biological Conservation* 129, 558–565.

Webb, A., French, D.D. & Flitsch, A.C.C. (1997) *Identification and Assessment of Possible Beaver Sites in Scotland.* Scottish Natural Heritage Research, Survey and Monitoring Report No. 94. Scottish Natural Heritage, Perth.

Williams, C.S. (1995) Conserving Europe's bees, why all the buzz? *Trends in Ecology and Evolution* 10, 309–310.

Wilson, K.A., McBride, M.F., Bode, M. & Possingham, H.P. (2006) Prioritizing global conservation efforts. *Nature* 440, 337–340.

Wolf, C.M., Griffith, B., Reed, C. & Temple, S.A. (1996) Avian and mammalian translocations: Update and reanalysis of 1987 survey data. *Conservation Biology* 10, 1142–1154.

Woodroffe, R. & Ginsberg, J.R. (1998) Edge effects and the extinction of populations inside protected areas. *Science* 280, 2126–2128.

Yalden, D.W. (1993) The problems of reintroducing carnivores. *Symposia of the Zoological Society of London* 65, 289–306.

Young, T.P. (2000) Restoration ecology and conservation biology. *Biological Conservation* 92, 73–83.

Index